Impact of Digital Transformation on the Development of New Business Models and Consumer Experience

Maria Antónia Rodrigues
CEOS, Polytechnic of Porto, Portugal & Sistemas de Interação e Inovação Social, Portugal

João F. Proença
Faculty of Economics, University of Porto, Portugal & Advance/CSG, ISEG, University of Lisbon, Portugal

IGI Global
PUBLISHER of TIMELY KNOWLEDGE

A volume in the Advances in Business Strategy and Competitive Advantage (ABSCA) Book Series

Published in the United States of America by
IGI Global
Business Science Reference (an imprint of IGI Global)
701 E. Chocolate Avenue
Hershey PA, USA 17033
Tel: 717-533-8845
Fax: 717-533-8661
E-mail: cust@igi-global.com
Web site: http://www.igi-global.com

Library of Congress Cataloging-in-Publication Data

Names: Rodrigues, Maria Antonia, 1977- editor. | Proença, João F., editor.
Title: Impact of digital transformation on the development of new business models and consumer experience / Maria Rodrigues, and João Proença, editor.
Description: Hershey, PA : Business Science Reference, [2022] | Includes bibliographical references and index. | Summary: "This book presents research findings and an innovative and multifaceted perspective of how digital transformation and other innovative technologies can drive new business models and create value experiences for consumers and/or firms"-- Provided by publisher.
Identifiers: LCCN 2021045721 (print) | LCCN 2021045722 (ebook) | ISBN 9781799891796 (hardcover) | ISBN 9781799891802 (paperback) | ISBN 9781799891819 (ebook)
Subjects: LCSH: Technological innovations--Economic aspects. | Information technology--Economic aspects. | Value. | New products. | Customer relations.
Classification: LCC HC79.T4 I4567 2022 (print) | LCC HC79.T4 (ebook) | DDC 338/.064--dc23/eng/20211101
LC record available at https://lccn.loc.gov/2021045721
LC ebook record available at https://lccn.loc.gov/2021045722

This book is published in the IGI Global book series Advances in Business Strategy and Competitive Advantage (ABSCA) (ISSN: 2327-3429; eISSN: 2327-3437)

British Cataloguing in Publication Data
A Cataloguing in Publication record for this book is available from the British Library.

For electronic access to this publication, please contact: eresources@igi-global.com.

Advances in Business Strategy and Competitive Advantage (ABSCA) Book Series

Patricia Ordóñez de Pablos
Universidad de Oviedo, Spain

ISSN:2327-3429
EISSN:2327-3437

Mission

Business entities are constantly seeking new ways through which to gain advantage over their competitors and strengthen their position within the business environment. With competition at an all-time high due to technological advancements allowing for competition on a global scale, firms continue to seek new ways through which to improve and strengthen their business processes, procedures, and profitability.

The **Advances in Business Strategy and Competitive Advantage (ABSCA) Book Series** is a timely series responding to the high demand for state-of-the-art research on how business strategies are created, implemented and re-designed to meet the demands of globalized competitive markets. With a focus on local and global challenges, business opportunities and the needs of society, the **ABSCA** encourages scientific discourse on doing business and managing information technologies for the creation of sustainable competitive advantage.

Coverage

- Balanced Scorecard
- Innovation Strategy
- Co-operative Strategies
- Outsourcing
- Value Creation
- Value Chain
- Cost Leadership Strategy
- Business Models
- Adaptive Enterprise
- Foreign Investment Decision Process

IGI Global is currently accepting manuscripts for publication within this series. To submit a proposal for a volume in this series, please contact our Acquisition Editors at Acquisitions@igi-global.com or visit: http://www.igi-global.com/publish/.

The Advances in Business Strategy and Competitive Advantage (ABSCA) Book Series (ISSN 2327-3429) is published by IGI Global, 701 E. Chocolate Avenue, Hershey, PA 17033-1240, USA, www.igi-global.com. This series is composed of titles available for purchase individually; each title is edited to be contextually exclusive from any other title within the series. For pricing and ordering information please visit http://www.igi-global.com/book-series/advances-business-strategy-competitive-advantage/73672. Postmaster: Send all address changes to above address.

Titles in this Series

For a list of additional titles in this series, please visit: http://www.igi-global.com/book-series/advances-business-strategy-competitive-advantage/73672

Cases on Survival and Sustainability Strategies of Social Entrepreneurs
Charles Oham (University of Greenwich, UK)
Business Science Reference • © 2022 • 312pp • H/C (ISBN: 9781799877240) • US $195.00

Career Re-Invention in the Post-Pandemic Era
Shalin Hai-Jew (Kansas State University, USA)
Business Science Reference • © 2022 • 332pp • H/C (ISBN: 9781799886266) • US $205.00

Handbook of Research on Cross-Disciplinary Uses of Gamification in Organizations
Oscar Bernardes (ISCAP, ISEP, Polytechnic Institute of Porto, Portugal & University of Aveiro, Portugal) Vanessa Amorim (ISCAP, Polytechnic Institute of Porto, Portugal) and António Carrizo Moreira (University of Aveiro, Portugal)
Business Science Reference • © 2022 • 657pp • H/C (ISBN: 9781799892236) • US $295.00

Critical Analysis and Architecture for Strategic Business Planning
James McKee (Independent Researcher, Australia)
Business Science Reference • © 2022 • 289pp • H/C (ISBN: 9781799880738) • US $215.00

Multidisciplinary Perspectives on Cross-Border Trade and Business
Asmat-Nizam Abdul-Talib (University Utara Malaysia, Malaysia) Norhayati Zakaria (University of Wollongong in Dubai, UAE) and Samshul-Amry Abdul-Latif (Universiti Utara Malaysia, Malaysia)
Business Science Reference • © 2022 • 375pp • H/C (ISBN: 9781799890713) • US $225.00

Cases on Digital Strategies and Management Issues in Modern Organizations
José Duarte Santos (Instituto Superior Politecnico, Spain)
Business Science Reference • © 2022 • 365pp • H/C (ISBN: 9781799816300) • US $195.00

Employee Share Ownership and Impacts on Organizational Value and Behavior
Sara Elouadi (Hassan II University, Casablanca, Morocco)
Business Science Reference • © 2022 • 255pp • H/C (ISBN: 9781799885573) • US $215.00

ICT as Innovator Between Tourism and Culture
Célia M.Q. Ramos (University of Algarve, Portugal) Silvia Quinteiro (University of the Algarve, Portugal) and Alexandra R. Gonçalves (University of the Algarve, Portugal)
Business Science Reference • © 2022 • 319pp • H/C (ISBN: 9781799881650) • US $215.00

IGI Global
PUBLISHER of TIMELY KNOWLEDGE

701 East Chocolate Avenue, Hershey, PA 17033, USA
Tel: 717-533-8845 x100 • Fax: 717-533-8661
E-Mail: cust@igi-global.com • www.igi-global.com

Table of Contents

Detailed Table of Contents

This chapter aims to clarify all mysteries about the term digital transformation. First, the focus will be understanding more about what is digital and what is transformational. The chapter will provide guidance on why we need digital transformation at all. What will be the penalties if the organizations try to pass? There are five key domains which will be covered: customers, competition, data, innovation, and value. After the domain, the chapter will introduce the six stages of digital transformation: business as usual, present and active, formalized, strategic, converged, and innovative and adaptive. Key topics that will be explained are the difference between digitization, process digitalization, and digital transformation. Finally, the chapter will end with more details on how to lead and embed the digital transformation in the organization.

The rise of tech-savvy consumers and their new demands pushes firms to transform their business strategies in order to respond to this changing consumer market. Digital transformation, in this regard, enhances the customer experience and satisfies digitally powered consumers by the integration of digital technology into all areas of a business that alters how a firm operates and delivers value to customers. Creation of value is replaced with co-creation that includes consumers as well as companies in the value creation process. Together with the emergence of digitalization, value creation is influenced again in terms of the uses of the digital tools by its participants. The first objective of this chapter is to give detailed information about the co-creation of value concept by explaining the drivers and the outcomes as well as the disadvantages and the benefits offered to consumers and to companies. The second objective is to examine the impact of digital transformation on the value co-creation process and to pay attention to the role of digital agility in this context.

This chapter describes the concept of a business model from the network perspective and examines the different types of business models. The author mentions the characteristics of a successful business model with the threats to a business model's success. A lean start-up process is explained, with an emphasis on the business model canvas technique. An organization's business model does not necessarily have to continue in perpetuity once it is launched. Accordingly, the business model change, characteristics of a transformative business model, and directions for future research are addressed. In this context, the chapter discusses the past, present, and future of e-business models.

Digital marketing and strategy are often thought of as using modern internet and communication technologies in a company's business operations. Companies have used such technologies to communicate with stakeholders, reduce costs, engage customers, and so on. Even today, many digital marketing courses focus on gathering views on brand content, gaining followers, or making users click on links and advertisements. Likewise, many companies wrongly understand that digital marketing is simply about using modern internet and communication technologies in conducting business or spreading their message. This chapter explains that digital technologies offer an opportunity to businesses to re-invent themselves by keeping customer experience firmly in focus. If they do so, they stand a much better chance of surviving and thriving in a considerably changed marketing environment. Transformation must occur in their business model, organisation structure and processes, people and culture, and above all, their focus on solving customer problems.

The eased access to new digital technologies allowed for new possibilities, with content streaming being one of the most expressive digital consumption and business models in the phonographic industry. Following, brand-new discussions regarding the consumption habits of its users took place. What is not yet clear is the consumption dynamics on these new platforms, particularly, when referring to exploration scenarios, the most relevant tools and what role factors such as familiarity and taste play in the discovery process of the existing catalogue. The intent is to comprehend the expressiveness of these music streaming platforms, what dynamics come to play referring to exploratory behaviours, and which tools or mechanisms are the most important in this process. Following data collection of 264 respondents through a survey, the results indicate both the popularity of streaming platforms and the respondents' high exploration tendencies, with existing features like playlists being the most significant tools to discover the catalogue.

This research chapter sheds light on the digital transformations that are happening in the medical industry and primarily focuses on how digital transformation processes are introduced and adapted into China's medical industry. Furthermore, the authors explore the characteristics, socio-economic impact, changes in business models and consumer experience, introduction, and restructuring of relevant government policies caused by these digital transformations. They also bring to light the opportunities, challenges, and risks that may present in the future. The authors take two case studies for demonstrating the impact: first, the intelligent assistance system that leverages 5G+AI and, second, the body temperature monitoring system that leverages the IoT and Bluetooth. Through the comparison of these two successful case-studies, they can realize that the impact of AI technologies and thereby the digital transformations will play a major role in the future of medical industry. They also explore the problems of digital transformation in the field of medical care with the help of a few case studies like IBM Watson.

The age of market globalisation and on-line presence allows companies to improve their relations with customers as well as to establish more direct communication. The different shopping acts may be related to a person's utilitarian and hedonic values. A study carried out by Hootsuite revealed that clothing and beauty products were the most on-line bought items in Portugal in 2017. The study aims at understanding the motivations behind choosing on-line channels for buying those types of products, with a special emphasis on the different generations of buyers. The authors use an exploratory methodology based on an on-line survey with 280 responses. There is a stronger association between the utilitarian value and the intention to repeat a purchase than between the hedonic value and that intention. Generation X is more associated to the repurchase intention to repeat a purchase based on utilitarian values and Generation Z shows a stronger association between hedonic values and being a repeat customer.

This chapter provides a qualitative case study of Pinduoduo: China's fastest-growing e-commerce firm. As a disruptive organization entering the retail industry in 2015, Pinduoduo has become the third largest e-commerce platform in China. The spectacular success of the company has caught the attention of entrepreneurs, business leaders, and investors across the world. This study demonstrates that digital technologies have enabled Pinduoduo to develop innovative business model and establish closer and diverse links with partners and experiences with customers. The innovative business model and strategy of Pinduoduo are worth studying. This chapter aims to provide an understanding of the strategies that underpin the innovative business models of Pinduoduo and the impact of digital innovation and technologies on consumer's experiences. The research results demonstrate how Pinduoduo addresses the needs of overlooked customers in their market spaces through leveraging advanced digital technologies and innovating platform business models and developing digital ecosystems.

Augmented reality (AR) try-on services have been proven to enhance customer engagement and purchase intentions by enabling users to experience the sense of flow. While few studies focused on the design principles of mobile AR services, little has been done regarding the role of flow in consumer experience whilst interacting with try-on services. This chapter reviews the current design principles of mobile AR and examines its influence in consumer flow state. Through a task-based semi-structured interview with consumers (n=9), it was possible to observe that all participants did not enter the flow state due to lack of perceived control and familiarity with the technology. Finally, this chapter provides recommendations for enhancing the flow experience of mobile AR try-on services. It is expected that this chapter might be of interest to retailers and researchers willing to explore mobile AR effectiveness through try-on-services such as the virtual fitting room (VFR).

Among technological changes currently influencing retail, the implementation of digital strategies to create more experiential retail stores has enriched customers' experiences. Interactive technologies such as augmented reality (AR) provide particularly promising possibilities. By using AR, retailers can develop strategies to attract existing and potential customers, while customers can experience shopping in augmented, immersive ways in which the digital and physical worlds are combined in an augmented one. Despite the several examples of the use of AR technology in retail, those instances have often been introduced with only a few specific features and with limited applicability. In response, this chapter introduces the concept of an augmented retail store as a more comprehensive integration of physical and digital elements. It may serve as a means to develop an augmented experience for customers and mutual benefits for retailers and consumers and thus provide value for both academics and practitioners.

The internet is a technology that has provided changes, giving rise to new trends and concepts applied in the most diverse areas. One of these trends is gamification, as it is a concept applied in several areas: education, information technology, management, communication, and marketing. Companies understand that gamification applied to marketing can be an opportunity to strengthen the relationship between brands

Preface

Digital transformation, also known as Industry 4.0, as a result of technological evolution, has brought a strong and accelerated change to businesses and consumers. At the organizational level, the concept of digital transformation relates to the use of digital technologies to improve business performance and consumer experience. Digital transformation, the main drive for a digital economy can be defined as an implementation of breakthrough changes in approach to customers and making business (Szopa and Cyplik, 2020). Digital transformation is revolutionizing the way business is conducted within industrial value chains using digital technologies devices (Parida *et al.*, 2019; Leme and Proenca, 2021). Moreover, in a broad sense, digital transformation is understood as any change in the organization and its business model due to the increasing use of digital technologies (Canestrino *et al.*, 2020).

At the academic level, digital transformation has been approached from different fields. Whether in the field of computer science, which is the leading area or in other fields as the human sciences, especially business, engineering, social sciences, information science, library science, education and educational research, decision science, medicine, protection of the environment, law, material science, etc. (Pihir *et al.*, 2019). From the historical point of view, the pioneers of digital transformation, as we know and understand the term today, come from medicine in the year 2001 and from the business area in the year 2003 (Pihir *et al.*, 2019). Another approach to digital transformation has been to identify the determinants to improve digital maturity and digitally transform an organization. Among the main determinants, the literature refers to customer-centricity, strategy orientation, innovation culture and organizational commitment, information and communication technologies (ICT), process infrastructure, talent, capability, and capacity-strengthening (Pihir *et al.*, 2019). This means that not all companies or organizations have the same conditions for digital transformation.

Among the technologies associated with digital transformation, we find artificial intelligence, internet of things, augmented reality, among many others. Each of these technologies can affect different organizations, different processes and require different changes and skills in the organization, its employees, and customers. In business, digital transformation has translated into improved efficiency and productivity, new business models, new services, and new consumer experiences.

This book focuses on digital transformation, especially at the business level. The book is entitled *Impact of Digital Transformation on the Development of New Business Models and Consumer Experience*, and it provides relevant theoretical and empirical research findings and innovative and multifaceted perspectives on how digital transformation can drive new business models and create valued experiences for consumers, and firms. Covering topics such as digital transformation, business models, consumer behavior, digital marketing, social media, e-commerce, communication, gamification, augmented reality, etc., this publication is ideal for industry professionals, managers, business owners, practitioners, researchers, professors, academics and students.

ORGANIZATION OF THE BOOK

The book is organized into 14 chapters. The book organization starts with chapters approaching a more general view of digital transformation followed by others focusing on digital transformation impact on business models and consumer experiences.

The first two chapters approach the main and basic concepts of digital transformation and discuss related concepts and issues. Chapters 3 and 4 address business models and customer experience from a general perspective and resulting from digital transformation. Chapters 5 and 6 discuss digital transformation in two concrete cases studies. Chapter 5 presents an innovative business model in the entertainment sector (the streaming platform) and chapter 6 the impact of digital transformation in the business model of the health sector. Moreover, as digital transformation has also allowed many companies to complement existing business models with e-commerce and new online sales channels, the following chapters approached the phenomenon. Chapters 7 and 8 focus on the online purchase motivations of consumers of generations X, Y, and Z and the Pinduoduo case, like an e-commerce business model. In addition, and considering that one of the most innovative technologies resulting from digital transformation is augmented reality, Chapters 9 and 10 focus on this topic. Chapter 9 addresses the mobile augmented reality service and Chapter 10 the augmented retail stores. Finally, digital transformation is occurring in different organizational areas using and implementing new technologies and devices, which in turn is providing new experiences and greater consumer engagement. Thus, the last four chapters discuss and show the opportunities, in terms of gamification, communication, and/or social media.

A brief description of each of the chapters follows:

Chapter 1 was written by Nikola Gaydarov and Roumiana Ilieva both from the Technical University of Sofia, Bulgaria, and is entitled "Digital Transformation Demystified: The Full Story About Digital Transformation." It presents a discussion about the term 'Digital Transformation' and related terms like, 'Digitalization' and 'Process Digitalization'. The chapter starts arguing why do we need Digital Transformation and puts in evidence six phases or periods of digital transformation: business as usual, present and active, formalized, strategic, converged, and last, innovative and adaptive. These steps allow organizations to find their position on the digitalization process and, then to proceed forward from there. The chapter ends by providing a section about how to lead and embed digital Transformation in the organization.

Chapter 2 was written by Meltem Çakici from Beykent University, Turkey, "Digital Transformation and Co-Creation of Value: The Role of Digital Agility," and links digital transformation to value co-creation literature. In this vein, and with digital transformation, value creation is replaced by co-creation value that includes the consumers and other companies in the value creation process. This chapter has two main goals. First, to discuss and give detailed information about value co-creation with firms and consumers and to relate the concept with digitalization. Second, to analyze the impact of digital transformation on the value co-creation process.

Beyza Gultekin from the Hacettepe University, Turkey, wrote Chapter 3, "The Past, Present, and Future of E-Business Models." This author argues that an organization's business model does not necessarily have to continue unchanged, and thus business models may or even should change according to the circumstances. In this context, the chapter discusses the past, the present, and the future of e-business models.

Dinesh Kumar from the Jagran Lakecity University, India, wrote Chapter 4, "Digital Transformation: Technology and New Business Models as Drivers of Customer Experience." This chapter focuses on the use of digital technologies as an opportunity for business, allowing companies to re-invent themselves by keeping customer experiences in focus. The authors draw attention to the fact that digital transformation is much more than using the internet and communication technologies. According to the authors, the transformation effects occur in firms' business models, organization structure and processes, people and culture, and above all, on focus to solve the customer's problems.

Chapter 5, "Music Streaming: Consumption Patterns in Digital Ambients," was written by Flávio Brito and Diana Vieira both from Polytechnic of Porto, Portugal, and focuses on one of the most expressive digital consumption and business models in the phonographic industry, the music streaming platforms. These researchers present an interesting empirical study using both quantitative and qualitative methodologies. The research tries to comprehend the expressiveness of music streaming platforms, what dynamics come into play referring to exploratory behaviors, and which tools or mechanisms are the most important in this process.

Chapter 6, "The Development and Impact of China's Digital Transformation in Medical Industry," was written by Poshan Yu from the Soochow University of China, by Wenye Xue from China, and by Ramya Mahendran from India and both independent researchers. This chapter explores and discusses the development and impact of the digital transformation of China's medical industry. The authors take two case studies to discuss and illustrate the digital transformation impact on China's medical industry business models. First, the authors explore the intelligent assistance system that leverages 5G and artificial intelligence (AI), and second, the body temperature monitoring system that leverages the internet of things (IoT) and bluetooth. Through the discussion of these two case studies, the authors considered that the future of smart healthcare under digital transformation is very promising. Given that the global society is now entering the big health technology revolution, smart medicine is bound to have a big market in the future. This Chapter shows that during the digital transformation of China's medical industry, the commercialization model of the medical industry has undergone specific changes. Although customers still have doubts about digital and intelligent medical treatment such as surgical robots, the upgrade of artificial intelligence and remote technology has improved customer experience and satisfaction.

Chapter 7 written by Ana Lima and Nicolau Monteiro both from the Polytechnic of Porto, Portugal, and entitled "E-Commerce: The Influence of Hedonic and Utilitarian Motivations on Generations X, Y, and Z," presents an empirical study focusing on consumer perspectives. The study aims to understand the motivations behind choosing online channels for buying products, with a special emphasis on the different generations of consumers, X, Y, and Z. Considering that the digital transformation allowed the development of new business models and sales channels, such as e-commerce, it is important to understand the consumer experiences in a digital environment. The research results show interesting differences between diverse generations and motivations.

Chapter 8 was written by Qiuyan Fan from the Western Sydney University, Australia, and presents "A Case Study of Business Innovation Through Digital Technologies." This chapter provides qualitative research based on a case study of a growing e-commerce firm, Pinduoduo. This research discusses and shows how digital technologies have enabled this business firm to develop an innovative business model impacting partners' and consumers' experiences.

Shuo-Yun Yang, Vanissa Wanick, Eirini Bazaki, and YuanYuan Yin, all from the Winchester School of Art, University of Southampton, United Kingdom were the authors of Chapter 9, entitled "Exploring the Role of Flow in Augmented Reality for Mobile Retailing: Implications for Practice and Research." This research follows the idea that traditional stores are being transformed to adapt to digital changes and organizations are modifying the way they interact with customers during the shopping process. Accordingly, augmented reality (AR) is an innovative technology becoming utilized by different businesses, particularly in retail providing news experiences for the customers. Although the relevance of this technology for services and customers, these researchers highlight that literature about AR users' experience is scarce. This chapter addresses two main research questions: Does the mobile augmented reality service trigger the user to engage in the flow status? And, what kinds of design elements in mobile augmented reality service will influence a user's flow status? The author's conclusion points out that organizations must understand the value that such technologies can bring. Although there is a trend in the market, many challenges remain.

Chapter 10 was written by Federica Caboni from the University of Cagliari, Italy, and by Johan Hagberg from the University of Gothenburg, Sweden, and is entitled "The Augmented Retail Store for Augmented Customer Experiences." This chapter also focuses on augmented reality, particularly in retail stores. Augmented retail stores combine the benefits of physical stores and augmented reality technology to create immersive places based on the combination of the physical elements typical of traditional stores and the features of digital technology. This technology can be useful for practitioners as a way to create and develop immersive shopping experiences. Thus, this chapter presents and develops the notion of augmented retail stores as places that combine the benefits of the physical and digital worlds to create augmented experiences for consumers.

Then Chapter 11 was written by Albérico Rosário, from IADE, European University, Portugal: "Understanding the Application of Gamification to Business When Applied to Marketing." This chapter presents a systematic literature review to explore the knowledge about the application of gamification to business when applied to marketing. Although games were previously perceived as entertainment tools only, the current digital transformation era has expanded its use in several areas. This expansion led to the development of the term 'gamification,' which refers to the use of game-design elements in non-game environments including marketing and promotional activities. This researcher concluded that gamification has become a significant value co-creation tool in modern-day marketing. In sum, this chapter shows the main purposes of gamification applied to marketing and the state of the art about the topic.

Chapter 12, "Digital Evolution in Brand Communication," was written by Esra Güven from the Celal Bayar University, Turkey. This chapter supports digital transformation at the business level in the evolution of technology and changes in the world and focuses, in particular, on digital transformation in marketing. Digital transformation occurs when traditional marketing is replaced by digital marketing and is manifested in terms of the purchase process, consumer behavior, and as a differentiating element among competitors. Then, the authors present the study of Turkish Airlines and Toyota to highlight and discuss the digital transformation changes in these companies' marketing and communication areas.

Vandana Ahuja from Amity Business School and Shirin Alavi from the Jaypee Institute of Information Technology, both from India wrote Chapter 13, entitled "Leveraging Social Media Tools for Business Purposes." This chapter enables readers to appreciate the concept of social media, detailing the most significant social media tools that can be used by business organizations and brands. Finally, this chapter identifies the main benefits of social media to businesses and individuals.

Finally, Anthony Bolton, Leila Goosen, and Elmarie Kritzinger, all from the University of South Africa, end the book with Chapter 14, entitled "Impact of Digital Transformation via Unified Communication and Collaboration Technologies: Productivity and Innovation at a Global Enterprise." These authors used the case study research methodology to show the impact of digital transformation on one of the world's largest automotive manufacturing and sales enterprises, General Motors. Under the scope of the study, the unified communication and collaboration (UC&C) framework was developed and tailored to guide the establishment of a technical and service architecture, facilitating broad digital transformation across multiple facets of employee-to-employee, employee-to-partner, employee-to-customer, and enterprise-to-employee communication and collaboration.

Maria Antónia Rodrigues
CEOS, Polytechnic of Porto, Portugal & Sistemas de Interação e Inovação Social, Portugal

João F. Proença
Faculty of Economics, University of Porto, Portugal & Advance/CSG, ISEG, University of Lisbon, Portugal

REFERENCES

Canestrino, R., C'wiklicki, M., Kafel, P., Wojnarowska, M., & Magliocca, P. (2020). The digitalization in EMAS-registered organizations: Evidences from Italy and Poland. *The TQM Journal*, *32*(4), 673–695. doi:10.1108/TQM-12-2019-0301

Leme, M., & Proenca, J. F. (2021). Digital Servitization as a New Research Stream: A Bibliometric Analysis. In *Digital Economy. Emerging Technologies and Business Innovation. ICDEc 2021. Exploring Service Science. Lecture Notes in Business Information Processing (LNBIP).* Springer Nature Switzerland AG.

Parida, V., Sjödin, D., & Reim, W. (2019). Reviewing literature on digitalization, business model innovation, and sustainable industry: Past achievements and future promises. *Sustainability*, *11*(2), 1–18. doi:10.3390u11020391

Pihir, I., Tomičić-Pupek, K., & Furjan, M. (2019). Digital Transformation Playground - Literature Review and Framework of Concepts. *Journal of Information and Organizational Sciences*, *43*(1), 33–48. doi:10.31341/jios.43.1.3

Szopa, Ł., & Cyplik, P. (2020). The concept of building a digital transformation model for enterprises from the SME sector – case study. *LogForum*, *16*(4), 593–601.

Acknowledgment

João Proença gratefully acknowledges financial support from FCT – Fundação para a Ciência e a Tecnologia (Portugal), national funding through research grant UIDB/04521/2020.

The editors would like to acknowledge the support of researchers and the IGI Global editor staff involved in this project. Among editors, authors, and reviewers, the book had the participation and commitment of thirty-nine researchers.

Twenty-eight authors from diverse countries or continents, namely from Australia, Bulgaria, China, India, Italy, Portugal, South Africa, Sweden, Turkey, and United Kingdom, have contributed to the book. The editors would like to thank each one of the authors.

All chapters were reviewed by two or more reviewers, which was a valuable work to enrich and improve the final result of the book. Thus, we gratefully acknowledge the support of the researchers that contributed to this book at the revision process of each chapter, which got the collaboration of Amélia Carvalho (Polytechnic of Porto), Ana Lima (Polytechnic of Porto), Anabela Ribeiro (Polytechnic of Porto), Eirini Bazaki (University of Southampton), Francisco Pedro (University of Minho), Flávio Brito (Polytechnic of Porto), Iolanda Vieira (Polytechnic of Viana do Castelo), Johan Hagberg (University of Gothenburg), José Santos (Polytechnic Institute of Gaia), Leila Goosen (University of South Africa), Luis Matosas-López (Rey Juan Carlos University), Mafalda Roxo (Maia University Institute), Marcela Leme (Católica Lisbon School and University of Porto), Meltem Çakıcı (Beykent University), Nikola Gaydarov (University of Sofia), Paulo Gonçalves (Polytechnic of Porto), Poshan Yu (University of Soochow), Raquel Almeida (University of Porto), Raquel Soares (European University and IPAM, Portugal), Shirin Alavi (Jaypee Institute of Information Technology), and Vanissa Wanick (University of Southampton).

The editors also appreciate IGI Global's support throughout the process.

João Proença gratefully acknowledges financial support from FCT – Fundação para a Ciência e a Tecnologia (Portugal), national funding through research grant UIDB/04521/2020.

Maria Antónia Rodrigues
CEOS, Polytechnic of Porto, Portugal & Sistemas de Interação e Inovação Social, Portugal

João F. Proença
Faculty of Economics, University of Porto, Portugal & Advance/CSG, ISEG, University of Lisbon, Portugal

Chapter 1
Digital Transformation Demystified:
The Full Story About Digital Transformation

Nikola Petkov Gaydarov
Technical University of Sofia, Bulgaria

Roumiana Ilieva
Technical University of Sofia, Bulgaria

ABSTRACT

This chapter aims to clarify all mysteries about the term digital transformation. First, the focus will be understanding more about what is digital and what is transformational. The chapter will provide guidance on why we need digital transformation at all. What will be the penalties if the organizations try to pass? There are five key domains which will be covered: customers, competition, data, innovation, and value. After the domain, the chapter will introduce the six stages of digital transformation: business as usual, present and active, formalized, strategic, converged, and innovative and adaptive. Key topics that will be explained are the difference between digitization, process digitalization, and digital transformation. Finally, the chapter will end with more details on how to lead and embed the digital transformation in the organization.

INTRODUCTION

Digital Transformation is a hot topic, so hot that everyone you meet is either speaking about it or has an opinion how it should be done. Many organizations have started programs and projects to pursue a major business transformation by using modern technology, latest applications, or elastic cloud platforms.

Sadly, often their efforts fail, and long-term transformation is hard to be achieved. The main reason for that is the complexity related to a major digital transformation is often not well assessed initially and the organizations are not prepared both theoretically and practically in advance.

DOI: 10.4018/978-1-7998-9179-6.ch001

There are many misunderstandings about Digital Transformation: is it a technological change or a cultural one or a combination of many different activities. To explain it as simple as possible the goal of a digital transformation isn't to become digital; it's to generate or improve value for the business. Value improvement must in the heart of all efforts, and this is something that is often forgotten on the way.

The question: Why do we need Digital Transformation? is often left without a clear answer where it should be easy to explain it. Clear and provable addition or improvement of business value for the current or new customers is a must. Sometimes simple actions to exchange paper with electronic applications are labeled as Digital Transformation.

Some organizations even don't make a difference between Transition with Transformation. Topics like affected domains within the organization are also to be clarified during the program preparation. Overall, there is no industry standard about what constitutes a Digital Transformation, so each organization makes their own interpretation of it. In the following lines we will try to provide a broad overview about this topic so that it gets a better understanding.

Leading a Digital Transformation is hard, and therefore many transformations ultimately fail in the end. There are many reasons to have a failure, sometimes the programs deliver the targeted results, but the culture does not change, or the organization as whole sees those initiatives as something temporary and does not embed this transformation as something permanent.

Embedding the transformation as something permanent is the hardest step. To achieve overall success, the topic must be demystified and taken as something native for the whole organization.

In the following paragraphs we will provide meaning for several key terms: Value, Transformation and Transition, and Business and IT Transformation.

Then we will provide more details on why we need the digital transformation after all. Topics like "what is Digital" and then "what is Digital Transformation" will be explained in detail as well.

With all this information at hand the different domains where the digital transformation is applicable will be covered. The levels of digitalization will be explained as well before finalizing the chapter with more details on how to lead a digital transformation and embedded on the long term in the organization.

BACKGROUND

Value

As mentioned above every Digital Transformation should be about improving the value delivered to the customers. So, let's first clarify what is Value? We will use the definition in ITIL4 as per (Axelos.com, 2022), where value refers to "The perceived benefits, usefulness, and importance of something".

The term Value is key especially when delivering services because it is the consumer who perceives the benefits created by the service delivery and defines the usefulness and the importance, thus defining the value itself. This means that value is subjective and is not defined as one-time off exercise by the provider, but by each customer on each interaction. Some customers might find certain outputs very useful, where another group of customers can be indifferent to those.

Having this definition, once a Digital Transformation starts there must be a mechanism set to measure is the value delivered being improved or not. This can be done in many ways: direct contact with customers, surveys, focus groups etc.

Transformation vs. Transition

After the definition of Value, the next key question to answer is "What is a Transformation?" and how it is different from a transition. In the service management world, a transformation would mean to start from a state A and move to state B by making noticeable changes in the way services are delivered and their value.

Sabri (2019) states that "Transformation: Is the journey of taking an organization in a new direction and reaching an entirely different level of effectiveness. It is a change to processes, systems, structure, and culture"

The goal of each transformation must be to improve as much as possible the value proposition by using all means available currently and in the near future. This improvement can be in form of additional outcomes that the service supports so that new markets can be reached or making it easier for the service to be consumed by the clients via new technology or new way of delivery.

"Every digital transformation is going to begin and end with the customer, and I can see that in the minds of every CEO I talk to." - Marc Benioff (Chairman and Co-CEO, Salesforce).

In short, a transformation is about redesigning what you currently have, maybe even from scratch to deliver better value to clients.

Now, what is a Transition? It is also a movement, but without the major redesign. For example, if you exchange one service management tool for another, but don't change your processes or anything else significantly, this is a transition. If take the time to review and update your processes, make trainings and provide additional new outcomes then it is a Transformation.

As you can see it is easy to make a mistake if you don't know where to look. To recap Transition looks at exchanging what the organization currently has with another but very similar tool or a concept, where Transformation takes a more holistic approach and tries to improve processes, tools and culture on a permanent base.

To make it more clear here are some examples on how to distinguish Transformation and Transition.

Online Hotel Reservation vs. Airbnb

Some years ago, to book a hotel one had to make a call and reserve a room. Pre-payment was not possible, so everything had to be done onsite at the reception. With the digitalization the hotels have developed web pages so that people can easily see room availability and prices and make a reservation if all fits their desires. Even when web-portals like Booking.com have emerged this was still a Transition. It was so because no real change in the business model was present. Hotels were offering rooms and services and people were reserving those rooms.

With the introduction of the Airbnb portal, it all has changed. The people were now not only customers, but they were also now landlords, leasing their own apartments to other people for a better price. This has truly revolutionized the industry, thus making it one of the most famous Transformation examples.

Online Banking Platforms vs. Crypto Currencies

Again, when the first online banking platforms were introduced, this was a major step towards digitalization. People were able to see their current balance, order payments, apply for loans etc. For sure this led to new business for the banks as it was easier for the people to operate with their money, but in the of day those services were already there so it was only the channel that changed. Thus, we can mark this as well as a Transition.

On another hand what was an exotic domain: the world of cryptocurrencies is now a growing phenomenon. There are hundreds and hundreds new currencies being offered, and the size of the capitalization is growing. This change was triggered and led by a technology called Blockchain, but it was not the technology that was the focus, it was how we think about money and how we can use them better. Clearly this is a Transformation, rather than a Transition.

Business Transformation and IT Transformation

After giving more light to the term Transformation, the next big confusion that we want to demystify in this book is about the general transformation types which are present in most organizations. In short there are two main types of transformation: Business and IT.

Business Transformation

Business Transformation is about making significant changes in whole businesses or business units. This change can include architectures, applications, platforms, processes, culture and relationships with partners. Such an initiative would usually require a program that will include many projects underneath it. Best will be to also have a governing body to support this transformation all the way.

McKeown and Philip (2003) provide similar definition: 'Business transformation' is an overarching concept encompassing a range of competitive strategies which organizations adopt in order to bring about significant improvements in business performance.

IT Transformation

Now the IT transformation can and must not happen without an ongoing business transformation. As previously started transformations are about improving the value delivery not only exchanging technology. So, the IT transformation must align to the Business transformation. Doing it separately can lead to major failures.

MAIN FOCUS OF THE CHAPTER

Why We Need Digital Transformation

This question can have many answers, but there is one which both very simple and very accurate. The main reason why we need to continuously do digital transformation is that the rate by which the technology changes is becoming bigger and bigger. We now experience extremely short cycles between an idea and its realization. The first article about Blockchain was written in 2008 by a person calling himself Satoshi Nakamoto, he or she also wrote about Bitcoin and in 2009 the first digital cryptocurrency was a fact. Now 10 years later Bitcoin is becoming even an official currency in some countries. The best way to think about the technology change is that it happens exponentially.

On another hand we have the organizational development. It involves attitudes, behavior, organizational change management and most of all culture as a mix of everything. It is not written in stone, but in general if we exclude fast growing start-ups the rate by organizations changes and evolves is logarithmic, which by the way is the exact opposite of exponential change in technology that we are now observing.

On Fig. 1 we have shown a visual comparison between and exponential and logarithmic function. The exponential function is given by $f(x) = ex$, whereas the logarithmic function is given by $g(x) = \ln x$, and former is the inverse of the latter.

As it can be seen on the figure in the long term the two lines go away from each other, which in practical terms mean that the technology cycles will become shorter and shorter, giving us more often new technical advancements, whereas the organizations will continue to have a steadier change which will obviously not correspond to the technology trend.

This is the simplest and most accurate reason why we need to adapt to the circumstances. Because if we don't, then the technological advancement will continue and overrun our organizational capabilities.

Figure 1. provide us with another critical insight: organizations need to have a digital transformation strategy so that they can keep up the pace with the technology changes. If this does not occur, then the organizations risk to have an outdated technology stack that can be vulnerable to security attacks and also demotivate the employees to do their daily work.

Many organizations are still trying to avoid this adaptation. They are waiting until a crisis is presented to do what was obvious long time ago. When this crisis happens usually it will take more efforts to implement this transformation and not only that, but it might even happen that the crisis cannot be fixed and so the organization will cease to exist.

It is also worth mentioning that when a crisis hit it is not only money being spent but also the reputation of the organization is at stake. What follows is now an example of such an organization and the problem they run into after neglecting their digital strategy.

Figure 1. Exponential vs. Logarithmic

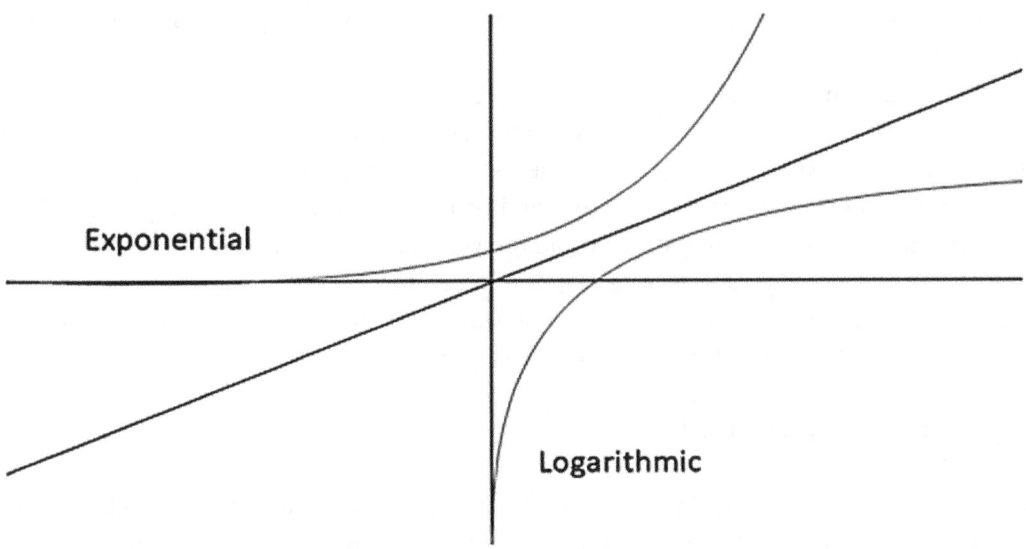

Maersk and NotPetya

According to Ritchie (2019) on the 27th of June 2017 Maersk, one of the world largest logistics companies has suffered one of the biggest ransomware attacks in history. In a single day all end-user devices including 49 000 laptops and printers were made useless.

All of their 1200 applications were inaccessible and about thousands of them were totally destroyed. More than 3000 servers were gone and couldn't be used again. All this due to a single ransomware called NotPetya. The virus was allegedly drafted in Ukraine, by a small software company.

It spread like a wildfire. It was unstoppable and they were not prepared for it. There was no plan what to do and all seamed lost until by pure luck they were rescued by a server in Nigeria that went down just minutes before the attack. On that server was the information they needed to restore the information about the millions of containers around the world.

After the attacked was stopped and finally things got back to normal, an investigation showed that NotPetya has exploited not only technological but also procedural and behavioral weaknesses.

The price tag for the recovery is estimated at about 250 to 300 million USD.

What Is Digital?

After defining the term Transformation, it is time to demystify the term Digital as well.

The word itself is simple enough, but within a single organization it can have many meanings. Therefore, it is key that each new employee is onboarded with the way the organization understands this term. In this way everyone will share the same understanding and goals will be easily achievable. If you don't do that you will get into a situation where everyone will have different understanding and communication will be hard.

There are many definitions that will go around mobile devices, videos, interactions with clients etc. The oldest one comes from decades ago when there was a shift from analog signals to digital ones and zeros. David Rogers (2016) clarifies the term: A method of getting information from one place to another that is not analog. This act is now often called Digitalization or to be more precise Digitization, but we will come to this later.

In the last decades the term Digital has been more and more connected to using applications and platforms in our day-to-day life. It has grown up from the concept of exchanging to digital what was done on paper and manually to using technology assisted solutions on a large scale to transform businesses.

The term digital is now connected to culture and behavior as well. There are terms like digital nomads – people who live anywhere in the world and remotely earn their salaries. Technology has changed dramatically our lives. Being digital is not an option but a must.

Once the culture has changed it means that new ways of management and governance must be developed. Senior management must be tech savvy, has to be and think digital.

Defining Digital Transformation

In his book "Building the Agile Business through Digital Transformation" Perkin and Abraham (2017) says something very important: "The digital native organization might be considered to be one that has grown up in, and has been very much shaped by, a digitally empowered world. As such, their view on the world is not tainted by legacy technologies, thinking, culture, strategies, or approaches".

Following up all the previous definitions and terms it must be now clear that there several key points regarding Digital Transformation.

First one is that no matter what the industry of an organization is, the digital transformation is a must. Perkin and Abraham (2017) says "Digital transformation is inevitable". No one can sit and wait. Technology is blooming, so is the competition. If an organization does not transform with the help of modern technology, it will most probably cease to exist.

The second key point is that Digital Transformation is not only about technology, but about changing the whole organization, its strategy and governance. Perkin and Abraham (2017) has said "Digital transformation is about more than technology". Often a new platform is bought, and senior management expects the people to just start using it without any guidance or any cultural changes. Imagine that your work was dependent on paper forms. Employees and clients were used to them, the way they look, the layout of the sections etc. Once those forms get into electronic form the previous knowledge on both sides will vanish. Phones or tablets will be used. Chargers will be needed. Software upgrades will be needed. Usernames and passwords to access the platform will be a must. In short what was before will never come back.

The third point to stress is that Digital Transformation is about making a significant change. Perkin and Abraham (2017) coins another key statement "Digital transformation involves fundamental and comprehensive change". So, it is not about changing one application with another one. It is about rethinking how value is delivered to clients. Technology should give an organization the possibility to provide services in new ways or new outcomes to existing services which were previously impossible.

In 2014, digital and business consultancy Altimeter defined digital transformation as the realignment of, or new investment in, technology and business models to more effectively engage digital customers at every touchpoint in the customer experience lifecycle.

Clearly this definition shows that the focus should not be only on technology, but also on new business models and customer experience.

What Are the Different Domains of Digital Transformation?

After clarifying what do we mean by Digital Transformation, the next step is to think where this transformation should take place in the organization. This is a key question as many organizations still see the Digital Transformation as an IT initiative. This is very wrong and leads to long term disappointments. Note that the Digital Transformation must be embraced by the whole organization.

According to Rogers (2016) there are five key domains: customers, competition, data, innovation, and value (Figure 2).

Figure 2. Digital Transformation Domains

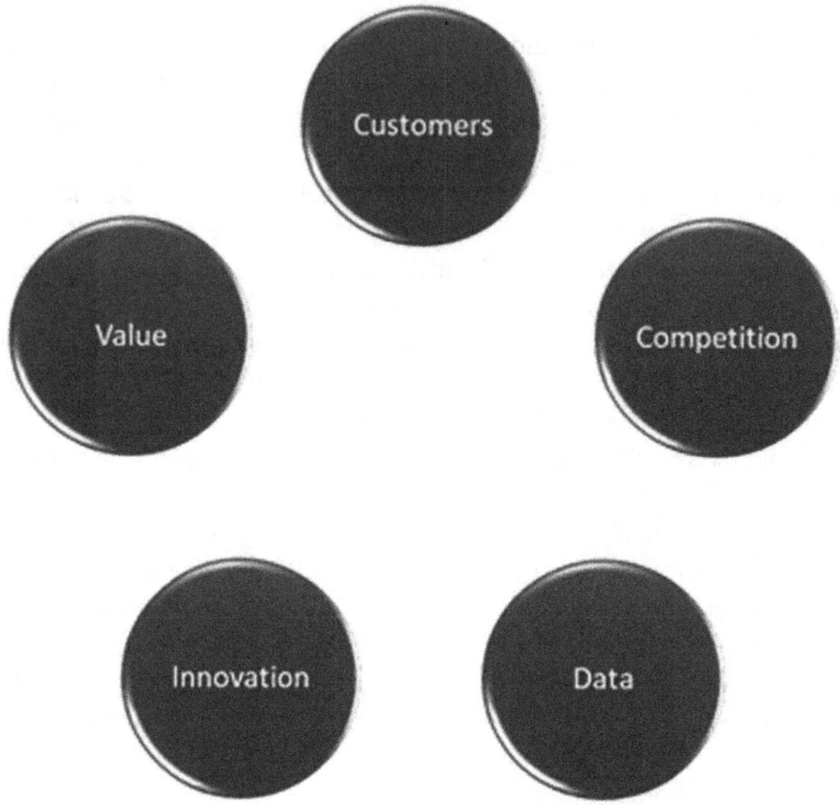

Customers

This is the first domain of Digital Transformation. And by customers we mean literally every single person or organization that is paying in any form for the services or products that the organization delivers. Traditionally most organizations are trying to achieve an economy of scale. This means simply that if you produce more or serve many customers in the same time your costs will be spread over this big demand and thus more profit will be achieved. Following this target the organization will try to specialize more and more in the domain where its services are applicable and try to become a leader in the segment. Now with the rise of digitalization it is becoming easier for an organization to not win more customers in its own domain but "steal" some from competitors which are active in other domains.

Another major point to consider here is that we are now interacting with or customers over many channels: phone, email, online platforms, social media etc. Not only that but the customers are also interacting with each other. There are numerous online platforms where users can exchange wisdom with each other without going to the official support channels provided by the vendor. This is key to understood and acted upon, because reputation can be easily damaged, if a customer request is not acted on and it goes viral over a social media.

All these omnichannel interactions with customers lead to a change in how business deliver their marketing initiatives. It also brings new possibilities on the table. Customers are now not only consumers but can also act as advocates, support or even salespersons. The goal of the digital transformation should be to nourish this behavior and if possible, even add more to it.

Competition

The next domain in digital transformation is about competition. Here the main point is how organizations understand and act against competitive entities. Back in the days everyone who is producing the same goods or delivering the same services was seen as a direct competition. On another hand the cooperation was done only with vendors who produce goods which were needed for the organization's products and services.

This classic situation has changed dramatically in the last decade. Now as mentioned above there are competitors which are outside the organization's domain. Not only that but often when an application is built upon a cloud platform and its business starts to thrive, the platform vendor copies the idea and becomes a direct competitive. Thus the relationship quickly changes from partnership to competition.

On another hand customers are expecting more and more regarding features, outcomes, support channels and delivery methods so sometimes even competitors make partnerships to respond to certain complex customer requirements.

There is an interesting example – drop shipping. This model is built upon the idea that online shops do not have the items they sell on stock. When a customer makes an order, the seller contacts the vendor who has the item on stock, and it gets shipped directly or via the seller to the customer. The cooperation starts when a vendor who has items on stock becomes also a reseller of other vendors. Though they are sometimes in direct competition each of these vendors is happy to share profit if there is a sell. The idea here is that it is a lot easier for the customer to shop from one place then from couple different ones.

Data

When we speak about Digital Transformation there is no way we can skip Data. It is the underlying force that drives everything we do. Based on the data we get information. This simple fact is often forgotten, but key for each organization. Information has to be produced by working on raw data, it has to be managed and guarded and, in the end, it must be used. Information that is not used is a waste of resources.

Traditionally data was generated on a pull basis. It was gathered from internal processes and was used mostly for evaluating, forecasting and decision making. Today data is generated on a push basis. We are literally swimming in data and this has become one of the major challenges of our generation. This data is not coming solely from internal sources, but from every conversation in a social media or support platform, from every customer interaction which can be phone call, online feedback forms etc and also from a universe of devices which can be professional or home appliances. The IoT has brough up an unprecedented amount of data points for each vendor out there. Following the trend, it is not a surprise that the applications related to Big Data have become a mandatory tool for each organization. Those applications help to make predictions or identify patterns in business activity by corelating multiple sources of data which was previously impossible.

Data has become vital part of every organization. It has even become a tradable asset. Many organizations now gather and sell data which can be used for achieving business goals.

Innovation

As written already each transformation is about making a significant and noticeable change. To achieve this usually an innovation of some kind will be needed. Thus, the fourth domain of Digital Transformation is Innovation.

Innovation is the process of gathering ideas, evaluating them against organization's vision, mission and objectives and finally brough to the customers in the form of products and services. The major cost point in those initiatives was testing. Making a pilot or a dummy model was a significant investment, so in the end decisions were made based on a "educated guess" over some scarce data. There were cases where the cost of failure led to closing the whole business, so in some companies this was a bad word.

Today innovation is the fuel that drives every Start-up forward. We live in times where fail fast and learn is a moto for many organizations. This is because building pilots and testing has become a lot easier and less expensive. Minimum valuable prototypes are now released on fast pace even to live environments and customers are paying to use them even though they are far away from the final version. Once assumptions can be verified and tested with real customers the risk of failure is minimized. Thus, the organizations appetite for innovation is growing and customers can enjoy more and more features to their products or services. The fear of failure is now gone.

Value

In the end each Digital Transformation should be about the value the organization provides to its customers. The last domain is about Value, the value proposition that each organization has.

Traditionally the value an organization is offering is closely related to the industry it is part of. If you hear a big car manufacturing company name the first association will be that if offers vehicles which help its customers obtain value via transportation of themselves or goods. To succeed in a such a competitive market the car manufacturers need to have a clear value proposition, some clear differentiator like price or safety and put extra efforts to deliver this value with each new model.

In the last decades the car manufactures have invested a lot in new value propositions. They are now becoming lifestyle suppliers, which can sell you not only cars, but clothes, shoes, perfumes etc. Brands are now focusing now so much on the cars themselves but on the connectivity, it can provide, the time it can save by driving itself on the high-way and many more.

Markets change, customer needs as well. There is a saying by Heraclitus which states: "The only Constant in Life is Change". Therefore, the drive for improving value should never stop, because if it does then this will lead to competition taking over customers from the organization. Digital technology should be a key tool in the Innovation toolbox.

Six Stages of Digital Transformation

When we think about where we are in the journey of Digital Transformation it would be great if there was a benchmark or a scale that we can easily measure our progress against. Well, there isn't such a thing, but in this chapter we will provide some guidance based on six stages approach proposed by a consulting company called Altimeter and modified a bit by a one of the biggest online technology platforms TechRepublic. (Altimeter, 2016; Forrest, 2016)

Figure 3. Digital Transformation Stages

As depicted on Figure 3. the first level is Business as Usual, then the organization will move though Present and Active, Formalized, Strategic, Converged and finish on the highest level Innovative and Adaptive.

Business as Usual

There are organizations that are just fine with where they are in their digital journey. For them taking risks should be set to minimum, thus their innovation potential is close to zero. For them Digital Transformation is something that they plan to do, but in the future. They are focused on their delivery and not on their customers. This stage is called "Business as usual".

On individual level the employees of those organizations are afraid to take risks and propose innovations. They don't get support from the organization for their self-development, so they must do it on their own. The teams are also usually working in silos and with different goals. This is a major roadblock for any Digital Transformation initiatives.

Major point to consider is that cross functional teams and cross collaboration are a must for the success of each modern organization, so the senior management should take actions in advance.

Present and Active

The second stage "Present and active" is for organizations which are not so adherent to risk, but are ready to test new technologies and make organizational changes as needed. Those organizations are willing to try "new things", by starting pilot projects or programs. Success is visible to some extent, but often there are still organizational silos and results are treated as local and not global.

At this stage the organizations start to also an outside-in approach as well. They start to think about their customers and their needs. Social media platforms and other digital ways of collecting feedback will be used to channel this information. A major step in the skills improvement initiatives will be taken as well so that the skills match the level of the newly acquired technologies. Those initiatives will lead to a creation of a pool of early adopters or pioneers, which will then spread the word and help rest of the organization.

Formalized

When the early adopters are allowed to work for some time a momentum can be gained, and the success can be sustained. As this stage which is called "Formalized" the organizations will not see the Digital Transformation efforts as some random exotic events but as a normal part of daily life. The level of maturity will rise and there will enough documentation and training available for each new employee that joins the organization. On top data will be collected and analyzed so that the results are also formalized.

Most of this data will be related to customers. This will lead to discussion of the digital customer experience as well. Clearly if an organization is making a Digital Transformation and the channels by which it interacts are changing along to digital, then the customer's experience will be mostly digital.

At this stage the Digital Transformation must become an official strategic goal. It must be confirmed by senior management and if needed the vision and mission statements have to be adjusted.

Strategic

At this next stage after the senior management has made it official, the Digital Transformation has reached most of the departments and teams. They are aware of the initiatives and the reasons behind them. There are new roles which are being staffed: Chief Digital Officer (CDO) and Chief Customer Officer (CCO). Those roles will advocate in the board meetings the new digital culture.

All the data gathering, and analysis is now at its best. Data is not gathered meaningless but with clear objectives which follow the vision of the senior management. Key achievement is that there are roadmaps for technology and digital transformation initiatives which allow the whole organization to plan accordingly. At this stage called "Strategic" the digital initiatives are also being evaluated properly so that each one has a ROI, that can be later accounted for.

Converged

In stage five, the companies previously separate efforts converge into a more streamlined approach to digital transformation. Analytics begin to improve and streamline operations, and the efforts made to improve the customer experience begin to improve the back-office as well. Change agents often become formal leaders at this point and executive leadership takes a vital role in supporting an agenda for transformation. A governing body is often established to oversee transformation as well.

At this stage which is called "Converged" the organizations have a streamlined approach to digital transformation. Will all the data being analyzed and the customer experience being captured the whole organization is changing as well. As noted many times before Digital Transformation means not only new technology but a significant change in how we deliver services.

This is the moment where the IT department within the organization will need to absolutely align to the overall strategy and thus form a partnership with all the business departments. All employees are now educated from day one on the digital strategy of the organization. This education is not one time but a continuous effort. Again, major focus will be held on the customer experience, which at this stage should be mostly if not 100% digital.

Innovative and Adaptive

This stage is not the last one. At this last step the Digital Transformation should be a well-known topic and all related to it activities formalized, and employees educated. The customer experience will be at its best due to a constant data gathering and feedback loops. The roles and responsibilities will be set, but if needed new positions will be opened to add new ideas or expand in new topics.

What Are the Different Levels of Digital Transformation?

Digitalization is a word that is used on many occasions and with different context within each organization. One can use it to denote an exchange of a paper form that is used for quality assurance with an application that can do the same. Another organization can use the same term for changing how a whole business line operates. Clearly the level of change in those two examples is different, but the same word is used to describe it. In the next lines the different levels of Digital Transformation will be explained, so that a common perception can be gained.

Digitization

The first level of Digital Transformation is Digitization. Gobble (2018) provides a short explanation about the term "Digitization is the straightforward process of converting analog information to digital – turning pages into bytes, for instance, by scanning a document or uploading a sound recording.". Figure 4. shows this classical digitization scenario: paper to digital.

This term can be used when a part or a step in a process can be changed to a digital format. Many organizations will put such banners on their pages. "We have removed paper; we are now signing electronically our documents". It often the case that this removal is valid only for a single document and the whole process related to it stays as non-digital or analog as before. Such actions can be part of a bigger Digital Transformation, but their scope is limited and their value for the organization or the clients is quickly absorbed.

Figure 4. Digitization

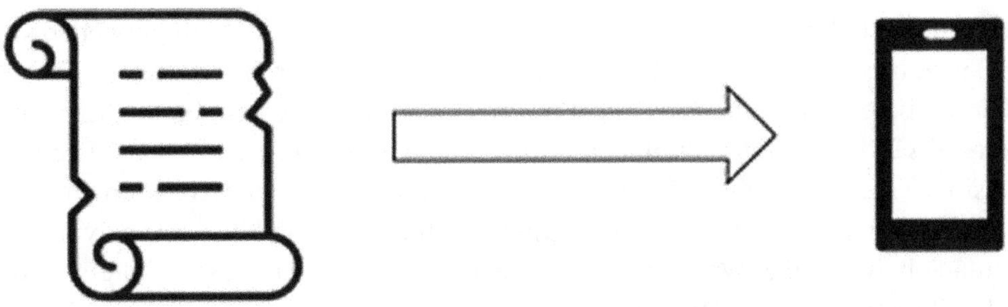

There are pitfalls which need to be addressed here as well. When a small change is done, the effect can be seen quickly, which in long run raises the organization appetite for more and more such small changes. The risk here is that the more the small changes are the bigger the risk of failure. When the failures become more and more the organization and the employees can reach a level, called Change Fatigue or just being tired of all those daily changes.

There is also one more perspective here – Value. In the end all changes must contribute to sustaining the current value proposition or improving it. When you make a series of small changes their contribution to the overall value can be hard to be understood and measured. Often by improving one step of a process the other steps are becoming worse than before, which leads to an overall negative result. In a big organization the processes and the steps within them are interconnected, so if a certain step is modified then maybe another process will be affected, again if not done properly the overall result can be negative.

Figure 5. Process Digitalization

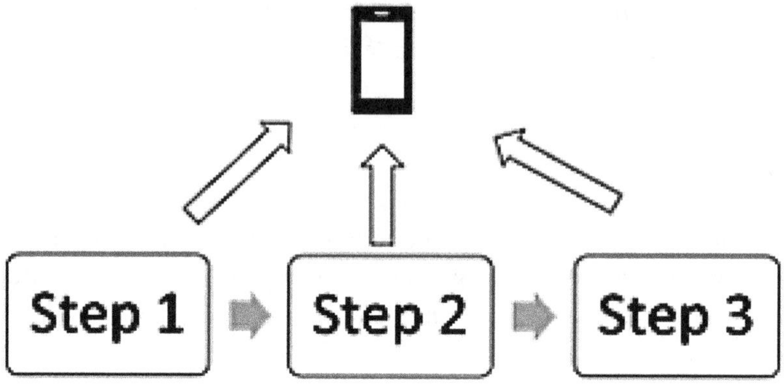

Process Digitalization

The next level of Digital Transformation is Process Digitalization. This term is used when a process from input to output is to be done a new digital way as depicted on Figure 5. To get to this point the process will need first to be analyzed, issues will need to be fixed, and all the steps will need to have a clear description which includes who, what, where. The whole exercise will need to be done as efficient as possible. When working on the process the integrations with other processes must be documented and an investigation needs to be done how the new process design will affect them. If needed simulations or prototyping can be used to ensure the changes will not introduce overall negative results.

As main driver here as well, the focus must be on value. It must be sustained or improved. Here it is key that the organization's Vision is used to guide the whole initiative. Each Process Digitalization must follow the Vision. This is the biggest difference between the Process Digitalization and Digitization as the latter is focused on a single step and the mapping to the Vision will be extremely hard.

The difference between the two levels can be seen of course easily also by the way the initiatives are delivered. When the scope is lower the level of documentation and testing will be lower as well. Key point to be considered here is that each process must have an owner. This owner will need to play a major role in the process digitalization. Sadly some times the processes are known only to the people that deliver them, which makes the whole initiative hard to be finalized.

Digital Transformation

The goal of the Digital Transformation is to improve the organization. As such this is the ultimate level, where the change should affect all layers from top to bottom. Not only this but the clients will need to be considered as well. After all they will be the ones who are going to be most affected by the transformation.

As stated above each transformation should have a clear Vision statement. This statement must be drafted by the most senior levels of the organization and communicated to everyone both internally and externally. By external stakeholders here it is meant but not limited to the clients of the organization, vendors, partners, regulatory institutions etc. Once this is done the Vision must be turned into Goals and Objectives. This exercise is very important because it can lead to a roadmap where all current and future activities can be planned. The reporting of progress will also be done on this base.

Figure 6. People, Processes and Technology

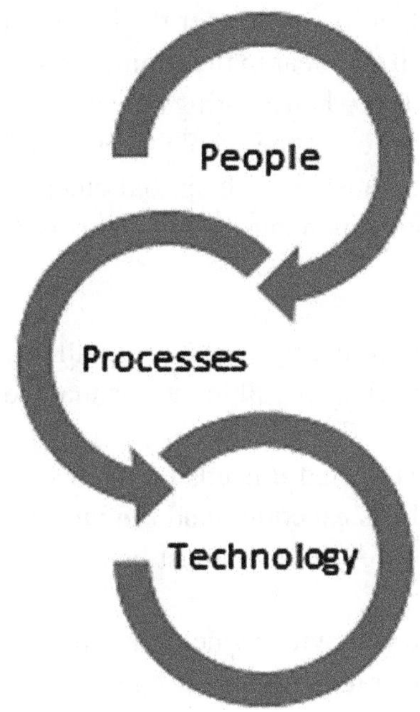

As depicted on Figure 6. for a true transformation to succeed there are three key focus areas:

- People – Each transformation is about change and not only the technology needs to change, but also the employees. Most importantly the culture of the organization needs to change, because if it stays the same then the whole work might be for nothing. In short when doing a Digital Transformation change in Culture is a must.

The 8-Step Process for Leading Change developed by Kotter (2012) is proving an approach that can help:

1. Create a sense of urgency.
2. Build a guiding coalition.
3. Form a strategic vision and initiatives.
4. Enlist a volunteer army.
5. Enable action by removing barriers.
6. Generate short-term wins.
7. Sustain acceleration.

8. Institute change.

This process urges the organization to explain as good as possible to each employee why the current situation is so bad or why the new state after the transformation will be better. This will create a desire in the organization for a change and not fear. It is common that when a new change is announced people's first reaction is fear. This needs to be expected and managed. So to be successful a group of supporters needs to be gathered and they must be active part of the transformation. Remember that a transformation is a big initiative, so the more people join a supporter the better. To unite the people even more and to convert to positive the ones which still not clear in their minds, a strong Vision statement will be needed. This statement can serve as guiding light when creating the goals and the objectives. Senior management will need to be there for the people thru out the whole transition. Town-howl meetings or one to ones can be used to allow for questions and answers. The initial quick wins must be communicated as much as possible and used to create a positive momentum. Once this is done it needs to be sustained until the transformation is undergoing.

- Processes – From input to output and by considering all interfaces with other processes. There should be efficiency gains as much as possible: no manual work or no manual checks.

When a Digital Transformation is started it needs to be checked what is the level of process documentation. The details about procedures execution and the interfaces with between the processes must be clear to everyone involved. All process owners must be taken on board so that all dependencies are pointed out as early as possible.

As mentioned above one of the key activities when digitalizing a process is to update the documentation. All the details about steps, diagrams, procedures and working instructions must be checked and updated. Also, a must is to check about interfaces to other processes within the organization. This task is often forgotten or done in a hurry which leads to major issues in the long run.

- Technology –. When most people think about Digital Transformation they think about technology. The technology is everywhere around us and it supports organizations and people in all kinds of activities. There are onsite solutions, cloud solutions, open source, and many more other options to choose from.

Figure 7. Digital Transformation Overview

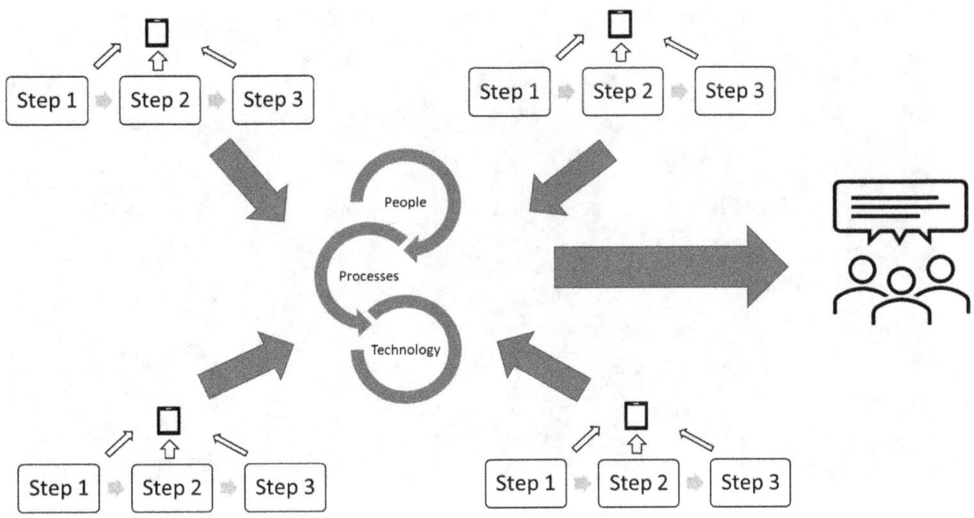

Figure 7. tries to depict the complexity of the Digital Transformation on the organization level. In each moment in time there will be many Digitization activities on step-by-step level. On parallel there will be Process Digitalization efforts within different parts of the organization. In the heart of this whole model there will be the mixture of People, Processes and Technology which will glue the whole Digital Transformation efforts together.

Application Portfolio Analysis (APA) is a great tool that can be used to cover the application assessment part of a Digital Transformation. The approach looks like this:

- List all applications:
  - Define sub-criterias (min 3) to measure the Business Value of each application.
  - Define sub-criteria (min 3) to measure the IT Value of each application.
  - Calculate the Operational Cost (the total spent on a yearly base) of each application.

The Gardner TIME method is great way to finalize this application analysis:

T – Tolerate. Those are applications that provide high Technical Value but moderate Business Value.
I – Invest. High on both. Those are applications that the company needs to invest in.
M – Migrate. Those are applications that have high business value but have issues the with the technology side of them, like data or platform used.
E – Eliminate. Those are applications that no longer provide business value and are technically performing very bad.

Figure 8. Gardner TIME Analysis

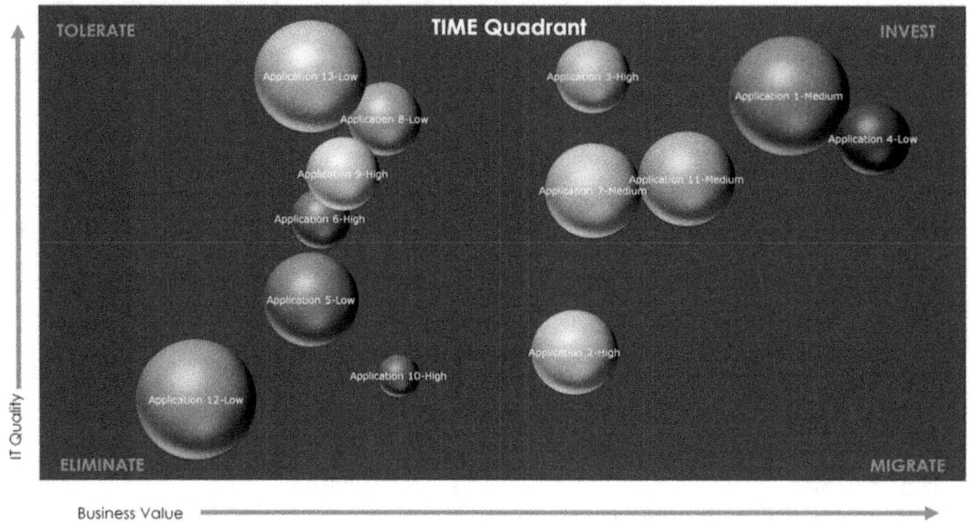

On Figure 8. is shows an example of Gardner TIME application analysis done over 12 applications. As an additional information each application Risk level can be added. Here in this example there are 3 levels: High, Medium and Low. Also the size of the bubbles shows the Operational cost levels. For the example the levels were 9. Application 12 is a clear candidate for elimination as it provides both low Business Value and low IT Quality. On top it has high level of operational cost and is not critical for the business (low Risk level). Application 2 for example is a good candidate for migration. The Business Value is there but the IT Quality is low. If possible a new technology should be introduced to increase the IT Quality level.

Lead the Digital Transformation

Organizations that excel in the Digital Transformation initiatives have two critical capabilities says Westerman (2014) in Leading Digital:

- Digital Capabilities – Being able to master any technology. Have skills and capacity to spend time on learning and implementing this technology in the organization
- Leadership Capabilities – Being able to lead a significant organizational change which includes but is not limited to use of new technology

Those organizations see new technologies as an opportunity to change the way they do business. They are not afraid of those technologies but on opposite they embrace them and use them to their advantage. Still, they never forget that Digital Transformation is not only about technology, so they invest and focus a lot in the employees. After all a tool is as good as the hand that uses it.

Commitment to Leadership must be shown. Everyone in the organization must understand that this is not just a PR statement, but a true strategic goal. The senior management has to steer the Digital Transformation top-down. They have to set direction, build a momentum and ensure the middle level management is following their direction. Still the middle level management should be allowed for some freedom in actions. This will take off some burden off the senior management and provide opportunities for new leaders to emerge.

Key point to stress on is Vision. Having common goals among employees on all levels is only possible when the organization's vision is communicated properly. Vision must be built step by step. After the message is sent to the organization real actions must follow. Best is if there a quick wins, projects that can show to everyone that leadership is committed to the Digital Transformation. Vision statements must be bold, but not a total miracle. If an organization has never provided a certain service or a product, reaching first place among competitors can take more than couple of months.

To lead properly the Digital Transformation is also strongly advised to create new roles within the organization. This was touched before in the chapter. Accountability is key factor for success. There is a saying that shared responsibility is no ones accountability. By having dedicated people for certain activities, the organization will ensure that quality will improve over time. Following the best practice, we know that for a process or a task to have the right level of quality someone needs to account for it.

Also remember that in the modern world of digitalization you must lead and not follow.

Embed the Digital Transformation

After the level of understanding about the different aspects of Digital Transformation is there, the next step is to make it more permanent or to embed it in the organization's culture.
Here are some possible actions to perform:

A. Define the Overall Business Strategy for at Least Two Years Ahead

- What are all the services that are being offered (portfolio of services)?
- What are the target customers?
- What is the technology architecture now and in the near future?
- Which areas need improvement?

B. Identify a Core Team of Supporters That Will Lead or Be Part of the Transformation All the Way

- Use outside consultants only if needed
- Outside leadership help might be used in the beginning but later on should be avoided if possible
- Train the core team as the work on the transformation progresses.

C. Form a Customer Community Around Key Clients That Can Be Trusted

- Use the community to quickly get feedback, by creating feedback loops
- Use the community to identify beta testers which can be used in the long run

D. Educate All Employees as Much as Possible and Provide Them Ongoing Support When Needed

- Don't forget that people fear the unknown, so employees must receive trainings and documentation
- If there will be people that will be left without work, they can receive trainings and be grow into other roles within the organization

E. The Digital Transformaiton Must Have a Company Wide Process Set Up to Manage and Direct the Activities

- In the end like or not the Digital Transformation activities must never stop, so a governing body and a process related to it will be needed.

F. Embrace Agility as Mindset and a Cultural Shift

- Agile mindset and agility in actions will be needed in every part of the organization.
- Everyone must be able to understand and articulate the value of iteration and increments.

To embed the Digital Transformation and not see it as a one-time off initiative, the transformation needs to happen on all levels. All teams should be involved, and everyone will need to participate as much as possible.

Change in the culture is a corner stone in such a transition. This change needs to be planned and managed, so that there are no surprises. Fear is a normal reaction to change, so no one should be blamed about it. If people overcome their fear they will be highly motivated to support the transformation. This motivation needs to be cultivated and sustained as the changes will become part of the organization's daily life.

CONCLUSION

This chapter has set a goal to demystify the term Digital Transformation, as there are many interpretations about its nature, goals, and applicable domains. To do so in the beginning the chapter revealed several key terms about Digital Transformation and one key fact: each transformation must lead to value as perceived by the client. The difference between Transformation and Transition plus also the difference between Business and IT Transformation was covered afterwards as well to conclude the Background section.

The main focus of the chapter started with one key question: Why do we need Digital Transformation? This question was answered with a graphical representation of how the technology changes over time and how the organizations. This visualization made it clear that there is a big difference between both and to fill it up each organization must embrace the Digital Transformation.

Once the path forward has been chosen it was shown in the chapter that there are five key domains which have to be covered - customers, competition, data, innovation, and value. After the applicable domains the chapter has introduced the six stages of Digital Transformation: Business as usual, Present and Active, Formalized, Strategic, Converged and Innovative and adaptive. Those stages are very important so that every organization can find its current position and proceed forward from there.

Key topic that was covered in the chapter was the difference between Digitization, Process Digitalization and Digital Transformation. Many organizations claim there are undergoing Digital Transformation, but do they really understand what this means? It was shown that often mere Digitization is considered as Digital Transformation and not only this but there are many pitfalls to watch for.

Finally, in the end of the chapter details were provided on how to lead and embed the Digital Transformation in the organization. Not only this, but also the Gardner TIME approach was included so that practical analysis can be made and actions taken.

REFERENCES

Altimeter. (2016). *The Six Stages of Digital Transformation.* https://www.prophet.com/2016/04/the-six-stages-of-digital-transformation/

Forrest, C. (2016). *Altimeter report outlines 6 stages necessary for digital transformation in business.* https://www.techrepublic.com/article/altimeter-report-outlines-6-stages-necessary-for-digital-transformation-in-business/

Gobble, M. (2018). Digitalization, Digitization, and Innovation. *Research Technology Management, 61*(4), 56–59. doi:10.1080/08956308.2018.1471280

ITIL4. (2022). *ITIL 4: the framework for the management of IT-enabled services.* https://www.axelos.com/certifications/itil-service-management

Kotter, J. (2012). Leading Change. *Harvard Business Review.*

McKeown, I., & Philip, G. (2003). Business transformation, information technology and competitive strategies: Learning to fly. *International Journal of Information Management, 23*(1), 3–24. doi:10.1016/S0268-4012(02)00065-8

Perkin, N., & Abraham, P. (2017). *Building the Agile Business through Digital Transformation.* Kogan Page.

Ritchie, R. (2019). *Maersk: Springing back from a catastrophic cyber-attack.* I-CIO.com

Rogers, D. (2016). *The Digital Transformation Playbook: Rethink Your Business for the Digital Age.* Columbia Business School Publishing. doi:10.7312/roge17544

Sabri, E. (2019). *Technology Optimization and Change Management for Successful Digital Supply Chains.* IGI Global

Westerman, G. (2014). Leading Digital: Turning Technology into Business Transformation. *Harvard Business Review.*

ADDITIONAL READING

Herbert, L. (2017). *Digital Transformation: Build Your Organization's Future for the Innovation Age*. Bloomsburry Business.

Raskino, M. (2015). *Digital to the Core: Remastering Leadership for Your Industry, Your Enterprise, and Yourself*. Taylor & Francis.

Siebel, T. (2019). *Digital Transformation: Survive the Thrive of an Era of Mass Extinction*. RosettaBooks.

KEY TERMS AND DEFINITIONS

Digital: The day-to-day and a cultural change implied by technology.

Digital Transformation: Significant technology and organizational change of state which is supplemented by latest technology achievements and digital savvy leadership.

Digitization: The exchange of non-digital items with their digital analogues.

Transformation: This is the movement from one defined state to another by making significant improvement in the value delivery. Focus is to provide more value to clients by improving the organization.

Transition: This is the movement from one defined state to another without making any significant improvement of the value delivered to clients. Focus is mostly on efficiency and effectiveness gains.

Value: The perceived improvement in one's life or work efforts due to a service consumption.

Vision: A clearly defined point in the future of the organization that is both achievable and desirable.

Chapter 2
Digital Transformation and Co-Creation of Value:
The Role of Digital Agility

N. Meltem Çakıcı
Beykent University, Turkey

ABSTRACT

The rise of tech-savvy consumers and their new demands pushes firms to transform their business strategies in order to respond to this changing consumer market. Digital transformation, in this regard, enhances the customer experience and satisfies digitally powered consumers by the integration of digital technology into all areas of a business that alters how a firm operates and delivers value to customers. Creation of value is replaced with co-creation that includes consumers as well as companies in the value creation process. Together with the emergence of digitalization, value creation is influenced again in terms of the uses of the digital tools by its participants. The first objective of this chapter is to give detailed information about the co-creation of value concept by explaining the drivers and the outcomes as well as the disadvantages and the benefits offered to consumers and to companies. The second objective is to examine the impact of digital transformation on the value co-creation process and to pay attention to the role of digital agility in this context.

INTRODUCTION

Consumers today can choose among many products and services that are offered by companies. They are also more powerful than before thanks to the existence of multiple technological tools for getting and sharing information with others easily. Shortly, it has become more difficult to satisfy customers during their purchase journeys. Previous studies include several factors that influence and are related to customer satisfaction such as customer loyalty (Donio' et al., 2006), cross-national determinants (Morgeson et al., 2011), business-to-business (Molinari et al., 2008), and online purchasing behavior (Tzeng et al., 2021).

One of the factors that plays a key role in understanding customer satisfaction and purchase intentions is customers' perceptions of value. Sweeney and Soutar (2001) proposed a four dimensional PERVAL

DOI: 10.4018/978-1-7998-9179-6.ch002

scale that includes emotional, social, quality, and price elements. The fact that value can be seen from various perspectives results in a group of studies examining perceived value together with satisfaction and loyalty (Flint et al., 2011) while others including perceived risk (Agarwal & Teas, 2001), perceived product value (Snoj et al., 2004), switching costs (Yang & Peterson, 2004) and other related variables for the analysis of perceived value.

However, most of the previous research about value considers customers as inactive actors who only play the role of perceiving value during their purchase activities though customers can also participate in the creation of value (Vargo & Lusch, 2008). Service-dominant (S-D) logic (Vargo & Lusch, 2004), in this regard, triggers the need for a radical change in the marketing strategy perspective by considering customers as the co-creators of value (Lusch & Vargo, 2006; Vargo & Lusch, 2004) since value is created not only by the company but also by the actions of the customers. This process is called as "value co-creation" and is defined as the joint creation of value by the company and the customer (Prahalad & Ramaswamy, 2004). Value co-creation is also explained as a process that includes consumers who have active roles and create value together with companies across one or more stages of production and consumption (Sugathan et al., 2017; Ranjan & Read, 2016). It is also defined as the collective activities of the directly interacting participants that aim to create value for each party (Grönroos, 2012). This means that the customer is an active player instead of a passive audience (Payne et al. 2009; Prahalad & Ramaswamy, 2000) and that the customer's role in the marketing process is redefined (Xie et al., 2008). It is also argued that value co-creation is not optional since value is always co-created (Vargo & Akaka, 2009).

Within today's competitive market conditions, consumers' dynamic roles as co-creators of value can be realized and monitored if firms acquire and use real-time data about consumers provided by the latest digital tools (Chawla & Goyal, 2021). Traditional ways of offering products and communicating with consumers can not be satisfactory for the digitally-powered dynamic consumers since they expect their actions to be seen instantly. In other words, co-creation of value requires companies to revise their business models in numerous ways such as digitalization of personalised offerings to consumers (Nambisan et al., 2017) and use of intelligent operating systems (Choudhury et al., 2021).

Digital transformation, in this respect, refers to the use of digital technologies in order to enhance customer experience by transforming company-wide business practices and operations (Vial, 2019). It has gained increased importance among scholars shown by a substantial growth of literature in multiple research domains such as new business models (Choudhury et al., 2021), strategic leadership (Tumbas et al., 2018), and firms' innovative activities (Mishra et al., 2018; Muhuri et al., 2019). It is argued that digital transformation requires firms not only to explore new digital technologies but also to make necessary changes in their organizations (Steiber et al., 2020). This means that digital transformation includes the use of digital innovations that are shaped by both organizational and technological innovations (Hinings et al., 2018).

This chapter focuses on the dynamics of value co-creation and presents the consumer- and firm-specific elements that are related to the creation of value. How value co-creation benefits consumers and companies will be discussed. Besides, management of value co-creation by firms will be explained with a concentration on the roles of newly proposed business models. Finally, the emergence and the uses of multiple digital channels during consumers' purchase journeys and the way companies respond to this changing buying environment will be examined by defining and explaining digital transformation and digital agility.

BACKGROUND

Value co-creation literature includes several topics such as customer loyalty (Cossío-Silva et al., 2016), new product development (Bonner, 2010), customer-firm interactions (Grönroos & Voima, 2013), customers' initiation efforts for value co-creation (Chen et al., 2018), the factors that motivate customers to be co-creators (Ranjan & Read, 2019), value co-creation process (Prahalad & Ramaswamy, 2004), how co-creation of value benefits firms (Alves et al., 2016), and many other concepts within the marketing field. The involvement of many different concepts in order to explain value co-creation process already shows its multidimensional nature. The inclusion of customers in the value creation process is no more a choice but a necessity within today's competitive market conditions since customers want their voices to be heard and actions to be taken into account seriously.

An important concept that is also influenced by value co-creation and examined by scholars is customer value proposition (CVP hereafter). CVP is defined as a firm's strategic tool that is used to communicate its ability to offer superior value to customers (Payne et al., 2017). Scholars have been suggesting diverse approaches to CVPs (Rintamäki & Saarijärvi, 2021) since they argue that value propositions decided by firms should be replaced with mutually determined propositions due to tough competition and changing market dynamics (Payne et al., 2017).

Co-creation of value is also studied within the context of brands. Merz et al. (2018) develop Customer Co-creation Value scale with a focus on brand value. How customers can contribute to a company's efforts for brand value creation is examined. The multidimensional nature of their scale including various customer-specific features such as knowledge, commitment, and skills demonstrates the difficulty of measuring customers' participation in the value co-creation process.

The multifaceted characteristic of value co-creation causes researchers to suggest different conceptual dimensions in order to explain this concept. The difficulty in proposing a widely accepted definition for value co-creation is due to the intertwined roles and actions of customers and companies in the value co-creation process (Vargo & Lusch, 2017). In other words, both customers and companies may have changing roles in creating value during the production and the consumption of products/services. Consideration of this complex nature of value co-creation in the previous studies results in a focus on mainly two dimensions: co-production and value-in use (Ranjan & Read, 2016; Xie et al. 2008).

Co-Production and Value-In-Use

Co-production, which is defined as the customer's participation in the performance of the various activities that take place in one or more of the steps of the production process (Etgar, 2008; Lusch & Vargo, 2006), has been an important topic of discussion in the marketing field (Prahalad & Ramaswamy, 2004; Vargo & Lusch, 2004). Its dynamic characteristic, as proposed by Etgar (2008), requires research on co-production to take into account multiple variables as either the antecedents or the outcomes of it. For example, all customers may not want to engage in co-production because of lack of time or skills needed to perform a task. Customer's motivation to join co-production activites is also affected by the product category. These examples show that specific preconditions should be met in order to observe customers as active participants in the production process. Co-production is also examined in terms of the changing roles of customers during the traditional consumer journey. Conceptualized as the "consumer production journey" (Dellaert, B.G.C, 2019), consumers become active by co-designing new products, selling products through online platforms, co-producing experiences for other consumers, and evaluating their consumption experiences via technological tools.

On the other hand, value co-creation includes not only co-production but also value-in-use since value extends beyond co-production and exists through the process of consumption (Grönroos, 2006). This means that consumers' active roles as co-creators of value starts with production and continues during their experiences (Sugathan et al., 2017). The physical, affective, and cognitive dimensions that form customer experience influence how value is created and the multidimensional characteristic of experience results in different outcomes of value creation (Lemon & Verhoef, 2016). The consideration that value is created during consumption as well- instead of assuming it only as being embedded in a product or a service- creates increased emphasis on consumers' roles as value creators. This also means that companies can collaborate with and learn from customers rather than considering them as passive individuals who are waiting their needs to be satisfied by the firms (Vargo & Lusch, 2004).

Benefits and Disadvantages of Value Co-creation

As the emerging value co-creation paradigm suggests, companies are not the only actors in the creation of value and consumers play important roles through their interactions with other consumers, firms, and brands. During these interactions, consumers can act as beneficiaries by co-creating value for themselves. At this point, consumers' level of participation in the value co-creation process depends very much on how they perceive the tangible and the intangible benefits that can be gained by their value co-creation efforts (Roberts et al., 2014). For example, consumers perceive products that they design as unique which in turn creates an intangible benefit- in addition to the tangible benefit provided by the functional value of the product- since their need for uniqueness is satisfied (Snyder, C.R., 1992). Co-creation of value benefits consumers since value is created not only by firms but also by consumers' active participation in the value creation process. Consumers know that their value creation activities during production help in creating the products and services that will satisfy their needs. Consumers also evaluate value during their consumptions of products and services which means that they continue to be co-creators of value during their experiences.

Co-creation of value also provides advantages to firms in many ways. Value co-creation is an important determinant of attitudinal loyalty which refers to personal attitudes and emotions towards products. Consumers' perceptions of brands are influenced positively and their brand experiences are enhanced (Payne et al., 2009). If a firm plans market development as a growth strategy, co-creation leads to increased brand awareness in the new markets. Co-creation is also a source of knowledge for firms during new product or service development (Kozinets et al., 2008). During the value co-creation process, companies can learn from consumers which in turn provides them to come up with innovative ideas.

However, value co-creation may also create problems to consumers and to firms. For example, consumers' suggestions for a product may be impractical or not applicable. This may create tension since consumers may think that their opinions are not valuable and the feeling after being rejected will act as a barrier for their continuous participation in the creation of value afterwards. Another issue is consumers' tendencies to suggest familiar products and solutions instead of coming up with innovative ideas. Therefore, dependence on consumers' suggestions may limit firms to offer attractive and competitive products. One other risk is the possibility that consumers may demand exclusive rights to the created product or service offering (Gassmann et al., 2010). These possible negative outcomes of value co-creation are the signals that warn managers for carefully analyzing the expected gains and losses so that the results are satisfactory in terms of the tangible and the intangible assets of the company.

Value Co-creation Management and Digital Transformation

The explanations so far show that most of the previous research on value co-creation process examines how value co-creation emerges, consumer- and company-related factors that influence the value co-creation process and how co-creation of value benefits and challenges consumers and companies (Anker et al., 2015; Heinonen et al., 2010; Xie et al., 2008). However, understanding how firms can manage the dynamic value co-creation process is also very important since quality should be the major concern not only for the product or service offered but also for the co-creation experience shared by the customer and the company. Due to its complex nature that demands newly added relationships and roles, value co-creation requires firms to develop new business models (Priem et al., 2018).

Prahalad and Ramaswamy (2004), in this respect, proposed the DART model stating that dialogue, access, risk assessment, and transparency can help companies in engaging customers as collaborators effectively. Previous studies, in this regard, analyzed the components of DART in terms of their effects on customer satisfaction (Solakis et al., 2021). Companies can not achieve their goals if they don't take into account the dimensions of DART since value co-creation management requires managers to look from different angles while developing strategies. For example, when a customer becomes active in the value creation process, a company not only benefits from this situation in terms of increased satisfaction and loyalty but also takes a risk since a problem or an unexpected outcome may occur for the customer. Therefore, a company should adopt a multifaceted perspective for value co-creation that considers both the benefits and the risks. Payne et al. (2008) developed a process based conceptual framework for value co-creation management. Their framework includes customer, supplier, and encounter processes, each of them being characterized by different uses of resources and practices to manage activities and relationships. For instance, supplier value-creating processes involves the use of resources to manage relationships with customers and other stakeholders.

On the other hand, value co-creation process has become more difficult for companies due to consumers' many types of interactions among complex array of networks, each of which includes consumers, firms and even objects brought by the entrance of Internet of Things (IoT). Understanding these networks within an increasingly global- and mobile-oriented market demands firms newly developed strategies in order to enhance customer satisfaction (Verhoef et al., 2021). The rise of the Internet and the emergence of the new digital channels created complex customer experiences since customers can interact with firms and other customers through rapidly increasing number of digital touch points (Lemon & Verhoef, 2016). Today, it is almost impossible to have competitive advantage in the dynamic market if a company does not take consumers' active roles- strengthened by lots of digital touch points enabling customers to share and to get information effortlessly- seriously. Therefore, firms are required to transform their businesses digitally in order to acquire the tools to manage complicated customer journeys and to handle the reduced control over them.

Also called as a company-wide change, digital transformation, in this regard, forces firms to revise their strategies in all areas such as human resources, information technology, logistics, service operations, and marketing (Verhoef et al., 2021). During digital transformation, it is crucial to consider not only the required digital resources and the compatible organizational structures but also the customers as co-creators of value (Vargo & Lusch, 2008). It is important to consider the fact that just because a firm implements digital transformation strategy does not guarantee advantages for that company since multiple factors should be considered beforehand in order to succeed.

First of all, the skills and the orientation of the top management, the structure of the organization, and the overall digital transformation strategy of the firm influence the success of digital transformation. Top management should have the knowledge, skills, and vision to make use of newly developed digital technologies. Commitment to traditional ways of doing business and being rigid in terms of accepting latest technologies will be the obstacles during digital transformation. Top management should confirm the reasonable and justifiable proposals of other managers and employees within the organization. At the same time, top management should encourage employees to challenge old ways of working since digital transformation, by nature, requires new ways of doing business. Besides, replacement of the traditional recruitment methods with new ones that demand specific digital skills and education is also crucial since digital transformation requires full participation by all of the employees in the organization.

Secondly, the organizational culture should be compatible with the underlying logic of digital transformation: quick decision making by multiple participants. Mindset of employees should be ready to adopt new digital tools and changing responsibilities within the firm so that they can serve as contributors rather than obstacles during the transformation. Employees at all levels of the organization should understand the need and the meaning of digital transformation. Their motivation and willingness is very important. There are several factors to be considered by the organizations in order to provide this work environment. Firstly, the company should pay attention to its employees' opinions and suggestions instead of relying only on outside consultants. Empowering employees to play key roles during transformation will increase their motivations. Secondly, it is crucial to recognize fears if employees perceive digital transformation as a threat to their jobs (Tabrizi et al., 2019).

Thirdly, companies that are using recent sophisticated technologies such as hybrid clouds, artificial intelligence, augmented reality, Internet of Things, and data analytics achieve success in digital transformation. Revision of the standard operating procedures by the latest technologies and implementation of digital tools to facilitate analysis of complex information are the requirements of digital transformation. Digital transformation as a company strategy is inevitable since companies can handle exponentially growing data only by using technological tools. Customer Data Platforms (CDP), for example, help firms to organize fragmented data from multiple sources by collecting data from all available sources, organizing it, and making it accessible to anyone who needs it (Newman, 2020).

A company can implement a successful digital transformation strategy if the factors mentioned above are taken into account. Another element that plays a key role for a successful digital transformation strategy is digital agility. Adoption of a digital transformation strategy influences the whole company and its ways of doing business. Digital agility, in this respect, helps firms to increase the likelihood of success during this transformation.

Digital Agility

Continuously changing consumer preferences, emergence of new markets, fast technological advances, dynamic business markets and competition have been the challenges for companies. These challenges force organizations to become more efficient and agile in order to survive. Agility is defined as the ability to sense and to respond to business opportunities and unexpected changes in the market (Brown & Bessant, 2003) or as one of the capabilities that can help firms in the development of new business models by continuously sensing and seizing market opportunities (Teece, 2010). As a key business requirement for firms in order to stay competitive and innovative (Teece, et al., 2016), agility pushes firms for a combination of speed, flexibility and dynamic configuration of all available resources.

Previous studies on organizational agility concentrate on the required firm-level capabilities to achieve agility (Eshlaghy et al., 2010; Ren et al., 2009), the role of agility in firms' operations (Gehani, 2010; Sherehiy et al., 2007) and strategies within changing environments (Sambamurthy et al., 2003; Singh & Sharma, 2013). Agility is also examined by its relationship with information technology capabilities and innnovativeness capacities of firms as well as the effect of individual-level factors on the adaptation of agility in an organization (Mikalef & Pateli, 2017).

The emergence of digital transformation requires digital agility that is conceptualized as the ability to quickly and easily revise existing processes by applying and leveraging digital technology tools, processes and softwares. Companies should be digitally agile in order to continuously modify existing digital capabilities (Eggers & Park, 2018). Companies are required to be quick, flexible and innovative so that they can respond to the emergence of new digital technologies, changing consumer needs, and tough competition. Within today's dynamic and unpredictable markets, firms have to rapidly enable, update, change or adapt their business processes. They need dynamic and easy-to-use technological tools so that employees can easily adapt to the transforming business. Thanks to digital agility, firms can quickly develop and test new systems.

During digital transformation, digital agility is an important adaptation tool for the employees of an organization. Digital agility motivates employees to acquire knowledge, skills, and technical know-how to do their jobs effectively under changing working conditions. Digital transformation can give positive outcomes and contribute to value co-creation in terms of increased customer satisfaction and loyalty only if agility is taken into account seriously by a firm. An important element that is a prerequisite for this condition is being characterized as a "learning organization" since it is this learning characteristic that leads an organization to continuously expand employees' agile capability through systematic thinking and sharing information (Lim et al., 2014).

One of the big challenges for organisations in becoming more agile is a widespread fear of failure. However, failure is an essential part of digital transformation and agility since agility itself means trying something new and evaluating whether the desired results are achieved. Companies that are using their resources for innovativeness and trying to find new solutions for their customers already accept a certain level of risk in their efforts. Therefore, a corporate culture that does not tolerate failure will prevent employees to take steps towards discovering and implementing brand new strategies.

FUTURE RESEARCH DIRECTIONS

Co-creation of value is a multi-dimensional and complex process that includes the participation of several members. On the other hand, creation of value has changed not only by the inclusion of consumers as well as firms in the value creation process but also the unavoidable effects of digitalization on both parties. Digitalization requires firms digitally enabled customer service capabilities because of the increasing uses of digital technologies and tools by consumers. These capabilities can be acquired by firms by the successful implementation of a digital transformation strategy within the dynamic and competitive market conditions.

An important point to be considered for successful value creation and digital transformation is the fact that consumers differ in terms of their willingness to participate in the value creation process and uses of digital tools. This means that a customer-centric strategy for the co-creation of value and digital transformation may create satisfaction for certain customer groups while not influencing the others positively. For this reason, companies' market segmentation and targeting strategies should include the newly added factors of co-creation of value and digital transformation. Therefore, further academic research should examine the varying levels of consumer participation in the value creation process and the factors that influence their decisions. How consumers differ in terms of their uses of digital tools and the impact of these differences on their expectations of value should be questionned. Finally, alternative business models should be suggested to firms for a successful digital transformation strategy in the value creation process.

CONCLUSION

Consumers are more demanding than ever by their ability to use multiple digital tools to search and to share information about products and services. They are also participating in the value creation process that gives them extra power in terms of quick response about their complaints, added features to products and services, and alternative solutions for their problems. Digital transformation and agility, in this regard, helps companies to manage this multi-dimensional and complex market with several actors in it.

Management of the value co-creation process in today's digital environment can be effective only if firms can achieve success in digital transformation. Success in digital transformation requires organizations preparations about several topics such as human resources, information technology infrastructure, and corporate culture. Digital transformation includes a series of steps each of which demands careful analysis and plan. The steps of the customer journey and the roles of digital tools in each step should be carefully analyzed. Digital transformation strategy creates a dynamic environment in which companies develop new business models, transform their cultures and empower their teams with flexible and innovative technology. A responsive and agile approach embedded in the business strategy leads firms for offering brand new solutions to consumers. Digital agility, as an enabler of digital transformation, triggers managers to be proactive, taking steps quickly and going ahead of consumers instead of being only reactive and giving feedback by offering solutions to consumers' requests and problems.

REFERENCES

Agarwal, S., & Teas, R. K. (2001). Perceived value: Mediating role of perceived risk. *Journal of Marketing Theory and Practice*, *9*(4), 1–14. doi:10.1080/10696679.2001.11501899

Alves, H., Fernandes, C., & Raposo, M. (2016). Value co-creation: Concept and contexts of application and study. *Journal of Business Research*, *69*(5), 1626–1633. doi:10.1016/j.jbusres.2015.10.029

Anker, T. B., Sparks, L., Moutinho, L., & Grönroos, C. (2015). Consumer dominant value creation: A theoretical response to the recent call for a consumer dominant logic for marketing. *European Journal of Marketing*, *49*(3/4), 532–560. doi:10.1108/EJM-09-2013-0518

Bonner, J. M. (2010). Customer interactivity and new product performance: Moderating effects of product newness and product embeddedness. *Industrial Marketing Management*, *39*(3), 485–492. doi:10.1016/j.indmarman.2008.11.006

Brown, S., & Bessant, J. (2003). The manufacturing strategy-capabilities links in mass customisation and agile manufacturing—An exploratory study. *International Journal of Operations & Production Management*, *23*(7), 707–730. doi:10.1108/01443570310481522

Chawla, R. N., & Goyal, P. (2021). Emerging trends in digital transformation: A bibliometric analysis. *Benchmarking*, 1463–5771. doi:10.1108/BIJ-01-2021-0009

Chen, T., Drennan, J., Andrews, L., & Hollebeek, L. D. (2018). User experience sharing: Understanding customer initiation of value co-creation in online communities. *European Journal of Marketing*, *52*(5/6), 1154–1184. doi:10.1108/EJM-05-2016-0298

Choudhury, A., Behl, A., Sheorey, P. A., & Pal, A. (2021). Digital supply chain to unlock new agility: A TISM approach. *Benchmarking*, *28*(6), 2075–2109. doi:10.1108/BIJ-08-2020-0461

Cossío-Silva, F.-J., Revilla-Camacho, M.-Á., Vega-Vázquez, M., & Palacios-Florencio, B. (2016). Value co-creation and customer loyalty. *Journal of Business Research*, *69*(5), 1621–1625. doi:10.1016/j.jbusres.2015.10.028

Dellaert, B. G. C. (2019). The consumer production journey: Marketing to consumers as co-producers in the sharing economy. *Journal of the Academy of Marketing Science*, *47*(2), 238–254. doi:10.100711747-018-0607-4

Donio', J., Massari, P., & Passiante, G. (2006). Customer satisfaction and loyalty in a digital environment: An empirical test. *Journal of Consumer Marketing*, *23*(7), 445–457.

Eggers, J. P., & Park, K. F. (2018). Incumbent adaptation to technological change: The past, present, and future of research on heterogeneous incumbent response. *The Academy of Management Annals*, *12*(1), 357–389.

Eshlaghy, A. T., Mashayekhi, A. N., Rajabzadeh, A., & Razavian, M. M. (2010). Applying path analysis method in defining effective factors in organisation agility. *International Journal of Production Research*, *48*(6), 1765–1786.

Etgar, M. (2008). A Descriptive model of the consumer co-production process. *Journal of the Academy of Marketing Science*, *36*, 97–108.

Flint, D. J., Blocker, C. P., & Boutin, P. J. (2011). Customer value anticipation, customer satisfaction and loyalty: An empirical examination. *Industrial Marketing Management*, *40*(2), 219–230.

Gassmann, O., Kausch, C., & Enkel, E. (2010). Negative side effects of customer integration. *International Journal of Technology Management*, *50*(1), 43–63.

Gehani, R. R. (2010). Time-based management strategic roles. *International Journal of Operations & Production Management*, *15*, 19–35.

Grönroos, C. (2006). Adopting a service logic for marketing. *Marketing Theory*, *6*(3), 317–333.

Grönroos, C. (2012). Conceptualising value co-creation: A journey to the 1970s and back to the future. *Journal of Marketing Management*, *28*(13-14), 1520–1534.

Grönroos, C., & Voima, P. (2013). Critical service logic: Making sense of value creation and co-creation. *Journal of the Academy of Marketing Science*, *41*(2), 133–150.

Heinonen, K., Strandvik, T., Mickelsson, K., Edvardsson, B., Sundström, E., & Andersson, P. (2010). A customer-dominant logic of service. *Journal of Service Management*, *21*(4), 531–548.

Hinings, B., Gegenhuber, T., & Greenwood, R. (2018). Digital innovation and transformation: An institutional perspective. *Information and Organization*, *28*(1), 52–61.

Kozinets, R. V., Hemetsberger, A., & Schau, H. J. (2008). The wisdom of consumer crowds: Collective innovation in the age of networked marketing. *Journal of Macromarketing*, *28*(4), 339–354.

Lemon, K. N., & Verhoef, P. C. (2016). Understanding customer experience throughout the customer journey. *Journal of Marketing*, *80*(6), 69–96.

Lim, D. H., Song, J. H., & Yoon, S. W. (2014). Trends and issues in integrating knowledge management and organizational learning for workplace performance improvement. In N. Chalosfki & M. L. Morris (Eds.), *Handbook of HRD: Theory and application* (pp. 369–385). Jossey-Bass.

Lusch, R. F., & Vargo, S. L. (2006). Service-dominant logic: Reactions, reflections and refinements. *Marketing Theory*, *6*(3), 281–288.

Merz, M. A., Zarantonello, L., & Grappi, S. (2018). How valuable are your customers in the brand value co-creation process? The development of a Customer Co-Creation Value (CCCV) scale. *Journal of Business Research*, *82*, 79–89.

Mikalef, P., & Pateli, A. (2017). Information technology-enabled dynamic capabilities and their indirect effect on competitive performance: Findings from PLS-SEM and fsQCA. *Journal of Business Research*, (70), 1–16.

Mishra, D., Gunasekaran, A., Papadopoulos, T., & Childe, S. J. (2018). Big data and supply chain management: A review and bibliometric analysis. *Annals of Operations Research*, *270*(1), 313–336.

Molinari, L. K., Abratt, R., & Dion, P. (2008). Satisfaction, quality and value and effects on repurchase and positive word-of-mouth behavioral intentions in a B2B services context. *Journal of Services Marketing*, *22*(5), 363–373.

Morgeson, F. V., Mithas, S., Keiningham, T. L., & Aksoy, L. (2011). An investigation of the cross-national determinants of customer satisfaction. *Journal of the Academy of Marketing Science*, *39*, 198–215.

Muhuri, P. K., Shukla, A. K., & Abraham, A. (2019). Industry 4.0: A bibliometric analysis and detailed overview. *Engineering Applications of Artificial Intelligence*, *78*, 218–235.

Nambisan, S., Lyytinen, K., Majchrzak, A., & Song, M. (2017). Digital innovation management: Reinventing innovation management research in a digital world. *Management Information Systems Quarterly*, *41*(1), 223–238.

Newman, D. (2020). *Top ten digital transformation trends for 2021.* https://www.forbes.com/sites/danielnewman/2020/09/21/top-10-digital-transformation-trends-for-2021/?sh=3c85f180c6f4

Payne, A., Frow, P., & Eggert, A. (2017). The customer value proposition: Evolution, development, and application in marketing. *Journal of the Academy of Marketing Science, 45*, 467–489.

Payne, A., Storbacka, K., Frow, P., & Knox, S. (2009). Co-creating brands: Diagnosing and designing the relationship experience. *Journal of Business Research, 62*(3), 379–389.

Payne, A. F., Storbacka, K., & Frow, P. (2008). Managing the co-creation of value. *Journal of the Academy of Marketing Science, 36*, 83–96.

Prahalad, C. K., & Ramaswamy, V. (2000). *Co-opting customer competence.* https://hbr.org/2000/01/co-opting-customer-competence

Prahalad, C. K., & Ramaswamy, V. (2004). Co-creating unique value with customers. *Strategy and Leadership, 32*(3), 4–9.

Priem, R. L., Wenzel, M., & Koch, J. (2018). Demand-side strategy and business models: Putting value creation for consumers center stage. *Long Range Planning, 51*(1), 22–31.

Ranjan, K. R., & Read, S. (2016). Value co-creation: Concept and measurement. *Journal of the Academy of Marketing Science, 44*, 290–315.

Ranjan, K. R., & Read, S. (2019). Bringing the individual into the co-creation of value. *Journal of Services Marketing, 33*(7), 904–920.

Ren, J., Yusuf, Y. Y., & Burns, N. D. (2009). A decision-support framework for agile enterprise partnering. *International Journal of Advanced Manufacturing Technology, 41*(1–2), 180–192.

Rintamäki, T., & Saarijärvi, H. (2021). An integrative framework for managing customer value propositions. *Journal of Business Research, 134*, 754–764.

Roberts, D., Hughes, M., & Kertbo, K. (2014). Exploring consumers' motivations to engage in innovation through co-creation activities. *European Journal of Marketing, 48*(1/2), 147–169.

Sambamurthy, V., Bharadwaj, A., & Grover, V. (2003). Shaping agility through digital options: Reconceptualizing the role of information technology in contemporary firms. *Management Information Systems Quarterly, 27*(2), 237–263.

Sherehiy, B., Karwowski, W., & Layer, J. K. (2007). A review of enterprise agility: Concepts, frameworks, and attributes. *International Journal of Industrial Ergonomics, 37*(5), 445–460.

Singh, J., & Sharma, G. (2013). Organizational agility: What it is, what it is not, and why it matters. *Academy of Management Proceedings, 2013*(1), 1–40.

Snoj, B., Pisnik Korda, A., & Mumel, D. (2004). The relationships among perceived quality, perceived risk and perceived product value. *Journal of Product and Brand Management, 13*(3), 156–167.

Snyder, C. R. (1992). Product scarcity by need for uniqueness interaction: A consumer catch-22 carousel? *Basic and Applied Social Psychology, 13*(1), 9–24.

Solakis, K., Peña-Vinces, J., Lopez-Bonilla, J. M., & Aguado, L. F. (2021). From value co-creation to positive experiences and customer satisfaction. A customer perspective in the hotel industry. *Technological and Economic Development of Economy*, *27*(4), 948–969.

Steiber, A., Alänge, S., Ghosh, S., & Goncalves, D. (2020). Digital transformation of industrial firms: An innovation diffusion perspective. *European Journal of Innovation Management*, *24*(3), 799–819.

Sugathan, P., Ranjan, K. R., & Mulky, A. G. (2017). Atypical shifts post-failure: Influence of co-creation on attribution and future motivation to co-create. *Journal of Interactive Marketing*, *38*, 64–81.

Sweeney, J. C., & Soutar, G. N. (2001). Consumer perceived value: The development of a multiple item scale. *Journal of Retailing*, *77*(2), 203–220.

Tabrizi, B., Lam, E., Girard, K., & Irvin, V. (2019). *Digital transformation is not about technology.* https://hbr.org/2019/03/digital-transformation-is-not-about-technology

Teece, D., Peteraf, M., & Leih, S. (2016). Dynamic capabilities and organizational agility: Risk, uncertainty, and strategy in the innovation economy. *California Management Review*, *58*, 13–35.

Teece, D. J. (2010). Business models, business strategy and innovation. *Long Range Planning*, *43*(2-3), 172–194.

Tumbas, S., Berente, N., & Brocke, J. V. (2018). Digital innovation and institutional entrepreneurship: Chief digital officer perspectives of their emerging role. *Journal of Information Technology*, *33*(3), 188–202.

Tzeng, S.-Y., Ertz, M., Jo, M.-S., & Sarigöllü, E. (2021). Factors affecting customer satisfaction on online shopping holiday. *Marketing Intelligence & Planning*, *39*(4), 516–532.

Vargo, S. L., & Akaka, M. A. (2009). Service-dominant logic as a foundation for service science: Clarifications. *Service Science*, *1*, 32–41.

Vargo, S. L., & Lusch, R. F. (2004). Evolving to a new dominant logic for marketing. *Journal of Marketing*, *68*(1), 1–17.

Vargo, S. L., & Lusch, R. F. (2008). Service-dominant logic: Continuing the evolution. *Journal of the Academy of Marketing Science*, *36*, 1–10.

Vargo, S. L., & Lusch, R. F. (2016). Institutions and axioms: An extension and update of service-dominant logic. *Journal of the Academy of Marketing Science*, *44*, 5–23.

Vargo, S. L., & Lusch, R. F. (2017). Service-dominant logic 2025. *International Journal of Research in Marketing*, *34*, 46–67.

Verhoef, P. C., Broekhuizen, T., Bart, Y., Bhattacharya, A., Qi Dong, J., Fabian, N., & Haenlein, M. (2021). Digital transformation: A multidisciplinary reflection and research agenda. *Journal of Business Research*, *122*, 889–901.

Vial, G. (2019). Understanding digital transformation: A review and a research agenda. *The Journal of Strategic Information Systems*, *28*(2), 118–144.

Xie, C., Bagozzi, R. P., & Troye, S. V. (2008). Trying to prosume: Toward a theory of consumers and co-creators of value. *Journal of the Academy of Marketing Science, 36*(1), 109–122.

Yang, Z., & Peterson, R. (2004). Customer perceived value, satisfaction, and loyalty: The role of switching costs. *Psychology and Marketing, 21*, 799–822.

ADDITIONAL READING

Eigenraam, A. W., Eelen, J., Van Lin, A., & Verlegh, P. W. (2018). A consumer-based taxonomy of digital customer engagement practices. *Journal of Interactive Marketing, 44*, 102–121. doi:10.1016/j.intmar.2018.07.002

Hoffman, D. L., & Novak, T. P. (2018). Consumer and object experience in the internet of things: An assemblage theory approach. *The Journal of Consumer Research, 44*(6), 1178–1204. doi:10.1093/jcr/ucx105

Jain, G., Paul, J., & Shrivastava, A. (2021). Hyper-personalization, co-creation, digital clienteling and transformation. *Journal of Business Research, 124*, 12–23. doi:10.1016/j.jbusres.2020.11.034

Kane, G. C., Palmer, D., Phillips, A. N., Kiron, D., & Buckley, N. (2015). Strategy, not technology, drives digital transformation. *MIT Sloan Management Review and Deloitte University Press, 14*, 1–25.

Lamberton, C., & Stephen, A. T. (2016). A thematic exploration of digital, social media, and mobile marketing: Research evolution from 2000 to 2015 and an agenda for future inquiry. *Journal of Marketing, 80*(6), 146–172. doi:10.1509/jm.15.0415

Sklyar, A., Kowalkowski, C., Tronvoll, B., & Sörhammar, D. (2019). Organizing for digital servitization: A service ecosystem perspective. *Journal of Business Research, 104*, 450–460. doi:10.1016/j.jbusres.2019.02.012

Sun, X., & Zhang, Q. (2021). Building digital incentives for digital customer orientation in platform ecosystems. *Journal of Business Research, 137*, 555–566. doi:10.1016/j.jbusres.2021.08.068

Wielgos, D. M., Homburg, C., & Kuehnl, C. (2021). Digital business capability: Its impact on firm and customer performance. *Journal of the Academy of Marketing Science, 49*(4), 762–789. doi:10.100711747-021-00771-5

KEY TERMS AND DEFINITIONS

Co-Creation of Value: Joint creation of value by companies and customers.

Customer Value Proposition: A firm's strategic tool that is used to communicate its ability to offer superior value to customers.

Digital Agility: A firm's ability to rapidly enable, update, change or adapt its business processes.

Digital Transformation: An overall change in a firm's strategy and perspective in terms of using digital technologies and adapting business models for the digital environment.

Internet of Things (IoT): Advanced technology that connects physical and virtual world.

Tech-Savvy: Well-informed about modern technology and takes advantage of it by using skills and knowledge.

Value-in-Use: An outcome or objective that is acquired by the creation of value.

Chapter 3
The Past, Present, and Future of E-Business Models

Beyza Gultekin
Hacettepe University, Turkey

ABSTRACT

This chapter describes the concept of a business model from the network perspective and examines the different types of business models. The author mentions the characteristics of a successful business model with the threats to a business model's success. A lean start-up process is explained, with an emphasis on the business model canvas technique. An organization's business model does not necessarily have to continue in perpetuity once it is launched. Accordingly, the business model change, characteristics of a transformative business model, and directions for future research are addressed. In this context, the chapter discusses the past, present, and future of e-business models.

INTRODUCTION

The term "business model" was first used in a late 1950s academic journal article to refer to a reproduction of an actuality or reality guided by a model (DaSilva & Trkman, 2014). Since then, it has not caught the academic world's interest until the rise of technology-based companies in the 1990s (DaSilva & Trkman, 2014). Business models emerged with the widespread use of personal computers, spreadsheets (Magretta, 2002), and the emergence of the internet (Chatterjee, 2013). In 2000, over 500 articles in prestigious magazines and journals used the term "business model" three or more times, compared to just one in 1990 (Shafer, Smith, & Linder, 2005). Between 2000 and 2021, Web of Science (n.d.) lists 15.473 and Scopus (n.d.) lists 36.524 results for the term "business model".

While conducting a search for "business models" on search engines, it is not uncommon to come across terms such as Business-to-Business (B2B), Business-to-Customer (B2C), Business-to-Government (B2G), Government-to-Customer (G2C), and Customer-to-Customer (C2C). The marketplaces (e.g., Amazon, eBay, Trendyol), once named as market makers (Mahadevan, 2000), which connect multiple suppliers, producers, intermediaries, and customers, could provide some of the raw materials necessary in the manufacture of a product without putting any limits on other businesses, intermediaries, or

DOI: 10.4018/978-1-7998-9179-6.ch003

end-customers. For example, Airbnb enhanced its business model by adding cleaning and maintenance services. Are these models then identified only as B2B and B2C, or as B2C2B2C? It is not viable to envision business models exclusively as B2B or B2C in this context, as business models operate as networks. Accordingly, the business model is examined and considered in this chapter via the perspective of a network. Defining and classifying business models in this environment necessitates a more holistic view of distribution channels. As such, this chapter analyzes the business model in terms of distribution channels, including structure-based distribution strategies such as single, multi-, cross-, and omni-channel distribution (Gultekin & Erdem, 2021).

Business models are frequently web-based systems made of interconnected components in this aspect (Magretta, 2002). The business model describes how an organization develops and employs its resources in order to provide higher value to its customers and generate revenue (Afuah & Tucci, 2003). Additionally, a successful business model includes a good story and continuous revenue streams (Magretta, 2002). The story component of a business model is not about discussing the model's history, but about delivering value. Different types of value are incorporated into business models. There are several strategies for offering value, such as cost-benefit analysis, quality standards, low prices, and value judgments (Gultekin & Kement, 2018: 91–107), as well as numerous revenue generation methods, such as subscriptions, advertising, and free services. Hence, the business model is a critical factor in determining a firm's performance (Afuah & Tucci, 2003).

Previously, the terms "business model" and "strategy" were frequently used interchangeably. (Magretta, 2002). Contemporary business models, on the other hand, eschew strategy and planning in favor of the lean start-up approach (Blank, 2013). This chapter discusses the characteristics of a lean start-up after examining several business models and successful examples from around the world.

To be successful, conventional e-business models (Mahadevan, 2000) must contain revolutionary aspects or transformative elements (Kavadias, Ladas, & Loch, 2016). Finally, this chapter explores the transformative components of e-business models through relevant examples.

THE CONCEPT OF A BUSINESS MODEL

All businesses, either explicitly or implicitly employ a particular business model. (Teece, 2010, p. 191). Desperately seeking definition: Identity crisis of the business model. (Shafer, Smith, & Linder, 2005, p. 200)

The foundations of network approach to business models and the conceptualization perspectives to the business model are discussed in this part.

The Foundations of Network Approach to Business Models

As simple as this framework may seem, its power lies in the complex interdependencies of its parts. (Johnson et al., 2008: 61)

While conceptualizations exist for the term "business model," none are universally accepted, and there is no consensus on a definition. This lack of agreement could be explained by the concept's widespread appeal across disciplines (i.e., e-business, strategy, technology, and information systems)(Shafer et al., 2005). As a result, present and future business models need to place a emphasis on an holistic network perspective that takes into account all distribution channel members. A dyadic relationship (Harwood,

Garry, & Broderick, 2008: 27) resembles the B2B and B2C perspectives. B2B and B2C perspectives resemble single-channel and multi-channel distribution systems. In single-channel distribution, a company prefers to use just one channel of distribution and chooses sole channel from many channels such as a website, supermarket, department store, telephone, and television. For example, Amazon was initially operating as a single channel, selling books via the website or solely based on the internet channel, in its launch on July 5, 1994 (Hartmans, 2021) [1], as given in Figure 1.

Figure 1. Single channel distribution

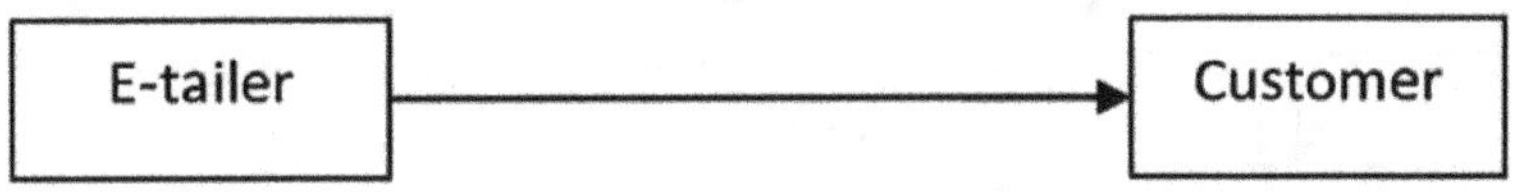

A multi-channel distribution system enables businesses to distribute their products through many channels. However, as illustrated in Figure 2, no integration exists between channels. For example, when a consumer places an order online and there is no option for pickup, or when a customer adds an item to the basket via a company's website, the item does not appear in the mobile application's basket.

Figure 2. Multi-channel distribution

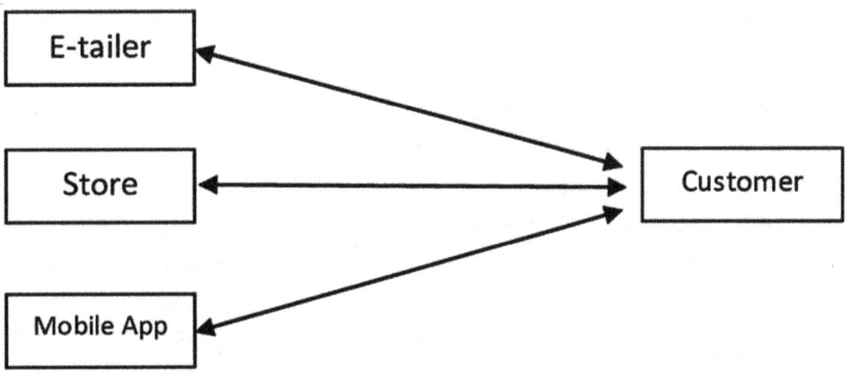

Because of their network-centric structure, cross- and omni-channel distribution should be investigated in addition to single- and multi-channel distribution. While the cross-channel distribution system integrates the channels, however, the integration between them is limited. Amazon's launch of the Amazon Go store and Treasure Truck, in addition to its website, may be considered cross-channel instances due to the integration of the channels; nonetheless, the relationship between those channels is limited. Customers access the Amazon Go store via the Amazon app and pay for their purchases directly through the app, alleviating the need for a cashier. Customers who opt-in to the Treasure Truck service receive an SMS or email and continue their buying experience away from the company's website. There is some degree of integration between channels in a cross-channel distribution system, but not across all channels, as illustrated in Figure 3.

Figure 3. Cross-channel distribution

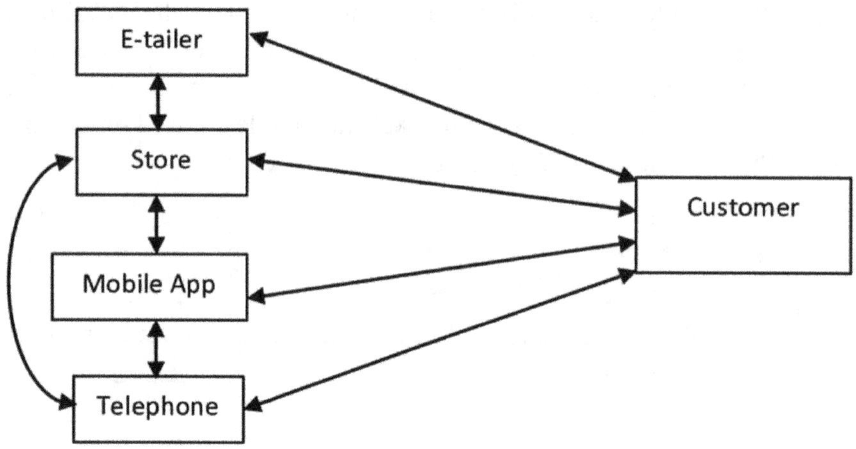

Therefore, most of the business models are and going to be more complicated then it was in the past. They operate like an omni-channel system as presented in Figure 4. In the omni-channel distribution system, customers have a seamless channel experience (Gultekin & Erdem, 2021). Customers are unaware of the many channels (i.e. internet, mobile application, store, telephone, and television) that serve them since they move seamlessly among them in omni-channel distribution.

Figure 4. Omni-channel Distribution

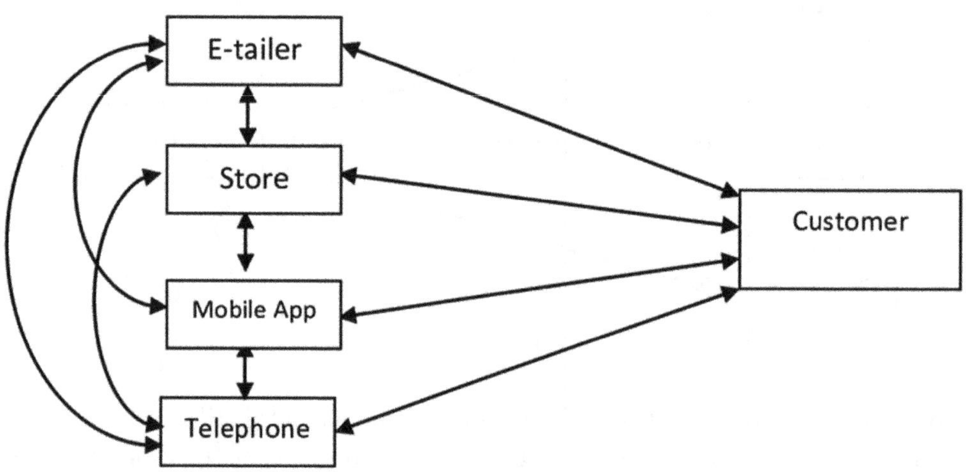

They can place an order online and pick it up in store; if there is a problem with the transaction, they can contact the call center for assistance. Consumers do not submit comprehensive transaction information because the database records the date and time of the order, the amount, and the channel of purchase.

Business Model Conceptualizations

Business model is defined as "the story that explains how an enterprise works" (Casadesus-Masanell & Ricart, 2011: 4-5) or "the way of doing business" (DaSilva & Trkman, 2014: 384). A business model is a simplified and consolidated view of a company's activities (Wirtz, Pistoia, Ullrich, & Göttel, 2016). "A business model is a configuration (activity systems) of what the business does (activities) and what it invests in (resources) based on the logic that drives the profits for a specific business" (Chatterjee, 2013: 97). The business model is a picture of the company and explains in what way the pieces of the work operate at a specific time (DaSilva & Trkman, 2014), and defines how the various components of a firm work together as a system (Magretta, 2002). Business models exist to generate and manage value exchange system (Liu, Tong, & Sinfield, 2021).

A business model is made up of diverse but related parts that contribute to the value creation of a business (Johnson et al., 2008). Similarly, Chesbrough (2010) state that business models include value proposition, market segment and revenue generation method, structure of the value chain, costs, and competitive strategies. More specifically, Peter Drucker defined the business model as identifying customers, creating value for the customers, and reaching appropriate cost (Casadesus-Masanell & Ricart, 2011). Accordingly, business models utilize the commercialization of the new products and technologies (Chesbrough, 2010).

In this sense, business model refers to a system whose many characteristics interact to create and capture value. The model's characteristics describe the customer value proposition and price mechanism, identify how the business will structure itself and with whom it will collaborate to create value, and indicate how the supply chain will be formed (Kavadias, Ladas, & Loch, 2016)

According to Shafer et al. (2005: 202), a business model is a reflection of a firm's fundamental "core logic and strategic choices for creating and capturing value within a value network". Creating and capturing value occurs within the context of a value network, which may include suppliers, distribution channel members, and alliances, and end customers that enrich the company's own resources (Shafer et al., 2005).

While the term "business model" has a variety of definitions, most people agree that it refers to a system whose many characteristics interact to create and capture value. The model's characteristics describe the customer value proposition, identify how the business will structure itself and with whom it will collaborate to create value, and indicate how the supply chain will be formed and prices (Shafer et al., 2005). Most of the research in the literature has emphasized the significance of value creation in business models (Niemimaa, Järveläinen, Heikkilä, & Heikkilä, 2019). Accordingly, a business model is a description of the structure or architecture of the value creation, distribution, and capturing processes being used that provides a means of achieving a competitive advantage (Teece, 2010). The function that a business decides to play in its value network is critical to its business model (Shafer et al., 2005). In other words, consistent with the perspective of this chapter, the term "business model" is not exclusive to any form of organization, whether offline or online; it encompasses a network of relationships.

FEATURES OF A SUCCESSFUL BUSINESS MODEL

This section discusses the characteristics of a successful business model once venturing into the reasons for failure.

Success of the Business Model

Business models should have a story to tell (Magretta, 2002). A business model should be accompanied by a narrative. That story, on the other hand, is not one like Don Quixote, a novel by Miguel de Cervantes. The value that was created is included in the story and in the network of operations.

Mutlubiev.com create value by its service quality, whereas Armut.com may create value through its diversity of offers from various service providers at different price levels. *Mutlubiev.com* is a Turkish pipeline business model that creates value by connecting its home-cleaning professionals with consumers. Employees receive training from the company. Employees and consumers are both protected by the AXA insurance company's assurance. Consumers have different service options in terms of professional cleaning. *Armut.com* is a marketplace for service providers and customers. There are several cleaning, repair, cooking, and other services that a consumer need and can choose from. Consumers can rank and review providers in both models following their use of the service. These business models success relies on the value they create.

An enterprise's ability to create value cannot be explained by a single theory (Morris, Schindehutte, & Allen, 2005). There are numerous ways of creating value for customers via economic (i.e. lowest price), functional (features and quality of the products), emotional (positive feeling, hedonic consumption), and symbolic (social prestige, status, personal achievement) value propositions (Yi, Wang, & Shu, 2020).

Successful business models create a value proposition, generate value, and have key resources and processes (Johnson et al., 2008). A value proposition is a strategic tool that enables an organization to communicate its capabilities to share resources and to provide a superior value to the target market (Payne, Frow, & Eggert, 2017). Payne, Frow, and Eggert (2017) identify value propositions in three ways: supplier-determined, transitional, and mutually determined. Supplier-determined value propositions are value-in-exchange or in-side-out in nature, as the value is delivered from the company to the customer. Transitional value has a one-way focus, in which the firm determines the value and creates an offer that takes into consideration the customer's experience. However, this approach continues to focus on demonstrating and documenting how the company delivers superior value to its customers, and the value is embedded in the product. Mutually defined value propositions focus on co-creation of value and seeks the active engagement of a customer, through sharing selected resources and contributing to win-win outcomes. For example, customers of Uber are not passive receivers of value. Customers participate by selecting from a variety of options (e.g., Uber X, Uber Black, and Uberlux) with varying prices and tracking their ordered car in real time. Drivers frequently offer water or candy to passengers and also volunteer to help load and unload bags from the trunk and do not charge a tip. Both parties submit quantitative feedback (Payne et al., 2017).

Lindič & Marques da Silva (2011) emphasize the importance of customers in the value proposition, considering the Amazon.com case and innovations. As customers (e.g. end consumers, shopping infrastructure customers, and developers) ultimately make the decision, the value proposition should be examined through their viewpoints (Lindič & Marques da Silva, 2011). Ziaie, ShamiZanjani, & Manian (2021) demonstrate the critical role of customer-centric digital value propositions such as vividness, mobility, peer communication, personalization, interactivity, connectivity, value co-creation, telepresence, and information availability in delivering superior customer experiences that differentiate retailers from established and startup competitors.

Business models create value by employing assortment, reducing costs (i.e. price, search costs, and transaction costs), customer service, convenience, and values (Gultekin & Kement, 2018). Successful business models follows the changes in the consumer preferences and values (value judgments). Values have shifted among consumers. For example, cars were most often combined with a way of communicating personal accomplishment, status, luxury and freedom in 1994. However, in 2014, people attributed automobiles to saving time, ease of commuting, high costs, and pollution (Kathan, Matzler, & Veider, 2016). So, the value judgment phrase "you are what you possess" translates into "you are what you share," as evidence of the impact of value shifts' on business models. As a result, new business models such as sharing platforms arise to create value in this segment.

However, most of the business models do not focus on creating value, value propositions, and doing their job. Companies, besides doing their job, strive to do various jobs and underestimate their focus because of "insufficient wealth, access, skill, and time" (Johnson et al., 2008: 63). Ratan Tata overwhelms the insufficient wealth barrier by introducing low price cars for families using scooters (Johnson et al., 2008). Enrico Piaggio overcome the access barrier inspired by a scooter and launched Vespa especially for women wearing skirts and could not drive motorcycles because of the barrier or unavailable space on the traditional motorcycles (Marino, 2019). Medical Park introduced an online examination process for some medical branches and Zoom introduced a base or freemium model during COVID-19 pandemic against access and time barriers.

Besides creating value, gathering revenue is an important component fo the success of the business model (DaSilva & Trkman, 2014). Initially the price should be determined consistent to the customer value proposition and then variable costs and gross margins identified which in turn determines the scale of the business model (Magretta, 2002). Moreover, a successful business model should integrate itself to its goals, have internal consistency (e.g., a low cost airline having low levels of service), and be robust or sustain its effectiveness (Casadesus-Masanell & Ricart, 2011). Bego Demir, who launched the clean fashion movement in 2013 and is the founder of the 100% recyclable jeans (e.g. the buttons of the jeans are made of rice) "Bego Jeans"(Bego Jeans, n.d.), for example, does not distribute internationally owing to his vision and values surrounding sustainability (Örnek, 2021).

Furthermore, the success of business models depend on the competitive environment (Casadesus-Masanell & Ricart, 2011). When Zeng (2018), dean of Hupan School of Entrepreneurship, presents 10 corporate executives and asks students to identify them. Even they are familiar with Elon Musk and Steve Jobs; yet, no one recalls the CEOs of Citigroup, Toyota, or General Electric. Instead of managing, digital leaders need to encourage people to innovate and integrate the user feedback system to firm decisions and practice. Their aim is to raise the success rate of innovation, not to boost operational efficiency since that is achieved by the machine-learning algorithms (Zeng, 2018). In contrast to Citigroup, Toyota, and GE, Zeng (2018) asserts that digital firms must build a network to implement their vision.

Threats to the Business Model

When business models fail, it's because they don't pass the narrative (i.e. not creating value) or financial tests (determining the optimal costs and profit margins) (Magretta, 2002). Using a system that concentrates entirely on creating and delivering value, without also accounting for capturing value, will almost certainly lead to an economic failure (Chatterjee, 2013). In other words, presumptions concerning the creation and capture of value is another reason of the business model failure. Some businesses might place more emphasis on value creation than on value capture (e.g. Yahoo) and others get confused with potential value to actual value (e.g., paying more attention on the number of customers instead of cash flow) (Shafer et al., 2005).

Other treats to the success of a business model arise from: "flawed assumptions underlying the core logic", "limitations in the strategic choices considered", and "flawed assumptions about the value network." (Shafer et al., 2005: 204). Treats to a business model's success arise as a result of incorrect assumptions behind the key logic (Shafer et al., 2005: 204). For example, an entrepreneur is to start a company that will provide integrated services across wireless networks in numerous regions throughout the United States. However, such a network did not exist at that time and is unlikely to develop for several years. In addition, limited strategic choices might result in a business model failure. In other words, focusing on only some aspects (i.e., target market and value proposition) in the business model is a shallow view. Strategic choices should include many elements such as mission, target market, value proposition, capabilities and competencies, revenue/pricing, competitors, offering, strategy, branding, differentiation (Shafer et al., 2005). Some businesses may base their decisions on faulty assumptions about the value network (Shafer et al., 2005).

Most managers are perplexed by concepts such as business model, strategy, and tactics, which might be a reason for their failure (Casadesus-Masanell & Ricart, 2011). Casadesus-Masanell and Ricart (2011) give examples of the strategy, business model, and tactics. Accordingly, "strategy is designing and building the car, the business model is the car, and tactics are how you drive the car" (Casadesus-Masanell & Ricart, 2011: 9). Business model is not a strategy, although it incorporates several features of strategy. Likewise, it is not an activity set, while activity sets encompass all facets of a model (Morris et al., 2005).

The business model is commonly confused with the strategy in two ways. First, creating dynamic capabilities that can adjust to changes in the business model is part of strategy. Second, while strategy describes what a business aspires to be, business models define what a business actually is at any specific moment in time. (DaSilva & Trkman, 2014: 383). Besides value-creating resources, strategy deals with positioning (Casadesus-Masanell & Ricart, 2011). These are formed by virtuous cycles, which stimulate business models. This is difficult for the companies to operate in this environment that includes the interaction with competitors, intermediaries, and customers (Casadesus-Masanell & Ricart, 2011).

Business models' failure may also be influenced by the competitive environment (Casadesus-Masanell & Ricart, 2011). For example, when a company is bankrupt, the contingency to be considered by a competitor should not be to change its running business model but to enhance dynamic capabilities to benefit from this opportunity in the environment (DaSilva & Trkman, 2014).

TYPES OF E-BUSINESS MODELS

Business models are classified in a variety of ways and there is no universally acknowledged categorization. While it is obvious that the number of possible business models is limitless, academics focus on model taxonomies (Morris et al., 2005). This study considers establishing a standardized classification system for business models as challenging.

Traditional classifications starts in the beginning of 2000s. There are numerous traditional classification systems for business models. Pipeline or suppliers is a business model that includes traditional value chain members (e.g. like Walmart, Nike, General Electric) and value is created in pipeline business models by managing a sequential set of operations (the classic value chain model). Apple's smartphone business is primarily a pipeline (Alstyne, Parker, & Choudary, 2016). Apple creates value through this pipeline business model, which involves the use of their own website and other intermediaries over which they have more control. Business models have altered in recent decades to accommodate new consumption practices that are gradually threatening sole ownership (Kathan et al., 2016).

Platform strategy requires an understanding of the ecosystem's relationships and is no longer managed internally (Alstyne et al., 2016) and one partner having the complete control. The platform business model (e.g., Uber, Airbnb) enables the resources of the community and its members to be pooled together for cooperation in terms of value and data exchange and feedback. A platform is the backbone of a marketplace that connects providers and customers. Even though there are various kinds of platforms, the platforms all have an ecosystem that follows the same general premise, made up of four types of players. The players in the platform ecosystem are the owner, provider, producer, and consumer, however they can swiftly alter roles. Google is the *owner* of Android, applications on Android are the *producers* of the platform's offerings for the *consumers* (buyers or users) via *providers* (interfaces like mobile devices) (Alstyne et al., 2016). The basic issue inherent in this attempt is migrating from a world in which you have complete control over the goods and services given to your clients to one in which you can only influence the value created for them ("by third parties or by interactions among themselves") (Hagiu & Altman, 2017).

In addition, various companies demonstrate that firms can be pipelines and platforms at the same time. When Apple combined with the App Store, the marketplace that connects app creators and iPhone owners, a platform emerges (Alstyne et al., 2016). Pipeline companies remain competitive in the marketplace, but when platforms enter the same industry, platforms almost always emerge victorious. Relying on this Walmart, Nike, and GE are all moving to include platforms in their models (Alstyne et al., 2016). Similarly, the platform is defined as an upper level concept like "a flat surface that is raised higher than the floor or ground and that people stand on when performing or speaking" (Merriam-Webster Dictionary, n.d.). Amazon also illustrated how it is possible to bypass the supply chain and derive new value (Mahadevan, 2000) for the customers and ecosystem.

Apple's iTunes serves as an intermediary or a reseller (e.g. supermarkets) (Hagiu, 2013). Consumers purchase or rent music and movies directly from Apple, which maintains complete control over pricing and is ultimately liable for the merchandise available. On the other hand, Apple's App Store performs the function of a multi-sided platform (MSP). The relationship between consumers and app developers is contractual, with pricing and design being at the control of the developers (Hagiu, 2013). Multi-sided platforms enable the coexistence of two or more distinct but interdependent customer segments. By fostering interactions between various groups, the platform creates value. To generate value, the platform must appeal to and serve all groups concurrently (Osterwalder & Pigneur, 2010: 78). Apple, Alphabet, Amazon, Facebook, and Microsoft are five of the ten most valuable firms in the world today. They get a large portion of their value from their multisided platforms (MSPs), which enable inter-party interactions or transactions. Companies would take advantage of integrating platform business components into their offerings (Hagiu & Altman, 2017).

Getir is a Turkish e-commerce platform that allows customers to place purchases solely using a mobile application. Customers make payments via credit card or when the order delivered to the client. The order appears on the warehouse's computer screen. The warehouse personnel prepares and delivers the order to the motorbike courier employee. Within minutes and, the courier delivers the order to the specified address using the GPS application on their mobile phone for time-conscious customers (Başlangıç Noktası, 2019). Moreover, Getir delivers within 10 minutes and 7/24 in some locations. This model is stated to be the first in the world (Getir, 2021) which is currently serves in UK (London, Birmingham,

Manchester, Cardiff, Liverpool, Bringhton, Bristol), Netherlands (Amsterdam), Germany (Berlin), and France (Paris) (Wikipedia, 2021).

Numerous multisided platforms (MSPs) are more valuable than businesses that provide simply products or services in similar industries: Airbnb, for example, is now more valuable than Marriott, the world's largest hotel company (Hagiu & Altman, 2017). Airbnb's platform-based business model fundamentally alters and threatens the traditional hotel business model. Airbnb enables clients to rent any type of sleeping or living space (from a mattress to an entire house) using an online platform that links visitors with homeowners willing to share a room or a whole house (Kavadias et al., 2016)

Lawson Chain, a convenience store in Japan, and Trendyol, marketplace owned by Alibaba, are other examples of multisided platform. At Lawson, customers can obtain services such as invoice payment, package sending and receiving, and acting as the delivery point for orders placed on e-commerce websites (Hagiu & Altman, 2017). To ease the delivery, Trendyol introduced the delivery point system in Turkey. Customers preference to receive their order via a delivery point (cargo companies, laundry and tobacco shops) ensures them gain a coupon of ₺10. A multisided platform is an illustration of a network and omnichannel distribution system.

Not only do sharing platforms (e.g. Uber, Airbnb, Lyft,) connect users to owners in the most convenient location and at a significantly lower cost than purchasing a good, they also act as a way for developing trust through individual authentication, feedback mechanisms, and online payment processing (Kathan et al., 2016).

Moreover, three types of business models based on cost value, experience value, and platform value exist. Cost value includes "price transparency, consumption-based pricing, reverse auctions, buyer aggregation, rebates and rewards" business models (Aagaard, 2019: 6). Experience value includes business models on "customer choice, personalization, automation, lower latency and any device any time" (Aagaard, 2019: 6). Platform value business model relies on marketplaces, crowdsourcing, peer-to-peer, sharing economy and data monetization (Aagaard, 2019).

Another type of business model is the portal. A portal is a "door", "entrance to a bridge or tunnel", and "a website serving as a guide or point of entry to the World Wide Web and usually including a search engine or a collection of links to other sites arranged especially by topic" (Merriam-Webster Dictionary, n.d.). A portal business model is a website that provides users with online information and information-related services, such as search, community-building, business opportunities, personal productivity apps, and a means of communication with the site owner and other users (Eisenmann & Pothen, 2000). A portal is a site that serves as a starting point for accessing the web and from which the user may access many other sites. The most important function is the collecting of buyers and suppliers to make the transaction easier for the buyer and more efficient for the suppliers (Hartman and Sifonis, 2000). The presentation layer (generally an internet web site) gives the user of the portal access to certain information, dependent upon the user's level of security clearance and/or need to know. Thus, this layer can be personalized, based on the requirements of the user. The data are extracted from different sources and are transmitted from the partners to the portal, wirelessly, over fiber optic cable or via satellite. It is estimated that traffic from portals (search engines-(e.g., Google, Bing, Yandex, Baidu, DuckDuckGo) to content sites is 300% more than traffic from social media (Eroğlu, 2019). In 2013, Google experienced an outage that lasted approximately 5 minutes. The amount of worldwide internet traffic has decreased by around 40% as a result of this process. This may indicate a reliance on search engines (Eroğlu, 2019).

Mark Johnson presented an analogy for the business models. In that analogy, Wikipedia and Youtube resembles crowdsourcing (i.e., outsourcing content creation). Airbnb and Uber are alike digital platforms;

Spotify, LinkedIn, Dropbox resembles freemium system, car2go is alike pay-as-you-go, and Facebook is like data-into-assets (Johnson et al., 2008). Numerous portals (e.g. cimri.com is a gateway to price comparison) have evolved into marketplaces in addition to serving as portals.

Weill & Woerner (2015) based their classification on the company's level of control over the value chain and its desire to engage in understanding the end consumer. Accordingly, businesses should determine if they want complete power over the value chain, become a part of that linear value chain or to take a part in a more complex ecosystem (Weill & Woerner, 2015). Then, they should decide how much time and money they are willing to devote in discovering about their final consumers (Weill & Woerner, 2015). Relying on this, companies have four options: Omni channel business, ecosystem driver, supplier, and modular producer. Omni channel business and ecosystem driver have a comprehensive understanding of their clients, whereas suppliers and modular producers only have a partial insight. With regards to business design, omni channel businesses and suppliers view themselves as part of a value chain, whereas ecosystem drivers and modular producers view themselves as ecosystem members (Weill & Woerner, 2015).

Suppliers (e.g., insurance via agent) have only a superficial understanding of their final consumers, and they work within the value chain of another large corporation. For example, P&G realizes the pitfall of losing power if they do not make an effort to understand its end users and is endeavoring to shift from a supplier model to an omni channel model. By means of omni channel model (e.g. banks, retailers), customers can access the products they need via a variety of channels, including physical and digital, providing them with wider choice and a seamless experience. Ecosystem drivers (e.g. Amazon, Apple, Microsoft) provide a business platform for partners. The platform can be configured to be more or less open (i.e., Google vs. Apple). Modular producers (PayPal) offer plug-and-play items that can adapt to a number of ecosystems (Weill & Woerner, 2015). Alibaba operates an ecosystem in which businesses and consumers interact with each other and the environment (the online platform and the larger off-line physical elements) (Zeng, 2018). In other words, Alibaba is a combination of "Amazon, eBay, PayPal, Google, FedEx, wholesalers, and a good portion of manufacturers do in the United States" which is called smart business, a technology driven platform that synchronizes the interactions of many business participants within an ecosystem (i.e., Taobao, Aliexpress (global marketplace), Ant Financial Services (includes Alipay), Ele.me (delivery), Cainiao Network (logistics), Alibaba Cloud (cloud computing), 1988.com (whosaling-China), Alibaba.com (whosaling-global), Alibaba Pictures/Music/Sports (digital media and entertainment)) (Zeng, 2018). To become a smart business, companies need to enable automation to make more operational choices than individuals accompanied by their own research methodology (Zeng, 2018).

LEAN START-UP

Although it sounds incredible to people who haven't been to one, some businesses are formed on a Friday evening and are generating actual revenue by Sunday afternoon. (Blank, 2013, p. 94)

Traditionally, each entrepreneur is required to create a business plan outlining their revenue, profit, and cash flow projections for the next five years (Blank, 2013) in the past. Similarly, Morris et al. (2005) argues that although business model encapsulates critical components of a business plan, the business plan addresses a variety of start-up and operating challenges that go beyond the model (Morris et al., 2005). However, nowadays it is reported that except for venture capitalists and the former Soviet Union, no one needs five-year forecasts (Blank, 2013). Plans can easily be out of date in turbulent environments, and regulatory uncertainty makes forecasting challenging (Reeves, Zeng, & Venjara, 2015).

A lean start-up, which does not engage in months of planning and research and instead summarizes the enterprise's projections into a framework known as a business model canvas. The business model canvas, developed by Alexander Osterwalderand Yves Pigneur, depicts nine fundamental components - value propositions, key partners, key activities, key resources, customer relationships, customer segments, channels, cost structure, and revenue streams- of a business on one page (Osterwalder & Pigneur, 2010: 44). Osterwalder and Pigneur (2010) take their inspiration from the human brain. On the center there is the value proposition. On the left canvas (logic of the brain) efficiency components of key partners, key assets, key resources, and cost; on the right canvas value (emotions of the brain) customer relationships, customer segments, channels and revenue streams exist (Osterwalder & Pigneur, 2010: 49).

Then, lean start-ups begin testing hypotheses by gathering and soliciting input on all aspects of the business model from potential users, purchasers, and partners. Agile development is used in lean start-ups to save time and resources by rapidly and continuously developing the offering (Blank, 2013). Although start-ups are not scaled-down versions of established firms, Alibaba, like many other companies, employs a continuous "replanning" method to deal with the volatile environment in which it operates (Reeves et al., 2015). Therefore, the lean start-up approach is not specific to startups in the technology sector and the majority of large corporations (e.g. General Electric) acknowledge their need to innovate in order to address ever-increasing external threats (Blank, 2013).

Morris et al. (2005) reported that a business model is composed of six components, many of which resemble a lean startup's business model canvas: *Value creation via offering* component (e.g. goods, services or mixture; standardized, some personalization, high personalization; product lines being narrow/ shallow, medium, broad/deep), *customer component* (e.g. B2B-B2C-both; local-regional-national- international; transactional-relational), *source of competence component* (e.g. production/operation systems, supply chain management, technology/R&D/creative or innovative capability/intellectual), *positioning component* (e.g. product quality/selection/features/availability; innovation leadership; low cost/efficiency), *economic or capturing value component* (e.g. fixed/mixed/flexible pricing and revenue sources; high/ medium/low volumes; high/medium/low margin), *personal/investor component* (e.g. subsistence model; income model; growth model. This framework is regarded as a flexible tool that helps entrepreneurs create value in each of the six areas of focus (Morris et al., 2005).

Social enterprises also uses Business Model Canvas by expanding the questions as follows: "What is the value proposition of the service?, What need is being addressed?, Who is the targeted customer?, Who are potential partners?, Who are our competitors? Can we turn them into partners?, What are associated costs/revenues?, How can we design the service to best serve the client?" (Gorissen, Vrancken, & Manshoven, 2016).

Triple layer business model canvas incorporates economic, environmental, and social considerations into an organization's business model. Economic layer is the same as classical canvas business model of Alexander Osterwalderand Yves Pigneur. Environmental layer includes functional value, supplies and outsourcing, production, end-of life, use phase, distribution, environmental impacts and environmental benefits. The social layer is composed of social value, local communities, governence, employees, societal culture, end-user, scale of outreach, social impacts, and social benefits (Joyce & Paquin, 2016).

Besides, business model canvas and its different versions there are other models. *St Gallen Business Model Navigator* (i.e. offering, value proposition, revenue model, value chain, target market), *value design model* (value drivers, value extracts, value nodes, value exchanges), *DNA* (Design-key partners, key resources, and key activities, Needs-channels, customer relationship, customer segments, Aspirations- value proposition, revenue, cost) model, and *IoT Business Model Framework* (collobrators, inputs, network, service/processing packaging, content/information product, benefits, strategy, tactic) are among the examples of business model canvas (Aagaard, 2019) and they commonly are composed of similar components as the business model canvas.

BUSINESS MODELS' CHANGE AND TRANSFORMATIVE FEATURES

"One secret to maintaining a thriving business is recognizing when it needs a fundamental change" (Johnson et al., 2008, p. 59).

The change is defined as "to make different in some particular." and transformative is "causing or able to cause an important and lasting change in someone or something" (Merriam-Webster Dictionary, n.d.). This section begins by discussing the changing nature of business models; it then discusses the transformative or radical differences and characteristics of business models.

Change in Business Models

As a result of the environmental changes throughout time, it is likely that business model evolution or business model innovation will be essential (Wirtz et al., 2016). However, detailed planning is not possible in business models (Hienerth, Keinz, & Lettl, 2011). Identifying factors that contribute to the success of a business model and sustainable value creation helps managers to decide. For example, comparison of manufacturer-centric value creation versus user-centric value creation opens a sight for the business model (Hienerth et al., 2011). Manufacturer- centric value is created by the company and derived from using a product and regarded as a traditional way of doing business. User-centric value creation examines the impact of users on business model improvements. It is the value derived from usage of the product which also involves customers in new product development, production, and marketing process (co-creation of value) (Hienerth et al., 2011). Firm-user co-creation is crucial in every step of the business model change from idea generation to evaluation of the alternative ideas and commercialization (Hienerth et al., 2011).

On the path to profitability, successful new enterprises often revise their business models at least four times (Johnson et al., 2008). According to a survey, more than half of the companies (7 out of 10) are trying to form new business models and nearly all of them (98%) are changing the current business model (Casadesus-Masanell & Ricart, 2011). Rovio, founder of the Angry Birds game, has continually revised its business model by various updates and different versions of the game (i.e., Angry Birds Rio and Angry Birds Seasons) to satisfy the existing customers and capture new ones (DaSilva & Trkman, 2014). Accordingly, change in the business model is inevitable. However, how to make this change is a vague concept since it cannot be predicted in advance and can be determined as the company experiences and as the time passes like "trial-and-error learning" period (Achtenhagen, Melin, & Naldi, 2013: 428).

During this period, Achtenhagen et al. (2013: 441) mention "that there is no one best way" to achieve the sustained value creation. However, what is crucial in change or whether the company needs this development and change depends on the answers of the managers to the formed questionnaire. The questionnaire includes questions first in value creation strategy actions: "Do you know where and how value is generated in the company?, Do you know which capabilities and competences your company possesses and which it lacks?" (Achtenhagen et al., 2013: 440). Then, managers identify and experiment with new business opportunities by answering the following questions: "Do you systematically interpret major economic and regulatory trends?, Do you systematically retrieve information about changes in the marketplace?" (Achtenhagen et al., 2013: 440). Balanced use of resources is evaluated by answering the questions which are given as follows: "Do you focus on achieving steady cash flows for current and future activities? Are you actively managing and developing your human resources?" (Achtenhagen et al., 2013: 440). Leadership, culture and employees are evaluated by the following questions: "Is an important role of top management to facilitate processes and coach employees?, Can you define your company's culture and what is special about it?" (Achtenhagen et al., 2013: 440). Questions about complementaries are as follows: "Do you have interlinked performance measures, which include quantitative and qualitative targets?, Do you actively monitor how different strategizing actions and critical capabilities interact for value creation?" (Achtenhagen et al., 2013: 440)

Companies determine when a change is required relying on the customer needs and/or environmental opportunities (i.e., unmet needs because of high prices, complex or insufficient available product alternatives in the market, a company's low-cost advantage, new use of existing technology such as adapting a military technology to end-consumers, adapting to the changes in the competitive environment) (Johnson et al., 2008: 58).

Business models resemble "virtuous cycles" and those could not be successful forever because of the competition (Casadesus-Masanell & Ricart, 2011: 6). Three different virtuous cycles of Ryanair is given as an example. All cycles starts with low fares and finishes with even lower fares. In the first and virtuous cycle of low fares is followed by high volumes. The high volumes would cause greater bargaining power over suppliers and lower fixed costs then the company reaches even lower fares. As time passes other competitors imitate this business model. Then the second virtuous cycle starts like the first cycle in terms of low fares, high volumes. High volumes results in high aircraft utilization and low fixed cost per passenger and even lower fares. In the last virtuous cycle, low fares are followed by expectations of low quality service and offering no meals, which lowers costs and ensures even lower fares (Casadesus-Masanell & Ricart, 2011: 6). Then business model of the Ryanair is presented which again offers low fares with no free products that creates a "reputation for fair fares" and lowers costs.

Thus, company's change decisions need to be in coordination with the company's goals. Companies have three alternatives in creating competitive advantage via business models: establishing stronger virtuous cycles, demolish competitors' virtuous cycles, and cooperation with the competitors (Casadesus-Masanell & Ricart, 2011).

Transformative Features of a Business Model

These characteristics are common in transformative business models: (1) personalization, (2) a closed-loop process, (3) asset sharing, (4) usage-based pricing, (5) a collaborative ecosystem, and (6) an agile and adaptive organization." (Kavadias et al., 2016: 5).

- **Personalization:** Several emerging models bring more adaptive or customized products to their clients at competitive pricing by employing technology.
- **A closed-loop process:** Many models replace a linear consumption process with a closed loop. In the linear consumption process, products are manufactured, utilized, and disposed of. However, in a closed loop, used products are recycled, which minimizes overall resource costs.

- **Asset Sharing:** Certain new business models are successful because they enable the sharing of costly assets. Airbnb enables home owners to rent out their properties to visitors, and Uber helps car owners to share their assets.
- **Usage-based Pricing:** As an alternative to requiring customers to purchase an item completely, many business models charge customers on a per-use basis.
- **Collaborative Ecosystem:** Several business models succeed because they improve supply chain collaboration and risk management, resulting in cost savings and more value for customers.
- **Agile and Adaptive Organization:** Successful new business models use technology to make decisions instead of conventional hierarchical structures, allowing for real-time responses to changes (Kavadias et al., 2016).

Three or more of the six characteristics are present in the most transformational company models. No company model, however, possesses all six of these attributes concurrently (Kavadias et al., 2016). Similar to Uber, Martı (a Turkish electric scooter sharing business model, www.marti.tech) possesses five of those characteristics: personalization (e.g., closest car, rating), asset sharing, usage-based pricing, collaborative ecosystem, and agility. When it comes to the Letgo business model, which is defined as a platform that allows for the exchange of used products, personalization, closed loop pricing, usage-based pricing, and a collaborative ecosystem are key features.

These features are tied to technological trends (i.e., optimization (AI, big data) and cloud technologies, platforms) and the needs of the market (i.e., increased demand, increasing input costs, diversified preferences of consumers, pressure of regulations) (Kavadias et al., 2016).

Typical business models focus heavily on creating and capturing value. Besides this, sustainable transformative business models incorporate unmonetized value (negative or positive externalities). A diverse stakeholder network is essential in transformational business models. Beyond the typical consumer emphasis, transformative business models consider all stakeholders' ideas and preferences. More than legislations and regulations transformative business models might alter and possibly even structure market and communities. Transformative business models are those that successfully shape their context by developing alternatives in existing industries (Proka, Beers, & Loorbach, 2018).

FUTURE RESEARCH DIRECTIONS

The COVID-19 pandemic has compelled businesses to seek digital replacements or methods of delivering their products with minimum physical interaction and in a safe manner. Firms can now be more creative in redesigning existing products, creating new digital products, rethinking delivery channels and processes, and looking for strategic positions and partners in the new ecosystem. To succeed in the new ecosystem, businesses must be agile and have dynamic capabilities that enable them to react to changing conditions (Seetharaman, 2020). In addition, in the future research the influence of digitalization on non-monetary outcomes could be investigated (i.e., "the creation of shared value for stakeholders interested in the firm's activities") (Caputo, Pizzi, Pellegrini, & Dabić, 2021: 498). Finally, future studies field studies are expected in the technological innovation, strategic management, and digital transformation aspects (Caputo et al., 2021).

CONCLUSION

Business models are conceptualized and classified in a variety of ways. This chapter defines a business model as a system and network of interactions that enable the creation and capture of value. Additionally, this chapter underlines the infinite possibilities for classifying business models and the complexities inherent in doing so. However, basically most of the successful business models operate relying on a network relations approach whether it is a pipeline, platform, multisided platform, and/or portal.

Besides a narrative method of value creation, a successful business model must also generate revenue or capture value in return. Moreover, lean start-up is discussed in the context of business model canvas, stakeholders' feedback, and agility.

Change is an unavoidable part of any business model. There is, however, a misunderstanding between the concepts of "change" and "transformation". This chapter discusses the characteristics of change in a business model and the business model's transformational characteristics.

REFERENCES

Aagaard, A. (2019). The Concept and Frameworks of Digital Business Models. In A. Aagaard (Ed.), *Digital Business Models Driving Transformation and Innovation* (pp. 1–26). Palgrave Macmillan. doi:10.1007/978-3-319-96902-2_1

Achtenhagen, L., Melin, L., & Naldi, L. (2013). Dynamics of Business Models – Strategizing, Critical Capabilities and Activities for Sustained Value Creation. *Long Range Planning*, *46*(6), 427–442. doi:10.1016/j.lrp.2013.04.002

Başlangıç Noktası, W. (2019). *Getir'in Sosyolojisi* [The Sociology of Getir]. Retrieved July 25, 2021, from https://baslangicnoktasi.org/getirin-sosyolojisi/

Bego Jeans. (n.d.). Retrieved December 14, 2021, from https://www.begojeans.com/

Blank, S. (2013). Why the Lean Start-Up Changes Everything. *Harvard Business Review*, *91*(5), 63–72.

Caputo, A., Pizzi, S., Pellegrini, M. M., & Dabić, M. (2021). Digitalization and business models: Where are we going? A science map of the field. *Journal of Business Research*, *123*, 489–501. doi:10.1016/j.jbusres.2020.09.053

Casadesus-Masanell, R., & Ricart, J. E. (2011, Jan.). How to design a winning business model. *Harvard Business Review*.

Chatterjee, S. (2013). Simple rules for designing business models. *California Management Review*, *55*(2), 97–124. doi:10.1525/cmr.2013.55.2.97

Chesbrough, H. (2010). Business Model Innovation: Opportunities and Barriers. *Long Range Planning*, *43*(2–3), 354–363. doi:10.1016/j.lrp.2009.07.010

DaSilva, C. M., & Trkman, P. (2014). Business Model: What It Is and What It Is Not. *Long Range Planning*, *47*(6), 379–389. doi:10.1016/j.lrp.2013.08.004

Eroğlu, O. (2019). *2018 Yılı Arama Motoru İstatistikleri* [Search Engine Statistics for 2018]. Retrieved September 22, 2021, from https://www.motionb.com/blog/2018-yili-arama-motoru-istatistikleri

Getir. (2021). *Kurucularımız*. Retrieved July 25, 2021, from https://getir.com/hakkimizda/kurucularimiz/

Gorissen, L., Vrancken, K., & Manshoven, S. (2016). Transition Thinking and Business Model Innovation—Towards a Transformative Business Model and New Role for the Reuse Centers of Limburg, Belgium. *Sustainability*, *8*(112), 1–23. doi:10.3390u8020112

Gultekin, B., & Erdem, S. (2021). Omni-Channel Strategy in the Framework of the Search Engines. In T. Dirsehan (Ed.), *Managing Customer Experiences in an Omnichannel World*. Emerald Publishing Limited.

Gultekin, B., & Kement, U. (2018). *Müşteri İlişkileri Yönetimi (Customer Relationship Management)* (1st ed.). Nobel Academic Publishing.

Hagiu, A. (2013). *Multi-Sided Platforms: Foundations and Strategy*. Academic Press.

Hagiu, A., & Altman, E. J. (2017, July). Finding the Platform in Your Product. *Harvard Business Review*.

Hartmans, A. (2021). *Jeff Bezos originally wanted to name Amazon "Cadabra," and 14 other little-known facts about the early days of the e-commerce giant*. Retrieved September 9, 2021, from https://www.businessinsider.com/jeff-bezos-amazon-history-facts-2017-4

Harwood, T., Garry, T., & Broderick, A. (2008). *Relationship Marketing: Perspectives, Dimensions and Contexts*. McGraw-Hill Higher Education.

Hienerth, C., Keinz, P., & Lettl, C. (2011). Exploring the Nature and Implementation Process of User-Centric Business Models. *Long Range Planning*, *44*(5–6), 344–374. doi:10.1016/j.lrp.2011.09.009

Johnson, M. W., Christensen, C. M., & Kagermann, H. (2008). Reinventing your business model. *Harvard Business Review*, *86*(12), 58–68.

Joyce, A., & Paquin, R. L. (2016). The triple layered business model canvas: A tool to design moresustainable business models. *Journal of Cleaner Production*, *135*, 1474–1486. doi:10.1016/j.jclepro.2016.06.067

Kathan, W., Matzler, K., & Veider, V. (2016). The sharing economy: Your business model's friend or foe? *Business Horizons*, *59*(6), 663–672. doi:10.1016/j.bushor.2016.06.006

Kavadias, S., Ladas, K., & Loch, C. (2016). The Transformative Business Models. *Harvard Business Review*, *94*(10), 90–98.

Lindič, J., & Marques da Silva, C. (2011). Value proposition as a catalyst for a customer focused innovation. *Management Decision*, *49*(10), 1694–1708. doi:10.1108/00251741111183834

Liu, J., Tong, T. W., & Sinfield, J. V. (2021). Toward a resilient complex adaptive system view of business models. *Long Range Planning*, *54*(3), 102030. doi:10.1016/j.lrp.2020.102030

Magretta, J. (2002). Why business models matter. *Harvard Business Review*, *80*(5), 86–92. PMID:12024761

Mahadevan, B. (2000). Business models for Internet-based e-commerce: An anatomy. *California Management Review*, *42*(4), 55–69. doi:10.2307/41166053

Marino, U. (2019). *Enrico Piaggio: Vespa (Enrico Piaggio: Un Songo Italiano)*. Moviheart RAI Fiction.

Merriam-Webster Dictionary. (n.d.). *Definition*. Retrieved September 22, 2021, from https://www.merriam-webster.com/dictionary

Morris, M., Schindehutte, M., & Allen, J. (2005). The entrepreneur's business model: Toward a unified perspective. *Journal of Business Research, 58*(6), 726–735. doi:10.1016/j.jbusres.2003.11.001

Niemimaa, M., Järveläinen, J., Heikkilä, M., & Heikkilä, J. (2019). Business continuity of business models: Evaluating the resilience of business models for contingencies. *International Journal of Information Management, 49*, 208–216. doi:10.1016/j.ijinfomgt.2019.04.010

Örnek, N. (2021). *Nasıl Olunur? Bego Abdulhalim Demir*. Retrieved December 18, 2021, from https://spoti.fi/3sbcF86

Osterwalder, A., & Pigneur, Y. (2010). *Business Model Generation A Handbook for Visionaries, Game Changers, and Challengers*. John Wiley & Sons, Inc.

Payne, A., Frow, P., & Eggert, A. (2017). The customer value proposition: Evolution, development, and application in marketing. *Journal of the Academy of Marketing Science, 45*(4), 467–489. doi:10.100711747-017-0523-z

Proka, A., Beers, P. J., & Loorbach, D. (2018). Transformative Business Models for Sustainability Transitions. In L. Moratis, F. Melissen, & S. Idowu (Eds.), *Sustainable Business Models. CSR, Sustainability, Ethics & Governance*. Springer. doi:10.1007/978-3-319-73503-0_2

Reeves, M., Zeng, M., & Venjara, A. (2015, June). The Self-Tuning Enterprise. *Harvard Business Review*.

Scopus. (n.d.). *Scopus (keyword: "business model")*. Retrieved December 14, 2021, from https://bit.ly/3DUwX86

Seetharaman, P. (2020). Business models shifts: Impact of Covid-19. *International Journal of Information Management, 54*, 102173. doi:10.1016/j.ijinfomgt.2020.102173 PMID:32834338

Shafer, S. M., Smith, H. J., & Linder, J. C. (2005). The power of business models. *Business Horizons, 48*(3), 199–207. doi:10.1016/j.bushor.2004.10.014

Teece, D. J. (2010). Business Models, Business Strategy and Innovation. *Long Range Planning, 43*(2–3), 172–194. doi:10.1016/j.lrp.2009.07.003

Van Alstyne, M. W., Parker, G. G., & Choudary, S. P. (2016). Pipelines, Platforms, and the New Rules of Strategy. *Harvard Business Review*, (April), 2–9.

Web of Science. (n.d.). *Web of Science (keyword: "business model")*. Retrieved December 14, 2021, from https://bit.ly/3231OCd

Weill, P., & Woerner, S. L. (2015). Thriving in an Increasingly Digital Ecosystem. *MIT Sloan Management Review, 56*(4), 27–34.

Wikipedia. (2021). *Getir*. Retrieved July 25, 2021, from https://tr.wikipedia.org/wiki/Getir

Wirtz, B. W., Pistoia, A., Ullrich, S., & Göttel, V. (2016). Business Models: Origin, Development and Future Research Perspectives. *Long Range Planning*, *49*(1), 36–54. doi:10.1016/j.lrp.2015.04.001

Yi, Y., Wang, Y., & Shu, C. (2020). Business model innovations in China: A focus on value propositions. *Business Horizons*, *63*(6), 787–799. doi:10.1016/j.bushor.2020.07.002

Zeng, M. (2018, Sept.). Alibaba and the Future of Business Lessons from China's innovative digital giant. *Harvard Business Review*.

Ziaie, A., ShamiZanjani, M., & Manian, A. (2021). Systematic review of digital value propositions in the retail sector: New approach for digital experience study. *Electronic Commerce Research and Applications, 47*, 101053.

ADDITIONAL READING

Currie, W. L. (2004). Value creation from e-Business models: issues and perspectives. *Value Creation from E-Business Models*, 3–10. doi:10.1016/B978-075066140-9/50003-5

de Faria, V. F., Santos, V. P., & Zaidan, F. H. (2021). The Business Model Innovation and Lean Startup Process Supporting Startup Sustainability. *Procedia Computer Science*, *181*, 93–101. doi:10.1016/j.procs.2021.01.106

Guo, L., Wei, S. Y., Sharma, R., & Rong, K. (2017). Investigating e-business models' value retention for start-ups: The moderating role of venture capital investment intensity. *International Journal of Production Economics*, *186*, 33–45. doi:10.1016/j.ijpe.2017.01.021

Larosa, F., & Mysiak, J. (2020). Business models for climate services: An analysis. *Climate Services*, *17*, 100111. doi:10.1016/j.cliser.2019.100111

Osterwalder, A., & Pigneur, Y. (2004). An ontology for e-Business models. *Value Creation from E-Business Models*, 65–97. doi:10.1016/B978-075066140-9/50006-0

Palmaccio, M., Dicuonzo, G., & Belyaeva, Z. S. (2021). The internet of things and corporate business models: A systematic literature review. *Journal of Business Research*, *131*, 610–618. doi:10.1016/j.jbusres.2020.09.069

Radenković, M., Bogdanović, Z., Despotović-Zrakić, M., Labus, A., & Lazarević, S. (2020). Assessing consumer readiness for participation in IoT-based demand response business models. *Technological Forecasting and Social Change*, *150*, 119715. doi:10.1016/j.techfore.2019.119715

Shin, J., & Park, Y. (2009). On the creation and evaluation of e-business model variants: The case of auction. *Industrial Marketing Management*, *38*(3), 324–337. doi:10.1016/j.indmarman.2007.06.017

KEY TERMS AND DEFINITIONS

Business Model: An interdependent system and network of operations and decisions for the purpose of creating and capturing value, which may require change or transformation over time.

Business Model Canvas: One page summary of a business model which is a part of the lean start-up. It includes the headings of value propositions, key partners, key activities, key resources, customer relationships, customer segments, channels, cost structure, and revenue streams.

Business Model Change: To make an incremental difference in a business model.

Ecosystem: Interrelated parts, dimensions, and organizations acting as a unit.

Lean Start-Up: To develop an agile business model focusing on the quick response of the consumers and associated partners without the necessity of a long-term business plan.

Multisided Platforms: Connect two or more independent but mutually dependent client segments. To generate value, the platform must appeal to and serve all groups concurrently.

Pipeline Business Model: The traditional value chain structure consists of suppliers, producers, intermediaries, and customers, and is characterized by a hierarchy and unequal distribution of power among the participants.

Platform: A comprehensive type of business model (e.g., marketplaces, freemiums, and multisided platforms) that integrates owner, provider, producer, and consumer.

Portal: A business model which is a point of entry into a content, communication, and/or commerce channel.

Transformative Business Model: A crucial and lasting change in a business model.

Value: A concept that can be defined and expressed in a variety of ways. Value can be established through cost-benefit analysis, or it can be obtained primarily from product quality, low price, assortment, convenience, customer service, and ethical judgments. Value can be created in the factory, by the consumer, or through the company's collaboration with the client (co-creation).

ENDNOTE

1 Jeff Bezos wanted Amazon brand name be "Cadabra" or "Relentless". Brand name could not be "Cadabra" since it resembles "cadaver" "especially over the phone". In addition, when you type "Relentless.com", it directs you to Amazon (Hartmans, 2021).

Chapter 4
Digital Transformation:
Technology and New Business Models as Drivers of Customer Experience

Dinesh Kumar
Jagran Lakecity University, India

ABSTRACT

Digital marketing and strategy are often thought of as using modern internet and communication technologies in a company's business operations. Companies have used such technologies to communicate with stakeholders, reduce costs, engage customers, and so on. Even today, many digital marketing courses focus on gathering views on brand content, gaining followers, or making users click on links and advertisements. Likewise, many companies wrongly understand that digital marketing is simply about using modern internet and communication technologies in conducting business or spreading their message. This chapter explains that digital technologies offer an opportunity to businesses to re-invent themselves by keeping customer experience firmly in focus. If they do so, they stand a much better chance of surviving and thriving in a considerably changed marketing environment. Transformation must occur in their business model, organisation structure and processes, people and culture, and above all, their focus on solving customer problems.

INTRODUCTION

Businesses thrive when they deliver the customer experience expected of them. Since customers like to shop at places where they feel good, delivering and surpassing customer expectations is the path to long term loyalty and higher consumer spends.

Customer experience is a function of people, processes and technology, which are guided by corporate vision. As technology has advanced, it offers ways to provide customer experience in many ways, supporting people and creating processes that enhance every interaction that a customer has with a company. The value of digital marketing and strategy, often thought of as using modern internet and communication technologies in a company's business operations, actually offers unique ways by which to enhance customer experience. Kumar (2021) writes that though many digital marketing courses even

DOI: 10.4018/978-1-7998-9179-6.ch004

today focus on gathering views on brand content, gaining followers or making users click on links and advertisements, its actual contribution is much richer if we deploy it to deliver and surpass expectations of customers.

This chapter explains that digital technologies provide a way to re-imagine businesses. Old methods of doing business give way to new ones as companies adopt digital transformation. The idea is to have a clear digital strategy that is able to change its existing culture and style of working and invent a completely new way of doing business, transforming processes, talent engagement and business models. Companies that are not digitally mature focus on operational technologies, whereas those that are digitally mature look to transforming the business.

The chapter is organised as follows. We first explain the concept of digital transformation. Usually companies treat digital as just another department in the organisation, but it actually means re-inventing business models. Companies have to use digital to develop ecosystems that exert gravitational pull. After digital transformation, companies must strive for digital mastery, which is explained in the next section. Digital mastery is obtained by building four pillars, embedding digital technologies in business operations and the organisation's DNA.

Next, we look at how companies reinvent their business models and try to optimise consumer decision journeys. This leads us to the next step – rebuilding the organisation. The next section describes how new business models must be oriented towards delivering customer experience at all times. We illustrate this with the help of several companies that have successfully transformed themselves.

We have selected two case studies to show how companies must transform themselves. The first is that of Asian Paints, an old economy company founded in 1942. The case study describes how the company has transformed itself and build digital technologies into its DNA. The second case study shows that being digital savvy is not enough – even a modern, highly digital company like Microsoft can hurtle towards extinction if the focus on customer experience is lost. The case study describes how it became a digital master again.

The case studies highlight our argument that companies must constantly reinvent themselves. Being digital is not enough – it is important to use digital technologies to enhance customer experience. Only companies that marry digital transformation with an obsession with customer experience can hope to survive in an environment marked by Volatility, Uncertainty, Complexity and Ambiguity, which is remembered by the acronym VUCA.

The objective of this chapter is to show that digital technologies are not simply "add-ons" or tools to conduct business. They have the potential to completely transform business models. Companies that can build digitally transform and change their DNA have a better chance to deliver customer experience than ones who merely treat digital intervention as a separate unit or department.

We hope to draw attention to a gap that exists in many companies: their efforts of using technology are limited to digitising some functions or using social media messages. Yet, a majority of companies mistake digitising a few functions as being digitally savvy. But, as pointed out by Leinwand & Mani (2021), digitising is not the same as digital transformation. The "accelerated wave of digital initiatives must not be confused with the real business transformation needed for success in the digital age," they write. Digital strategy must be about building real, long-term competitive advantage.

DIGITAL TRANSFORMATION

Digital transformation or strategy consists of integrating digital technologies such as social, mobile, analytics and cloud. Individually they cannot contribute meaningfully to company strategy but the real strength arises from integrating them into the business model. Hanelt et al (2021) explain that digital transformation means continuous adaptation which is driven by digital business ecosystems, resulting in malleable organizational designs. They find that such a transformation is only partially covered by conventional frameworks on organizational change. Further, it calls for a change in a company's culture. A review by Nadkarni & Prügl (2021) reveals that certain aspects, such as the pace of transformation, the culture and work environment, or the middle management perspective are significantly underdeveloped in most companies.

Benkler (2006) writes that the new information and communications technologies do not simply introduce efficiency into traditional ways of doing business, but also support fundamentally new ways of doing things. It is up to businesses to discover ways to go beyond operational efficiencies and use technology creatively providing a deeper connect with consumers. The opportunity is to use digital transformation by using technology and new business models as drivers of customer experience.

Indeed, customers' expectations have also been changing. Verhoef et al (2021) find that digital transformation has fundamentally altered consumers' expectations and behaviors. They too stress that digital transformation requires specific organizational structures and different metrics than the ones used earlier.

Many companies make the mistake of treating digital as another functional department. They use it as a way of communicating with customers through their social media and other channels, posting content and encouraging customer engagement. Such efforts bypass the tremendous benefits that can be achieved by a complete digital transformation, or integrating technology into each operation of a business. Tabrizi et al (2019) write that digital transformation is not about technology, but also about people's mindsets and organisational practices. Matarazzo et al (2021) studied organisations in Italy and found that digital instruments contribute to innovation of their business model, creating new distribution channels and new ways to create and deliver value to customer segments.

Today, competition is also not limited to existing competitors but can come from unimagined sources. An app that solves customer problems on the basis of deep customer knowledge can threaten existing businesses. For example, in the digital world the competition to a travel agency is not with other travel agencies but with a search engine that is able to provide information better than agencies. In this way, new business models based on data are created that create value in many new ways.

Digital technologies can help create new and better ways of delivering customer experience if companies can transform themselves to:

1. Expand the scope of their businesses
2. Re-invent their business models
3. Invest in creating ecosystems that pull customers

As these are new strategies, they are further elaborated here.

A. Expand the Scope of Business: Digital marketing is generally misunderstood as promoting and branding business through digital media. However, digital technologies allow expansion of scope of business. Johnson et al (2008) describe ways in which the scope of business can be expanded:

- **Accomplish tasks in better ways.** When companies analyse data streams, they are not merely data crunching transactional data, but can discover past patterns, write Meyer & Schwager (2007). For example, companies need not invest in surveys to understand consumer behaviour but can get accurate insights by data analytics.
- **Solve a long standing problem.** Businesses are not just supplying products and services. Those businesses stand to gain who solve customer problems. For example, e-wallets and micro payments have helped the poor to have accounts and keep their money securely. Similarly, Netflix has solved a problem of delivering entertainment to people's homes. By solving problems, companies are able to expend their scope and tap new customers.
- **Expand markets and help tap new market segments.** Digital transformation helps companies go beyond their traditional markets and segments. For instance, books now publish electronic versions today, helping expand their reach to areas where they are not available. Restaurants use home delivery apps to expand their business.

B. Reinvent the Business Model: Customer experience is enhanced when business models are reinvented. Digital technologies lead to reinvention of business models in four ways, write Johnson et al (2008):

- **Changing the customer value proposition:** Digital technologies allow companies to anticipate customer needs. E-commerce companies, for instance, track purchase data and offer subscription services which saves customer time for re-ordering.
- **Changing the profit formula:** Companies can alter their revenue and cost structures by using new technologies. Digitising supply chains changes the profit formula. For instance, companies can use artificial intelligence and just-in-time methods to save inventory costs while also helping customers by real time tracking of their orders.
- **Key resources**: Key resources refer to elements that create value and differentiation. These are a combination of people, facilities, equipment and channels, which are modified by technology to have a consistent focus on customers.
- **Key processes:** Companies build processes that help them achieve competitive advantage. A simple process like helping customers track shipments, for example, becomes a key process in achieving differentiation. Similarly, companies can use digital techniques to automate or improve recurrent tasks that are either efficient or help customers in some way.

Pull strategy: Companies use the web to develop an ecosystem which exerts a pull on customers. In the digital age, the focus of marketing has shifted from *push to pull*: while push ads and notifications are increasingly blocked, consumers seek out products themselves. Boncheck (2017) explains that in such an ecosystem, "the new challenge is to have influence from a distance." He draws a parallel to how gravity exerts a force of pull from a distance. Like the solar system, the company's digital strategy is at the centre and customers are like planets. They are in orbit and feel the gravitational pull. This implies that the company's core – or digital strategy – must exert a strong enough influence to pull them in towards the company. To achieve this, new business models must achieve three objectives: (a) *attract* customers by exerting an influence that pulls them towards it; (b) *observe and influence* consumers from a distance, understanding them without being too pesky and without interfering in their lives; and (c) *be ubiquitous* by participating in the larger culture, using technologies to be everywhere the customer expects them to be.

This is how customer experience is impacted by companies. The gravity analogy sums up how companies must exert influence in the online space. The focus of companies changes from products to purpose through a strong focus on customer experience, which exerts a pull influence on consumers to get them into the brand's orbit just as gravity pulls an object closer. Influence is gained by going beyond products, encouraging interactions among people without controlling them. Companies must develop *gravity generators*, *experiential orbits* and *force multipliers* so that customers do not leave the orbit of the brand and the pull becomes stronger successively.

- **Gravity generators**: People feel attracted to a company if they feel a shared purpose with it. They may or may not be customers but people who are attracted to the company for a shared reason or common ground.
- **Experiential orbits**: Keeping customers in orbit means maintaining ongoing relationships with them. The company does not focus on individual transactions but on having long term relationships with their customers.
- **Force multipliers**: As customers and stakeholders start getting closer, they start exerting their own gravitational pull, becoming force multipliers. The company can be visualised a solar system with the core of shared purpose and stakeholders orbiting around that purpose.

The shared purpose builds customer experience through emotional connect. This is something that a company must develop over time. Companies that do so are referred to as digital masters.

DIGITAL MASTERY

Though every company is using digital technology in one way or the other, companies that have achieved digital maturity do so much better than everyone else and are referred to as "Digital Masters" by Westerman (2014). Hence they remain ahead of their competitors. It is not a matter of which technology or software package they are using, but how they make use of technology to implement business practices. Customer experience is developed through two capabilities that every company must excel in:

- **Digital capabilities:** Digital masters invest in digital capabilities that contribute directly in improving business processes and customer engagements that shorten consumer decision journeys. They are always looking for technologies that help in solving business problems.
- **Leadership capabilities:** Digitally mature companies have the capability of leading change. They use data streams and combine them with technology solutions for future growth, make better decisions, and build efficiency in their supply chains. They are better able to understand customers and use their leadership capabilities to drive transformation and modify their business models.

Digital Masters are not technology companies but those companies that are able to use digital technologies to improve their customer experience. Examples of digital masters are Asian Paints and Nike, which illustrate how a paint manufacturer and a sports goods company reinvented their models and to come closer to its customers by using technology. Such companies report better profits than others in the same industry. On the other hand, even a digitally native company like Microsoft can lose track of its customers and miss out on growth opportunities. It was only after the company reinvented itself that it could become a master again, as our case study at the end of the chapter shows.

Digital masters can be distinguished from other companies in their use of technology. For example, many companies simply follow the latest trend and adopt it because everybody else is doing it. So they invest in publishing blogs, creating branded content, engage on social media and so on without any clear strategy. Such companies are dubbed as *fashionistas* who flaunt technology but it does not contribute to profits. Unfortunately there are a large number of companies that fall in this category.

On the other extreme are *conservatives* who are very careful in deploying technology. They invest in a few functions but an integrated approach or a leadership role is missing. Conservative companies stress on control and thereby miss opportunities in business. Usually there are no digital leaders on their boards.

Digital masters get over the limitations of both fashionistas and conservatives. Digital masters drive their strategy from the boardroom rather than adding digital components to their functions. This is an important distinction. It helps not just gain efficiencies from new technologies but shows the company a path to tap new markets and to reinvent itself.

Carr (2013) writes that companies fall in the trap of focusing on technology as an end in itself, whereas technology must be used as a means to achieve strategic objectives. Apart from tracking customer behavior and enhancing experience across channels, digital technologies help increase reach, engagement and customer experiences. Digital transformation happens across supply chains in order to improve customer experience across platforms.

Another reason to achieve digital mastery is the volatile business environment that companies operate in these days. Fletcher & Griffiths (2020) write that the Covid pandemic showed that digitally immature organisations were fragile. Business organisations would be foolish to ignore the VUCA environment – (Volatility, Uncertainty, Complexity and Ambiguity). The authors mention three key lessons learned from the pandemic period: (i) organisations must improve their digital maturity, (ii) digitally immature organisations are more fragile, and (iii) digitally mature organisations tend to be more flexible. Organisations can ignore VUCA and digital transformation at their own peril.

FOUR PILLARS OF DIGITAL TRANSFORMATION

Sahu, Deng, and Mollah (2018) write that digital transformation consists of data analytics, trends analytics, process analytics, strategic execution, business model, value proposition, customer processes, customer collaboration, customer services, customer engagement, integration, capability, and capacity.

Rather than follow digital fads, digital strategy consists of integrating online marketing activities to deliver seamless customer experience. Gupta (2018) explains that successful companies do not treat digital strategy as separate from their overall strategy so it is important to integrate all aspects of business. He writes that companies must embed digital technologies into their operations and DNA. For example, companies may implement electronic payments because of ease of use, but rather than function as stand-alone systems, they can be integrated into the company's cash and credit management system and also into the sales and order system.

Digital strategy is a plan to achieve competitive advantage through improved customer experience by making use of data assets and technology-based initiatives. It has four pillars as summarised in Table 1.

Table 1. Four pillars of digital strategy

Re-imagine the Business	Value Chain	Customer Connect	Rebuild the Organization
Expand the scope	Open Innovation	Engaging and acquiring customers	Managing Digital Transition
Reinvent the business model	Industry 4.0	Optimizing consumer decision journeys	Designing an Organization for Innovation
Use a pull strategy through platforms and ecosystems	Omnichannel Strategy	Measuring marketing ROI for each intervention	Skills, Capability, and Talent Management

Source: Adapted from Gupta (2018)

As the world shifts to digital, new business models emerge. Table 1 shows that businesses are able to expand much beyond their traditional scope, enhancing their value chains at every stage, developing a laser focus on their customers and re-inventing their business that keeps customer at the heart of operations. Traditional structures like bureaucracies and strict departmentalisation are demolished.

REINVENTING BUSINESS MODELS

Traditional business models focus on selling goods and services and thereby making a profit. The customer was an entity to be served at a price that ensured profits for the corporation. But digital technologies promise to change the way companies create and deliver value. Johnson et al (2008) describe three components of the business model:

- **Customer value proposition**: How the company serves its customers better than others. Instead of product offerings, new business models describe the problem that they solve for customers.
- **Profit formula:** A company traditionally generated value both for the customer and for itself by improvements in its product offerings. Now it can segment markets better, offer dynamic prices and acquire flexibility in product offerings. The profit formula has therefore become much more complex than in the past.
- **Key resources and processes:** A combination of key resources that deliver the value proposition to customers.

Business models are re-invented in order to improve customer connect, which results in better customer experience. Companies know which customers to acquire by analysing long term profitability and customer lifetime value (CLV). Engaging customers by influencing moments of truth (MOT) and story-telling is possible in the digital era. Interactions at each stage can be measured through metrics and marketing spends can be optimised. Customer-connect must have the objective of moving consumers along their decision journeys to purchase and post-purchase recommendations.

Digital technologies enable companies to engage their customers. Companies adopt various methods such as encouraging two way communication, providing platforms for reviews and comments, using social media and so on. Emotional connections are established for long term bonding with brands.

More important, the new business models help in optimizing consumer decision journeys. The consumer decision journey (CDJ) shows the interactions with brands as the prospect moves towards deciding what to buy. This means optimizing cross-channel experiences. Technologies must be used to "lead rather than follow customers on their digital journeys," write Edelman and Singer (2015). CDJs are a source of competitive advantage in the digital era. By optimising CDJs and making them innovative, compelling and interesting, companies can earn their customers' loyalty. Hence companies must invest in automation to personalize their interactions and journeys and deliver content that customers appreciate. Companies can measure the effectiveness of each intervention through real-time marketing metrics.

REBUILDING THE ORGANIZATION

The new business organisation must have a sharp focus on customers. Every department is focused on enhancing customer experience, and the new organisation does not have walls between departments. The formulation of digital strategy leads to developing new capabilities of both digital and traditional businesses. Favaro (2016) writes that digital technology can be used to:

- Expand companies' boundaries upstream or downstream
- Add value to the business through information and delivery
- Change target consumers and find new segments
- Enhance value proposition to target customers through products or services
- Differentiate from competition – use social media or big data to differentiate

Every company must therefore turn into a "math house," writes Ram Charan (2016). "Every winning company will be using algorithms, or mathematical rules for processing information, to shape end-to-end customer experience," he writes. As the volume of data increases exponentially, companies must process streaming information from various sources: sensors, search engines, social media, retail stores, and so on. Algorithms process this huge data to produce amazing results, and help businesses with insights that would not be available otherwise.

The first important change is that companies think beyond their products and build platforms that involve all partners, including customers and outsiders: Metcalfe's law states that the more the people associated with the platform, the more will be its value. General Electric (GE), for instance, which is a traditional company, has created a platform for the entire energy industry.

The second change required is to break silos that traditional industry is comfortable with. All departments must operate as one. Companies must digitize all operations across channels: customers may interact with product design or manufacturing, then move to partner channels for delivery, and then on to service. Customer experience across all units and channels must be unified, which requires breaking of department silos. Very often, managers will have to overcome cultural resistance as well.

Digital transformation must result in strong customer focus and breakdown of rigid structures that are created to achieve functional efficiency. That is why they face difficulty in adapting to the digital revolution. Gürkan & Tükeltürk (2017) write that decentralization, autonomy and managing risk are required. However, these are difficult to achieve in present organisations that encourage departmental empires. Zacca and Dayan (2017) say that large organizations are focused on maintaining status quo making administrators out of managers and hence the resistance to change. But reinventing business models requires a redesign of traditional organisations. Managers have to be geared to new technologies to keep track of marketing metrics. Further, what is required in today's world is "enterprise agility" so as to respond to changes quickly, respond and adapt to customer needs, increase efficiency in operations, engage customers and empower employees.

The challenges before companies are to recruit people who act like venture capitalists rather than managers. Traditional hierarchies have to be dismantled and freedom has to be given to teams. Performance indicators rest on agile practices that gain digital talent and leadership. To retain talent, career paths and growth avenues have to be designed. HR, which traditionally manages things like recruitment, compensation and similar functions, has to acquire new capabilities. For example, to be customer-centric, organisations must keep their employees happy, motivated and dedicated. Above all, a culture has to be established that achieves two things: first, it must empower people to deliver customer experience, and second, it must attract, retain and reward talent.

Digital transformation, thus, goes much beyond adopting technologies. It includes developing people and processes, organisational redesign and customer-centricity.

To achieve customer centricity, companies use customer oriented branded content, site optimisation and inbound links, investing in keywords, and building communities. Techniques like just-in-time marketing, artificial intelligence and programmatic marketing are also part of digital strategy. Finally companies are able to achieve segment-of-one marketing by deploying data analytics.

In doing this, companies have to move beyond their focus on branded content. A plethora of digital marketing articles has led companies to believe that developing content is the way to get engaged audiences. Called "content marketing," it led to a great push toward branded content. Content marketing is a marketing technique that involves the creation and sharing of online material such as videos, blogs, infographics, podcasts, social media posts and other types of content so that it drives interest in the company's products or services. It looks like ads, but does not add to customer experience.

The online content that is consumed widely contains stories, characters, entertainment or delivers value of some kind. A list of the 100 most popular youtube channels based on subscriber count (socialblade.com) shows that brand content is not popular; only TV channels, celebrities, entertainers, and other types of content providers dominate the list. Similarly, Instagram top rankings (hyperauditor.com) are also dominated by entertainers, many of them unknown. As the list is updated based on the number of followers, it shows popularity of young entertainers from all over the world who have gained viewers. There are no brands or companies on the top-rankers list, showing that brand content does not figure in the reckoning on social media sites. Without customer experience, most viewers skip advertising videos or simply abandon the content. Platforms like Netflix and Amazon offer advertising-free content and are thus gaining traction worldwide.

The main problem that branded content faces is that users can opt out of ads. Companies cannot buy fame on the Internet as they were able to in traditional media. Now they have to compete directly with real entertainment. Brand content is seen as spam. Social media platforms charge companies if they want to push their "sponsored" content into the feeds of people who are following them or are defined by the companies. This shows the need to use a combination of digital elements.

CREATING NEW BUSINESS MODELS FOR CUSTOMER EXPERIENCE

While customer experience can be enhanced by using a combination of methods influencer marketing, site optimisation, inbound links and keyword advertising, digital transformation requires innovation in business models.

The entire activities of a business corporation must be transformed. Some of these are described below:

- **Customer acquisition:** Some digital business models suggest that services are offered free with the hope of monetising the large network thus built.
- **Value Chains:** Value chains are now focused on customer needs rather than being limited to supply chains.
- **Key activities and resources:** The company's key activities and resources undergo a change, as the case studies cited in this chapter show.
- **Key partners:** There are no competitors. New business models demand that competitors be turned into key partners.
- **Value proposition:** New business models build value propositions on the basis of how they solve problems for customers and are not focused on products.
- **Customer relationships:** Digital technologies provide the opportunity to redefine and build customer relationships. Very often customers are turned into partners and consultants.
- **Revenue streams:** Earlier revenue streams were limited to what companies could sell. New models help discover new revenue streams arising from network value.
- **Segments of one:** Market segments are usually thought of as grouping of customers with common characteristics. Today business models focus on individuals, turning each customer into a segment that can be served individually.

Deloitte's (2017) report on future digital readiness concludes that the digital lends strength to all the key characteristics of a successful organisation: agility, flexibility, mobility, flat hierarchy and adaptability. Large scale change can be undertaken only by companies that are geared to take advantage of the shift to digital.

Several companies have achieved digital mastery. These companies have integrated digital technologies in their business models rather than using them to improve functional efficiencies. For instance, the newspaper industry has been struggling since the advent of digital. News are available on social media; there is no need to buy a newspaper. The newspaper reading habit has been declining over the years. Both circulation of papers and their advertising revenues has been drying up. Newspapers are struggling, and some have folded up. *The New York Times* did not fall into this trap. Realising that people would pay for independent journalism, analysis and opinion, it went beyond the news. It followed a subscription model so that users pay for its online content. By 2019 it reported more than $800 million in digital revenue, with over 500 million digital subscribers, far greater than any other newspaper group.

Companies that succeed in the digital era have invested in the omnichannel approach.

A mobile app that provides ease of trading experience has helped Zerodha achieve success in India. Disney has installed IoT sensors in their parks. A RFID band called MagicBand wristband is provided to its guests. These bands are connected to the sensors and act as payment, hotel room keys and even ride tickets. In this way, Disney is able to collect data about its customers that are used to improve UX. Walmart launched a mobile app can be used by customers to calculate the costs of their shopping lists. At the store, the app's 'store assistant' guides them to items on their list via a map.

These companies have used different strategies for their digital transformation. At the heart of their transformation is a strong focus on the customer. They borrow wisdom from the physical world, in which customer experience keeps companies one step ahead of the competition or changing technology.

We further illustrate how technology and new business models act as drivers of customer experience with the help of two case studies. Asian Paints, a paint manufacturer, was founded in 1942. It re-invented itself to provide a unique experience to people who wanted to redecorate their homes. In contrast, the second case of Microsoft shows that a digital leader lost its way by concentrating on products rather than customers, and how it bounced back after discovering its customers again. The first case shows that a traditional company could change its culture and model to serve customers, the send shows that re-discovering the customer pays rich dividends.

CASE STUDIES

Asian paints: Digital masters need not be technology companies but those that are able to use digital technologies effectively to transform themselves for growth and profits. Asian Paints is a leading paint manufacturer and one of India's most valuable brands. It has re-invented itself by weaving "a modern digital backbone into the fabric of its organization," according to a report by Cognizant (2018). In 2013 the company decided to 'Go Digital'.

Its focus shifted from being a paints manufacturing company to a provider of home improvement services. It realised that while customers could buy paint from anywhere, they needed help and advice when they were redecorating their homes. By providing a strong customer experience, it provided Easycolour Consultancy to guide customers about the colour decor and even *vastu* (traditional Indian system of architecture).

By mapping customer journeys and touchpoints, the company found that customers wanted advice when they wanted to redo their homes. It decided to offer consultancy services, thus differentiating from other paint companies.

The exercise began by understanding the customer. It found that customers did not buy paint directly but looked for help about colours and styles when they decided to re-do their homes. The company identified two lucrative segments: (a) the upper middle class and the newly rich who wanted to show off their wealth through lavishly decorated houses, and (b) the educated, foreign returned Indian who wanted a high-end home in India.

The company's CRM system connects with customers, analyses data for loyalty, calculates Net Promoter Score (NPS) and measures Customer Satisfaction (SAT). A seamless experience to customers, dealers and influencers is provided by connecting all channels—physical, digital and human. The omnichannel approach helped the company to develop seamless customer journeys, helping to generate unique offers to each customer. An integrated view provides data to the call centres, consultants and dealers for responding to customer needs and queries.

One major achievement was to be able to get over the resistance from employees and partners and to change its culture towards adopting digital technology across physical channels.

The company used social media initially to address customer complaints and later for campaigns to educate customers about home décor solutions. In this way, the company has transformed itself from being a bricks-and-mortar business into a 'click-and-mortar' business.

Along with its digital initiatives, the company undertook a physical transformation as well. To meet the needs of the modern customers, the company launched large showrooms with an average area of 10,000 square feet in partnership with dealers. Equipped with 3D visualization and virtual reality, these stores provide customers with a visual experience, allowing them to experience different colours and textures. Consultants assist in the decision-making process. IoT, AI, chatbots and natural language translation capabilities are also used.

The company has a strong web presence with sites such as asianpaints.com, sleekworld.com and beautifulhomes.com. These serve as platforms for consumers looking for advice on painting and decorating their homes. Asian Paints tracks customer interaction data and leverages the data with advanced web analytics and personalization technology to position content with customer offers.

Although Asian Paints is known as a paint manufacturer, it has acquired companies dealing in modular kitchen space and bathroom fittings that fit perfectly with its thrust on the home improvement business. It has integrated technology into its operations, with the IT head as part of the corporate advisory board, which has helped the company to use modern technology in its business operations, keeping it ahead of the curve.

Given that Asian Paints is an 'old economy' company, it has managed the transition to technology very well. It has invested in people, culture and technology, using its legacy to build its brand equity. The company uses 3D visualization for showing various home décor options to customers. Partners use this to create visual models for customers, speeding up their purchase decision cycles. Customers can also interact with bots that assist them in their choices. The company uses the 'Eureka' app for generating new product ideas, which has been very successful.

Using an omnichannel approach, Asian Paints uses digital technologies to engage customers, dealers and influencers by supporting CDJs in the physical world using Colour Ideas and Signature Stores, and in the virtual world using websites and mobile technologies. It adds a human touch by providing colour consultancy through partners and dealers. Pain points of customers are eased by various means. One is a colour visualizer app, and another is the Signature Stores where the whole family can experience their home upgradation. An ecosystem has been created for contractors who play a key role in delivering services. Today, a contractor can engage with customers and the company through the mobile app.

Microsoft: Microsoft is well known for the computer revolution it spawned by providing the operating systems that made personal computers useful for millions of people around the world. It was the most valuable company for many years but lost out to other companies like Google, Amazon and Apple. People started talking of Microsoft's demise: in 2007, a blog post "Microsoft is Dead" became highly popular. Having missed out on the mobile revolution, it seemed that the company which gave the world Windows would slowly vanish as other companies and technologies continued to gain favour.

It didn't happen that way. In 2018, Microsoft briefly became the most valuable company in the world once again, pushing Apple to second place. Naughton (2019) explains that behind Microsoft's comeback is an excellent use of strategy that encompasses using digital technologies, company culture, and transformation. The company had changed course when Satya Nadella had taken over as CEO, replacing Steve Ballmer in 2014.

With its focus on Windows, Microsoft had let the mobile and social media revolution pass it by. It had not been able to capitalise on its OS capability, leaving the advantage to Google's Android system. Microsoft came back in the reckoning by re-inventing not only its business model but changing the way it did business.

Microsoft revelled it its Windows domination. Bill Gates had articulated his dream of a computer on every desk, each running Microsoft software. The dream had been realized and Windows had become ubiquitous. However, the company could not capitalise on developments that came about later. The rise of the internet, cloud computing, the arrival of smartphones – all had pushed Microsoft aside. The late arrival of the Nokia mobile phone running on Windows operating system did nothing for the company.

Under Nadella, Microsoft gave up its obsession with Windows. Instead, it opted for open-source software projects using Linux and cloud technologies. Shifting focus from Windows, it put sales emphasis on Microsoft's Azure cloud services. Today, it competes with Amazon Web Services, which is the market leader in the commercial cloud.

At the same time, Microsoft moved away from pushing its Windows monopoly and instead focused on developing partners. This has ensured expansion of Azure's portfolio and also ensures ability to work with companies' existing data centres. Instead of competing, Microsoft has formed partnerships with competitors like Dropbox, Red Hat, Salesforce and even Amazon.

Microsoft's new way of doing business was to become a horizontally diversified company. It developed its cloud computing capabilities, and the open source helped target its services at users of iPhone, Android and Linux. Developers were freed from building systems compatible with Windows only and instead Microsoft became a more customer focused company, developing products for them rather than for Windows.

In the process, the image of the company also changed – from being a monopolistic threat, it is now seen as a responsible corporation in the networked world. While Google and Facebook face heavy fines for data misuse and their use of monopoly power, Microsoft has not faced such controversies in recent years.

The rebound of Microsoft provides lessons for companies operating in the digital world, becoming important lessons in digital strategy. In becoming a digital master again, Microsoft shifted focus on customers. Microsoft looked for new ways to serve customers, changing its product focus. There's a lesson to be learnt from Microsoft – companies must change and adapt (*The Economist*, 2019). Long term survival depends on how new opportunities are used.

FUTURE RESEARCH DIRECTIONS

Many companies still treat digital marketing as an add-on to their traditional marketing efforts and are not well prepared for digital transformation. A survey of digital future readiness of Swiss companies by Deloitte (2017) confirms this. It found that 61% of the companies were correctly positioned for digital transformation as far as business models and organisational DNA was concerned. 57% had the requisite culture to do so, 42% had the right people policies geared towards transformation, and 32% had the right digital environment. These figures show that companies struggle to achieve digital transformation.

Further, the case studies in this chapter show that digital natives may not be well geared for digital transformation, even as traditional companies can achieve this with the right organisation, people, culture, and digital infrastructure. The failure of digital start-ups shows that it is not enough to be a digital native to reap the benefits of technology.

Researchers can focus their attention on what companies can do for effective digital transformation. They can study both successful and unsuccessful start-ups to understand what works and what does not. Another line of research could be – what prevents companies from transforming themselves even though they know that the future lies in digital integration. The drivers of digital transformation and the hurdles could be identified in the future.

Innovating customer service is another area for future research. Technologies are being developed daily that promise to add to customer service initiatives. Integrating them into a company's working remains a challenge. How companies can do so is an interesting line of future research.

CONCLUSION

This chapter shows how digital transformation can be affected to improve all aspects of customer experience. It explains that the transformation is not about using digital marketing methods or tools, but must alter all aspects of the corporation. In doing this, corporations depend on traditional wisdom: companies must keep customer in their focus at all times. If they don't they are in danger of becoming defunct, as the case of Microsoft shows. On the other hand, the case of Asian Paints shows that even a company founded more than 80 years ago can transform itself with digital tools and re-invent itself.

Unfortunately, many companies still do not understand this. Digital marketing is still treated as sharing content on social media sites and engaging customers. Such companies treat digital as any other department, and hence reap incremental benefits, if at all. Other companies find their digital investments a waste. Tabrizi et al (2019) point out that 70% of all digital transformation initiatives fail. They estimate that of the $1.3 trillion that was spent on digital in 2018, some $900 billion went to waste. That is why companies must approach digital transformation as an opportunity to innovate each stage of their value chains, business processes and organisational structure. Companies that do so will thrive, others may find the going difficult as digital technologies promise to change the entire marketing framework.

SUGGESTIONS AND RECOMMENDATIONS FOR MANAGERS

This paper has practical implications. Managers not only have to be digital-ready or incorporate digital technologies for customer service, but have to prepare for a complete transformation of the business. They have to build digital DNA into their systems, consisting of building an agile organisation, changing the mindset of the people through training, building a customer-obsessed culture, and creating a digital infrastructure.

The case studies presented in the paper show that digital transformation can be done by traditional organisations, while digital natives can lose their way if they do not keep customers firmly into focus. Ultimately it is about marrying marketing with digital technologies but the mistake made by many managers is to treat digital as a separate department. The digital readiness survey shows that companies are often not ready to embrace digital transformation. Managers of the future thus need to take a neutral view of their organisations and assess whether they are future-ready.

Companies have to develop both digital initiatives as well as organizational culture to achieve digital mastery. They have to improve their engagement with customers as also with all stakeholders.

This chapter describes a road map for managers. Many managers do not obsess over customer orientation: according to a 2014 research by the Chief Marketing Officer (CMO) Council, only 14 percent of marketers think that their company is customer-centric. This shows that though companies introduce modern technologies they have a long way to go to become customer-centric. It just means going back to traditional marketing wisdom – keep customer needs at the centre of all plans, digital or not.

REFERENCES

Benkler, Y. (2006). *The Wealth of Networks—How Social Production Transforms Markets and Freedom*. Yale University Press.

Bonchek, M. (2017). A Good Digital Strategy Creates a Gravitational Pull. *Harvard Business Review*. Retrieved from https://hbr.org/2017/01/a-good-digital-strategy-creates-a-gravitational-pull

Carr, N. G. (2003). IT Doesn't Matter. *Harvard Business Review*. Retrieved from https://hbr.org/2003/05/it-doesnt-matter

Charan, R. (2016). How to Transform a Traditional Giant into a Digital One. *Harvard Business Review*. Retrieved from https://hbr.org/2016/02/how-to-transform-a-traditional-giant-into-a-digital-one

Council, C. M. O. (2014). *Mastering Adaptive Customer Engagements*. Retrieved from https://www.cmocouncil.org/thought-leadership/reports/286

Deloitte. (2017). *Digital Future Readiness*. Retrieved from https://www2.deloitte.com/content/dam/Deloitte/ch/Documents/consumer-business/ch-cip-en-swiss-transformation.pdf

Edelman, D. C., & Singer, M. (2015). Competing on Customer Journeys. *Harvard Business Review*. Retrieved from https://hbr.org/2015/11/competing-on-customer-journeys

Favaro, K. (2016). Don't Draft a Digital Strategy just because everyone else is. *Harvard Business Review*. Retrieved from https://hbr.org/2016/03/dont-draft-a-digital-strategy-just-because-everyone-else-is

Fletcher, G., & Griffiths, M. (2020). Digital transformation during a lockdown. *International Journal of Information Management*, *55*, 102185. doi:10.1016/j.ijinfomgt.2020.102185 PMID:32836642

Gupta, S. (2018). *Driving Digital Strategy: A Guide to Reimagining Your Business*. Harvard Business Review Press.

Gürkan, G. C., & Tükeltürk, S. A. (2017). Strategies for Innovative Organization Structure: Innovative Culture and Open Innovation. In Ü. Hacioğlu, H. Dinçer, & N. Alayoğlu (Eds.), *Global Business Strategies in Crisis: Strategic Thinking and Development* (pp. 185–199). Springer. doi:10.1007/978-3-319-44591-5_13

Hanelt, A., Bohnsack, R., Marz, D., & Antunes Marante, C. (2021). A systematic review of the literature on digital transformation: Insights and implications for strategy and organizational change. *Journal of Management Studies*, *58*(5), 1159–1197. doi:10.1111/joms.12639

Johnson, M.W., Christensen, C. M., & Kagermann, H. (2008). Reinventing Your Business Model. *Harvard Business Review*.

Johnson, M. W., Christensen, C. M., & Kagermann, H. (2008). Reinventing Your Business Model through Disruptive Innovation. *Innosight*. Retrieved from https://www.innosight.com/insight/reinventing-yourbusiness-model/

Kumar, D. (2021). *Marketing in the Digital Age*. Sage.

Leinwand, P., & Mani, M. M. (2021). Digitizing Isn't the Same as Digital Transformation. *HBR Org*. Retrieved from https://hbr.org/2021/03/digitizing-isnt-the-same-as-digital-transformation

Matarazzo, M., Penco, L., Profumo, G., & Quaglia, R. (2021). Digital transformation and customer value creation in Made in Italy SMEs: A dynamic capabilities perspective. *Journal of Business Research*, *123*, 642–656. doi:10.1016/j.jbusres.2020.10.033

Meyer, C., & Schwager, A. (2007). Understanding Customer Experience. *Harvard Business Review*. PMID:17345685

Nadkarni, S., & Prügl, R. (2021). Digital transformation: A review, synthesis and opportunities for future research. *Management Review Quarterly*, *71*(2), 233–341. doi:10.100711301-020-00185-7

Naughton, J. (2019). How Microsoft reinvented itself. *The Guardian*. Retrieved from https://www.theguardian.com/commentisfree/2019/may/12/how-microsoft-was-resurrected-as-the-third-most-valuable-tech-company-1-trillion-dollars

Perspectives, C. (2018). *Asian Paints: The Digital Odyssey of a Serial Reinventor*. Retrieved from https://www.cognizant.com/perspectives/asian-paints-the-digital-odyssey-of-a-serial-reinventor

Sahu, N., Deng, H., & Mollah, A. (2018). Investigating the Critical Success Factors of Digital Transformation for Improving Customer Experience. *CONFIRM 2018 Proceedings*. Retrieved from https://aisel.aisnet.org/confirm2018/18

Tabrizi, B., Lam, E., Girard, K., & Irvin, V. (2019). Digital Transformation is not about Technology. *HBR Org*. Retrieved from https://hbr.org/2019/03/digital-transformation-is-not-about-technology

The Economist. (2019). *What Microsoft's revival can teach other tech companies*. Retrieved from https://www.economist.com/leaders/2019/07/25/what-microsofts-revival-can-teach-other-tech-companies

Verhoef, P. C., Broekhuizen, T., Bart, Y., Bhattacharya, A., Dong, J. Q., Fabian, N., & Haenlein, M. (2021). Digital transformation: A multidisciplinary reflection and research agenda. *Journal of Business Research*, *122*, 889–901. doi:10.1016/j.jbusres.2019.09.022

Westerman, G., Bonnet, D., & McAfee, A. (2014). *Leading Digital: Turning Technology into Business Transformation*. Harvard Business Review Press.

Zacca, R., & Dayan, M. (2017). Entrepreneurship: An Evolving Conceptual Framework. *International Journal of Entrepreneurship and Innovation Management*, *21*(1/2), 2–26. doi:10.1504/IJEIM.2017.081495

ADDITIONAL READING

Bonnet, D., & Westerman, G. (2020). The New Elements of Digital Transformation. *MIT Sloan Management Review*. https://sloanreview.mit.edu/article/the-new-elements-of-digital-transformation/

Chamorro-Premuzić, T. (2021). The Essential Components of Digital Transformation. *HBR Org*. https://hbr.org/2021/11/the-essential-components-of-digital-transformation

Kraus, S., Palmer, C., Kailer, N., Kallinger, F. L., & Spitzer, J. (2019). Digital entrepreneurship: A research agenda on new business models for the twenty-first century. *International Journal of Entrepreneurial Behaviour & Research*, *25*(2), 353–375. doi:10.1108/IJEBR-06-2018-0425

McKinsey & Co. (2021). *Elevating digital customer experience in the next normal*. https://www.mckinsey.com/featured-insights/mckinsey-live/webinars/elevating-digital-customer-experience-in-the-next-normal

McQuivey, J. (2013). *Digital Disruption: Unleashing the Next Wave of Innovation*. Amazon Publishing.

Van Alstyne, M. W., & Parker, G. G. (2021). Digital Transformation Changes How Companies Create Value. *HBR Org*. https://hbr.org/2021/12/digital-transformation-changes-how-companies-create-value

Wirtz, B. W. (2019). *Digital Business Models: Concepts, Models, and the Alphabet Case Study*. Springer Nature. doi:10.1007/978-3-030-13005-3

Zhang, J. J., Lichtenstein, Y., & Gander, J. (2015). *Designing Scalable Digital Business Models, Business Models and Modelling. Advances in Strategic Management* (Vol. 33). Emerald Group Publishing Limited. doi:10.1108/S0742-332220150000033006

KEY TERMS AND DEFINITIONS

Business Model: A business model is how a company creates and delivers customer value.

Consumer Decision Journey (CDJ): A model that shows how consumers make purchase decisions. The process is a circular journey with four phases: initial consideration; active evaluation, closure, and post-purchase.

Digital Mastery: Companies that use digital technologies to drive significantly higher levels of customer engagement and service. It consists of building both digital and leadership capabilities.

Digital Strategy: A plan to achieve competitive advantage through improved customer experience by making use of data assets and technology-based initiatives.

Digital Transformation: Digital transformation is the process of integrating digital technologies into all areas of a company's business model to fundamentally alter how customer value is created and delivered. It involves changing business processes, culture, and customer experiences.

Omnichannel: An approach in which companies use all its channels to provide customers with a seamless shopping experience.

VUCA: An acronym that describes the business environment in modern times, consisting of Volatility, Uncertainty, Complexity, and Ambiguity.

Chapter 5
Music Streaming:
Consumption Patterns in Digital Ambients

Flávio Augusto Brito
Porto Accounting and Business School, Polytechnic of Porto, Portugal

Diana Aguiar Vieira
Porto Accounting and Business School, Polytechnic of Porto, Portugal

ABSTRACT

The eased access to new digital technologies allowed for new possibilities, with content streaming being one of the most expressive digital consumption and business models in the phonographic industry. Following, brand-new discussions regarding the consumption habits of its users took place. What is not yet clear is the consumption dynamics on these new platforms, particularly, when referring to exploration scenarios, the most relevant tools and what role factors such as familiarity and taste play in the discovery process of the existing catalogue. The intent is to comprehend the expressiveness of these music streaming platforms, what dynamics come to play referring to exploratory behaviours, and which tools or mechanisms are the most important in this process. Following data collection of 264 respondents through a survey, the results indicate both the popularity of streaming platforms and the respondents' high exploration tendencies, with existing features like playlists being the most significant tools to discover the catalogue.

INTRODUCTION

Technological evolution brought a series of changes to various social sectors. These changes paved the way for new music consumption forms relying on digital formats at the expense of physical ones. Existing research has shown that some of the main advantages of digital music platforms include comfort, convenience and access to an extensive catalogue. These advantages result from technological innovations, the pervasive nature of the Internet, the appearance of social networks and, later, the appearance of multiple streaming platforms (Mendes, 2019; Charron, 2017). It has previously been observed that digital sources of music consumption play a vital role in the phonographic industry, with streaming plat-

DOI: 10.4018/978-1-7998-9179-6.ch005

forms like Spotify and others being crucial regarding music consumption and revenue income sources. Accordingly, it is stated that streaming as a business model made up more than 60% of the total revenue generated in the global phonographic industry during 2020, with subscription services playing a central role in this field. On the other hand, more traditional digital consumption models, like iTunes or other downloading platforms, have shown a steady decline over the years, similar to the physical format as well (IFPI, 2021; Nielsen Music, 2020; Audiogest, 2020; Maasø, 2018; Mendes, 2019; Eiriz & Leite, 2017). Over the years, consumption practices have shifted from unit-based models to an access-based model, propelled by the appearance of various music streaming platforms on the market (Coelho & Mendes, 2019). Table 1 summarizes the evolution of revenue source income in the international phonographic industry during the last three years.

Table 1. International revenue distribution in the phonographic industry between 2018 and 2020

Revenue Models	2018	2019	2020
Subscription streams	37%	42%	46%
Ad-supported streams	10%	14.10%	16.2%
Physical format	25%	21.60%	19.5%
Downloads	12%	7.20%	5.8%
Performance rights	14%	12.60%	10.6%
Synchronisation	2%	2.40%	2%
Total Revenue (in billions of American dollars)	18.7	20.2	21.6

Source: (IFPI, 2021)

In the literature on digital platforms, consumption practices and dynamics have been subject to considerable discussion. Some scholars point to a shift in consumption patterns (Datta et al., 2018). However, others claim a possible reinforcement of existing or similar ones (Kamehkhosh, 2019; Weingartner, 2020). The general purpose of this chapter is to examine different scholars' contributions and viewpoints regarding the digital transformation of the phonographic industry, its implications on music consumption patterns in digital platforms and, through field research, further understand the uses of streaming platforms as consumption tools and their prominence in exploration scenarios.

The theoretical background will focus on the industry changes over the years, the appearance of streaming platforms, the characteristics of social and cultural dynamics and how these might manifest in digital ambients, especially in exploration scenarios. Additionally, this chapter will provide insight into how social dynamics influenced streaming services' business approach and their subsequent focus on creating branded experiences. Furthermore, field research aims to investigate the frequency of usage of streaming services, the general impressions users share regarding these, how relevant they are in exploratory use cases and the most used tools or sources in this process. Additionally, this chapter aims to explore the age and consumption practice correlations on the collected sample.

This chapter will follow a four-section structure. First, the general background will provide insight on P2P networks and the transition to the digital market, the emergence of streaming platforms, taste and consumption patterns, opportunities and issues posed by digital services, the value proposition of streaming services and finally, digital ownership and consumption patterns. The second part will focus on the field research conducted through a survey, its analysis and how the findings correlate with the existing theoretical background presented here. Finally, the last two sections of this chapter will suggest future research directions and highlight general conclusions.

BACKGROUND

P2P Networks and Transition to a Digital Market

Previous research has established P2P (peer-to-peer) networks as a pivotal aspect regarding the shift to a digital form of music consumption. Additionally, P2P networks proved to be challenging for record labels at the time due to their disruptive nature.

Arditi (2014) argues that P2P networks were challenging because they facilitated the distribution process by theoretically eliminating the mediators that helped keep existing dominant positions by big record labels. The former author mentions these mediators as "brick-and-mortar" (p. 409). Since independent artists or smaller labels could not compete with big players unless they had invested in expensive distribution networks, the only viable solution was to sign a deal with a big record label. Accordingly, big record labels had great control over distribution mediums due to their vast capital power. On a side note, Arditi (2014) claims there should not expect a significant change in existing power structures solely because of changes in the distribution systems (p. 411). Moreover, the distribution process is still one of the main barriers for artists, even if the Internet made it easier than it previously was.

Seeing their dominant position threatened by these new technologies, record groups were quick to move resources to stop P2P services as much as possible and maintain their dominant position. Considering that digital distribution systems would not disappear anytime soon, Arditi (2014) mentions record labels adopting a two-way action plan. The first step was to pursue legal action against those who used P2P networks and other illegal sources of music consumption. The second one was to quickly develop alternative proprietary technologies as fast as possible before losing their dominance over the market. At the same time, the adoption of technological distribution models meant the maintenance of the presence of mediators to record labels will.

The result was the surge and massive adoption of platforms like iTunes, which preserved the necessary entry-level barriers to sustain already existing power structures. These barriers meant that users or artists could not upload their content freely, unlike P2P services, unless they paid a fee to compete on the market or signed a deal with a big record label that would cover such costs for them (p. 419). As with other similar services, like Rhapsody or Napster, iTunes presents itself as a digital storefront where millions of individual songs are available for download (Tepper & Hargittai, 2009).

The Emergence of Streaming

The term "streaming" was applied in the late 80s to define various services that did not require the user to download files to the local hard drive to access them. Instead, those files were accessible through a subscription or an Internet connection (Morris & Powers, 2015). Therefore, music streaming services follow a distinct approach that dismisses the purchase of CDs or any physical media, offering instead access to a vast catalogue hosted on digital networks (Kischinhevsky et al., 2015). Scholars also describe the consumption practice on these services as being access-based instead of unit-based (Marshall, 2015; Coelho & Mendes, 2019). Streaming revenue models divide into three main categories. These are on-demand services, radio or webcasting services and, finally, cloud-based storage services. The first category consists of services that allow the user to choose which tracks to play at any time. The second one consists of those that only allow track playback without any user interaction. Finally, the third one consists of services like Amazon Cloud Player, in which users upload and access content to their cloud through various gadgets (Marshall, 2015).

As these services gained more market traction, questions started raising concerning streaming as a business model. Several entities have expressed their dissatisfaction with such services, mainly due to the apparent low revenue they generate. Other means of concern relate to questions like ethical issues derived from the access-based model itself and the negative impact on sales of digital files. Marshall (2015) points out that some artists claim that on-demand streaming services are not a capable financial model to sustain their careers. Additionally, moral arguments regarding music value and how micro-payments contribute to devaluing music itself are also relevant on this matter.

However, Spotify does not appear to be cheating on its payment distribution with digital suppliers. Instead, it seems to be carrying out rather conventional rates, similar to other competitors such as iTunes (Marshall, 2015). Analysing their business model practices, Spotify generates revenue through advertising displays and subscriptions. After that, Spotify distributes a fixed income amount to rights holders by dividing the generated revenue by the number of streams on their service. As Marshall (2015) points out, Spotify answers the revenue model criticism by using the scalability argument as a shield and incentivising users to pay for their service. Therefore, Spotify claims that the more people use their service and generate income, the better it will pay artists and labels for the streams they get on the platform.

In addition to business model concerns, other questions regarding the possible reinforcement of existing consumption habits, what Weingartner (2020) called the "bubble effect", have risen. On the other hand, Datta et al. (2018) point to broader consumption patterns on several dimensions, such as the number of tracks, artists or music genres. More in-depth considerations regarding these viewpoints will be presented later in this chapter.

Taste and Consumption Patterns

Different theories exist in the literature regarding taste, its manifestation and how it moulds consumption patterns.

Bourdieu (1984) argues that the taste for cultural goods operated following a specific, hierarchical and economy-like logic. Furthermore, he claims that educational and social factors influence expressions of taste for cultural goods. Therefore, Bourdieu (1984) proposes that socially higher individuals appreciated artistic expressions seen as superior. On the other hand, inferior art expressions would be seen with disregard by high-status individuals. Similarly, lower-class individuals would appreciate popular aesthetic manifestations seen as accessible and, instead, dismiss those that rejected this idea. In sum, different social classes would express liking towards specific styles or genres, being educational factors the most prominent and influential ones.

Posing questions regarding Bourdieu's viewpoints, Peterson (1992) provides additional insight on the matter, arguing that elitism in taste consumption goes beyond selecting specific artistic forms. Furthermore, elitism is defined as the appreciation of distinct aesthetic manifestations and social activities, with higher-class individuals manifesting omnivorous consumption tendencies (Peterson, 1992). On the other hand, lower-class individuals express univorous association tendencies, having few different activities or aesthetic dispositions and focusing on similar ones instead (Peterson, 1992). Following a similar approach, Bryson (1996) points to the existence of selective taste patterns where individuals would incorporate distinct music genres seen as prestigious by other cultures while rejecting those that were not. Moreover, to be omnivorous is considered as a mechanism to obtain social and political status (Bryson, 1996).

Even though Bourdieu's observations regarding associations between taste and social hierarchies have been subject to various discussions, Nowak (2016) argues that the "habitus" concept proposed by Bourdieu is still relevant. The "habitus" is defined as both a disposition system and a "structuring structure", in the sense that it follows a scheme of organising classes and influences an individual's inclination towards some practices (Nowak, 2016; Bourdieu, 1984).

Drawing upon the idea of taste as being reflexive, Hennion (2007) proposes various considerations regarding this concept. According to the author, taste is not an attribute of the objects themselves. Instead, it is found by the contact with them, by applying a series of dispositions originated from various social determinants, to feel and make feel, to let it flow. In sum, Hennion (2007) argues that taste is a reflexive activity and not an attribute of the objects themselves. Transposing this concept to the discovery process, Nowak (2016) argues that such can solely happen when it affects the listener, whether it is a good experience or a bad one. More than assuming discovery as a consequence of technological tools and the dematerialisation of music, as mentioned by Belk (2013), Eiriz & Leite (2017) or Coelho & Mendes (2019), it has to be memorable.

Several are the factors that influence music consumption practices. Some are related to characteristics such as familiarity or taste in itself. These factors relate strictly in the sense that the existence of high levels of familiarity relates closely to high levels of appreciation for certain music (Taylor & Dean, 2019, 2021). Another important aspect related to consumption practices and influences is the various social figures or influencers. Several authors refer to these social actors as leader opinions and mavens, pointing to slight differences between them. Ruvio & Shoham (2007) define opinion leaders as individuals who concentrate their knowledge on specific products or lines of products. Moreover, mavens display broader market knowledge, search actively for information and buy new products or brands. Additionally, mavens are said to take more risks on their quests (p. 714).

Verboord (2019) claims the existence of different consumption practices and cultural influences. Moreover, this author sustains that interactions between individuals follow a reciprocal dynamic, meaning that the more the individuals make recommendations, the more recommendations they will receive. Furthermore, Verboord (2019) argues that there exist similar taste dispositions to other individuals in a group and a negative influence towards different taste manifestations. Another vital point this author makes is that, while traditional media are slowly losing ground to newer forms of recommendation and interpersonal contacts, there is no clear evidence that existing aesthetic dispositions are becoming irrelevant Verboord (2019, p.17).

Opportunities and Issues in Digital Ambients

As indicated previously, technological innovations had a massive influence on various sectors. Likewise, it is stated that new technologies facilitated fan and artist interactions and how they listen to music in general. As the International Federation for the Phonographic Industry (IFPI, 2019) points out, fans express high engagement levels, looking for new ways to share and interact with music in their daily lives through new consumption practices made possible by technology (p.5). During a time where live music was severely affected, digital tools allowed for innovation and brand-new experiences for music fans. Additionally, these experiences go beyond sharing practices, allowing for global and immersive experiences, with record labels searching for ways to integrate music into various forms of entertainment. Accordingly, these new forms follow a co-creation model between fans and artists (IFPI, 2021, p.5). Likewise, Charron (2017) pointed earlier to similar conclusions. However, this author mentions the physical presence in live events as suggestive of a sense of community and authenticity that digital ones are yet to offer.

However, with the rise of such technologies in daily lives, new discussions regarding phenomena such as data collection and information overload in digital ambients arose. Proposing a two-dimensional definition, Davis (2011) splits the concept of information overload into macro and micro dimensions. The first one refers to the incapacity of systems to process excessive informational volumes, while the second one refers to the user's inability to operate the system itself. Furthermore, this author points to the complex nature of this problem, especially regarding the micro-level. Attempting to provide a guide on understanding this problem, Davis (2011) presents several questions, such as "(...) is there too much text? Are there too many graphics? Are we expressing too many ideas? Are there too many sounds?" (p. 48).

On this matter, it is relevant to mention some of the strategies adopted by streaming platforms to deal with the vast catalogue they possess, their value proposition and what use they make with users' data. Beer (2010) is one of the authors whose contributions are essential to understanding data collection and processing practices regarding consumption habits in mobile devices. This author points to a transition to a more "permeable" and connected consumption reality, in sync with capitalist organizations' wills. As a result, data on the users' consumption practices are collected and processed to present musical products they might be interested in (Beer, 2010, p. 479).

Value Proposition of Streaming Services

According to Nowak (2016), digital music technologies allow content discovery thanks to the possibility of accessing a vast catalogue. On the other hand, such a possibility does not eliminate social context or influences, given that individuals now deal with more mediators during their music discovery journey on digital ambients. Such dynamics become more plausible when considering the gradual shift that Spotify made towards a more focused approach on the social aspects available on the platform, such as following users and Facebook integrations, instead of focusing on its catalogue size.

Indeed, the social dimension observed on streaming platforms influences their strategy to distinguish themselves from competitors by offering branded experiences that invite users to see their traits and personality reflected on their service of choice (Morris & Powers, 2015). Therefore, data on the users' tastes and activity is stored and processed to create segmented audiences and suggest new content (Beer, 2010).

One of the most prominent features of music streaming services is playlists, with scholars mentioning these as proof of the existence of a social and affective dimension manifested on these platforms. Morris & Powers (2015) argue that playlists are a tool with multiple use cases. For streaming services, playlists serve to distinguish themselves among competitors by offering branded experiences on their platforms. For outlets, playlists allow them to focus on the promotion and curation business aspect. For users, playlists function as a tool to curate, control and discover new musical products and manage their social identity. Automated playlists, tailored towards certain moods or occasions, or human-generated ones, are the materialisation of the emphasis on music as a social experience.

Playlists are products of versatile nature, used on diverse occasions or contexts, which can manifest in different ways such as temporary or permanent, static or dynamic (Hagen, 2015). The following section describes in greater detail how playlists reflect various social dynamics, including psychological ownership.

Digital Ownership and Consumption Practices

According to Belk (2013), the individual's possessions make part of what he describes as the extended self. Those possessions might include physical objects like pictures, texts, music or others, and individuals see them as a part of themselves (p. 477). Turning now to digital ambients, this author poses a series of questions regarding what extent digital objects would have the same emotional attachment as their physical counterparts. Belk (2013) concludes that the extended self still exists on these new ambients, although its manifestation differs slightly from pre-digital ones. These differences occur mainly due to brand-new interaction and aggregation possibilities offered by digital mediums, in addition to the individual's feeling of being part of something bigger than themself.

Turning now to music consumption in digital platforms, Sinclair & Tinson (2017) share similar thoughts. As the aforementioned authors point out, digital music can also serve as a psychological possession and a form of expressing one's extended self through social media. Moreover, Sinclair & Tinson (2017) mention the possibility of keeping track of another's consumption practices on several digital platforms like Spotify or Facebook. Such practice impulses the necessity of social identity management. This can manifest through practices like choosing consciously not to share one's listening habits by activating the "private session" feature on Spotify, for instance (Sinclair & Tinson, 2017, p. 7).

Hagen & Luders (2017) also mention such management practices regarding playlists, claiming that these serve as impression management tools through selective sharing practices on the user's social circles. Regarding personal connections on digital platforms, said authors argue that these provide the weaker or absent social ties with a new level of importance thanks to the social features available on these platforms, such as connecting and sharing capabilities. On a side note, the aforementioned authors also argue that connections with weaker or absent ties relate strongly to exploratory behaviours, while those with existing strong ones are usually associated with maintenance purposes through selective sharing practices (pp. 652- 653).

Given the versatile nature of playlists, Hagen (2015) claims that these might reflect the need to collect objects and control them. This urge in control derives from the necessity of ordering a vast catalogue on a generic platform. As Hagen & Lüders (2017) point out, playlist curation might reflect daily tasks and emotions or personal experiences (p. 648).

Moreover, Hagen (2015) claims that playlists represent both the user's unique character and the fluidity of technology. Thanks to the tools available on multiple platforms, content edition, reorganisation and the creation, or almost instant elimination of the playlist itself are some of the possibilities in these digital ambients (p.16). While Hagen (2015) mentions the fluid nature and the new catalogue manipulation and organisation possibilities brought by brand-new technological tools, Morris & Powers (2015) point out the existence of a control illusion derived from the eased access to an extensive content library.

Turning now to content variety on digital media, a much-debated question is whether consumption habits have changed resulting from access to such a vast catalogue. Datta et al. (2018) showed that streaming services cannibalise other consumption mediums, including iTunes. In addition, they cause less concentration on consumption patterns regarding both the number of artists or tracks and the number of music genres. While the aforementioned authors claim a broader content variety consumption, they do not point to specific mechanisms that might trigger such patterns, suggesting playlists as one of the possible reasons for such.

Adopting a distinct position from the previous authors, Weingartner (2020) claims existing similar consumption compositions, even on different platforms. Additionally, he defends that users in digital ambients might be more inclined to stay within the borders of their socially structured preferences. As mentioned previously, the author suggests the existence of a potential bubble effect on such platforms, derived from the presence of automatic recommendation systems (Weingartner, 2020, p. 9). While the focus of his study relates to movie consumption, the author claims that "movies and music are both cultural products" (Weingartner, 2020, pp. 2- 3).

Other scholars had shared similar conclusions to Weingartner (2020). Kamehkhosh et al. (2019) point to homogeneity as having a significant level of importance when creating playlists. While diversity is also relevant in this context, it should not exceed desired levels. Additionally, the aforementioned authors claim a negative correlation between the adoption rate of a recommendation and the high diversity level of artists suggested by recommendation systems. It is also important to stress out that users want to simultaneously discover new music they might find relevant when creating a playlist and receive already known song recommendations that might be relevant to the context in question (pp. 316- 317).

Examining the association links between different content forms available on YouTube, Airoldi et al. (2016) point to a similarity-based logic regarding content groups produced by uploaders and listeners, thanks to technologically mediated aggregation practices or algorithms. This similarity-based logic manifests in two ways. On the one hand, the prevalence of more conventional music genres is still one of the most relevant structuring forces of the orientation process for users in a platform. On the other hand, new content classification forms based on functional or situational characteristics are becoming more relevant over time. These new classification schemes do not rely on traditional attributes or genres to classify music by focusing instead on the effect music has on daily tasks. Considering the importance of music as a situational object (Airoldi et al., 2016), this phenomenon might help to sustain the claims made by Datta et al. (2018) regarding their allegations of broader volume and variety consumption patterns.

Scholars also address other relevant points regarding consumed content. Among these are the dominant position big record labels hold the charts of the most popular tracks on Spotify, the short timespan of such on these charts, the long-term relevancy of the so-called superstar tracks, and the issue of the tyranny of choice. The latter consists of low choice levels, even if before a huge library volume to choose from in a platform (Coelho & Mendes, 2019). On this matter, custom computer-generated playlists are tools that help to lower uncertainty when searching for new music through features like "Discover Weekly" and "Daily Mix" on Spotify or "Flow" on Deezer (Kaimann et al., 2021). Other features like the "new releases" section on Spotify highlight the recently released materials, similar to a physical record store (Werner, 2020). On the other hand, while big record labels amplified their dominant position thanks to streaming platforms, Coelho & Mendes (2019) claim that music digitalisation, along with more significant exposure of long-tail products, allows for new diversification opportunities. Additionally, record labels can pursue diversification strategies without sacrificing existing superstar-focused efforts.

FIELD RESEARCH

Methodological Approach

To additionally contribute to previously discussed topics, field research was conducted through a survey on Google Forms. This survey was composed of multiple-choice questions based on a seven-degree Likert scale from 1 to 7. On the disagreement side of the scale, level 1 degree corresponds to total disagreement, level 2 corresponds to general/considerable disagreement, and level 3 corresponds to minor or slight disagreement. Level 4 corresponds to a neutral or ambivalent answer. On the agreement side of the scale, level 5 corresponds to a minor or slight agreement, level 6 corresponds to a general or considerable agreement, and level 7 corresponds to total agreement. According to Bhattacherjee (2012), Likert scale questions allow for more granular answers when compared to binary-based items, including neutral ones.

Before publication on social media, existing errors and other clarity issues were identified and corrected through pilot testing on three individuals from different age groups following a convenience sample procedure. After making the necessary corrections, the data collection process began. During four weeks, the survey was available and open to collect as many answers as possible through a snowball procedure (Bhattacherjee, 2012), being shared various times during those weeks.

This study aimed to primarily analyse the use frequency and relevancy of streaming services in discovery scenarios and the most relevant tools and sources for such purposes. To further complement the investigation on this matter, this research followed a descriptive statistical methodology procedure, except for age where Pearson correlation tests were carried out. All analyses were based on individual questions.

Reported Results

In total, 264 respondents answered the survey in question. Regarding the participants' gender, 103 respondents identified as female, 98 identified as male, and 63 preferred not to tell. Percentage-wise, 39% were female, 37.1% were male, and 23.9% did not report their gender, respectively. Furthermore, young individuals compose the most significant part of the gathered sample. The age gap reported by the survey ranges from 16 to 57-year-olds, with age groups divided into five sections, these being 11 to 20 year-olds, 21 to 30 year-olds, 31 to 40 year-olds, 41 to 50 year-olds and 51 to 60 year-olds. The bar chart in figure 1 indicates the age gap among respondents.

Regarding their occupation status, most respondents were either students or employees. Specifically, 78 reported being students, 108 were employees, 40 were working students, 27 were self-employed, and 11 were unemployed. Percentage-wise, 29.5% were students, 40.9% were employees, 15.2% were working students, 10.2% were self-employed, and finally, 4.2% were unemployed.

Figure 1. Total respondents by age groups

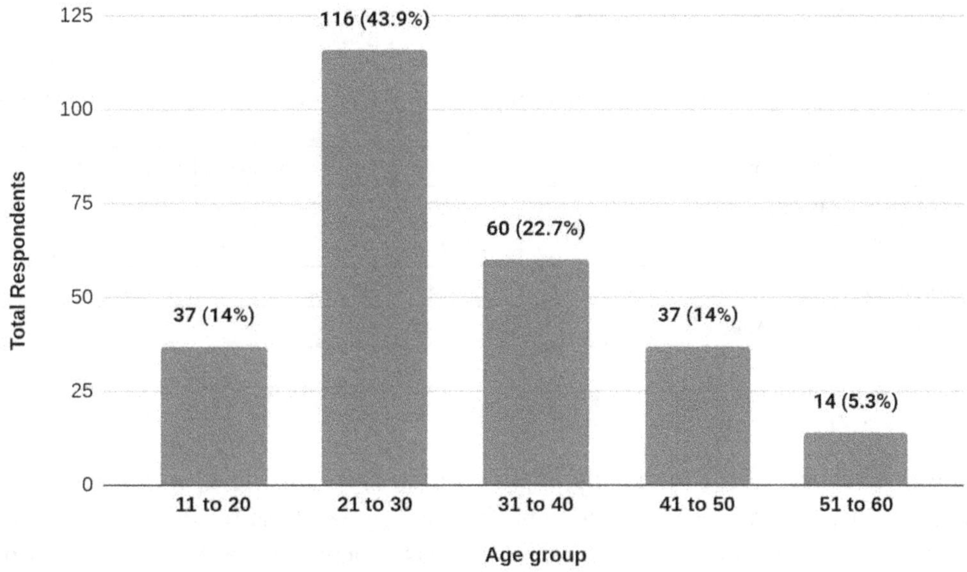

When asked about how recurrent the use of streaming services during their listening sessions was, respondents reported frequent use rates. Accordingly, 57.7% of respondents reported daily usage of streaming services, while 39.6% reported weekly usage. Contrastingly, only 1.9% and 0.8% of respondents reported sporadic and monthly usage, respectively. Participants also reported the usage of a wide range of streaming services, with YouTube/YouTube Music, Spotify and Deezer being the most popular platforms among respondents. Figure 2 shows the most relevant streaming platforms for the gathered sample.

Figure 2. Distribution of platform usage among respondents

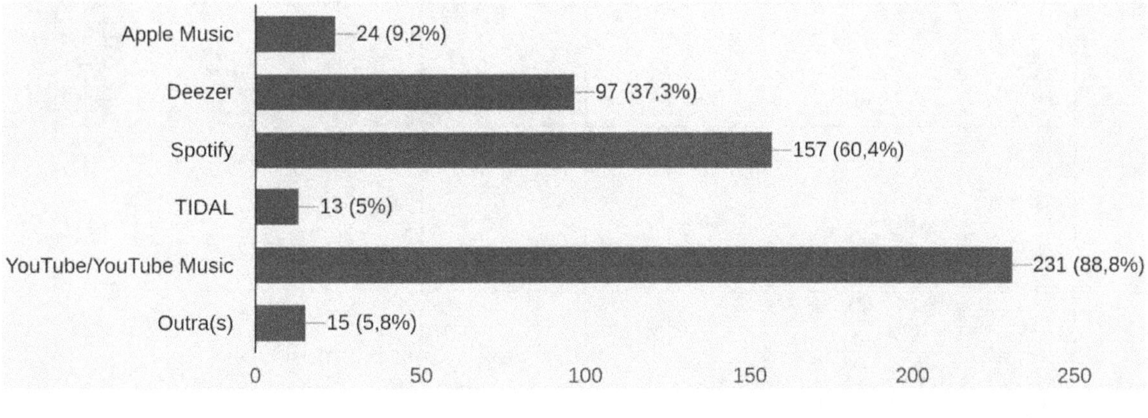

Given that respondents could select more than one streaming platform as their preferred based on their use case, it is important to stress out that platform combination was frequent in the sample. Table 2 shows that the most recurrent combination choices were Spotify with YouTube/YouTube Music and

Deezer with YouTube/YouTube Music. However, the combination of three or more platforms during listening habits was not frequent.

Table 2. Number of respondents by the usage of most frequent services and cross-service combinations

Platform	Number of Respondents
Spotify, YouTube/YouTube Music	98 (37.7%)
Deezer, YouTube/YouTube Music	50 (19.2%)
YouTube/YouTube Music	23 (8.8%)
Deezer, Spotify, YouTube/YouTube Music	21 (8.1%)
Spotify	14 (5.4%)

Regarding their experience, respondents reported high agreeance levels when asked if streaming platforms provide fast and easy access to content. Figure 3 shows these results in greater detail.

On the other hand, respondents did not report expressive agreeing levels when asked if streaming platforms offer access to a limited catalogue. On this matter, feelings of neutrality were the most expressive, followed by disagreeing patterns. Figure 4 shows these results.

Figure 3. Distribution of respondents regarding agreeance on whether or not streaming platforms provide fast and easy access to content

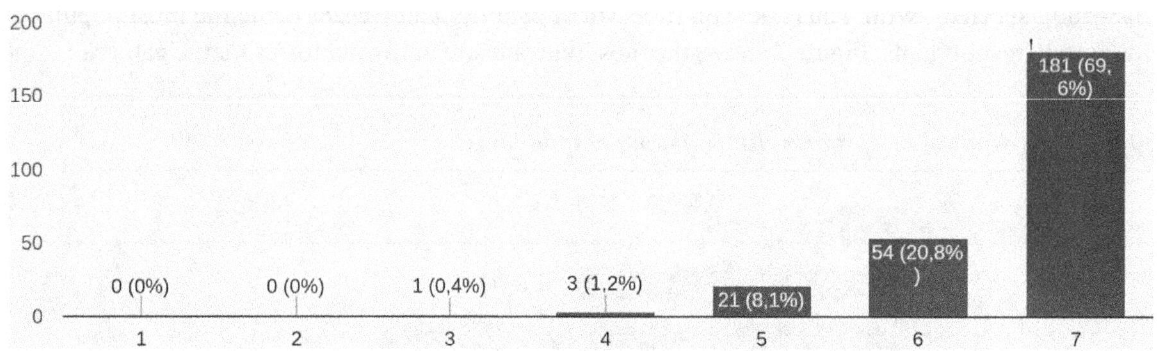

Figure 4. Distribution of respondents regarding agreeance on whether streaming platforms have a limited catalogue

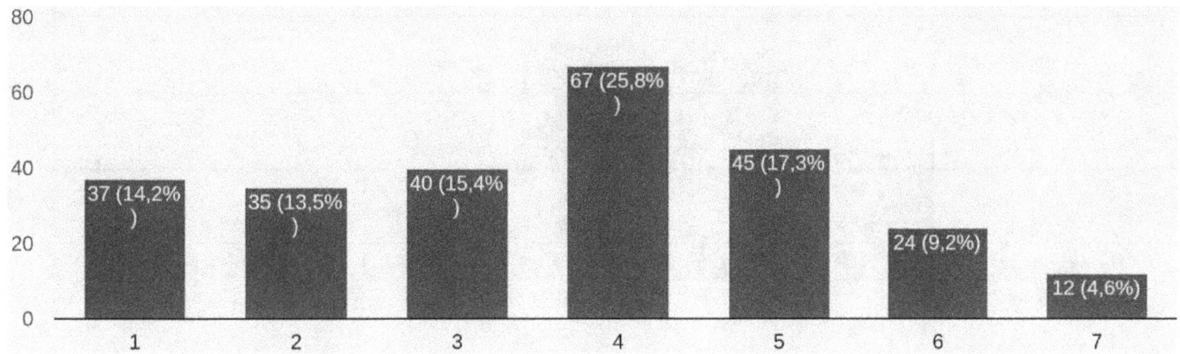

Respondents reported considerable satisfaction patterns regarding the music streaming platform of their choice. However, neutrality was the most significant pattern observed regarding this question. These results are shown in figure 5.

Figure 5. Distribution of respondents regarding their satisfaction levels with their preferred platform of usage

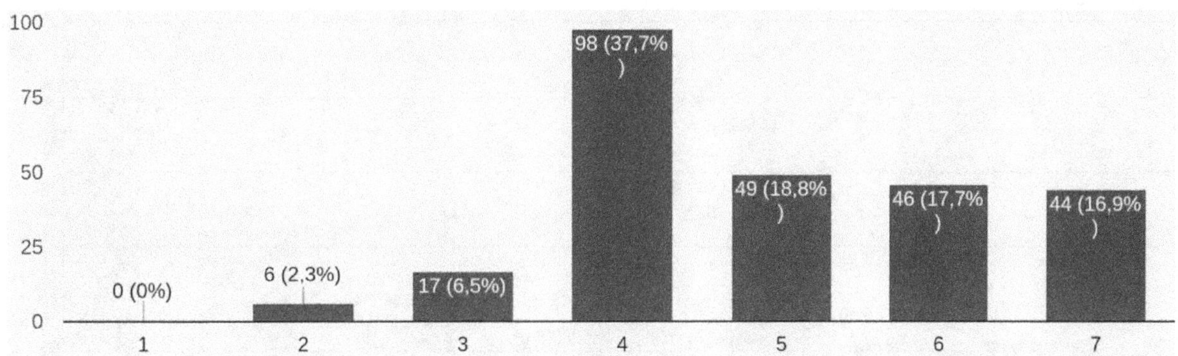

Contrastingly, figure 6 shows that respondents did not report high control patterns with their experience using music streaming platforms.

Figure 6. Distribution of respondents regarding their sense of control on streaming platforms

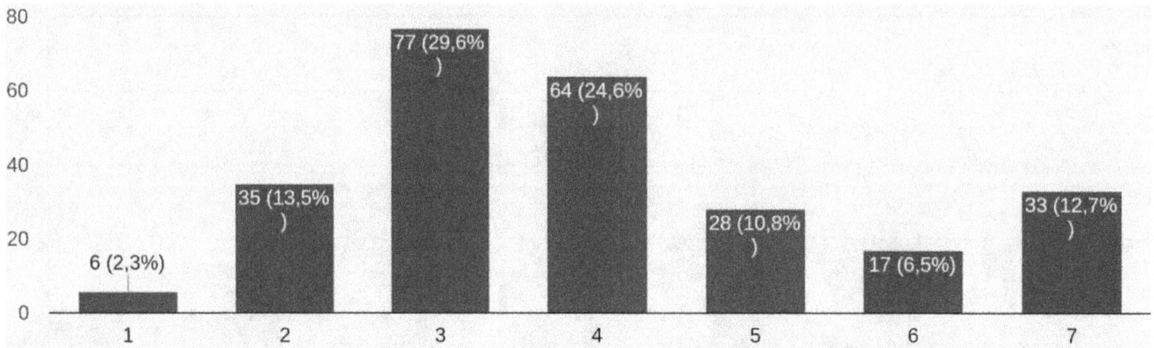

discover new music and explore the available catalogue on such. Figure 7 shows these results in greater detail.

Additionally, when asked if respondents ignore the recommended or suggested tracks on these platforms, results show significant disagreeing patterns, which might further highlight their willingness to explore the existing library. Figure 8 shows these results in greater detail.

Figure 7. Distribution of respondents regarding their tendency of using streaming platforms to discover new music

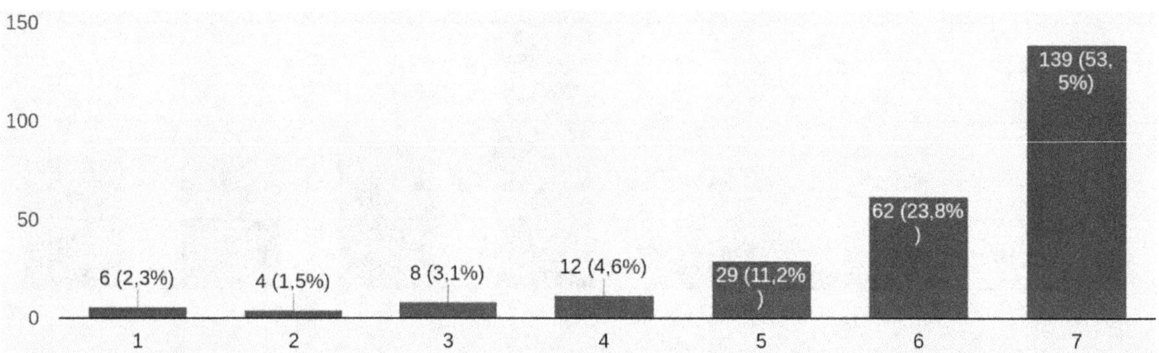

Figure 8. Distribution of respondents when asked if participants do not engage in exploratory behaviour in streaming platforms

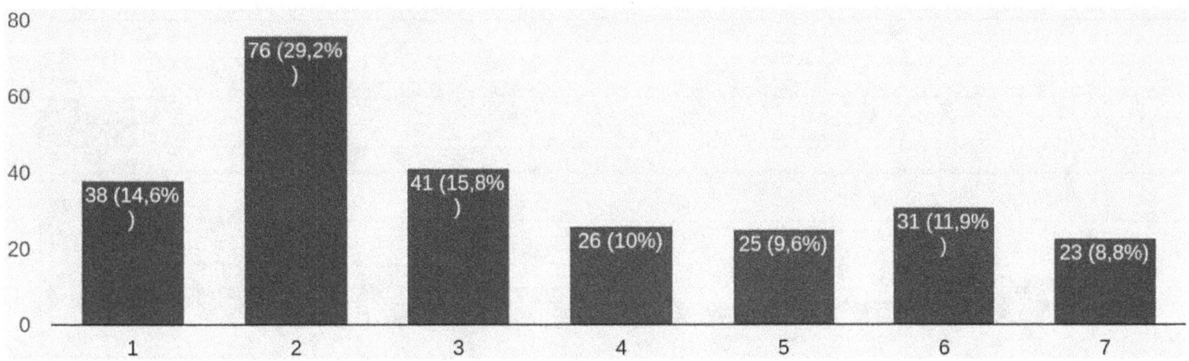

When asked if respondents ignore automatic recommendations presented in streaming platforms, results show expressive disagreeing patterns, indicating that participants take into consideration track suggestions in their listening habits. Figure 9 shows these results.

Figure 9. Distribution of respondents when asked if participants ignore suggested tracks on streaming platforms

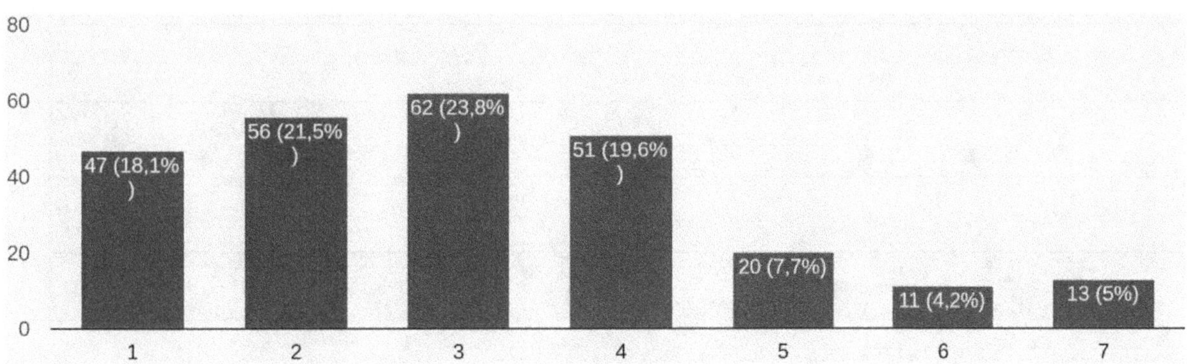

The most relevant tools for exploration purposes are the already existing ones in streaming platforms. Features such as "Discover Weekly" on Spotify or "Flow" on Deezer were the most significant ones that respondents reported using for discovery practices. Figure 10 shows these results in greater detail.

Figure 10. Distribution of respondents regarding their use of features like "Discover Weekly" to discover new music

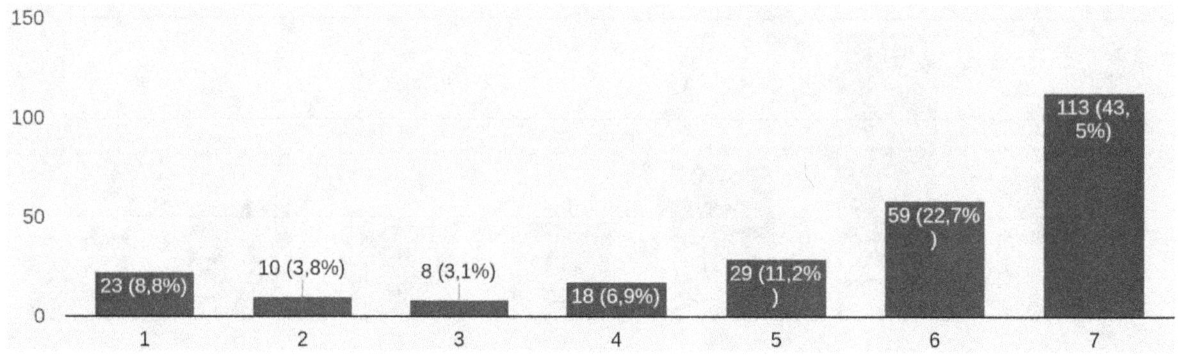

Similarly, figure 11 shows that participants also reported high agreeance when asked if they use the "new releases" sections during their listening habits. In summary, respondents take into consideration internal sources of recommendation in their listening and exploration experiences.

Figure 11. Distribution of respondents regarding their use of the "new releases" section to discover new music

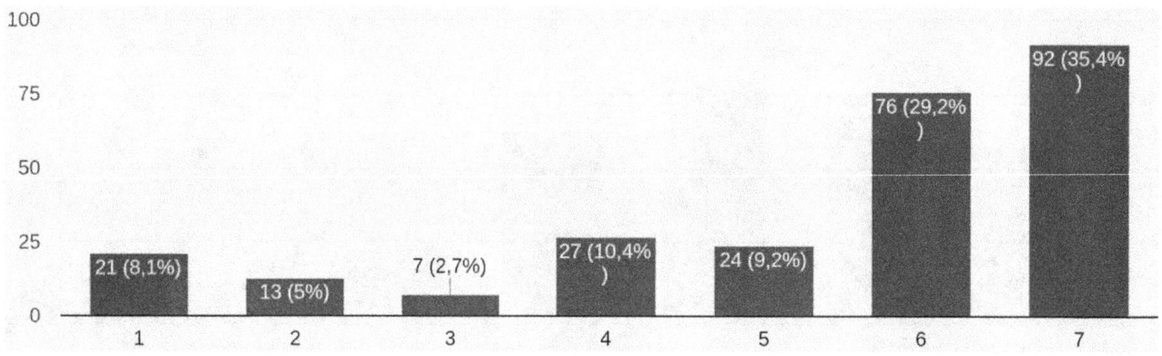

Contrastingly, external recommendation sources were not significant in a positive manner. Figure 12 shows that respondents reported expressive disagreeing patterns when confronted if they asked for friends or family members' opinions during their exploration journey.

Similarly, figure 13 shows that the recurrence of forums or critic lists to discover new music was not relevant for respondents. On the other hand, the disagreeing pattern regarding these sources, in particular, was more evenly distributed in comparison to the recurrence of friends and family's opinions.

Figure 12. Distribution of respondents when asked if participants search for friend suggestions to discover new music

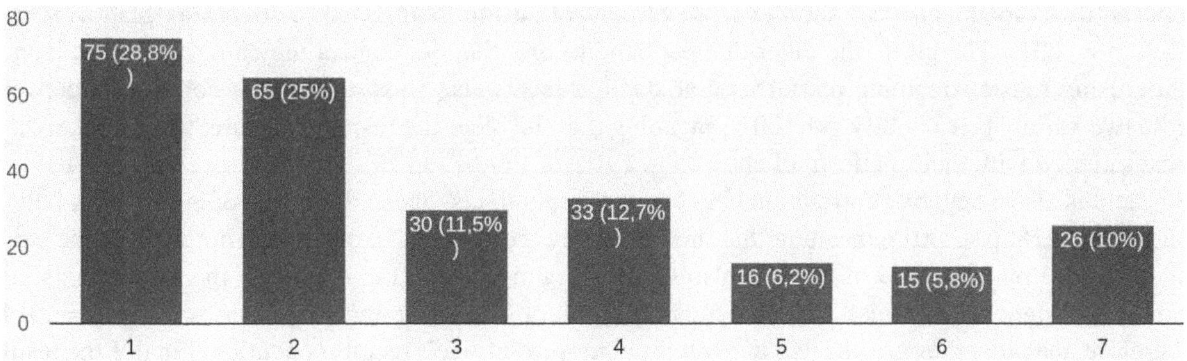

Figure 13. Distribution of respondents when asked if participants use forums or critic lists to discover new music

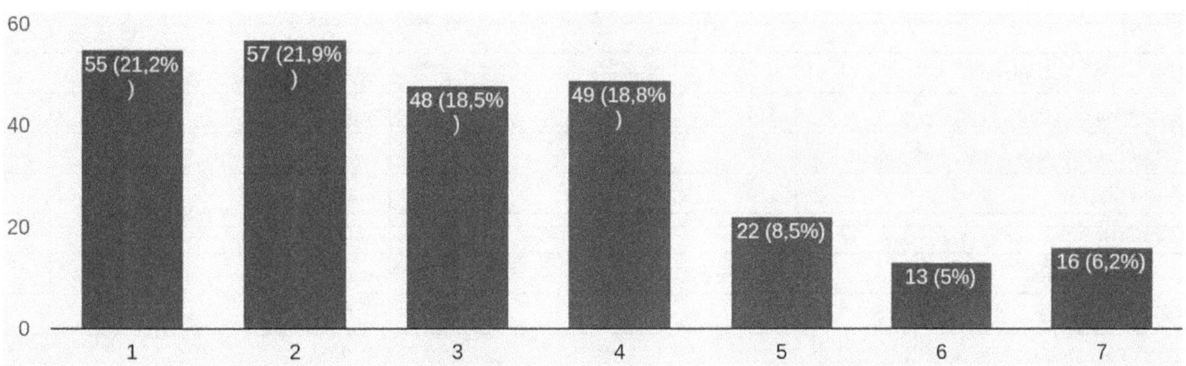

Age and Consumption Correlations

Having presented the general impressions on streaming platforms, their relevancy and various use cases, the next part of this section will highlight the correlations between consumption practices and age.

The results show a significantly positive correlation between respondents' age and the perception of a limited catalogue on streaming platforms ($r = .314$, $p < .001$). Therefore, the older the respondents are, the more likely they are to consider the existing library as limited. Results also show a significantly positive correlation between respondents' age and the use of the new releases section ($r = .209$, $p = .001$). Therefore, the older the respondents are, the more likely they are to use these sections when searching for new music. Additionally, it is also important to point out the positive correlation between respondents' age and the use of playlists ($r = .159$, $p = .010$). Therefore, the older the respondents are, the more likely they are to use these tools in exploration scenarios.

On the other hand, there are several negative correlations to point out as well. The results show negative correlation patterns between respondents' age and the use of streaming services themselves (r = -.315, p < .001). Hence, the older the respondents are, the more likely they are to not incorporate streaming services into their music listening habits. Another negative correlation shown by results is between the respondents' age and the sense of control during their usage of streaming platforms (r = -.236, p < .001). Therefore, the older the respondents are, the less control they are to perceive having while using music streaming platforms. Satisfaction levels also show a negative correlation between these two variables (r = -.294, p < .001), meaning that the older the respondents are, the less likely it is to be satisfied with their platform of choice.

There is also a negative correlation between the respondents' age and the lack of exploratory behaviours (r = -.218, p < .001), meaning that the older they are, the less likely it is to not explore the existing catalogue on the platform. Results also show a negative correlation between the respondents' age and the willingness to dismiss unknown music suggestions on streaming services (r = -.153, p = .014). Therefore, the older they are, the less likely it is to ignore a service's recommendation. Finally, the results show a negative correlation between the respondents' age and asking for a friend's or family member's suggestions during exploration scenarios (r = -.292, p < .001). Therefore, the older the respondents are, the less likely it is to ask for music suggestions from friends or family members.
Table 3 summarizes the reported results regarding respondents' age and variable correlations.

Table 3. Respondents' age and variable correlations

Variable	r	Sig.
Perception of a limited catalogue	.314	< .001
Use of the new releases section	.209	< .001
Use of playlists	.159	< .010
Use of streaming platforms	-.315	< .001
Control perception	-.236	< .001
Satisfaction level	-.294	< .001
Lack of exploratory behaviour	-.218	< .001
The dismissiveness of automatic recommendations	-.153	< .014
Asking for a friend or family member's opinion	-.292	< .001

DISCUSSION

Consistent with the claims made in the literature, this study found that participants reported high usage levels of music streaming platforms on their consumption practices, in addition to the frequent usage of these. Moreover, respondents reported high agreeance levels regarding streaming platforms allowing for quick and easy access to content. These results corroborate previous findings (e.g. Mendes, 2019; IFPI, 2019).

Another important finding was the combined use of different platforms simultaneously. Indeed, the most frequently reported answers pointed to the combined use of two distinct streaming platforms. In particular, Spotify or Deezer, combined with YouTube/YouTube Music, were the most popular combinations. On the other hand, parallel usage of three or more streaming platforms was not relevant. These results show that while participants reported cross-platform behaviours, this tendency does not translate into a wide range of usage of streaming platforms together. While Moschetta (2017) pointed to consumption behaviours distributed between different physical gadgets, there is no awareness of a study indicating combined usage of distinct streaming platforms. Moreover, given the results pointed to a lack of listening habits distributed between three or more platforms, these findings seem unique to date.

In accordance with studies from the IFPI (2019, 2021) and Datta et al. (2018), this study has demonstrated that participants express broad consumption patterns, using streaming platforms to discover new music while also engaging in exploratory behaviour. On this matter, existing tools in streaming services, like playlists, new release sections or automatic suggestions, were the most relevant to the gathered sample. On the other hand, participants mostly do not rely on the advice of their social circles or other promotion media like critics lists when engaging in exploratory behaviours. In sum, external sources of recommendation do not seem very relevant to the gathered sample. While some external sources in particular, like forums and critics' lists, presented a more evenly distributed disagreeing pattern, this makes it impossible to corroborate with Hagen & Luders' (2017) findings regarding weak or absent ties to an extent. While there was evidence for disregarding stronger ties during exploration practices, similar behaviour happened with weak or absent ones.

Despite displaying such exploratory tendencies, the results of this study did not show either a strong sense of control or satisfaction regarding participants' experience with streaming platforms. When asked if participants are satisfied or feel in control while using their platform of choice, they express high neutrality levels. On the other hand, while displaying very similar outcomes, the feeling of lack of control seems slightly more relevant when compared to the dissatisfaction with the platform of choice. Furthermore, respondents expressed high neutrality levels when asked if streaming platforms have a limited catalogue.

The inexistence of strong agreeing or disagreeing levels regarding these topics could indicate a sense of information overload while using streaming services, as pointed out by Davis (2011). If this is the case, there is a considerable probability that respondents could not fully comprehend the available tools and their features, which would translate into a poor user experience. However, considering that respondents claim expressive usage of available features in streaming platforms during exploration scenarios, this seems unlikely. Alternatively, these findings could indicate a sense of catalogue pollution pointed out by Coelho & Mendes (2019). Another factor that could influence answers is advertising, even though it was impossible to assess if this was true or not. Thus, it remains unclear what factors might trigger such outcomes.

Nevertheless, considering that playlists were the most relevant tools in exploration scenarios, it is worth mentioning observations shared by Kaimann et al. (2021). According to the aforementioned authors, an artist's chart performance can benefit considerably by associating with a major label. Therefore, it is possible that respondents feel presented content on streaming platforms to be influenced by major record labels. Although Coelho & Mendes (2019) claim that digital tools provide new opportunities for long-tail products, said authors also stress that the superstar effect hasn't gone irrelevant.

Concerning age and consumption correlations, this study pointed to both positive and negative correlations. There were positive correlations between age and the belief of existing limited catalogues, the usage of new-release sections and the use of playlists. In contrast, there were negative correlations between age and frequency of use of streaming platforms, sense of control, satisfaction levels, the lack of exploratory behaviour, the dismissiveness of automatic recommendations and asking for a friend or family member's opinion. Concerning the less frequent usage of streaming services by older age groups, these results seem consistent with the IFPI (2019) report.

FUTURE RESEARCH DIRECTIONS

In this investigation, the aim was to examine the phenomenon of digital music, particularly streaming services and the various social and consumption dynamics that might influence the overall experience on these digital platforms. While this chapter aimed to explore the yet largely unknown world of discovery tools and mechanisms and their role on music streaming services, some limitations are worth mentioning. For one, it was impossible to assess the existing habits of the participants before taking part in the survey, nor how they define a catalogue as being limited. It was also impossible to examine what role new situational forms of music classification play during the exploration process. Additionally, it was impossible to determine if the exploration process is bound to happen on the so-called superstar tracks or if it expands to long-tail territories. Future research could provide better insight into these topics.

Notwithstanding these limitations, this study suggests qualitative investigation to determine what criteria respondents use to define a catalogue as limited in a music streaming platform. One possible reason for such finding could correlate with the dominance of big record labels on these platforms pointed by Kaimann et al. (2021), although this was not possible to assess. Another possible reason could be related to the information overload phenomenon pointed out by Davis (2011). If so, their experience on digital platforms would possibly be affected in some way. Another possible factor that might have influenced the respondents' answers could be advertising display on these platforms. Therefore, some relevant topics for future investigation include a better understanding of the presence of advertisements as possible factors that contribute to lower satisfaction or control levels on streaming platforms, especially in older age groups.

Other relevant areas for future investigation include a better understanding of a possible correlation between the high exploratory and the satisfaction levels. Considering the observations pointed by Datta et al. (2018), a negative correlation between high discovery levels and the long-term consumption practice might be possible.

CONCLUSION

This chapter aimed to present a broad overview of the digital ambients, specifically music streaming platforms. By examining existing literature on social dynamics and general consumption patterns, this chapter intended to provide comprehensive insight on various fundamental factors that help to understand the contexts and behaviours that take place in such new scenarios. This chapter highlights that, while it is undeniable that technologies had a significant impact on various social aspects, it is vital to keep in mind the importance of existing social backgrounds. As for the field research, survey results have shown that streaming services are widely and frequently used, with results indicating both the high exploration tendencies and the use of internal sources to explore the available library. On the other hand, external sources, such as friends or family, are not considered primary sources for music exploration practices as a whole. Another crucial finding reported on field research was the cross-use of streaming platforms on the respondents' listening habits. As far as it is able to tell, this is a brand-new finding in the literature regarding the matter. Finally, this chapter highlights a need for further investigation on topics such as satisfaction and experience control levels and their correlation with advert display, especially on older age groups. Other relevant topics for further research are related to a better understanding of the frontiers of exploration practices, specifically, if these are bound to happen on the superstar tracks or expand to long-tail songs.

REFERENCES

Airoldi, M., Beraldo, D., & Gandini, A. (2016). Follow the algorithm: An exploratory investigation of music on YouTube. *Poetics*, *57*, 1–13. doi:10.1016/j.poetic.2016.05.001

Arditi, D. (2014). ITunes: Breaking barriers and building walls. *Popular Music and Society*, *37*(4), 408–424. doi:10.1080/03007766.2013.810849

Audiogest. (2020). *Números de mercado da música.* Audiogest. http://www.audiogest.pt/documents/files/Dados%20Mercado%20ano%202019%20P%C3%BAblico%20Final%285%29.pdf

Audiogest. (2021). *Números de mercado da música.* Audiogest. https://www.audiogest.pt/documents/files/Dados%20Mercado%20CY%202020%200303vrp%281%29.pdf

Beer, D. (2010). Mobile music, coded objects and everyday spaces. *Mobilities*, *5*(4), 469–484. doi:10.1080/17450101.2010.510331

Belk, R. W. (2013). Extended self in a digital world. *The Journal of Consumer Research*, *40*(3), 477–500. doi:10.1086/671052

Bourdieu, P. (1984). *A Social Critique of the Judgement of Taste*. Academic Press.

Bryson, B. (1996). "Anything but heavy metal": Symbolic exclusion and musical dislikes. *American Sociological Review*, *61*(5), 884–899. doi:10.2307/2096459

Charron, J.-P. (2017). Music Audiences 3.0: Concert-Goers' Psychological Motivations at the Dawn of Virtual Reality. *Frontiers in Psychology*, *8*, 800. doi:10.3389/fpsyg.2017.00800 PMID:28588528

Coelho, M. P., & Mendes, J. Z. (2019). Digital music and the "death of the long tail.". *Journal of Business Research*, *101*, 454–460. doi:10.1016/j.jbusres.2019.01.015

Datta, H., Knox, G., & Bronnenberg, B. J. (2018). Changing Their Tune: How Consumers' Adoption of Online Streaming Affects Music Consumption and Discovery. *Marketing Science*, *37*(1), 5–21. doi:10.1287/mksc.2017.1051

Davis, N. (2011). Information overload, reloaded. *Bulletin of the American Society for Information Science and Technology*, *37*(5), 45–49. doi:10.1002/bult.2011.1720370513

Eiriz, V., & Leite, F. P. (2017). The digital distribution of music and its impact on the business models of independent musicians. *Service Industries Journal*, *37*(13–14), 875–895. doi:10.1080/02642069.2017.1361935

Hagen, A. N. (2015). The Playlist Experience: Personal Playlists in Music Streaming Services. *Popular Music and Society*, *38*(5), 625–645. doi:10.1080/03007766.2015.1021174

Hagen, A. N., & Lüders, M. (2017). Social streaming? Navigating music as personal and social. *Convergence*, *23*(6), 643–659. doi:10.1177/1354856516673298

Hennion, A. (2007). Those things that hold us together: Taste and sociology. *Cultural Sociology*, *1*(1), 97–114. doi:10.1177/1749975507073923

International Federation of the Phonographic Industry (IFPI). (2019). *Music Listening 2019- A look at how recorded music is enjoyed around the world*. Author.

International Federation of the Phonographic Industry (IFPI). (2021). *Global Music Report 2021*. https://gmr2021.ifpi.org/assets/GMR2021_State%20of%20the%20Industry.pdf

Kaimann, D., Tanneberg, I., & Cox, J. (2021). "I will survive": Online streaming and the chart survival of music tracks. *Managerial and Decision Economics*, *42*(1), 3–20. doi:10.1002/mde.3226

Kamehkhosh, I., Bonnin, G., & Jannach, D. (2019). Effects of recommendations on the playlist creation behavior of users. *User Modeling and User-Adapted Interaction*. Advance online publication. doi:10.100711257-019-09237-4

Kischinhevsky, M., Vicente, E., & de Marchi, L. (2015). Em busca da música infinita: os serviços de streaming e os conflitos de interesse no mercado de conteúdos digitais. *Fronteiras - Estudos Midiáticos*, *17*(3). doi:10.4013/fem.2015.173.04

Maasø, A. (2018). Music Streaming, Festivals, and the Eventization of Music. *Popular Music and Society*, *41*(2), 154–175. doi:10.1080/03007766.2016.1231001

Marshall, L. (2015). 'Let's keep music special. F—Spotify': On-demand streaming and the controversy over artist royalties. *Creative Industries Journal*, *8*(2), 177–189. doi:10.1080/17510694.2015.1096618

Mendes, T. T. J. (2019). *A música online : o uso de plataformas streaming e a sua influência na descoberta e no gosto*. http://hdl.handle.net/10071/19085

Morris, J. W., & Powers, D. (2015). Control, curation and musical experience in streaming music services. *Creative Industries Journal*, *8*(2), 106–122. http://10.0.4.56/17510694.2015.1090222. doi:10.1080/17510694.2015.1090222

Nielsen Music. (2020). *Year-End Music Report U.S. 2019*. Author.

Nowak, R. (2016). When is a discovery? The affective dimensions of discovery in music consumption. *Popular Communication*, *14*(3), 137–145. doi:10.1080/15405702.2016.1193182

Peterson, R. A. (1992). Understanding audience segmentation: From elite and mass to omnivore and univore. *Poetics*, *21*(4), 243–258. doi:10.1016/0304-422X(92)90008-Q

Ruvio, A., & Shoham, A. (2007). Innovativeness, exploratory behavior, market mavenship, and opinion leadership: An empirical examination in the Asian context. *Psychology and Marketing*, *24*(8), 703–722. doi:10.1002/mar.20180

Sinclair, G., & Tinson, J. (2017). Psychological ownership and music streaming consumption. *Journal of Business Research, 71*, 1–9. doi:10.1016/j.jbusres.2016.10.002

Taylor, J. R., & Dean, R. T. (2019). Encouraging Attention and Exploration in a Hybrid Recommender System for Libraries of Unfamiliar Music. *Musicae Scientiae, 2*. doi:10.1177/2059204319893179

Taylor, J. R., & Dean, R. T. (2021). Influence of a continuous affect ratings task on listening time for unfamiliar art music. *Journal of New Music Research, 50*(3), 1–17. doi:10.1080/09298215.2020.1867588

Tepper, S. J., & Hargittai, E. (2009). Pathways to music exploration in a digital age. *Poetics, 37*(3), 227–249. doi:10.1016/j.poetic.2009.03.003

Verboord, M. (2019). Music mavens revisited: Comparing the impact of connectivity and dispositions in the digital age. *Journal of Consumer Culture*. Advance online publication. doi:10.1177/1469540519846203

Weingartner, S. (2020). Digital omnivores? How digital media reinforce social inequalities in cultural consumption. *New Media & Society*. Advance online publication. doi:10.1177/1461444820957635

Werner, A. (2020). Organizing music, organizing gender: Algorithmic culture and Spotify recommendations. *Popular Communication, 18*(1), 78–90. doi:10.1080/15405702.2020.1715980

ADDITIONAL READING

Aguiar, L., & Waldfogel, J. (2019). Platforms, Power, and Promotion: Evidence from Spotify Playlists. https://conference.nber.org/confer/2021/DTs21/joel3.pdf

Aguiar, L., Waldfogel, J., & Waldfogel, S. (2021). Playlisting favorites: Measuring platform bias in the music industry. *International Journal of Industrial Organization, 78*, 102765. doi:10.1016/j.ijindorg.2021.102765

Anderson, A., Maystre, L., Anderson, I., Mehrotra, R., & Lalmas, M. (2020, April). Algorithmic effects on the diversity of consumption on spotify. In *Proceedings of The Web Conference 2020* (pp. 2155-2165). https://dl.acm.org/doi/pdf/10.1145/3366423.3380281

Barata, M. L., & Coelho, P. S. (2021). Music streaming services: Understanding the drivers of customer purchase and intention to recommend. *Heliyon, 7*(8), e07783. doi:10.1016/j.heliyon.2021.e07783 PMID:34458619

Hansen, C., Mehrotra, R., Hansen, C., Brost, B., Maystre, L., & Lalmas, M. (2021, March). Shifting consumption towards diverse content on music streaming platforms. In *Proceedings of the 14th ACM International Conference on Web Search and Data Mining* (pp. 238-246). https://dl.acm.org/doi/pdf/10.1145/3437963.3441775

Hesmondhalgh, D. (2021). Is music streaming bad for musicians? Problems of evidence and argument. *New Media & Society, 23*(12), 3593-3615. https://journals.sagepub.com/doi/pdf/10.1177/1461444820953541

Mehrotra, R., Shah, C., & Carterette, B. (2020, September). Investigating listeners' responses to divergent recommendations. In *Fourteenth ACM Conference on Recommender Systems* (pp. 692-696). https://dl.acm.org/doi/pdf/10.1145/3383313.3418482

Park, S. Y., & Kaneshiro, B. (2021). Social Music Curation That Works: Insights from Successful Collaborative Playlists. *Proceedings of the ACM on Human-Computer Interaction, 5*(CSCW1), 1-27. https://dl.acm.org/doi/pdf/10.1145/3449191

KEY TERMS AND DEFINITIONS

Brick-and-Mortar: A term used to describe physical stores that sell a range of products, such as CDs and music merchandise.

Dematerialisation: A term used to describe the process of transposing an object to an equivalent digital counterpart. One such example is digital music files or photos, being equivalent to existing physical objects. These can be stored, processed, and retrieved through various technological gadgets.

Long-Tail: Also mentioned by some authors as "heavy tail" or "power-law tail". It describes a series of products that usually do not make part of the well-known or best-selling categories, being instead part of a niche market.

Mediators: A series of actors sometimes referred to as middlemen. They function as sellers or connectors between the customer and the producer of a good or product.

P2P: Abbreviation for "peer-to-peer". This term describes a range of social networks in which users can share content without requiring any mediators.

Performance Rights: Refers to the rights to play songs in live venues or by broadcasters.

Superstar Tracks: A term used to describe music tracks that stand out as having a large consumption volume.

Synchronisation: as defined by the IFPI, it refers to music that is used in films, games and television.

Chapter 6
The Development and Impact of China's Digital Transformation in the Medical Industry

Poshan Yu
Soochow University, China & Krirk University, Thailand

Wenye Xue
Independent Researcher, China

Ramya Mahendran
Independent Researcher, India

ABSTRACT

This research chapter sheds light on the digital transformations that are happening in the medical industry and primarily focuses on how digital transformation processes are introduced and adapted into China's medical industry. Furthermore, the authors explore the characteristics, socio-economic impact, changes in business models and consumer experience, introduction, and restructuring of relevant government policies caused by these digital transformations. They also bring to light the opportunities, challenges, and risks that may present in the future. The authors take two case studies for demonstrating the impact: first, the intelligent assistance system that leverages 5G+AI and, second, the body temperature monitoring system that leverages the IoT and Bluetooth. Through the comparison of these two successful case-studies, they can realize that the impact of AI technologies and thereby the digital transformations will play a major role in the future of medical industry. They also explore the problems of digital transformation in the field of medical care with the help of a few case studies like IBM Watson.

1. INTRODUCTION

To evolve and re-invent themselves enterprises use innovative technologies like the Internet of things (IoT), artificial intelligence (AI), cloud computing, big data as their driving forces. This process of self-evolution is called 'digital transformation' (Vial, 2019, p. 118). In recent decades, China's medical

DOI: 10.4018/978-1-7998-9179-6.ch006

industry has undergone a tremendous digital transformation. This digital transformation has improved the customer and user (doctors, patients, care takers) experience in many ways. Technology breakthroughs in medical science such as AI powered virtual assistant systems, integrated mining of big data and intelligent imaging has significantly enhanced customer experience (Jin & Qiu, 2019). The gradual maturity of telemedicine systems meet the needs of specific patients and nursing staff (Liu et al., 2019). Digital transformation enables consumers to seamlessly connect with information and data from anywhere, anytime and on any device (CB insights, 2021). According to National Internet Emergency Center (2021), the Chinese government has accordingly invested on related platforms, infrastructure development projects and played a regulatory role to enable the healthy and wholistic development of smart medical care. According to AI Research Institute of Shanghai Jiaotong University (2019), the change in medical business models, also promotes the decentralization of medical resources.

During the COVID-19 pandemic, AI medicine has started playing a significant role in patient care and recovery. This article compared two case-studies for demonstrating the impact, first, the intelligent assistance system that leverages 5G+AI (5th Generation wireless technology and Artificial Intelligence) that is being used at the Zhongnan Hospital in Wuhan University and second, the body temperature monitoring system that leverages the Internet of Things (IoT) and Bluetooth technologies that are being used at the Shenzhen Longhua District Central Hospital. Through the comparative analysis of these two successful case-studies, the significance and impact of AI medical care under the digital transformation have been discovered. According to 2020 China Health Statistics Yearbook (2020), Medical technologies undergoing digital transformation has greatly contributed to the reduction of the urban-rural health disparities. There is a gaining prospect for smart medical market in the future. However, these digital transformations are also facing huge challenges like public opinion, skepticism and ethical conflicts between traditional and digital medical practices (Rezaei et al., 2021). Apart from this, there are other implementational challenges such as resource interoperability, sensitive data sharing, doctor-patient confidentiality, market feasibility and economic viability.

This chapter aims to explore the development and impact of the digital transformation of China's medical industry by analyzing the institution level changes that are promoted by Chinese regulatory agencies. This chapter will also assess the impact of such changes on the industry.

2. BACKGROUND

Starting in early 2000s, China's medical field has gone on an extensive digital exploration. According to Xiong (2020), the development of Internet medical care in China is relatively slow due to the influence of regulations, policies, and resistance of the existing medical systems to adapt and change. However, after the COVID-19 outbreak in 2019, China's Internet medical services ushered in new opportunities for technology development. With the help technologies like IoT, AI and Robotics the nation's medical systems are undergoing speedy digital transformation. In a way the pandemic has made us rethink and reimagine the systems of today. Pushed all stakeholders to think differently and improvise on the go. Technology has especially played a crucial role during these times, as we had to work around constraints like contactless patientcare. Xiong (2020) pointed out that the pandemic has promoted changes in the behavior of doctors and patients at both the diagnosis and the treatment phase. In China, the uneven distribution of medical resources and the mismatch between patients and doctors are important factors for friction in doctor-patient relationship (Zhang et al., 2020). At the same time, the rapid development of medical digitalization is expected to achieve efficiency improvement and resource integration to a certain extent, alleviating the imbalance between China's medical resources and service supply and demand. According to China Academy of Information and Communications Technology (2021), the outbreak of COVID-19 is expected to prompt the Internet medical industry to break through the bottleneck and usher in explosive growth in 2021. Under the dual influence of favorable policies and the COVID-19, digital transformation in the medical field will be the trend of the times.

There are many medical technology innovations through the application of machine learning that are aiding the digital transformation. Machine learning is being used to assess the risk of disease and estimate the success rate of treatment. It is used to manage or relieve complications. It also plays a role in continuous patient care, health monitoring, and ongoing pathology or therapeutic efficacy research (Becker, 2019).

Many different fields including medicine are undergoing in-depth integrations of digital technologies. However in the field of medical care it is more related to social economy, human behavior and rapid urbanization of people's lives in recent years. Kunaviktikul et al. (2021) found that the emerging reality of social change through digital technology is central to eHealth (over the internet) and mHealth (over mobile). The usage of AI and ML with different medical application is increasing drastically. It can be seen from Figure 1 that the overall trend of investment and financing of China's AI medical companies from 2015 to 2021 is on the rise. The decrease in investment and financing from 2020 to 2021 is due to COVID-19. As can be seen from Figure 2, driven by national policies and the needs of various medical fields, the market size of China's medical AI industry has rapidly expanded. The digital medical market has promoted economic and social development to a certain extent. The continuous improvement of market value has not only brought huge economic profits, but also new promises to the people's livelihood, employment opportunities and social stability.

Figure 1. 2015-2021 China AI medical company investment and financing situation
Source: Essence Securities Research Center

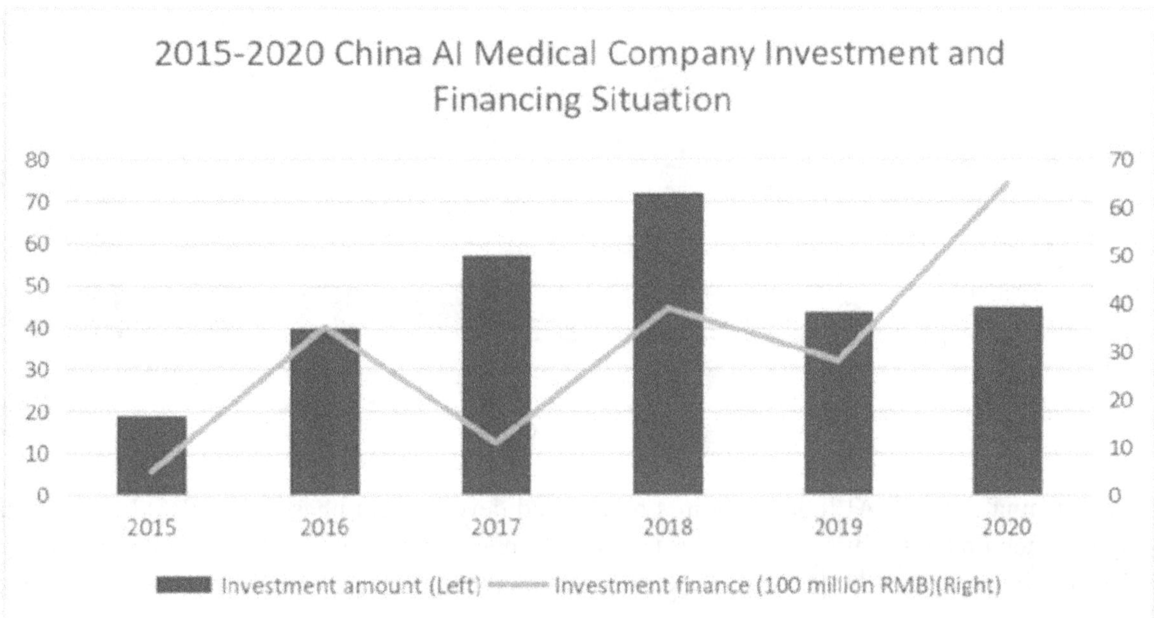

Figure 2. The development index of digital medical industry
Sources: Desk research, KPMG analysis

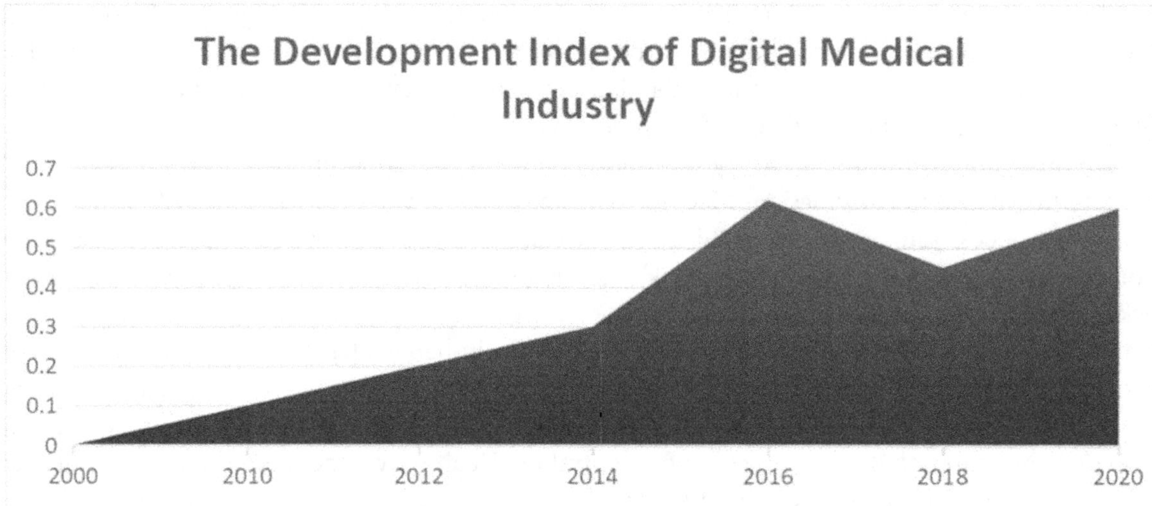

Figure 3. China's AI medical market scale
Source: Essence Securities Research Center

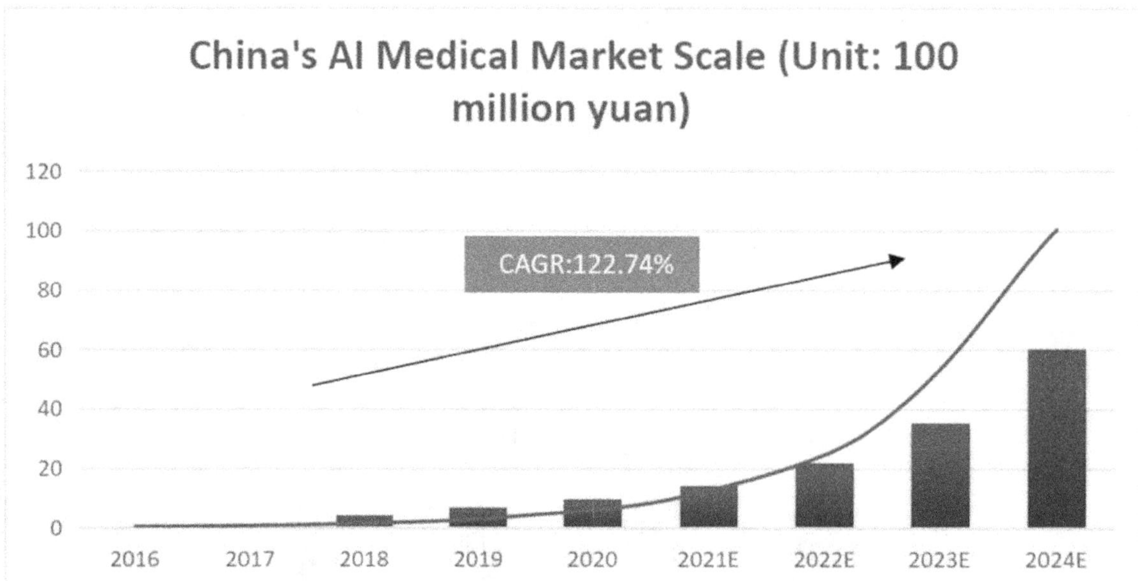

While China's overall AI Industry is in a high-speed development phase, China's AI medical care is playing catch up too (Figure 4). The investment and financing market is developing rapidly (Figures 1 & 7), and the number of projects are increasing. Among them, medical robots, was and is one of the most important sub-application areas of AI medical applications with a market size of 4.32 billion yuan as of 2019. Rehabilitation robots, surgical robots, assistive robots, and medical service robots accounted for 47%, 17%, 23% and 13%, respectively. As can be seen from Figure 3, the compound annual growth rate (CAGR) of the medical industry from 2017 to 2019 reached 31.98%, showing that the industry has great potential. According to Essence Securities Research Center's forecast for 2021-2024, the compound growth rate of the medical industry from 2016 to 2024 reached 122.74%. According to statistics from the Chinese Institute of Electronics, the market size of the medical AI industry will reach 7.53 billion yuan by 2021.

Figure 4. The development history of China's artificial intelligence industry
Sources: McKinsey Global Institute (MGI), White Paper on China's AI Intelligence Industry

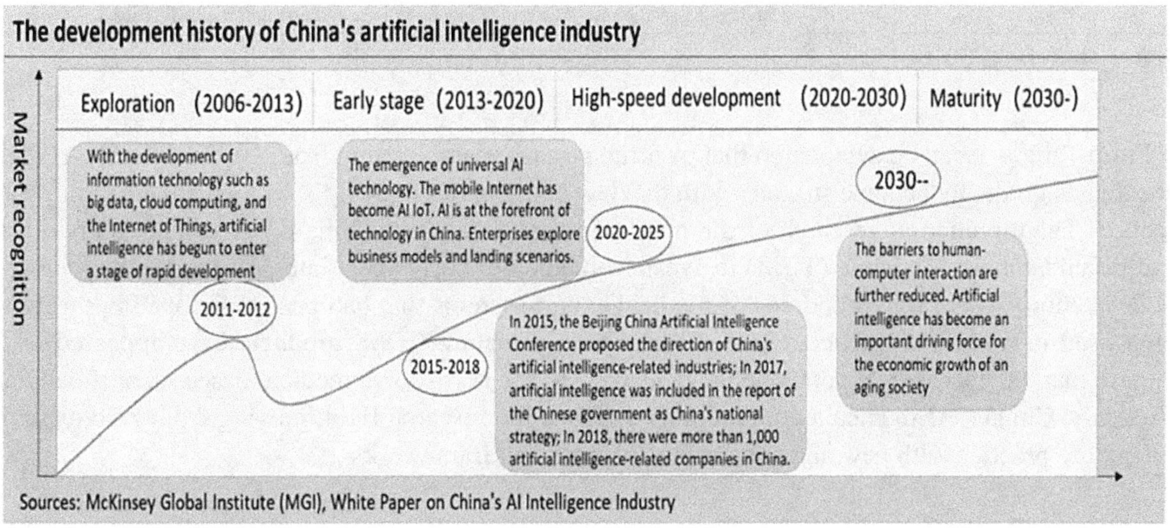

As a service, AI will play an increasing role in the technological infrastructure of the society, enabling many application functions to be realized, promoted, and supported (Cobbe & Singh, 2021). According to data from the China Academy of Information and Communications Technology and International Data Corporation (IDC), the scale of China's AI industry has reached 310 billion yuan in 2020 and the AI infrastructure market will reach 3.93 billion dollars, with a year-on-year increase of 26.8%.

Table 1. China's AI Digital Medical Development

	China's AI Digital Medical Development
1960-1980	In 1978, Beijing Hospital of Traditional Chinese Medicine developed the country's first medical expert system.
1980-2000	In 1980s, the direction of research was in building expert system and was mostly explored by traditional Chinese medicine. In 1990s, the direction of research in building expert systems slowly transferred to the field of western medicine.
2000-2010	Hundreds of expert systems were developed by the Chinese research society, but almost none of them were adopted and used in real-time clinics.
2010-2020	In 2015, researchers carried out study on the impact of Al in healthcare. From 2016 to 2017, relatively mature Clinical Decision Support System (CDSS) products started appearing in the Chinese market. From 2018, AI was applied in the field of genetic testing. In 2019, researchers learned to use AI to solve more complex and difficult medical cases.

Source: iResearch (2021)

From Table 1 it can be deciphered that over the past 60 years, starting from 1960s, China's AI medical care has gradually become stronger with the development of the world's AI medical technology and practice. The direction of research of the medical expert system in China has gradually shifted from Traditional Chinese Medicine (TCM) to Western medicine. Forty years later, during the beginning of the 21st century, there were hundreds of medical expert systems that had been developed but were not being used in real-time practice. Since then, relatively mature CDSS products have appeared in the Chinese market and medical personnel have learned to use AI to solve medical cases scientifically and efficiently. China's AI medical care gradually expands the research field, moving from zero expertise to a mature practice with new and enhanced processes and frameworks.

Figure 5. 2011-2019 China's total medical expenditure and GDP share
Sources: National Bureau of Statistics, Wind database

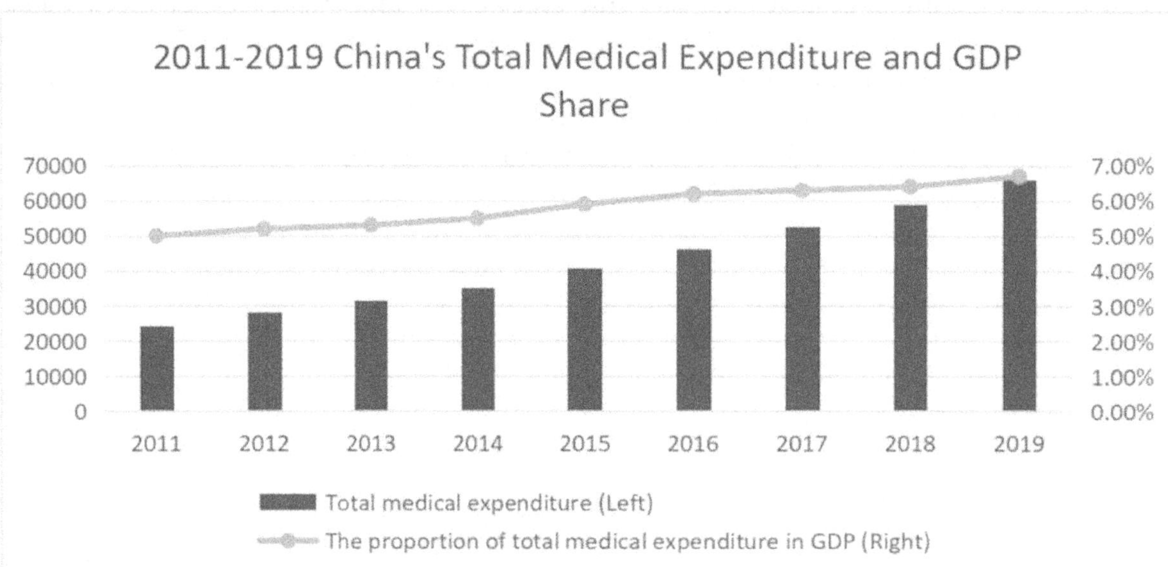

It can be seen from Figure 5 & 6 that AI is an inevitable choice to fix the imbalance between the supply and demand of medical resources. As of 2019, China's total medical and health expenditure reached 6.6 trillion yuan and the CAGR of total medical and health expenditure in 2011-2019 reached 6.9% (Figure 5). As far as the consumption expenditure of China's population is concerned, medical consumption accounts for about 6%-8% of the total consumption expenditure of urban population and about 9%-11% of the total consumption expenditure of rural population (Figure 6). To a certain extent, this reflects the greater demand for medical resources in rural areas and the urgency of improving the efficiency of medical care. AI medical care can not only improve the management and R&D of hospitals and pharmaceutical companies, but also improve the medical level and efficiency of primary healthcare and medical institutions on a large scale without differentiation (Xingye Securities, 2021). According to IDC statistics, the global AI application market is expected to reach 127 billion dollars by 2025 and the medical industry will account for one-fifth of it. It will be one of the fastest growing tracks in the next five years.

Figure 6. 2014-2019 Medical consumption expenditure of urban and rural residents in China
Sources: National Bureau of Statistics, Wind database

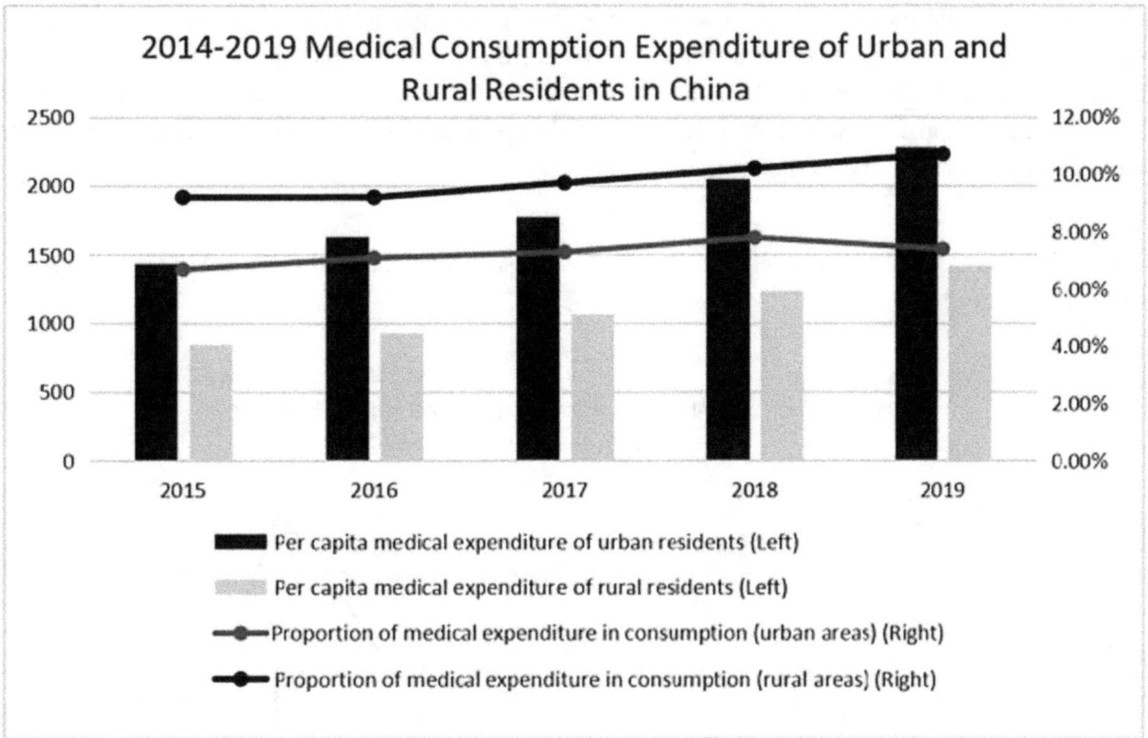

3. CHARACTERISTICS OF CHINA'S DIGITAL TRANSFORMATION IN MEDICAL INDUSTRY TO ENHANCE CONSUMER EXPERIENCE

a. Changes in Medical Business Models: Decentralization of Medical Resources

The digital transformation of China's medical industry has triggered specific changed in its business models. The digital transformation of healthcare mainly relies on the Internet and other internet-based technologies like cloud, IoT, AI, and so on (Kunaviktikul et al., 2021). Internet medical care includes five major tracks: smart hospitals, online consultation platform, medical pharmacy, medical insurance, and other related health services. Figure 7 shows the distribution of China's AI+ medical financing scale from 2010 to 2020, with AI+ new medical research and AI+ auxiliary examination accounting for the largest proportion. The core of medical care in digital transformation is to realize the decentralization of medical resources. The changes in business models can solve the problems of uneven distribution of regional resources, differences in level of consumer convenience and skewed doctor patient ratio in various locations (Kraus et al., 2021). Decentralization enables effective averaging of medical resources, reducing regional differences in medical standards and enhancing consumer's experience. After the transformation of the medical field, new business models and products have emerged, such as online to offline (O2O, Table 2), business to business (B2B), business to consumer (B2C) and prescription circulation (Huatai Securities, 2020). These new business models combine innovations of the internet and medicine; to improve customer convenience. Highly personalized and contextualized doctor-patient relationships are formed due to these advancements.

Figure 7. 2010-2020 China's AI+ medical total financing amount, number of financing and distribution of financing scale
Source: iResearch

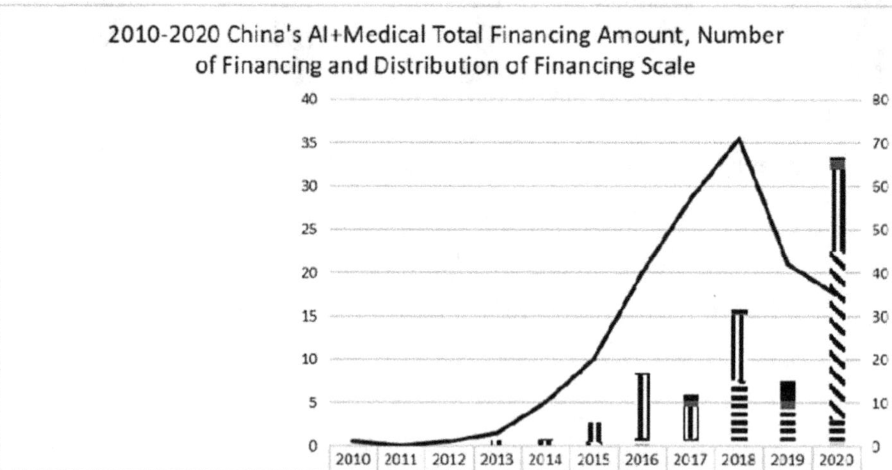

	2010	2011	2012	2013	2014	2015	2016	2017	2018	2019	2020
Wisdom medical record	0	0	0	0	0.1	0	0.2	0.7	0.5	2.2	0.2
Clinical decision support system (CDSS)	0	0	0	0	0	0	0	0.7	0.2	1.8	1.2
AI+auxiliary examination	0	0	0	0.6	0.6	2.3	7.8	3.6	7.5	3.6	9.5
AI+new medical research	0	0	0	0	0	0.5	0.5	1	7.7	0	22.5
Other	0	0	1	0	0	0	1.4	1.3	14.6	8.4	5.2
AI+genetic test	0	0	0	0	0	0	0.5	0.2	0	0.2	0
Surgical robot	0	0	0	0	0	0	0	0	0	0	1.2
Number of financing events	1	0	1	3	10	20	40	57	71	42	35

Table 2. China's AI Digital Medical Development

Three Platforms in O2O Mode		
Type	**Mode**	**Representative Company**
Self-operated platform	It is a self-operated app, where the patient can order on app (or online) and the medicine is home delivered	Ding Dong Quick Medicine
Third-party platform	Cooperate with chain of pharmacies where patient orders on app and the medicines are home delivered	Ali Health JD Health Home
Takeaway platform	Cooperate with chain pharmacies where the patient orders on app and picks up the delivery at the nearest location	ELEME Takeout Meituan-Dianping Takeout

Sources: Kantar Consulting, Huatai Securities Research Institute

b. A Breakthrough in AI Medical Care: Greatly Enhance the Customer Experience

In recent years, machines have surpassed human performance in many cognitive tasks (Whiting et al., 2021). AI is likely to revolutionize the field of healthcare (Kunaviktikul et al., 2021). Xing et al. (2021) concluded that AI can be applied to many health-related fields, from hospital care and clinical research to drug discovery and diagnostic prediction. There are three main applications of AI in digital medicine: virtual assistant systems; integration and mining of big data; smart imaging. The virtual assistant system can help doctors, nurses, and technicians to quickly diagnose and administer care (Choi et al., 2021). According to Choi et al. (2021), the system can greatly improve efficiency and accuracy of diagnosis by reducing the number of steps and saving time; the integration and mining of big data makes medical shared resources more effective and open. At the same time, the development, infrastructure and security of the data terminals have improved to a great extend; AI imaging greatly improves the accuracy, reduces the omissions and enhances the experience of customers. Spyropoulos (2000) noted that AI planning and scheduling methods can provide a lot of support for hospital management and help improve service levels and efficiency.

Virtual assistant systems and big data integration platforms are being developed and extensively used in China (Liu et al., 2019). According to National Internet Emergency Center (2021), in 2017, Guangxi People's Hospital began using the esophageal cancer screening system developed by Tencent that assists doctors in clinical diagnosis with an accuracy rate of 90%; Chinese AI company iCarbonX established a large-scale data platform specialized in health management, called MiWo. The platform can analyze the health of users based on sports activities, diets, and their skin conditions (Daxue Consulting, 2020).

Figure 8. Market size of AI for medical imaging industry in China from 2019 to 2022
Source: Statista

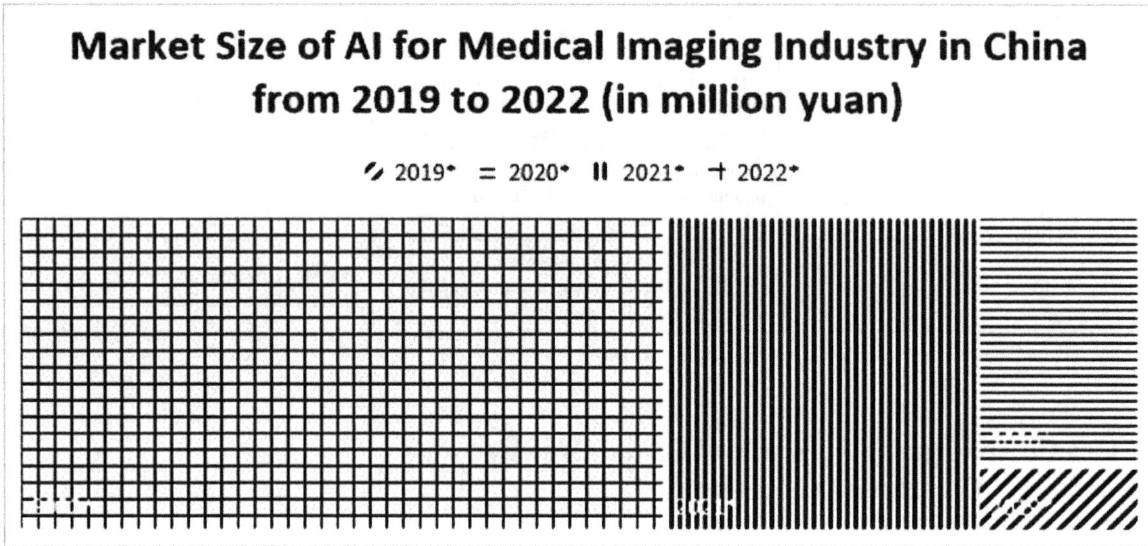

It can be seen from Figure 8 that the AI market in China's medical imaging industry is expected to have exponential increase year on year from 2019 to 2022. Cheng et al. (2021) discuss the application of AI in nuclear medicine imaging. This application has focused on the diagnosis, treatment monitoring, and correlation analyses with pathology of specific gene mutations (Table 3). It can also be used for image generation to shorten the time of image acquisition, reduce the dose of injected tracer, and enhance image quality. In short, the application has greatly promoted medical imaging technology, thereby enhancing the efficiency and accuracy levels of doctors' diagnosis (Kraus et al., 2021).

Besides, advances in AI technology raise the question of whether additional semi-automatic image analysis (i.e., AI assisted reporting) will reduce the number of missed secondary discoveries in a time and life-saving manner. The available AI algorithms usually have a very narrow clinical focus and are evaluated only by quantifying the diagnostic indicators achieved compared by radiologists (Rueckel, 2021).

China's new technology to combat the COVID-19 includes the ability to read Computed Tomography (CT) scans. A CT scan of the chest is indeed a key method for diagnosing coronavirus. Alibaba and health insurance company Ping An collaboratively developed an intelligent image reading system that can provide results within 15 seconds with an accuracy rate of over 90% (Daxue Consulting, 2020). Technological advancements have significantly improved the efficiency of the medical industry (Kraus et al., 2021), as radiologists can spend up to 15 minutes reading CT images of patients suspected of being infected with COVID-19, increasing waiting time, heightening the anxiety of the patient and the spread of infection due to prolonged exposure for the healthcare professionals.

Figure 9. Number of AI-related companies established in China in 2018, by industry
Source: Statista

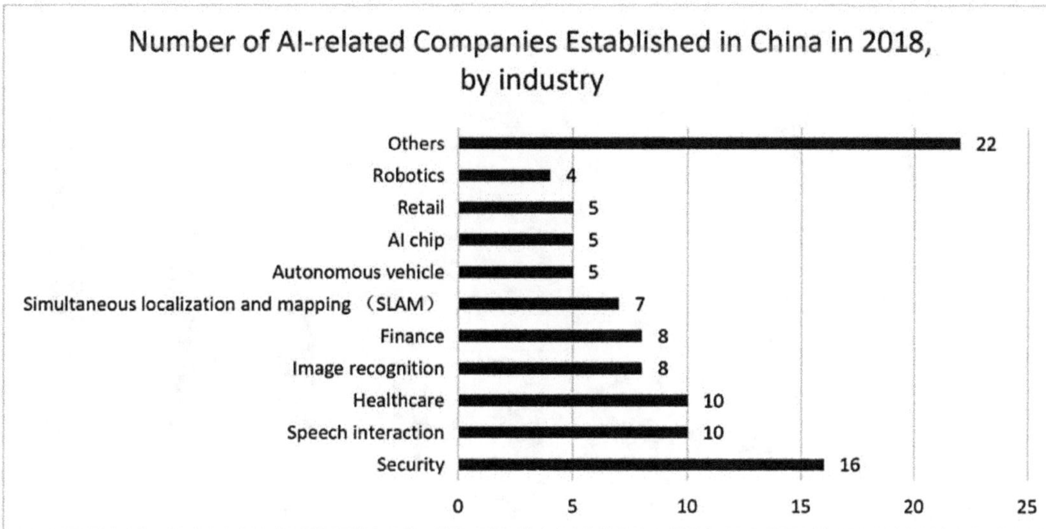

Table 3. The application of AI in the field of medical imaging

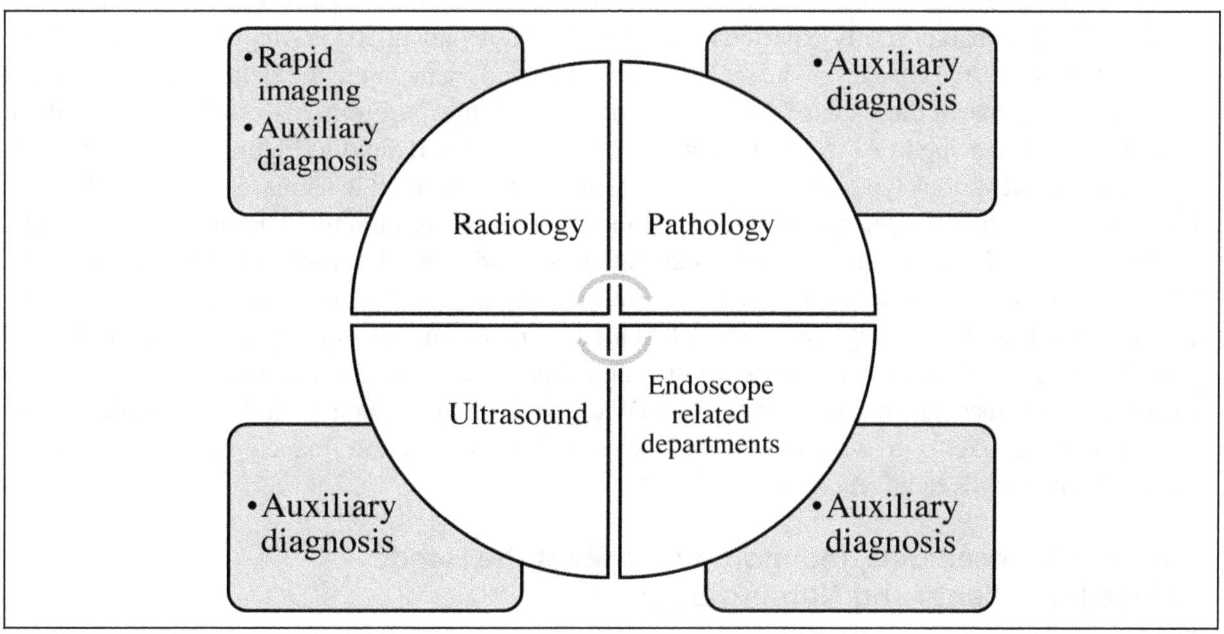

Figure 10. 2015-2023E China's AI medical imaging market size
Sources: Head Leopard Research Institute, Xingye Securities Research Institute

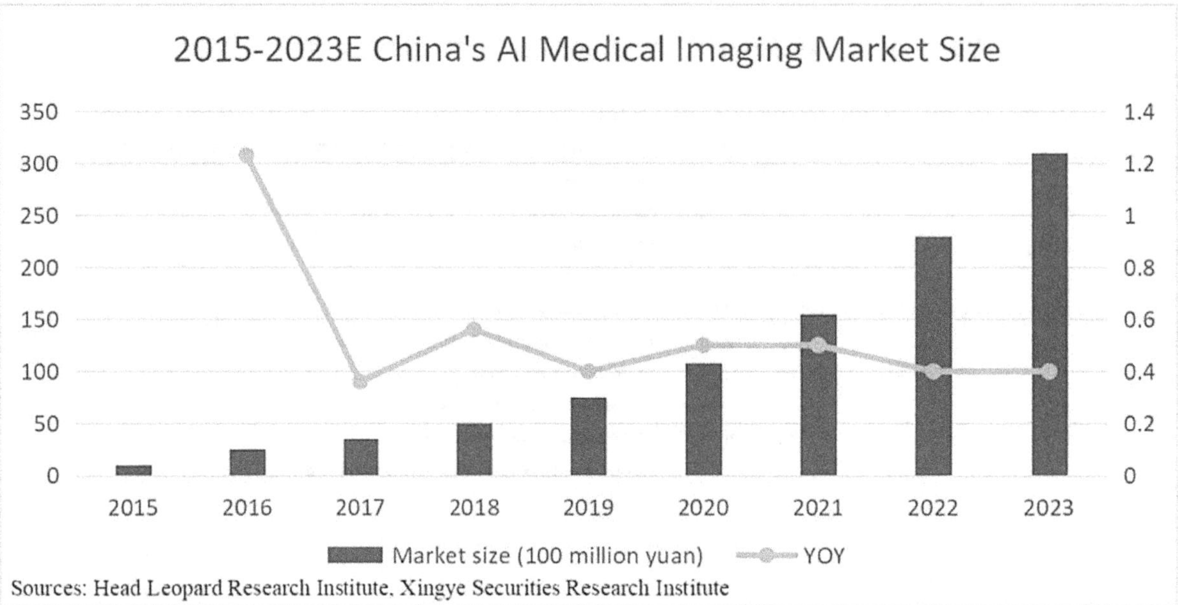

The traditional AI medical imaging industry in China began to take shape in 2015. The market size increased from 1.09 billion yuan in 2015 to 4.97 billion yuan in 2018, with a compound annual growth rate of 65.8%. The market size is expected to reach 30.7 billion yuan in 2023 (Xingye Securities, 2021). In the past ten years, the changes in the scale of investment and financing in the field of AI medical care in China roughly match the scale of AI medical imaging (Figure 7). From 2015 to 2018, the scale of investment and financing in AI medical imaging industry has grown rapidly (Figure 10). It can be seen from Figure 9 that various types of medical AI companies have emerged in China. Since 2019, the scale of investment and financing has dropped significantly, the market has gradually returned to rationality, and the medical AI industry has entered a stage of steady and rapid development (Xingye Securities, 2021). The key aspects of medical imaging AI technology innovation are robustness, usability, and safety (Xiao & Liu, 2019). In the future, digital AI medical treatment will not only change the traditional medical imaging methods, but also improve the clinical practices of medical treatment, enabling many aspirations of the medical society to be realized (Wang & Shi, 2019). On the whole, the medical imaging AI industry market is growing rapidly and the overall investment and financing enthusiasm for the medical AI industry is relatively high.

c. Mature Telemedicine Technology: To Meet the Needs of Specific Patients and Nursing Staff

In recent years, many health systems in China have begun to implement telemedicine programs. According to Zhang et al. (2020), telemedicine includes remote teleradiology, remote ultrasound diagnostics, telesurgery, telemedicine consultation, and other forms of remote healthcare. Telemedicine consultation is the most used form of telemedicine. The COVID-19 has made more hospitals aware of the importance of telemedicine platforms. According to Xiong (2020), digital leaders are not just focusing on leveraging digital technologies during the coronavirus situation but are also redefining their telemedicine plans to achieve longer-term goals, and hopefully prepare the medical professionals to be able to proactively respond and manage such situations that might occur in the future. According to Rezaei et al. (2021), the advancement of telemedicine technology promotes the continuous development of telemedicine platforms. Related functional branches of telemedicine encompass teleconsultation, telecare, telemonitoring or telehealth, and tele diagnoses (Arni & Laddha, 2017; Ford et al., 2017; Tuzii, 2017). At present, some telemedicine systems have integrated functions linked to the electronic health record (EHR) system (Choi et al., 2021). According to Choi et al. (2021), these platforms will also enhance their functions based on the type of medical service, the number of patients, and geographic location to meet some new needs of patients like offering real-time language translation to non-Chinese speakers. However, telemedicine technology still has some specific problems in practice, such as the pressure on doctors & nurses and the problem of staffing arrangements (Rezaei et al., 2021). The future telemedicine platform will consider the needs of nursing staff and patients (Zhang et al., 2020). For instance, constantly training and updating the staff to attain technological and digital literacy, could bridge the gap that telemedicine is facing.

Telemedicine technology can also be combined with AI robots. Through remote control technology, hospitals can leverage robots to carry and dispense medicines to patients (Villaronga & Mahler, 2021). During the corona pandemic robots were used to collect samples, provide food and medicine, and UV robots were used to sanitize and disinfect the rooms. Robots can also be programmed to interface with smart elevators, to reach any floor and return to the hospital pharmacy to refill (Daxue Consulting, 2020).

Digital pathology remote consultation promotes the sinking of resources of high-quality pathologists and facilitates the advancement of hierarchical diagnosis and treatment (Kraus et al., 2021). Traditional pathological consultations generally include two methods: In the first method, local basic-level hospitals mail the pathological slices or wax blocks applied for consultation to the pathology department of the higher-level hospital; In the second method, patients or their family members carry the pathological slices or wax blocks to a large local or remote hospital for consultation (Xingye Securities, 2021). Both methods need to send solid pathology specimen materials to the consulting hospital, which usually face problems such as insufficient timeliness, low efficiency, risk of damage or loss of specimens, high transportation costs, etc. (Zhang et al., 2020).

With the vigorous development of digital slice scanning technology and the Internet, digital and remote pathology consultation has taken root across the country and is becoming more and more accurate, efficient and the market for remote pathology is maturing. The key word for digital pathology remote consultation is "digital + remote". The former is a prerequisite for the realization of the entire process. Pathological slices and other case data must be digitized before they can be transmitted via the Internet; the latter is for pathological consultations. The production scan (converting physical file to digital file for easier management) and medical consultation of pathological slices can cross the limitation of time and place (Xingye Securities, 2021). Remote pathology consultation can effectively utilize the technical advantages of the pathology department of higher-level hospitals, promote the sinking of resources of high-quality pathology experts, and facilitate the advancement of hierarchical diagnosis and treatment.

Figure 11. Proportion of medical institutions in China
Source: 2020 China Health Statistics Yearbook

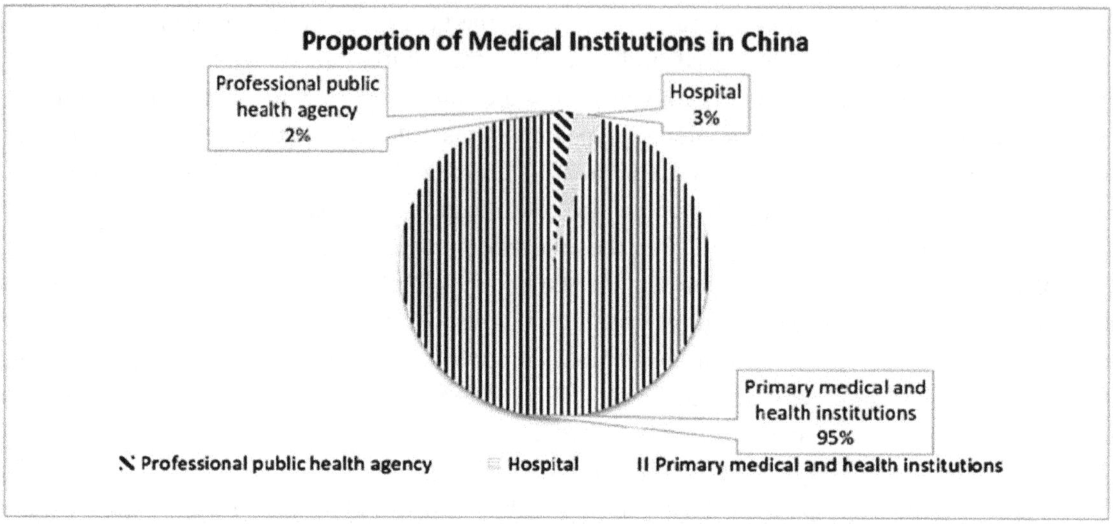

There has always been a big gap between the level of medical care in China's urban and rural areas. As of 2019, the total number of medical institutions in China was 1,007,579, of which primary medical and health institutions accounted for 95% (Figure 11). As the modern medical situation becomes more and more complex, the existing rural health practitioners have a certain risk of insufficient knowledge reserves (Jin & Qiu, 2019). AI healthcare can assist doctors in identifying more complicated medical conditions through CDSS, medical record maps, medical condition dictionaries, etc. (Essence Securities, 2021). By providing AI medical standardized products to rural areas, the gap between urban and rural areas will be gradually bridged (Liu et al., 2019). According to the National Bureau of Statistics, the diseases with higher mortality rates in rural China in 2019 were malignant tumors, heart disease, cerebrovascular diseases and respiratory diseases. Diseases with higher mortality rates in urban and rural areas are roughly the same. AI medical remote auxiliary diagnosis system can alleviate the lack of experience of technical personnel in rural areas and improve the medical level of rural areas through remote collaboration (Alshamrani, 2021).

Figure 12. The structure of urban and rural health personnel in 2019
Source: 2020 China Health Statistics Yearbook

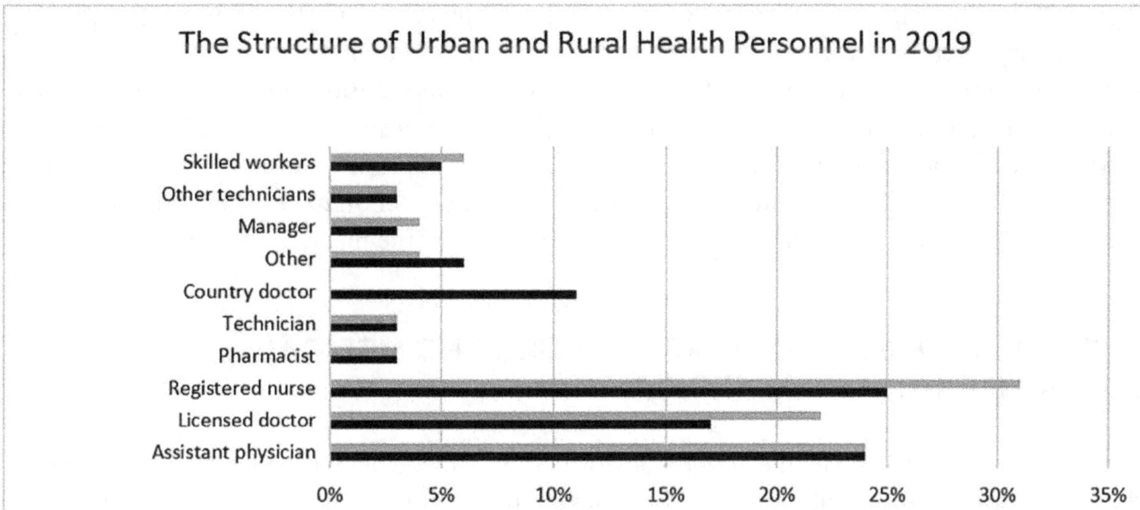

	Assistant physician	Licensed doctor	Registered nurse	Pharmacist	Technician	Country doctor	Other	Manager	Other technicians	Skilled workers
Urban health personnel	24%	22%	31%	3%	3%	0%	4%	4%	3%	6%
Rural health personnel	24%	17%	25%	3%	3%	11%	6%	3%	3%	5%

In addition to remote consultation and treatment, consumers can also purchase medicines and pay online, which will further reduce the gap in the levels of medical care between urban and rural areas (Huang & Wu, 2020). Whether online medical services can be paid directly by the medical insurance determines the breadth of the Internet medical audience (Zhang et al., 2020). According to 2020 China Health Statistics Yearbook (2020), medical insurance could not be used to pay for medical treatment on the Internet previously. According to Rezaei et al. (2021), this has led to patients to see a doctor online at their own expense, which greatly affected the frequency of patients using the telemedicine option. The liberalization of the online medical insurance payment policy will enhance the patient's medical experience (Essence Securities, 2021). In February 2020, the National Medical Insurance Administration and the Health Commission issued relevant documents, clarifying that eligible "Internet +" medical services can be included in the scope of medical insurance reimbursement. Many provinces and cities in China temporarily included online consultations in medical insurance payments. The realization of online diagnosis and treatment is expected to provide application scenarios for AI inquiries and AI prescriptions (Zhang et al., 2020).

d. Digital Transformation Enables Consumers to Seamlessly Connect With Information and Data: Stimulate Product Innovation to Improve Consumers' Medical Experience

Consumers under digital transformation can quickly obtain relevant patient information and data in a variety of ways (Kraus et al., 2021). These data are limited at present because the Medicare and Medicaid Services Center's (MSC) final ruling on interoperability requires consumers to have access to their limited medical records (Liu et al., 2019). Due to the COVID-19, the deadline to comply with the new ruling has been postponed to 2021. However, certain health plans and health systems are implementing some necessary reforms. These reforms may enable consumers in digital medical care to inquire about personal information data more comprehensively (National Internet Emergency Center, 2021). On the other hand, once consumers have access to their own data, a new wave of IT innovations in the medical field will seize this opportunity to create new products which improve consumers' medical experience (Beninger, 2020). According to Mardani et al. (2020), the stimulus of digital medical product innovation will promote more competition and increase the transparency of the medical industry.

3. THE ROLES OF GOVERNMENT IN PROMOTING MEDICAL INDUSTRY'S DIGITAL TRANSFORMATION

Since the government developed the digital transformation of medical industry in 2015, its policies have gradually shown a trend of continuous support from top to bottom. According to China National Health Commission (2018), the main policies focus on the development of diagnostic assistance and disease prevention. During the COVID-19, Internet medical services were connected to medical insurance payment policies (Beninger, 2020). The pilot projects were launched in Hangzhou and Shanghai.

The development of China's AI medical policy has shown the characteristics of "top to bottom". The guiding documents and development plans are issued at a national macro level, proposing guidelines for the research and application of AI (National Internet Emergency Center, 2021). Local governments will issue relevant implementation documents in accordance with corresponding guidance. This kind of targeted guidance often plays a major role in practice. For example, the document, "Three-year Action Plan to Promote the Development of the New Generation in Artificial Intelligence Industry (2018-2020)", proposes the use of medical imaging and intelligent service robots. This instruction directly indicates the direction of development for digital medicine. In the 2017 "New Generation Artificial Intelligence Development Plan", the government set up a "three-step" action plan to be achieved by 2030. It includes two major items related to smart healthcare in the new generation AI plan (China Industry and Information Technology Department, 2017). This document prompted an explosive development in digital healthcare in 2018. In addition to setting goals and playing a guiding role, the government should also aid the construction of relevant platforms and play a regulatory role in the process of digital transformation to enable the stable development of medical care (Beninger, 2020; CB insights, 2021). At the same time, the development of new medical business models also depends on the degree of openness of local policies.

Table 4. China's Policies about AI Medical

China's Policies About AI Medical		
Date	**File Name**	**Content**
July, 2015	Guiding Opinions on Actively Promoting the "Internet +" Action	Rely on the Internet platform to provide AI public innovation services; Accelerate the breakthrough of core AI technologies; List AI as one of the 11 key fields of digital development.
March, 2016	Outline of the Thirteenth Five-Year Plan for National Economic and Social Development	Focus on breakthroughs in new areas of AI technology; Vigorously develop industrial robots, service robots, surgical robots and military robots; Promote the commercial use of AI technology in various fields.
March, 2016	The Development Plan in Robotic Industry (2016-2020)	Realize serialization of the service robots; Realize the commercialization of personal and home service robots.
May, 2016	The Three-year Action Implementation Plan on "Internet+" AI	Support the pilot demonstration of AI applications in important areas such as commerce, education, environment, health care, network security, manufacturing, social governance, and transportation; Promote the large-scale application of AI.
June, 2016	Guiding Opinions on Promoting and Regulating the Application and Development of Big Data in Health Care	Support the Research and Development (R&D) of AI technology related to health care; Accelerate the transformation of R&D results; Improve the manufacturing level of digital medical platforms, IoT devices and other medical equipment; Promote the upgrade of the health and intelligent medical equipment industry.
September, 2016	Special Action for Innovative development of Smart Hardware Industry (2016-2018)	Encourage medical institutions to accelerate the process of informatization; Promote the application of smart medical and health equipment in diagnosis, treatment, nursing, and rehabilitation.
November, 2016	Planning Guide on Pharmaceutical Industry Development	Develop mobile medical products and wearable devices with cloud services and AI functionality, various types of health management software based on mobile internet, remote medical systems that can perform short-range monitoring and enable remote consultation.
December, 2016	"Thirteenth Five-Year" National Informatization Plan	Promote the application of technologies and products such as AI, biological 3D printing, medical robots, wearable devices and relevant micro-sensors related to health care in disease prevention, trauma and emergency health care and daily medical care.
January, 2017	"Thirteenth Five-Year" Plan for National Population Health Information Development	Give full play to the leading role of advanced technologies and equipment products such as AI, virtual reality (VR), augmented reality, biological 3D printing, medical robots, and wearable devices in the development of population health information and big data health care applications; Promote the transformation from medical treatment to healthcare service transformation; Realize the transformation from treatment-centered to health-centered.
June, 2017	"Thirteenth Five-Year" Special Plan for Health and Health Technology Innovation	Promote medical AI technology; Carry out technical research such as medical big data analysis and machine learning; Develop a variety of technical solutions such as centralized intelligence and distributed intelligence; Support machine intelligence to assist personalized diagnosis, precision treatment, assisted decision support systems and assisted rehabilitation & nursing; Support the development of smart medical care.

Continued on following page

Table 4. Continued

China's Policies About AI Medical		
Date	**File Name**	**Content**
July, 2017	Plan for New Generation AI Development	Promote the application of new models of AI treatment; Establish a fast and accurate medical intelligence system. Explore the construction of smart hospitals; develop equipment such as surgical robots with man-machine collaboration. Carry out the intelligentization of pharmaceutical supervision based on AI research.
December, 2017	Three-year Action Plan to Promote the Development of a New Generation of AI Industry (2018-2020)	By 2020, a certain scale of industry application data will be collected in the medical, finance, transportation, and other fields to support entrepreneurship and innovation. Promote the standardization of medical imaging data collection; Accelerate clinical assistance application and the commercialization of medical imaging auxiliary diagnosis system.
April, 2018	Opinions on Promoting the Development of "Internet + Medical Health"	Improve the "Internet + medical and health" service and support systems
April, 2018	Norms and Standards of National Hospital Informatization Construction (Trial Implementation)	Use AI technology to predict disease risks, realize medical image-assisted diagnosis, clinical auxiliary diagnosis & treatment, intelligent health management, intelligent hospital management and virtual assistants.
July, 2018	Notice on the In-depth Development of "Internet + Medical and Health" activities to benefit and facilitate medical care for the people	Accelerate the construction of smart hospitals, transform and optimize the diagnosis & treatment process; Promote the application of intelligent medical image recognition, pathological classification, multidisciplinary consultation and intelligent voice technology in various medical and health scenarios to improve the efficiency of medical services.
March, 2019	Guiding Opinions on Promoting the Deep Smart Integration of AI and the Real Economy	Steadily promote the internal integration, sharing and opening of data in the fields of education, energy, medical care, public security, etc.; Formulate data resource lists and open plans; Encourage high-quality institutions to provide AI services and resources to local governments.
August, 2019	Guidelines for the Construction of the National New Generation of AI Open Innovation Platform	Encourage leading companies in the AI fields to build open source and open platforms, open AI technology R&D resources to the public and export artificial technology intelligent service capabilities to the society; Promote the industry application of AI technology, cultivate industry leaders and help small, medium and micro enterprises grow.
October, 2019	Catalogue for the Guidance of Industrial Structure Adjustment (2019)	From the perspective of industry, four industries including "Human Resources and Human Capital Services", "AI", "Elderly Care and Childcare Services", and "Housekeeping" were added to the encouraged category.

AI medical is gradually becoming compliant and commercialized under the promotion of policies (Beninger, 2020). On November 13, 2020, the National Medical Products Administration (NMPA) provided the approval certificate for the first pulmonary nodule CT imaging-assisted software medical device which is based on deep learning technology, and it was the first pulmonary nodule AI certificate it issued. According to National Internet Emergency Center (2021), the issuance of the certificate means that the National Medical Products Administration has a clearer approval path for these types of AI medical products, and that the approval of compliant medical AI products has begun to accelerate.

In the future, the R&D and sales of AI medical companies will continue to grow smoothly. AI medical solutions can also be market-tested and commercialized faster. The issuance of the certificate will also help enterprises to carry out large-scale sales of their innovative solutions. 2020 was the concentration period for NMPA to issue certificates for AI medical care, laying the foundational policies for commercial launch in 2021 (China Academy of Information and Communications Technology, 2021). On January 15, 2020, after Keya Medical obtained the first AI medical certificate, the review of NMPA was accelerated. Figure 13 shows the proportion of AI medical disciplines reviewed by NMPA. As of the end of 2020, a total of 9 products have passed the audit. Combined with statistics and analysis based on the high incidence rates of urban and rural areas, AI medical products can assist in the faster diagnosis of these high incidence cases, thereby reducing the uneven distribution of medical resources to a certain extent (Kraus et al., 2021).

Figure 13. Proportion of AI medical disciplines reviewed by NMPA
Source: China National Medical Products Administration

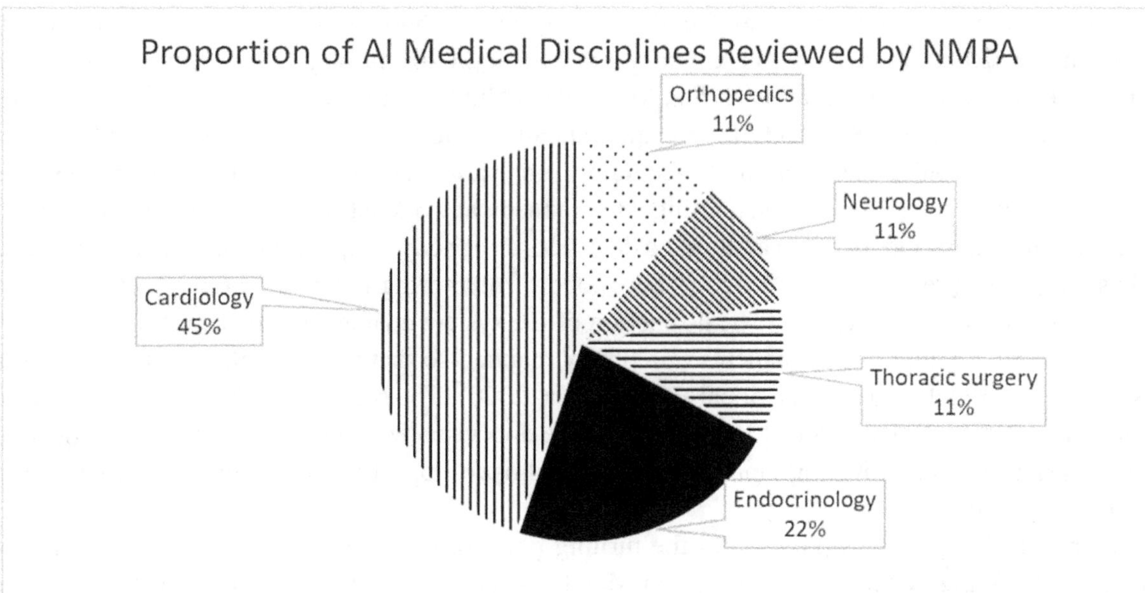

4. CASE ANALYSIS OF CHINA'S MEDICAL DIGITAL TRANSFORMATION

a. Comparison of Two Successful Cases of China's Medical Digital Transformation: The 5G+AI Based Assistance of Wuhan Zhongnan Hospital and the Bluetooth IoT Enabled Body Temperature Monitoring System of Shenzhen Longhua District Central Hospital

The sudden outbreak of the COVID-19 in 2019 prompted the national medical system to accelerate the change and adapt under pressure. In the fight against the pandemic many successful cases of medical digital transformation have emerged all over China. According to the People's Daily (2020), the team of

Professor Xu Haibo from the Medical Imaging Department of Wuhan Zhongnan Hospital developed a new coronary pneumonia CT AI diagnosis system with Tencent. This 5G+AI intelligent diagnosis system uses 5G wireless network to connect imaging equipment. According to National Party Media (2020), it relies on the technology and concept of remote medical services to interconnect imaging examination equipment and remote experts in different hospitals. At the most severe stages of the pandemic, the hospital arranged 4 strategic medical checkpoints and nearly 5,400 beds for the treatment of patients with severe new coronary pneumonia (People's Daily, 2020). Zhongnan Hospital was the hospital with the largest number of patients suffering from the new coronary pneumonia condition in Wuhan (Chinanews, 2021). By using digital technology, the system realizes the automatic transmission of images and diagnosis reports across hospitals, greatly improving the accuracy and efficiency of diagnosis in primary hospitals (National Party Media, 2020).

As an equally successful digital transformation case, unlike the former using AI+5G to achieve telemedicine, Shenzhen Longhua Central Hospital used IoT based technology to achieve medical monitoring (People's Daily, 2020). During the epidemic, to detect the body temperature of patients safely, quickly, and efficiently in the isolation ward, Shenzhen Longhua Central Hospital developed the "Bluetooth IoT Body Temperature Monitoring System" collaborating with technology companies (Longhua District Health Bureau, 2020). According to National Party Media (2020), through a lightweight and compact wearable smart body temperature patch that looks like a "button", this system is docked with the hospital's Health Information System (HIS) to automatically retrieve patients' information and create the body temperature monitoring function. By accurately monitoring the patient's body temperature with the IoT patch at regular intervals and transmitting it to the medical workstation via Bluetooth, the hospital is able to monitor, share and maintain authorized data records of body temperature information throughout the hospital, 24x7 (People's Daily, 2020). "Zero-touch" monitoring improves the work efficiency and safety of the medical staff. The statistical function of the system enables the medical staff to know the distribution and condition of the patients in a timely manner, so that they can allocate the work of the nursing staff more intelligently (National Party Media, 2020). The big data analysis of the IoT devices continuously monitors the patient's body temperature and visualizes the change of body temperature through various charts, providing more powerful visual data support for the clinical frontline, prompting appropriate action.

The case of Longhua Hospital seizes the turning point of digital transformation to help fight the pandemic. Since the system was launched on March 11, 2020, its advantages have gradually become prominent. The features listed below refer to the "2020 China Digital Transformation Successful Case Collection (National Party Media, 2020) ". The first feature is real-time monitoring. The system uses big data to improve the efficiency of diagnosis and treatment. The system can automatically measure once every 3 minutes for observing patients in fever wards. The highest number of patients monitored at the same time in a single day reached 21. The longest continuous monitoring time for a single patient in the system is 72 hours. The system starts from practical application and organically integrates informatization and clinical first line. Medical staff can view the temperature changes of each patient in the observation ward in real time through computers, large nursing screens, and mobile iPad terminals in the office area (People's Daily, 2020). They can also quickly view the temperature distribution of patients in the ward according to the statistical function module, and reasonably allocate the work for the nursing staff. They can test the curative effect of the treatment and medicines administered based on the patient temperature changes that is visualized as data charts, and promptly treat the patient on time, in case there is a no or negative development. The second feature is that it saves time and effort. The system helps to make up for the shortcomings of manpower and materials. According to People's Daily (2020), medical staff was in short supply and medical protective materials (Personal Protection Equipment, PPE, like gloves, scrubs, and masks) were limited during the pandemic. Sealed protective gear causes a lot of inconvenience to medical staff in terms of breathing, walking, and performing complex tasks. After the system went live, its "zero-touch" feature greatly reduced the labor intensity of nursing staff, the risk of infection, and the consumption of medical supplies (Longhua District Health Bureau, 2020). The third feature has a strong reproducibility. The prospect of application of the system is extensive and can be extended to other departments and use cases, benefiting inpatients, especially at the intensive care unit (ICU), pediatrics, neonatology, etc. In addition, it can also be extended to home use. People with fever can be connected to the hospital or the medical community to monitor their body temperature right from the comfort of their home, which can prove useful for elderly, immobile, chronically ill or auto-immune patients. The Bluetooth IoT enabled body temperature monitoring system provides a brand-new, advanced, and effective method of body temperature measurement, which may replace the mercury thermometer and bring about the unification of economic and social benefits (People's Daily, 2020).

b. Unsuccessful Cases and Problems Behind the Medical Digital Transformation

In recent years, the digital transformation of healthcare has seen more and more breakthroughs in the development process (Kunaviktikul et al., 2021). Prior to this, the highly acclaimed IBM Watson has been questioned by the outside world during its development and is considered a failed transformation case. IBM claims to be able to surpass human doctors by focusing on intractable diseases such as tumors (Rundle et al., 2020). The lack of medical data and practical experience makes such a declaration extremely unreliable (Strickland, 2019). Digital transformation in the medical field requires a large amount of data for machine learning. However, these data need to accumulate over time. According to Mann (2021), one of the major problems with large health care datasets is they lack a common infrastructure, so it can be difficult to harmonize data across different platforms. IBM wanted to achieve absolute machine accuracy, which cannot be done in a short time. In the product development stage, IBM Watson was out of touch with market promotion and cutting-edge technology research (Mathur, 2019). In fact, the number of people involved in product development within IBM and the number of real medical records available were very small (Strickland, 2019). In August 2015, IBM spent $1 billion to acquire Merge Healthcare, a medical imaging company. However, in the field of medical image recognition, IBM did not make some subsequent achievements, nor had it integrated text analysis and image recognition into its product development (Mann, 2021). This shows that its planned development path is very confusing. This unsuccessful transformation case has also prompted the follow-up medical digital transformation to gain some reference and experience, which will help them to enter the digital transformation process more quickly (Mathur, 2019).

There are also many problems and consumers' doubts in the digital transformation of medical care in China. Among them, the case where surgical robots replace surgeons to perform operations causes a wider concern (Yao et al., 2020). Patients and their families generally question the safety and reliability of surgical robots. According to Yao et al. (2020), robotics has made huge leaps in improving healthcare services in various medical fields, including oncology and surgical interventions. Robots are replacing human assistants. However, the use of medical robots in diagnosis and intervention still must deal with some challenges (Xing, 2021). Compared with medical robots, consumers are more willing to accept traditional doctors or robots to assist doctors in performing operations (Boada et al., 2021). The acceptance of surgery operated entirely by surgical robots is relatively low. Psychologically speaking, compared to a doctor, robots will increase the nervousness of patients (Villaronga & Mahler, 2021). According to Fan (2019), more than 70 Da Vinci surgical systems have been in clinical use in mainland China. The official website of the State Food and Drug Administration showed that the agent of the "Da Vinci Surgical Robot" released an incident report. According to the report, 981 endoscopic surgical instrument control systems sold in China needed to be recalled. Many technical and psychological challenges make it difficult to design machines that effectively cooperate with people (Whiting et al., 2021). Zhang (2018) pointed out that surgical robots have some very significant shortcomings, such as no tactile feedback and inability to perceive. According to Villaronga & Mahler (2021), when nursing robots are in close contact with children, the elderly and the disabled, malfunctions of the robots or threats to network information security may affect the health and well-being of said people.

5. OPPORTUNITIES AND CHALLENGES FOR PROMOTING MEDICAL SECTOR'S DIGITAL TRANSFORMATION IN CHINA

a. Opportunities

At present, there are both opportunities and challenges in the development of digital medical care in China.

Figure 14. Average change in AI investment in global companies due to COVID-19 2020, by industry
Source: Statista

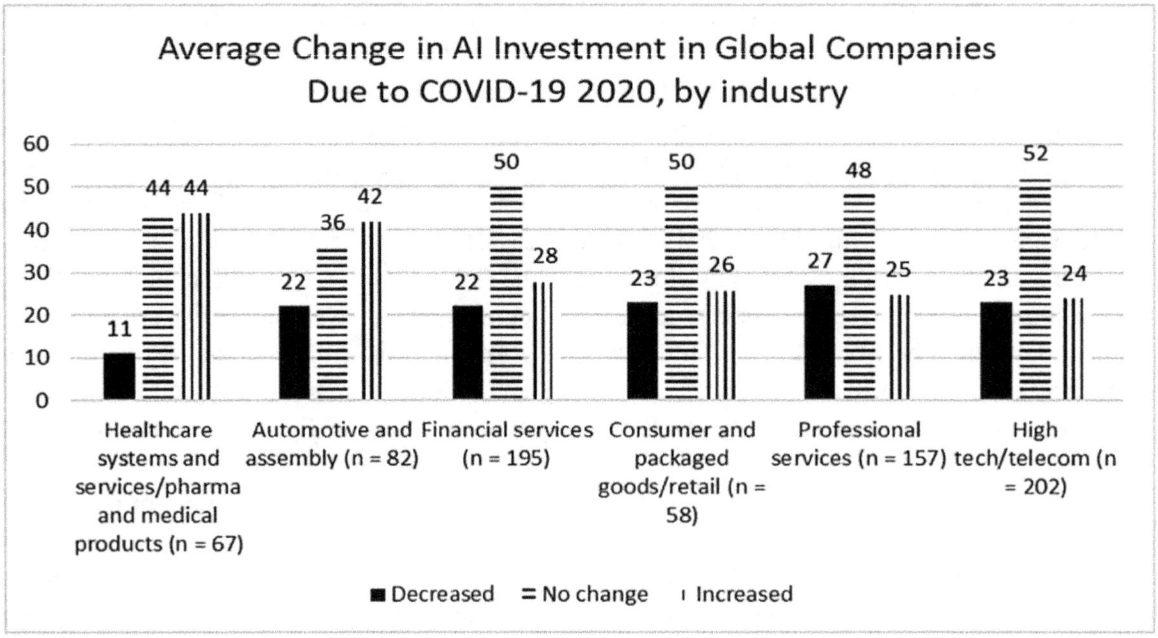

Due to the COVID-19 pandemic in 2020, investment in the global AI industry has changed. As can be seen from Figure 14, by industry, the growth of investment in the healthcare systems and services/ pharma and medical products ranked first in the AI segment. Compared with other AI sub-industries, the medical field has great confidence in investment and financing (Figure 14).

From the comparison of the distribution of medical resources between China and the United States, 95% of China's medical resources are allocated to hospital services, while the proportion in the United States is only 19% (China Academy of Information and Communications Technology, 2021). In the future, China will mobilize more medical resources in the areas of disease prevention, disease rehabilitation, elderly care, family health care and health risk management (Jin & Qiu, 2019). According to Liu et al. (2019), the upgradation of technologies like AI, robot, blockchain (for the security and reliability of medical data) and 3D printing will continue to influence changes of traditional technologies, processes and frameworks both in the products and the services side. It would thereby continue to promote the digital transformation of China's medical treatment. This shows that the future of the smart medical market is promising.

b. Challenges

The first challenge is the public opinion and ethical conflict between traditional medicine and digital medicine. According to Rezaei et al. (2021), through the survey and analysis of customer satisfaction, it is known that some people have a skeptical attitude towards digital smart medical care. They question its reliability and security. For said customers, it is much easier to accept the traditional medical care than smart medical care (Boada et al., 2021). According to Boada et al. (2021), the continuous development of intelligent robots in the field of technology and science has aroused widespread ethical concerns about its disruptive potential. In addition to its potential contribution to nursing practice, Social Assistance Robots (SAR) also have major ethical issues. The patient's doubts sometimes exacerbate the tension in the doctor-patient relationship. Studies have shown that tensions between patients and doctors, due to conflicts of interest, can have a negative impact on patients' wellness (Jefferies et al., 2019). The major challenge for digital medical industry now is how to make the people generally accept and promote the application of new AI treatment models (Rezaei et al., 2021).

Model design and verification of transparency in all aspects should be used in digital medical transformation to help ensure the reliability of medical AI. When applied to the healthcare field, some current models cannot meet the transparency needs of clinicians and patients (Kraus et al., 2021). Medical models that lack transparency cannot gain the trust of consumers (Senadeera et al., 2021). These models lack quality assurance, thus restricting doctor-patient dialogue.

Secondly, the transition from traditional medical care to smart medical care is facing the challenge of resources, data and linking systems (Colnar et al., 2020; Schneebergerb et al., 2021). Because medical data involves patient privacy, data barriers are difficult to break (Villaronga & Mahler, 2021). On the one hand, the internal health data of the Chinese hospital system lacks structured planning. Medical institutions at all levels have established independent information systems, with many scattered medical data such as patient cases, medical test results, imaging reports, and financial data (Liu et al., 2019). However, these data information lack structural application and the channels for data flow. The development of a digital medical system requires a large amount of clinical data. Many hospitals in China still use traditional databases. They do not effectively use and integrate medical information. Once the sharing of information is hindered, the technological development and product research will be greatly restricted (Colnar et al., 2020). On the other hand, external institutions in the hospital system such as university, scientific research institutions, pharmaceutical companies and insurance companies, are getting more and more expensive to obtain data from hospitals, causing a large amount of waste of medical data resources and greatly hinders the development of medical industry (Kraus et al., 2021). How to achieve multi-party medical data sharing and improve the efficiency of medical data mining is a huge challenge in the current medical field (Xingye Securities, 2021). However, as technologies such as big data, cloud computing and blockchain mature, these databases will gradually become cloud based (Singh et al., 2021). On the premise of protecting the privacy of patients and the authority of doctors, medical resources must be interoperable.

In addition to data sources and circulation issues, data quality has also become an important issue for the normal operation of medical AI applications. Many medical AI applications are trained based on ideal laboratory data or available open data rather than real-time data based on actual applications (Schneebergerb et al., 2021). As more and more AI applications operate based on real-time data, the medical industry urgently needs to find solutions that can solve erroneous data related problems.

Finally, as the digital medical market continues to expand, it will also face the scrutiny of market economic value. Due to the huge investment capital and labor costs for the research and development of digital medical products, the market valuation of smart medicine will be affected to a certain extent. For example, smart wearable products are being developed in recent years (Sun et al., 2021). Although it is a large innovation for the medical field, its audience is not wide. It has not produced considerable economic value. Xing et al. (2021) conducted a research on smart wearable devices for the elderly. The study investigated the social and technological barriers affecting the large-scale deployment of AI wearable devices for the elderly in China. They found that this challenge was triggered by a series of clinical, financial, legal, management and technical issues, which is greatly preventing the large-scale deployment and use of wearable medical devices in China (Xing et al., 2021). Once the R&D of digital medical products ignore their economic value and market consumer, they will fall into an endless loop and cannot truly bring about the development and progress of digital medical treatment (Colnar et al., 2020).

The gradual implementation of digital smart medical care needs to solve the problems pertaining to resource integration, data sharing, public opinion guidance and closed-loop operations.

6. CONCLUSION AND RECOMMENDATIONS

The past few years China has witnessed the digital transformation of the medical field through technologies like AI, robotics, blockchain (data security and reliability), 3D printing technology and medical big data. According to Mardani et al. (2020), the COVID-19 has prompted the entire medical and health industry to accelerate digital transformation, achieving many breakthroughs. Digitization is gradually occupying a pivotal position in the medical field. With the current development of China's AI and other technologies entering a new stage, China's medical digital transformation has also entered a key phase. Medical digital transformation is not only the new focus of current international competition, but also a new engine for China's future economic development.

The future of smart healthcare under digital transformation is very promising. Given that the global society is now entering the big health technology revolution, and smart medicine is bound to have a big market in the future. During the digital transformation of China's medical industry, the commercialization model of the medical industry has undergone specific changes. The core of China's medical digital transformation is to realize the decentralization of medical resources. Although customers still have doubts about digital and intelligent medical treatment such as surgical robots, the upgrade of AI and remote technology has improved customer experience and satisfaction to a certain extent.

According to Straw (2020), Medical inequality in the global population will continue to exist, and the impact of medical bias on different patient groups is still being bought to light by the research community. As the clinical AI system expands in response to Covid19, the role of AI in exacerbating the health gap must be scrutinized (Huang & Wu, 2020). In the face of various opportunities and challenges in the future digital medical transformation, the government and industry need to take some countermeasures. In addition to setting goals and playing a guiding role, the government should also aid the construction of related platforms, play a regulatory role, and enable the development of smart healthcare (National Internet Emergency Center, 2021). Facing the gradual implementation of digital smart medical care, the entire medical industry ought to solve problems such as resource integration, data sharing, public opinion guidance and closed-loop operations.

For individuals in the era of digital transformation, they must develop the ability to understand and distinguish the different smart products that are launched in the market. The authoritative tone and misleading nature of new products requires further demonstration. The transformation of the traditional medical model to new digital model still needs a structured process. According to China Academy of Information and Communications Technology (2021), the Chinese medical system should establish a sharing platform to interconnect health and medical data in the future. It will not only spread the concept of healthy lifestyle, wholistic, proactive and preventive healthcare but also bring life and health management services to ordinary people and improve the employment ecosystem of medical staff.

ACKNOWLEDGMENT

The authors extend sincere gratitude to:

• Our colleagues from Soochow University, the Australian Studies Centre of Shanghai University and Krirk University as well as the independent research colleagues who provided insight and expertise that greatly assisted the research, although they may not agree with all of the interpretations/conclusions of this chapter.

• China Knowledge for supporting our research.

• The Editor and the International Editorial Advisory Board (IEAB) of this book who initially desk reviewed, arranged a rigorous double/triple blind review process and conducted a thorough, minute and critical final review before accepting the chapter for publication.

• All anonymous reviewers who provided very constructive feedbacks for thorough revision, improvement, extension and fine tuning of the chapter.

REFERENCES

Alshamrani, M. (in press). IoT and artificial intelligence implementations for remote healthcare monitoring systems: A survey. *Journal of King Saud University - Computer and Information Sciences*.

Arni, P., & Laddha, S. (2017). Adoption of digital marketing in health industry. *SIES Journal of Management, 13*(1).

Balagurunathan, Y., Mitchell, R., & Naqa, I. E. (2021). Requirements and reliability of AI in the medical context. *Physica Medica, 83*, 72–78. doi:10.1016/j.ejmp.2021.02.024 PMID:33721700

Becker, A. (2019). Artificial intelligence in medicine: What is it doing for us today? *Health Policy and Technology, 8*(2), 198–205. doi:10.1016/j.hlpt.2019.03.004

Beninger, P. (2020). COVID-19: Regulatory Landscape of Medicinal and Medical Device Products for Human Use. *Clinical Therapeutics, 42*(8), 1444–1450. doi:10.1016/j.clinthera.2020.06.014 PMID:32651020

Boada, J. P., Maestre, B. R., & Genís, C. T. (2021). The ethical issues of social assistive robotics: A critical literature review. *Technology in Society, 67*, 101726. doi:10.1016/j.techsoc.2021.101726

Catania, L. J. (2021). 6 - Current AI applications in medical therapies and services. In *Foundations of Artificial Intelligence in Healthcare and Bioscience*. Academic Press.

Cheng, Z. B., Huang, G., Wen, J. H., & Yan, J. H. (2021). Applications of artificial intelligence in nuclear medicine image generation. *Quantitative Imaging in Medicine and Surgery, 11*(6), 2792–2822. doi:10.21037/qims-20-1078 PMID:34079744

China Academy of Information and Communications Technology. (2021). *White Paper on China's Digital Economy Development*. Beijing: Author.

China Academy of Information and Communications Technology. (2021). *Artificial Intelligence Core Technology Industry White Paper*. Beijing: Author.

China Comprehensive Deepening Reform Commission. (2019). *Guiding Opinions on Promoting the Deep Smart Integration of Artificial Intelligence and the Real Economy*. China General Office of the State Council.

China Industry and Information Technology Department. (2016). Special Action for Innovative development of Smart Hardware Industry (2016-2018) (China Ministry of Industry and Information Technology [2016] No. 302). Beijing: China General Office of the State Council.

China Industry and Information Technology Department. (2017). Three-year Action Plan to Promote the Development of a New Generation of Artificial Intelligence Industry (2018-2020) (China Ministry of Industry and Information Technology [2017] No. 315). Beijing: China General Office of the State Council.

China National Development and Reform Commission. (2016). *The Development Plan in Robot Industry (2016-2020)* (Beijing ICP No. 05052393). Beijing: China General Office of the State Council.

China National Development and Reform Commission. (2016). The Three-year Action Implementation Plan on "Internet+" Artificial Intelligence (China Development and Reform Commission [2016] No. 1078). Beijing: China General Office of the State Council.

China National Development and Reform Commission. (2016). Planning Guide on Pharmaceutical Industry Development (Beijing ICP No. 05070218). Beijing: China General Office of the State Council.

China National Development and Reform Commission. (2017). "Thirteenth Five-Year" Plan for National Population Health Information Development (Beijing ICP No. 05052393). Beijing: China General Office of the State Council.

China National Development and Reform Commission. (2019). *Catalogue for the Guidance of Industrial Structure Adjustment (2019)* (China National Development and Reform Commission Publication No. 29). Beijing: China General Office of the State Council.

China National Health Commission. (2018). Norms and Standards of National Hospital Informatization Construction (Trial Implementation) (China National Health Office Planning Publication [2018] No. 4). Beijing: China General Office of the State Council.

China National Health Commission. (2018). Notice on the In-depth Development of "Internet + Medical and Health" Activities to Facilitate the People and Benefit the People (China National Health Office Planning Publication [2018] No. 22). Beijing: China General Office of the State Council.

Chinanews. (2021). *Wuhan Zhongnan Hospital 5G mobile CT assists Hebei*. https://www.chinanews.com/sh/2021/01-11/9383897.shtml

Choi, K., Gitelman, Y., Leri, D., Deleener, M. E., Hahn, L., & Lang, E. (2021). Insourcing and scaling a telemedicine solution in under 2 weeks: Lessons for the digital transformation of health care. *Health Care*, *9*(3), 100568. PMID:34293616

Cobbe, J., & Singh, J. (2021). Artificial intelligence as a service: Legal responsibilities, liabilities, and policy challenges. *Computer Law & Security Review*, *42*, 105573. doi:10.1016/j.clsr.2021.105573

Colnar, S., Penger, S., Grah, B., & Dimovski, V. (2020). Digital transformation of integrated care: Literature review and research agenda. *IFAC-PapersOnLine*, *53*(2), 16890–16895. doi:10.1016/j.ifacol.2020.12.1221

Daxue Consulting. (2020). *The AI in China 2020 White Paper*. https://daxueconsulting.com/ai-in-china-white-paper/

Essence Securities. (2021). *2021: Smart flowers bloom, AI is all over the world.* https://m-robo.datayes.com/report/summary?id=4421892

Essence Securities. (2021). *Welcome to the first year of AI medical commercialization-Smart Flower 2021 Series Report 4.* https://mp.weixin.qq.com/s/Gh8BLJsTqffeO5Hlzw37SA

Fan, D. D. (2019). *Surgical robot is warned! FDA does not recommend robotic tumor surgery and mastectomy*. https://med.sina.com/article_detail_103_2_61748.html

Ford, G., Compton, M., Millett, G., & Tzortzis, A. (2017). *The Role of Digital Disruption in Healthcare Service Innovation*. Academic Press.

Habuza, T., Navaz, A. N., Hashim, F., Alnajjar, F., Zaki, N., Serhani, M. A., & Statsenko, Y. (2021). AI applications in robotics, precision medicine, and medical image analysis: An overview and future trends. *Informatics in Medicine Unlocked*, *24*, 100596. doi:10.1016/j.imu.2021.100596

Haleem, A., Javaid, M., & Khan, I. H. (2019). Current status and applications of Artificial Intelligence (AI) in medical field: An overview. *Current Medicine Research and Practice*, *9*(6), 231–237. doi:10.1016/j.cmrp.2019.11.005

Huang, X., & Wu, B. X. (2020). Impact of urban-rural health insurance integration on health care: Evidence from rural China. *China Economic Review*, *64*, 101543. doi:10.1016/j.chieco.2020.101543

Huatai Securities. (2020). *Internet Medical Industry Depth: Analysis Framework of Internet Medical Industry*. https://m-robo.datayes.com/report/summary?id=4173915

Insights, C. B. (2021). *China Industry Digital Development Report*. http://www.cbdio.com/node_2567.htm

Jefferies, J. G., Bishop, S., & Hibbert, S. (2019). Customer boundary work to navigate institutional arrangements around service interactions: Exploring the case of telehealth. *Journal of Business Research*, *105*, 420–433. doi:10.1016/j.jbusres.2019.03.052

Jin, Y. H., & Qiu, M. J. (2019). *China Artificial Intelligence Medical White Paper*. Shanghai: Artificial Intelligence Research Institute of Shanghai Jiaotong University.

Kraus, S., Schiavone, F., Pluzhnikova, A., & Invernizzi, A. C. (2021). Digital transformation in healthcare: Analyzing the current state-of-research. *Journal of Business Research*, *123*, 557–567. doi:10.1016/j.jbusres.2020.10.030

Kunaviktikul, W., Juntasopeepun, P., Soriano, G. P., Locsin, R. C., & Evangelista, L. S. (in press). Social transformation and social isolation of older adults: Digital technologies, nursing, healthcare. *Collegian (Royal College of Nursing, Australia)*.

Li, X. L. (2019). "Surgical robot" medical accident liability consultation. *Democracy and the Rule of Law Times*. Retrieved May 24,2021, from http://www.mzyfz.com/cms/benwangzhuanfang/xinwenzhongxin/zuixinbaodao/html/1040/2019-09-27/content-1406397.html

Liu, D., Zhao, J., He, K. L., Wang, Z. Q., Wei, B., & Huang, Y. H. (2019). *White Paper on Smart Healthcare in the 5G Era*. Internet Healthcare Industry Alliance.

Longhua District Health Bureau. (2020). *Longhua District Central Hospital's Bluetooth IoT body temperature monitoring system: one of China's Top 10 Technological Battles*. Government office of Longhua.

Mann, D. L. (2021). Will Artificial Intelligence Transform Translational Medicine: (Not So) Elementary, My Dear Watson. *JACC. Basic to Translational Science*, *6*(4), 400–401. doi:10.1016/j.jacbts.2021.03.005 PMID:33997527

Mardani, A., Saraji, M. K., Mishra, A. R., & Rani, P. (2020). A novel extended approach under hesitant fuzzy sets to design a framework for assessing the key challenges of digital health interventions adoption during the COVID-19 outbreak. *Applied Soft Computing*, *96*, 106613. doi:10.1016/j.asoc.2020.106613 PMID:32834799

Mathur, N. (2019). *IEEE Spectrum: IBM Watson has a long way to go before it becomes an efficient AI doctor*. https://hub.packtpub.com/ieee-spectrum-ibm-watson-has-a-long-way-to-go-before-it-becomes-an-efficient-ai-doctor/

Ministry of Science and Technology of China. (2019). Guidelines for the Construction of the National New Generation of Artificial Intelligence Open Innovation Platform (Ministry of Science and Technology Publication [2019] No. 265). Beijing: China General Office of the State Council.

National Internet Emergency Center. (2021). Digital China Development Report in 2020 (Beijing ICP No. 14042428). Beijing: China National Internet Information Office.

National Party Media. (2020). *2020 China Digital Transformation Successful Case Collection*. https://www.hubpd.com/c/2020-05-13/960082.shtml

People's Daily. (2020). *China's Digital Transformation Successful Cases Announced in 2020*. http://ip.people.com.cn/n1/2020/0529/c136655-31728749.html

Rezaei, M., Vahid, J. S., Cao, D. M., & Mahdiraji, H. A. (2021). Key indicators of ethical challenges in digital healthcare: A combined Delphi exploration and confirmative factor analysis approach with evidence from Khorasan province in Iran. *Technological Forecasting and Social Change*, *167*, 120724. doi:10.1016/j.techfore.2021.120724

Rueckel, J., Sperl, J., Kaestle, S., Hoppe, B., Fink, N., Rudolph, J., Schwarze, V., Geyer, T., Strobl, F., Ricke, J., Ingrisch, M., & Sabel, B. (2021). Reduction of missed thoracic findings in emergency whole-body computed tomography using artificial intelligence assistance. *Quantitative Imaging in Medicine and Surgery*, *11*(6), 2486–2498. doi:10.21037/qims-20-1037 PMID:34079718

Rundle, A. G., Torsiello, N. E., Davis, B. M., Griffin, B., Neugut, A. I., & Levy, D. L. (2020). Analyses of Employer Medical Claims Data to Assess Receipt of High-Priority Preventive Health Services. *American Journal of Preventive Medicine*, *58*(5), 715–723. doi:10.1016/j.amepre.2019.12.016 PMID:32173164

Schneebergerb, D., Stögera, K., Kiesebergc, P., & Holzingerd, A. (2021). Legal aspects of data cleansing in medical AI. *Computer Law & Security Review*, *42*, 105587. doi:10.1016/j.clsr.2021.105587

Senadeera, M. P., Quinn, T., Jacobs, S., Le, V., & Coghlan, S. (2021). The three ghosts of medical AI: Can the black-box present deliver? *Artificial Intelligence in Medicine*, 102158. PMID:34511267

Singh, P., Singh, G., & Kaur, G. (2021). Integrating Artificial Intelligence/Internet of Things Technologies to Support Medical Devices and Systems. In G. Kaur (Ed.), *Artificial Intelligence to Solve Pervasive Internet of Things Issues* (pp. 331–349). Academic Press. doi:10.1016/B978-0-12-818576-6.00017-4

Smith, M. J., & Bean, S. (2019). AI and Ethics in Medical Radiation Sciences. *Journal of Medical Imaging and Radiation Sciences*, *50*(4), S24–S26. doi:10.1016/j.jmir.2019.08.005 PMID:31563532

Spyropoulos, C. D. (2000). AI planning and scheduling in the medical hospital environment. *Artificial Intelligence in Medicine*, *20*(2), 101–111. doi:10.1016/S0933-3657(00)00059-2 PMID:10936748

State Council of China. (2015). Guiding Opinions on Actively Promoting the "Internet +" Action (China National Publication [2015] No. 40). Beijing: China General Office of the State Council.

State Council of China. (2016). Guiding Opinions on Promoting and Regulating the Application and Development of Big Data in Health Care (China State Council [2016] No. 47). Beijing: China General Office of the State Council.

State Council of China. (2016). "Thirteenth Five-Year" National Informatization Plan (China National Publication [2016] No. 73). Beijing: China General Office of the State Council.

State Council of China. (2017). "Thirteenth Five-Year" Special Plan for Health and Health Technology Innovation (China National Publication [2016] No. 77). Beijing: China General Office of the State Council.

State Council of China. (2017). Plan for New Generation Artificial Intelligence Development (China National Publication [2017] No. 35). Beijing: China General Office of the State Council.

State Council of China. (2018). Opinions on Promoting the Development of "Internet + Medical Health" (China State Council [2018] No. 26). Beijing: China General Office of the State Council.

Straw, I. (2020). The automation of bias in medical Artificial Intelligence (AI): Decoding the past to create a better future. *Artificial Intelligence in Medicine*, *110*, 101965. doi:10.1016/j.artmed.2020.101965 PMID:33250145

Strickland, E. (2019). *How IBM Watson overpromised and underdelivered on AI health care*. https://spectrum.ieee.org/biomedical/diagnostics/how-ibm-watson-overpromised-and-underdelivered-on-ai-health-care

Sun, R. J., Yu, Y., Zhang, Z. H., Liu, H. P., Yuan, S. W., Jiang, T., & ... . (2021). AI-guided resource allocation and rescue decision system for medical applications. *Future Generation Computer Systems*, *118*, 485–491. doi:10.1016/j.future.2020.12.010

Tuzii, J. (2017). Healthcare information technology in Italy, critiques and suggestions for European digitalization. *Pharmaceuticals Policy & Law*, *19*(3/4), 161–176.

Vial, G. (2019). Understanding digital transformation: A review and a research agenda. *The Journal of Strategic Information Systems*, *28*(2), 118–144. doi:10.1016/j.jsis.2019.01.003

Villaronga, E. F., & Mahler, T. (2021). Cybersecurity, safety and robots: Strengthening the link between cybersecurity and safety in the context of care robots. *Computer Law & Security Review*, *41*, 105528. doi:10.1016/j.clsr.2021.105528

Wang, Q., & Shi, Y. H. (2019). The Artificial Intelligence-Enabled Medical Imaging: Today and Its Future. *Chinese Medical Sciences Journal*, *34*, 71–75. PMID:31315746

Whiting, T., Gautam, A., Tye, J., Simmons, M., Henstrom, J., Oudah, M., & Crandall, J. W. (2021). Confronting barriers to human-robot cooperation: Balancing efficiency and risk in machine behavior. *iScience*, *24*(1), 101963. doi:10.1016/j.isci.2020.101963 PMID:33458615

Wisdom Innovation Development Institute. (2021). *In-depth, China's digital medical development trend and outlook*. Retrieved May 23,2021, from https://baijiahao.baidu.com/s?id=1688775674315855921&wfr=spider&for=pc

Xiao, Y., & Liu, S. Y. (2019). Collaborations of Industry, Academia, Research and Application Improve the Healthy Development of Medical Imaging Artificial Intelligence Industry in China. *Chinese Medical Sciences Journal*, *34*, 84–88. PMID:31315748

Xing, F., Peng, G. C., Zhang, B. Q., Li, S. Y., & Liang, X. T. (2021). Socio-technical barriers affecting large-scale deployment of AI-enabled wearable medical devices among the ageing population in China. *Technological Forecasting and Social Change*, *166*, 120609. doi:10.1016/j.techfore.2021.120609

Xingye Securities. (2021). *In-depth report on the pathological diagnosis industry: Tracing the origin, the long-ignored "fundamental of medicine"*. https://m-robo.datayes.com/report/summary?id=4526796

Xingye Securities. (2021). *Privacy Computing: The New Blue Ocean in the Era of Data Security.* https://mp.weixin.qq.com/s/VU4Zl4QK3mpzrhOTNAI6Xg

Xinhua News Agency. (2016). Outline of the Thirteenth Five-Year Plan for National Economic and Social Development (Beijing ICP No. 05070218). Beijing: China General Office of the State Council.

Yao, Y. B., Liu, Y., Li, Z., Yi, B., Wang, G. H., & Zhu, S. H. (2020). Chinese surgical robot micro hand S: A consecutive case series in general surgery. *International Journal of Surgery*, *75*, 55–59. doi:10.1016/j.ijsu.2020.01.013 PMID:31982634

Zhang, J. Y., Gao, F., & Ye, Z. W. (2020). Remote consultation based on mixed reality technology. *Global Health Journal*, *4*(1), 31–32. doi:10.1016/j.glohj.2020.01.001 PMID:33614179

Zhang, M., Zhang, Z. C., Wang, X., Yu, H., Xia, Y. F., Tan, K. R., Wang, X., & Wang, F. Y. (2021). From AR to AI: Augmentation Technology for Intelligent Surgery and Medical Treatments. *IFAC-PapersOnLine*, *53*(5), 792–796. doi:10.1016/j.ifacol.2021.04.174

ADDITIONAL READING

Ann, A., & Martin, D. B. (2021). Leveraging data and AI to deliver on the promise of digital health. *International Journal of Medical Informatics*, *150*, 104456. doi:10.1016/j.ijmedinf.2021.104456 PMID:33866232

Elsa, N. C., Natasha, A. M., Ramesh, S. K., & David, N. O. (2021). Technological progress in electronic health record system optimization: Systematic review of systematic literature reviews. *International Journal of Medical Informatics*, *152*, 104507. doi:10.1016/j.ijmedinf.2021.104507 PMID:34049051

Erling, B., James, C. D., Richard, B. F., & Kristina, M. (in press). Twisting the demand curve: Digitalization and the older workforce. *Journal of Econometrics*.

Fei, H., Qu, X., & Kaye, C. (2020). COVID-19 and China's Hotel Industry: Impacts, a Disaster Management Framework, and Post-Pandemic Agenda. *International Journal of Hospitality Management*, *90*, 102636. doi:10.1016/j.ijhm.2020.102636 PMID:32834356

Katja, G., Julia, H., & Chiara, O. (2021). Emotional support from a digital assistant in technology-mediated services: Effects on customer satisfaction and behavioral persistence. *International Journal of Research in Marketing*, *38*(1), 176–193. doi:10.1016/j.ijresmar.2020.06.004

Mehran, E. T., Manu, S., Louise, R., & Leila, C. W. (2022). Understanding the potential of emerging digital technologies for improving road safety. *Accident; Analysis and Prevention*, *166*, 106543. doi:10.1016/j.aap.2021.106543 PMID:34971922

Michelle, H. V., Carlos, C., & Goutam, C. (2019). Digitization of healthcare organizations: The digital health landscape and information theory. *International Journal of Medical Informatics, 124*, 49–57. doi:10.1016/j.ijmedinf.2019.01.007 PMID:30784426

Praveen, K. K., Manish, G., Andreas, K., Divya, R., Werner, R., & Aric, R. (in press). Examining artificial intelligence (AI) technologies in marketing via a global lens: Current trends and future research opportunities. *International Journal of Research in Marketing*.

KEY TERMS AND DEFINITIONS

Clinical Decision Support System (CDSS): A clinical assistant decision-making system that follows evidence-based medicine by learning from a large number of clinical guidelines, pharmacopoeia and high-quality medical records of tertiary hospitals, based on natural language processing, knowledge graph and other AI technologies.

Contextualized Doctor-Patient Relationship: A special relationship between physicians and patients in the medical field. This kind of interpersonal relationship is presented in a concrete form in medical situations, involving the communication between medical staff and patients.

Computed Tomography (CT): A medical diagnosis method that uses X-ray beams, gamma rays, ultrasound and other technologies and highly sensitive detectors to scan a cross-section around a certain part of the human body to check various diseases.

Rehabilitation: The action of restoring someone to health or normal life through training and therapy after imprisonment, addiction, or illness.

Semi-Automatic Image Segmentation Analysis: One of the methods of image segmentation. The image is divided into the target area and the background area, and then the edge of the target area of the image is optimized by the relevant algorithm, and accurate object shape information is obtained through a large number of experiments.

Teleconsultation: A new type of medical treatment method that uses modern communication tools such as emails, websites, telephones, and faxes to complete medical record analysis, disease diagnosis, and determine treatment plans for patients.

Ultrasound: Sound or other vibrations having an ultrasonic frequency, particularly as used in medical imaging.

Virtual Assistant Systems: A system that can help doctors, nurses, and technicians to quickly diagnose and administer care by reducing the number of steps and saving time. For example, the voice electronic medical record system is a virtual assistant system that helps doctors quickly enter medical records through voice-to-text.

Chapter 7
E-Commerce:
The Influence of Hedonic and Utilitarian Motivations on Generations X, Y, and Z

Ana Pinto de Lima
Porto Accounting and Business School, Polytechnic of Porto, Portugal

Nicolau Almeida Monteiro
Porto Accounting and Business School, Polytechnic of Porto, Portugal

ABSTRACT

The age of market globalisation and on-line presence allows companies to improve their relations with customers as well as to establish more direct communication. The different shopping acts may be related to a person's utilitarian and hedonic values. A study carried out by Hootsuite revealed that clothing and beauty products were the most on-line bought items in Portugal in 2017. The study aims at understanding the motivations behind choosing on-line channels for buying those types of products, with a special emphasis on the different generations of buyers. The authors use an exploratory methodology based on an on-line survey with 280 responses. There is a stronger association between the utilitarian value and the intention to repeat a purchase than between the hedonic value and that intention. Generation X is more associated to the repurchase intention to repeat a purchase based on utilitarian values and Generation Z shows a stronger association between hedonic values and being a repeat customer.

INTRODUCTION

Consumers appreciate their brand experiences and, especially when they are in a digital environment. There are certain customer motivations associated to purchases, which make them buy the desired goods. Those motivations can either be utilitarian or hedonic. The main problem nowadays is the diversity of stimulus that brands can undertake and how this can affect the consumers' choice.

The objective of this study is to understand the motivations for on-line shopping behavior, using generations X, Y and Z as the backdrop. The authors aim at understanding how the utilitarian and he-

DOI: 10.4018/978-1-7998-9179-6.ch007

donic purchase motivations influence shopping on-line, while also considering the possible relationship between the perceived risk and the repurchase intention with transactions in the on-line channel.

The authors used a quantitative methodology through the use of a survey. Results show that the utilitarian value has a greater association with repeat purchase intention than the hedonic value and the same intention.

BACKGROUND

The Internet and Its Growth

Nowadays, the internet represents powerful information technology capable of creating new business opportunities for organizations, namely in the creation of positioning strategies, something that was not possible before because of the information technologies available then (Porter & Michael, 2001).

From a commercial point of view, Dijesh and Babu (2016) consider that the Internet brings benefits both to sellers (as it can help organizations reach a narrower market segment, which in turn may result in sales and then profit) and buyers, as it allows searching for products/services from different sellers.

The market is becoming increasingly attractive, not only for buyers who have a huge variety of products/services available, but also for sellers who have access to new customers, thus reducing the costs inherent to these transactions for everyone involved (Kaplan & Sawhney, 2000; Srinivasan, Anderson & Ponnavolu, 2002).

Gunasekaran, Marri, McGaughey and Nebhwani (2002) consider that nowadays people feel more comfortable using the Internet, and its worth is emphasized by the amount of information it makes available to users worldwide. Websites are just a click away and they have become a new kind of information technology (Liu & Arnett, 2000).

To determine the current importance of the internet at a global level, the North American consultant Hootsuite has published global digital data for the year 2017 when, as shown in Figure 1, around 4,021 billion people were Internet users. The world population is circa 7,593 billion.

Figure 1. World population using the Internet regularly
Source: Hootsuite - The Global State of digital in 2018

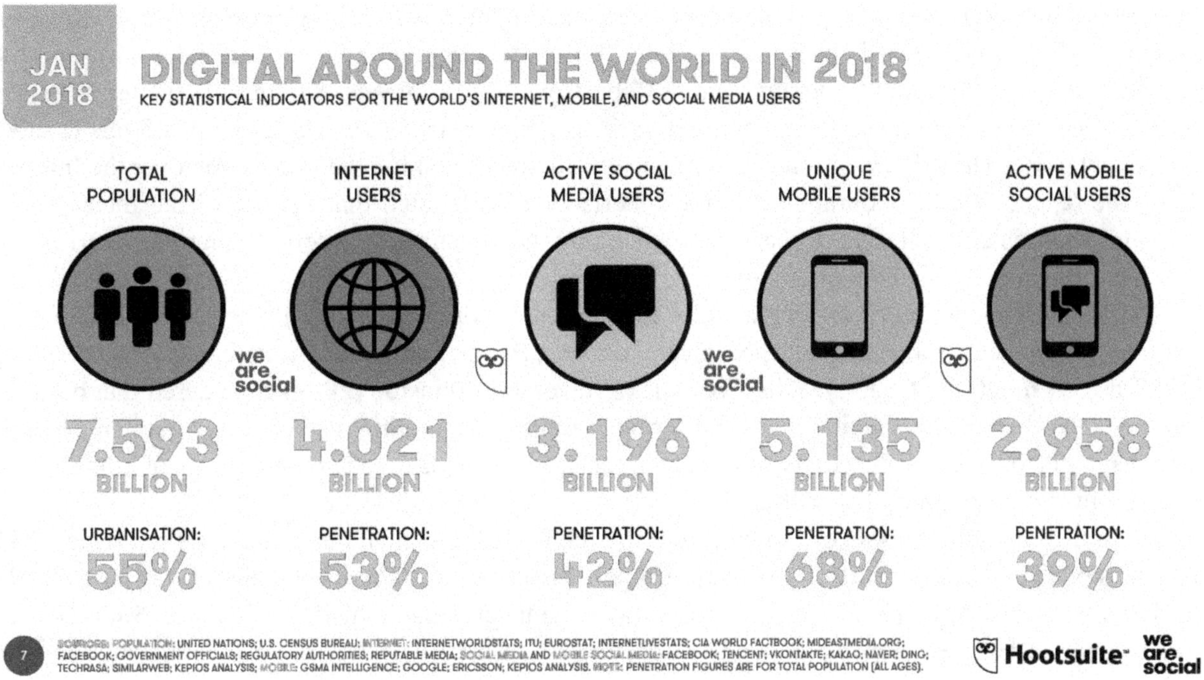

According to the same marketing consultant, the number of Internet users is around 7.73 million in Portugal, with 78% of those aged between 16 and 74 using the mobile/smartphone for access, while 73% use laptop computers (INE, 2016). This data is shown in Figure 2.

Figure 2. Proportion of people between the ages of 16 and 74 that use the internet and the equipment used to access it, Portugal, 2016.
Source: INE (Statistics Portugal) - Information and Knowledge Society. Survey on the Use of Information and Communication Technologies by families, 2016

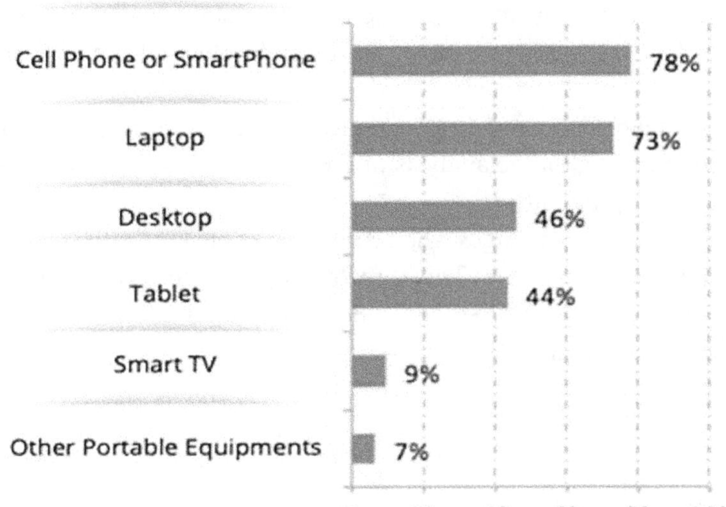

The On-line Channel Evolution

At present, the Internet has a large number of users and the trend is for it to grow even more. However, using it does not mean one is buying something. Both shoppers and browsers are internet users, but they are using it differently (Soopramanien & Robertson, 2007). *Internet Shoppers* is the term used to define users who have purchased something over the Internet, whereas *Internet Browsers* refers to those who search for products/services on-line but who ended up not making the transaction over the Internet (Forsythe & Shi, 2003). Soopramanien and Robertson (2007) stated that the use of the Internet as a medium of purchase is, in a first phase, influenced by the consumer's accepting that the Internet is a new interactive medium and a means of communication.

The on-line channel has evolved gradually and garnered more and more followers. Contrary to what happens in physical stores, buying through the on-line channel represents a new way of purchasing (To, Liao & Lin, 2007). Chaffey, Ellis-Chadwick, Mayer and Johnston (2009) considered that both the Internet and other existing digital media have revolutionized Marketing, because they made it possible for consumers to have a wide variety of products, services and a place to compare prices of other brands more easily, while enabling faster shopping.

When dealing with the sale of products through the on-line channel, the authors are referring to the sale of goods via the Internet itself, which is also known as '*brick and click*' (Yang, Lu & Chau, 2013). Hulland, Wade and Antia (2007) defined it as a way to connect with the market. Voorveld, Smit, Neijens and Bronner (2016) gave as examples of on-line channels the e-mail, websites, social media, search engines and feedback on on-line products. According to Korper and Ellis (2001), the sale of products through this channel cannot be based solely on website creation and then wait for customers to find and visit it. Organizations that have been successful and achieved a high return on investment have a specifically defined e-commerce strategy focused on customers, inventory, and profits. Korper and Ellis (2001) also considered that companies using an e-commerce system do not see it as something unusual or mystical, but rather as another avenue that can help leverage their business. For Sterne (2002), an organization that does not have a website is similar to trying to conduct business without a mobile phone or fax.

Being present on the on-line channel has gradually been considered essential, as it is where stakeholders more easily find information about consumers and/or prospective buyers, their aim being to customize the offer. Verhagen and Van Dolen (2009) stated that consumers used both the on-line and off-line channels when they were involved in their purchasing process.

Buying on-line does not allow consumers to touch the product or try it out, they can only observe it virtually. This is one of the reasons why prices in different channels can be different (Fruchter & Tapiero, 2005).

The use of the on-line channel by consumers is, therefore, based on the search for information about the products, on price comparison, on the analysis of customer reviews, on the selection of the desired products and, finally, on placing the order.

Thus, on-line stores have many advantages when compared to physical stores, as they allow customers to buy what they want anywhere, any time. This directs people to time and cost savings, which would not happen if they had to go to a physical store to get the intended good (Moshrefjavadi, Dolatabadi, Nourbakhsh, Poursaeedi & Asadollahi, 2012).

E-Commerce Evolution and Its Typologies

Trade is considered one of the main drivers of the world economy. Thanks to the digital revolution and the development of Information Technologies, new business opportunities and challenges have emerged, as was the case of on-line transactions, and will continue to arise (Nazir, 2017). The main reasons behind this Digital boom that human beings enjoy presently are related to Internet penetration, social media, the possibility of price comparison, the emergence of smartphones and constant innovation in logistics. After that revolution and the emergence of the Internet itself, the world is now experiencing a second Internet revolution, called e-commerce (Gunasekaran, et al., 2002). Delone and McLean (2003) defined e-commerce as the use of the Internet to facilitate, materialize and process business transactions. Such transactions imply a buyer, a seller and the exchange of products or services for money.

The development of e-commerce cannot be seen only as a local phenomenon, given that more and more consumers like to buy on foreign websites the products they cannot find on national ones. This is becoming ever easier and more accessible for buyers all over the world (Strzębicki, 2017). When companies integrate the on-line channel into their environment, they are trying to create a competitive advantage to increase their revenue and market share (Yang, et al. 2013). However, Yang, et al. (2013) stated that the benefits of adopting an e-commerce strategy will only become clear in a market where the public clearly understands and welcomes the new on-line channels in their environment seamlessly.

The development of e-commerce brought about new types of transactions. The new typologies range from business done between companies and their customers and the interactions happening between governments. Nemat (2011) put forward 12 types of e-commerce, with some better known and used more frequently than the others:

- Business to Business -one of the best-known types, refers to transactions done between businesses, as is the case between wholesalers and retailers.
- Business to Consumer - Business to Consumer (or Business to Customer) pertains to product and service transaction between businesses and the end consumer.
- Business to Employee - This type of e-commerce includes, according to Nemat (2011), businesses selling goods and services to their staff through an Intranet.
- Business to Government -Business to Government is another of the e-commerce types available. It focusses on the transactions happening between companies and the public sector, with the internet being used specifically for public procurement, licensing procedures and other government-related operations (Gupta, 2014).
- Business to Manager - According to Nemat (2011), Business to Manager is a recent model of business where organizations conduct business with professional managers.
- Consumer to Business - The authors previously described Business to Consumer (B2C), but there is also the possibility of the consumer doing business with the company (B2C).
- Consumer to Consumer - One of the types of business that evolved because of the Internet growth was *Customer-to-Customer* (C2C), also known as *Citizen-to-Citizen*. This refers to consumers trading goods among them, using a platform (Nemat, 2011).
- Government to Business - Generally speaking, the on-line transactions carried out by organizations are of a commercial nature. Thus, some transactions are carried out between companies and consumers, between organizations themselves and among consumers.

- Government to Consumer - Another type of e-government referred by Wang and Liao (2008) is *Government to Consumer* (G2C) or *Government to Citizen*. According to Nemat (2011), G2C is characterized by communication between the government and the citizen, which usually takes place through Information and Communication Technologies, but it can also be carried out by sending a direct e-mail or communication through the media.
- Government to Government - The third and last type of e-government is, according to Wang and Liao (2008), *Government-to-Government* (G2G). This refers to non-commercial interactions between governmental organizations (Nemat, 2011); Joia (2004) further defined it as the collaboration and cooperation between different governmental organizations in a digital structured format.
- Government to Employees - As said before, Wang and Liao (2008) described three types of e-government systems. But, Nemat (2011) added, yet another type of business in which government agencies are involved, namely *Government-to-Employees* (G2E). Apart from Nemat (2011), Rao (2011) also referred to four types of e-government business, including G2E. This includes the on-line interactions that exist through appropriate communication tools between governmental units and their staff.
- Peer to Peer - The last type of business described by Nemat (2011) was *Peer-to-Peer* (P2P). This type consists of a network that allows the sharing of information and resources between the different members belonging to a circle, without those members being concentrated on a single server. (Parameswaran, Susarla & Whinston, 2001; Ripeanu, 2001).

Generational Concept

Each generation has its own characteristics and lifestyles. The authors used the study carried out by Levickaite (2010) to describe Generations X and Y.

Generation X includes people who were born in the early 1960s up until 1974; Levickaite (2010) stated that this generation is characterised by the arrival of household computers, as well as the use of the Internet for social and commercial purposes. Generation X consumers are looking for greater shopping convenience as well as relationships between communities and brands.

Then comes generation Y, which encompasses those born between 1975 and 1989 (Parment, 2013). This generation grew up influenced by the political, technological and trends/fashion aspects of that period. Generation Y belongs to a time when buying was not just a simple act, but an experience in itself (Lissitsa & Kol, 2016).

Generation Z is characteristically the most technological one, and the consumers are on-line. It comprises people born between the mid-90s up until the end of the first decade of the 21st century. They are digital natives, the only generation to have been raised in a completely digital environment, and are constantly on-line from any device (Turner, 2015; Bencsik, Horváth-Csikós & Juhász, 2016; Chicca & Shellenbarger, 2018).

Purchase Motivations

Many purchases are related to the customers' utilitarian and hedonic values (Babin, Darden & Griffin, 1994). On the one hand, the utilitarian dimension results from a more thought-out action and has an intended outcome where the shopping experience is also valued. On the other hand, the hedonic dimension is the result of spontaneous responses related to personal pleasure and one in which the purchase of products can be accidental to the shopping experience. According to To, Liao and Lin (2007) products that are purchased for pleasure have a different impact compared to those that are purchased for a particular purpose.

The utilitarian dimension is related to the cognitive and non-emotional scope of a shopping experience (Albayrak, Caber & Çömen, 2016). Kesari and Atulkar (2016) reported that buyers value a utilitarian purchase highly only when they need to buy something.

Generally speaking, in a utilitarian behaviour, the purchase is made rationally, with the customer carefully analysing the product/service before making the purchase (Sarkar & Das, 2017).

On the other hand, the hedonic behavior is assessed based on the satisfaction derived by the customer (Batra & Ahtola, 1991). For To, *et al.* (2007) the main reason why consumers with hedonic values like to buy results from their joy/excitement with the purchase process itself and not from the achievement of a goal/task (a feature of the utilitarian dimension). In a way, more relaxed customers long for strong hedonic values (Babin, *et al.*, 1994).

Kesari and Atulkar (2016) argued that the different types of consumer segments lead to different purchase behaviors and values, because while the buying behavior of the younger segment is oriented towards entertainment and exploration, in the older segment there is a greater focus on convenience shopping and financial savings. Wolfinbarger and Gilly (2001) argued that if an individual has a certain amount of time available and some longing it will make the buying behavior more focused on experience.

Chandon, Wansink and Laurent (2000) considered that the benefits of a sales promotion can be considered as utilitarian given that they help consumers improve the usefulness, efficiency and economy of their search and purchase, but also as hedonic because they can provide an internal stimulus, fun and self-esteem. Thus, the authors considered that monetary savings, product quality and convenience are benefits of a sales promotion, which can be categorized as utilitarian, as they help the consumer both in the usefulness of the purchase and in improving the shopping experience. On the other hand, Chandon, et al. (2000) pointed to the possibility of both the benefits related to entertainment and exploration being classified as hedonic, as they are linked to emotions, experiences, satisfaction, and self-esteem.

Utilitarian Purchase Motivations

As already mentioned, utilitarian purchase motivations are related to buying what is necessary. Wolfinbarger and Gilly (2001) put forward four purchase motivations related to utilitarian buying:

- **Accessibility/Convenience**: Convenience results from the fact that you may buy the intended good where it is most convenient for you, without being concerned about possible restrictions.
- **Selection**: The on-line medium is perceived as a potential source of inventory when physical stores are out of stock. On-line stores have a wide selection of items, and the price is usually lower when compared to physical stores (To, et al., 2007).
- **Available Information**: Searching for information on the Internet has a much lower cost compared to collecting information in physical stores, if one takes into account that the latter implies transport costs.
- **No social presence**: Some customers do not like to be bothered when shopping, either by employees or family members.

Apart from saving time, the mentioned costs also include the financial costs when opting for an on-line purchase (To, et al., 2007). Chiu, et al. (2014) and Simonson (1999) argued that the available offer is also a utilitarian benefit to be considered when purchasing on-line. For example, clothing purchases mostly are driven by a utilitarian motive; however, consumers can be interested in new styles of clothing, so they will be more driven by a hedonic motivation (Shao & Li, 2021). For the purpose of this study, the authors adopted four utilitarian dimensions, as put forward by Chiu, et al. (2014), namely: available supply, available information, monetary savings and convenience.

Hedonic Purchase Motivations

Hedonic motivation is closely associated with buying for pleasure rather than necessity. Arnold and Reynolds (2003) considered there were 6 hedonic motivations associated with buying:

- **Adventure:** Buying because of a created stimulus, experiencing an adventure and the feeling like being in a world completely apart.
- **Social:** The Internet allows on-line customers to share information about brands, products/services and create experiences with other individuals with similar interests (To, et al., 2007).
- **Gratification:** Shopping is a form of stress relief and individual relaxation (Arnold & Reynolds, 2003)
- **Idea:** Customers find it easy to search for, evaluate and understand information about brands, products, and market novelties on the Internet (To, et al., 2007).
- **Buyer's role:** This refers to the fun and joy one feels when buying products for other people and not for their own use (Arnold & Reynolds, 2003).
- **Best deal:** Internet shopping can provide greater sensory engagement and excitement. When customers find discounted products they take it as a personal achievement (To, et al., 2007).

Hedonic purchase motivations is associated with customer satisfaction and loyalty (Vieira et al., 2018) and in the virtual context, is defined as fun or pleasure that results from technology use (Venkatesh et al., 2012).

Perceived Risk and Repurchase Intention in E-Commerce

There is a certain level of risk associated to any transaction whenever someone buys something. According to Wai, Dastane, Johari and Ismail (2019), the on-line purchase process implies research, selection, purchase, and use – in order to meet the needs of individuals – and, along that process, buyers are exposed to several risks, from the moment they visit the website to when the purchase is finalized.

Sitkin and Pablo (1992) established that risk is a characteristic of decision-making, which can be defined as uncertainty in relation to the results. These in turn may be positive or disappointing, according to the decisions that will be made. Risk decision-making refers to choosing between alternatives. For risk to exist, one of the possible consequences must be less desirable than the others (Weber & Bottom, 1989).

Chiu, et al. (2014) considered that there are four dimensions associated with perceived risk, namely financial risk, product performance, privacy, and product delivery. Hong (2015) added psychological and social risks as dimensions of perceived risk. In addition to those already mentioned, Forsythe and Shi (2003) also considered the time/convenience risk as another type of perceived risk.

- **Performance Risk:** This risk refers to refers to the probability that the purchased product does not meet the expectations.
- **Financial Risk:** Garner (1986, cited by Ko, Jung, Kim and Shim, 2004) and Forsythe and Shi (2003) stated that financial risk refers to the perception that a certain amount of money will need to be spent for the product to work properly.
- **Privacy Risk:** This concerns the customers' loss of control over personal information that has been posted on-line.
- **Product Delivery Risk:** This risk refers to losses that may result from the failure to deliver the product or if it is delivered after the due date (Chiu, Wang, Fang & Huang, 2014).
- **Social and Psychological Ris ks:** According to Jacoby and Kaplan (1972), the social risk is that which may affect the idea and/or opinion of those surrounding the person who bought the product. The psychological risk concerns what the customer feels when he/she buys a product that does not fit his/her image, i.e., the way one sees oneself.
- **Risk associated to time/convenience:** This risk is focused on the loss of time and the inconvenience experienced by the person because it was difficult to browse, submit the order, discover appropriate websites and there was a delay in getting the products.
- **Repurchase Intention:** The concept of repurchase intention is based on the idea the customer will buy another product/service from the same brand, considering his/her present situation and circumstances (Hellier, Geursen, Carr & Rickard, 2003). Hume, Mort and Winzar (2007), on the other hand, defined the repurchase intention as the decision made by the consumer to relate in the future with an activity carried out by the service/product provider, i.e., the brand, and the way in which this activity will happen. From a company's perspective, the repurchase intention has an impact on sales growth (Ali, 2019). Repurchase intention is relevant because the cost of retaining customers is much less than finding new ones; therefore, repeatedly buying from existing customers create more profit for companies (Maharani et al., 2020).

Factors Leading to Repurchase Intention

Tsai and Huang (2007) highlighted four basic factors leading to the intention of repeating on-line purchases:

- **Building a community:** a community can be made up of customers or other stakeholders, all sharing a certain connection. Communities share a lot of common interests and knowledge.
- **Customization:** Internet allows retailers to get to know their customers in more detail, thus having the opportunity to create customized offers.
- **Total satisfaction:** what the customer feels when the product/service meets all his/her needs and expectations (Hellier, et al., 2003).
- **Obstacles associated to change:** this refers to the costs associated to the time and effort the customer would have to put in if the relation with the brand was terminated and a new one had to be established.

Table 1 summarizes each variable, their definition, and the authors.

Table 1. Study variables

Constructs	Description	Authors
	Utilitarian	
Accessibility / Convenience	Time and effort saved in an on-line purchase, as one is not constrained by location or working hours.	Childers, Carr, Peck and Carson (2001)
Available Information	Information is more widespread on the Internet, which is one of the reasons why buyers look for and buy products on that same channel, according to a utilitarian activity.	Wolfinbarger and Gilly (2001)
Cost savings	Time saved by consumers when they use the on-line channel. Consumers have the possibility of purchasing products with the same quality as those in the physical store, sometimes for a lower price.	Keeney (1999); To, Liao and Lin (2007)
Available Offer	The total of products/services offered by the retailer, showing the breadth and depth of the product line available for purchase.	Simonson (1999)
	Hedonic	
Adventure	Purchases resulting from a given stimulus, experiencing an adventure and the feeling of being in a totally different world. Adventure purchase motivation is related to other findings that show that consumers look for sensory input while shopping.	Arnold and Reynolds (2003).
Social	Social motivation refers to the satisfaction of shopping with friends/family, socialisation and the bonds created with strangers. For many people, the transaction is seen as an opportunity for fun and an escape from the daily routine.	Arnold and Reynolds (2003)
Gratification	Going shopping is seen as a way to relieve stress and to relax during a less positive phase the person may be going through. This motivation refers to a form of personal treatment. The consumer is acting emotionally and not rationally.	Arnold and Reynolds (2003)
Idea	Motivation that refers to shopping as a way of monitoring new trends/fashions and analysing current innovations;	Arnold and Reynolds (2003)
Buyer's Role	This type of hedonic motivation refers to the enjoyment someone has when buying products for other people and not for their own use. This activity impacts the feelings of those who buy, there is an enormous inner joy when discovering the perfect product for others.	Arnold and Reynolds (2003)

RESEARCH METHODOLOGY

In order to understand the on-line purchase motivations of different generations regarding the purchase of clothing and beauty products, we used a quantitative methodology and conducted a survey with the objective of collecting information on the behavior of the digital consumer when shopping on-line. Based on the literature review presented, the conceptual research model used was based on the work of Chiu, et al. (2014) changing two research hypotheses, namely H4 and H5.

Apart from the already referred constructs, the conceptual model also has four variables, namely age, gender, past transactions, and experience on the Internet, in order to verify their influence on the repurchase intention.

Both the utilitarian value and hedonic value are presented in the Figure 3 model as secondary constructs in order to understand their relative importance in determining the repurchase intention (Chiu, Wang, Fang & Huang, 2014). The first value is made up of four dimensions: available supply, available information about the product, monetary savings and convenience. The hedonic value, on the other hand, is constituted by six dimensions: adventure,gratification, buyer's role, searching for the best deals, social and idea.

In their study, Chiu Wang Fang and Huang (2014) noticed that both the utilitarian dimensions and the hedonic dimensions affect the repurchase intention, hence our adoption of this model as a way of confirming whether this condition was also verified in our exploratory study. Hypotheses H4 and H5 were changed comparatively to those in the article by Chiu Wang Fang and Huang (2014).
The conceptual model is shown in Figure 3.

Figure 3. Conceptual Model.
Source: Chiu, et al. (2014)

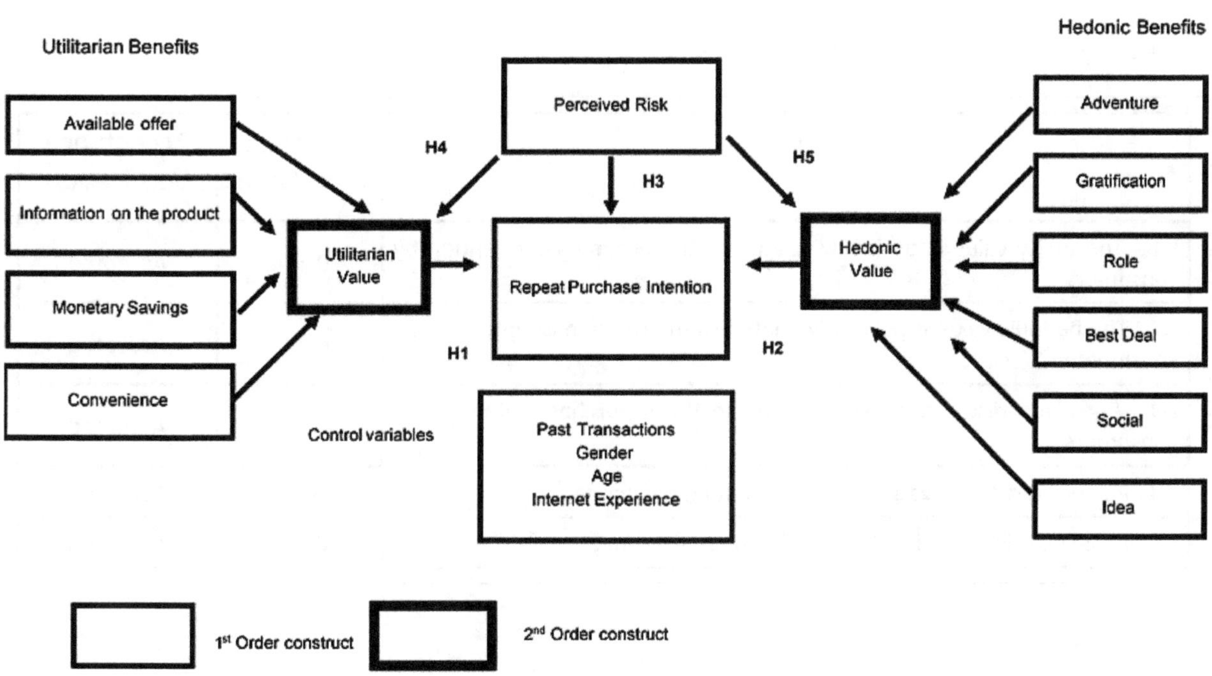

Therefore, the hypotheses of this study are as follows:

H1 - The utility value is positively related to the repurchase intention by consumers.
H2 - The hedonic value is positively related to the repurchase intention by consumers.
H3 - Perceived risk is negatively related to the repurchase intention by consumers.
H4 - Perceived risk is negatively related to utilitarian value.
H5 - Perceived risk is positively related to hedonic value.

These hypotheses aim at confirming the existence of a relationship between the utilitarian and hedonic purchase motivations and risk perception and repurchase intention.

Data Collection and Results

The survey was online during two months and disseminated via email and social media, obtaining 280 responses. The sample was for convenience, in which the survey had an initial question as a filter in order to obtain responses from people who actually shopped online for at least 6 months. Thus, a valid sample of 137 respondents who met the objective of the study was obtained. For the analysis of the responses obtained, the Statistical Package for the Social Sciences (SPSS) software was used.

The Figure 3 shows the complete structural model with the values referring to the correlations that validate the research hypotheses. This model derives from the conceptual model presented in the literature review, where one may confirm it contains the correlated values, both positive and negative ones. None of the correlations is either positively perfect or negatively perfect, since none of the coefficients obtained the values 1 or -1, respectively. Likewise, Table 2 presents the results of the correlations and the corresponding acceptance of the research hypotheses.

Table 2. Hypotheses verification

Hypotheses	Pearson's Correlation	Acceptance Verification
H1 - The utility value is positively related to the repurchase intention by consumers.	0.544	Accepted
H2 - The hedonic value is positively related to the repurchase intention by consumers.	0.273	Accepted
H3 - Perceived risk is negatively related to the repurchase intention by consumers.	-0.202	Accepted
H4 - Perceived risk is negatively related to utilitarian value.	-0.207	Accepted
H5 - Perceived risk is positively related to hedonic value.	0.303	Accepted

CONCLUSION

This study aimed at understanding how utilitarian and hedonic motivations influence the repurchase intention and which ones are the most important for the generations X, Y and Z. Our findings contribute to the improvement of new business models in Digital Transformation as it brings relevant insights for consumer experience.

The utilitarian and hedonic values result in consumers' rational and emotional acts. In this study, the authors found a greater correlation between the utilitarian value and the repurchase intention than between the hedonic value and the same intention, indicating that consumers value aspects related to the utilitarianism of the purchase.

The authors found that in generation X (44-53 year olds), as the utilitarian value increased, the repurchase intention also increased, indicating that for this generation the utilitarian value is an important driver for repeat purchase and relationship with the brand. On the other hand, the relation between hedonic value and repurchase intention in Generation Z (<=28) was higher, although not very explanatory and limited to the study sample.

The hedonic motivations that most reinforce the repurchase intention was Adventure, with the greatest impact on the repurchase intention for Generation Z, and this is where there was a higher correlation value in the motivations Gratification, Buyer's Role, Idea and Social.

Concerning Best Deal, generation X registered a higher value compared to the others, indicating that a huge attention was paid to sales and lower prices by individuals of this generation and that this is reflected on their repurchase intention. As far as the hedonic dimension is concerned, it is only in the best deal motivation that Generation Z does not have a higher value in the correlation with the repurchase intention.

With the analysis of the motivations in the hedonic dimension completed, it is time to address the data relating to the motivations that belong in the utilitarian dimension. As for the utilitarian dimension, the authors concluded that the value of the correlation between the Accessibility/Convenience Motivation and the Repurchase Intention is strong in generation X. This shows that the convenience of purchasing, including aspects such as saving time and the fact that the person can buy anywhere, lead to a more evident intention of repeat purchases in this generation.

Regarding the correlation between the cost savings motivation and the repurchase intention, the figures for generation Z and generation X are quite similar, probably underlying the fact that shopping from websites can be considered cheap and saves money, which reinforces the repurchase intention. Anyway, the highest correlation value was registered in generation X.

As for the available offer motivation, the study showed that generation X is the one with a higher correlation value between that motivation and the repurchase intention. This shows that for this generation the available offer is an important factor for the repurchase intention.

Finally, from the available information, the authors could determine that generation X had a greater correlation with the repurchase intention. Although the value was considered weak, the authors concluded that, for this motivation, information about the products is a "driver" for the repurchase intention.

These results, together with those concerning the correlation between the utilitarian value and the repurchase intention, are conclusive since the authors found that in all four items that make up the utilitarian value, there was always a higher correlation in Generation X. Thus, it is clear in this research that Generation X highly values utilitarianism in purchases.

It is also important to point out that generation Y did not register any greater correlation in relation to the other generations, for any of the motivations.

In terms of hedonism, there was also a greater relationship in Generation Z with the repurchase intention, indicating that in this age group there is greater emotion when buying than rationality. It was only in the best deal motivation that Generation Z did not have a higher correlation value. This goes to show that, in this study, generation Z came across as driven by hedonic values, meaning that the search for a low price or the existence of sales does not affect the repurchase intention for this generation. It is also a generation that likes to buy whenever it is feeling not so well, that appreciates buying for other people, that admires socialization and that likes to be aware of new fashions and trends. The authors may thus conclude that generation Z highly appreciates the hedonic value of purchasing.

LIMITATIONS, RECOMMENDATIONS AND FUTURE RESEARCH

This work has some limitations, one of which is the convenience sample, which does not guarantee representativeness of generations of consumers. Another limitation is the purchase and possible change in behavior, since the initial question of the survey was based on online purchases in the last 6 months.

This chapter intends to contribute to future studies related to the online buying behavior of digital consumers. It contains information that reinforces the studies already carried out on the subject, thus adding value and keeping the subject up to date.

This work can serve as a motto for conducting future studies that focus on investigating the purchasing behavior of only one generation and correlating it with geodemographic aspects.

In the managerial view, it allows organizations that have an online channel in their environment or that intend to create a collection of ideas on how to approach this same channel. This study can lead brands to a better assessment of their target audience and understand in what motivations they should pay more attention and encouragement to complete an online sale and win over customers.

A suggestion for further investigation will be the in-depth study of just one generation and analysis of the motivations that lead to an intention to repeat purchase.

ACKNOWLEDGMENT

This work was financed by national funds through the FCT – Foundation for Science and Technology, I.P., under the project UIDB/05422/20.

REFERENCES

Albayrak, T., Caber, M., & Çömen, N. (2016). Tourist shopping: The relationships among shopping attributes, shopping value, and behavioral intention. *Tourism Management Perspectives*, *18*, 98–106. doi:10.1016/j.tmp.2016.01.007

Ali, H. (2019). Building Repurchase Intention and Purchase Decision: Brand Awareness and Brand Loyalty Analysis (Case Study Private Label Product in Alfamidi Tangerang). *Saudi Journal of Humanities and Social Sciences*, *4*(09), 623–634. doi:10.36348/SJHSS.2019.v04i09.009

Almarashdeh, I., Jaradat, G., Abuhamdah, A., Alsmadi, M., Alazzam, M. B., Alkhasawneh, R., & Awawdeh, I. (2019). The difference between shopping online using mobile apps and website shopping: A case study of service convenience. *International Journal of Computer Information Systems and Industrial Management Applications*, *11*, 151–160.

Arnold, M. J., & Reynolds, K. E. (2003). Hedonic shopping motivations. *Journal of Retailing*, *79*(2), 77–95. doi:10.1016/S0022-4359(03)00007-1

Babin, B. J., Darden, W. R., & Griffin, M. (1994). Work and/or fun: Measuring hedonic and utilitarian shopping value. *The Journal of Consumer Research*, *20*(4), 644–656. doi:10.1086/209376

Bakos, Y. (1998). The emerging role of electronic marketplaces on the Internet. *Communications of the ACM*, *41*(8), 35–42. doi:10.1145/280324.280330

Ballantine, P. W. (2005). Effects of interactivity and product information on consumer satisfaction in an online retail setting. *International Journal of Retail & Distribution Management*, *33*(6), 461–471. doi:10.1108/09590550510600870

Batra, R., & Ahtola, O. T. (1991). Measuring the hedonic and utilitarian sources of consumer attitudes. *Marketing Letters*, *2*(2), 159–170. doi:10.1007/BF00436035

Bencsik, A., Horváth-Csikós, G., & Juhász, T. (2016). Y and Z Generations at Workplaces. *Journal of Competitiveness*, *8*(3), 90–106. doi:10.7441/joc.2016.03.06

Chaffey, D., Ellis-Chadwick, F., Mayer, R., & Johnston, K. (2009). *Internet marketing: strategy, implementation and practice*. Pearson Education.

Chandon, P., Wansink, B., & Laurent, G. (2000). A Benefit Congruency Framework of Sales Promotion Effectiveness. *Journal of Marketing*, *64*(4), 65–81. doi:10.1509/jmkg.64.4.65.18071

Chicca, J., & Shellenbarger, T. (2018). Connecting with Generation Z: Approaches in Nursing Education. *Teaching and Learning in Nursing*, *13*(3), 180–184. doi:10.1016/j.teln.2018.03.008

Childers, T. L., Carr, C. L., Peck, J., & Carson, S. (2001). Hedonic and utilitarian motivations for online retail shopping behavior. *Journal of Retailing*, *77*(4), 511–535. doi:10.1016/S0022-4359(01)00056-2

Chiu, C. M., Wang, E. T., Fang, Y. H., & Huang, H. Y. (2014). Understanding customers' repeat purchase intentions in B2C e-commerce: The roles of utilitarian value, hedonic value and perceived risk. *Information Systems Journal*, *24*(1), 85–114. doi:10.1111/j.1365-2575.2012.00407.x

Dawes, J. (2008). Do data characteristics change according to the number of scale points used? An experiment using 5-point, 7-point and 10-point scales. *International Journal of Market Research*, *50*(1), 61–77. doi:10.1177/147078530805000106

Delone, W. H., & McLean, E. R. (2003). The DeLone and McLean model of information systems success: A ten-year update. *Journal of Management Information Systems*, *19*(4), 9–30. doi:10.1080/07421222.2003.11045748

Dijesh, P., & Babu, S. S. (2016, March). Electronic commerce process as a method to improve the product and process. In *Data Mining and Advanced Computing (SAPIENCE), Internationa Conference on* (pp. 378-381). IEEE. 10.1109/SAPIENCE.2016.7684126

Featherman, M. S., & Pavlou, P. A. (2003). Predicting e-services adoption: A perceived risk facets perspective. *International Journal of Human-Computer Studies*, *59*(4), 451–474. doi:10.1016/S1071-5819(03)00111-3

Flavián, C., & Guinalíu, M. (2006). Consumer trust, perceived security and privacy policy: Three basic elements of loyalty to a web site. *Industrial Management & Data Systems*, *106*(5), 601–620. doi:10.1108/02635570610666403

Forsythe, S. M., & Shi, B. (2003). Consumer patronage and risk perceptions in Internet shopping. *Journal of Business Research*, *56*(11), 867–875. doi:10.1016/S0148-2963(01)00273-9

Fruchter, G. E., & Tapiero, C. S. (2005). Dynamic online and offline channel pricing for heterogeneous customers in virtual acceptance. *International Game Theory Review*, *7*(02), 137–150. doi:10.1142/S0219198905000454

Gunasekaran, A., Marri, H. B., McGaughey, R. E., & Nebhwani, M. D. (2002). E-commerce and its impact on operations management. *International Journal of Production Economics*, *75*(1-2), 185–197. doi:10.1016/S0925-5273(01)00191-8

Hellier, P. K., Geursen, G. M., Carr, R. A., & Rickard, J. A. (2003). Customer repurchase intention: A general structural equation model. *European Journal of Marketing*, *37*(11/12), 1762–1800. doi:10.1108/03090560310495456

Hong, I. B. (2015). Understanding the consumer's online merchant selection process: The roles of product involvement, perceived risk, and trust expectation. *International Journal of Information Management*, *35*(3), 322–336. doi:10.1016/j.ijinfomgt.2015.01.003

Hulland, J., Wade, M. R., & Antia, K. D. (2007). The impact of capabilities and prior investments on online channel commitment and performance. *Journal of Management Information Systems*, *23*(4), 109–142. doi:10.2753/MIS0742-1222230406

Hume, M., Mort, G. S., & Winzar, H. (2007). Exploring repurchase intention in a performing arts context: Who comes? and why do they come back? *International Journal of Nonprofit and Voluntary Sector Marketing*, *12*(2), 135–148. doi:10.1002/nvsm.284

Jacoby, J., & Kaplan, L. B. (1972). *The components of perceived risk*. ACR Special Volumes.

Joia, L. A. (2004). Developing Government-to-Government enterprises in Brazil: A heuristic model drawn from multiple case studies. *International Journal of Information Management*, *24*(2), 147–166. doi:10.1016/j.ijinfomgt.2003.12.013

Kaplan, S., & Sawhney, M. (2000). E-hubs: The new B2B marketplaces. *Harvard Business Review*, *78*(3), 97–106. PMID:11183982

Ko, H., Jung, J., Kim, J., & Shim, S. W. (2004). Cross-cultural differences in perceived risk of online shopping. *Journal of Interactive Advertising*, *4*(2), 20–29. doi:10.1080/15252019.2004.10722084

Korper, S., & Ellis, J. (2001). *The E-Commerce Book: Building the E-Empire*. Morgan Kaufmann.

Levickaite, R. (2010). Generations X, Y, Z: How social networks form the concept of the world without borders (the case of Lithuania). *LIMES: Cultural Regionalistics*, *3*(2), 170–183.

Lissitsa, S., & Kol, O. (2016). Generation X vs. Generation Y–A decade of online shopping. *Journal of Retailing and Consumer Services*, *31*, 304–312. doi:10.1016/j.jretconser.2016.04.015

Liu, C., & Arnett, K. P. (2000). Exploring the factors associated with Web site success in the context of electronic commerce. *Information & Management*, *38*(1), 23–33. doi:10.1016/S0378-7206(00)00049-5

Maharani, N., Helmi, A., Mulyana, A., & Hasan, M. (2020). Factors Influencing Purchase Intention on Private Label Products. *The Journal of Asian Finance. Economics and Business*, *7*(11), 939–945. doi:10.13106/jafeb.2020.vol7.no11.939

Moshrefjavadi, M. H., Dolatabadi, H. R., Nourbakhsh, M., Poursaeedi, A., & Asadollahi, A. (2012). An analysis of factors affecting on online shopping behavior of consumers. *International Journal of Marketing Studies*, *4*(5), 81. doi:10.5539/ijms.v4n5p81

NAZIR, S. (2017). E-Commerce Perception and Adoption-A Study of Tour and Travel Operators of J&K State. *Amity Global Business Review, 12*(2).

Nemat, R. (2011). Taking a look at different types of e-commerce. *World Applied Programming*, *1*(2), 100–104.

Parameswaran, M., Susarla, A., & Whinston, A. B. (2001). P2P networking: An information sharing alternative. *Computer*, *34*(7), 31–38. doi:10.1109/2.933501

Parasuraman, A., Zeithaml, V. A., & Malhotra, A. (2005). ES-QUAL: A multiple-item scale for assessing electronic service quality. *Journal of Service Research*, *7*(3), 213–233. doi:10.1177/1094670504271156

Parment, A. (2013). Generation Y vs. Baby Boomers: Shopping behavior, buyer involvement and implications for retailing. *Journal of Retailing and Consumer Services*, *20*(2), 189–199. doi:10.1016/j.jretconser.2012.12.001

Pires, G., Stanton, J., & Eckford, A. (2004). Influences on the perceived risk of purchasing online. *Journal of Consumer Behaviour: An International Research Review*, *4*(2), 118–131. doi:10.1002/cb.163

Porter, M. E. (2001). *Strategy and the Internet*. Ilustraciones Gibbs.

Rao, V. R. (2011). Collaborative government to employee (G2E): Issues and challenges to e government. *Journal of e-Governance, 34*(4), 214-229.

Rintamäki, T., Kanto, A., Kuusela, H., & Spence, M. T. (2006). Decomposing the value of department store shopping into utilitarian, hedonic and social dimensions: Evidence from Finland. *International Journal of Retail & Distribution Management*, *34*(1), 6–24. doi:10.1108/09590550610642792

Ripeanu, M. (2001, August). Peer-to-peer architecture case study: Gnutella network. *Peer-to-Peer Computing, 2001. Proceedings. First International Conference on IEEE*, 99-100.

Sarkar, R., & Das, S. (2017). Online shopping vs Offline shopping: A comparative study. *International Journal of Scientific Research in Science and Technology, 3*(1).

Shao, A., & Li, H. (2021). How do utilitarian versus hedonic products influence choice preferences: Mediating effect of social comparison. *Psychology and Marketing, 38*(8), 1250–1261. doi:10.1002/mar.21520

Simonson, I. (1999). The Effect of Product Assortment on Buyer Preferences. *Journal of Retailing, 75*(3), 347–370. doi:10.1016/S0022-4359(99)00012-3

Sitkin, S. B., & Pablo, A. L. (1992). Reconceptualizing the determinants of risk behavior. *Academy of Management Review, 17*(1), 9–38. doi:10.5465/amr.1992.4279564

Soopramanien, D. G., & Robertson, A. (2007). Adoption and usage of online shopping: An empirical analysis of the characteristics of "buyers""browsers" and "non-internet shoppers". *Journal of Retailing and Consumer Services, 14*(1), 73–82. doi:10.1016/j.jretconser.2006.04.002

Srinivasan, S. S., Anderson, R., & Ponnavolu, K. (2002). Customer loyalty in e-commerce: An exploration of its antecedents and consequences. *Journal of Retailing, 78*(1), 41–50. doi:10.1016/S0022-4359(01)00065-3

Sterne, J. (2002). *World Wide Web marketing: integrating the Web into your marketing strategy*. John Wiley & Sons.

Strzębicki, D. (2017). Development factors for cross-border b2c e-commerce in the world and in Poland. *Acta Scientiarum Polonorum. Oeconomia, 16*(4), 161–168. doi:10.22630/ASPE.2017.16.4.55

Szymanski, D. M., & Hise, R. T. (2000). E-satisfaction: An initial examination. *Journal of Retailing, 76*(3), 309–322. doi:10.1016/S0022-4359(00)00035-X

To, P. L., Liao, C., & Lin, T. H. (2007). Shopping motivations on Internet: A study based on utilitarian and hedonic value. *Technovation, 27*(12), 774–787. doi:10.1016/j.technovation.2007.01.001

Tsai, H. T., & Huang, H. C. (2007). Determinants of e-repurchase intentions: An integrative model of quadruple retention drivers. *Information & Management, 44*(3), 231–239. doi:10.1016/j.im.2006.11.006

Turner, A. (2015). Generation Z: Technology and social interest. *Journal of Individual Psychology, 71*(2), 103–113. doi:10.1353/jip.2015.0021

Venkatesh, V., Thong, J. Y. L., & Xu, X. (2012). Consumer Acceptance and Use of Information Technology: Extending the Unified Theory of Acceptance and Use of Technology. *Management Information Systems Quarterly, 36*(1), 157–178. doi:10.2307/41410412

Verhagen, T., & Van Dolen, W. (2009). Online purchase intentions: A multi-channel store image perspective. *Information & Management, 46*(2), 77–82. doi:10.1016/j.im.2008.12.001

Vieira, V., Santini, F. O., & Araujo, C. F. (2018). A meta-analytic review of hedonic and utilitarian shopping values. *Journal of Consumer Marketing, 35*(4), 426–437. doi:10.1108/JCM-08-2016-1914

Voorveld, H. A., Smit, E. G., Neijens, P. C., & Bronner, A. F. (2016). Consumers' cross-channel use in online and offline purchases. *Journal of Advertising Research, 56*(4), 385–400. doi:10.2501/JAR-2016-044

Wai, K., Dastane, O., Johari, Z., & Ismail, N. B. (2019). Perceived risk factors affecting consumers' online shopping behaviour. *The Journal of Asian Finance. Economics and Business*, *6*(4), 246–260.

Wang, Y. S., & Liao, Y. W. (2008). Assessing eGovernment systems success: A validation of the DeLone and McLean model of information systems success. *Government Information Quarterly*, *25*(4), 717–733. doi:10.1016/j.giq.2007.06.002

Weber, E. U., & Bottom, W. P. (1989). Axiomatic Measures of Perceived Risk: Some Tests and Extensions. *Journal of Behavioral Decision Making*, *2*(2), 113–131. doi:10.1002/bdm.3960020205

Wolfinbarger, M., & Gilly, M. C. (2001). Shopping online for freedom, control, and fun. *California Management Review*, *43*(2), 34–55. doi:10.2307/41166074

Yang, S., Lu, Y., & Chau, P. Y. (2013). Why do consumers adopt online channel? An empirical investigation of two channel extension mechanisms. *Decision Support Systems*, *54*(2), 858–869. doi:10.1016/j.dss.2012.09.011

Yang, Z., Cai, S., Zhou, Z., & Zhou, N. (2005). Development and validation of an instrument to measure user perceived service quality of information presenting web portals. *Information & Management*, *42*(4), 575–589. doi:10.1016/S0378-7206(04)00073-4

ADDITIONAL READING

Akram, U., Junaid, M., Zafar, A. U., Li, Z., & Fan, M. (2021). Online purchase intention in Chinese social commerce platforms: Being emotional or rational? *Journal of Retailing and Consumer Services*, *63*, 102669. doi:10.1016/j.jretconser.2021.102669

Anand, T., Ramachandran, J., Sambasivan, M., & Batra, G. S. (2019). Impact of hedonic motivation on consumer satisfaction towards online shopping: Evidence from Malaysia. *e-Service Journal*, *11*(1), 56–88. doi:10.2979/eservicej.11.1.03

Rahayu, R., & Day, J. (2017). E-commerce adoption by SMEs in developing countries: Evidence from Indonesia. *Eurasian Business Review*, *7*(1), 25–41. doi:10.100740821-016-0044-6

Rohm, A. J., & Swaminathan, V. (2004). A typology of online shoppers based on shopping motivations. *Journal of Business Research*, *57*(7), 748–757. doi:10.1016/S0148-2963(02)00351-X

Swinyard, W. R., & Smith, S. M. (2003). Why people (don't) shop online: A lifestyle study of the internet consumer. *Psychology and Marketing*, *20*(7), 567–597. doi:10.1002/mar.10087

Trusov, M., Bucklin, R. E., & Pauwels, K. (2009). Effects of word-of-mouth versus traditional marketing: Findings from an internet social networking site. *Journal of Marketing*, *73*(5), 90–102. doi:10.1509/jmkg.73.5.90

KEY TERMS AND DEFINITIONS

Buying Motives: A motive is defined as a drive for which individuals can seek satisfaction. It becomes a buying motive when the individual seeks satisfaction through the purchase of something.

E-Commerce: Refers to a business model that allows companies and individuals to buy and sell goods and services over the Internet.

Generations: Refers to a specific generation of people based on birth, preferences, attitudes, and upbringings that distinguish them from other groups.

Hedonic Motives: Attributes that deal with the experiences of sensory, appeals, which include emotion and gratification.

Perceived Risk: Refers to the customer's perception of the risks associated with any purchase.

Repurchase Intention: Is the process of an individual purchasing goods or services from the same brand.

Utilitarian Motives: Are directed toward achieving goals, and they relate to efficiency and rational decision-making.

Chapter 8
A Case Study of Business Innovation Through Digital Technologies

Qiuyan Fan
Western Sydney University, Australia

ABSTRACT

This chapter provides a qualitative case study of Pinduoduo: China's fastest-growing e-commerce firm. As a disruptive organization entering the retail industry in 2015, Pinduoduo has become the third largest e-commerce platform in China. The spectacular success of the company has caught the attention of entrepreneurs, business leaders, and investors across the world. This study demonstrates that digital technologies have enabled Pinduoduo to develop innovative business model and establish closer and diverse links with partners and experiences with customers. The innovative business model and strategy of Pinduoduo are worth studying. This chapter aims to provide an understanding of the strategies that underpin the innovative business models of Pinduoduo and the impact of digital innovation and technologies on consumer's experiences. The research results demonstrate how Pinduoduo addresses the needs of overlooked customers in their market spaces through leveraging advanced digital technologies and innovating platform business models and developing digital ecosystems.

INTRODUCTION

Businesses are increasingly turning towards digital as it is the future of the global economy. Digitally driven business innovations are shaping the future of business. Digital business innovations are significant changes to organisational processes and in the way to engage and interact with business partners and customers using disruptive digital technologies such as artificial intelligence, big data and cloud computing technologies as well as Internet of Things (Chaffey, Hemphill & Edmundson-Bird, 2019). Deploying these disruptive digital technologies has offered opportunities for businesses to develop innovative products and services in the global market space and establish closer and diverse links with partners and customers. Attempts at digital business innovation have led to both repeated failures and

DOI: 10.4018/978-1-7998-9179-6.ch008

successes. This chapter offers a case study of Pinduoduo (PDD) that stresses contributing factors to its success in business innovation through digital technology. PDD is China's fastest-growing e-commerce firm to date and it is now the third largest e-commerce platform in China. The spectacular success of the company has caught the attention of many entrepreneurs, business leaders and investors. PDD, founded in 2015, has become one of China's largest online business in its short life. How PDD became one of China's top e-commerce platforms within such a short period of time? This chapter investigates what is behind the success and discussed the challenges facing PDD and future prospect. This research aims to provide an insight of PDD's business and market strategy with a focus on business innovation through digital technology and to demonstrate how start-ups can create a significant disruption in the value chain and business models of established firms. The main objectives of the chapter are to understand the value of platforms and ecosystems through the success of PDD and to discover best practices of a digital platform and ecosystem in this particular case study.

The chapter is structured as follows. First, the researcher reviews the literature in relation to the topics and presents the profile of the case company. The researcher subsequently describes the methodology used in the research. Then, the results and discussion are presented and followed by the solutions and recommendations. Finally, the chapter concludes with a discussion of future research direction and a summary of the research.

BACKGROUND

In the following sections, the researcher reviews the literature on platform business model and business ecosystem and discuss the challenges and trends and customer experiences in relation to platforms and provides the evolving profile of PDD.

Platform Business Model and Business Ecosystems

Companies are increasingly innovating their business models through digital technology and they have demonstrated particular interests in digital platforms and ecosystems (Hoch & Brad, 2021). Researchers observed that companies that developed innovative business models utilising digital technologies were more competitive and productive (Fan & Ouppara, 2021; Hoch & Brad, 2021). In recent years, much research has been devoted to study of digital platforms and business ecosystems. Hoch and Brad (2021) defined platforms as intermediaries by bringing buyers and sellers together, connecting groups of users, facilitating transaction and interaction between them. Kim (2016, p2116) suggested 'a business ecosystem as a system in which platform providers, value suppliers and consumers interact with each other'. Bughin, Catlin & Dietz (2019, p2) argue, "Digital platforms and ecosystems define the new competition and the lines between the platforms and ecosystems are blurring and will continue to blur". The power of platforms lies in ecosystems of producers, consumers, suppliers and other participants creating and sharing in value (Falk & Riemensperger, 2019).

A digital platform strategy has become increasingly prevalent in times of uncertainty and disruption (e.g. during the Covid-19 crisis). Platform companies are in nearly every market. Platform based markets are often described as multi-sided in that platform owners provide access to and support interaction among multiple groups of participants such as consumer, sellers, suppliers, third-party service providers (Fan & Ouppara, 2021). Platform companies must be able to identify which stakeholders that they need to bring together to generate revenue that exceed their costs. Falk and Riemensperger (2019, p2) revealed that the majority of the companies studied in Germany were taking advantage of platform business model but "only 16% of the platforms studied in Germany were being run as open, networked ecosystems that connect multiple players". Indeed, the majority of the companies studied were discounting the power of network effects as their platforms were closed or one-sided and they failed to think strategically and look beyond just selling products on the platforms (Falk & Riemensperger 2019). Companies should take an innovative approach to designing a digital ecosystem and multi-sided platform that enable customers, suppliers, and partners to share and create value. Companies are turning to digital technologies such as artificial intelligence, Internet of Things; cloud computing and mobile Internet to improve operational efficiencies and to enhance customer experiences (Fan & Ouppara, 2021). However, digital technologies, on their own, do not guarantee success in creating value to customers and gaining competitive advantage if they are not fully integrated into innovative business models (Hoch & Brad, 2021). A platform strategy must be taken in building a successful platform model and business ecosystem. Fan and Ouppara (2021,p11) states that "a platform ecosystem strategy is an approach to entering a market that revolves around the task of allowing platform participants to develop a trust-based relationship with each other on the platform and connect disparate parties such producers, consumers and other stakeholders". It is important to include all participants into the system from the outset of any platform business initiative. Kim (2016, p2113) argues, "Platforms evolve through the connection and interaction of participants, and act as ecosystems of coexistence that can provide values and benefits to all participants". Platform companies are required to establish a business ecosystem to enable all market participants to create value and enjoy benefits in the system.

The creation of a digital platform is no guarantee of business success. Cusumano, Yoffie and Gawer (2020) revealed that some platform businesses yield a competitive advantage with positive financial result to match while others are struggling to generate sales growth and profits. Their research shows that most platforms lose money but successful platform companies were growing twice as fast and valuable as their conventional counterparts were (Cusumano, Yoffie & Gawer, 2020). Platform companies face the increasing market competition and business challenges as the ecosystems and digital technologies that drive platforms are constantly changing and evolving. They must be able to anticipate "the trends that will determine platform success versus failure in the coming years and the technologies that will spawn tomorrow's disruptive platform battlegrounds" (Cusumano, Yoffie & Gawer, 2020, p3). According to McKinsey's latest survey of Chinese e-commerce, "purchases initiated from social media platforms, the uptake of online shopping among consumers in low-tier cities and e-commerce penetration beyond first-mover product categories such as apparel" are the potential sources of major e-commerce growth in China (Wang, Lau & Gong, 2016, p1). The survey shows that the e-commerce activity of low-tier cities has surpassed that of tiers 1 and 2 cities since 2015 and consumers have used social media as a powerful platform not just for searching product information but also for initiating online purchases (Wang, Lau & Gong, 2016). Many surveys show that consumers at large want brands to be socially active (McKinsey & Company, 2020; Wang, Lau & Gong, 2016). The trend is clear that consumers are empowered by digital platforms such as e-commerce, social media and mobile apps to do their shopping (Fan & Ouppara, 2021). This requires companies to focus on orchestrating and facilitating external participants and building engaged communities through platform structures and ecosystems (Dawson, 2018). It is critical to deliver better customer services and enhance user experience in platforms through consistent data gathering and analysis using digital technologies. Platform companies increasingly integrate AI and big data analytics to create a seamless shopping experience and predict a customer's future worth. AI allows platform companies to identify which customers are more interested in their products and services, more loyal and profitable. They then can create targeted approaches for each group to provide personalized shopping experiences. With the help of AI and big data, platforms can provide individualised products recommendation to meet customer's needs. This not only helps their operations become smarter and more streamlined but also assist their customers to benefit from more convenient and personalized shopping experiences. Research has shown that companies that build relationship with consumers first and sell to them second will be well positioned for success. A hybrid model as the dominant strategy for platform business has become positive trends (Cusumano, Yoffie & Gawer, 2020). The most valuable global companies such as Amazon and Apple all follow hybrid strategies. A hybrid platform model not only connects buyers and sellers, advertisers and consumers, or users of social networks but also encourages third parties to create complementary apps and services (Cusumano, Yoffie & Gawer, 2020).

The Evolving Profile of Pinduoduo

PDD was established in 2015 to provide e-commerce services with a wide range of products from groceries to home appliances. The company started with a handful of people and it now has over 5000 employees (PDD, 2020a). Digital technology plays an important role in the business growth of PDD. More than 50% of its 5000 employees are engineers (PDD, 2020a). PDD combines social media and e-commerce into a mobile platform allowing consumers to buy together as a "team" to receive discounts on their purchase. PDD has established an inclusive business ecosystem where all relevant participants in the process of value creation trade with them.

PDD is one of the fastest growing businesses in recent years in China. PDD was listed on NASDAQ in July 2018 and only three years after its launch in 2015, PDD is now the top five overseas-listed Chinese internet company (China International Capital Corporation, 2019). PDD has experienced huge growth since 2015. Total revenue for the quarter in 2020 was increased by 89% from RMB14, 209.8 million (US$2,092.9 million) in the same period in 2019. The company ranked the 2nd most popular e-commerce platform by monthly active users and the 3rd most popular apps by gross mechanise value (GMV) in China (Kubala, 2019). The average monthly active user for the quarter was 643.4 million (PDD, 2020b), up 50% from 429.6 million in the same period in 2019 (PDD, 2019). Active buyers for the 12 months ended September 30, 2020 were 731.3 million (PDD, 2020b), compared to 536.3 million for the 12 months ended September 30, 2019 (PDD, 2019). There was an increase of 36% in the 12-month period. According to the PDD (2020b) financial report, as of third quarter 2020, there was a big increase of gross mechanise value (GMV) from RMB 840.2 billion in September 2019 (PDD, 2019) to RMB1,457.6 million (US$2214.7 billion) in September 2020, which was up over 70%. Annual expenditure per active buyer was RMB1, 566.7 for the 12 months ended September 30, 2019 (PDD, 2019) and RMB1, 993.1 (US$293.6) for the 12 months ended September 30, 2020 (PDD, 2020b). It has gone up by 27% within the 12 months. The rapid growth of PDD is in line with the outcomes of the research conducted by Cusumano, Yoffie and Gawer. Their research confirmed that "successful platform yield a powerful competitive advantage with financial results to match" (Cusumano, Yoffie & Gawer, 2020, p.5).

As the most popular social commerce platform in China, the innovative business model and strategy of PDD are worth studying. The successful experience of PDD can provide best practices, guidelines, and implications for e-commerce management in practice, which could be applicable for new entrants, suppliers, manufacturers, platform providers, marketing and sales managers, service or product developers and supply chain managers with limited capabilities to compete in the digitally disruptive business environment. This chapter would be useful for business leaders, professionals and researchers.

RESEARCH METHODOLOGY: A CASE STUDY APPROACH

This research took a qualitative approach to investigate the case of PDD. A case study was used as the research methodology in this chapter, as it fits well with the aim and objectives of the research. Moreover, social commerce is a relatively new industry in China where most Chinese social commerce companies were established after 2014. Case study methodology is particularly helpful to provide observations of new social phenomena and explain how and why of specific business model and development (Yin, 1994). The researcher conducted extensive web-based document analyses and literature review and experienced the PDD App first hand as a user and a "participant observer" during the research. A small field work was undertaken to engage with some of the PDD' customers and suppliers in 2019 to enhance the research. A total of 10 semi-structured interviews of the participating suppliers and online shoppers of PDD were conducted between September and November 2019. Each session lasted about two hours. All interviews were digitally recorded and transcribed. In addition to the interview data, the researcher gathered the data on the case company and information in the areas of digital innovation, platforms and ecosystems. These data and information were collected from industry, government and media reports as well as internal documents of the selected company to complement the interview data and assist the researcher in developing a comprehensive understanding of the phenomenon under investigation and achieving data triangulation and verification through cross references. Data analysis was performed in an iterative manner which allow researchers to iterate between the primary interview data and the relevant secondary sources of data on digital platforms and ecosystems. The researcher used categorizing, coding, and contextualization techniques to look for patterns and themes in the process of data analyses. The findings and discussion were presented in the next section in an effort to offer insights on how the platform business model can help PDD drive business growth, improve efficiency of operations, and enhance customer experiences.

RESULTS AND DISCUSSION

This section analyses the primary and secondary data collected in the case study and presents the main findings. The data analysis draws on the interview data, field observation and company documents as well as industry data and professional literature. Based on the analysis of the data, the aspects of the main findings perceived as important factors of PDD's success include:

Developing an Innovative Business Model

PDD created an innovative team purchase model to meet users' needs. Users can buy a large portfolio of items in bulk at a discount price through team purchase and have fun while doing it. How does the PDD's team purchase model work? There are two different prices for each item listed on the site: a market price and a group price. If consumers share products with their friends and buy them together, they can get a group price for the products they purchase as a team. The price of a group purchase is usually cheaper than the market price for an individual purchase. The usual discount can reach 70 to 90%. The more people that sign up to buy it, the larger the discount gets. Although it is a group purchase, the items are delivered to each group member separately. The interviewees told the researcher that they shared PDD's product information with their friends and family members via WeChat and invited them to form a shopping team to get a lower price for their purchases. A regular online shopper said: "I really enjoyed these dynamic and fun shopping experiences as the platform kept me motivated and better connected with my friends and extended family to get the best prices for the products we purchased."

The app allows customers to browse a list of people who are looking to fill their groups and join them when they are unable to find enough friends. Users can log in at any time to see products that the Artificial Intelligence (AI) engine has tailored specifically to them, and quickly get a group together to score great deals. A large proportion of the purchases on PDD platform in the past few years were team purchases according to the company report (PDD, 2020a). In addition, the app includes many mini programs and games. These mini programs enable users to discover value-for-money products through interactions and connections among them (Graziani, 2018). The PDD users shared their experiences with the Bargain with Friends Game. They said to the researcher "this game enables us to slash price by sharing with our friends and receive product for free".

Developing Effective Marketing and Pricing Strategies for Users

PDD has developed an effective marketing strategy. It focuses on identifying a niche market and capitalizing on a new source of users in lower-tiered cities. Sixty percent of PDD users are married middle-age women living in lower-tier Chinese cities and doing most of the shopping for the family (Nie & Feng 2019). They are price sensitive and eager to snap up a good deal. PDD provides subsides or coupons or discount to these users through various games and mini programs. These users often have more free time to play with apps and games and search for cheap products and are more likely to share with friends on social media to win discounts. The PDD's consumer said "I am sending the production information through WeChat precisely to my friends or family members as I know their consumption preferences and affordability". The approach is both cost-saving and effective as "the costs for advertising and marketing are also lowered through user sharing to social media" (Lee, 2018). PDD also is leveraging viral marketing to build the identity of all the lesser-known brands on its platform. Choosing lesser-known brands over famous brands for their users enables PDD to avoid any costs that come from branding (China potion, 2020). The interviewee told the researcher "I have recently retired from work. I care less about products brands but more on discounts on everyday items when shopping at the PDD platform. I bought tissue paper at less than $2 for 10 boxes and paid $1.5 for an umbrella the other day". The low pricing strategy of PDD is compelling attraction to their target users as most of customers from lower tier cities consider price as the most important factor in their purchasing decision. The main challenge for PDD lies in sustaining its advantage of extremely low prices through digital innovation.

Leveraging Artificial Intelligence and Big Data Analytics and Ecosystems

PDD leverages distributed AI to understand customer behaviours in their sharing and purchasing activities, which assist manufacturers in producing customised products to meet customer demands and purchasing preferences (PDD, 2019a). Unlike the conventional search model used by other e-commerce platforms, PDD addresses user demands through a personalized recommendation model and the most popular Chinese social media WeChat (Kubala, 2019). It constantly recommends customised products or popular products with lower prices to stimulate purchasing desires and promote sales. PDD is leveraging AI and Big data to reduce user decision-making costs and guide users to place orders quickly. Consumers can share their experiences and see the whole process of product manufacturing through the visual platform of a live broadcast (Xie, 2018). All production information of the factory is synchronised to the platform of PDD through digital partnering in the ecosystems (PingWest 2018). PDD is partnering with Tencent, whose app WeChat with 1 billion users is the main driver of traffic to the site (Graziani, 2017). Moreover, the majority of PDD's transactions and payments are made through WeChat Pay. These ecosystems with a strong digital partnering capability not only help offer the best value-based products and satisfies consumers' needs but also improve the relationship between manufacturers and consumers (PDD, 2019a). The increased data from consumers' purchasing behaviours and connections and interactions among them would be valuable for further analysis to enhance and improve the products and services through customized production.

Disrupting Traditional Agriculture Supply Chain

Traditionally farmers in China sell their fresh produce through a long and inefficient supply chain, which includes multiple tiers of distributors, wholesalers and retailers. PDD connects customers directly with farmers by cutting out intermediaries. It delivers fresh fruit and vegetables directly from farmer to customers' home. By doing so, farmers can sell their fresh produce via the PDD platform at a higher price while customers can get better value for their purchases. The online shopper said: "I regularly buy a few boxes of fresh fruits with a group of people via PDD's app as seasonal fruits sold on PDD platform are much cheaper than buying them in the supermarkets or the city's fruit stands". PDD use a bulk-selling model with a focus on the bestseller produces to attract more consumers. As the platform aggregated user's demand and simplified the supply chain, it not only creates a larger number of orders for the farmers but also leaves the farmers more room to cut prices for buyers.

Developing a Consumer to Manufacturer Model

PDD expanded its Consumer to Farmer model (C2F) into other products categories such as apparel, cosmetics, furniture, household goods and electronics. It developed a Consumer to Manufacture (C2M) business strategy, which benefits both sides. PDD is integrating with this C2M model to perform a full circle of "production + distribution + transaction + consumption" (Zhao, Wang & Chen, 2019). This new business model focuses on the growth of SMEs, especially those manufacturers who were the upstream suppliers of the international supply chain have quality production capability but without a famous brand in China (China Potion, 2020). As the manager of one of the PDD's suppliers said, "PDD takes user data on its platform and packages it up for us to create our own high margin products". PDD gather consumer demand and bring it to the upstream supply chain or small manufacturers through leveraging AI, big data analytics and other digital technologies.

In a nutshell, PDD's platform business model enables the emergence of new, large-scale, and multi-sided markets that cut across the traditional industries and cooperation appear to be at the across sector level. Farmers, manufacturers, and SMEs have built businesses and sell products and services on PDD's platform and collectively they create significant business value for the case company. PDD's ecosystem has leveraged company's core functionality and value proposition to attract large number of customers and create network effect. The platform integrates multiple companies services together to holistically address customer needs and allow users to interact with end-users socially to attract as many customers and social interactions as possible.

Issues and Challenges of Pinduoduo Moving Forward

Major e-commerce platforms that historically engage online shoppers on high-tier cities have invested heavily to acquire customers and build logistics networks in low tier cities (Wang, Lau & Gong, 2016). Alibaba's B2C marketplace Taobao and JD.com have recently penetrated into less developed areas in China through successfully launching special buy programme on their apps to target a part of PDD users. PDD is becoming increasingly difficult to maintain high growth and its dominance in third and fourth tier cities. To address these challenges, PDD was adapting its strategy to grow customer base in first and second tier cities. However, these citifies do not have huge potential for e-commerce growth driven by user penetration (Wang, Lau & Gong, 2016). Furthermore, PDD launched a "10 billion subsidies" promotion in an effort to expand into more expensive and luxury product categories. However, this effort was ineffective and largely failed. As the regular shopper of PDD said, "I do not buy expensive products on the platform. My friends and I only buy cheap stuff on their app. I guess this what has made PDD successful." People's perception of PDD as low-end will not change easily or quickly. It is vital for PDD to address the issues associated with low-quality perception in order to compete with their major competitors such as Alibaba's Taobao and JD.com in the future. Clearly, PDD's heavy investment in marketing through promotions and coupons will not make its competitive advantages sustainable. As the e-commerce market in lower-tier cities became saturated, how to grow its customer base and maintain sustainable development of its business platform is a major challenge for PDD moving forward.

SOLUTIONS AND RECOMMENDATIONS

Although it is critical to understand e-commerce market and major competitors, equally crucial is the need to maintain focus on business strengths and customer expectations. PDD's core strengths rest in their commitment to bringing its innovative business model and platform to both sell side (China's lower tier and rural Internet users) and buy side (China's small suppliers or manufacturers and farmers). PDD's C2M and C2F model will continue to give them the advantages of achieving its business growth.

This research recommends that PDD continue to maintain its low-price strategy but remove low quality public image through quality control of products and services such as raising the threshold of merchants to enter the platform and increasing new branding through further implementing C2M initiatives. It suggests that PDD develop its own brand strategy, which aims to support the growth of small manufacturers and address low quality image. Research demonstrates "the product itself has no brand advantage but the platform unique channel represents the brand which make consumers believe that the industrial products and agricultural products sold on the platform represent good quality, design and favourable prices" (Zhao, Wang and Chen, 2019, p16). PDD should empower merchants and manufacturers with e-commerce knowhow through training, traffic and brand-building support to promote their products to customers and realize seamless connection between production and sales and in turn increase customer's satisfaction and trust.

This chapter also recommends that PDD increase its focus on building a more sustainable and innovative platform and ecosystem to meet the need for different stakeholders in the agriculture value chain. It suggests that PDD combine transaction and innovation platforms into a hybrid model. A hybrid strategy enables PDD to "shift the traditional model of value creation from inside organizations to enabling external value-creation from an extended ecosystem of participants" and their interactions (Bughin,Catlin, & Dietz, 2019, p.3). By addressing farmer pain points, the company announced a strategic partnership with the National Engineering Research Centre for Information Technology in Agriculture to explore the use of AI and 5 G for precision farming and develop smart agriculture solutions (PDD, 2020a). Armed with this strategic initiative, it suggest that PDD develop a hybrid business model that offers significant value to all participants in the value chain. Through this model, farmers can get aggregated customer demand, preferences, and market pricing so that they can quickly sell their products on the platform at a reasonable price. For customers they are able to enjoy lower prices for high quality products. Leveraging data analytics and digital technologies has been a critical component of the growth and success of PDD. PDD should continue to integrate demand and supply through digital technologies such AI, IoT and Big data to make it easy for both buy and sell side of the supply chain. Building a more innovative ecosystem from multi-stakeholders in the agriculture value chain such as government agencies, farmers, and technology and finance providers would be essential for the growth of the sector and the customer base of PDD.

FUTURE RESEARCH DIRECTIONS

Digital technology advances are accelerating the pace of disruptive innovations. However, most SMEs are slow to adopt digital innovation, technology, and lack of strategies to respond to disruptors and disruptive innovations in a market space. Research has found that SMEs with a high level of digital engagement are more profitable, survive longer and grow larger (Deloitte Access Economics, 2013). The proposed future research will provide insights into how digital platform service providers such as PDD can help SMEs transform and compete in digitally disruptive and globally competitive environment.

This study acts as a starting point and provide a foundation for a future research project that will include a number of Australian SMEs intending to do business in China to carry out a more comprehensive study on how an Australian SMEs to partner with PDD, along with other Chinese businesses to develop and distribute products for the Chinese market. The rise of cross border e-commerce platforms such as PDD and Tmall presents a huge opportunity to reach the Chinese consumer base. It allows foreign brands without a physical presence in China to sell to Chinese consumers. This will not only benefit the participating SMEs to get the most out of the China's cross border e-commerce opportunity and but also contribute to the economic development of Australia.

CONCLUSION

By analysing the case of PDD, this study provides insights into the critical factors of a successful e-commerce firm. This study demonstrates that digital ecosystems and innovation have led to the success of PDD. Digital technologies have enabled PDD to develop innovative business model and establish closer and diverse links with partners and customers.

PDD has been particularly successful in business innovation through digital technology. The company creates an innovative business model with a fusion of social and mobile commerce. Compared to other e-commerce sites and apps, which have designed their user-experience around searching for products, PDD has built their user experience based around sharing and interaction between themselves rather than searching for products (Kubala, 2018). PDD's business model innovation lies in its integration of social components into the traditional online shopping process. It appears that PDD's customers enjoy the social approach to shopping.

E-commerce market in China is highly consolidated but PDD is not competing on the same term with the giant companies such as Amazon, Alibaba or JD in China. PDD has been targeting niche market with price sensitive consumers from the lower tier cities in China and older demographics. PDD takes advantage of games and social media such as WeChat and QQ to acquire new customers and identify target user profiles. The case of PDD just proved that start-ups can disrupt the market as long as they are innovating the incumbent's business model and addressing the needs of the targeting customer segments.

The success of PDD platform shows that the importance of digital innovation on both buy and sell sides of supply chain. PDD's competitive advantage is in its innovative C2M and C2F model, which allow it to get rid of layers of distributors and ship directly from the manufacturers or farmers to consumers. These business models not only allow consumers to buy cheaper goods and products but also enable manufacturers to get greater profits. The ecosystem approach is particularly effective for the sale of perishable agricultural products and fresh products because it can provide quick and effective matching of supply and demand (Lee, 2018). PDD's case illustrates that they have developed an open ecosystem to bring more value to customers and drive innovation in the agriculture and manufacturing industry through digital partnering and ecosystems.

This chapter recommends that PDD maintain focus on their business strengths and develop a hybrid business model to address the issues and challenges of PDD moving forward.

PDD achieves high growth through developing ecosystems with digital partnering capabilities, capture value from ecosystems, and create value for all of their partners and users through disruptive digital technology. PDD's business model is not only a social e-commerce platform but also a networked ecosystem. The lessons learnt from the case study can be helpful for companies intending to adopt a platform business model into their business.

REFERENCES

Bughin, J., Catlin, T., & Dietz, M. (2019, May 7). The right digital-platform strategy. *The McKinsey Quarterly*.

Chaffey, D., Hemphill, T., & Edmundson-Bird, D. (2019). *Digital business and e-commerce management* (7th ed.). Pearson Education.

China International Capital Corporation (CICC). (2019). *China E-commerce Industry in 2019*. Retrieved August 2020 from https://research.cicc.com/index

China Potion. (2020). *Breakdown of PDD's business model to overtake Alibaba*. https://www.kidostech.com/post/breakdown-of-PDDs-business

Cusumano, M., Yoffie, D. B., & Gawer, A. (2020). The Future of Platforms. *MIT Sloan Management Review*, *61*(3).

Dawson, R. (2018). *The six elements of platform strategy.* Retrieved from https://rossdawson.com/new-framework-the-six-elements-of-platform-strategy/

Deloitte Access Economics. (2013). *Connected Small Businesses: how Australian small businesses are growing in the digital economy*. Retrieved October 10, 2014 from https://www.deloitteaccesseconomics.com.au/uploads/File/Connected%20Small%20Busin ss.pdf

Falk, S., & Riemensperger, F. (2019, August 5). Three Lessons From Germany's Platform Economy. *MIT Sloan Management Review*. Retrieved November 2021 from https://sloanreview.mit.edu/article/three-lessons-from-germanys-platform-economy/

Fan, Q., & Ouppara, N. (2021). Surviving Disruption and Uncertainty Through Digital Transformation: A Case Study on Small to Medium-Sized Enterprises (SME). In T. Semerádová & P. Weinlich (Eds.), *Moving Businesses Online and Embracing E-Commerce: Impact and Opportunities Caused by COVID-19* (pp. 1–22). IGI Global. doi:10.4018/978-1-7998-8294-7.ch001

Graziani, T. (2017, June 13). WeChat Official Account: A Simple Guide. *WalktheChat*. Retrieved August 2019 from https://walkthechat.com/wechat-official-account-simpleguide/

Graziani, T. (2018). *PDD: A closer look at the Fastest Growing E-commerce App in China*. Retrieved October 10, 2014 from https://www.techinasia.com/talk/PDD-fastest-growing-appchina

Hoch, N. B., & Brad, S. (2021). Managing business model innovation: An innovative approach towards designing a digital ecosystem and multi-sided platform. *Business Process Management Journal*, *27*(2), 415–438. doi:10.1108/BPMJ-01-2020-0017

Kim, J. (2016). The platform business model and business ecosystem: Quality management and revenue structures. *European Planning Studies*, *24*(12), 2113–2132. doi:10.1080/09654313.2016.1251882

Kubala, M. (2019). *China's second biggest e-commerce player: PDD*. Retrieved October 10, 2014 from https://www.drwealth.com/chinas-second-biggest-e-commerce-player-PDD/

Lee, E. (2018, July 26). The Incredible Rise of Pinduoduo, China's Newest Force in E Commerce. *TechCrunch*. Retrieved August 2019 from https://techcrunch.com/2018/07/26/the-incredible-rise-of-pinduoduo/

McKinsey & Company. (2020). *McKinsey COVID-19 US digital Sentiment Survey (April 25-28, 2020).* McKinsey & Company. Retrieved from https://www.mckinsey.com

Nie, W., & Feng, Y. F. (2019, February). PDD: E-Commerce for the Underserved – A Chinese Online Merchant at the Crossroads. *IMD*. Retrieved October 2020 from https://www.imd.org/research-knowledge/articles/pdd-ecommerce-for-the-underserved/

PDD. (2019b, September 30). *PDD Inc. Q3 2019 financial report*. Retrieved March 2021 from https://investor.PDD.com/financial-information/quarterly-results

PDD. (2020a). *PDD Inc. 2019 annual report.* Retrieved March 2021 from https://investor.PDD.com/financial-information/annual-reports

PDD. (2020b, September 30). *PDD Inc. Q3 2020 financial report.* Retrieved March 2021 from https://investor.PDD.com/financial-information/quarterly-results

Pinduoduo (PDD). (2019a, June 28). *PDD Inc. Pinduoduo's "New Brand Initiative" Reshapes Retail Industry by Prioritizing Consumers' Needs.* Retrieved August 2021 from https://investor.pinduoduo.com/node/6831/pdf

PingWest. (2018). *PDD's Factory of Creation.* Retrieved August 2019 from https://www.pingwest.com/a/160720

Wang, K. W., Lau, A., & Gong, F. (2016, April 15). *How savvy social shoppers are transforming Chinese e-commerce.* McKinsey Survey.

Xie, K. Y. (2018) *Uncover the secret of Pinduoduo popularity.* Retrieved July 2019 from http://finance.jrj.com.cn

Yin, R. K. (1994). *Case Study: Design and Methods.* Sage Publications.

Zhao, W., Wang, A. Q., & Chen, Y. (2019, November). How to maintain the sustainable development of a Business Platform: A case study of PDD Social Commerce Platform in China. *Sustainability.* Retrieved August 2020 from https://www.mdpi.com/journal/sustainability

ADDITIONAL READING

Attaran, M. (2020, July). Digital technology enablers and their implications for supply chain management. In Supply Chain Forum. *International Journal (Toronto, Ont.)*, *21*(3), 158–172.

Chan, C. M., Teoh, S. Y., Yeow, A., & Pan, G. (2019). Agility in responding to disruptive digital innovation: Case study of an SME. *Information Systems Journal*, *29*(2), 436–455. doi:10.1111/isj.12215

Giones, F., & Brem, A. (2017). Digital Technology Entrepreneurship: A Definition and Research Agenda. *Technology Innovation Management Review*, *7*(5), 44–51. doi:10.22215/timreview/1076

Xu, Y., Ahokangas, P., Turunen, M., Mäntymäki, M., & Heikkilä, J. (2019). Platform-Based Business Models: Insights from an Emerging AI-Enabled Smart Building Ecosystem. *Electronics (Basel)*, *8*(10), 1150. doi:10.3390/electronics8101150

Zangiacomi, A., Pessot, E., Fornasiero, R., Bertetti, M., & Sacco, M. (2020). Moving towards digitalization: A multiple case study in manufacturing. *Production Planning and Control*, *31*(2-3), 2–3, 143–157. doi:10.1080/09537287.2019.1631468

KEY TERMS AND DEFINITIONS

Digital Ecosystem: A business system that goes beyond digital platform and enables all participants to create and deliver value to their target audience and share value and enjoy benefits from the presence of each other in the system.

Digital Innovation: The applications of digital technology to facilitate existing business processes efficiency, improve customer experience, develop new products and services, or create new business models.

Digital Technology: Any electronic tools, systems, devices, and resources that generate, transmit, store, or process data recorded in binary code of combinations of the digits 0 and 1.

Digital Transformation: The change that occurs when digital technologies are applied to organisational processes, structure, and systems to improve business performance and competitiveness.

E-Commerce: All electronically mediated transactions between business and its stakeholders.

Chapter 9
Exploring the Role of Flow in Augmented Reality for Mobile Retailing:
Implications for Practice and Research

Shuo-Yun Yang
University of Southampton, UK

Vanissa Wanick
University of Southampton, UK

Eirini Bazaki
University of Southampton, UK

YuanYuan Yin
University of Southampton, UK

ABSTRACT

Augmented reality (AR) try-on services have been proven to enhance customer engagement and purchase intentions by enabling users to experience the sense of flow. While few studies focused on the design principles of mobile AR services, little has been done regarding the role of flow in consumer experience whilst interacting with try-on services. This chapter reviews the current design principles of mobile AR and examines its influence in consumer flow state. Through a task-based semi-structured interview with consumers (n=9), it was possible to observe that all participants did not enter the flow state due to lack of perceived control and familiarity with the technology. Finally, this chapter provides recommendations for enhancing the flow experience of mobile AR try-on services. It is expected that this chapter might be of interest to retailers and researchers willing to explore mobile AR effectiveness through try-on-services such as the virtual fitting room (VFR).

DOI: 10.4018/978-1-7998-9179-6.ch009

INTRODUCTION

Digital transformation brings opportunities to develop new business models, by reshaping the way organisations deliver customer value. The ability to integrate different channels is a core strategy that allows consumers to make decisions across several platforms, switching between physical and digital touchpoints (Berman, 2012). Digital transformation also brings new challenges for organisations, such as the alignment of business goals with new strategies (Matt et al., 2015), quick learning capabilities (Mattila, Yrjölä and Hautamäki, 2021), consumer privacy concerns (de Ruyter et al., 2020) and employee adoption (Alavi and Habel, 2021). Thus, it is imperative to learn how the adoption of new technologies can change established business practices and models.

Under the wave of digital transformation, the retailing industry is seeing an impact on its brick-and-mortar physical stores. The traditional stores are being transformed to adapt to digital changes and organisations are modifying the way they interact with customers during the shopping process (Yadav and Pavlou, 2014). The high connectivity and interactivity levels of new technologies can enhance customer's shopping experience (Javornik, 2016). For instance, Lee and Xu (2020) acknowledged that Augmented Reality (AR) has a great potential, minimising the gap between physical and online stores (Beck and Crié, 2016), and enhancing both hedonic and utilitarian consumer values during the shopping experience (Lee and Xu, 2020).

Since AR is becoming each time more mainstream and utilised by different businesses (particularly in retail), there is a need to understand which practices need to be changed or adapted in order to provide consumer and business value. AR has been predicted to provide a vast increment in productivity and efficiency for retailing. For instance, 54% of retailers have planned to implement this technology into their business (Microsoft, 2019). AR combines both real and virtual environments, allowing the user to interact with 3D objects in real-time (Azuma, 1997). AR has the potential to adapt to new consumer needs (Caboni and Hagberg, 2019; Lee and Xu, 2020) since it combines virtual objects with consumer's physical environment through the use of mobile technology. This AR shopping experience provides a more intuitive way for the customer to obtain product information such as product size, colour and fitness and encourages consumers to try the product on by interacting with a product virtually (Cook et al., 2020).

AR applications for retailing could be divided into three types: (i) online web-based applications, (ii) in-store applications and (iii) mobile applications (Caboni and Hagberg, 2019). Mobile AR applications have great potential to increase profits and market share (Lee and Leonas, 2018; Scholz and Duffy, 2018; Caboni and Hagberg, 2019) since it evokes ubiquitous shopping behaviour. One example is the mobile application "IKEA Place'' from the Swedish furniture company IKEA. This application allows users to evaluate where they prefer to place the company's products using their mobile phone and camera (Rese et al., 2014; Lee and Leonas, 2018). Other examples are the accessory brand Ray-Ban and the makeup brand Sephora (Caboni and Hagberg, 2019). Since consumers are shopping more online, interactive mobile AR applications are considered to be a new method for optimising the customer journey (Lee and Leonas, 2018; Scholz and Duffy, 2018; Caboni and Hagberg, 2019).

Although AR shopping has captured the attention of retail researchers and practitioners, there are still two major challenges remaining: (i) technical problems regarding accuracy and calibration (Pachoulakis and Kapetanakis, 2012; Javornik, 2016) and (ii) lack of optimal user experience (Beck and Crié, 2016; Yaoyuneyong et al., 2016; Hilken et al., 2017; Poushneh and Vasquez-parraga, 2017a; Caboni and Hagberg, 2019; Javornik et al., 2019). While research indicates that AR would positively impact customer experience (Wedel et al., 2020;Romano et al., 2020) there is still an opportunity to study AR and its design elements (Chen, 2020). Since flow mediates consumer perception of AR and purchase intentions (Javornik, 2016), there is a need to understand which design elements influence consumers' flow state in AR.

This chapter starts by reviewing the role that AR plays in digital transformation. This is followed by a literature review on customer experience in AR services. AR design elements from leading technology companies like Google, Facebook and Apple are further analysed. Flow theory is subsequently reviewed to gain more detail about how customers perceive AR. This is followed by a task-based semi-structured interview, in which participants were asked to interact with a specific application ("IKEA Place") and asked questions related to flow status and experience. The results showed that although participants were familiar with the technology, there were many challenges related to lack of control and high complexity levels when manipulating 3D objects. The main contributions of this study are the mapping of design elements for mobile AR try-on retailing services and recommendations for further business application (e.g., rely on AR try-on services to enhance hedonic values) and improvement of consumer experience (e.g., through the enhancement of usability elements in the User Interface (UI), adoption of familiar gesture metaphors in the 3D environment, etc.).

BACKGROUND

The Role of AR in Digital Transformation

Digital transformation has four common elements, such as changes in value creation, structural changes, use of technologies (including attitude of the organisation towards new technologies) and financial aspects (Matt, Hess and Benlian, 2015). Particularly in B2B sales, digital transformation has left its mark by forcing organisations to quickly learn and relearn new practices. By identifying the need to unlearn and what needs to be changed, managers need to be aware of new technologies that can facilitate digital selling (Mattila, Yrjölä and Hautamäki, 2021). Since AR overlays reality with digital content, there is a huge opportunity to understand how AR can be effectively integrated within organisational practices. Current AR practices in mobile involve sensors and perceptions towards the environment and interactions (Qiao et al., 2019). With the adoption of 5G, the rendering of these digital layers and the quality of the experience might be improved. As Qiao et al. (2019) mention, upcoming 5G interactions might make current issues such as latency and tracking more effective. AR also provides opportunities for consumers to "see" a product in its context of use (de Ruyter et al., 2020). For example, the "IKEA Place" app allows consumers to visualise the products in their own living room. Thus, a crucial element for AR (particularly applied in advertising) is context mapping (de Ruyter et al., 2020). However, due to its high contextual nature and integration with user data, privacy concerns emerge as an important aspect to be considered when adopting AR applications. Also, since the connections with consumers are now cross-channel, AR becomes another touchpoint that can converge the consumer towards a meaningful experience (Ernst & Young, 2011). Due to its interactive nature, AR can be promising for retailers, particularly for fashion and cosmetics brands to engage with consumers (Watson, Alexander and Salavati, 2018), moving away from the transactional nature of consumer-brand relationship (Scholz and Duffy, 2018).

Customer Experience in AR Service

The term "customer experience" or "consumer experience" (CX) refer to consumer's dynamic reaction of multidimensional, cognitive, emotional, behavioural, sensorial and social responses, while interacting with a product or service, particularly across all phases of the customer journey (Wedel et al., 2020). Since CX involves consumer behavioural and affective reflections during the consumer journey, User Experience (UX) is also part of CX. In this context, UX is about the user interaction with a product or service through a particular User Interface (UI), which can include AR (Irshad and Rambli, 2014). The customer journey is conveyed through the orchestration of several touch points (Kietzmann et al., 2018) and is divided into the pre-purchase, purchase and post-purchase phases (Sands et al., 2016).

During the pre-purchase phase, consumers are influenced by internal and external stimuli (Pine and Gilmore, 2011); the former is derived from individuals, which includes purchase and involvement (Puccinelli et al., 2009) and the latter comes from environmental factors such as design elements and technology (Jain and Bagdare, 2009). The key element in the purchase stage is consumer decision making (Wedel et al., 2020). When consumers pay more attention to the product features, it contributes to product choice (Garaus & Wagner, 2016). Due to that, consumers learn more about the product and that raises their confidence (Romano et al., 2021, Wedel et al., 2020). Consumers could also decide to complain about the product, which can influence negative behaviour such as product return or negative WOM (Wedel et al., 2020).

AR allows consumers to try products virtually, which narrows down the consumer choice (Wedel et al., 2020). During the pre-purchase stage the main factors of consumer experience are recognition, consideration and search (Lemon & Verhof, 2016). AR helps consumers to browse, try and find suitable products. After trying the product, consumers can decide. AR plays a crucial role in outfit curation (Wedel et al., 2020), providing real-time visual representations that can be easily changed. Outfit curation has a similar role to the salesperson in the physical store. Since AR plays a similar function, it enhances the shopping experience (Bazaki and Wanick, 2019). Subsequently, hedonic value is delivered through AR try-on interactions. Consumers can have a playful experience during the purchase stage (Wedel et al., 2020). However, in the post-purchase stage, there might be some discrepancy between the "virtual" and the actual product. This means that consumers' utilitarian value is not always satisfied (Wedel et al., 2020).

User Experience (UX) in Mobile AR

AR services aim at enhancing customer experience through customer value (Chen, 2020). Hedonic and utilitarian (Olsson and Salo, 2011; Poncin and Mimoun, 2014; Rese et al., 2014; Dacko, 2017; Hilken et al., 2017; Yim et al., 2017) values positively impact the process when people experience AR.

Research is relatively vast in AR and User Interface (UI). Most UI design guidelines focus on usability and tangible UI principles (Dünser et al., 2007; Kim et al., 2017). Yet, specific solutions are not explored. Providing an easy and intuitive interface is the main target of academic and business areas. For instance, Apple (2020) proposed hiding some unnecessary UI design when guiding users through AR systems. Also, keeping screen space to a minimum could enhance users' perceived ease of use. However, onboarding and instruction features should be included in order to immerse users to the AR experience.

From the perspective of hedonic values, Chen (2020) found that AR can provide enjoyment and playful experiences to consumers. Javornik (2016) concluded that AR provides more hedonic values than utilitarian ones. The same point was pointed out by Guo (2013), who emphasised that hedonic values enhanced by UX are a great *stimulus* for people to feel entertained during the process. For instance, offscreen exploration and sensory feedback, such as audio or haptic design, can enhance the consumer experience.

In order to follow industrial standards, AR design guidelines from leading technology companies such as Apple, Google and Facebook/Meta were used to capture key design elements. These include the design guidelines from ARCore (Google, 2020), ARKit (Apple, 2020) and SparkAR (Facebook, 2020). The main elements contain components from both physical and virtual worlds. For example, the user's space is crucial since it determines where the object should be placed and how the interactions happen (Facebook, 2020).

Users who install AR applications in their devices are curious (Olsson and Salo, 2011). Olsson (2012) indicated that users want to see the content embedded with real-world objects. This implies that the object should include real-world information, providing utilitarian values for the user and further impacting consumer purchase intention (Olsson and Salo, 2011; Olsson et al., 2013; Dacko, 2017; Yim et al., 2017). Google listed texture, modelling, shadows, lighting, and depth as design elements that help users perceive the object's density.

In order to place the 3D object into the physical environment, AR systems request the user to detect a plane where the object would be placed. Typically, the system provides an instruction to guide the user to place the virtual plane in a particular position in the physical world. In this case, ARCore, ARKit and SparkAR considered providing visual instructions to guide the user more intuitively. This stage includes selection, translation, rotation, scaling gesture and proximity (Google, 2020).

Gesture is considered the most crucial element during the manipulation stage since the user uses familiar gestures to interact with the AR experiences (Apple, 2020). Users' familiar gestures can come from smartphone habits, based on 2-dimensional (2D) surfaces.

Flow Theory and Its Development

Flow is "a state in which an individual is completely immersed in an activity without reflective self-consciousness but with a deep sense of control." (Engeser and Schiepe- Tiska, 2012, p.1). The state of flow occurs when two conditions are met: (i) an individual would engage with a challenge at the appropriate level when their capacities are matched; and (ii) an individual has clear goals and receives feedback immediately regarding the progress they make (Nakamura and Csikszentmihalyi 2014). These conditions are mediated by seven components: action awareness, attention, loss of self-consciousness, feeling of control, clear and logically ordered actions, goal and feedback, autotelic experience (i.e. when an individual is motivated to progress or explore more automatically) and temporal distortion (i.e. when an individual has a sense that time passes faster than usual) (Csikszentmihalyi,1975; Nakamura and Csikszentmihalyi, 2014).

Flow has been acknowledged to play an essential role in web e-commerce (Hoffman and Novak, 2009; Carlson and O'Cass, 2011; van Noort et al., 2012). Online shopping can be a great space to achieve the flow state since online customer behaviour is usually grounded in goal-directed and non-directed motivation (Hoffman and Novak 2009). There is a relationship between AR and flow experience that requires attention. Javornik, (2016) found that the way people perceive AR technologies impacts the user's flow state and purchase intentions associated with affective and cognitive responses. The study from Javornik (2016) and Parise et al. (2016), for instance, also acknowledged that flow is a factor that mediates AR services.

MAIN FOCUS OF THE CHAPTER

From our initial literature review, we have identified that AR services can positively impact customer experience and evoke both utilitarian and hedonic consumer values. However, the lack of optimal user experience is the main reason why people cannot immerse themselves in this new service, which may result in a negative experience. Therefore, this chapter addresses two main research questions:

- **RQ1:** Does the mobile AR service trigger the user to engage in the flow status?
- **RQ2:** What kinds of design elements in mobile AR service would influence a user's flow status?

Although people perceive AR as essential to understanding the user's experience, literature on this field is scant. Hence, this research aims at providing suggestions for businesses that plan to adopt AR as a digital transformation strategy to enhance the customer experience in the retail industry. Consequently, the research objectives for this paper are: (i) To understand which current mobile AR design elements would positively influence people to engage in flow status, and (ii) to explore what design elements would affect the user's flow status while interacting with AR mobile try-on retail services.

Research Design

This study adopts a qualitative approach via an in-depth case study of an existing app and semi-structured interviews through a task-based activity. Seifert and Hedderson (2010) argued that interviews could provide a more vivid interpretation of flow experience perceptions. Semi-structured interviews are often used in earlier research for examining flow experiences (Nakamura and Csikszentmihalyi 2014). Also, quantitative methods such as self-reporting questionnaires can be efficient to measure flow. Guo and Poole (2009) developed and tested a scale focused on the holistic aspect of online-based activities. They identified the measure properties for the online shopping activity and portrayed 28 questions from eight flow characteristics.

For the purpose of our study we have utilised the flow characteristics from Guo and Poole's scale (2009) since they have been developed around online shopping experiences. These characteristics were used as criteria for reviewing the design elements of a popular existing app ("IKEA Place") and categorising the findings from the semi-structured interviews. Figure 1 shows the integration of the flow characteristics from Guo and Poole's (2009) questionnaire with the key points from the design guidelines.

Figure 1. Research design

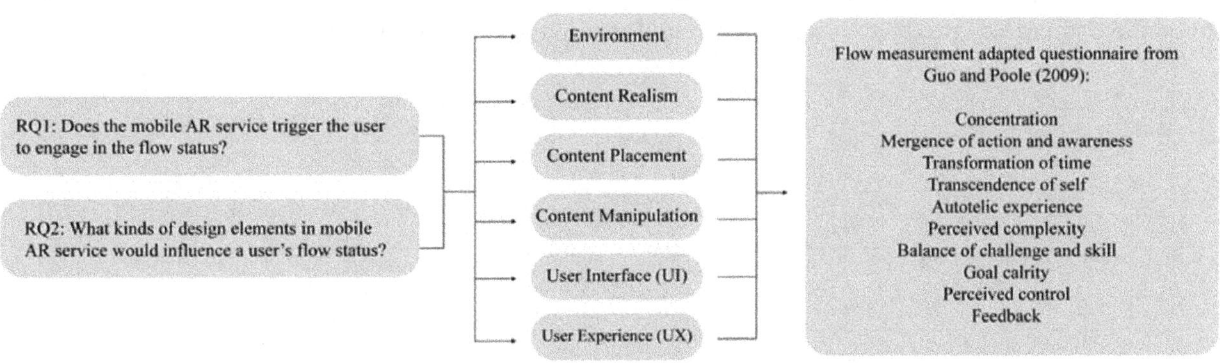

The design guidelines have been categorised into six main elements, emerged from our initial literature review (see Figure 1):

- Environment;
- Content Realism;
- Content Placement;
- Content Manipulation;
- User Interface (UI);
- User Experience (UX) (including users' expectations, needs, desires towards the type of interaction presented)

Sampling Strategy and Research Process

Digital natives (e.g., Millennials and Generation Z consumers) tend to be more favourable towards cutting-edge services such as AR technologies (Microsoft, 2019). Since this is an exploratory study, a sample size of 5-7 participants should be sufficient to indicate if a problem exists in a product (Nielsen, 2000). Considering this, a convenient sample strategy was utilised and the criteria for the participant selection was based on age (e.g., 22-36 years old).

The next step was the selection of a mobile AR application. Previous studies discussed the app "IKEA Place", which portrays a decent prospect since its first version in 2014 (Huang and Liao, 2015; Scholz and Smith, 2016; Javornik et al., 2016; Caboni and Hagberg, 2019; Davidavičienė et al., 2019; Heller et al., 2019; Alves and Luís Reis, 2020; Ozturkcan, 2021). Since this app attracted attention in both academic and business areas, this study utilises "IKEA Place" as a case study.

Figure 2. The research process of this study

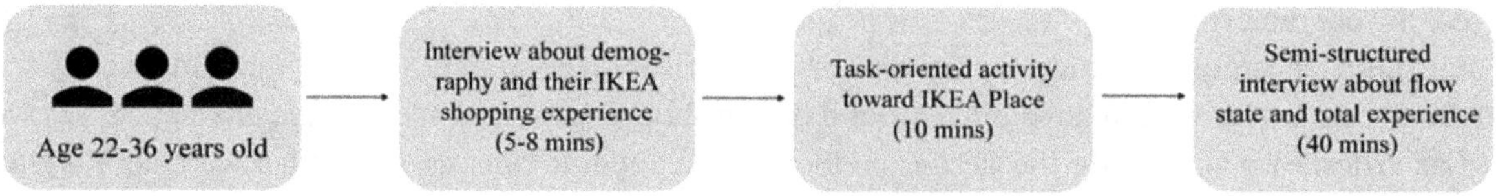

Since flow experience occurs the application's challenge meets the user's skills, we assigned a task for participants. In the first stage of the interview, participants were asked about their shopping experience in IKEA (e.g., frequency of going to IKEA and what kinds of products they usually buy). After overviewing the function and the products that "IKEA Place" offers, the speaker (Figure 3) was selected to be the compulsory product participants should manipulate during the interview.

Figure 3. Compulsory product selection during the task
(IKEA, 2020; screenshot by the authors)

After the task, we conducted a semi-structured interview through a set of predefined questions. Finally, a thematic analysis was utilised by grouping information through codes derived from Guo and Poole's list of preconditions of flow experiences.

Issues, Controversies, Problems

In total, 9 participants (aged 22-36 years, 3 male, 6 female, living in the UK) took part in the study. Most of the participants worked in retail. The results showed that perceptions about being negatively under control and high complexity levels occurred after participants manipulated the 3D object using the app. The most reported issue was the difficulty to control two objects that were closely placed. The second issue was object scale and rotation. This implies that proximity and gesture issues influenced perceived control and perceived complexity. The lack of feedback reported by participants was also related to perceived control and complexity, since the app did not provide sufficient instruction or messages to guide participants. In the next subsections we highlight the issues, controversies and problems according to each design element.

Issue in Environment Design Element

In order to understand the influence of AR in the physical space, we have categorised the *environment design element* into two sub-codes: virtual and physical. 3 participants mentioned that the "Room Set" function from the app was not suitable to preview one specific product in the physical environment.

Another issue discovered was the product size unreliability. Due to that, participants lost trust and motivation to continue using the app. A participant noticed that the virtual object size was not in a 1-to-1 scale in comparison with a physical object (e.g., a fan) (see Figure 4).

Figure 4. Putting virtual object into physical world (screenshot by the participants)

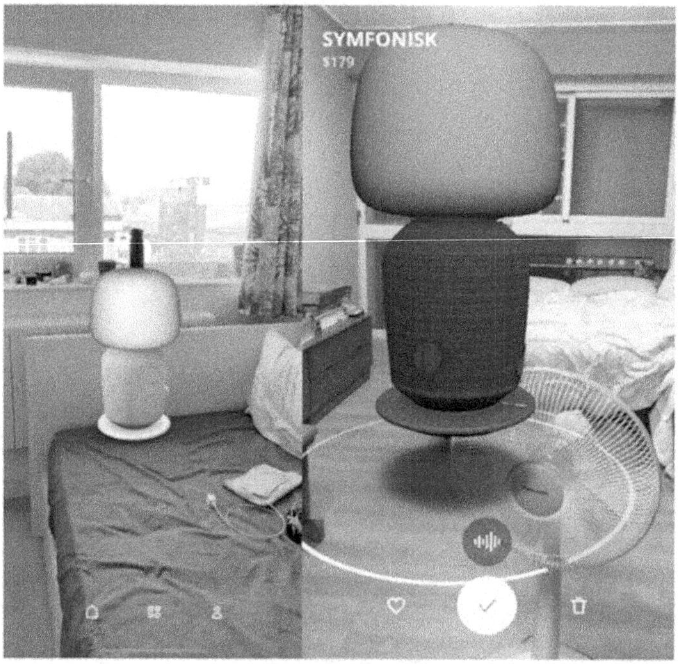

Issue in Content Realism Design Element

Modelling and content detail are the sub-codes for the *content realism design element*. When negative experiences occurred during the autotelic experience, participants reported that the virtual product was out of control. The same issue occurred in the environment design element. The 3D object size was unreliable. Another issue was the lack of product information such as texture, shadows and lighting since participants found it hard to judge the product information only by the virtual features.

Issue in Content Placement Design Element

Before placing a virtual object, the system had to calibrate and detect the space in the physical world. In "IKEA Place", this is done through plane detection (see Figure 5). In the app, a short animation is played and the user needs to follow it to achieve correct detection. Due to that, the sub-codes of *content placement* are *plane detection* and *optimal placement*.

Figure 5. Plane detection in "IKEA Place" (screenshot by the authors)

Participants reported flow issues during the plane detection stage. They reported that they did not understand the instructions and detection points. Since participants were not familiar with this process, the instructions did not guide them effectively.

Another issue occurred when participants saw objects "floating in the air" (see Figure 6). This was caused by a failure of the system during the plane detection stage. This impacted the sense of realism and object size reliability.

Figure 6. Virtual objects placed in the wrong position due to flawed plane detection (screenshot by the participants)

Issue in Content Manipulation Design Element

The sub-codes utilised for *content manipulation* are *content selection and proximity*, *content scaling and translation* and *gesture*; these sub-codes are based on Apple (2020), Google (2020) and Facebook/ Meta (2020) design guidelines.

The design element that addresses *gesture* was widely reported as participants utilised familiar 2D gestures in the 3D environment. This happened particularly when participants wanted to enlarge the object, by using two fingers to enlarge it. However, scaling products in "IKEA Place" is not allowed since each furniture has a fixed size. Since gesture issues occurred when people scaled and rotated the object, this provided an unbalance of skills and challenge as it did not work as expected. Another issue was proximity when participants selected two closed objects and it was hard to select only one.

Issue in User Experience Design Element

User experience (UX) includes user perception and responses (ISO, 2018) that occurs before, during and after user interaction. Hence, *offscreen exploration* and *total experience description* are the sub-codes for the *UX design element*; the former focuses on the user's behaviours such as their emotion, and the latter focuses on the whole shopping process.

Participants stated that "IKEA Place" did not assist them to know more details about product information; thus, they would not only rely on "IKEA Place" for purchasing goods online. Participants considered the app more suitable for hedonic values rather than utilitarian ones. As a result, participants would not explore the app's functions since it will not assist their practical needs. The app only gave them the ability to preview "what product will be suitable a space" by trying several furniture rather than "how would the product fit in this space" by product size and its materials. Participants also reported that the current app version showed only a corner rather than a wider view of space such as the view of the whole kitchen or room. By contrast, participants acknowledged that "IKEA Place" concretised their imagination about the space and provided a visual reference in the planning process.

Issue in User Interface (UI) Design Element

The sub-code references in *User Interface (UI)* design elements are *condition*, *error*, *onboarding and instruction*, and *browsing product*. All participants reported that finding a product was hard. The logic for classification was complicated and participants mentioned that they needed to browse several times to understand the product category. Since this research asked participants to find the speaker as a product, the product (speaker) could only be found in a particular collection (audio), which is named as "SYMFONISK" (a Swedish name). When participants looked for the product, they ignored the audio collection due to unfamiliarity with the Swedish name. There was one similar category called "TV & Media furniture", but the speaker did not belong to it, which made participants feel confused.

The other issue reported when looking for products was the cover image. Participants mentioned that the cover image for a collection named SÖDERHAMN (see Figure 7) showed carpet, cushion and sofa, but there were only sofas in this category. This issue shows how important that cover image is in order to provide guidance for users to find the product efficiently.

Figure 7. Cover image and product browsing (screenshot by the participants)

Secondly, participants also mentioned that the icons in the app did not provide enough user guidance. This happened after a system error. When participants had to go back to the app, they found all the products they have interacted previously were gone.

SOLUTIONS AND RECOMMENDATIONS

Although it is suggested that online environments can enable flow experiences due to their high level of interactivity and the type of activity (shopping) (Hoffman and Novak 2009), the same did not happen in mobile AR try-on services. In this study, participants reported usability issues that influenced the goal-oriented behaviour of buying goods online. In fact, this study reinforced the idea that mobile AR try-on applications can enhance hedonic and experiential behaviours, but the actual purchase might not happen.

As RQ1 enquired whether participants would engage in the flow experience, the results show that the majority of participants did not enter into a "flow" state. It is possible that there was a peak of concentration at the beginning of the task, but after encountering many issues regarding perceived control and complexity with the app, participants lost their motivation and goal. Our finding explains that standards and design guidelines that AR services play should be discussed first, since it is suggested that hedonic and utilitarian values are hard to co-exist when usability issues exist. The main reason for that was due to inaccuracy, as participants could not ensure that the virtual product size was the same as the physical product. Participants reported they would not rely only on AR before buying the product. This has a significant impact on businesses looking at having AR try-on services as a digital touchpoint. Since there could be a risk that experiences like these could evoke negative feelings due to usability issues, it is crucial that businesses invest time and resources in user experience design. This chapter suggests that the design elements proposed in Figure 1 (environment, content realism, content placement, content manipulation, UI and UX) should be followed and embedded in try-on AR mobile services.

On the other hand, there was a positive relationship between the experience in AR try-on services and hedonic values due to its interactivity, as AR can be seen as playful and entertaining. However, this interactivity and object manipulation might not be enough to convey engaging user experiences. For instance, participants utilised the mental model from the 2D mobile environment when interacting with 3D in the AR environment, which resulted in disappointment.

The findings revealed that proximity and gesture influenced the sense of perceived complexity as participants found that the app was hard to control. The two design issues identified were: (i) UI elements related to product categories and user instruction and; (ii) problems in the content placement when participants did not understand the visual guidance and failed to calibrate the app via the plane detection process.

Another aspect that could be improved is product browsing. Our findings suggest mobile AR try-on services should provide an option to browse for a specific product at a time. Product classification was also problematic product discoverability. The cover image should also reflect the information that symbolises the product category to facilitate product browsing; this image should be familiar to the user. Another point for improvement is the familiarity with icon design. Icon and instruction design should be based on the user's online experience to reduce cognitive load. Users should be able to quickly recover from error and be rewarded by their progress.

Since the findings show that the floating placement and unreal product scale result from unsuccessful plane detection, the app must have an excellent initial and intuitive calibration. For that, the design of the instructions should be clear for users.

If considering the five layers of UX (surface, skeleton, structure, scope and strategy) proposed by Garrett (2010), we have addressed surface, skeleton and structure, which are usually related to visual design. In our study, participants had issues with plane detection, which is a function that reflects the app UI. Since UX entails more layers (e.g., user needs, product objectives, content requirements and functional specifications), the whole user journey needs to be clarified. The findings also revealed that the information architecture in the AR service should be designed based on the user's interactive experience in 2D environments. Thus, it is suggested that the role AR services play in the whole experience should be identified from the beginning (e.g., from user needs and product objectives) as a tool for customers to obtain practical help and enhance the brand image.

Our finding indicated that the current AR services have problematic issues that can influence all aspects of the consumer journey. Since participants reported the AR app did not make them purchase the product straightaway, it is suggested that whole customer journey should be reviewed since there is a lack of connection between the pre-purchase and purchase phases. Thus, companies should develop a holistic customer journey to link all stages of the consumer journey by merging the online touchpoint with the offline touchpoint (physical store) to achieve omnichannel experiences (Lee and Leonas, 2018).

FUTURE RESEARCH DIRECTIONS

Managerial Implications

If considering all customer journey stages (e.g., pre-purchase, purchase and post-purchase) (Lemon and Verhoef, 2016), AR services can be highly utilised in the pre-purchase phase, providing a platform for users to browse and try products. According to our research, the app "IKEA Place" was difficult to use due to 3D object flaws and usability problems. This can affect the customer journey since it might influence the pre-purchase stage, stopping users from entering the purchase and post-purchase phases.

Since this problem was exposed, other questions emerged: How can businesses optimise the user experience of AR services? What is the value that AR services might bring to businesses? Managers should account for issues AR services might bring, especially when consumers browse and try virtual products online. For example, in the browsing stage, AR services can be improved by providing more effective product classifications that users can understand. Other enhancements should include making the 3D object manipulation easier to understand and addressing technical aspects such as the plane detection process. If the AR try-on service is a tool that aims at helping customers, businesses need to address these problems first.

The majority of the participants mentioned that the idea of using AR try-on services is promising, but it can be useless to make a final product purchase. Participants did not know whether they needed to buy the product online or in the physical store while using "IKEA Place". This suggests that just the use of AR might not be enough to motivate customers to purchase a product. Based on this, organisations need to express their values and goals first and then extend this to the purchase stage. This shows that the customer experience in mobile AR try-on services has flaws and that each touchpoint needs to be more connected.

Theoretical Implications

Our study reviewed the features of AR try-on services, which includes surface elements such as UI and product contents. The issues identified in each of these elements provided insights about what strategies AR try-on services should have in order improve the customer experience. However, if considering Garrett's (2010) UX layers, AR try-on services lack strategy and scope. This means that businesses willing to utilise this type of technology should include AR services within the business model. Thus, businesses should define the AR service's scope first and do more research on what strategy it represents.

Another implication is the alignment of consumer behaviour needs with the type of interactions the AR try-on services provide. Our study showed that the browsing process needs to be easy and quick since consumers would not use AR try-on retailing services just for entertainment. Thus, consumer's values need balance both hedonic and utilitarian consumer needs.

Our research indicated that AR services can have non-addressed usability issues. When a product is represented in the 3D world, users can feel disappointed when there is a lack of visual precision. Since users are more familiar with 2D digital environment gestures and manipulations, future research could study the process when the users manipulate devices in 2D and apply them into 3D to decrease cognitive overload.

Businesses should also provide an aligned strategy. AR try-on services should offer design features that reflect the business model and consumer expectations. For instance, in our study participants mentioned they would not utilise "IKEA Place" before buying an IKEA product due to usability and lack of product information (e.g., texture and size). Those factors blocked the customer journey and prevented the business to build an effective omnichannel strategy. Thus, future research should look at the factors that businesses need to address in order to orchestrate the touchpoints influenced by AR try-on services.

CONCLUSION

This chapter revealed users' issues while manipulating AR try-on services through the lens of the flow theory. By doing so, the elements "perceived complexity" and "control" emerged as primary concerns. Our findings indicated that participants were not familiar with the mobile 3D environment due to UI and content placement problems. As a result, participants felt disappointed since they felt lost in the AR service. Based on that, we suggest that businesses define the core value they want to express by AR try-on services beforehand. Flavián et al. (2019) also mentioned that managers should define the AR design features first, in order to make the consumer journey more seamless, connecting both online and offline channels. Since Hilken et al. (2021) found that AR would positively impact purchase intentions, future research should look at improving problems found in UI and content placement in order to optimise positive feedback and purchase intention. AR technology is expected to flourish when 5G contributes to ease its technical problem. With huge business investments in AR and Virtual Reality (VR) technologies, boosted by 2021's Facebook/Meta (2021) announcements concerning the metaverse, it is imperative that organisations understand the value that such technologies can bring. Although there is a trend in the market, many challenges still remain.

Limitations

This study was conducted during the pandemic of COVID-19 through an online-based research that requested participants to use the app remotely. This may result in the quality of observation when participants interacted with the "IKEA Place" app. Also, the quality of the experience could have been affected by network issues and potentially unsupported devices. For instance, the number of participants recruited was impacted as some of them did not have the required hardware. Hence, our future research would recruit more participants and add observation notes for bringing more insights into this topic.

ACKNOWLEDGMENT

This research received no specific grant from any funding agency in the public, commercial, or not-for-profit sectors.

REFERENCES

Alavi, S., & Habel, J. (2021). The human side of digital transformation in sales: Review & future paths. *Journal of Personal Selling & Sales Management*, *41*(2), 83–86. doi:10.1080/08853134.2021.1920969

Alves, C., & Reis, J. L. (2020, February). The Intention to Use E-Commerce Using Augmented Reality-The Case of IKEA Place. In *International Conference on Information Technology & Systems* (pp. 114-123). Springer. 10.1007/978-3-030-40690-5_12

Apple Inc. (2020). *Augmented Reality-System Capabilities-IOS-Human Interface Guidelines - Apple Developer.* https://developer.apple.com/design/human-interface-guidelines/ios/system-capabilities/augmented-reality/

Azuma, R. T. (1997). A survey of augmented reality. *Presence (Cambridge, Mass.)*, *6*(4), 355–385. doi:10.1162/pres.1997.6.4.355

Bazaki, E., & Wanick, V. (2019). *Unlocking the potential of the salesperson in the virtual fitting room: Enhancing the online retail experience for fashion brands*. Academic Press.

Beck, M., & Crié, D. (2018). I virtually try it… I want it! Virtual Fitting Room: A tool to increase on-line and off-line exploratory behavior, patronage and purchase intentions. *Journal of Retailing and Consumer Services*, *40*, 279–286. doi:10.1016/j.jretconser.2016.08.006

Berman, S. J. (2012). Digital transformation: Opportunities to create new business models. *Strategy and Leadership*, *40*(2), 16–24. doi:10.1108/10878571211209314

Caboni, F., & Hagberg, J. (2019). Augmented reality in retailing: A review of features, applications and value. *International Journal of Retail & Distribution Management*, *47*(11), 1125–1140. doi:10.1108/IJRDM-12-2018-0263

Carlson, J., & O'Cass, A. (2011). Creating commercially compelling website-service encounters: An examination of the effect of website-service interface performance components on flow experiences. *Electronic Markets*, *21*(4), 237–253. doi:10.100712525-011-0073-z

Chen, R. (2020). *The Role of Augmented Reality in Retail Settings: A Systematic Literature Review and Research Agenda* (Doctoral dissertation). The University of Manchester.

Cook, A. V. (2020). *Augmented shopping : the quiet revolution.* Deloitte. https://www2.deloitte.com/content/dam/insights/us/articles/6367_Augmented-shopping/DI_Augmented-shopping.pdf

Csikzentimihalyi, M. (1975). Beyond boredom and anxiety: Experiencing flow in work and play. Academic Press.

Dacko, S. G. (2017). Enabling smart retail settings via mobile augmented reality shopping apps. *Technological Forecasting and Social Change*, *124*, 243–256. doi:10.1016/j.techfore.2016.09.032

Davidavičienė, V., Raudeliūnienė, J., & Viršilaitė, R. (2019). User experience evaluation and creativity stimulation with augmented reality mobile applications. *Creativity Studies, 12*(1), 34-48.

de Ruyter, K., Heller, J., Hilken, T., Chylinski, M., Keeling, D. I., & Mahr, D. (2020). Seeing with the Customer's Eye: Exploring the Challenges and Opportunities of AR Advertising. *Journal of Advertising*, *49*(2), 109–124. doi:10.1080/00913367.2020.1740123

Dünser, A., Grasset, R., Seichter, H., & Billinghurst, M. (2007, March). *Applying HCI principles to AR systems design* [Conference contribution]. MRUI'07: 2nd International Workshop at the IEEE Virtual Reality 2007 Conference, Christchurch, New Zealand.

Engeser, S., & Schiepe-Tiska, A. (2012). Historical lines and an overview of current research on flow. In Advances in flow research (pp. 1-22). Springer Publishing. doi:10.1007/978-1-4614-2359-1_1

Ernst & Young. (2011) *The digitisation of everything*. Available at: https://www.ey.com/Publication/vwLUAssets/The_digitisation_of_everything_-_How_organisations_must_adapt_to_changing_consumer_behaviour/%24file/EY_Digitisation_of_everything.pdf

Facebook. (2020). *Introducing The Spark AR Design Guidelines.* https://sparkar.facebook.com/blog/introducing-spark-ar-design-guidelines/

Facebook. (2021). *Connect 2021: Our vision for the metaverse.* Retrieved 28 November 2021, from https://tech.fb.com/connect-2021-our-vision-for-the-metaverse/

Garaus, M., & Wagner, U. (2016). Retail shopper confusion: Conceptualization, scale development, and consequences. *Journal of Business Research, 69*(9), 3459–3467. doi:10.1016/j.jbusres.2016.01.040

Garrett, J. J. (2010). *The elements of user experience: user-centered design for the web and beyond.* Pearson Education.

Google. (2020). *Augmented Reality Design Guidelines.* https://designguidelines.withgoogle.com/ar-design/augmented-reality-design-guidelines/introduction.html

Guo, F. (2013). *More Than Usability: The Four Elements Of User Experience, Part IV, UX matters.* https://www.uxmatters.com/mt/archives/2013/11/more-than-usability-the-four-elements-of-user-experience-part-iv.php

Guo, Y. M., & Poole, M. S. (2009). Antecedents of flow in online shopping: A test of alternative models. *Information Systems Journal, 19*(4), 369–390. doi:10.1111/j.1365-2575.2007.00292.x

Heller, J., Chylinski, M., de Ruyter, K., Mahr, D., & Keeling, D. I. (2019). Touching the untouchable: Exploring multi-sensory augmented reality in the context of online retailing. *Journal of Retailing, 95*(4), 219–234. doi:10.1016/j.jretai.2019.10.008

Hilken, T., Chylinski, M., Keeling, D. I., Heller, J., de Ruyter, K., & Mahr, D. (2021). How to strategically choose or combine augmented and virtual reality for improved online experiential retailing. *Psychology and Marketing*, 1–35.

Hilken, T., de Ruyter, K., Chylinski, M., Mahr, D., & Keeling, D. I. (2017). Augmenting the eye of the beholder: Exploring the strategic potential of augmented reality to enhance online service experiences. *Journal of the Academy of Marketing Science, 45*(6), 884–905. doi:10.100711747-017-0541-x

Hoffman, D. L., & Novak, T. P. (2009). Flow online: Lessons learned and future prospects. *Journal of Interactive Marketing, 23*(1), 23–34. doi:10.1016/j.intmar.2008.10.003

Huang, T. L., & Liao, S. (2015). A model of acceptance of augmented-reality interactive technology: The moderating role of cognitive innovativeness. *Electronic Commerce Research, 15*(2), 269–295. doi:10.100710660-014-9163-2

International Organization for Standardization. (2010). *Ergonomics of human-system interaction — Part 210: Human-centred design for interactive systems* (ISO/DIS Standard No. 9241-210). Retrieved from: https://www.iso.org/obp/ui/#iso:std:iso:9241:-210:ed-1:v1:en

Irshad, S., & Rambli, D. R. B. A. (2014, September). User experience of mobile augmented reality: A review of studies. In *2014 3rd international conference on user science and engineering (i-USEr)* (pp. 125-130). IEEE. 10.1109/IUSER.2014.7002689

Jain, R., & Bagdare, S. (2009). Determinants of customer experience in new format retail stores. *Journal of Marketing Communications, 5*(2).

Javornik, A. (2016). 'It's an illusion, but it looks real!'Consumer affective, cognitive and behavioural responses to augmented reality applications. *Journal of Marketing Management, 32*(9-10), 987–1011. doi:10.1080/0267257X.2016.1174726

Javornik, A., Kostopoulou, E., Rogers, Y., Fatah gen Schieck, A., Koutsolampros, P., Maria Moutinho, A., & Julier, S. (2019). An experimental study on the role of augmented reality content type in an outdoor site exploration. *Behaviour & Information Technology, 38*(1), 9–27. doi:10.1080/0144929X.2018.1505950

Kietzmann, J., Paschen, J., & Treen, E. (2018). Artificial intelligence in advertising: How marketers can leverage artificial intelligence along the consumer journey. *Journal of Advertising Research, 58*(3), 263–267. doi:10.2501/JAR-2018-035

Kim, H. Y., Lee, J. Y., Mun, J. M., & Johnson, K. K. (2017). Consumer adoption of smart in-store technology: Assessing the predictive value of attitude versus beliefs in the technology acceptance model. *International Journal of Fashion Design. Technology and Education, 10*(1), 26–36.

Lee, H., & Leonas, K. (2018). Consumer experiences, the key to survive in an omni-channel environment: use of virtual technology. *Journal of Textile and Apparel, Technology and Management, 10*(3).

Lee, H., & Xu, Y. (2020). Classification of virtual fitting room technologies in the fashion industry: from the perspective of consumer experience. *International Journal of Fashion Design, Technology and Education, 13*(1), 1-10.

Lemon, K. N., & Verhoef, P. C. (2016). Understanding customer experience throughout the customer journey. *Journal of Marketing, 80*(6), 69–96. doi:10.1509/jm.15.0420

Matt, C., Hess, T., & Benlian, A. (2015). Digital Transformation Strategies. *Business & Information Systems Engineering, 57*(5), 339–343. Advance online publication. doi:10.100712599-015-0401-5

Mattila, M., Yrjölä, M., & Hautamäki, P. (2021). Digital transformation of business-to-business sales: What needs to be unlearned? *Journal of Personal Selling & Sales Management, 41*(2), 113–129. doi:10.1080/08853134.2021.1916396

Microsoft Corporation. (2019). *Retail trends report, 2019 Retail Trends Report.* https://info.microsoft.com/rs/157-GQE-382/images/2019%20Retail%20Trends%20Report.pdf

Nakamura, J., & Csikszentmihalyi, M. (2014). The concept of flow. In Flow and the foundations of positive psychology (pp. 239-263). Springer Publishing. doi:10.1007/978-94-017-9088-8_16

Nielsen, J. (2000). *Why You Only Need to Test with 5 Users, NN/g Nielsen Norman Group.* https://www.nngroup.com/articles/why-you-only-need-to-test-with-5-users/

Olsson, T. (2012). *User expectations and experiences of mobile augmented reality services* (Doctoral dissertation). Tampere University of Technology.

Olsson, T., Lagerstam, E., Kärkkäinen, T., & Väänänen-Vainio-Mattila, K. (2013). Expected user experience of mobile augmented reality services: A user study in the context of shopping centres. *Personal and Ubiquitous Computing*, *17*(2), 287–304. doi:10.100700779-011-0494-x

Olsson, T., & Salo, M. (2011, October). Online user survey on current mobile augmented reality applications. In *2011 10th IEEE International Symposium on Mixed and Augmented Reality* (pp. 75-84). IEEE. 10.1109/ISMAR.2011.6092372

Ozturkcan, S. (2021). Service innovation: Using augmented reality in the IKEA Place app. *Journal of Information Technology Teaching Cases*, *11*(1), 8–13. doi:10.1177/2043886920947110

Pachoulakis, I., & Kapetanakis, K. (2012). Augmented reality platforms for virtual fitting rooms. *The International Journal of Multimedia & Its Applications*, *4*(4), 35–46. doi:10.5121/ijma.2012.4404

Parise, S., Guinan, P. J., & Kafka, R. (2016). Solving the crisis of immediacy: How digital technology can transform the customer experience. *Business Horizons*, *59*(4), 411–420. doi:10.1016/j.bushor.2016.03.004

Pine, B. J., & Gilmore, J. H. (2011). *The experience economy*. Harvard Business Press.

Poncin, I., & Mimoun, M. S. B. (2014). The impact of "e-atmospherics" on physical stores. *Journal of Retailing and Consumer Services*, *21*(5), 851–859. doi:10.1016/j.jretconser.2014.02.013

Poushneh, A., & Vasquez-Parraga, A. Z. (2017a). Customer dissatisfaction and satisfaction with augmented reality in shopping and entertainment. *Journal of Consumer Satisfaction, Dissatisfaction & Complaining Behavior*, 30.

Puccinelli, N. M., Goodstein, R. C., Grewal, D., Price, R., Raghubir, P., & Stewart, D. (2009). Customer experience management in retailing: Understanding the buying process. *Journal of Retailing*, *85*(1), 15–30. doi:10.1016/j.jretai.2008.11.003

Qiao, X., Ren, P., Dustdar, S., Liu, L., Ma, H., & Chen, J. (2019). Web AR: A Promising Future for Mobile Augmented Reality-State of the Art, Challenges, and Insights. *Proceedings of the IEEE*, *107*(4), 651–666. doi:10.1109/JPROC.2019.2895105

Reinartz, W., Wiegand, N., & Imschloss, M. (2019). The impact of digital transformation on the retailing value chain. *International Journal of Research in Marketing*, *36*(3), 350–366. doi:10.1016/j.ijresmar.2018.12.002

Rese, A., Schreiber, S., & Baier, D. (2014). Technology acceptance modeling of augmented reality at the point of sale: Can surveys be replaced by an analysis of online reviews? *Journal of Retailing and Consumer Services*, *21*(5), 869–876. doi:10.1016/j.jretconser.2014.02.011

Romano, B., Sands, S., & Pallant, J. I. (2021). Augmented reality and the customer journey: An exploratory study. *Australasian Marketing Journal*, *29*(4), 354–363. doi:10.1016/j.ausmj.2020.06.010

Sands, S., Ferraro, C., Campbell, C., & Pallant, J. (2016). Segmenting multichannel consumers across search, purchase and after-sales. *Journal of Retailing and Consumer Services*, *33*, 62–71. doi:10.1016/j.jretconser.2016.08.001

Scholz, J., & Duffy, K. (2018). We ARe at home: How augmented reality reshapes mobile marketing and consumer-brand relationships. *Journal of Retailing and Consumer Services*, *44*, 11–23. doi:10.1016/j.jretconser.2018.05.004

Scholz, J., & Smith, A. N. (2016). Augmented reality: Designing immersive experiences that maximize consumer engagement. *Business Horizons*, *59*(2), 149–161. doi:10.1016/j.bushor.2015.10.003

Seifert, T., & Hedderson, C. (2010). Intrinsic motivation and flow in skateboarding: An ethnographic study. *Journal of Happiness Studies*, *11*(3), 277–292. doi:10.100710902-009-9140-y

Van Noort, G., Voorveld, H. A., & Van Reijmersdal, E. A. (2012). Interactivity in brand web sites: Cognitive, affective, and behavioral responses explained by consumers' online flow experience. *Journal of Interactive Marketing*, *26*(4), 223–234. doi:10.1016/j.intmar.2011.11.002

Wedel, M., Bigné, E., & Zhang, J. (2020). Virtual and augmented reality: Advancing research in consumer marketing. *International Journal of Research in Marketing*, *37*(3), 443–465. doi:10.1016/j.ijresmar.2020.04.004

Yadav, M. S., & Pavlou, P. A. (2014). Marketing in computer-mediated environments: Research synthesis and new directions. *Journal of Marketing*, *78*(1), 20–40. doi:10.1509/jm.12.0020

Yaoyuneyong, G., Foster, J., Johnson, E., & Johnson, D. (2016). Augmented reality marketing: Consumer preferences and attitudes toward hypermedia print ads. *Journal of Interactive Advertising*, *16*(1), 16–30. doi:10.1080/15252019.2015.1125316

Yim, M. Y. C., Chu, S. C., & Sauer, P. L. (2017). Is augmented reality technology an effective tool for e-commerce? An interactivity and vividness perspective. *Journal of Interactive Marketing*, *39*, 89–103. doi:10.1016/j.intmar.2017.04.001

ADDITIONAL READING

Peddie, J. (2017). *Augmented reality: Where we will all live*. Springer. doi:10.1007/978-3-319-54502-8

Pettersson, I., Lachner, F., Frison, A. K., Riener, A., & Butz, A. (2018, April). A Bermuda triangle? A Review of method application and triangulation in user experience evaluation. In *Proceedings of the 2018 CHI Conference on Human Factors in Computing Systems* (pp. 1-16). ACM.

Saunders, M., Lewis, P., & Thornhill, A. (2009). *Research methods for business students*. Pearson education.

KEY TERMS AND DEFINITIONS

Augmented Reality: Augmented reality (AR) is the interactive experience when people interact with the virtual object, AR experience integrates the real environment with a virtual object and performs in the device.

Customer Behaviour: Customer behaviour is a study regarding a group of people, individuals and organisations, which links with purchase behaviours, and it further relates to customers' satisfaction, emotion and attitude toward their purchase experience.

E-Retailing: E-retailing or electronic retailing is processed when people sell or buy goods through electronic media, normally via the internet.

Flow Experience: The state when an individual immerses in activity and loses self-consciousness but has a deep sense of control.

Mobile Augmented Reality: Mobile augmented reality is the AR service that is designed for mobile devices, people could interact with virtual objects on the mobile screen, which is a mixture display with the real environment and virtual 3D objects.

User Experience (UX): User experience is about the user's needs and requirements, which approaches to enhance user totally experiences when the user is interacting with the product or service.

Virtual Fitting Room: The virtual fitting room supports by the virtual product, which is generally made of 3-dimension objects and simulates those virtual objects to overlap on customer's body measurement.

Chapter 10
The Augmented Retail Store for Augmented Customer Experiences

Federica Caboni
University of Cagliari, Italy

Johan Hagberg
University of Gothenburg, Sweden

ABSTRACT

Among technological changes currently influencing retail, the implementation of digital strategies to create more experiential retail stores has enriched customers' experiences. Interactive technologies such as augmented reality (AR) provide particularly promising possibilities. By using AR, retailers can develop strategies to attract existing and potential customers, while customers can experience shopping in augmented, immersive ways in which the digital and physical worlds are combined in an augmented one. Despite the several examples of the use of AR technology in retail, those instances have often been introduced with only a few specific features and with limited applicability. In response, this chapter introduces the concept of an augmented retail store as a more comprehensive integration of physical and digital elements. It may serve as a means to develop an augmented experience for customers and mutual benefits for retailers and consumers and thus provide value for both academics and practitioners.

INTRODUCTION

The wide availability of technological tools such as smartphones, other mobile devices, virtual reality, and augmented reality (AR) has increasingly reconfigured the retail landscape (Fuentes et al., 2017; Shankar et al., 2021; Qin et al., 2021) in ways that have not only digitalized the physical environment but also physicalized the digital environment. In parallel, amid ever-growing competition between retailers, the increased use of online commerce (Fuentes et al., 2017) and digital technologies (Shankar et al., 2021), along with the general acceleration of retail digitalization (Hagberg et al., 2016; Pantano, 2020;

DOI: 10.4018/978-1-7998-9179-6.ch010

Amankwah-Amoah et al., 2021), have forever altered the structure of retail. For customers, today's shopping journeys (i.e., pre-purchase, purchase, and post-purchase) (Lemon & Verhoef, 2016) thus typically involve integrating various online and offline channels and touchpoints. The journeys may start at home as consumers search for, collect, and compare information about products before completing purchases in physical retail stores in city centers, or what is called *webrooming* (Arora & Sahney, 2017). Alternatively, consumers may start by seeking out and evaluating products in physical stores before purchasing them online, which is known as *showrooming* (Gensler et al., 2017), possible due to the lower prices and greater convenience sometimes afforded by shopping online. Similar to entire shopping journeys, post-purchase activities such as services and returns can also be conducted via numerous channels and touchpoints.

Such changes have altered the conditions of brick-and-mortar retailers, who have been affected by transformations in shopping due to changing technologies and shifting behavior among consumers (Hagberg et al., 2017; Pantano, 2020; Grewal et al., 2021). Some retailers have been forced to close their physical stores, whereas others have struggled to adapt to new patterns of consumption. Facing those circumstances, retailers with physical stores now seek to find new ways to interact with their customers and to attract new categories of customers. Thus, now more than ever before, understanding consumers' experiences and customers' journeys (Lemon & Verhoef, 2016; Bonetti et al., 2019) is essential for retailers' strategic performance. A common response of retailers has been to create new kinds of shopping experiences that consider consumers' changing needs and shopping journeys (Holbrook & Hirschman, 1982; Gentile et al., 2007; Meyer & Schwager, 2007). As stated by Reinartz et al. (2019), "a shift in stationary retailing from a transaction-oriented POS [Point of Sale] to one that is experience-oriented" has occurred (p. 362), which requires retailers to acknowledge that consumers shop for several reasons, which may or may not include the need for a specific product or service (Puccinelli et al., 2009).

This chapter explores how AR enables digital and physical elements to coexist in retail environments and to be combined in ways that generate new experiences for customers (Azuma, 1997; Azuma et al., 2001; Reinwald et al., 2014; Bonetti et al., 2019; Caboni & Hagberg, 2019). In particular, the chapter presents and develops the notion of what we call *augmented retail stores* as places that combine the benefits of the physical and digital worlds thanks to augmented content offered by AR. In our thinking, augmented retail stores offer a way to adapt to the changing needs and desires of consumers seeking immersive experiences by facilitating the development of immersive store environments (Mankodiya et al., 2013) augmented by merged physical and digital elements. Augmented retail stores may thus represent the evolution of physical retail stores in prioritizing not the quality of goods but the quality of experiences (Chen & Chen, 2010). Along those lines, the chapter analyses the physical and digital elements that constitute augmented environments and exploit AR technology to meet consumers' need for entertainment, social interaction, and intellectual stimulation during their shopping journeys (Arnold & Reynolds 2003) and contribute to creating augmented experiences for them.

The chapter next presents a review of literature on AR along with practical examples of AR applications. Based on that combination, it proposes a new form of retail store in which physical, digital, and augmented elements coexist and where the customers' experience is considered to be an augmented experience (Caboni & Hagberg, 2019). The chapter also proposes a definition of *augmented retail store* and discusses future prospects and opportunities for further research.

AR AND RETAIL

AR was first used in the mid-1990s during its development for the assembly and installation of electronic cables in airplanes (Caudell & Mizell, 1992). Over time, the technology found application in various sectors, including medicine, the military, retail, and games (Hwangbo et al., 2017). Although computer science and engineering were the primary fields in which early studies on AR emerged (Azuma, 1997; Azuma et al., 2001), scholars' have since branched out into the retail sector (Kang, 2014; Yim et al., 2017; Pantano et al., 2017; Pantano & Gandini, 2017, 2018; Scholz & Duffy, 2018; Hilken et al., 2018; Hilken et al., 2021; Caboni & Hagberg, 2019). The principal element that characterizes AR is its potential to merge physical and digital elements into one augmented environment, which allows users to interact with virtual objects in real-life contexts (Ramadan & Farah, 2017), including in brick-and-mortar retail stores and in their homes. Given today's consumers' profound digital skills and access to a wealth of information about the products that they want to buy, functional qualities provided by physical stores may be insufficient if consumers seek more enriched, memorable experiences than those stores offer. The great promise of AR for retail is thus based on its capacity to combine physical environments with virtual content and elements reproduced in three dimensions (Azuma, 1997) to enhance immersive experiences for consumers (Bonetti et al., 2019; Hilken et al., 2021).

Table 1. Recent studies on AR, their main themes and context

Source	Themes	Contexts
Javornik, 2016	Consumers' affective, cognitive and behavioral responses to augmented reality applications	Online
Poushneh & Vasquez-Parraga 2017	User experience, satisfaction and willingness to buy	Online
Scholz &Duffy, 2018	Consumer brand relationship	Online and mobile
Bonetti et al., 2019	Consumers' experiences and interactions with immersive technologies	Offline
Caboni & Hagberg, 2019	Features, applications and value of AR	Online and offline
Flavian et al., 2019	Impact of augmented and mixed reality on the customer experience	Online
Heller et al., 2019	Multisensory online retailing	Online and offline
Pantano, 2020	Retail Futures	Online and offline
Pizzi et al., 2020	Utilitarian and hedonic value perceptions of the shopping experience	Offline
Hilken et al., 2021	Stimulation of customers purchasing intention	Online to offline
Kumar, 2021	Consumer behaviors	Online
Nikhashemi et al., 2021	Continuous intention to use AR	Mobile
Qin et al., 2021	Purchase intention and continuous use	Mobile
Qin et al., 2021	Consumer decision making	Mobile

In the last decade, while several definitions and frameworks of AR related to the retail sector have been developed (e.g., Carmignani & Furth, 2011; Sood, 2012; Olsson et al., 2013; Scholz & Smith, 2016; Javornik 2016a, 2016b; Grewal et al., 2017; Hwangbo et al., 2017; Pantano et al., 2017; Poushneh & Vasquez-Parraga 2017; Rese et al., 2017; Ukawauani & Bashir, 2017; Brengman et al., 2018; Lee & Leonas, 2018; Watson et al., 2020; Hilken et al., 2018; Caboni & Hagberg, 2019; Hilken et al., 2021), there is still a paucity of literature that outline AR as a more integrated feature of retailing. Table 1 provides an overview of recent studies published in retail journals that analyzed various themes of AR in different retail contexts. The literature has so far particularly explored consumer attitudes and behaviors related to AR in online, mobile and offline contexts, while there is still a lack of literature that conceptualize a more holistic integration of AR in a physical store setting and how it may affect customer experiences.

Based on the principal frameworks of AR (e.g., Carmignani & Furth, 2011; Sood, 2012; Olsson et al., 2013; Scholz & Smith, 2016; Javornik 2016a, 2016b; Grewal et al., 2017; Hwangbo et al., 2017; Pantano et al., 2017; Poushneh & Vasquez-Parraga 2017; Rese et al., 2017; Ukawauani & Bashir, 2017; Brengman et al., 2018; Lee & Leonas, 2018; Watson et al., 2020; Hilken et al., 2018; Caboni & Hagberg, 2019; Hilken et al., 2021), four primary elements that characterize AR can be identified (Table 2): time, environment, interaction, and content. As for the first, all kinds of AR applications are based on contextualization in real time such that users can stay in touch and interact with other users, elements, and content in real time in real networked experiences (Pantano & Gandini, 2018). In view of the customer journey, it is relevant to consider "time" as fundamental to offering memorable experiences during shopping processes in physical places such as traditional stores. Additionally, in order to create a memorable shopping experience for customer both online and offline (Hilken et al., 2021) the "environment" appears as a crucial element during the customer journey. Specifically, this element refers to a physical place where people are immersed during the shopping process. Whereas the environment in virtual reality is artificial and unnatural—namely, a computer-generated place reproduced via digital devices (Burdea & Coiffet, 2003)—the immersive environment in AR is entirely natural and real but simply augmented by additional features. The environment could be considered as a crucial element able to modify the entire experience into an augmented shopping experience (Caboni & Hagberg, 2019). The third element to consider, largely because AR is an interactive technology, is interaction between users and object and/or features reproduced in their natural environments. Always present in AR, interaction is the element that drives and adds value to shopping experiences as they shift from being static to interactive. Interaction could be considered as a specific element able to co-create value both for consumer and retailers throughout the entire customer journey. Fourth and last, the content of AR is based on objects, elements, and features categorized in terms of their digital characteristics. All in all, the content could be representing the common thread of all digital elements characterizing the augmented shopping experience (Caboni & Hagberg, 2019).

Table 2. Characteristics of Augmented Reality (AR)

	Characteristics of Augmented Reality (AR)
AR	Real time
	Physical Environment
	Interaction
	Digital Content

AR can be a valuable, practical technology when applied in retail to develop interactive, immersive, networked shopping experiences (Watson et al., 2020; Cruz et al., 2018; Pantano & Gandini, 2018; Flavián et al., 2019; Hilken et al., 2021). From the other direction, the retail sector offers strong potential for AR, especially AR with characteristics that modify and enrich the shopping experience with new elements (Watson et al., 2020). The adoption of AR in retail has also been aided by the spread of smartphones (Fuentes et al., 2017) and other devices able to support the adoption of AR. Most of today's consumers are equipped with smartphones, thanks to which they can use AR to discover, for example, augmented content related to products. Studies on the possible application of AR in retail that have emerged during the last decade (Pantano, 2010, 2014, 2016; 2020; Pantano & Naccarato, 2010; Pantano & Laria, 2012; Pantano & Servidio, 2012; Pantano & Timmermans, 2014; Pantano et al., 2017, 2018; Hilken et al., 2021) have particularly focused on the technology's potential for that sector. During that time, awareness has risen among scholars and practitioners of the need to create an attractive place and transform shopping based on social contacts between humans (Pantano & Gandini, 2017, 2018). The future of retail (Grewal et al., 2017, 2021) could be thus redefined by the new and different ways of applying digital technology, especially AR.

Retail firms in different retail subsectors have developed several AR applications in recent years (Caboni & Hagberg, 2019). They include brands such as Benefit Cosmetics, Estée Lauder, L'Oréal, Mac Cosmetics, Sephora, Shiseido, and Rimmel in the beauty sector; Adidas, GAP, Nike, Topshop, Burberry, Zara, and Converse in the apparel and footwear sector; and DeBeers and Swarovski in the jewelry sector. Other examples include Ray-Ban in the accessories sector, BMW in the automotive sector, and IKEA in the home furnishings sector (Lee & Kim, 2019). Although the benefits derived from using AR in retail continue to be investigated (Pantano et al., 2017; Pantano, 2020), several benefits for consumers and retailers can clearly be achieved by implementing AR, as shown in Table 3.

Table 3. Benefits of applying AR for retailers and consumers

AR's Benefits for Retailers	AR's Benefits for Consumers
Developing an immersive shopping experience	Enhancing interaction with retailers, people, elements, and content
Sharing a positive brand image	Experiencing positive feeling
Offering augmented services	Gaining a broad volume of information
Refining the information system	Facilitating the shopping process
Improving technological skills	Improving engagement during the shopping experience

From the retailer's side, implementing AR appears to be helpful in developing immersive experiences in physical environments that unite the best of the physical and digital worlds (Hilken et al., 2021). AR also makes it possible to share positive brand images by involving people in the brand's world thanks to augmented content. With AR, it is additionally possible to offer various services during the shopping journey, including before, during, and after purchases. Moreover, increasingly tapping into AR's potential increasingly improves familiarity with the digital technology and allows consumers to experience new types of interactions between retailers and other consumers. AR moreover enables interacting with objects and content, which allows experiencing new positive feelings and new levels of engagement. Thanks to AR, it is also possible to gain specific information about products and their use and, consequently, enjoy a more straightforward shopping process in all phases of the shopping journey. Considering those benefits of AR for retailers and consumers, the next section outlines the notion of augmented retail stores—that is, physical retail stores that integrate AR in comprehensive, holistic ways.

AUGMENTED RETAIL STORES

One way to provide customers with an enhanced shopping experience is to develop a new kind of store where people can interact with each other and with the products therein. The development of such an augmented retail store should be regarded as a hypothetical concept of a viewpoint in retail that can enrich shopping experiences (Pantano, 2020; Hilken et al., 2021). At base, the envisioned augmented retail stores represent physical places where various outcomes (e.g., interaction, sharing, novelty, hedonism, and pleasure) are enabled and enhanced by the use of AR, specifically by merging the physical elements of traditional stores with digital ones. AR stores holistically enclose and complement several elements that characterize traditional retail stores—physical environment, human–human interaction, physical products, touch, aesthetics, and authenticity—with digital elements enabled by AR (Hilken et al., 2021). Above all, the characteristics of traditional stores enclosed in AR stores are the physical environment where the shopping journey usually takes places, human–human interaction with retailers and other people, the presence of physical products, and, consequently, all feelings related to real experiences with products involving touching, aesthetics, and authenticity. Those elements are merged with the digital and augmented ones, including interaction in real-time and in a real environment and with digital objects, elements, and other content, through all of which people can add value to their shopping experiences.

Augmented retail stores combine the benefits of physical stores and AR technology to create immersive places based on the combination of the physical elements typical of traditional stores and the features of digital technology. In fact, the principal value of augmented retail stores is based on the characteristics and features derived from the union of physical elements and digital ones enabled by AR. From that combination, it is possible to enhance customers' experiences by facilitating their abilities to interact with people and products, share their shopping experiences with others, and have novel, hedonic, and pleasurable experiences. Augmented retail stores offer customers the possibility of undertaking their shopping journeys in a physical place by physically trying on products, touching them, and otherwise interacting with them before completing the purchase. If all of those elements are matched with AR, then it is possible to offer customers superior shopping experiences, one that permits people to try on products by using applications such as virtual mirrors and digitally discovering whether there are other colors or sizes of clothing that they want to buy. In the case of furniture stores, for another example, consumers could shop for a sofa or bookcase by using AR to see other colors of the same product. Furthermore, in the case of beauty and cosmetic retail, customers could experiment with different colors of beauty products before pinpoint the ones that suit their needs and preferences. Although augmented retail stores thus have all characteristics of traditional retail stores, they moreover enable people to use digital means activated by AR and can thus contribute to creating engaging atmospheres and interactive, multisensory places in which to shop. Inside augmented retail stores, both the physical and digital elements are strongly and intrinsically interconnected to develop an augmented, more memorable retail experience for customers (Tung & Ritchie, 2011). Thus, they can be characterized as retail stores where customers can have a unique, augmented experience while browsing or buying products in an augmented or physical retailscape (Fuentes et al., 2017) and while interacting with several different augmented elements and features (Caboni & Hagberg, 2019).

FACILITATING AUGMENTED CUSTOMERS' EXPERIENCES

Developing an immersive experience for customers offers retailers a way to handle the increasingly intense competition between online and offline retailers. Owing to that development, technological changes increasingly influence how retail is conducted (Amankwah-Amoah et al., 2021; Shankar et al., 2021), particularly in the planning and implementation of strategies to create physical stores that combine digital and physical elements. In creating such immersive shopping experiences, however, retailers also need to consider consumers' perceptions of retail environments and their satisfaction or dissatisfaction with certain experiences (Pantano & Viassone, 2015; Pantano & Laria, 2012) that play out along a continuum of the physical and digital worlds, which are becoming increasingly irrelevant to consider as separate spheres. Even then, the same retail environment may produce starkly different outcomes and feelings depending on each consumer's goal (Puccinelli et al., 2009). Although a primary motive of consumers during the shopping process can be experience-oriented, such experiences may differ concerning values related to for example functional aspects, hedonism (Holbrook & Hirschman, 1982), emotions, aesthetics, ethics, escapism (Varshneya & Das, 2017) and memorability (Zimmerman & Kelley, 2010). To those ends, adopting digital technologies can be a way to provide consumers with opportunities for new shopping experiences. After all, creating vibrant, interactive retail stores by implementing new technology can transform the physical places where people shop into increasingly attractive spaces (Komninos et al., 2013) for not only shopping but also living out shared, networked experiences (Pantano & Gandini, 2018).

The interactive technology analyzed in this chapter offers different solutions and benefits for consumers and retailers. Augmented retail stores offer several opportunities to intensify shopping experiences for consumers by accommodating a high level of interaction between the real environment and the augmented content and context. Via AR, consumers can experience immersive shopping journeys in physical environments. At the same time, AR allows retailers to hone their retail strategies and overcome restrictions related to the enrichment of shopping experiences traditionally associated with physical stores. One way to encourage retailers to introduce AR into their physical stores is to stress the different kinds of experiences that can be realized in stores with and without AR. Table 4 shows the differences between a regular shopping experience, a digital shopping experience, and an augmented shopping experience.

In the regular shopping experience, customers enter stores to buy or search for something that they need or to find inspiration based on their interaction with products, staff, and/or other customers. In that process, their level of interaction is modest and can including engaging with staff members to locate different product varieties and information about products that they want to buy and/or using various senses (e.g., touch and smell) to experience the products. Overall, the regular shopping experience can be considered to primarily involve physical interaction and the absence of technology. By comparison, the digital shopping experience also affords a modest level of experience inasmuch people can interact with digital devices and gain more in-depth information about product characteristics. At that moderate level of experience, consumers operate at a discrete level of interaction based of what the digital technology affords. However, the digital shopping experience also presents some shortcomings in relation to the regular shopping experience, for it precludes touching products, for instance, and trying on several different colors of the same cloth. On top of that, the digital shopping experience often involves gaps in time and space, including between actual purchases and their fulfilment.

The augmented shopping experience, by contrast, can be considered to represent an entirely different level of shopping experience, one that combines the regular and digital shopping experiences. In the augmented shopping experience, the experiential quality is intensified because customers can interact with people and products in the store during their shopping journey as well as via digital means. Consequently, the augmented shopping experience allows customers to access richer information about products without the help of employees or retail assistants but instead via AR technology. It also allows customers to enrich their realities in retail environments by affording multisensorial experiences (Poushneh & Vasquez-Parraga, 2017) in a retail environment during the shopping process by enhancing their shopping experience into a multisensorial one. By using AR, customers can experience overlap and interaction with the augmentation enabled by the combination of digital and physical elements in real time and space (Ramadan & Farah, 2017; Carmignani & Furth, 2011).

Table 4. Differences between the regular shopping experience (RSEX), digital shopping experience (DSEX), and augmented shopping experience (ASEX)

	RSEX	DSEX	ASEX
Level of experience	Moderate	Moderate	Intense
Interaction	Physical	Digital	Digital and physical
Product information	Sensorial	Informative	Multisensorial

CONCLUSION

This chapter has introduced the concept of augmented retail stores as retail stores that integrate physical and digital elements by using AR in order to create augmented shopping experiences. The concept is based on a shift of the physical store from being transaction-oriented to being experience-oriented (Reinartz et al., 2019). In such stores, the act of the purchase becomes secondary to the primary reason of visiting stores, which is to interact with technology and have an enhanced, more intense customer experience. Thus, augmented retail stores could be understood as part of the evolution of traditional brick-and-mortar stores in which the quality of products is preceded by the quality of experience (Chen & Chen, 2010; Reinartz et al., 2019). Augmented retail stores are based on the trend that some customers seek enhanced, intensified shopping experiences possibly enriched with hedonic, emotional, aesthetic, ethical, and/or escapist values (Varshneya & Das, 2017). Likewise, the development of the augmented shopping experience can be mobilized as a way to allow customers to explore their emotions, fantasies, and memories (Zimmerman & Kelley, 2010). In that light, augmented retail stores can transform traditional, static retail stores into more attractive, dynamic environments through the implementation of AR technology (Komninos et al., 2013; Azuma, 1997; Azuma et al., 2001).

Bearing in mind the potential benefits for consumers and retailers that may derive from the application of AR in retail settings, it is also important to underscore some challenges and limitations. For one, implementing AR may require in-store investments with uncertain outcomes. For another, although consumers may appreciate the use of augmented technology as an initial novelty, they are liable to soon find the experience dull. Added to that, it is important to consider digital divides among retailers and consumers; what some customers may experience as value adding can for others be experienced as discouraging. Augmented retail stores allow for constant change and improvement via novel uses and combinations of physical and digital elements afforded by AR technology. However, there is also the risk that such development may not be sustainable or that such efforts provide few benefits for customers in terms of their experiences, which needs to be further tested and evaluated in both practice and research.

FUTURE RESEARCH DIRECTIONS

Future could be oriented toward exploring the opportunities for and challenges of introducing AR technology in retail in greater depth. In particular, because most AR applications have been developed by major retailers, some of those efforts could particularly focus on independent retailers, especially in urban areas. Several such retailers have experienced particularly challenging times and are seeking ways to attract customers by new means. Among other things, research can be oriented toward identifying suitable strategies for independent retailers to integrate AR into their total offerings in order to create more intense and memorable shopping experiences. Researchers could also examine the level of knowledge about AR among independent retailers as well as the economic impacts experienced by implementing AR technology. Although applying digital technologies is not always considered to be beneficial due to fears of high investments associated with technology, the widespread use of smartphones means that AR can be a relatively inexpensive technology when applied in retail. Indeed, in increasingly digitalized retail environments, it is difficult to abstain from using technology to improve customers' experiences, and AR is not only comparatively affordable but also shows great potential to be integrated through the development of augmented retail stores.

MANAGERIAL IMPLICATIONS

The concept of augmented retail stores can be useful for practitioners as a way to create and develop immersive shopping experiences using digital technologies. More specifically, digital technologies are significantly changing the retail world (Shankar et al., 2021) not least visible throughout the changing retail and shopping practices during the COVID-19 pandemic. In that sense, retail managers involved in orchestrating customer's shopping process and experiences could find suitable solutions in the applications of AR in order to coordinate and enhance the customer experience both online and offline. By focusing their attention on augmented experiences, retailers have the possibility to attract customers with specific strategies based on the concept of the augmented retail store. All in all, the analysis of the differences between the regular shopping experience (RSEX), digital shopping experience (DSEX), and augmented shopping experience (ASEX) can help retailers to seek and develop new dimensions of customer experiences. The possibility to develop an augmented retail store can be useful for traditional brick and mortar retailers, online retailers and particularly in the continuing integration of physical and online that increasingly characterizes contemporary retailing.

REFERENCES

Amankwah-Amoah, J., Khan, Z., Wood, G., & Knight, G. (2021). Covid-19 and digitalization: The great acceleration. *Journal of Business Research, 136*, 602–611. doi:10.1016/j.jbusres.2021.08.011 PMID:34538980

Arnold, M. J., & Reynolds, K. (2003). Hedonic Shopping Motivations. *Journal of Retailing*, *79*(2), 77–95. doi:10.1016/S0022-4359(03)00007-1

Arora, S., & Sahney, S. (2017). Webrooming behaviour: A conceptual framework. *International Journal of Retail & Distribution Management*, *45*(7/8), 762–781. doi:10.1108/IJRDM-09-2016-0158

Azuma, R., Baillot, Y., Behringer, R., Feiner, S., Julier, S., & Macintyre, B. (2001). Recent advances in augmented reality. *IEEE Computer Graphics and Applications*, *21*(6), 34–47. doi:10.1109/38.963459

Azuma, R. T. (1997). A survey of augmented reality. *Presence (Cambridge, Mass.)*, *6*(4), 355–385. doi:10.1162/pres.1997.6.4.355

Bonetti, F., Pantano, E., Warnaby, G., & Quinn, L. (2019). Augmenting reality: Fusing consumers' experiences and interactions with immersive technologies in physical retail settings. *International Journal of Technology Marketing*, *13*(3-4), 260–284. doi:10.1504/IJTMKT.2019.104592

Brengman, M., Willems, K., & Van Kerrebroeck, H. (2018). Can't touch this: The impact of augmented reality versus touch and non-touch interfaces on perceived ownership. *Virtual Reality (Waltham Cross)*, 1–12.

Burdea, G., & Coiffet, P. (2003). *Virtual reality technology*. MIT Press. doi:10.1162/105474603322955950

Caboni, F., & Hagberg, J. (2019). Augmented reality in retailing: A review of features, applications and value. *International Journal of Retail & Distribution Management*, *47*(11), 1125–1140. doi:10.1108/IJRDM-12-2018-0263

Carmignani, J., & Furht, B. (2011). Augmented Reality: An Overview. In B. Furht (Ed.), *Handbook of Augmented Reality. Heidelberg/Dortrecht/London/New York* (pp. 3–46). Springer Verlag. doi:10.1007/978-1-4614-0064-6_1

Caudell, T. P., & Mizell, D. W. (1992). Augmented reality: an application of heads-up display technology to manual manufacturing processes. *Proceedings of the 25th Hawaii International Conference on System Sciences*, *2*, 659-669. 10.1109/HICSS.1992.183317

Chen, C. F., & Chen, F. S. (2010). Experience quality, perceived value, satisfaction and behavioral intentions for heritage tourists. *Tourism Management*, *31*(1), 29–35. doi:10.1016/j.tourman.2009.02.008

Cruz, E., Orts-Escolano, S., Gomez-Donoso, F., Rizo, C., Rangel, J. C., Mora, H., & Cazorla, M. (2018). An augmented reality application for improving shopping experience in large retail stores. *Virtual Reality (Waltham Cross)*, 1–11.

Flavián, C., Ibáñez-Sánchez, S., & Orús, C. (2019). The impact of virtual, augmented and mixed reality technologies on the customer experience. *Journal of Business Research*, *100*, 547–560. doi:10.1016/j.jbusres.2018.10.050

Fuentes, C., Bäckström, K., & Svingstedt, A. (2017). Smartphones and the reconfiguration ofretailscapes: Stores, shopping, and digitalization. *Journal of Retailing and Consumer Services*, *39*, 270–278. doi:10.1016/j.jretconser.2017.08.006

Gensler, S., Neslin, S. A., & Verhoef, P. C. (2017). The showrooming phenomenon: It's more than just about price. *Journal of Interactive Marketing*, *38*, 29–43. doi:10.1016/j.intmar.2017.01.003

Gentile, C., Spiller, N., & Noci, G. (2007). How to sustain the customer experience: An overview of experience components that co-create value with the customer. *European Management Journal*, *25*(5), 395–410. doi:10.1016/j.emj.2007.08.005

Grewal, D., Gauri, D. K., Roggeveen, A. L., & Sethuraman, R. (2021). Strategizing Retailing in the New Technology Era. *Journal of Retailing*, *97*(1), 6–12.

Grewal, D., Roggeveen, A. L., & Nordfält, J. (2017). The future of retailing. *Journal of Retailing*, *93*(1), 1–6. doi:10.1016/j.jretai.2016.12.008

Hagberg, J., Jonsson, A., & Egels-Zandén, N. (2017). Retail digitalization: Implications for physical stores. *Journal of Retailing and Consumer Services*, *39*, 264–269.

Hagberg, J., Sundstrom, M., & Egels-Zandén, N. (2016). The digitalization of retailing: An exploratory framework. *International Journal of Retail & Distribution Management*, *44*(7), 694–712.

Hilken, T., Chylinski, M., Keeling, D. I., Heller, J., de Ruyter, K., & Mahr, D. (2021). How to strategically choose or combine augmented and virtual reality for improved online experiential retailing. *Psychology and Marketing*, 1–13.

Hilken, T., Heller, J., Chylinski, M., Keeling, D. I., Mahr, D., & de Ruyter, K. (2018). Making omnichannel an augmented reality: The current and future state of the art. *Journal of Research in Interactive Marketing*, *12*(4), 509–523.

Holbrook, M. B., & Hirschman, E. C. (1982). The experiential aspects of consumption: Consumer fantasy, feelings and fun. *The Journal of Consumer Research*, *9*(2), 132–140.

Hwangbo, H., Kim, Y.S. & Cha, K.J. (2017). Use of the smart store for persuasive marketing and immersive customer experiences: a case study of Korean apparel enterprise. *Mobile Information System*, 1-17.

Javornik, A. (2016a). Augmented reality: Research agenda for studying the impact of its media characteristics on consumer behavior. *Journal of Retailing and Consumer Services*, *30*, 252–26.

Javornik, A. (2016b). It's an illusion, but it looks real! Consumer affective, cognitive and behavioural responses to augmented reality applications. *Journal of Marketing Management*, *32*(9-10), 987–1011.

Kang, M. J. Y. (2014). Augmented reality and motion capture apparel e-shopping values and usage intention. *International Journal of Clothing Science and Technology*, *26*(6), 486–499.

Komninos, N., Pallot, M., & Schaffers, H. (2013). Smart Cities and the Future Internet in Europe. *Journal of the Knowledge Economy*, *4*(2), 119–134.

Lee, H., & Leonas, K. (2018). Consumer experiences, the key to survive in an omni-channel environment: Use of virtual technology. *Journal of Textile and Apparel Technology Management*, *10*(3), 1–23.

Lee, J. H., & Kim, S. I. (2019). Evaluation of User Experience in AR-based shopping Applications Focused on Ikea Place and Amazon AR View. *Journal of Digital Convergence*, *17*(10), 411–416.

Lemon, K. N., & Verhoef, P. C. (2016). Understanding Customer Experience throughout the Customer Journey. *Journal of Marketing*, *80*(6), 69–96.

Mankodiya, K., Martins, R., Francis, J., Garduno, E., Gandhi, R., & Narasimhan, P. (2013). Interactive shopping experience through immersive store environments. In *International Conference of Design, User Experience, and Usability*. Springer.

Meyer, C., & Schwager, A. (2007). Understanding customer experience. *Harvard Business Review*, *85*(2), 116.

Olsson, T., Lagerstam, E., Kärkkäinen, T., & Väänänen-Vainio-Mattila, K. (2013). Expected user experience of mobile augmented reality services: A user study in the context of shopping centres. *Personal and Ubiquitous Computing*, *17*(2), 287–304.

Pantano, E. (2010). New technologies and retailing: Trends and directions. *Journal of Retailing and Consumer Services*, *17*(3), 171–172.

Pantano, E. (2014). Innovation drivers in retail industry. *International Journal of Information Management*, *34*(3), 344–350.

Pantano, E. (2016). Benefits and risks associated with time choice of innovating in retail settings. *International Journal of Retail & Distribution Management*, *44*(1), 58–70.

Pantano, E. (Ed.). (2020). Retail Futures: The Good, the Bad and the Ugly of the Digital Transformation. Emerald Group Publishing.

Pantano, E., & Gandini, A. (2017). Exploring the forms of sociality mediated by innovative technologies in retail settings. *Computers in Human Behavior*, *77*, 367–373.

Pantano, E., & Gandini, A. (2018). Shopping as a 'networked experience': An emerging framework in the retail industry. *International Journal of Retail & Distribution Management*, *46*(7), 690–704.

Pantano, E., & Laria, G. (2012). Innovation in retail process: From consumers' experience to immersive store design. *Journal of Technology Management & Innovation*, *7*(3), 198–206.

Pantano, E., & Naccarato, G. (2010). Entertainment in retailing: The influences of advanced technologies. *Journal of Retailing and Consumer Services*, *17*(3), 200–204.

Pantano, E., Priporas, C. V., & Dennis, C. (2018). A new approach to retailing for successful competition in the new smart scenario. *International Journal of Retail & Distribution Management*, *46*(3), 264–282.

Pantano, E., Rese, A., & Baier, D. (2017). Enhancing the online decision-making process by using augmented reality: A two-country comparison of youth markets. *Journal of Retailing and Consumer Services*, *38*, 81–95.

Pantano, E., & Servidio, R. (2012). Modeling innovative points of sales through virtual and immersive technologies. *Journal of Retailing and Consumer Services*, *19*(3), 279–286.

Pantano, E., & Timmermans, H. (2014). What is smart for retailing? *Procedia Environmental Sciences*, *22*, 101–107.

Pantano, E., & Viassone, M. (2015). Engaging consumers on new integrated multichannel retail settings: Challenges for retailers. *Journal of Retailing and Consumer Services*, *25*, 106–114.

Pizzi, G., Vannucci, V., & Aiello, G. (2020). Branding in the time of virtual reality: Are virtual store brand perceptions real? *Journal of Business Research*, *119*, 502–510.

Poushneh, A., & Vasquez-Parraga, A. Z. (2017). Discernible impact of augmented reality on retail customer's experience, satisfaction and willingness to buy. *Journal of Retailing and Consumer Services*, *34*, 229–234.

Puccinelli, N. M., Goodstein, R. C., Grewal, D., Price, R., Raghubir, P., & Stewart, D. (2009). Customer experience management in retailing: Understanding the buying process. *Journal of Retailing*, *85*(1), 15–30.

Qin, H., Osatuyi, B., & Xu, L. (2021). How mobile augmented reality applications affect continuous use and purchase intentions: A cognition-affect-conation perspective. *Journal of Retailing and Consumer Services*, *63*, 102680.

Qin, H., Peak, D. A., & Prybutok, V. (2021). A virtual market in your pocket: How does mobile augmented reality (MAR) influence consumer decision making? *Journal of Retailing and Consumer Services*, *58*, 102337.

Ramadan, Z. B., & Farah, M. F. (2017). The Pokémonisation of the first moment of truth. *International Journal of Web Based Communities*, *13*(2), 262–277.

Reinartz, W., Wiegand, N., & Imschloss, M. (2019). The Impact of Digital Transformation on the Retailing Value Chain. *International Journal of Research in Marketing*, *36*(3), 350–366.

Reinwald, F., Berger, M., Stoik, C., Platzer, M., & Damyanovic, D. (2014). Augmented reality at the service of participatory urban planning and community informatics – a case study from Vienna. *The Journal of Community Informatics*, *10*(3).

Rese, A., Baier, D., Geyer-Schulz, A., & Schreiber, S. (2017). How augmented reality apps are accepted by consumers: A comparative analysis using scales and opinions. *Technological Forecasting and Social Change*, *124*, 306–319.

Scholz, J., & Duffy, K. (2018). We are at home: How augmented reality reshapes mobile marketing and consumer-brand relationships. *Journal of Retailing and Consumer Services*, *44*, 11–23.

Scholz, J., & Smith, A. N. (2016). Augmented reality: Designing immersive experiences that maximize consumer engagement. *Business Horizons*, *59*(2), 149–161.

Shankar, V., Kalyanam, K., Setia, P., Golmohammadi, A., Tirunillai, S., Douglass, T., ... Waddoups, R. (2021). How technology is changing retail. *Journal of Retailing*, *97*(1), 13–27.

Sood, S. (2012). The death of social media in start-up companies and the rise of s-commerce: Convergence of e-commerce, complexity and social media. *Journal of Electronic Commerce in Organizations*, *10*(2), 1–15.

Tung, V. W. S., & Ritchie, J. B. (2011). Exploring the essence of memorable tourism experiences. *Annals of Tourism Research, 38*(4), 1367–1386.

Ukwuani, N., & Bashir, E. (2017). Emerging technologies: An exploration of novel interactive technologies. *International Journal of Information Systems in the Service Sector*, *9*(4), 30–43.

Varshneya, G., & Das, G. (2017). Experiential value: Multi-item scale development and validation. *Journal of Retailing and Consumer Services*, *34*, 48–57.

Watson, A., Alexander, B., & Salavati, L. (2020). The impact of experiential augmented reality applications on fashion purchase intention. *International Journal of Retail & Distribution Management*, *48*(5), 433–451.

Yim, M. Y. C., Chu, S. C., & Sauer, P. L. (2017). Is augmented reality technology an effective tool for e commerce? An interactivity and vividness perspective. *Journal of Interactive Marketing*, *39*, 89–103.

Zimmerman, C. A., & Kelley, C. M. (2010). I'll remember this! Effects of emotionality on memory predictions versus memory performance. *Journal of Memory and Language*, *62*, 240–253.

KEY TERMS AND DEFINITIONS

Augmented Customer Experience: A memorable shopping experience generated through the exploitation of augmented reality technology.

Augmented Reality: An interactive technology which combines digital elements in real environments.

Augmented Retail Store: A physical place where various outcomes are enabled and enhanced by the use of AR, specifically by merging the physical elements of traditional stores with digital ones.

Digital Shopping Experience: A shopping experience where people primarily interact with digital devices.

Physical Store: A traditional brick and mortar retail store usually placed in a commercial shopping area.

Regular Shopping Experience: A shopping experience that involves physical interaction within a physical store setting.

Shopping Experience: Customer experiences throughout a shopping journey.

Chapter 11
Understanding the Application of Gamification to Business When Applied to Marketing

Albérico Travassos Rosário
GOVCOPP, IADE, Universidade Europeia, Portugal

ABSTRACT

The internet is a technology that has provided changes, giving rise to new trends and concepts applied in the most diverse areas. One of these trends is gamification, as it is a concept applied in several areas: education, information technology, management, communication, and marketing. Companies understand that gamification applied to marketing can be an opportunity to strengthen the relationship between brands and consumers, increasing consumer engagement and loyalty. Marketing strategy based on gamification can boost marketing results, increase brand engagement, generate more motivation among users, promote knowledge retention, encourage cooperation, and provide a competitive advantage and valuable feedback. It becomes pertinent to understand how gamification can attract, engage, and understand a brand's audience. This chapter is based on the methodology of a systematic bibliometric literature review with a qualitative approach to understand the application of gamification to business when applied to marketing in order to verify research themes and development patterns.

INTRODUCTION

Research and new technologies have made gamification methods and tools transferable in commerce to benefit organizations in most economic sectors. Games can influence players' attitudes and behaviors due to high engagement levels (Yang et al., 2017). Therefore, companies use games to create compelling experiences for achieving competitive advantage and successful branding, a process Berger et al. (2018) term as gamified interactions. People voluntarily choose games and their enjoyable activities to avoid ordinary routines and create playful experiences. Thus, companies adopt gamified interactions to build a brand by providing consumer entertainment (Vos, 2015). Berger et al. (2018) explain that marketing in gamification occurs in two dimensions: advergames and in-game advertising. While advergames

DOI: 10.4018/978-1-7998-9179-6.ch011

involve custom-made games specifically designed for product or brand promotion, in-game advertising involves brand or product placements in an existing game. Although there is an increase in the adoption of games as a promotional strategy, academic literature on the effectiveness of gamification in marketing is not enlightening. This Systematic Review of Bibliometric Literature (LRSB) aims to build with knowledge to fill the gap, understanding the main purpose of gamification when applied to marketing, thus improving decision making.

METHODOLOGICAL APPROACH

The research uses a Systematic Bibliometric Literature Review (LRSB) with a qualitative approach to collect, analyze, and synthesize data on the application of gamification in marketing.

However, we must consider that the scope is limited by the definition of the question and the selection criteria. Furthermore, most of the time, the questions reformulate alternatives that are not answered by the chosen central question. Although it involves gathering data from existing literature, a systematic review is considered an original work (Rosário, 2021, Raimundo & Rosário, 2021, Rosário et al., 2021; Rosário & Cruz, 2019). It consists of identifying, selecting, appraising, and synthesizing high-quality studies that explicitly indicate precise contexts and research intentions through rigorous and explicit design (Bettany-Saltikov, 2016). It involves summarizing and combining relevant individual studies, thus, developing knowledge usable in decision-making and strategizing. In addition, a qualitative approach was adopted to provide in-depth data analysis on factors influencing branding and promotional activities in games. Bilgin (2017) explains that in-depth character is the main advantage of qualitative market research since it allows data collection and analysis of factors such as the quality of interaction determining consumer satisfaction. Huotari and Hamari (2017) indicate that gamification in marketing literature is illustrated as a communicative stage that conceptualizes consumers as co-producers. In recent commerce activities, consumer engagement in business processes has become rampant due to increasing empowerment platforms, such as social media, that facilitate user-generated content. Therefore, this methodology can build knowledge on the context of gamification, its goals, affordances, and psychological mediators that make it an appropriate marketing strategy.

LRSB process was carried out, divided into 3 phases and 6 steps (Table 1), as proposed by Rosário, 2021, Raimundo & Rosário, 2021, Rosário et al., 2021; Rosário & Cruz, 2019.

Table 1. Process of systematic LRSB.

Phase	Step	Description
Exploration	Step 1	formulating the research problem
	Step 2	searching for appropriate literature
	Step 3	critical appraisal of the selected studies
	Step 4	data synthesis from individual sources
Interpretation	Step 5	reporting findings and recommendations
Communication	Step 6	Presentation of the LRSB report

The database of scientific and/or academic articles used was SCOPUS, the most important peer-review in the scientific and academic world. However, we consider that the study has the limitation of considering only the SCOPUS database, excluding the other scientific and academic bases. The bibliographic search includes peer-reviewed scientific and/or academic documents published until June 2021.

The initial search involved the keyword "gamification" to screen abstracts, titles, and keywords. A total of 8,223 documents were identified, which were reduced to 255 by adding the keyword "marketing." The search was later limited to the search area "Business, Management and Accounting" to ensure that only the most relevant research was integrated into the report for accuracy and applicability in the marketing field (Table 2).

Finally, content and theme analysis techniques were used to identify, analyze and report the various documents as proposed by Rosário, (2021), Raimundo & Rosário, (2021), Rosário et al. (2021); Rosário & Cruz, (2019).

Table 2. Screening Methodology.

Database Scopus	Screening	Publications
Meta-search	keyword: Gamification	8,223
First Inclusion Criterion	keyword: Gamification, Marketing	255
Second Inclusion Criterion	keyword: Gamification, Marketing Subject area Business, Management and Accounting	96
Screening	keyword: Consumer, Marketing Subject area Business, Management and Accounting Published until June 2021	

The 96 scientific and/or academic documents indexed in SCOPUS are later analysed in a narrative and bibliometric way to deepen the content and possible derivation of common themes that directly respond to the research question (Rosário, 2021, Raimundo & Rosário, 2021, Rosário et al., 2021, Rosário & Cruz, 2019). Of the 96 selected documents, 60 are articles, 15 are book Chapters, 14 are conference papers, 4 are reviews, 2 are books, and 1 is an Erratum.

PUBLICATION DISTRIBUTION

Peer-reviewed articles on understanding the application of gamification to business when applied to marketing until 2021. The year 2019 had the highest number of peer-reviewed publications on the subject, reaching 24.

Figure 1 summarizes the peer-reviewed literature published in 2021.

The publications were sorted out as follows: with 6 Journal Of Business Research; with 3 (Business Of Gamification A Critical Analysis; Journal Of Interactive Marketing; Journal Of Marketing Education; Journal Of Research In Interactive Marketing; Journal Of Social Marketing; Lecture Notes In Business Information Processing); with 2 (2019 16th International Conference On Service Systems And Service Management Icsssm 2019; Contributions To Management Science; European Journal Of Marketing; Gamification In Education And Business; Journal Of Retailing And Consumer Services;

Marketing Intelligence And Planning; Social Enterprise And Special Events; Vision 2020 Sustainable Growth Economic Development And Global Competitiveness Proceedings Of The 23rd International Business Information Management Association Conference Ibima 2014); with 1 (2015 12th International Conference On Service Systems And Service Management Icsssm 2015; 2018 IEEE Conference On E Learning E Management And E Services Ic3e 2018; Accounting Education; Advances In Crowdsourcing; Australasian Marketing Journal; Business Horizons; Cities; Consumption Markets And Culture; Cultural Heritage In A Changing World; Electronic Commerce Research And Applications; Electronic Markets; Engaging Consumers Through Branded Entertainment And Convergent Media; Engineering Economics; Espacios; Fundamentals Of Software Startups Essential Engineering And Business Aspects; Handbook Of Engaged Sustainability; Handbook Of Research On Effective Advertising Strategies In The Social Media Age; Hospitality Marketing And Consumer Behavior Creating Memorable Experiences; Industrial Management And Data Systems; Industrial Marketing Management; Innovation Organization And Management; Innovative Marketing; Intangible Capital; International Journal Of Bank Marketing; International Journal Of Business Excellence; International Journal Of Industrial Engineering And Production Research; International Journal Of Information Management; International Journal Of Internet Marketing And Advertising; International Journal Of Recent Technology And Engineering; International Journal Of Retail And Distribution Management; International Journal Of Tourism Cities; Journal For Advancement Of Marketing Education; Journal Of Brand Management; Journal Of Business And Industrial Marketing; Journal Of Business Ethics; Journal Of Communication Management; Journal Of Destination Marketing And Management; Journal Of Managerial Psychology; Journal Of Policy Research In Tourism Leisure And Events; Journal Of Retailing; Journal Of Service Theory And Practice; Journal Of Tourism Futures; Journal Of Travel And Tourism Marketing; Marketing Health Services; Marketing Theory; Marketing Zeitschrift Fur Forschung Und Praxis; Proceedings Of The 16th European Conference On Management Leadership And Governance Ecmlg 2020; Proceedings Of The 2020 IEEE International Conference Quality Management Transport And Information Security Information Technologies IT And Qm And Is 2020; Proceedings Of The European Conference On Innovation And Entrepreneurship Ecie; Proceedings Of The International Conference On Electronic Business Iceb; Proceedings Vrcai 2019 17th ACM SIGGRAPH International Conference On Virtual Reality Continuum And Its Applications In Industry; Public Relations Review; Self Tracking Empirical And Philosophical Investigations; Simulation And Gaming; Strategic Direction; Tourism Management).
As of 2013 there is interest in the topic with a drop from 2019.

Figure 1. Documents by year

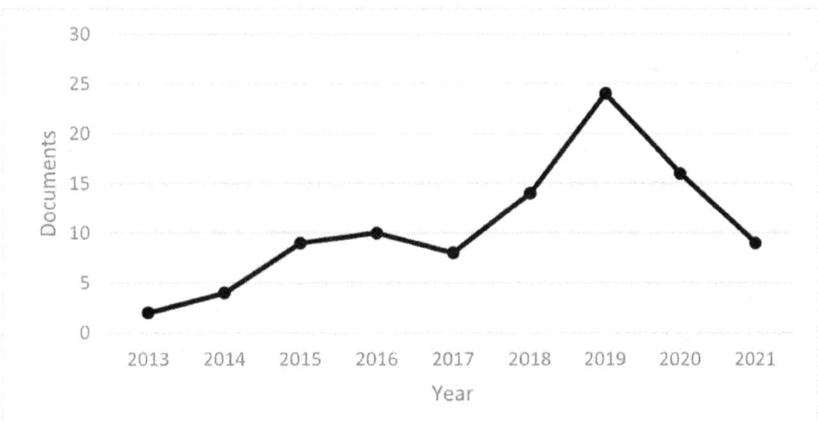

In Table 3 we analyze for the Scimago Journal & Country Rank (SJR), the best quartile and the H index by publication. Management Science is the most quoted publication with 5,940 (SJR), Q1 and H index 127.

There is a total of 26 publications on Q1, 12 publications on Q2 and 5 publications on Q3 and 3 publications on Q4. Publications from best quartile Q1 represent 37% of the 71 publications titles; best quartile Q2 represents 17%; best quartile Q3 represents 7%; and finally, best Q4 represents 4% each of the 71 publications.

Finally, 25 publications without indexing data represented 35% of publications.

As evident from Table 3, the significant majority of publications on the application of gamification to business when applied to marketing rank on the Q1 best quartile index.

Table 3. Scimago journal & country rank impact factor.

Title	SJR	Best Quartile	H Index
Tourism Management	3,330	Q1	199
Journal Of Retailing	3,180	Q1	136
International Journal Of Information Management	2,770	Q1	114
Journal Of Interactive Marketing	2,610	Q1	106
Journal Of Business Ethics	2,210	Q1	187
Business Horizons	2,170	Q1	87
Journal Of Business Research	2,050	Q1	195
Industrial Marketing Management	2,020	Q1	136
Journal Of Travel And Tourism Marketing	1,860	Q1	73
Cities	1,770	Q1	90
Journal Of Destination Marketing And Management	1,700	Q1	39
Marketing Theory	1,640	Q1	65
Journal Of Retailing And Consumer Services	1,570	Q1	89
Public Relations Review	1,570	Q1	82
European Journal Of Marketing	1,200	Q1	100
Electronic Commerce Research And Applications	1,180	Q1	74
Journal Of Service Theory And Practice	1,170	Q1	85
Industrial Management And Data Systems	0,990	Q1	103
Journal Of Marketing Education	0,980	Q1	55
Journal Of Communication Management	0,980	Q1	38
Journal Of Managerial Psychology	0,880	Q1	80
Accounting Education	0,870	Q1	37
Electronic Markets	0,850	Q1	35
Consumption Markets And Culture	0,830	Q1	29
Journal Of Business And Industrial Marketing	0,740	Q1	67
International Journal Of Retail And Distribution Management	0,730	Q1	78
Journal Of Research In Interactive Marketing	0,910	Q2	35

Continued on following page

Table 3. Continued

Title	SJR	Best Quartile	H Index
International Journal Of Bank Marketing	0,790	Q2	81
Journal Of Brand Management	0,780	Q2	50
Marketing Intelligence And Planning	0,750	Q2	70
Australasian Marketing Journal	0,630	Q2	37
Journal Of Social Marketing	0,600	Q2	24
Journal Of Tourism Futures	0,530	Q2	15
International Journal Of Tourism Cities	0,520	Q2	12
Journal Of Policy Research In Tourism Leisure And Events	0,510	Q2	23
Simulation And Gaming	0,510	Q2	60
Journal For Advancement Of Marketing Education	0,410	Q2	8
Engineering Economics	0,300	Q2	29
International Journal Of Business Excellence	0,290	Q3	18
Marketing Zeitschrift Fur Forschung Und Praxis	0,280	Q3	3
Intangible Capital	0,250	Q3	14
Innovative Marketing	0,240	Q3	5
Lecture Notes In Business Information Processing	0,210	Q3	49
International Journal Of Internet Marketing And Advertising	0,170	Q4	19
International Journal Of Industrial Engineering And Production Research	0,150	Q4	2
Strategic Direction	0,120	Q4	12
Proceedings Of The European Conference On Innovation And Entrepreneurship Ecie	0,130	-*	6
2018 IEEE Conference On E Learning E Management And E Services Ic3e 2018	0,120	-*	3
Proceedings Of The International Conference On Electronic Business Iceb	0,120	-*	7
Proceedings Vrcai 2019 17th ACM SIGGRAPH International Conference On Virtual Reality Continuum And Its Applications In Industry	0,120	-*	2
2019 16th International Conference On Service Systems And Service Management Icsssm 2019	0,110	-*	2
International Journal Of Recent Technology And Engineering	-*	-*	20
Marketing Health Services	-*	-*	19
Espacios	-*	-*	17
Contributions To Management Science	-*	-*	14
Vision 2020 Sustainable Growth Economic Development And Global Competitiveness Proceedings Of The 23rd International Business Information Management Association Conference Ibima 2014	-*	-*	5
Business Of Gamification A Critical Analysis	-*	-*	-*
Gamification In Education And Business	-*	-*	-*
Social Enterprise And Special Events	-*	-*	-*
2015 12th International Conference On Service Systems And Service Management Icsssm 2015	-*	-*	-*
Advances In Crowdsourcing	-*	-*	-*
Cultural Heritage In A Changing World	-*	-*	-*
Engaging Consumers Through Branded Entertainment And Convergent Media	-*	-*	-*

Continued on following page

Table 3. Continued

Title	SJR	Best Quartile	H Index
Fundamentals Of Software Startups Essential Engineering And Business Aspects	-*	-*	-*
Handbook Of Engaged Sustainability	-*	-*	-*
Handbook Of Research On Effective Advertising Strategies In The Social Media Age	-*	-*	-*
Hospitality Marketing And Consumer Behavior Creating Memorable Experiences	-*	-*	-*
Innovation Organization And Management	-*	-*	-*
Proceedings Of The 16th European Conference On Management Leadership And Governance Ecmlg 2020	-*	-*	-*
Proceedings Of The 2020 IEEE International Conference Quality Management Transport And Information Security Information Technologies IT And Qm And Is 2020	-*	-*	-*
Self Tracking Empirical And Philosophical Investigations	-*	-*	-*

Note: *data not available.

The subject areas covered by the 96 scientific and/or academic documents were: Business, Management and Accounting (96); Social Sciences (23); Economics, Econometrics and Finance (21); Computer Science (14); Decision Sciences (14); Engineering (8); Mathematics (5); Environmental Science (3); Psychology (3); Arts and Humanities (2); and Medicine (2).

The most quoted article was "Transforming homo economicus into homo ludens: A field experiment on gamification in a utilitarian peer-to-peer trading service" from Hamari (2013) with 370 quotes published in the Electronic Commerce Research and Applications 1.180 (SJR), the best quartile (Q1) and with H index (74), reports the "results of a field experiment, which gamifies a utilitarian peer-to-peer trading service by implementing the game mechanism of badges that users can earn from a variety of tasks".

In Figure 2 we can analyze the evolution of citations of the documents published until 2021. The number of citations shows positive net growth with R2 of 78% for the period ≤2010-2021, with 2020 reaching 537 citations.

Figure 2. evolution of citations between ≤2010 and 2021.

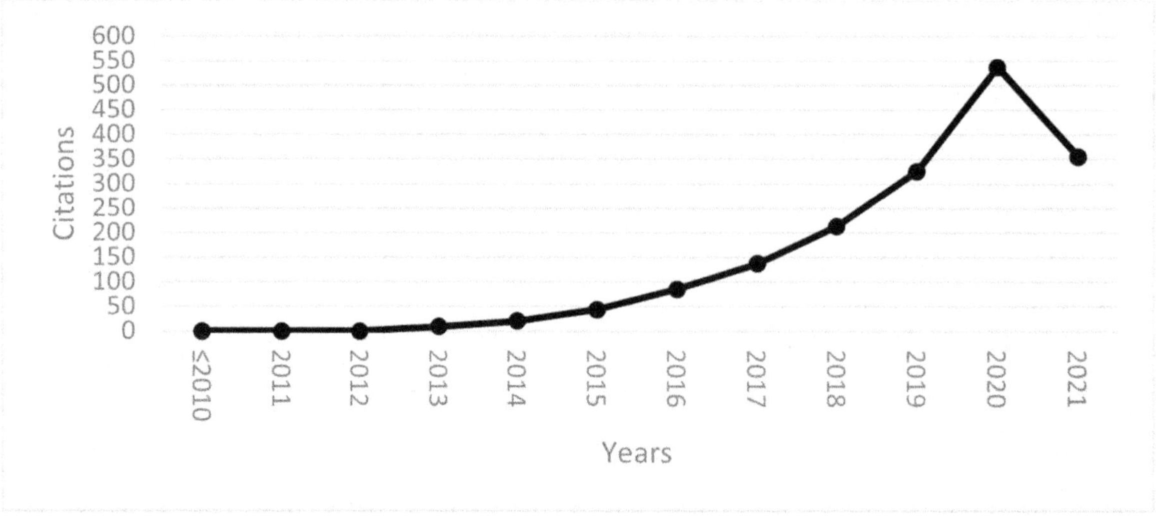

The h-index was used to ascertain the productivity and impact of the published work, based on the largest number of articles included that had at least the same number of citations. Of the documents considered for the h-index, 20 have been cited at least 20 times.

In Annex I, citations of all scientific and/or academic documents from the period 2010 to 2021 are analyzed, with a total of 1725 citations, of the 96 documents 26 were not cited.

Annex II examines the self-citation of the document during the period ≤2010 to 2021, 9 documents were self-cited 116 times, the document "A definition for gamification: anchoring gamification in the service marketing literature" by Huotari & Hamari (2017) published in Electronic Markets has been cited 27 times.

The bibliometric study was carried out to investigate and identify indicators on the dynamics and evolution of scientific and/or academic information in documents based on the main keywords (Figure 3). The results were extracted from the scientific software VOSviewe, which aims to identify the main search keywords "Gamification" and "Marketing".

The research was based on scientific and/or academic documents on the application of Gamification to Business When Applied to Marketing. In Figure 4, we can examine the linked keywords, and thus, it is possible to highlight the network of keywords that appear together / linked in each scientific article, allowing to identify the topics studied by research and identify trends in future research. Finally, in Figure 5, a profusion of co-citation with a unit of analysis of the cited references is presented.

Figure 3. network of all keywords

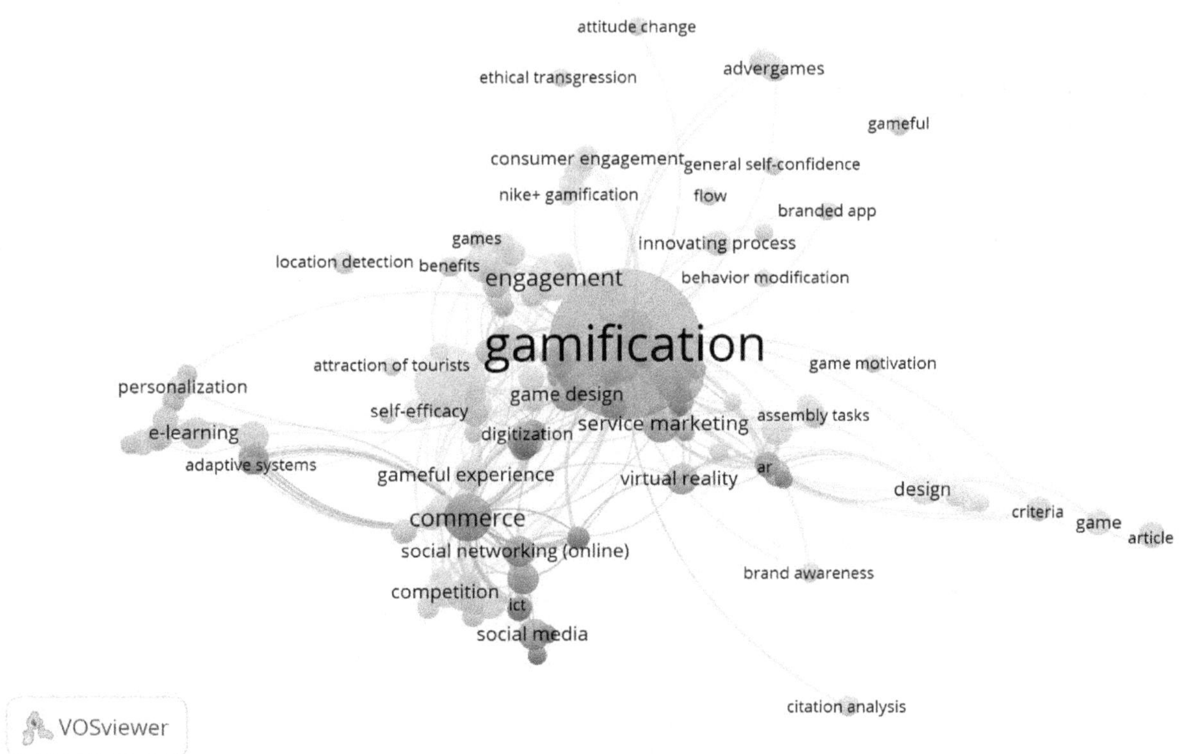

Figure 4. network of Linked Keywords

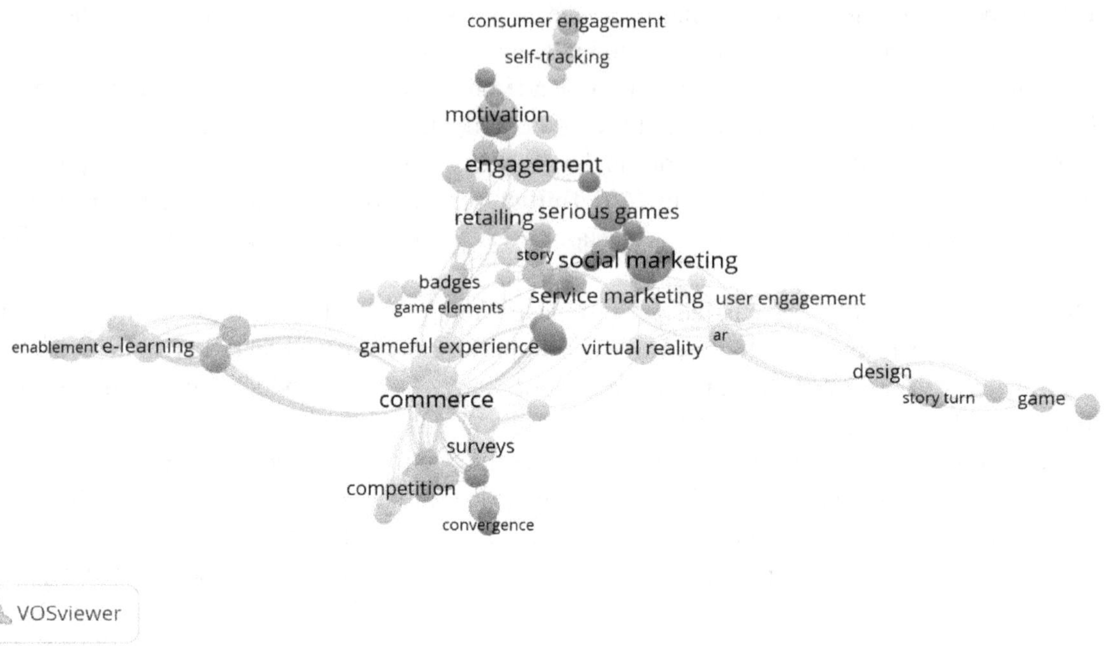

Figure 5. network of co-citation

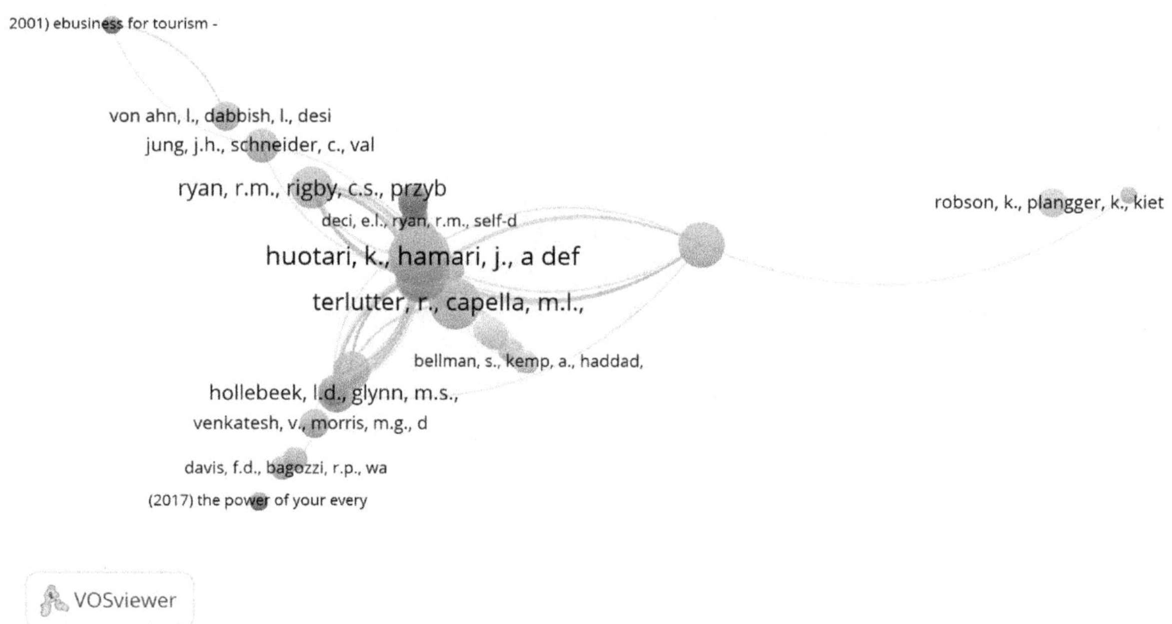

THEORETICAL PERSPECTIVES

Although games were previously perceived as entertainment tools only, the current digital era has expanded its use to include promotional activities. The challenges and rewards increase players' engagement and enthusiasm to progress and create compelling experiences. The expansion led to the development of the term 'gamification,' which refers to the use of game-design elements in non-game environments. Çeker and Özdaml (2017) define gamification as non-game activities created through game principles and rules to increase and motivate participation and encourage gamified thinking and game mechanics for problem-solving. Similarly, Landers (2019) defines it as the design process used to add game elements to an existing non-game system. For the marketing context, game elements can be integrated into a current marketing strategy to increase target consumer engagement by creating a sense of immersion and gathering data to predict future behaviors and attitudes that might affect purchasing decisions (Shpakova et al., 2020). Therefore, the game elements identified and added should be meaningful and impactful to achieve the desired marketing outcomes. According to Yang et al. (2018), gamification in marketing involves integrating game design elements in promotional activities to realize marketing-related objectives through game-like experiences that appeal to target consumers. The components may include rewards, competition, challenges and constraints, points, badges, cooperation, progression, and emotions (Helmefalk & Marcusson, 2019).

Different game elements have varying implications on players' experiences and decision-making. For instance, the rewards are often perceived as incentives to encourage using an app or purchasing from a particular brand (Silva et al., 2019). Awarding redeemable points to the players after achieving specific game-related goals can encourage more engagement. As a result, the players will use this experience to evaluate a brand or product, encouraging more purchases. Therefore, gamification has the potential to improve organizational performance through game advertising.

GAMIFICATION IN MARKETING

Marketing involves searching and stimulating consumers to interact with the company in promotions, product development, communication, pricing, and distribution to satisfy their needs. Innovative technologies, such as games and social media, have enabled organizations to create and maintain deep and meaningful relationships with existing and potential customers within targeted locations (Thorpe & Roper, 2019). E-commerce is a significant business development that recognizes and integrates gamification to increase user engagement and excitation (Noorbehbahani et al., 2019). The success of e-commerce is strongly dependent on consumers' online interactions and activities since they influence their online purchasing decisions and intentions. In this context, companies add game dynamics and mechanics to computer programs to create an interactive design and enhance digital advertising to influence consumer behaviors (Vasilevski et al., 2019). Examples of gaming tools applied in the gamified marketing systems include points, badges, quests/challenges, rewards, levels, and engagement loops that increase player involvement, enjoyment, and activities. The choice of gaming elements should depend on the company's target market dynamics to ensure they are relatable and enhance user experience and stickiness (Timchenko et al., 2020). Consequently, gamification as an element of e-commerce and e-marketing can lead to data collection on consumer background and interests for future projections and improvements, increased e-commerce platform visits, and increased sales (Wolf et al., 2020). Therefore, gamification can significantly contribute to customer value creation if the tools and methods are appropriately incorporated into an organization's existing marketing strategy.

Gamification has become an effective tool of social marketing. Mitchell et al. (2017) explain that social marketing is a long-term approach used to change people's behaviors by improving their welfare and the social, economic, and physical environment they live in. It targets behaviors that consumers may find disagreeable, characterized by difficulties in performing them and fewer benefits (Xu et al., 2017). Social marketers have adopted game elements to increase consumers' motivation to participate in these pro-social behaviors, such as exercising (Widawska-Stanisz, 2018). Gamification can improve social behaviors through intrinsic and extrinsic motivation (Xu et al., 2016). Ultimately, the interest and enjoyment experienced through games create inherent motivation that leads to behavioral changes.

Similarly, rewards and punishments can encourage behavioral changes to gain particular benefits or avoid penalties associated with failure to achieve a quest. However, Mitchell et al. (2017) argue that intrinsic motivation supports the maintenance of behavior change, that is, players are more likely to maintain behaviors achieved during gaming if they enjoyed or had interests in the gaming activities. Since social marketing behaviors are challenging to achieve and slow to accumulate than other competing behaviors, social marketers must provide actual goods and services offering real value and positive exchange. Mulcahy et al. (2018) explain that gamification in social marketing achieves behavioral impact since it creates positive value for players through game design elements that are more rewarding and motivating. For instance, an exercise app enables players to perform a behavior, i.e., exercising, while increasing enjoyment through entertainment gaming elements (Högberg et al., 2019). Thus, social marketers should create gaming systems that offer benefits incorporating multiple consumer needs, such as the desire for entertainment while maintaining a healthy lifestyle.

Gamification in social marketing integrates gaming principles and technology that goes beyond entertainment to include other life aspects, such as health and wellbeing. Mulcahy et al. (2018) indicate that it contains 'serious games' with broader goals and purposes, including healthcare, learning, marketing, and behavior change. For example, Pokémon Go encourages players to build relationships and exercise while the Nike+ app enables them to monitor their physical activities to score points (Mitchell et al., 2017). Social marketers develop game design elements based on the targeted behaviors. For instance, a game that aims to encourage moderate alcohol consumption can have different features than one that targets reducing household energy usage (Yamakami, 2015). Therefore, organizations and marketers should study their target populations and understand game elements' functionalities to ensure that the designs and systems developed address the specific social behaviors intended (Kassabli Al Fakhry, 2019). In addition, this process ensures that the game is relatable and appealing to the target audience to encourage repetitive participation. Thus, the game developed should integrate multiple features that encourage players to keep playing by creating intrinsic motivation and stimulating interest in specific activities and behaviors.

Gamification has become a significant value co-creation tool in modern-day marketing. The digital era has changed consumers' status as the passive target of firms' offerings to an active knowledge and skills contributor to help them realize these offerings (de Jong et al., 2021). Technological developments have led to consumer empowerment through increased informational resources and consumer-to-consumer interactions that allow information exchange regarding experiences, opinions, and intentions (Yen et al., 2019). In addition, the increase in promotional information online has significantly reduced consumers' trust in their accuracy and reliability. Instead, they favor peer reviews and recommendations to make purchasing decisions (Dietrich et al., 2019). This shift has significantly created the need for value co-creation to ensure that the goods and services produced and offered match consumers' specific needs and develop a sense of association in the innovation process that influences attitudes towards an organization and its offerings. Gamification contributes to this value co-creation process by providing a platform to voluntarily navigate themselves through numerous affordances and consumption propositions (Charitsis et al., 2019). Through an organization's resources and systems, consumers can co-produce subjectivities, such as life forms, affects, relations, and networks and communications needed to influence individual or group lifestyles. Thus, game elements in marketing are more emotional, symbolic, affective, and communal to ensure that players can relate to the goals and objectives and to lead to eventual behavioral changes.

Game apps downloadable in mobile phones have significantly promoted marketing strategies. Given the recent technological advancements and mobile phone affordability, companies can reach global populations through mobile marketing. Dymek (2016) explains that gamification has been introduced as a core communication strategy in mobile phone marketing campaigns in an attempt to reach wider audiences and enhance digital adaptation. It creates a new method of improving consumer engagement with a brand or products through challenges and quests, and rewards that encourage critical thinking, problem-solving, and enjoyment (Dillon & Olberding, 2016). Mobile Apps and advertising ensure that target consumers are always engaged. The discovery of the fun element in gamification can increase consumers' willingness to buy and lead to increased sales. Dymek (2016) indicates that gamification in mobile marketing applies the universally acknowledged marketing communications dynamics that integrate various factors ranging from high engagement, a sense of community, fun and playful activities, and passion. It is perceived as a cost-effective mass media approach that allows companies to generate consumer attention to achieve specified marketing goals (Drell, 2014). As global populations increasingly adopt mobile phones in their daily lives, the effectiveness of gamification in mobile marketing will continue to grow. Thus, marketers and organizations should optimize this opportunity to ensure the provision of gamified products and services that appeal to target populations.

In addition, some marketers use game entertainment to educate and train players on various skills or to impart necessary knowledge. It has become a critical tool for creating awareness regarding various life aspects such as environmental, social, and economic issues that can potentially affect human life. This tool is incredibly fundamental for companies using corporate social responsibility (CSR) as a core marketing and management aspect to provide positive social value (Dymek, 2018). For instance, gamification has become an appealing marketing method used to reduce over-indulgence in activities that are harmful to human beings and can lead to adverse implications (Eppmann et al., 2018). Some organizations use advergames to minimize the impact of commercial advertising that leads to alcohol over-consumption among teens and adults.

Dietrich et al. (2018) recommend that marketers adopt a user-oriented approach in creating the game design to ensure that the players' value is explicitly understood. Achieving specific behavioral changes require users to understand the goals of the game's activities and the impacts of their achievements (Dymek & Zackariasson, 2016). According to the principle of operant conditioning, external rewards provided after achieving specific desired outcomes can control behavior (Kim & Ahn, 2017). Rewards are positive reinforcements that encourage participants to keep learning and improve until they reach the desired behaviors. In this context, the marketers can utilize this potential to award players after proof of understanding the various concepts taught through game features (Fernandes et al., 2018). It can lead to increased sensitivity on issues of absolute importance to their wellbeing and lead to brand loyalty for companies marketing sustainable products.

However, companies struggle with evaluating the effectiveness of gamification as a marketing tool (Eppmann et al., 2018). As a result, Eppmann et al. (2018) recommend using the gameful experience scale [GAMEX] to measure gameful experiences by capturing involving and emotional qualities of gamification that shape positive behaviors associated with increased buying and loyalty. The scale facilitates data collection and analysis to enable marketers to understand the various dimensions of gameful experience integrated when designing gamified applications (García-Magro & Soriano-Pinar, 2020). Besides, it can assist in predicting marketing outcomes to ensure strategies adopted are meaningful and create value for the organization. Yang et al. (2018) explained that the success of marketing activities in gamification depends on the marketer's understanding of gaming elements and their application in creating exciting experiences that stimulate intrinsic motivation to change behaviors or purchase advertised products. Therefore, the GAMEX can help evaluate gameful experiences and appropriate gaming elements needed to improve them for value creation and successful marketing.

CRITICAL GAME DESIGN ELEMENTS IN MARKETING

The Elemental Tetrad Model recommends design characteristics needed in gamification, including story, mechanics, aesthetics, and technology (Hofacker et al., 2016). They create the theme, structure, look and feel, and features that lead to attitude, engagement, purchase, retention, and repurchase.

Story

Storytelling is a marketing strategy used to persuade target consumers to purchase promoted products or services. Using a narrative in gamification prompts player's mental capabilities and systems to focus on the narrated occurrences, leading to immersion and engagement. Hofacker et al. (2016) explain that transporting narrative to influence players' attention involves two components; empathy and mental imagery. Empathy enables the listener to understand and relate to the story's character, while mental imagery enables them to imagine being a part of the story (Saleme et al., 2020). These aspects influence how the listener experiences the story. This game element in gamification enables developers to create relatable game characters with a relatable storyline that allows players to imagine they are experiencing and encountering similar challenges and emotions as the character they are playing (Gatautis & Vitkauskaite, 2014). Storytelling is a necessary human experience that enables marketers to develop deep connections with their target consumers. Therefore, this game element is fundamental in in-game advertising and advergames.

Mechanics

Comprehending game outcomes requires feedback that is often attained through mechanics. Hofacker et al. (2016) define game mechanics as game's rules and processes that determine how players achieve game goals and receive awards. The structures and the rules guide players towards making meaningful choices that are connected to the game outcomes. Examples of mechanics in games include leaderboards, badges, progress bars, and points that reflect the player's capability to pursue challenging goals (Aydin & Schnabel, 2016). They also describe incentives that motivate players and build loyalty to show goal achievement and progression. Incentives and rewards in marketing are essential in encouraging people to purchase from a specific brand since they provide additional value. They influence consumers' views on a product or service, leading to higher marketing outcomes.

Aesthetics

Appearance is essential in creating an impactful and gameful experience. Game developers should thoroughly consider physical aspects such as colors, facial expressions, movements, and character shapes when designing games that align with the desired theme and narrative. Hofacker et al. (2016) indicate that character quirks and aesthetic features determine the creative vision that influences players' engagement and the effectiveness of gamification. In addition, visual semiotics influences how players interpret messages represented in the graphical images through signs and symbols (Vashisht et al., 2019). For instance, the brand, product, or service promoted in the gamified app or system should be clearly identified and connected to the game objectives (Bayuk & Altobello, 2019). The game elements and features should include visual symbols and patterns that explicitly identify the product to ensure the interactions and engagements are meaningful and related to the promotional goals and outcomes.

Technology

Technology represents the infrastructure used to communicate promotional messages. According to Hofacker et al. (2016), the technology game element represents the channel used to tell the story, operate the mechanics, and present the aesthetics. Therefore, achieving gamification goals would be impossible without the appropriate technologies (Bitrián et al., 2021). Consumers engaging experiences depend on the capability to use technological features developed. Game developers should ensure that the technical characters achieve compatibility with multiple devices (Sigala, 2015). Technological advances have availed multiple personal devices such as smartphones, tablets, and laptops, which differ in size and technical features (Brownell et al., 2015). Players should be able to experience the intended functionalities and adventures regardless of the devices they are using. Thus, the technical elements' quality should not frustrate the players' attempts to achieve game goals.

GAMIFICATION TO IMPROVE CONSUMER EXPERIENCES, ATTITUDES, AND INTENTIONS IN MARKETING

Businesses use gamification as a strategic resource to influence target consumer behaviors in online and offline environments. Olaison and Taalas (2016) indicate that gamification aims to increase employee or consumer engagement to enhance collaboration and innovation. The use of game elements in non-game environments can lead to brand awareness, loyalty, engagement, and motivation since players are consistently engaged in tasks and challenges that are fun and require high involvement (Feng et al., 2019). According to Gartner Inc. gamification strategies budget amounted to $2.8 billion in 2014, while gamified applications were predicted to account for 70% of the Forbes Global 2000 (Olaison & Taalas, 2016). These statistics highlight the significance of increased consumer engagement in fun activities as a marketing strategy in the modern digital era. The realization of marketing goals associated with these financial figures requires companies to align their gamification goals with consumer needs and expectations to create appealing experiences. This strategy ensures that players do not use the game features in an unintended way that does not benefit the company or promote its promotional activities (De Canio et al., 2021). Players' perceptions of a game and their interpretations of intended purposes depend on their gameful experiences that are often experienced through achievements, a sense of collaboration/community, and transparency (Bennett & Vijaygopal, 2018). Therefore, the game features selected and integrated into gamified marketing applications and strategies should consider the target audience's preferred game elements for improved experiences and intentions to play.

Additionally, a successful and influential advergame improves consumer experiences, attitudes, and intentions by ensuring it's designed from a consumer's perspective. Advergames are advertising techniques that use games for advertising products or services (Hu & Wise, 2021). The advertising games are designed by or collaborating with an organization to promote a brand (Gutt et al., 2020). The most critical factors in ensuring the success of advergame include Game design, Players' personality-related, Technical, and Brand/product-related aspects ("A gamified marketing strategy…," 2021). These factors affect a player's experiences and utilize the game features to satisfy personal needs.

Game Design Factors

Game design elements influence the usability and performance of the advergames, consequently affecting marketing outcomes. When designing the gamified applications for brand promotions, some elements include the narrative, game goals, mechanisms, fantasy, challenges, interaction and sociality, and the value acquired from playing (Wasan, 2017). These factors determine the players' gameful experiences that define long-term commitment. Although game design elements are essential in all marketing strategies, they are more significant in social marketing strategies that aim to achieve behavioral impacts associated with complex changes (Hadar, 2016). Game design factors are considered the most critical elements in determining the game's success ("A gamified marketing strategy…," 2021). Thus, poor design can lead to consumer resistance, frustrations, and reluctance to play, limiting the success of the advergames. Olaison and Taalas (2016) indicate that the game design and mechanics must be designed to align with players' multiple objectives and emotional levels to enhance engagement and motivate them to play. Yang et al. (2017) further explain that failed gamification projects often occur due to companies increased focus on technology instead of the targeted users. Therefore, gamified applications should be based on the developers' understanding of the consumers and their needs.

Players' Personality-Related Factors

An individual's personality defines their pattern of thinking, feelings, and behaviors. Player engagement is significantly dependent on individual characteristics such as gender, age, and interests. It is recommendable for advergames to include personalization features that modify experiences based on individual factors and differences to increase dependency on the game ("A gamified marketing strategy…," 2021). Abou-Shouk and Soliman (2021) contribute to this argument by indicating that companies should optimize customer data gathered from social media and gamification apps to understand the target population's preferences and needs and enhance value co-creation strategies. The spread of mobile technologies has created an opportunity for organizations to increase engagement and sales by providing personalized services and experiences (Hu & Wise, 2021). Aligning the game goals and objectives with consumer needs and preferences can lead to intrinsic motivation to build long-lasting implications. According to Mitchell et al. (2017), consumers are likely to drop newly acquired behaviors once they stop playing the game unless stimulated by intrinsic motivations such as interest and enjoyment. Personalizing advergames and in-game advertising create a sense of connection with the game. Brand promotion can lead to long-lasting brand awareness and loyalty and translate to increased sales and revenues (Yang et al., 2019). Therefore, like other forms of marketing such as emails and newsletters, gamification should be customized to ensure alignment and connection with target consumers.

Technical Factors

The technologies used to design the game and promote its features should be user-friendly to encourage consistent engagement. Various technical factors that should be considered when designing advergames include high-quality graphics, game reliability, compatibility with multiple devices, performance suggestions, appropriate soundtrack, the capability to play online and offline, interactivity with other players, and small game size ("A gamified marketing strategy…," 2021). Högberg et al. (2019) recommend that companies using gamification should integrate tools that hedonic and utilitarian value to the consumers to create gameful experiences and shape their attitudes towards the marketing practices. In addition, Piligrimiene et al. (2015) state that brand management depends on interactive and co-creative aspects of customer experiences that are determined through interactions with various objects or focal agents. In this context, game developers should ensure that the technical features developed and offered to layers do not frustrate their efforts to achieve certain gaming milestones (Samar & Mazuri, 2019). For instance, exercise apps include technical features, such as personal informatics tools that gather and track individuals' everyday activities to generate positive experiences (Jang et al., 2018). They monitor and manage personal health records and can lead to emotional and psychological needs satisfaction. In addition, they should ensure effective interactions with the brand features such as names, logos, or trademarks to influence their impressions.

Factors Related to the Brand / Product

Product features, such as price, packaging, and brand name, significantly contribute to an individual's purchasing decisions. The brand or product information provided in the advergames through product placement determines players' acceptance of the marketing content contained in the game ("A gamified marketing strategy…," 2021). Making purchasing decisions requires a comprehensive understanding of the products or services offered, often through available informational resources (Lieberoth et al., 2015). The game's relevance to the brand promoted depends on consumers' understanding of the brand-related information provided and its influence in shaping behaviors and buying decisions. Ögel Aydın and Argan (2021) indicate that the game's content should offer the brand's functional and lifestyle features to increase awareness and influence attitudes. While technical and game design features are more likely to influence individual gameful experiences, personality and brand/product-related factors influence attitudes and intentions (Bennett & Vijaygopal, 2018). Consumers can only purchase a product or service if its perceived and actual benefits address their needs (Kumar & Ravi Kumar, 2019). Therefore, the theme of the game should be aligned with the product category. For instance, games promoting dietary products should integrate features related to healthy lifestyles and health conditions (Hamari, 2013). The alignment influences how consumers process information and their attitudes towards the products or brand. Therefore, it is fundamental to ensure that players understand the game's purpose from the beginning to maintain interest and commitment.

GAMIFICATION AS A TOOL

A gamified system creates an avenue for value co-creation that leads to brand innovation. Branding is a marketing technique used to create designs, symbols, or names that differentiate brands from their competitors. The primary goal of integrating gamified apps and systems into an organization's marketing strategy is to increase existing and potential customers' engagement with its products or services (Nobre & Ferreira, 2017). The process involves voluntary participation in value co-creation since consumers interact with various game elements to improve their gameful experiences. In addition, gamification enables organizations to optimize modern data collection practices and analysis to understand players' interests and preferences indicated in their online activities (Harman et al., 2014). Consumer information enhances the organization's innovativeness by building a brand image based on target consumers' perceptions and expectations. Florenthal (2019) explains that online environments in the digital era have become fundamental in building consumer-brand relationships. Kemell et al. (2020) attribute this development to the increased engagement and consistent promotion of a brand's and its associated products and services online presence. Advergames and in-game advertising require companies to publish brand-related content that initiates communication and engagement (Kachniewska, 2015). As a result, marketers and firms can track and monitor the player's activities and interactions to understand their perceptions and attitudes towards specific products or services advertised (Shpakova et al., 2019). This data can improve the brand or branding initiatives to ensure they align with consumers' interests for enhanced adoption and purchasing intentions.

Gamification plays a critical role in increasing brand engagement to facilitate positive marketing outcomes. Xi and Hamari (2020) define brand engagement as the outcomes of the co-creative customer experience built through interactions with the brand's service portfolio and providers. It involves three primary dimensions; social, emotional, and cognitive (la Cuadra et al., 2020). The emotional aspect describes the positive brand-related affects, feelings, and reactions occurring from consumer-brand interactions (Kuznetsova & Sos, 2020). Social engagement refers to the meaning of communications and connections experienced during the interactions (Seiffert-Brockmann et al., 2018). In gamified systems, social brand engagement is achieved through collaborations and communities, where players work with other players to attain a particular game goal or gain certain rewards (Landers et al., 2020). Cognitive engagement involves the players' mental investments in the interactions and is reflected through an individual's degree of interest and conscious attention. Xi and Hamari (2020) indicate that gamified interactions are positively related to cognitive and social engagement dimensions since they are optimally challenging and highly challenging. A company can evaluate cognitive brand engagement by tracking players' patterns of thought processes, duration of focus, and frequency of using the gamified apps and systems.

Consequently, players who frequently visit a gamified site or spend a lot of time playing the game can be described as cognitively engaged. The degree of an individual's social, emotional, or cognitive brand engagement is dependent on their perceived value gained from participation and the ease of use of the game features (Robson, 2019). Therefore, game developers should consider the functionalities and benefits of game design and technical elements in gamified apps and systems to increase brand engagement (Landers et al., 2018). They should be based on a comprehensive analysis of target consumer needs and characteristics to ensure they are relatable and appealing to capture their interests and long-term commitment to participate.

Brand engagement in gamification facilitates customer-based brand equity, which stimulates an organization's financial gains from a marketing strategy. According to Xi and Hamari (2020), brand equity refers to brand loyalty, awareness, and assets such as names and symbols that make a brand memorable among target consumers. Game developers achieve this branding aspect by integrating a brand's significant symbols into the design to increase players' interactions and ensure they remain memorable (Meng & Hamzah, 2014). Consequently, players can easily recognize and identify a brand as part of particular product categories and prioritize it when purchasing decisions (Tseng et al., 2021). Games that are fun and create compelling experiences for players are likely to increase customers' willingness to invest more time, money, and energy, leading to brand loyalty (Seiffert & Nothhaft, 2015). In addition, the positive emotions built through gamified experiences can lead to positive attitudes and a desire to maintain a good relationship with a brand (Mishra & Malhotra, 2020). As a result, these consumers are more likely to frequently purchase from the specific company associated with the game by willingly expanding their activities beyond game functionalities. For example, suppose a player consistently interacts with a product while playing the game and often achieves positive experiences. In that case, they are more likely to purchase other products related to the brand for everyday use (Moncrief et al., 2015). Therefore, engagement and experience in gamification increase brand awareness and loyalty, which are critical elements of brand equity.

GAMIFICATION IN MARKETING EDUCATION

Social interactions significantly contribute to high academic performance among marketing learners and professionals. According to social exchange theory (SET), people make conscious and unconscious decisions after evaluating the costs and benefits of an action or relationship (Moscardo, 2020). Therefore, gamification in marketing education can be perceived as an approach of encouraging learners to maximize the rewards of technology adoption to improve their knowledge and skills (Canhoto & Murphy, 2016). While some students may or may not anticipate rewards, gamification has been significantly adopted in online learning as a measure of increasing student engagement to establish a positive, intrinsically motivating experience (Dikcius et al., 2020). Game elements such as digital points reflect an individual student's academic progress throughout the course and can be used to personalize teaching strategies and course content for better outcomes (Mulcahy et al., 2020). The games make the learning experiences more entertaining and enjoyable, thus, increasing learning motivation, performance, engagement, and emotional skills. Educators can use these positive outcomes to predict the effectiveness of the learning process and consequent student satisfaction.

The need for personalization in learning has been a significant driver for gamification in marketing education. Personalized learning involves tailoring learning materials and strategies to individual learners' specific traits and requirements (Nguyen & Meixner, 2020). Since the gamified websites, applications, and systems are based on specific individual needs and preferences, learning outcomes are often higher and ensure that marketing professionals have the current knowledge and skills required to optimize new opportunities (Aljabali & Ahmad, 2019). The performance results from customization that considers a learner's existing skills, knowledge level, preferred learning style, and objectives (Schiele, 2018). Gamification tools enable game designers to gather and analyze data related to the learner's past experiences connected to the current knowledge and skills (Olberding, 2016). As a result, the strategy enhances learning effectiveness by improving engagement, teaching new concepts, and ensuring knowledge retention.

In this digital era, technologies have transformed marketing by ensuring promotional strategies are more personalized and immersive. Digital marketing has also created more targeted and integrated ecosystems through advanced infrastructures and value (Séraphin et al., 2017). Consequently, academic researchers argue engaging marketing professionals in gamified learning environment enables them to familiarize themselves with technologies employed in the practical marketing field (Bechkoff, 2019). Therefore, the use of game mechanisms, elements, and technologies in marketing education can help bridge the gap between theoretical learning and marketing practice (Paknejad et al., 2021). It can create a pool of marketing professionals with skills and knowledge that relate to the modern approach and business environment.

Young generations, such as Gen Y and Z, are exposed to technologies at young ages, prompting educators to move beyond traditional learning environments. These populations have significantly adopted technologies as part of daily lives and have embedded them in knowledge production, communication, networking, and creative expression (Robson, 2019). They need them to learn, play, and maintain social communications during peer activities. Thus, educators understand that integrating gamification in learning is essential in ensuring student engagement and increasing motivation to learn (Panasenko et al., 2018). The combination of games and education led to the formulation of the "edutainment" concept, which balances students' entertainment and education needs (Séraphin, 2019). While videogames might not solve the diverse educational needs of students, educators continue to implement games-based curriculum structures that focus on increasing engagement and creating immersive learning experiences.

However, academic researchers noticed that the development and application of particular games didn't specifically influence learning outcomes. As a result, gamification in the classroom has been expanded to include using structural elements of the games to improve educational experiences by integrating existing curricula, processes, and practices (Séraphin, 2019). Benefits of gamification in marketing education can include increased class attendance, higher quality student participation, increased engagement, and higher motivation and autonomy (Robson, 2019). These can reduce the potential disruptions associated with technologies that undermine learners' capability to focus on school work for a long time. In addition, technological advancements have shifted human interactions from the physical to the virtual world (Ruffino, 2017). Despite the need for social and communication skills, current generations' reliance on online platforms such as social media for communication has caused significant changes in marketing communications (Richter et al., 2015). Modern-era marketers need the knowledge and skills required to create and maintain online relationships. Therefore, integrating gamified learning experiences exposes these professionals to the virtual world, preparing them for their after-school roles.

CONCLUSION

Gamification refers to the use of game elements in non-game contexts, such as marketing. It involves high engagement as players solve puzzles and challenges to achieve certain rewards or incentives. These activities often create compelling experiences that influence attitudes and behaviors. In the marketing context, gameful experiences can affect players' perceptions and attitudes towards a brand, product, or service, leading to increased sales and revenues. Given the increasing rate of technology adoption among global populations, gamification provides marketers with an opportunity to promote products in entertaining and enjoyable ways. Therefore, the integrated gaming elements should be based on the target audience's interests and preferences to increase their willingness to engage in value co-creation strategies. The success of gamified marketing depends on the game's capability to create long-lasting impressions and behaviors. For instance, some players are likely to drop some behaviors the moment they stop playing a game. Therefore, the primary goal of gamification in marketing should be to stimulate intrinsic motivations and intentions to build a relationship with the company. This process will ensure loyalty and retention, thus, proving the effectiveness of gamification as a marketing tool.

ACKNOWLEDGMENT

I would like to express gratitude to the Editor and the Arbitrators. They offered extremely valuable suggestions or improvements. The authors were supported by the GOVCOPP Research Center of the University of Aveiro and IADE, European University.

REFERENCES

A gamified marketing strategy to create emotional customer connection: Success factors for irresistible advergame design. (2021). *Strategic Direction, 37*(1), 25-27. doi:10.1108/SD-10-2020-0182

Abou-Shouk, M., & Soliman, M. (2021). The impact of gamification adoption intention on brand awareness and loyalty in tourism: The mediating effect of customer engagement. *Journal of Destination Marketing & Management, 20*, 100559. Advance online publication. doi:10.1016/j.jdmm.2021.100559

Aljabali, R. N., & Ahmad, N. (2019). *A review on adopting personalized gamified experience in the learning context.* Paper presented at the 2018 IEEE Conference on e-Learning, e-Management, and e-Services, IC3e 2018. 10.1109/IC3e.2018.8632635

Aydin, S., & Schnabel, M. A. (2016). The museum of gamers: Unmediated cultural heritage through gaming. In Cultural heritage in a changing world (pp. 125-141). doi:10.1007/978-3-319-29544-2_8

Bayuk, J., & Altobello, S. A. (2019). Can gamification improve financial behavior? The moderating role of app expertise. *International Journal of Bank Marketing*, *37*(4), 951–975. doi:10.1108/IJBM-04-2018-0086

Bechkoff, J. (2019). Gamification using a choose-your-own-adventure type platform to augment learning and facilitate student engagement in marketing education. *Journal for Advancement of Marketing Education*, *27*(1), 13–30.

Bennett, R., & Vijaygopal, R. (2018). Consumer attitudes towards electric vehicles: Effects of product user stereotypes and self-image congruence. *European Journal of Marketing*, *52*(3-4), 499–527. doi:10.1108/EJM-09-2016-0538

Berger, A., Schlager, T., Sprott, D. E., & Herrmann, A. (2018). Gamified interactions: Whether, when, and how games facilitate self–brand connections. *Journal of the Academy of Marketing Science*, *46*(4), 652–673. doi:10.100711747-017-0530-0

Bettany-Saltikov, J. (2016). *How to do a Systematic Literature Review in Nursing: A step-by-step guide* (2nd ed.). McGraw-Hill Education.

Bilgin, Y. (2017). Qualitative method versus quantitative method in marketing research: An application example at Oba restaurant. *Qualitative Versus Quantitative Research*, 1-28.

Bitrián, P., Buil, I., & Catalán, S. (2021). Enhancing user engagement: The role of gamification in mobile apps. *Journal of Business Research, 132*, 170–185. doi:10.1016/j.jbusres.2021.04.028

Brownell, B., Cechanowicz, J., & Gutwin, C. (2015). Gamification of survey research: Empirical results from gamifying a conjoint experiment. In Gamification in education and business (pp. 569-591). doi:10.1007/978-3-319-10208-5_29

Canhoto, A. I., & Murphy, J. (2016). Learning from simulation design to develop better experiential learning initiatives: An integrative approach. *Journal of Marketing Education*, *38*(2), 98–106. doi:10.1177/0273475316643746

Çeker, E., & Özdaml, F. (2017). What" Gamification" Is and What It's Not. *European Journal of Contemporary Education*, *6*(2), 221–228. doi:10.13187/ejced.2017.2.221

Charitsis, V., Yngfalk, A. F., & Skålén, P. (2019). 'Made to run': Biopolitical marketing and the making of the self-quantified runner. *Marketing Theory*, *19*(3), 347–366. doi:10.1177/1470593118799794

De Canio, F., Fuentes-Blasco, M., & Martinelli, E. (2021). Engaging shoppers through mobile apps: The role of gamification. *International Journal of Retail & Distribution Management*, *49*(7), 919–940. Advance online publication. doi:10.1108/IJRDM-09-2020-0360

de Jong, A., de Ruyter, K., Keeling, D. I., Polyakova, A., & Ringberg, T. (2021). Key trends in business-to-business services marketing strategies: Developing a practice-based research agenda. *Industrial Marketing Management*, *93*, 1–9. doi:10.1016/j.indmarman.2020.12.004

Dietrich, T., Mulcahy, R., & Knox, K. (2018). Gaming attribute preferences in social marketing programs: Meaning matters more than rewards. *Journal of Social Marketing*, *8*(3), 280–296. doi:10.1108/JSOCM-06-2017-0038

Dietrich, T., Rundle-Thiele, S., Kubacki, K., Durl, J., Gullo, M. J., Arli, D., & Connor, J. P. (2019). Virtual reality in social marketing: A process evaluation. *Marketing Intelligence & Planning*, *37*(7), 806–820. doi:10.1108/MIP-11-2018-0537

Dikcius, V., Urbonavicius, S., Adomaviciute, K., Degutis, M., & Zimaitis, I. (2020). Learning marketing online: The role of social interactions and gamification rewards. *Journal of Marketing Education*. Advance online publication. doi:10.1177/0273475320968252

Dillon, K., & Olberding, J. C. (2016). Promoting events: Through cause marketing, social media, and "gamification." In Social enterprise and special events (pp. 37-51). doi:10.4324/9781315673219

Drell, L. (2014). Let the gamification begin. *Marketing Health Services*, *34*(1), 24–27. PMID:24741765

Dymek, M. (2016). Inside the gamification case of a mobile phone marketing campaign: The amalgamation of game studies with marketing communications? In The business of gamification: A critical analysis (pp. 99-121). doi:10.4324/9781315740867

Dymek, M. (2018). Expanding the magic circle–gamification as a marketplace icon. *Consumption Markets & Culture*, *21*(6), 590–602. doi:10.1080/10253866.2017.1361153

Dymek, M., & Zackariasson, P. (2016). The business of gamification: A critical analysis. In The business of gamification: A critical analysis (pp. 1-229) doi:10.4324/9781315740867

Eppmann, R., Bekk, M., & Klein, K. (2018). Gameful experience in gamification: Construction and validation of a gameful experience scale. *Journal of Interactive Marketing*, *43*, 98–115. doi:10.1016/j.intmar.2018.03.002

Eppmann, R., Klein, K., & Bekk, M. (2018). WTG (way to go)! how to take gamification research in marketing to the next level. Marketing. *Zeitschrift Fur Forschung Und Praxis*, *40*(4), 44–52. doi:10.15358/0344-1369-2018-4-44

Feng, Y., Liu, Z., Qian, W., Guo, M., & Chen, J. (2019). *Research on the influence mechanism of gamification elements on users' willingness to continue using in interest-based virtual communities - based on ECM-ISC model*. Paper presented at the 2019 16th International Conference on Service Systems and Service Management, ICSSSM 2019. 10.1109/ICSSSM.2019.8887645

Fernandes, J., Martins, J., Teixeira, M. S., Branco, F., Gonçalves, R., Au-Yong-Oliveira, M., & Moreira, F. (2018). Incorporating innovative ICT in child-oriented marketing - A retail sector case study. *Proceedings of the European Conference on Innovation and Entrepreneurship, ECIE*, 1006-1014.

Florenthal, B. (2019). Young consumers' motivational drivers of brand engagement behavior on social media sites: A synthesized U&G and TAM framework. *Journal of Research in Interactive Marketing*, *13*(3), 351–391. doi:10.1108/JRIM-05-2018-0064

García-Magro, C., & Soriano-Pinar, I. (2020). Design of services in servitized firms: Gamification as an adequate tool. *Journal of Business and Industrial Marketing*, *35*(3), 575–585. doi:10.1108/JBIM-12-2018-0413

Gatautis, R., & Vitkauskaite, E. (2014). Gamification in marketing activities. *Proceedings of the 23rd International Business Information Management Association Conference, IBIMA 2014, 1*, 1875-1881.

Gutt, D., von Rechenberg, T., & Kundisch, D. (2020). Goal achievement, subsequent user effort, and the moderating role of goal difficulty. *Journal of Business Research*, *106*, 277–287. doi:10.1016/j.jbusres.2018.06.019

Hadar, E. (2016). *Mobile gamification principles applied to social engagement: Short paper of industry experience*. doi:10.1007/978-3-319-40515-5_15

Hamari, J. (2013). Transforming homo economicus into homo ludens: A field experiment on gamification in a utilitarian peer-to-peer trading service. *Electronic Commerce Research and Applications*, *12*(4), 236–245. doi:10.1016/j.elerap.2013.01.004

Harman, K., Koohang, A., & Paliszkiewicz, J. (2014). Scholarly interest in gamification: A citation network analysis. *Industrial Management & Data Systems*, *114*(9), 1438–1452. doi:10.1108/IMDS-07-2014-0208

Helmefalk, M., & Marcusson, L. (2019). Gamification in a servicescape context: A conceptual framework. *International Journal of Internet Marketing and Advertising*, *13*(1), 22–46. doi:10.1504/IJIMA.2019.097894

Hofacker, C. F., de Ruyter, K., Lurie, N. H., Manchanda, P., & Donaldson, J. (2016). Gamification and mobile marketing effectiveness. *Journal of Interactive Marketing*, *34*, 25–36. doi:10.1016/j.intmar.2016.03.001

Högberg, J., Ramberg, M. O., Gustafsson, A., & Wästlund, E. (2019). Creating brand engagement through in-store gamified customer experiences. *Journal of Retailing and Consumer Services*, *50*, 122–130. doi:10.1016/j.jretconser.2019.05.006

Högberg, J., Shams, P., & Wästlund, E. (2019). Gamified in-store mobile marketing: The mixed effect of gamified point-of-purchase advertising. *Journal of Retailing and Consumer Services*, *50*, 298–304. doi:10.1016/j.jretconser.2018.07.004

Hu, X., & Wise, K. (2021). How playable ads influence consumer attitude: Exploring the mediation effects of perceived control and freedom threat. *Journal of Research in Interactive Marketing*, *15*(2), 295–315. Advance online publication. doi:10.1108/JRIM-12-2020-0269

Huotari, K., & Hamari, J. (2017). A definition for gamification: Anchoring gamification in the service marketing literature. *Electronic Markets*, *27*(1), 21–31. doi:10.100712525-015-0212-z

Jang, S., Kitchen, P. J., & Kim, J. (2018). The effects of gamified customer benefits and characteristics on behavioral engagement and purchase: Evidence from mobile exercise application uses. *Journal of Business Research*, *92*, 250–259. doi:10.1016/j.jbusres.2018.07.056

Kachniewska, M. (2015). Gamification and social media as tools for tourism promotion. In Handbook of research on effective advertising strategies in the social media age (pp. 17-51). doi:10.4018/978-1-4666-8125-5.ch002

Kassabli Al Fakhry, C. (2019). *Marketing strategies in the age of technology*. doi:10.1007/978-3-030-30874-2_27

Kemell, K., Feshchenko, P., Himmanen, J., Hossain, A., Jameel, F., Puca, R. L., Vitikainen, T., Kultanen, J., Risku, J., Impiö, J., Sorvisto, A., & Abrahamsson, P. (2020). Software startup education: Gamifying growth hacking. In Fundamentals of software startups: Essential engineering and business aspects (pp. 269-277) doi:10.1007/978-3-030-35983-6_16

Kim, K., & Ahn, S. J. (2017). The Role of Gamification in Enhancing Intrinsic Motivation to Use a Loyalty Program. *Journal of Interactive Marketing*, *40*, 41–51. doi:10.1016/j.intmar.2017.07.001

Kumar, G. A., & Ravi Kumar, A. (2019). Employing gamification methods to increase customer engagement in digital marketing. *International Journal of Recent Technology and Engineering, 8*(2), 869-872. doi:10.35940/ijrte.B1366.0882S819

Kuznetsova, E., & Sos, P. J. (2020). Management education for digital natives in the 21st century. *Proceedings of the 16th European Conference on Management Leadership and Governance, ECMLG 2020*, 106-112. 10.34190/ELG.20.034

la Cuadra, M. T., Vila-Lopez, N., & Hernandez-Fernández, A. (2020). Could gamification improve visitors' engagement? *International Journal of Tourism Cities*, *6*(2), 317–334. doi:10.1108/IJTC-07-2019-0100

Landers, R. N. (2019). Gamification misunderstood: How badly executed and rhetorical gamification obscures its transformative potential. *Journal of Management Inquiry*, *28*(2), 137–140. doi:10.1177/1056492618790913

Landers, R. N., Auer, E. M., & Abraham, J. D. (2020). Gamifying a situational judgment test with immersion and control game elements: Effects on applicant reactions and construct validity. *Journal of Managerial Psychology*, *35*(4), 225–239. doi:10.1108/JMP-10-2018-0446

Landers, R. N., Auer, E. M., Collmus, A. B., & Armstrong, M. B. (2018). Gamification science, its history, and future: Definitions and a research agenda. *Simulation & Gaming*, *49*(3), 315–337. doi:10.1177/1046878118774385

Lieberoth, A., Møller, M., & Marin, A. C. (2015). Deep and shallow gamification in marketing: Thin evidence and the forgotten powers of really good games. In Engaging consumers through branded entertainment and convergent media (pp. 110-126). doi:10.4018/978-1-4666-8342-6.ch006

Meng, C. K., & Hamzah, M. (2014). A gamification model to motivate lecturers towards a satisfied job performance. *Proceedings of the 23rd International Business Information Management Association Conference, IBIMA 2014, 1*, 196-200.

Mishra, S., & Malhotra, G. (2020). The gamification of in-game advertising: Examining the role of psychological ownership and advertisement intrusiveness. *International Journal of Information Management*. Advance online publication. doi:10.1016/j.ijinfomgt.2020.102245 PMID:33012944

Mitchell, R., Schuster, L., & Drennan, J. (2017). Understanding how gamification influences behavior in social marketing. *Australasian Marketing Journal*, *25*(1), 12–19. doi:10.1016/j.ausmj.2016.12.001

Moncrief, W. C., Marshall, G. W., & Rudd, J. M. (2015). Social media and related technology: Drivers of change in managing the contemporary sales force. *Business Horizons*, *58*(1), 45–55. doi:10.1016/j.bushor.2014.09.009

Moscardo, G. (2020). The story turn in tourism: Forces and futures. *Journal of Tourism Futures*. doi:10.1108/JTF-11-2019-0131

Mulcahy, R., Russell-Bennett, R., & Iacobucci, D. (2020). Designing gamified apps for sustainable consumption: A field study. *Journal of Business Research*, *106*, 377–387. doi:10.1016/j.jbusres.2018.10.026

Mulcahy, R. F., Russell-Bennett, R., Zainuddin, N., & Kuhn, K. (2018). Designing gamified transformative and social marketing services: An investigation of serious m-games. *Journal of Service Theory and Practice*, *28*(1), 26–51. doi:10.1108/JSTP-02-2017-0034

Nguyen, D., & Meixner, G. (2020). *Comparison user engagement of gamified and non-gamified augmented reality assembly training*. doi:10.1007/978-3-030-37534-8_8

Nobre, H., & Ferreira, A. (2017). Gamification as a platform for brand co-creation experiences. *Journal of Brand Management*, *24*(4), 349–361. doi:10.105741262-017-0055-3

Noorbehbahani, F., Salehi, F., & Jafar Zadeh, R. (2019). A systematic mapping study on gamification applied to e-marketing. *Journal of Research in Interactive Marketing*, *13*(3), 392–410. doi:10.1108/JRIM-08-2018-0103

Ögel Aydın, S., & Argan, M. (2021). Understanding how gamification influences consumers' dietary preferences. *Journal of Social Marketing*, *11*(2), 82–123. doi:10.1108/JSOCM-09-2019-0137

Olaison, L., & Taalas, S. L. (2016). Game of gamification: Marketing, consumer resistance, and digital play. In The business of gamification: A critical analysis (pp. 59-80). doi:10.4324/9781315740867

Olberding, J. C. (2016). *Social enterprise and special events.* doi:10.4324/9781315673219

Paknejad, F., Mosaddad, S. H., & Naeini, H. S. (2021). Purchasing and consumption modification among Iranians throughout gamification. *International Journal of Industrial Engineering and Production Research*, *32*(1), 121–132. doi:10.22068/ijiepr.32.1.121

Panasenko, S. V., Nikishin, A. F., Mayorova, E. A., Boris, O. A., & Murtuzalieva, T. V. (2018). Innovative approach to fitness industry development. *Espacios, 39*(41).

Piligrimiene, Z., Dovaliene, A., & Virvilaite, R. (2015). Consumer engagement in value co-creation: What kind of value it creates for company? *The Engineering Economist*, *26*(4), 452–460. doi:10.5755/j01.ee.26.4.12502

Raimundo, R., & Rosário, A. (2021). Blockchain system in the Higher Education. *European Journal of Investigation in Health, Psychology and Education, 11*(1), 276-293. doi:10.3390/ejihpe11010002

Richter, G., Raban, D. R., & Rafaeli, S. (2015). *Studying gamification: The effect of rewards and incentives on motivation*. Gamification in Education and Business. doi:10.1007/978-3-319-10208-5_2

Robson, K. (2019). Motivating professional student behavior through a gamified personal branding assignment. *Journal of Marketing Education*, *41*(2), 154–164. doi:10.1177/0273475318823847

Rosário, A. (2021). Research-Based Guidelines for Marketing Information Systems. *International Journal of Business Strategy and Automation*, *2*(1), 1–16. doi:10.4018/IJBSA.20210101.oa1

Rosário, A., & Cruz, R. (2019). Determinants of Innovation in Digital Marketing, Innovation Policy and Trends in the Digital Age. *Journal of Reviews on Global Economics*, *8*, 1722–1731. doi:10.6000/1929-7092.2019.08.154

Rosário, A., Fernandes, F., Raimundo, R., & Cruz, R. (2021). Determinants of Nascent Entrepreneurship Development. In A. Carrizo Moreira & J. G. Dantas (Eds.), *Handbook of Research on Nascent Entrepreneurship and Creating New Ventures* (pp. 172–193). IGI Global. doi:10.4018/978-1-7998-4826-4.ch008

Ruffino, P. (2017). Engagement and the quantified self: Uneventful relationships with ghostly companions. In Self-tracking: Empirical and philosophical investigations (pp. 11-25). doi:10.1007/978-3-319-65379-2_2

Saleme, P., Dietrich, T., Pang, B., & Parkinson, J. (2020). A gamified approach to promoting empathy in children. *Journal of Social Marketing*, *10*(3), 321–337. doi:10.1108/JSOCM-11-2019-0204

Samar, R., & Mazuri, A. G. (2019). Does gamified elements influence on user's intention to adopt internet banking with integration of UTAUT and general self-confidence? *International Journal of Business Excellence, 19*(3), 394–414. doi:10.1504/IJBEX.2019.102835

Schiele, K. (2018). Utilizing gamification to promote sustainable practices: Making sustainability fun and rewarding. In Handbook of engaged sustainability (pp. 427-444). doi:10.1007/978-3-319-71312-0_16

Seiffert, J., & Nothhaft, H. (2015). The missing media: The procedural rhetoric of computer games. *Public Relations Review, 41*(2), 254–263. doi:10.1016/j.pubrev.2014.11.011

Seiffert-Brockmann, J., Weitzl, W., & Henriks, M. (2018). Stakeholder engagement through gamification: Effects of user motivation on psychological and behavioral stakeholder reactions. *Journal of Communication Management (London), 22*(1), 67–78. doi:10.1108/JCOM-12-2016-0096

Séraphin, H. (2019). *Marketing and diaspora tourism: Visual online learning materials as tools to attract the Haitian diaspora 'New generation'.* doi:10.1007/978-3-319-91095-6_25

Séraphin, H., Butcher, J., & Korstanje, M. (2017). Challenging the negative images of Haiti at a pre-visit stage using visual online learning materials. *Journal of Policy Research in Tourism, Leisure & Events, 9*(2), 169–181. doi:10.1080/19407963.2016.1261146

Shpakova, A., Dörfler, V., & MacBryde, J. (2019). *Gamifying innovation and innovating through gamification.* doi:10.1007/978-3-030-11542-5_10

Shpakova, A., Dörfler, V., & MacBryde, J. (2020). Gamifying the process of innovating. Innovation. *Organization and Management, 22*(4), 488–502. doi:10.1080/14479338.2019.1642763

Sigala, M. (2015). Gamification for crowdsourcing marketing practices: Applications and benefits in tourism. In Advances in crowdsourcing (pp. 129-146). doi:10.1007/978-3-319-18341-1_11

Silva, R., Rodrigues, R., & Leal, C. (2019). Play it again: How game-based learning improves flow in accounting and marketing education. *Accounting Education, 28*(5), 484–507. doi:10.1080/09639284.2019.1647859

Thorpe, A. S., & Roper, S. (2019). The ethics of gamification in a marketing context. *Journal of Business Ethics, 155*(2), 597–609. doi:10.100710551-017-3501-y

Timchenko, V. V., Trapitsin, S. Y., & Apevalova, Z. V. (2020). Educational technology market analysis. *Proceedings of the 2020 IEEE International Conference "Quality Management, Transport and Information Security, Information Technologies," IT and QM and IS 2020*, 612-617. 10.1109/ITQMIS51053.2020.9322982

Tseng, T. H., Hsieh, S. H., & Lee, C. T. (2021). How gamified branded applications drive marketing effectiveness? *Marketing Intelligence & Planning, 39*(5), 633–648. Advance online publication. doi:10.1108/MIP-09-2020-0407

Vashisht, D., Royne, M. B., & Sreejesh, S. (2019). What we know and need to know about the gamification of advertising: A review and synthesis of the advergame studies. *European Journal of Marketing, 53*(4), 607–634. doi:10.1108/EJM-01-2017-0070

Vasilevski, N., Brand, J., & Birt, J. (2019). Optimizing augmented reality outcomes in a gamified place experience application through design science research. *Proceedings - VRCAI 2019: 17th ACM SIGGRAPH International Conference on Virtual-Reality Continuum and its Applications in Industry.* 10.1145/3359997.3365747

Vos, L. (2015). Simulation games in business and marketing education: How educators assess student learning from simulations. *International Journal of Management Education, 13*(1), 57–74. doi:10.1016/j.ijme.2015.01.001

Wasan, P. (2017). Managing technologies for consumer engagement. In Hospitality marketing and consumer behavior: Creating memorable experiences (pp. 261-289) doi:10.1201/9781315366227-11

Widawska-Stanisz, A. (2018). Questing in city promotion on the example of the city of częstochowa. *Innovative Marketing, 14*(1), 7–12. doi:10.21511/im.14(1).2018.01

Wolf, T., Weiger, W. H., & Hammerschmidt, M. (2020). Experiences that matter? the motivational experiences and business outcomes of gamified services. *Journal of Business Research, 106*, 353–364. doi:10.1016/j.jbusres.2018.12.058

Xi, N., & Hamari, J. (2020). Does gamification affect brand engagement and equity? A study in online brand communities. *Journal of Business Research, 109*, 449–460. doi:10.1016/j.jbusres.2019.11.058

Xu, F., Buhalis, D., & Weber, J. (2017). Serious games and the gamification of tourism. *Tourism Management, 60*, 244–256. doi:10.1016/j.tourman.2016.11.020

Xu, F., Tian, F., Buhalis, D., Weber, J., & Zhang, H. (2016). Tourists as mobile gamers: Gamification for tourism marketing. *Journal of Travel & Tourism Marketing, 33*(8), 1124–1142. doi:10.1080/10548408.2015.1093999

Yamakami, T. (2015). *A gap analysis of enterprise gamification applications with social servicenics theory: Challenges and implications.* Paper presented at the 2015 12th International Conference on Service Systems and Service Management, ICSSSM 2015. 10.1109/ICSSSM.2015.7170189

Yang, P., Xu, T., Feng, Y., Zhao, Y., & Wang, X. (2018). The impact of gamification elements on the evaluation of marketing activities. *Proceedings of the International Conference on Electronic Business (ICEB),* 634-643.

Yang, P., Zhao, Y., Xu, T., & Feng, Y. (2019). *The impact of gamification element on purchase intention.* Paper presented at the 2019 16th International Conference on Service Systems and Service Management, ICSSSM 2019. 10.1109/ICSSSM.2019.8887654

Yang, Y., Asaad, Y., & Dwivedi, Y. (2017). Examining the impact of gamification on intention of engagement and brand attitude in the marketing context. *Computers in Human Behavior, 73*, 459–469. doi:10.1016/j.chb.2017.03.066

Yang, Z., Algesheimer, R., & Dholakia, U. (2017). When ethical transgressions of customers have beneficial long-term effects in retailing: An empirical investigation. *Journal of Retailing, 93*(4), 420–439. doi:10.1016/j.jretai.2017.09.005

Yen, B. T. H., Mulley, C., & Burke, M. (2019). Gamification in transport interventions: Another way to improve travel behavioral change. *Cities (London, England)*, *85*, 140–149. doi:10.1016/j.cities.2018.09.002

KEY TERMS AND DEFINITIONS

Co-Creation: Form of innovation that happens when consumers, suppliers and employees associate with the business or product or brand, adding value, content or marketing innovation, receiving the benefits of the contribution, whether through access to customized products or brands or, in promoting ideas.

Corporate Social Responsibility: A business model that encourages companies to be socially responsible.

Game Aesthetics: It is defined in three dimensions: the sensory phenomena that the player encounters in the game (visual, auditory, tactile, embodied); the digital aspects of games that share other art forms; and, as an expression of the game that experiencing pleasure, emotion, sociability (aesthetic experience).

Game Design Elements: The basic building blocks of gamification apps (badges, leaderboards, performance charts, meaningful stories, avatars and teammates).

Gameful Experience: Interactive state that occurs when the player realizes that the goals are achievable, through an experience, measured by a game experience scale, which translates into the game experience.

Gamification: Strategy to increase user involvement, improving performance by generating experiences similar to those experienced in playing games.

Gen Y: Also called millennium generation, internet generation, or millennia born between 1980 and 1996.

Gen Z: Individuals born between the mid-1960s and early 1980s, years following the post-war baby boom (1946-1964).

APPENDIX 1

Table 4. Overview of document citations period ≤2010 to 2021

Documents		≤2010	2011	2012	2013	2014	2015	2016	2017	2018	2019	2020	2021	Total
The impact of gamification adoption intention on brand aware ...	2021	-	-	-	-	-	-	-	-	-	-	-	1	**1**
Gamifying the process of innovating	2020	-	-	-	-	-	-	-	-	-	-	3	-	**3**
A gamified approach to promoting empathy in children	2020	-	-	-	-	-	-	-	-	-	-	-	2	**2**
Gamifying a situational judgment test with immersion and con ...	2020	-	-	-	-	-	-	-	-	-	-	-	2	**2**
Design of services in servitized firms: gamification as an a ...	2020	-	-	-	-	-	-	-	-	-	-	-	1	1
Does gamification affect brand engagement and equity? A stud ...	2020	-	-	-	-	-	-	-	-	-	-	8	12	**20**
The gamification ofin-game advertising: Examining the role ...	2020	-	-	-	-	-	-	-	-	-	-	-	5	**5**
Comparison User Engagement of Gamified and Non-gamified Augm ...	2020	-	-	-	-	-	-	-	-	-	-	-	1	1
Experiences that matter? The motivational experiences and bu ...	2020	-	-	-	-	-	-	-	-	-	-	13	**8**	**21**
Designing gamified apps for sustainable consumption: A field ...	2020	-	-	-	-	-	-	-	-	-	-	9	12	**21**
Geai achievement, subsequent user effort and the moderating ...	2020	-	-	-	-	-	-	-	-	-	-	1	2	**3**
Young consumers' motivational drivers ofbrand engagement be ...	2019	-	-	-	-	-	-	-	-	-	-	5	7	12
A systematic mapping study on gamification applied to e-mark ...	2019	-	-	-	-	-	-	-	-	-	-	3	3	**6**
Virtual reality insocial marketing: a process evaluation	2019	-	-	-	-	-	-	-	-	-	-	5	6	11
Play it again: how game-based learning improves flow in Acco ...	2019	-	-	-	-	-	-	-	-	-	1	5	6	12
Creating brand engagement through in-store gamified customer ...	2019	-	-	-	-	-	-	-	-	-	-	8	6	**14**
'Made to run': Biopolitical marketing and the making of the ...	2019	-	-	-	-	-	-	-	-	1	-	4	3	**8**
Gamified in-store mobile marketing: The mixed effect of gami ...	2019	-	-	-	-	-	-	-	-	-	1	9	10	**20**
Motivating Professional Student Behavior Through a Gamified ...	2019	-	-	-	-	-	-	-	-	-	2	4	5	11
Can gamification improve financial behavior? The moderating ...	2019	-	-	-	-	-	-	-	-	-	1	2	8	11
What we know and need to know about the gamification of adve ...	2019	-	-	-	-	-	-	-	-	-	-	4	4	**8**
The Ethics of Gamification in a Marketing Context	2019	-	-	-	-	-	-	-	-	-	4	5	4	13
Retraction notice to "lhe Role ofGamification in Enhancing ...	2019	-	-	-	-	-	-	-	-	-	-	-	1	1
Gamification in transport interventions: Another way to impr ...	2019	-	-	-	-	-	-	-	-	-	4	7	2	13
A Review on Adopting Personalized Gamified Experience in the ...	2019	-	-	-	-	-	-	-	-	-	-	1	-	1
Does gamified elements influence on user's intention to adop ...	2019	-	-	-	-	-	-	-	-	-	-	1	3	**4**
Gamification using a choose-your-own-adventure type platform ...	2019	-	-	-	-	-	-	-	-	-	-	2	-	**2**

Continued on following page

Table 4. Continued

Documents		≤2010	2011	2012	2013	2014	2015	2016	2017	2018	2019	2020	2021	Total
Marketing and Diaspora Tourism: Visual Online Learning Mater ...	2019	-	-	-	-	-	-	-	-	-	-	1	-	1
Gamification in a servicescape context: A conceptual framewo ...	2019	-	-	-	-	-	-	-	-	-	-	1	2	**3**
Expanding the magic circle--gamification as a marketplace ice ...	2018	-	-	-	-	-	-	-	-	-	1	3	-	**4**
The effects of gamified customer benefits and characteristic ...	2018	-	-	-	-	-	-	-	-	-	2	14	7	**23**
Gameful Experience in Gamification: Construction and Valida!...	2018	-	-	-	-	-	-	-	-	2	11	22	11	**46**
Gaming attribute preferences insocial marketing programmes: ...	2018	-	-	-	-	-	-	-	-	1	1	2	3	**7**
Utilizing gamification to promete sustainable pradices: Mak ...	2018	-	-	-	-	-	-	-	-	1		1	1	**3**
Gamification Science, lts History and Future: Definitions an ...	2018	-	-	-	-	-	-	-	-	5	13	24	21	**63**
Consumer altitudes towards electric vehicles: Effects of pro ...	2018	-	-	-	-	-	-	-	-	2	2	5	4	**13**
Designing gamified transformative and social marketing servi ...	2018	-	-	-	-	-	-	-	-	2	**4**	8	7	**21**
The impact of gamification elements on the evaluation of mar ...	2018	-	-	-	-	-	-	-	-			1		1
WTG (Way togo)! How to take gamification research in market ...	2018	-	-	-	-	-	-	-	-	1		1	1	**3**
Stakeholder engagement through gamification: Effects of user ...	2018	-	-	-	-	-	-	-	-	-	1	3		**4**
When Ethical Transgressions ofCustomers Have Beneficial Lon ...	2017	-	-	-	-	-	-	-	-	-	1	1	1	**3**
Engagement and the quantified self: Uneventful relationships ...	2017	-	-	-	-	-	-	-	-	-	-	1	1	**2**
Gamification as a platform for brand co-creation experiences	2017	-	-	-	-	-	-	-	1		2	5	11	**19**
Serious games and the gamification of tourism	2017	-	-	-	-	-	-	-	6	13	24	42	23	**108**
Challenging the negative images ofHaiti ata pre-visit stag ...	2017	-	-	-	-	-	-	-	5	6	8	5		**24**
Understanding how gamification influences behaviour in socia ...	2017	-	-	-	-	-	-	-	-	6	7	8	6	27
A definition for gamification: anchoring gamification in the ...	2017	-	-	-	-	-	-	2	9	31	57	82	43	**224**
Managing technologies for consumer engagement	2017	-	-	-	-	-	-	-	-	-	-	-	1	1
Social Enterprise and Special Events	2016	-	-	-	-	-	-	-	-	-	-	2	-	**2**
Tourists as Mobile Gamers: Gamification for Tourism Marketin ...	2016	-	-	-	-	-	-	1	3	12	23	22	12	**73**
Learning From Simulation Design to Develop Better Experienti ...	2016	-	-	-	-	-	-	-	2	5	7	9	2	**25**
Gamification and Mobile Marketing Effectiveness	2016	-	-	-	-	-	-	5	8	19	31	44	29	**136**
The business of gamification: A criticai analysis	2016	-	-	-	-	-	-	-	-	1	3	1	-	**5**
lnside the gamification case ofa mobile phone marketing cam ...	2016	-	-	-	-	-	-	-	-	1	-	-	-	1
Game of gamification: Marketing, consumer resistance and dig ...	2016	-	-	-	-	-	-	-	-	2	1	-	-	**3**
The museum of gamers: Unmediated cultural heritage through g ...	2016	-	-	-	-	-	-	1	1	1	1	3	-	**7**
Deep and shallow gamification in marketing: Thin evidence an ...	2015	-	-	-	-	-	-	2	-	2	2	-	-	**6**

Continued on following page

Table 4. Continued

Documents		≤2010	2011	2012	2013	2014	2015	2016	2017	2018	2019	2020	2021	Total
Gamification and social media as tools for tourism promotion	2015	-	-	-	-	-	-	-	-	-	1	-	-	1
Gamification of survey research: Empirical results from gami ...	2015	-	-	-	-	-	-	-	2	-	-	1	-	**3**
Studying gamification: The effect of rewards and incentives ...	2015	-	-	-	-	-	5	15	19	31	35	34	14	**153**
The missing media: The procedural rhetoric of computer games	2015	-	-	-	-	-	-	2	1	2	1	3	-	**9**
Consumer engagement in value co-creation: What kind of value ...	2015	-	-	-	-	-	-	2	1	6	3	3	1	**16**
Gamification for crowdsourcing marketing practices: Applicat ...	2015	-	-	-	-	-	-	1	6	3	8	2	1	21
Social media and related technology: Drivers of change in ma ...	2015	-	-	-	-	-	2	5	4	4	5	9	6	**35**
Scholarly interest in gamification: A citation network analy ...	2014	-	-	-	-	-	1	3	7	1	4	6	2	**24**
Gamification in marketing activities	2014	-	-	-	-	-	-	1	-	-	-	-	-	1
Let the gamification begin.	2014	-	-	-	-	-	-		3	1	-	-	-	**4**
[Gamification as a strategy ofinternal marketing, Gamificac ...	2013	-	-	-	-	-	-	-	-	1	1	1	-	**3**
Transforming homo economicus into homo ludens: A field exper ...	2013	-	-	-	9	20	36	45	59	50	52	68	31	**370**
	Total	**0**	**0**	**0**	**9**	**20**	**44**	**85**	**137**	**213**	**325**	**537**	**355**	**1725**

Source: own elaboration

APPENDIX 2

Table 5. Overview of document self-citation period ≤2010 to 2021

Documents		≤2010	2011	2012	2013	2014	2015	2016	2017	2018	2019	2020	2021	Total
Gamifying the process of innovating	2020	-	-	-	-	-	-	-	-	-	-	2	-	**2**
Does gamification affect brand engagement and equity? A stud ...	2020	-	-	-	-	-	-	-	-	-	-	1	-	**1**
The gamification ofin-game advertising: Examining the role ...	2020	-	-	-	-	-	-	-	-	-	-	-	1	**1**
Experiences that matter? The motivational experiences and bu ...	2020	-	-	-	-	-	-	-	-	-	-	2	1	**2**
Designing gamified apps for sustainable consumption: A field ...	2020	-	-	-	-	-	-	-	-	-	-	1	3	**4**
Young consumers' motivational drivers ofbrand engagement be ...	2019	-	-	-	-	-	-	-	-	-	-	1	1	**2**
A systematic mapping study on gamification applied to e-mark ...	2019	-	-	-	-	-	-	-	-	-	-	-	1	**1**
Virtual reality insocial marketing: a process evaluation	2019	-	-	-	-	-	-	-	-	-	-	5	3	**8**
Play it again: how game-based learning improves flow in Acco ...	2019	-	-	-	-	-	-	-	-	-	-	-	2	**2**
Creating brand engagement through in-store gamified customer ...	2019	-	-	-	-	-	-	-	-	-	-	2	-	**2**
'Made to run': Biopolitical marketing and the making of the ...	2019	-	-	-	-	-	-	-	-	-	1	-	-	**1**
Gamified in-store mobile marketing: The mixed effect of gami ...	2019	-	-	-	-	-	-	-	-	-	1	1	-	**2**
What we know and need to know about the gamification of adve ...	2019	-	-	-	-	-	-	-	-	-	-	-	1	**1**
Gameful Experience in Gamification: Construction and Valida!...	2018	-	-	-	-	-	-	-	-	1	-	-	-	**1**
Gaming attribute preferences insocial marketing programmes: ...	2018	-	-	-	-	-	-	-	-	-	1	1	1	**3**
Gamification Science, Its History and Future: Definitions an ...	2018	-	-	-	-	-	-	-	-	-	4	1	-	**5**
Consumer altitudes towards electric vehicles: Effects of pro ...	2018	-	-	-	-	-	-	-	-	1	-	-	1	**2**
Designing gamified transformative and social marketing servi ...	2018	-	-	-	-	-	-	-	-	-	2	2	4	**8**
WTG (Way togo)! How to take gamification research in market ...	2018	-	-	-	-	-	-	-	-	1	-	-	-	**1**
Engagement and the quantified self: Uneventful relationships ...	2017	-	-	-	-	-	-	-	-	-	1	-	-	**1**
Serious games and the gamification of tourism	2017	-	-	-	-	-	-	-	-		1	1	1	**3**
Challenging the negative images ofHaiti ata pre-visit stag ...	2017	-	-	-	-	-	-	-	5	4	5	5	-	**19**
Understanding how gamification influences behaviour in socia ...	2017	-	-	-	-	-	-	-	-	-	-	1	-	**1**
A definition for gamification: anchoring gamification in the ...	2017	-	-	-	-	-	-	-	1	4	9	8	3	**27**
Tourists as Mobile Gamers: Gamification for Tourism Marketin ...	2016	-	-	-	-	-	-	-	-	-	-	1	-	**1**
Learning From Simulation Design to Develop Better Experienti ...	2016	-	-	-	-	-	-	-	-	1	-	-	-	**1**
Gamification and Mobile Marketing Effectiveness	2016	-	-	-	-	-	-	-	1	-	1	2	1	**5**

Continued on following page

Table 5. Continued

Documents		≤2010	2011	2012	2013	2014	2015	2016	2017	2018	2019	2020	2021	Total
The business of gamification: A criticai analysis	2016	-	-	-	-	-	-	-	-	1	-	-	-	**1**
The museum of gamers: Unmediated cultural heritage through g ...	2016	-	-	-	-	-	-	1	1	-	-	3		**5**
Deep and shallow gamification in marketing: Thin evidence an ...	2015	-	-	-	-	-	-	1	-	1	-	-	-	**2**
The missing media: The procedural rhetoric of computer games	2015	-	-	-	-	-	-	-	-	1	-	-	-	**1**
	Total	**0**	**0**	**0**	**0**	**0**	**0**	**2**	**8**	**15**	**26**	**40**	**24**	**116**

Source: own elaboration

Chapter 12
Digital Evolution in Brand Communication

Esra Güven
Manisa Celal Bayar University, Turkey

ABSTRACT

The developing technology and the changing world in this context have led to a digital transformation in the business world as well as individual and social lives. Such a transformation has also manifested itself in the marketing world, and traditional marketing has now begun to be replaced by digital marketing. This transformation, which manifests itself effectively in purchasing processes and consumer behaviour, has also started to stand out as a difference-making element in the competition of brands. In this chapter, the changes in digitalization and brand communication are discussed, and the basic tools and usage patterns used in digital marketing are detailed. In order to exemplify the digital transformation experienced in the marketing world, the effective marketing studies of Turkish Airlines and Toyota brands that attract attention in the digital world have been considered as two sample cases.

INTRODUCTION

In the new era, in which a rapid digital transformation occurs in communication methods and platforms, a new kind of consumer in brand-new communication environments comes to the fore. This new consumer type can give a rapid reaction to the communication efforts of brands in online environments. Unlike traditional consumers, this digitalized consumer actively engages with the marketing processes and has a great power to direct brands and companies. The biggest power in the hands of this new type of consumer is the digital or online elements such as smartphones, social media, online games, online communities, influencers, or Second Life.

In order to keep up with the demands of today's consumer, and to communicate effectively with current or potential customers, brands and companies are in need of being active in these digital platforms. Unless they achieve effective contact with the consumers in this digital transformation age, it will be hard for them to gain competitive advantage or even survive.

DOI: 10.4018/978-1-7998-9179-6.ch012

In this chapter, starting from this point of view, the marketing communication process will be dealt with in all its details and information about the digital transformation of brand communication, its content, and the value from the aspect of both the brand and the consumers will be presented. So, as to help the brands about these new platforms and to highlight the digital marketing communications for the researchers, the new digital platforms for marketing communications will be handled together with their content and impacts on marketing world, as well as the Turkish and international brand examples, which are in the effort of taking active role in this digital communication channels.

Digitalization and Brand Communication

In this age of rapid technology and growing interest in the digital processes, the internet has become a crucial part of daily life, functioning both as a cause and a result of the developing technology. Internet-based technological developments, having a profound impact on every part of life, lead to radical changes and digital transformations in business processes, as well as lifestyles. In order to be able to realize the effect and the future potential of this rapid digital transformation, it will be important to understand the content and scope of this digital transformation concept.

Digital transformation is a concept that emphasizes on the integration of digital solutions into the business processes, business models and the business itself to transform cultural and organisational aspects. Such a transformation helps the brands, or the companies develop the ability to adapt to various environments and conditions rapidly (Capitalbank, 2020). In another point of view, digital transformation marks the radical evaluations about the product or service offerings, dealing with the customer, getting rid of internal challenges and other parts of business processes.

These digital transformations, which are felt deeply in business environments and markets, open the doors of new approaches. Additionally, they become the cause of a rapid and efficient transformation in the communication and interactions between both the individuals to the brand, and individuals to individuals. As the internet becomes a communication tool, which can be used as an integrated or independent way for the aims of marketing communications, the use of it is closely related with the process of informing consumers and establishing permanent relations with them.

As the basic component of marketing activities, communication is regarded as an element providing the brand with competition advantage over their competitors. Communication plays a significant role in managing the relations between the customers and the brand in the short, middle, or long runs (Popescu, 2003). Marketing communications can be defined as the way of informing, persuading, or reminding the consumers about the products or the brand directly or indirectly. These communications cover a complex process consisting of a wide range of methods and techniques or platforms. In any of these methods or platforms, marketing communications can be seen as the voice of the brand. By means of this brand voice, all the elements in the marketing mix are combined, and the general message of the brand is supported (Kotler and Keller, 2008).

Regarded as a kind of 'value exchange', brand-consumer relationships have undergone significant changes and developments through the digital transformations in recent years. These digital revolutions allow for the rise in popularity of digital platforms used by the brands in an effort to communicate with the consumers. Thus brands and companies are becoming progressively more visible in online environments. By means of these online environments, today's consumers not only know what the alternatives are for themselves, but they also become part of a chain, having a potential to contribute to the innovations. New consumers no longer expect brands or companies to adapt to the new digital age in their processes such as orders, process innovations, promotion, feedback, online payment, and many other activities (Ovodenko et al, 2020). These expectations have a deep impact on brands, leading to a transformation chain beyond the borders affecting the whole marketing world.

It is seen that the transition from marketing, known as traditional marketing, to digital marketing using new generation technology and internet, has led to significant changes in the communication and advertising methods. This transformation can be seen below in Table 1.

Table 1. Differences between traditional marketing and digital marketing

	Traditional Marketing	Digital Marketing
Advertising	Advertising is prepared as print, video, or audio records, and media such as TV, radio, and standard newspapers are used. Generally, very limited information can be offered.	By designing very broad information, a sharing is placed on the business's website. The right to place banners from other sites is purchased.
Customer Services	Individual interviews, focus groups by phone or letters, using surveys are performed.	Service is offered twenty-four hours a day, seven days a week. Desired solutions are sent by phone, fax, or e-mail. The online dialogue continues. Maintenance and repair service is provided by remote computer support.
Sale	Customers and prospects are called by phone. Product is introduced physically or by using projection machines	Communication is established through newsgroups, and contact information acquired through e-mail is used.
Marketing Research	The ideas or thoughts of the customers visiting the store or talking on the phone are taken into account, information is gathered through face-to-face interviews.	Information from customers or potential customers is collected through online conversations or correspondence.

Adapted from the source: Çağlar and Kılıç (2006), Pazarlama, Nobel Yayınları, Ankara

With the emergence of the Internet and digitalization, the transition from much more traditional advertising to digital advertisements has made it possible to reach more customers faster and more effectively. Today's digital media, which uses the power of the internet and technology to the fullest, has significantly increased the influence and area of advertising as well.

Unlike analogue communication mediums such as traditional TV, radio, or print media, digital media has an interactive character. Therefore, consumers can quickly reach the information they want to find through a search engine. Additionally, they can access plenty of alternative information. The ability to choose the correct and reliable information comes to the fore, rather than obtaining it anymore. Today, consumers not only seek information but they also share their experiences and ideas with others. Consumer opinions regarding products and services give great significance for consumers in the purchasing decision process. For many consumers, such reviews serve as the most important source of information (Kecskes, 2017). The messages that brands give through digital interactions should be addressed, not only with the effect of encouraging purchase, but also with their contribution to creating brand value and strengthening behavioural intentions (Castillo and Fernandez, 2019).

Digital Advertising

Many definitions used for advertising are similar to each other, but the rapid global changes we are facing make it necessary to update these definitions. Especially with the spread of the internet and digital tools, it is noteworthy that there have been significant changes in the content and types of advertisements (Gura and Gura, 2016).

According to Tuten (2008), advertising is a collection of integrated promotional strategies used to capture the attention of a target audience, whether it is for consumer or business-to-business items.

Jimring (1996), who works on the communication dimension of the advertisement with the consumer, draws attention to the need to analyse the advertisement from four aspects;

1. To create product awareness
2. To change people's thoughts
3. To reinforce individuals' thoughts about the product
4. Entertainment

As seen in these four aspects, the aim of the advertising activities during the 19th century and before have not changed up to today. On the other hand, the tools to activate these goals have transformed in a significant amount. One of the most important tools preferred by advertisers today is the internet. In this regard, it is necessary to carefully consider how consumers, especially young people, use the Internet. The most important feature of this age group is that they are intertwined with video games, smartphones, and computers. Additionally, they are constantly using internet-related media tools (Cappo, 2004).

Tuten (2008) points out that with the development of online advertising, many of the weaknesses of traditional advertising have vanished, allowing it to reach a wider audience and have a greater impact. Traditional advertising, for example, reaches a broad audience, whereas online advertising can reach a specific population with personalised messaging. Secondly, traditional advertising is usually expensive, whereas online advertising is not always. Thirdly, traditional advertising does not lend itself to the kind of engagement and connection that digital advertising allows. As a result, digital marketing allows marketers to generate appealing messages which can be sent to a specified target demographic for a low cost.

In recent years, advertising has developed in tandem with the digital transition, now employing new communication methods to reach target audiences on the internet. Several studies in this sector have been undertaken to back up this claim (Wally and Kosky, 2014).

The first advertisement published on the Internet was an advertisement for the online version of 'wired magazine' on the hotwired.com website in 1994. Later, fourteen more advertisements were placed on this web page by other advertisers. In the process, this magazine web page continued its advertising activities through banner advertisements (Kozlen, 2006). It is known that Netscape Navigator 1.0, the first Internet browser, was also launched in the same days (Moody, 2010).

DIGITAL MARKETING TOOLS

Digital marketing is a branch of marketing that uses technology intensively to promote products and increase awareness among consumers. Compared to traditional media, digital marketing is much more advantageous in terms of cost, targeting and results. However, since it is based on technology, it can fall off the agenda quickly and needs to be updated very frequently (Varma et al., 2020).

Online marketing communications are regarded as an opportunity, having the power to establish a strong relationship between the brand and the consumers if they achieve to support the brand message (Badau, 2011). To be able to take advantage of this opportunity, brands and companies are in search of digital communications with the consumers in digital environments. A comprehensive scan in the related literature clearly shows that there are many alternatives for the brands to be digital. Some of them are as follows.

Social Media

"A set of internet-based apps that build on the conceptual and technological underpinnings of Web 2.0, and allow the production and exchange of user-generated content" is how social media is defined (Kaplan and Haenlein 2010). Over the last decade or more, social networks have transformed communications and changed the way of interaction with information and the production. Social media platforms such as Instagram, Facebook, YouTube, and Twitter allow for brands to be in contact with the consumers, at any time or place. The huge growth of these platforms have led marketers to discover and explore social networking sites to use in their marketing activities. Consequently, social media has started to replace traditional consumer communication methods to a large extent.

Reduced marketing expenses, both monetary and manpower, is one of the key advantages of social networking for businesses. With the current economic slump, many businesses are looking for ways to save costs, and social networking sites are one way for them to do so while also marketing their company. With Facebook and other social networking sites, communication costs have dropped dramatically, allowing businesses to connect directly, swiftly, and reliably with millions of individual customers (Mize, 2009). The potential benefits of using social media by the brands are given by Jothie et al. (2011) as follows;

1. Popularizing the brand or service for the target consumers
2. Informing the target consumers about the products or service
3. Stimulating a healthy market competition
4. Providing social benefits from the brands
5. Creating a permanent brand-consumer interaction

As previously stated, brands use social media widely to make the brand, goods or services known by the target customers. This connection allows for the customer to recall the brand when needed, while also creating a brand image in the customers' minds. As in traditional advertising, social media use in advertising also aims at providing the required information about the products or services. Social media use in advertising is known to trigger market competition, thus lowering the prices for customers. Social media is widely used by the brands to inform the public about its social responsibility projects. Such kinds of projects can actively be announced through social media and, therefore, customers or the general public are informed about the projects. Both social responsibility projects and other promotional activities of brands in social media provide the brand with effective interaction toward potential customer.

Small businesses have made good use of social media as an alternative to costly and time-consuming marketing initiatives (Benwell 2014). It is a highly successful method for tracking consumer behaviour and identifying new marketing techniques (Tuten 2008). Along with increasing brand awareness, social media improves brand image, giving brands more trust. Last but not least, the most important benefit is the establishment of a communication link between brands and customers. These advantages are frequently reflected in sales data.

The brand benefits greatly from excellent word-of-mouth from friends. Meyerson (2010) highlights a variety of aspects of social media as a "weird baffling and paradoxical realm", explaining that it is all about people, and people are perplexing. It's all about figuring out what makes people tick, both individually and in groups, on social media.

On the other side, there are other parts of digital marketing that are lacking or are detrimental. The Internet plays a big role in digital marketing. Connectivity rates for Internet access that differ from one region to the next may cause marketing initiatives to be disrupted. Because of the barrage of advertising, marketers promoting their commercials, and customers being driven to start talking about an organization's brand image or products on the internet and social media platforms, people have amazing knowledge and expertise. Some businesses may be seen adversely by customers because they lack online trust because of adverts appearing on websites and social media that may be considered fraudulent. In other words, even whether they are an individual or a small group, unscrupulous people operating in digital environments can harm the image of a well-known company. Digital marketing simply disseminates information to potential customers, many of whom lack the authority/power to buy, but the idea that this information will be reflected in actual sales volume in the short term can also be deceiving (Desai, 2019).

One of the most significant disadvantages of digital marketing is that it exposes organizations to competition as "open books." Competitors may be able to quickly and easily reproduce your digital marketing efforts. To fool consumers and gain market share, they can duplicate trademarks and logos, as well as corporate identities. Furthermore, they may easily deceive customers by presenting inaccurate information about products, services, or brands, resulting in a company's reputation being harmed and client exodus. In digital marketing, you must build relationships with customers you don't encounter in person, which needs a solid understanding of the psychology of online customer behaviour. Many marketers, however, ignore this when it comes to digital marketing campaigns and rely on traditional consumer psychology. As a result, because it ignores the intricacies of consumer behaviour and the relationships that are created online, efficiency suffers. On the other hand, negative comments and information on products and services, as well as trademarks, are visible and accessible to all Internet users, causing significant damage to a company's image and leading to client exodus (Veleva and Tsvetanova, 2020). The most common social media tools used for digital marketing can be mentioned as follows;

1. Facebook
2. Instagram
3. YouTube
4. Twitter
5. Second Life Virtual Environment

1. Facebook: Customers are increasingly using social networks, according to Edelman (2007), and they are spending far more time with online marketing than with any other marketing medium. Facebook allows businesses to communicate with far more people and far more frequently than they could through phone calls, emails, or meetings (Luke, 2009). To better understand customers, Facebook data can be compared to a crystal ball (Casteleyn et al, 2009). Users' actions on Facebook appear in their news feed status, which is visible to all their friends. Notifications can be sent to email addresses directly

(Shannon et al., 2008). Furthermore, Facebook's growth as a marketing platform has ushered in a new era of targeted and personalized advertising. As a result, Facebook advertising has surged in popularity.

According to Yang et al. (2008), Facebook advertising has become a viable traffic generator and advertising choice for small and large enterprises due to the introduction of demographic targeting ads (age, sex, education, and so on), as well as tighter limits on ad quality. Facebook is considered an enticing platform for Internet marketing specialists and online advertising due to its large number of active users and amount of each user's participation on this social networking website (Francisco, 2006). In terms of economics, Facebook offers a comprehensive and competitive fee structure, charging advertisers per-click or per-impression.

However, because individuals can create their own profiles on Facebook and write whatever they like, it does not always provide accurate, up-to-date, and accurate information about them (Treadaway & Smith, 2010). Marketers could focus on Facebook communities where consumers are members (Casteleyn et al, 2009). Marketers may uncover consumer tastes and likes through these communities, which is helpful in developing market segmentation, targeting, and positioning strategies (Acar & Polonsky, 2007). Marketers may learn a lot about people by looking at their profiles and the news feed remarks they publish on their walls and pages. Thereafter, the information might be utilized for direct marketing (Casteleyn et al, 2009).

2. Instagram: Instagram is regarded as the most effective social media platform for fashion brands. It's no wonder that it's the most popular photo sharing software on both Android and Apple devices, thanks to its digital photo filters technology and distinctive, inventive design. These characteristics in this appealing software make it rather distinctive in terms of displaying and sharing moments from users' daily life (Sholeh and Rusdi, 2019).

Instagram is an app-only service with no distinct internet experience (they do have a website, but it simply accepts logins and converts to an app-like interface) (Guarnieri, 2018). Instagram Direct or Instagram Messaging (Huey & Yazdanifard, 2014) is widely regarded as the best function that Instagram offers for assisting everyone, with small companies at the top of the list. It also features a function that allows you to specify the video length you want to submit.

Instagram has been downloaded around two billion times and has a far greater user engagement rate than Facebook and Twitter, the two most popular social media platforms today. According to the study, a whopping 93 percent of premium businesses have a strong Instagram presence and use it extensively in their marketing plan (Sangvikar, et al, 2019). Instagram's main capability – photo and video sharing – aids in their goal of connecting businesses with their target customers. It also has a function for engaging with customers, as well as one-click redirection to company websites and different ad locations. According to Manovich (2017), these tools not only make up the application, but also the user's lifestyle.

3. YouTube: With over two billion subscribers, YouTube is the most popular online video media channel. Every day, over a million hours of YouTube videos are posted and viewed, with seven out of ten viewers accessing the site via mobile devices (Stokes, 2017). With the advent of professional video bloggers, YouTubers, YouTube has acquired a lot of popularity in recent years. A growing number of YouTubers use their YouTube channels as a full-time job, filming, producing, and publishing videos. There are YouTubers with millions of subscribers and watchers from all over the world (Viertola, 2018).

YouTube is expected to account for roughly a quarter of all free video advertising spending, with over one billion hours of video being watched every day (Foye, 2018). Informational value, entertainment value, and trendiness are all significant variables in increasing YouTube's advertising value. Moreover, this value has a favourable impact on customers' purchase intent (Firat, 2019).

Standard and display, discovery (in-search), overlay, sponsored cards, and video bumper advertisements are among the marketing communication forms available on YouTube. Organizations and their brands frequently utilize video advertisements, which show at the beginning and during YouTube videos (Vingilisa et al, 2018). Organizations may also post their television ads and other public relations content to brand channels, which has transformed how young consumers see advertising because they can watch them whenever they want. Because ads may be uploaded for free, and possibly watched by millions of young customers, if they are sufficiently entertaining to go viral, YouTube brand channels have become cost-effective conduits. (2020, Duffet). In addition, YouTube offers complete analytics/metrics, allowing businesses to learn more about who is watching their channel content, as well as other MC material, in terms of demographic, geographic, video use, and other consumer data (Wendt and Griesbaum, 2016). YouTube-sponsored activities fall into one of three categories:

1. explicit sponsorship, in which the sponsoring firm pays the YouTuber a fixed price, or a set amount, based on the number of views on a video made especially to promote a brand or product;
2. affiliate links, in which the YouTuber earns a commission on sales made through the link or coupon code provided by the YouTuber;
3. free product sampling, in which companies send products to YouTubers in hope they will create product reviews, advertorials, or just general exposure of the product.

Because most consumers/viewers do not consider YouTube videos as a source of advertisement, marketing via YouTube content may be significantly more successful than traditional marketing. This is due to the fact that customers are more likely to see such information without apprehension (Wu, 2016).

4. Twitter: In a world where brands compete for the attention of potential customers (Davenport & Beck, 2002), attention economy is a new paradigm for examining the continual connectedness of modern social networking services in the commercial sector. In this respect, microblogging is a new form of communication in this attention economy in which users can describe objects of interest and express sentiments in brief posts that they are prepared to share with others (i.e., microblogs). These messages are then disseminated by instant messaging, cell phones, email, and the Internet. Microblogging, as a kind of e-WOM, needs considerable consideration due to its specific communication properties (Jansen et al, 2009).

Twitter, as a micro blogging platform, can provide both sorts of interactivity: "interpersonal interactivity" through message exchanges between organizations and individuals, as well as "machine interactivity" by referring other people's messages. Contained hyperlinks, for example, allow a tweet recipient to obtain further information by clicking on links embedded within tweets (Toubia and Stephen, 2013).

Twitter is a prominent social media site that allows registered users to send "tweets" to their "followers" in the form of text messages up to 140 characters long (Toubia and Stephen, 2013). As a result, Twitter's founder, practitioners, and a few researchers in the field have labelled the service "an information corporation" (The Economist, 2010).

Because a response to a person or a one-to-one communication is visible to a much broader audience on Twitter, it might cause issues when used as a response medium (Burton & Soboleva, 2011). Twitter's popularity as a microblogging service peaked in 2009, when it surpassed 58.5 million global users, a growth of 949 percent since September 2008 (Schonfeld, 2009). It also began to gain marketer's interest in that year, particularly because of its e-wom potential. Because microblogging, like as Twitter, allows consumers to communicate socially.

5. Second Life Virtual Environment: Virtual worlds are part of a larger category of Internet-based apps known as "social media", which are built on Web 2.0's ideological and technological basis, allowing for the creation and exchange of user-generated content (Kaplan & Haenlein, 2010). Second Life, the most popular of the virtual worlds, is a three-dimensional virtual environment that was first made available to the public in 2003. It is maintained by Linden Research, Inc., based in the United States. Users (referred to as "residents") can engage with virtual representations, in the form of individualized avatars, by entering it via a downloaded client software.

The most interesting characteristic of this virtual environment is that it allows individuals to live a second, but virtual, life in an online platform and interact with other individuals by choosing an avatar which represents the individual in this virtual environment (Jin and Sung, 2010). This digital environment is a simulation of the real world and users can find anything existing in real world, ranging from shops, brands, houses to friends and even families. Realizing the impact of this environment on individuals, many brands like IKEA act as a virtual character or their brand identity in this digital simulation world (Iacobucci, 2000).

SL is one of a series of Internet programs known as "virtual hyperrealities" or "virtual worlds," which have exploded in popularity in recent years. Hyperrealities are one of postmodernism's five criteria, being founded on "the concept that reality is created, and therefore it is conceivable to build things that are more real than real" (Venkatesh & Firat, 1993). They are a fundamental expression of postmodern philosophy because they do not presume that everyone shares the same reality. Instead, they mimic an alternate world in which users can engage in behaviours that they would be unable to undertake in real life.

Hyperreality has long been considered in marketing, particularly in relation to tourist attractions and media goods, as well as methods to improve the pre-purchase service experience. The most common commercial use of virtual social worlds is communication, and there are four main methods for businesses to take advantage of the advertising possibilities of Second Life.

To begin, businesses can create virtual flagship stores, where they can display digital versions of their physical items. Toyota, for example, has a store in Second Life where it displays virtual copies of the Scion xB model. Secondly, you may communicate by purchasing ad space in virtual malls or radio stations. Companies like MetaAdverse, a Second Life advertising network, rent out virtual billboards to businesses and then track who visits them to offer data to marketers, similar to how data is collected in traditional TV or internet advertising.

IMAX Corporation of Canada employed this strategy to promote the fifth instalment of the Harry Potter franchise, Harry Potter, and the Order of the Phoenix, on Second Life, and was able to reach out to 15,000 unique visitors. Aside from being effective, this type of virtual communication is far less expensive than traditional forms of internet advertising. For example, a billboard with 200,000 impressions may be set up for around 8,000 Linden Dollars, which corresponds to a cost-per-thousands of US$.15, compared to Google Ad Words, which costs between $1 and $8 per thousand hits, depending on the type of chosen terms.

Sponsoring virtual world events, as done by the British Guardian newspaper and semiconductor manufacturer Intel when they funded the Second Fest, a virtual music festival, is a third form of promoting. Finally, businesses should remember that their activities in virtual social worlds can have a beneficial influence on real-world news coverage. Conducting any type of action within Second Life may be the greatest method to gain favourable news publicity these days.

Smartphone Applications

Smartphones, and thus new media consumption habits, are a phenomenon impossible to ignore in marketing communications. Following the more traditional mobile activities such as SMS, branded applications for smartphones offered new possibilities in marketing activities. In these branded app communications, brand identity is exhibited by using the brand names and logos. In this way brand familiarity is increased, which allows a more effective and powerful communication between the brand and the consumers (Bellman et al., 2013).

By means of the branded apps, 'pushing' strategies has been replaced by 'pulling' ones, thus eliminating the permission of consumers for the marketing communications. This is because consumers themselves download the applications and show eagerness to the communication with the brand. Users of these branded apps willingly take the messages from the brand and process these messages more deeply and permanently than other messages coming from other sources.

Online Consumption Communities

Derived from the proliferation of social networking sites, there is now a trend in academia and practice to refer to any online group or Facebook page as a community, which is conceptually irresponsible and potentially misleading. Boorstin (1973) defines the consumption communities as the consumer groups sharing risks, interests and satisfactions. As those in the past, today's online consumption communities come together to share experience_or inform each other about the products or services with and adding of online environments. In these online communities, consumers can find or give opinions about the product or services independent of time or place limitations, and their size can range from small ones in locals to the international ones. Because of the huge potential of these communities to direct the consumers, brands and companies are in dire need of being present in these platforms and follow the message's content in detail.

Online consumption communities blur the lines between time and space, allowing consumers to interact, share knowledge, collaborate, and support one another at any time and from anywhere (Kozinets et al, 2008). An online group may only be considered a community, according to Muniz and O'Guinn (2001), if members develop shared rituals and traditions and feel a feeling of belonging and moral obligation to the group.

The brands, in an effort to listen to customers and provide solutions, need to play an active role in online consumption communities. By listening to the consumers and observing their behaviours and reactions in these platforms, brands can develop better strategies to deal with consumers and the market itself. An effective engagement with the online consumption communities gives the brand an opportunity to interact with the existing and potential customers, while helping to provide rapid and effective solutions when needed.

Online Games and Advergames

As entertainment is the main attraction factor in online environments, online games, one of the most widely preferred entertainment platforms, come to the fore in efforts of establishing an effective relationship with the consumers (Yuksel, 2007). Advergames are an entertainment and advertising system that can be a learning path in some cases, so it is constantly increasing around the world. According to many researchers, such advertising is an effective way to distribute the advertising message via the internet and mobile devices (Youn, et al. 2005). Advergames help consumers to perceive the advertising message positively and can create brand awareness. Entertainment is one of the main topics used in advertising today, and in this respect, gaming is accepted as a strong ad management (Gura and Gura, 2016).

Calin (2010) defines advergames as online games that contain marketing messages. Such kind of advertisements have the advantage of being selected by the player of the game, thus not being disturbing or intrusive. Another significant emphasis in these advertisements is that the players interact with the game and also the brand itself. Moreover, these kinds of advertisements are known to encourage the players to share their experiences with their family and friends. Therefore, they have a word-of-mouth effect among potential consumers.

The concept of Advergame was first used by Wired magazine in 2001 to express a website-based game (Wired.com, 2001). However, the actual emergence of game advertising dates back to earlier years. Kool-Aid and Pepsi developed Atari 2600 game and used this game for the promotion of their products in 1980. The "American Home Foods" company also distributed games in floppy disks and introduced the Chef Boyardee product in these games (Obringer; 2007). He applied for product promotion with the game "NVision Design" Good Willie Hunting" (Sharma, 2014) in 1998. Thereafter, hundreds of companies applied for product and brand recognition in the same way.

Games and advergames not only contribute for the promotion of the product or brand, they also allow a richer database regarding target consumers. This two-way contribution attracts the brands to be visible in online games or create their own games as advergames (Yuksel, 2007).

Ghirvu (2012) also looks at advergames as a marketing activity and associates it with brand personality promotion, target group profile, internet friendly features, strategic goals of the communication campaign and business image. As seen in these associations, advergames serve as a promotion method to reflect the brand's personality. These kinds of games are also known to create and empower the business image.

Research on game advertisements reveals different classifications and features. Based on these classifications, it is thought that for a game advertisement to be effective, it must have some basic features (Gura & Gura, 2016). Accessibility is one of these features. Easy game access is always an advantage, both because of the game player's characteristics, as well as having an advantage in the advergame market. Another important point here is the intelligibility, which means that players can easily understand the instructions and the steps in the game. This feature prevents players from getting bored easily and giving up playing the game. In addition, all advergames should have different competition levels, allowing the player to level up and get satisfied during the process. One of the main, and possibly the most basic, feature of advergames is that the games should be associated with brands or products. Brand messages given directly or subliminally during the game should be designed and planned carefully. The capacity of the games to increase and keep concentration is another element of a good advergame. Finally, an effective advergame should have viral marketing feature, allowing the players, or the brand to spread the message to potential customers.

Academic literature deals with advergames in different ways in terms of being associated with the brand, classifying them from the lowest to the highest:

1. Mobile game
2. Advertisement in a mobile game
3. Sponsorship of a mobile game
4. Advergame mobile

The highest level of game in terms of brand association is the content of advertisements (Salo, 2009). Advergame increase both brand awareness and memory. If a consumer is willing to purchase the product, they will resort to searching for information on the Internet. Furthermore, game ads have the feature of promoting products to the consumer without any special effort (Lopatina, 2005).

Internet Influencers- Opinion Leaders

The brands regarding the digital world as a strategic communication way, have become aware of the individuals sharing their opinions and experiences with others. Some of these individuals have a great number of followers in online platforms, such as YouTube or Instagram, and thus have great influence on their followers as opinion leaders. According to the two-way flow theory by Katz and Lazarsfeld (1955), the shared information does not always reach the target directly. Sometimes there are intermediaries between the source and the receiver. These intermediaries are the influencers, or the opinion leaders, whose messages regarding the products are of great value for the receivers or the potential customers. As a result, the use of these influencers by the brands makes brand communications considerably effective (Uzunoglu and Kip, 2014). The emergence of digital influencers created significant changes in the relationships between businesses and customers in social media environments.

Practitioners are supposed to use a mix of visible and perceptible indicators that offer a holistic view of the potential strengths of digital influencers. Such mix will be helpful for businesses to identify, evaluate and select the right influencers for their promotional efforts. Brands can understand influencers' impact on followers by assessing followers' perceptions of the brand and its value, and by examining their intention to sell the recommended product. To do so direct follower surveys can be a useful tool (Castillo and Fernandez, 2019).

BRAND EXAMPLES IN DIGITAL MARKETING WORLD

Toyota

Toyota makes excellent use of digital marketing to improve customer engagement and retention. It appears that being present on many platforms, conducting multi-channel campaigns and connecting with followers, through social media postings, would help Toyota maintain its market position for a longer period of time.

In a lot of ways, Toyota's social media posts are on trend. The firm tries to generate emotional appeals for its cars through a methodology centered on who to contact and how to reach them. Therefore, they're able to increase trust and engagement with its consumers. Toyota's social media approach is centered on engagement with followers by asking open-ended questions and talking about their experiences with Toyota, rather than just uploading images of their vehicles and trucks. The more you connect with consumers, the more input you'll receive. Thus, it will help improve performance and retain customers. Toyota uses innovative social media postings to emphasize the expectations and requirements of its target demographic, making the brand more approachable without sounding like an advertising.

Toyota has a strong market position thanks to effective social media and commercial tactics. Toyota will undoubtedly remain one of the most favoured automobile businesses by producing innovative material that inspires people, engaging more through social media, being an eco-friendly brand, and producing appealing advertisements (digitalagencynetwork.com).

Toyota uses amazing pictures and videos to interact with its target audience on social media, which is at the heart of its digital marketing strategy. The brand has around 17.5 million Facebook fans and over two million Instagram followers. Toyota wants to develop the imagination of its followers, motivate them to chase their ambitions and make them come true, as desired through catchy slogans and innovative posts.

The narrative of a little child roaming across Tokyo, bringing to life a new way to move using Toyota's mobility goods is told in a commercial named "Start Your Impossible" on YouTube. The commercial's catchphrase is "When you are free to move, anything is possible."

Another example is one of the finest Toyota digital ads, which announced a fantasy vehicle art contest as in Figure 1 and Figure 2. The contest's slogan is "inspire the world with your aspirations," and it encourages children to imagine the automobile of their dreams. This is a fun method to allow kids' imagination to go wild, while also inspiring others to conjure up and design their own fantasy automobile.

Figure 1.
Source: toyota.com

Figure 2.
Source: toyota.com

Turkish Airlines

Turkish Airlines, the flag carrier of Turkey, offers the opportunity to travel to many destinations around the world. It is known as the airline with the world's highest number of destinations. It is also the country's leading company in terms of digital technologies. Digitalization is important for such large companies in terms of controlling their wide-spread network. The company offers mobile apps, loyalty cards, social media campaigns, email marketing, influencer marketing, website marketing, mobile marketing, etc. Various programs are used by Turkish Airlines, such as flight search engines to increase customer loyalty and retain customers. They effectively use marketing items, such as promotional sales and additional sales alternatives to the customer.

As a result of the cooperation and objective data analysis of BoomSonar and Marketing Turkey, Turkish Airlines was awarded the Social Media Awards 2017 Turkey, which measures the social media performance of brands and agencies. Approximately 350 companies, from 50 categories, were evaluated within the scope of SocialBrand data analysis. Turkish Airlines, on the other hand, was the airline company that won the grand prize in this competition, thanks to its social media activities. (Boomsonar; Marketing Turkiye, 2017).

In April 2015, BuzzFeed carried out a study to announce the direct flight to San Francisco in partnership with Turkish Airlines. THY created a brand account with Bullseye Worldwide in BuzzFeed. Additionally, a project was designed to highlight the common features and similarities of the two cities, with a theme called "15 Reasons Istanbul and San Francisco Are Long-Lost Sister Cities" posted on the channel.

Another worldwide impactful THY campaign was the "Batman vs. Superman" movie sponsorship (Figure 3 and Figure 4). The movie was screened for the first time on Turkish Airlines planes. In addition, the Turkish Airlines plane took part in some scenes of the movie, and the leading actor flew with Turkish Airlines as per the scenario. This sponsorship was announced to large audiences on many social media platforms. Turkish Airlines frequently uses the famous validator in its marketing strategy. Commercial films were shot with many celebrities, such as Lionel Messi, Morgan Freeman, internet phenomenon Zack King, Kobe Bryant and Didier Drogba. The commercials are available on the airline's official YouTube channel.

Figure 3.
Source: thy.com

Figure 4.
Source: thy.com

Furthermore, Turkish Airlines actively uses mobile applications in its marketing strategies. Turkish Airlines has decided to apply a 15 percent discount to all domestic and international tickets, if purchased via mobile application, on January 18-20, 2018. This application was also used to present different offers and customized preferences to the passengers. Ticket sales and reservations can be made through the mobile application. Moreover, the app also includes various services, such as extra baggage allowance, lounge, car rental and baggage tracking. Passengers who download the Turkish Airlines mobile application to their Android and iOS devices get a discount on domestic and international tickets, purchase tickets or miles, and transfer miles to other members. The application was downloaded by one million four hundred thousand people during the process. Turkish Airlines General Manager, Bilal Eksi, shared a post regarding the campaign on Twitter as "Time for mobile", saying the campaign resulted in a 5-fold increase in turnover and a 2-fold increase in application downloads when compared to the previous period. After the campaign, the usage rate continued to expand even more. Thanks to this campaign, more customers chose to download and interact with the mobile application (Isılar, 2021).

FUTURE RESEARCH DIRECTIONS

In our new digital age, it could be easily predicted that marketing would benefit from the advantages of digital world more and more in the future. Thus, we can say that this field needs further research. The researchers planning to study on digital marketing in the future can focus on the details of social media platforms and consumer behaviours in these platforms. In addition, a comparative analysis of the marketing styles of born-digital companies and traditional companies trying to become digital would be helpful for marketing literature.

CONCLUSION

Consumers are bored of being passive consumers of traditional media messages, and as a result have adopted an active role in which they may not only listen to the brand's messaging, but also express their own sentiments and views to the brand, as well as receive and exchange information as needed (Rowley, 2004). In this regard, social media has influenced the brand experience process by altering the structure of communication between the brand and the consumer. On the other hand, one of the most significant triggers of this digital marketing on the part of companies has clearly been the fact that consumers are spending more time on digital media.

Digital marketing is a popular way to promote products or services and reach out to customers via digital platforms. Digital marketing, sometimes known as internet marketing, social media marketing, display advertising or search engine marketing encompasses a wide range of channels that require the use of the internet by mobile phones, and a variety of other digital media. Consumers can obtain information through digital media at any time and from any location. (Yasmin et al., 2015). When it comes to digital marketing, businesses have a variety of options. Search engine optimization (SEO), email marketing, content marketing, social media marketing, Pay Per Click (PPC), web analytics, and mobile marketing are just a few of the marketing channels available.

Through social media, firms have been able to make their products and services more visible to consumers as the digitalization process continues to accelerate. Furthermore, it enhances client interest in the brand by connecting them to information that allows them to interact. Social media offers brands new chances not just in terms of communication, but also in terms of monitoring customer wants starting on Sunday. To put it another way, social media allows firms to do low-cost research and learn what their customers are saying about them and their competition.

In this way, the overall situation and the input collected directly from customers about the brand may be more clearly determined by the strategy that the company should pursue. However, it's worth nothing that brand communication in the digital age has its own set of traits and dynamics. It is critical for effective brand communication to create appropriate content for this new environment. In this setting, effective digital brand communication necessitates the capacity to efficiently manage the process of developing and sharing content in a way that encourages customer participation.

REFERENCES

Baday, H. M. (2011). *Tehnici de comunicare in social media*. Polirom Publishing House.

Bellman, S., Treleaven-Hassard, S., Robinson, J. A., Varan, D., & Potter, R. F. (2013). Brand communication with branded smartphone apps: First insights on possibilities and limits. *NIM Marketing Intelligence Review*, *5*(2), 24–27. doi:10.2478/gfkmir-2014-0014

Benwell, S. (2014). Capitalising on social media to grow your business. *The Guardian, 28*.

Boomsonar; Marketing Türkiye. (2017). *Social Medya Awards Turkey. Social Medya Awards*. https://www.socialmediaawardsturkey.com/

Boorstin, D. J. (2010). The Americans: The democratic experience (Vol. 3). Vintage. *Business Horizons*, *53*(1), 59–68.

Burton, S., & Soboleva, A. (2011). Interactive or reactive? Marketing with Twitter. *Journal of Consumer Marketing*, *28*(7), 491–499. doi:10.1108/07363761111181473

Çağlar, İ., & Kılıç, S. (2005). *Pazarlama*. Nobel Yayın Dağıtım.

Călin, G. (2010). Advergames: Characteristics, Limitations and Potential. Annals of the University of Oradea. *Economic Science Series, 19*(1).

Cappo, J. (2005). *Reklamcılığın geleceği* (Ö. Girnek, Ed.). MediaCat Kitapları.

Casteleyn, J., Mottart, A., & Rutten, K. (2009). How to use Facebook in your market research. *International Journal of Market Research*, *51*(4), 439–447. doi:10.2501/S1470785309200669

Davenport, T. H., & Beck, J. C. (2002). *The attention economy: Understanding the new currency of business*. Harvard Business Press.

Desai, V. (2019). Digital marketing: A review. *International Journal of Trend in Scientific Research and Development*, *5*(5), 196–200. doi:10.31142/ijtsrd23100

Dholakia, U. M., Bagozzi, R. P., & Pearo, L. K. (2004). A social influence model of consumer participation in network-and small-group-based virtual communities. *International Journal of Research in Marketing*, *21*(3), 241–263. doi:10.1016/j.ijresmar.2003.12.004

Duffett, R. (2020). The YouTube marketing communication effect on cognitive, affective and behavioural attitudes among Generation Z consumers. *Sustainability*, *12*(12), 5075. doi:10.3390u12125075

Edelman, D. C. (2007). From the periphery to the core: As online strategy becomes overall strategy, marketing organizations and agencies will never be the same. *Journal of Advertising Research*, *47*(2), 130–134. doi:10.2501/S0021849907070146

Firat, D. (2019). YouTube advertising value and its effects on purchase intention. *Journal of Global Business Insights*, *4*(2), 141–155. doi:10.5038/2640-6489.4.2.1097

Foye, L. (2018). *Global ad spend will reach $37bn in the next five years*. Retrieved from http://www.bizcommunity.com/Article/1/12/172893.html#more

Francisco, B. (2006). *Cracking the social network code*. Academic Press.

Ghirvu, A. (2011). Advergames: marketing advantages and risks involved. *International Conference "Marketing – from information to decision"*, 174-183.

Gould, S. J., Pola, B. G., & Grabner-Krauter, S. (2000). Product Placements in Movies: A Cross- Cultural Analysis of Austrian, French and American Consumers' Attitudes Toward This Emerging, International Promotional Medium. *Journal of Advertising*, *29*(4), 41–58. doi:10.1080/00913367.2000.10673623

Guarnieri, O. L. (2018). The role of Instagram in Fashion Communication: Analyse of Dolce & Gabbana's profile. Academic Press.

Gura, S., & Gura, K. (2016). The use of mobile advergame as brand communication tool: Case study "Vodafon City". *American Journal of Marketing Research*, *2*(2), 61–72.

Horea, M. B. (2016). *Tehnici de comunicare în social media*. Elefant Online.Editura Polirom.

Huey, L. S., & Yazdanifard, R. (2014). *How Instagram can be used as a tool in social network marketing. Center for Southern New Hampshire University.*

Iacobucci, D., Arabie, P., & Bodapati, A. (2000). Recommendation agents on the internet. *Journal of Interactive Marketing*, *14*(3), 2–11. doi:10.1002/1520-6653(200022)14:3<2::AID-DIR1>3.0.CO;2-J

Işılar, H. B. (2021). Havayolu Endüstrisinde Dijital Pazarlama Uygulamalarının Değerlendirilmesi. *Havacılık ve Uzay Çalışmaları Dergisi*, *1*(2), 42–63.

Jansen, B. J., Zhang, M., Sobel, K., & Chowdury, A. (2009). Twitter power: Tweets as electronic word of mouth. *Journal of the American Society for Information Science and Technology*, *60*(11), 2169–2188. doi:10.1002/asi.21149

Jiménez-Castillo, D., & Sánchez-Fernández, R. (2019). The role of digital influencers in brand recommendation: Examining their impact on engagement, expected value and purchase intention. *International Journal of Information Management*, *49*, 366–376. doi:10.1016/j.ijinfomgt.2019.07.009

Jin, S. A. A., & Sung, Y. (2010). The roles of spokes-avatars' personalities in brand communication in 3D virtual environments. *Journal of Brand Management, 17*(5), 317–327. doi:10.1057/bm.2009.18

Jothi, P. S., Neelamalar, M., & Prasad, R. S. (2011). Analysis of social networking sites: A study on effective communication strategy in developing brand communication. *Journal of Media and Communication Studies, 3*(7), 234-242.

Kaplan, A. M., & Haenlein, M. (2010). Users of the world, unite! The challenges and opportunities of Social Media. *Business Horizons, 53*(1), 59–68. doi:10.1016/j.bushor.2009.09.003

Katz, E., & Lazarsfeld, P. F. (1955). *Personal influence: The part played by people in the flow of mass communications*. Routledge.

Kecskes, R. (2017). Brand communication in a digitalized world. *NIM Marketing Intelligence Review, 9*(2), 55–58.

Kotler, P., Keller, K. L., & Martinović, M. (2008). *Upravljanje marketingom* (Vol. 14). Izdanje.

Kozinets, R. V., Hemetsberger, A., & Schau, H. J. (2008). The wisdom of consumer crowds: Collective innovation in the age of networked marketing. *Journal of Macromarketing, 28*(4), 339–354. doi:10.1177/0276146708325382

Kozinets, R. V., Sherry, J. F., DeBerry-Spence, B., Duhachek, A., Nuttavuthisit, K., & Storm, D. (2002). Themed flagship brand stores in the new millennium: Theory, practice, prospects. *Journal of Retailing, 78*(1), 17–29. doi:10.1016/S0022-4359(01)00063-X

Kozlen, K. (2006). *The value of banner advertising on the web* (Doctoral dissertation). University of Missouri - Columbia.

Lopatina, I. (2005). *Context-aware mobile gaming* (Unpublished Master's thesis). Faculty of Science, Department of Computer Science, University of Troms.

Luke, K. (2009). Marketing the new-fashioned way: Connect with your target market through social networking sites. *Journal of Financial Planning*, (November/December), 18–19.

Manovich, L. (2017). *Instagram and Contemporary Image*. Available at: http://manovich.net/index.php/projects/instagram-and-contemporary-image

Meyerson, M. (2010). *Success secrets of social media marketing superstars*. Entrepreneur Press.

Mize, S. R. (2009). *Social network benefits*. Academic Press.

Moody, G. (2007). The Netscape Story: From Mosaic to Mozilla. *Computerworld UK, 12*(1).

Muniz, A. M. Jr, & O'Guinn, T. C. (2001). Brand community. *The Journal of Consumer Research, 27*(4), 412–432. doi:10.1086/319618

Obringer, L. A. (2007). *How Advergaming Works*. http://money.howstuffworks.com/ advergaming.htm

Ovodenko, A. A., Peshkova, G. Y., & Zlobina, O. V. (2020). Digital Evolution of Consumer Behavior and its Impact on Digital Transformation of Small and Medium Business Sustained Development Strategy. In *2nd International Scientific and Practical Conference on Digital Economy (ISCDE2020)* (pp. 424-428). Atlantis Press. 10.2991/aebmr.k.201205.071

Piccinini, E., Gregory, R. W., & Kolbe, L. M. (2015). Changes in the producer-consumer relationship-towards digital transformation. *Changes (Hove, England)*, *3*(4), 1634–1648.

Popescu, I. C. (2003). *Comunicarea in marketing: Concepte, tehnici, strategii*. Editura Uranus.

Ring, J. (1996). *Reklam Dünyasının İçyüzü*. Milliyet Yayınları.

Salo, J. (2009). Mobile games advertising in international marketing context. *Journal of International Marketing and Exporting*, 14.

Sangvikar, B., Kolte, A., & Pawar, A. (2019). Competitive Strategies for Unorganised Retail Business: Understanding Structure, Operations, and Profitability of Small Mom and Pop Stores in India. *International Journal on Emerging Technologies*, *10*(3), 253–259.

Schonfeld, E. (2009, Oct. 26). Twitter finds growth abroad with 58.4 million global visitors in September. *TechCrunch*.

Shannon, R., Stabeler, M., Quigley, A., & Nixon, P. (2009). Profiling and targeting opportunities in pervasive advertising. *1st Workshop on Pervasive Advertising*.

Sharma, M. (2014). Advergaming–The Novel Instrument in the Advertising. *Procedia Economics and Finance*, *11*, 249. doi:10.1016/S2212-5671(14)00193-2

Sholeh, A., & Rusdi, A. (2019). *A New Measurement of Instagram Addiction: Psychometric Properties of The Instagram Addiction Scale*. TIAS.

Stokes, R. (2013). *eMarketing: The essential guide to marketing in a digital world*. Quirk eMarketing.

The Economist. (2010, Jan. 30). A world of connections – a special report on social networking. *The Economist*.

Toubia, O., & Stephen, A. T. (2013). Intrinsic vs. image-related utility in social media: Why do people contribute content to twitter? *Marketing Science*, *32*(3), 368–392. doi:10.1287/mksc.2013.0773

Treadaway, C., & Smith, M. (2010). *Facebook marketing an hour a day*. Wiley Publishing.

Tuten, T. L. (2008). *Advertising 2.0: Social Media Marketing in a Web 2.0*. ABC-CLIO.

Uzunoğlu, E., & Kip, S. M. (2014). Brand communication through digital influencers: Leveraging blogger engagement. *International Journal of Information Management*, *34*(5), 592–602. doi:10.1016/j.ijinfomgt.2014.04.007

Varma, M., Dhakane, N., & Pawar, A. (2020). Evaluation of Impact of Instagram on Customer Preferences: The Significance of Online Marketing. *International Journal of Scientific & Technology Research*, *9*(2), 548–554.

Veleva, S. S., & Tsvetanova, A. I. (2020). Characteristics of the digital marketing advantages and disadvantages. *IOP Conference Series. Materials Science and Engineering*, *940*(1), 012065. doi:10.1088/1757-899X/940/1/012065

Venkatesh, A., Sherry, J. F. J., & Firat, A. F. (1993). Postmodernism and the marketing imaginary. *International Journal of Research in Marketing*, *10*(3), 215–223. doi:10.1016/0167-8116(93)90007-L

Viertola, W. (2018). *To what extent does YouTube marketing influence the consumer behaviour of a young target group* (Bachelor's thesis). Helsinki Metropolia University of Applied Sciences.

Vingilis, E., Yildirim-Yenier, Z., Vingilis-Jaremko, L., Seeley, J., Wickens, C. M., Grushka, D. H., & Fleiter, J. (2018). Young male drivers' perceptions of and experiences with YouTube videos of risky driving behaviours. *Accident; Analysis and Prevention*, *120*, 46–54.

Vukasovič, T. (2015). Brand developing relationships through social media. *Europe*, *21*(5).

Wally, E., & Koshy, S. (2014). *The use of Instagram as a marketing tool by Emirati female entrepreneurs: An exploratory study*. University of Wollongong in Dubai.

Wendt, L. M., Griesbaum, J., & Kölle, R. (2016). Product advertising and viral stealth marketing in online videos: A description and comparison of comments on YouTube. *Aslib Journal of Information Management*, *68*(3), 250–264. doi:10.1108/AJIM-11-2015-0174

Wu, K. (2016). YouTube marketing: Legality of sponsorship and endorsements in advertising. *JL Bus. & Ethics*, *22*, 59.

Yang, T., Kim, D., & Dhalwani, V. (2008). Social networking as a new trend in e-marketing. In Research and Practical Issues of Enterprise Information Systems II (pp. 847-856). Boston: Springer. doi:10.1007/978-0-387-76312-5_7

Yasmin, A., Tasneem, S., & Fatema, K. (2015). Effectiveness of Digital Marketing in the Challenging Age: An Empirical Study. *International Journal of Management Science and Business Administration*, *1*(5), 69–80. doi:10.18775/ijmsba.1849-5664-5419.2014.15.1006

Youn, S., Lee, M., & Doyle, K. O. (2003). Lifestyles of online gamers: A psychographic approach. *Journal of Interactive Advertising*, *3*(2), 49–56. doi:10.1080/15252019.2003.10722073

Yüksel, M. (2007). Küreselleşme sürecinde yeni bir iletişim ortami. *Öneri Dergisi, 7*(28), 317-326. doi:10.14783/maruoneri.684439

ADDITIONAL READING

Jiménez-Castillo, D., & Sánchez-Fernández, R. (2019). The role of digital influencers in brand recommendation: Examining their impact on engagement, expected value and purchase intention. *International Journal of Information Management*, *49*, 366–376. doi:10.1016/j.ijinfomgt.2019.07.009

Piccinini, E., Gregory, R. W., & Kolbe, L. M. (2015). Changes in the producer-consumer relationship-towards digital transformation. *Changes (Hove, England)*, *3*(4), 1634–1648.

Uzunoğlu, E., & Kip, S. M. (2014). Brand communication through digital influencers: Leveraging blogger engagement. *International Journal of Information Management*, *34*(5), 592–602. doi:10.1016/j.ijinfomgt.2014.04.007

KEY TERMS AND DEFINITIONS

Advergames: A type of interactive marketing in which websites (typically as pop-ups) display free downloaded computer games to promote a brand or product.

Digital Marketing: Any type of marketing that makes use of electronic devices that may be utilized by marketing professionals to provide promotional messaging and track its effectiveness throughout the consumer journey.

E-Mail Marketing: The use of email to sell items or services while also building relationships with potential customers or clients.

Influencer: A person who can persuade potential customers to buy a product or service by promoting or recommending it on social media.

Search Engine Optimization (SEO): The process of optimizing brand website to make it more visible when people use Google, Bing, and other search engines to look for items or services related to business or brand.

Social Media: A type of computer-based technology that allows people to share their views, ideas, and information through virtual networks and communities.

Web 2.0: Contrast to its previous form, the current version of the internet, which includes more user-generated content and usability for end-users, Version 1.0 of the internet.

Chapter 13
Leveraging Social Media Tools for Business Purposes

Vandana Ahuja
Amity Business School, Amity University, Noida, India

Shirin Alavi
Jaypee Institute of Information Technology, Noida, India

ABSTRACT

Human beings are increasingly social, and the growth of social media is a function of increased urbanisation, internet penetration, and digitisation, which have witnessed an increase in the number of internet users, active social media users, unique mobile users, and active mobile social users. This chapter will enable readers to appreciate the concept of social media and details the most significant social media tools that can be used by business organisations and brands and then proceeds to identify the benefits of social media to businesses and individuals.

INTRODUCTION

Social media refers to a series of virtual channels, tools and platforms which enable people to come together in the virtual arena and interact with each other, collaborate or share content. This is termed as *social* because it primarily comprises of user generated content and constitutes a mechanism whereby communities or cliques can come together for information sharing and exchange of ideas. In the words of Andreas Kaplan, one of the early proponents of the concept of social media, it is a popular platform on which customers engage behaviourally with organisations. It is *a group of Internet-based applications that build on the ideological and technological foundations of Web 2.0, and that allow the creation and exchange of User Generated Content.*

DOI: 10.4018/978-1-7998-9179-6.ch013

BACKGROUND

Social Media Tools for Businesses

As web 1.0 paved way for web 2.0 or the read write web, individuals could create content online and connect with organisations as well as with each other. This has changed the way business is done. Social Networking Platforms, Blogs, Online Communities and Mobile Apps are the most significant social media tools used by businesses today. Their usage varies from one industry vertical to the other.

Figure 1. Social Media Tools For Businesses
(IGI, 2021)

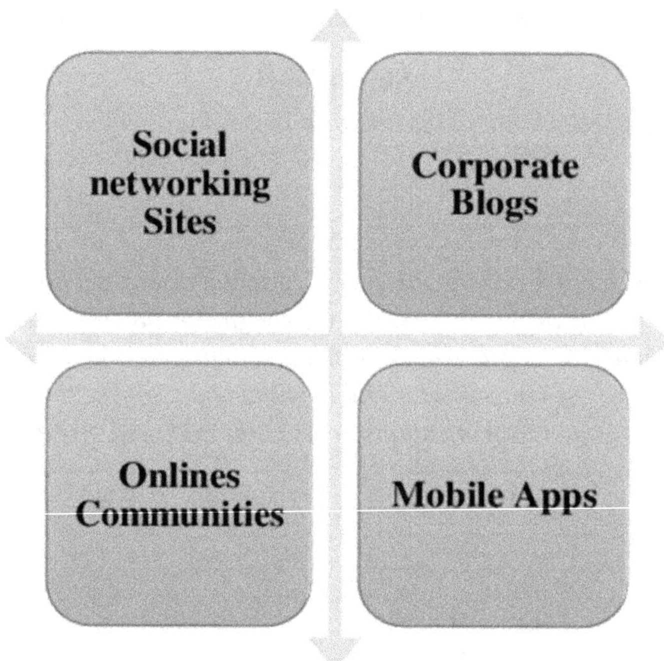

Social Networking Platforms

Social Networking Platforms are virtual domains where individuals can create personal profiles, build personal networks, connect with others, develop a social persona and create mutual value between associated entities. The actual evolution of this phenomenon stems from the offline interactivity of individuals, which when transferred online allows them to indulge in a convenient method for communication and exchange of information among their peers or people with whom they have some affinity or shared interests. This has helped transform these cliques into communities of significance. Contemporary times have witnessed the growth of several social networking platforms, like Facebook, Twitter, Instagram, Pinterest etc. The following section discusses how Facebook has developed as a social media platform with significant contributions to the field of Marketing. Facebook is not only limited to marketing, but it's usage can be extended to analysis and research as it gives insights into products and services and is able to generate immediate responses from customers (Gangadharbatla, 2008).

Twitter, Instagram and Pinterest are other examples of social networking platforms which help brands promote themselves. In an era where online reputations are hugely impacting brands, companies need to have well defined strategies in place for managing their virtual presence and diffusing information pertaining to innovative developments, promotional schemes and brand achievements. While companies need to have mechanisms to amplify positive consumer sentiment across their online social networks, they should also have appropriate methods for consumer redressal. Similarly, companies should be equipped to share meaningful information that will have some organisational, promotional or relational value for the consumers, and that will create a climate of participation. The success of the organisational endeavours on these platforms lies in achieving brand likeability, through the satisfaction of the self-gratification needs of consumers (Houk, Thornhill,2013). The idea of improving the effectiveness of marketing by allowing customers to participate in the marketing process has been recognized for at least 20 years. For consumers in the present times, gaining the functional benefit of using a product is simply insufficient and innovative involvement with brands adds value to the equation. Marketers must now understand how the latest digital tools can provide their customers with added value through their feeling of being involved in an experience shared by their peers in cyberspace (Hansson, Wrangmo, & Solberg Soilen, 2013). Brands need to engage customers by hosting social media content that is interesting to consumers and will help them engage in conversations with them. Brands need to identify what types of content appeal to what types of people. The objective is to build consumer engagement and ensure that people like content, share content and comment on the posts hosted by the organisation. This leads the consumers up the engagement continuum to a stage of involvement and loyalty towards a brand or organisation.

Blogs

A blog is a discussional online website which can be hosted for informational purposes. Several organisations make use of corporate blogs to share brand related knowledge and information. A blog is like an online diary where articles are uploaded in a chronological order and tagged based on the theme of the post. The idea here, is to create an online domain with very interesting content, so that consumers or other individuals can follow the content posted by the organisation or brand. Blogs hosted by brands or organisations are termed as corporate blogs and are used primarily for professional purposes. These blogs are used to host mainly three types of content-Organisational, Promotional and Relational. Organisational content is directed at sharing the achievements of the brand to enhance value perception and popularity. Promotional content aims at sharing information pertaining to promotional schemes, discounts and rebates to trigger consumer purchase intent. Relational content is directed towards showing the sensitive side of a brand and attempts to support brand-consumer relationships by showing that the brand cares for its consumers.

Once these consumers subscribe to the blog, the content uploaded by the brand reaches their feed regularly and ensures that the brand remains in the minds of the consumers. Brand visibility is enhanced through this process and consumer knowledge about the brand also improves. The blogs also have opportunities where consumers can like, comment or share the content, which further supports the process of enhancing the consumer-brand relationship, through an interactive affiliation. Brands benefit tremendously if consumers share their content on their own blogs or personal web spaces. Blogs are substantially popular in the healthcare industry and the fashion world.

Online Communities

These are virtual spaces created by individuals, brands or organisations, around some specific theme, product or cause. Each community has a set of participating members, who are actually individuals who are similar to each other by virtue of their affinity for the brand or support for the cause. Members possess a sense of community and socialisation. Members in a community engage in interaction and exchange of ideas, which results in the generation of trust and formulation of social relationships among participants. Online social networks have the potential to become business enablers (Swani, Milne, P. Brown 2013) Network ties, configuration, and stability help in building trust and developing a sense of shared goals and shared culture (Wang, Yu, Wei 2012). Brands can form communities around their products and through regular interaction and sharing of information, in a participatory environment, develop trust and affinity amongst the members. This enhances the value perception of the members, pertaining to the brand. A sense of kinship and belongingness amongst the members and this develops peer relationships, which influence consumer attitudes and behavior.

Mobile Apps

Internet-savvy smartphones supported by higher internet connectivity, are part of individual life styles in contemporary times. Hence organisations and brands need to make use of mobile technologies and these ubiquitous gadgets to sustain themselves, grow at a fast pace, become more competitive and reach out to as many consumers as possible. Anytime, anywhere connectivity makes it imperative for marketers to build a mobile footprint for their brands, as the digitally empowered consumer population has high expectations from brands. Mobile experiences are typically more unique and personalised and smartphones have now become a new way by which brands are communicating with their customers.

Mobile apps (applications) are innovative software programs designed to function on smartphones, tablet computers, and other handheld or mobile devices, have the ability to sync the data offline, and have changed the way business is done. The global mobile app market is growing at a very fast pace. As most brands launch their apps, to make their services available to the masses, App stores provide apps for IoS devices and Google play provides apps for android devices. Research studies have shown that on an average, smartphone users download 20-25 apps per month and it is in the interest of brands to make sure that consumers download their apps. Consumers can download a series of *utility-based apps* which help them make purchases from specific brands, perform certain transactions, as in the case of banking apps, book tickets or even download *social media apps* for faster access to their social media profiles. Marketers are constantly attempting to get more and more consumers to engage with them, through their apps, get interested in their brands and become loyal consumers.

Users can make use of mobile apps for shopping, downloading books, watching the news, for financial transactions, for ordering food, for enhancing workplace productivity, social networking and many more purposes.

USES OF SOCIAL MEDIA FOR BUSINESS

Social media can be used by businesses for several purposes (Figure 2). These include brand management, triggering sales, collecting customer intelligence, managing organisational reputations, building consumer brand relationships, understanding competitors, targeted advertising, analytics, for online payments and shopping. (Appel, Grewal, Hadi, & Stephen, 2020).

1. Brand Management

A Brand represents the symbols that help a customer distinguish an organisation or product form the competitors. Brands are used in the field of business, marketing and advertising. For instance, Amul represents a brand with a series of products under its umbrella.

Social media can be used by businesses to enhance brand awareness and visibility, brand identity, brand salience and resonance.

Brand awareness refers to the extent to which consumers know about the brand, are able to recognise it and are conscious about associated products and benefits. Awareness transforms to higher brand recall, once an individual is subjected to the brand related message a number of times. Social media is the perfect medium for hosting brand related messages multiple times, to ensure higher brand awareness, visibility and recall.

Figure 2. Uses of Social Media for Business Purposes
(IGI, 2021)

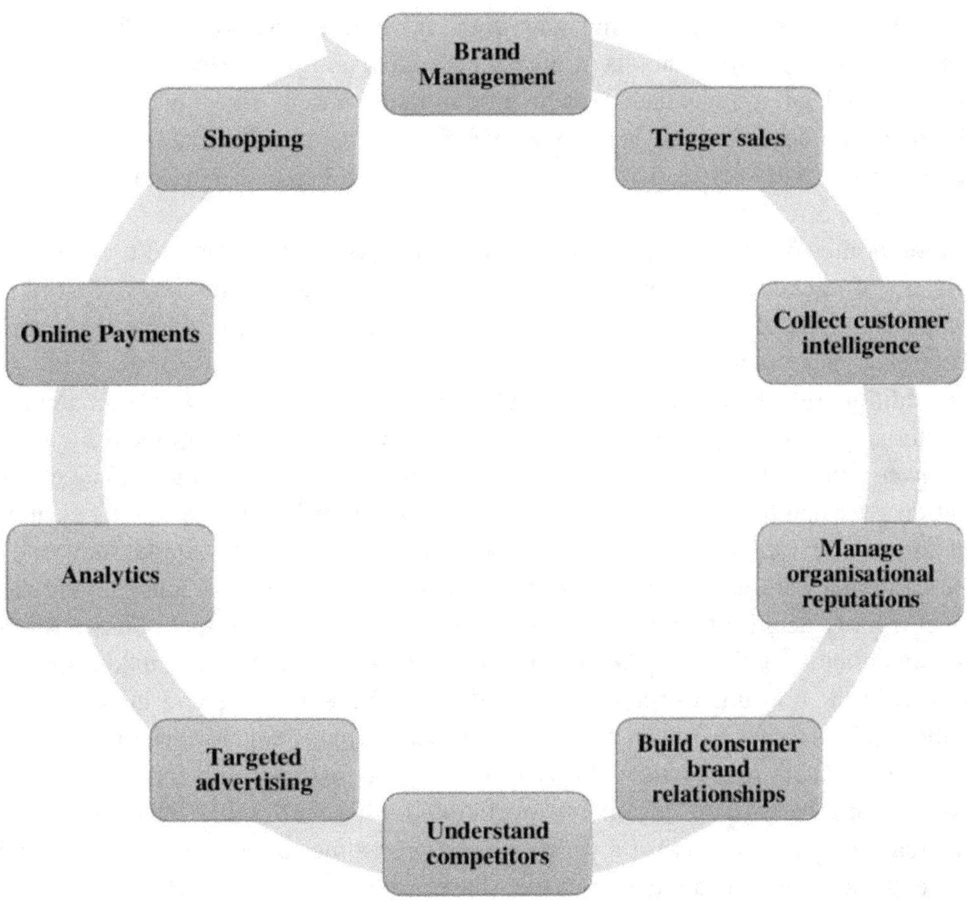

Brands can use social media to propagate and strengthen their brand identity and brand image. A brand identity constitutes the value proposition that a brand stands for, what the brand represents or wants to communicate to its customers. Brand image represents how the consumers perceive the brand, after consuming the content or information, shared by an organisation. By using social media to communicate their thoughts with the consumers, brands can host relevant content to shape an appropriate identity for themselves. For instance, if a commercial brand shares content pertaining to their corporate social responsibility endeavours, to shape an identity of a socially responsible brand, they can develop a brand image of a caring, accountable brand, in the consumer minds. Several brands in India, used their social media presence to condemn the terrorist attacks in Pulwama and express their solidarity with the armed forces. Similarly, posts pertaining to gender equality also enable organisations to depict what they feel about certain sensitive issues plaguing society, at large.

As travel and tourism becomes popular, the need for information pertaining to hotels and other places of stay, has increased. Search engines for hotels are getting popular. Trivago is a German transnational organisation which specialises in internet related services for the travel and tourism industry. Trivago allows users to compare hotel prices to compare deals in the same city, across several booking sites. The online platform grants users access to hotels in approximately 200 countries globally.

Double incomes in unit families has made weekend getaways popular and different consumer groups have different requirements. For some, an extremely stupendous hotel ambience is significant, while for others, pricing is a valuable determinant. Consumer expectations form the travel experience are diverse. Hence, there is a need for customisation in the travel planning process. Platforms like Trivago help visitors to locate appropriate hotels at a very fast pace, compare prices from different websites, simply by feeding in desired travel dates and helping in the search by filtering the process on the basis of price, distance from beach/airport, star categories, facilities etc. and throwing up responses ranging from budget hotels to luxury suites. Millions of aggregated hotel ratings and images allow travellers to complete their search after a thorough review.

A quick look at the social media presence of Trivago shows that Trivago id using the right mix of relevance (details of weekend getaways and associated hotels, city guides for food and drink, hotel lists), emotional appeal (details of places to love, valentine's day ideas, romantic getaways), perceived reliability (exceptional guest reviews).

However, additional efforts for generating social media content directed towards enhancing perceptual homophily, interactivity and experience-centricity need to be made by the company.

Brand salience represents the degree to which a brand appears in a consumer's choice set-the evoked or consideration set when he recognises a need for a product. For instance, when a consumer wants to buy a mobile phone, the top three choices that come into his mind, may be Apple, Samsung or Xiaomi. These top three choices are already in existence in the consumer subconscious and are retrieved, the moment the consumer decides to make a purchase. This is where social media has a role to play. As organisations and brands continuously keep on posting content into their social media spaces, they keep on interacting with the consumer eyeballs, across the social media feeds and inadvertently, enter the consumer subconscious space, based on the continuous perceptions being formed in the brain repeatedly.

Brand resonance refers to a brand's ability to relate to a customer and form a strong connection. Brands need to be in sync with the customer expectations. A higher brand resonance enables a brand to command increased loyalty because of a stronger brand-consumer bond. Social media can be used by businesses to educate customers about brands and share product knowledge which enables the formulation of a strong relationship between brands and consumers (O'Fallon, & Sullivan 2004).

By using social media, organisations can create humane brands that are emotional and sensitive to the consumer needs. Social media enables organisations to share their thoughts and communicate a lot of content which need not be marketing related material (Inkpen, A.C. & Tsang, E.W.K. 2005). By showcasing the ideology of the brand, its long-term mission and vision to benefit society at large, brands can generate the relevant goodwill for themselves. It is this goodwill that helps brands enter the consumer cognitive space and induces brand likeability. If a consumer likes a brand, he will remain loyal to the same, irrespective of promotional marketing message from competing brands.

2. Trigger Sales

Brands can continuously host information about their products and associated attributes, new offerings etc. on social media in a bid to increase sales. By enhancing visibility of their products, brands are trying to push more traffic onto their websites, as well as increase sales in the offline world. Details of promotional offers, when shared by brands on social media, garner consumer attention, stimulate intent and desire to purchase and sometimes trigger impulse purchases. Social media is like a persuasive salesperson-showing consumer the benefits of a purchase, and being convincing, till they actually do so. Social media can also help in viral marketing and influencer marketing. Certain social media content can be virally propagated to get a lot of views from consumers and this can result in enhanced popularity and visibility for the brand. Additionally, social media can be used to identify opinion leaders and brand influencers. These are people who have significant clout amongst the target consumer markets and brands can use these people for brand advocacy, recommendations and evangelism. A brand evangelist is a person whose opinion is respected in society, by virtue of his status, position or general popularity. Several social media analytics tools help brands identify popular influencers, who can be used for evangelism. These influencers not only endorse and support the brand themselves, also recommend the brands to others and in a subtle fashion ensure that their recommendations are honoured.

3. Collect Customer Intelligence

Figure 3. Collecting Customer Intelligence Using Social Media
(IGI, 2021)

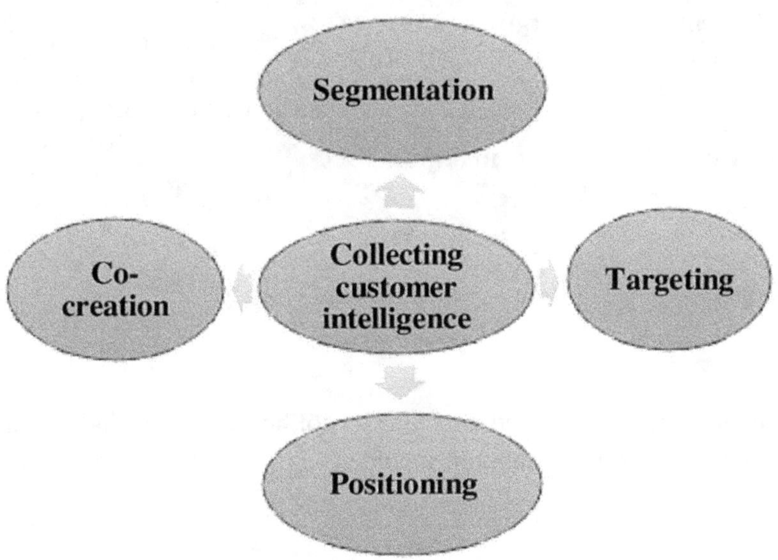

Organisations can make use of social media for collecting customer specific information for the purpose of Segmentation, Targeting, Positioning and Co-creation (Figure 3).

Consumers interact with a brand, by indulging in conversations, liking content hosted by the brand, sharing content and commenting on the content.

Banks can use their customers as their partners and solicit their ideas to generate value in the banking ecosystem. This is the process of co-creation. This usually results in more personalised experiences for the customer because of an improvement in the banking processes or unique experiences for the customers. Simultaneously, the process of co-creation results in improved revenue, enhanced learning and greater market performance drivers for the firm. For example, State Bank of India opened up its APIs for a hackathon. The hackathon was open to developers and start-ups from India, with the idea of tapping into a larger development pool for new technology innovations. By opening up the APIs, SBI attempted to create new services and products. By sharing this information on social media, the bank further showcased its commitment to increase user participation for the benefit of all.

The era of cookies allows organisations to track the various dimensions of consumer behaviour-time spent on a site, pages clicked and so on. Additionally, by using research techniques like netnography, social media analytics and text mining, (Figure 4) organisations can extract meaning out of the consumer conversations and aid decision making. One such aspect of decision-making is consumer segmentation.

Figure 4. Netnography, Social Media Analytics and Text mining
(IGI, 2021)

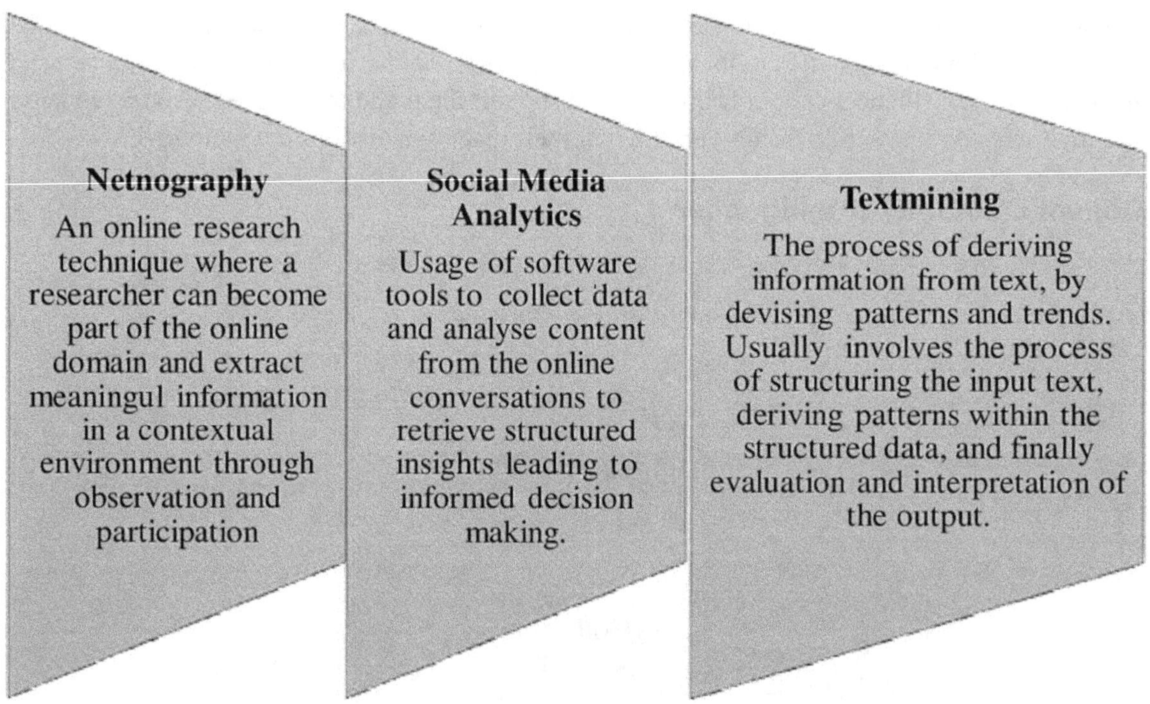

Segmentation involves grouping consumers into sets of homogeneous individuals who have certain similarities. Traditional basis of segmentation includes segmenting consumers on the basis of demographic variables, psychographic variables and behavioural variables. One example of how social media can aid segmentation is quantification of consumer sentiment for the brand, as is visible in the consumer comments, during their conversations with the brand. Consumers who have a positive sentiment for the brand (like, love, adore, happy, satisfied respect etc.) can be grouped into one segment and others who demonstrate a negative sentiment for the brand (hate, dislike, abhor, unhappy, dissatisfied) can be grouped into another segment. This way, brands can identify which consumers are satisfied with them and which are dissatisfied. While the satisfied consumers can be sent promotional messages, enticing them to buy more, dissatisfied consumers can be treated in a special, personalised way. Their problems should be resolved and special gifts or mementoes can help salvage the brand-consumer relationship. This is **consumer targeting**. In summary, while segmentation comprises grouping consumers on the basis of their similarities, targeting comprises which consumers are to be approached and in which manner.

Positioning involves creating specific perceptions in the consumer mind, about a brand. Social media can be used to do so. This can be done by creating a relevant differentiation about the brand, through a series of posts, showcase the competitive advantages of the brand and the core competencies of the brand. Additional posts can use subtle mannerisms to show the brand in a superior light, as compared to competition. Positioning can be done on the basis of product attributes, pricing, product benefits, usage occasions, social class and many more aspects. The customer intelligence harnessed through social media interactions with customers can help brands in understanding which positioning basis to use.

Social media can also be used for consumer co-creation. Co-creation refers to organisational endeavours centred around bringing consumers and brands together to jointly produce a mutually valued outcome. Consumers are invited to share their ideas about products and processes and after an associated due diligence, companies adopt those ideas. Social media can be used to source consumer ideas, which when implemented by a brand can result in improved, personalised and unique experiences for the customer, thereby enhancing his value perception. For the brand, these ideas need to spell higher revenue, enhanced market performance as well as learning and development to enhance value.

Hindustan Unilever Ltd (HUL) is a British-Dutch manufacturing company, producing food, beverages, cleaning agents, personal care products etc. A careful scrutiny of the brand's twitter presence shows that the brand is using the same to showcase its commitment to growing its business, reducing the negative environmental impacts of its operations, make sustainable living commonplace, and increasing its social impact. The virtual presence is directed towards two types of posts-Those directed at enhancing the perceived value of the brand by sharing organisational achievements and those directed towards enhancing the social image of the brand. The brand building posts include content pertaining to awards received by the company for use of artificial intelligence in consumer and marketing research, from the Market Research Society of India, company of the year award for its corporate social responsibility endeavours, CNBC India's business leadership awards, corporate governance awards, advertiser of the year awards etc. additional information pertaining to the organisation's collaborative ventures with other bodies like UNDP etc. further add to the company's accomplishments.

The social activities of the brand are documented across a series of posts including the #start a little good campaign, centred around water conservation, environmental cleanliness and sanitation. The #SafetyFirst campaign, #Gosafelyoutside campaign, the #helpa child reach five campaign are commendable efforts from HUL. Kwality Wall's drive promoting entrepreneurship, Lifebuoy's efforts towards consumer health, the social innovation drive and many more present HUL as an organisation, not directed towards making profits, but committed towards benefitting society at large.

Posts pertaining to enhancing consumer motivation, positivity, resilience and family bonds, further add value to the brand's image.

Interestingly, the social media presence seems to be less about building consumer engagement and more about brand positioning. The absence of content which can engage customers like contests and other promotional content clearly shows that the primary objective of the company's social media presence is less about building consumer relationships and more about securing respect of the consumer, society, media and other corporates, by making a statement about the brand-its identity and social standing.

4. Manage Organisational Reputations and Respond to Controversies

As the era of consumer generated media empowers consumers and all organisational stakeholders to create content in the online domain and share their views openly across platforms and review sites, it is vital for companies and brands to keep track of what is being said about them. Organisations have reputations to maintain and a constant monitoring practise can save them from a lot of embarrassment. If a brand is able to identify certain content being posted by a disgruntled customer or supplier or marketing intermediary, a proactive approach can help the brand in getting the situation blown out of proportion. As consumers find their voice, companies need to find a way to respond to them, pacify them and maintain a congenial relationship with them. As brands launch their social media presence, they can choose to moderate the brand-consumer conversations or let consumers say what they want to. A caring brand responds to consumers and attempts to resolve the issue that is causing them unhappiness. Interestingly, brands that have been able to maintain excellent brand-consumer relationships can benefit a lot when a satisfied customer posts positive content on the social media platform. The positivity is well received by the consumer's peers and it is the brand which benefits from the entire interaction. Social media platforms can also be used by brands to respond to any controversies that are circulating about them. Brands can also keep track of competitor strategies and attempt to stay ahead in the game.

5. Build Consumer Brand Relationships

Consumer-brand relationships are important for brands. Taking inspiration from Fournier's work (Fournier, 1998), there are six dimensions of a consumer-brand relationship. These are *love and passion, self-connection, interdependence, commitment, intimacy, and brand partner quality.* While the dimension of *love and passion* is focussed on building a strong emotional connection between brand and consumer, *self-connection* focusses on the ability of the brand to resonate with a consumer's identity and belief systems. The dimension of *interdependence* depicts intense cohesion between brand and consumer resulting in a synergistic relationship between the two. *Commitment* reflects the unsaid promise between consumer and brand which denotes dedication and longevity of the relationship. The dimension of *intimacy* shows the mutual understanding and empathy between consumer and brand and the dimension of *brand partner quality* depicts the consumer thoughts pertaining to brand reliability, trustworthiness and expectation fulfilment. Strong relationships are formed when all these six dimensions are working together, in harmony.

Long term relationships between consumer and brand spell consumer loyalty which implies higher profits for the brand. Research has shown that it costs five times more for organisations to acquire new consumers, than it costs to retain the older ones. Hence organisations should actively invest their time and energy in customer relationship management and partner relationship management. By building strong social, financial and structural bonds, with their consumers, organisations can ensure higher customer lifetime value. Customer lifetime value represents the net present value of the sum total of all future cash flows from one customer. For instance, an individual customer, aged 30, may buy around 5-6 laptops more, in his entire life span. It is in the interest of a brand that the customer buys all these laptops from the same brand. This can happen only if the consumer brand relationship is a very loyal one (Maraun, Wetterhall, Ireson, Chandler, Kendon,, Widmann, & Venema, 2010).

Known for its unique ethnic apparel options, Craftsvilla, is an e-commerce portal that sells fashion accessories as well as beauty and lifestyle products. Craftsvilla has successfully tied up with the Ministry of Textiles, in India for promoting handloom products and with several small players, by aggregating artisans, designers and retailers onto the platform. Craftsvilla maintains a commendable social media presence across a diverse range of platforms. In a bid to get its customers and partners to interact with the brand and share their experiences, Craftsvilla has launched two closed groups on social media. These are the Craftsvilla fashion group and the Craftsvilla style partner group. Both the groups focus on encouraging members to participate in conversations and share their experiences and ideas with brand Craftsvilla. In addition to this, explicit social media posts by the brand, pertaining to breezy tassel earrings, patiala suits, low hem kurtis, crepe sarees, floral designs, stylish jewellery, festive colors, lehenga goals, dazzling evening gowns, bright spring silhouettes, monochrome georgettes and charming classics help Craftsvilla in addressing the cognitive components in shaping consumer perceptions towards the brand. There is a significant opportunity for the brand to showcase its sensitive side to come across as an emotional brand to address the affective components in shaping consumer perceptions. The striking consumer appreciation of the content visible through the huge volume of likes, shares and retweets clearly indicate that Craftsvilla's social media presence has been successful in soliciting the appreciation of its consumers.

Organisations should focus on consumer satisfaction by having effective complaint handling mechanisms in place. A satisfied consumer demonstrates repurchase intent and recommends the product to others. A dissatisfied customer leaves the brand and buys products from the competing brands. Additionally, research has shown that while a satisfied customer only tells 5 more people about a brand, a dissatisfied customer tells 17 other people about his negative experience and the era of consumer generated media has given his voice the power to go viral, in online domains. Hence relevant brand investments in customer relationships, loyalty and satisfaction are a must.

Social media can be used by brands for building consumer brand relationships, garnering consumer loyalty and inducing consumer satisfaction (Margarida Barreto, A. 2013).

Table 1. Using social media to build consumer brand relationships, garnering consumer loyalty and inducing consumer satisfaction

Brand Objective	Social Media Strategy
Building consumer brand relationships	Brands can craft a humanistic image for themselves by sharing relevant social media content. This can trigger *love and passion* for the brand in the consumer mind. This can include simple social media messages like wishing consumers happy birthday, happy valentine's day etc. Social media content like discounts and sales, which appeals to a price sensitive customer can help a brand stimulate *self- connection. Interdependence* can be enhanced when a brand shares content which shows that the products are useful and beneficial to a consumer. Personalised social media messages or special posts for special consumer segments can enhance *commitment* and *intimacy* between brand and consumer. For instance, some brands regularly host contests on social media and share the names of the winners online. This enhances the consumer brand equation. Consumer testimonials hosted on social media or positive consumer views in the comments section can enhance the *brand-partner quality*.
Garnering consumer loyalty	Brand can develop online communities, invite customers to become members, and subsequently use these communities to trigger belongingness, participation and reciprocity in the consumer minds. This will lead to consumer loyalty. By finding ways to give recognition to members and enhance their self-esteem, these communities can lead consumers to be in the presence of others with similar goals, motivations, norms, values and interests, thereby stimulating faithfulness to the brand.
Consumer satisfaction	Brands can use effective complaint handling by responding to consumer complaints posted on social media and otherwise. Faster response to consumer queries using social media, makes consumers feel that the brand cares about them. Once a consumer complaints, brand should use social media conversations to instil trust in him regarding the brand's commitment towards resolution of his problem. This will lead to consumer satisfaction.

Source: (IGI, 2021)

Additionally, these relationships help organisations in cross selling and upselling to consumers. Cross-selling involves pushing a consumer who has bought one product from a brand, to purchase another product, from the same brand. This will ensure more share of money from a customer's wallet for an organisation. Upselling involves pushing a customer to buy an upgraded product from the same organisation or brand. Relevant social media content can aid brands in cross-selling and upselling to the consumer base.

6. Understand Competitors

By keeping abreast of the social media content hosted by its competitors, brands can gauge their marketing and relationship building strategies and formulate plans and tactics to stay ahead of their opponents. Brands can also get access to information pertaining to what consumers think about the other brands and react accordingly.

7. Targeted Advertising

The virtual world is witnessing an individualised form of advertising where brands are able to reach out to consumers on the basis of their traits, demographic, psychographic and behavioural factors. As a result, consumers who may be interested in a product are more likely to receive the associated information, as compared to those who may not have an interest in the same. The concept of targeting, in marketing, propagates a focussed approach by organisations, with the intention of identifying the consumers to be approached and in which manner, primarily, to enhance the efficiency of marketing and reducing wastage of marketing resources.

The digital epoch enables companies to track the online consumer activity, browsing history, keyword searches on search engines and contextual advertising (where appropriate advertisements are chosen and displayed by computerised systems based on user demographics, identity and specific pages displayed.) Once companies are aware of what sites consumers are visiting, they can gauge the interests and needs of consumers. Subsequently, relevant advertising messages can be served to the consumers, on their screens, based on their preference.

Social media targeting is about using the information that is available on social media, to target consumers with specific information. For instance, if a consumer has liked a specific fast-food brand, he will receive ads about the same brand, but according to his geographic location, as visible on social media. For instance, social media platforms like Facebook allow brands to target consumers on the basis of demographic information, consumer behaviour (as seen through online activity) and interests (Dwivedi, Ismagilova,, Hughes, Carlson, Filieri, Jacobson, & Wang, 2021) The low cost of this activity makes it an interesting option for marketers. Additionally, advertisers on social media can also make use of contextual targeting where they host a specific ad based on relative content, using and ad matching system which analyses contents on a webpage or presents ads through pop ups based on keywords used for search engine searches. In the recent times artificial intelligence (AI) have been applied to online advertising in order to augment the reach of target audiences (Choi, J. A., & Lim, K. 2020)
Brands can make use of social media for targeting consumers through

1. Geotargeting
2. Behavioural Targeting
3. Socio-psychographic targeting

The integration of marketing information involves using the same marketing messages, themes, stories and creative ideas across all media vehicles. A targeted marketing approach helps brands reach the right audiences with the right promotional messages. For instance, in the case of a financial services brand, which intends targeting younger consumers in the early thirties, targeting, based on location, age, gender, interests etc., can help the brand connect with consumers on a more personal level, by sending out advertising content that would be relevant and effective, by being in line with the consumer needs and expectations. For example, a brand trying to promote credit card purchase among college students can target them with free pizza coupons, whereas ads promoting financial stability can be used to push the same product onto professionals in the 30–40-year age group. The most significant benefit of targeting is that it helps brands reach users consumers who may have some affinity for the brand, rather than waste time and resources in reaching out to the masses who may not have any interest in purchasing the product at all.

Figure 5. Targeted Advertising Using Social Media
(IGI, 2021)

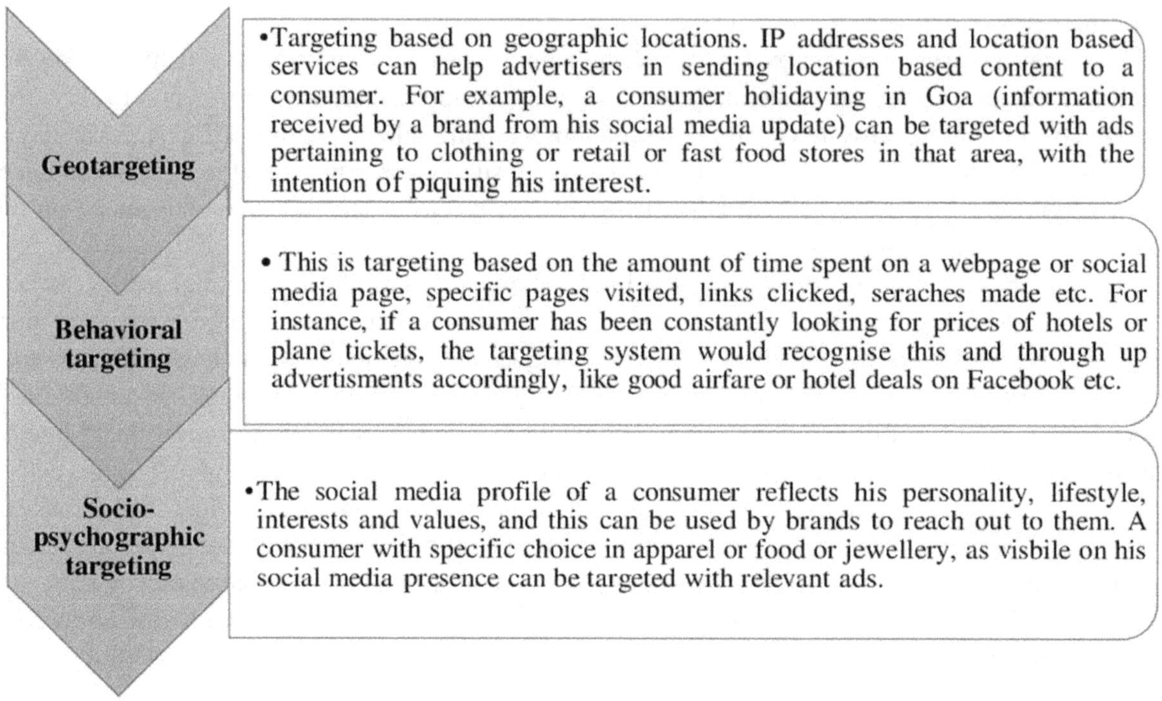

8. Analytics

Rapid technological evolution and universal connectivity has created new touchpoints between organisations and customers and there are several avenues for brands to collect consumer specific information. As large volumes of data become available to organisations, through customer mobile app usage, consumer generated media on social media, digital clicks and so on, businesses have the opportunity to start benefitting from the analysis of this data. The offline world has transformed as the internet of things (IoT) enters into all life arenas and IoT sensors, combined with products, individualise customer experiences across the world. Managers, business heads, policymakers and organisational stakeholders can use data driven methods for improved decision making. Several social media analytics tools are available for this. The chapter on social media analytics, discusses these concepts in detail. In a snapshot, the biggest benefits of analytics to the business world include-

1. Improved efficiency of processes and operations
2. Information into customer behaviours, lifestyles and preferences permit companies to personalise their messages to them. More individualised approaches bode well with the customers.
3. Better segmentation and targeting of customers, based on factual data around the online activity of the customer, time spent on a particular page, search history, number of clicks, browsing history, past purchasing patterns and online shopping behavior, number of unique items in the shopping cart-quantity and value etc.
4. Enhanced positioning of brands based on analysis of customers' expectations

5. Better customer experience management based on superior understanding of customer needs
6. Better customer relationship management
7. Development of new products after analysing data to derive consumer insights
8. Reduction of frauds and risks.
9. Reduction of costs

9. Online Payments

Contemporary times allow consumers to use their social media networks to transfer money to their friends or contacts, as well as perform some other banking operations. Several banks permit transfer of funds to a Facebook or Twitter friend once a consumer has registered using his email or social media credentials, merely by entering a one-time password or OTP. For example, ICICI bank permits users to make use of two applications-Pockets for Facebook and ICICI bank pay for Twitter. Individuals can make use of these apps for making payments, checking their bank balance, recharging mobiles, booking movie tickets and so on. As banks start appreciating the need to support the adoption of technology with the creation of social value, convenience and ease of use, the future of personal banking in a country like India, clearly looks humanistic, optimistic, responsive, immensely social and technology driven.

10. Shopping Using Social Media

Social media shortens the consumer's path to a purchase by acting like an online catalogue. As soon as a consumer likes a product, a *shop now* link on the social media platform, directs the consumer to the page from where they can make the purchase. Ease of access to the purchase venue in the online domain, convenience of the purchase activity, availability of choices, ability to make comparisons and consumer impulsiveness usher in quick sales for brands (Wilson, 2011).

CHAPTER SUMMARY

Social media refers to a series of virtual channels, tools and platforms which enable people to come together in the virtual arena and interact with each other, collaborate or share content. This is termed as *social* because it primarily comprises of user generated content and constitutes a mechanism whereby communities or cliques can come together for information sharing and exchange of ideas. Social Networking Platforms, Blogs, Online Communities and Mobile Apps are the most significant social media tools used by businesses. Social media can be used by businesses for the purposes of brand management, triggering sales, collecting customer intelligence, managing organisational reputations, building consumer brand relationships, understanding competitors, targeted advertising, analytics, for online payments and shopping.

REFERENCES

Appel, G., Grewal, L., Hadi, R., & Stephen, A. T. (2020). The future of social media in marketing. *Journal of the Academy of Marketing Science*, *48*(1), 79–95. doi:10.100711747-019-00695-1 PMID:32431463

Barreto, A. M. (2013). Do users look at banner ads on Facebook? *Journal of Research in Interactive Marketing*.

Choi, J. A., & Lim, K. (2020). Identifying machine learning techniques for classification of target advertising. *ICT Express*, *6*(3), 175–180. doi:10.1016/j.icte.2020.04.012

Dwivedi, Y. K., Ismagilova, E., Hughes, D. L., Carlson, J., Filieri, R., Jacobson, J., Jain, V., Karjaluoto, H., Kefi, H., Krishen, A. S., Kumar, V., Rahman, M. M., Raman, R., Rauschnabel, P. A., Rowley, J., Salo, J., Tran, G. A., & Wang, Y. (2021). Setting the future of digital and social media marketing research: Perspectives and research propositions. *International Journal of Information Management*, *59*, 102168. doi:10.1016/j.ijinfomgt.2020.102168

Fournier, S. (1998). Consumers and their brands: Developing relationship theory in consumer research. *The Journal of Consumer Research*, *24*(4), 343–373. doi:10.1086/209515

Gangadharbatla, H. (2008). Facebook me: Collective self-esteem, need to belong, and internet self-efficacy as predictors of the iGeneration's attitudes toward social networking sites. *Journal of Interactive Advertising*, *8*(2), 5–15. doi:10.1080/15252019.2008.10722138

Hansson, L., Wrangmo, A., & Søilen, K. S. (2013). Optimal ways for companies to use Facebook as a marketing channel. *Journal of Information, Communication and Ethics in Society*.

Houk, K. M., & Thornhill, K. (2013). Using Facebook page insights data to determine posting best practices in an academic health sciences library. *Journal of Web Librarianship*, *7*(4), 372–388. doi:10.1080/19322909.2013.837346

Inkpen, A. C., & Tsang, E. W. (2005). Social capital, networks, and knowledge transfer. *Academy of Management Review*, *30*(1), 146–165. doi:10.5465/amr.2005.15281445

Maraun, D., Wetterhall, F., Ireson, A. M., Chandler, R. E., Kendon, E. J., Widmann, M., Brienen, S., Rust, H. W., Sauter, T., Themeßl, M., Venema, V. K. C., Chun, K. P., Goodess, C. M., Jones, R. G., Onof, C., Vrac, M., & Thiele-Eich, I. (2010). Precipitation downscaling under climate change: Recent developments to bridge the gap between dynamical models and the end user. *Reviews of Geophysics*, *48*(3), RG3003. doi:10.1029/2009RG000314

O'Fallon, C., & Sullivan, C. (2004). Personalised marketing-improving evaluation. *Transport Engineering in Australia*, *9*(2), 85–101.

Punjaisri, K., & Wilson, A. (2011). Internal branding process: Key mechanisms, outcomes and moderating factors. *European Journal of Marketing*.

Swani, K., Milne, G., & Brown, B. P. (2013). Spreading the word through likes on Facebook: Evaluating the message strategy effectiveness of Fortune 500 companies. *Journal of Research in Interactive Marketing*, *7*(4), 269–294. doi:10.1108/JRIM-05-2013-0026

Wang, X., Yu, C., & Wei, Y. (2012). Social media peer communication and impacts on purchase intentions: A consumer socialization framework. *Journal of Interactive Marketing*, *26*(4), 198–208.

ADDITIONAL READING

Culnan, M. J., McHugh, P. J., & Zubillaga, J. I. (2010). How large US companies can use Twitter and other social media to gain business value. *MIS Quarterly Executive*, *9*(4).

Fraccastoro, S., Gabrielsson, M., & Pullins, E. B. (2021). The integrated use of social media, digital, and traditional communication tools in the B2B sales process of international SMEs. *International Business Review*, *30*(4), 101776. doi:10.1016/j.ibusrev.2020.101776

Kasemsap, K. (2019). Professional and business applications of social media platforms. In *Social entrepreneurship: Concepts, methodologies, tools, and applications* (pp. 824–847). IGI Global.

Kumar, A., & Ayedee, N. (2018). Social media tools for business growth of SMES. *Journal of Management*, *5*(3).

Lorenzo-Romero, C., Alarcón-del-Amo, M. D. C., & Constantinides, E. (2014). Determinants of use of social media tools in retailing sector. *Journal of Theoretical and Applied Electronic Commerce Research*, *9*(1), 44–55. doi:10.4067/S0718-18762014000100005

Maravilhas, S. (2018). Social media tools for quality business information. In Social Media Marketing: Breakthroughs in Research and Practice (pp. 883-912). IGI Global. doi:10.4018/978-1-5225-5637-4.ch044

Naim, M. F. (2014). Leveraging social media for Generation Y retention. *European Journal of Business and Management*, *6*(23), 173–179.

Veer, N., Pawar, P., & Kolte, A. (2019). Effectiveness of Social Media Tools and It's Impact on Promotions. *International Journal of Innovative Technology and Exploring Engineering, 8*(7S2), 224-230.

Wamba, S. F., & Carter, L. (2016). Social media tools adoption and use by SMEs: An empirical study. In *Social media and Networking: Concepts, methodologies, tools, and applications* (pp. 791–806). IGI Global. doi:10.4018/978-1-4666-8614-4.ch035

KEY TERMS AND DEFINITIONS

Blogs: A blog is a discussional online website which can be hosted for informational purposes. Several organisations make use of corporate blogs to share brand related knowledge and information. A blog is like an online diary where articles are uploaded in a chronological order and tagged based on the theme of the post.

Mobile Apps: Internet-savvy smartphones supported by higher internet connectivity, are part of individual lifestyles in contemporary times. Hence organisations and brands need to make use of mobile technologies and these ubiquitous gadgets to sustain themselves, grow at a fast pace, become more competitive and reach out to as many consumers as possible.

Online Communities: These are virtual spaces created by individuals, brands, or organisations around some specific theme, product, or cause. Each community has a set of participating members, who are actually individuals who are similar to each other by virtue of their affinity for the brand or support for the cause.

Online Payments: Contemporary times allow consumers to use their social media networks to transfer money to their friends or contacts, as well as perform some other banking operations. Several banks permit transfer of funds to a Facebook or Twitter friend once a consumer has registered using his email or social media credentials, merely by entering a one-time password or OTP.

Shopping Using Social Media: Social media shortens the consumer's path to a purchase by acting like an online catalogue. As soon as a consumer likes a product, a *shop now* link on the social media platform, directs the consumer to the page from where they can make the purchase.

Social Media Tools for Businesses: Social networking platforms, blogs, online communities, and mobile apps are the most significant social media tools used by businesses today.

Social Networking Platforms: Social networking platforms are virtual domains where individuals can create personal profiles, build personal networks, connect with others, develop a social persona and create mutual value between associated entities.

Chapter 14
Impact of Digital Transformation via Unified Communication and Collaboration Technologies:
Productivity and Innovation at a Global Enterprise

Anthony D. Bolton
University of South Africa, South Africa

Leila Goosen
University of South Africa, South Africa

Elmarie Kritzinger
University of South Africa, South Africa

ABSTRACT

In order to summarize and provide readers with an overview of the content, the purpose of this chapter is stated as describing the design of case study research developed for evaluating the impact of digital transformation on the development of new business models and consumer experiences, against the background of an empirical study into the effects of the introduction of unified communications and collaboration (UC&C) technologies on productivity and innovation within the context of the large-scale global automotive design, manufacturing, and business operations of General Motors (GM).

DOI: 10.4018/978-1-7998-9179-6.ch014

INTRODUCTION

This section will describe the general perspective of the chapter and end by specifically stating the objective.

Artificial Intelligence (AI) and other **emerging trends** regarding *technologies*, such as Virtual Reality (VR) and Augmented Reality (AR), are elements of differentiation and an important milestone in business development and *customer interactions*, particularly in terms of services. "The resulting enablement franchises the digital enterprise with a deep and broad set of functional data that can be applied across the value chain and lead to the creation of" several "**new business models** and sources of efficiency and innovation" (Bolton, Goosen, & Kritzinger, 2021b, p. 149). Anchored in using these digital *technologies* and institutional systems, as well as technological environments, enterprises are well-placed to make progress towards providing new **experiences** to *services* **customers** and/or enterprises in the cyber world (Goosen & Naidoo, 2014). The chapter makes a contribution towards fulfilling the need for an edited collection of original research in the area of service knowledge, by introducing the design of a *research methodology* developed with the **purpose** of evaluating the **impact of digital transformation on the development of new business models and consumer experiences**. This is done against the background of an empirical study into the effects of the introduction of Unified Communications and Collaboration (UC&C) technologies on **productivity and innovation** within the context of the large-scale **global** automotive design, manufacturing and business operations of General Motors (GM) as **enterprise** towards the post-COVID-19 era. Surviving the COVID-19 crisis (Sufi & Ahmed, 2021) and recovery demands results and **new** "**business models**, rapidly affecting the entire enterprise involved" (Bolton, Goosen, & Kritzinger, 2020a, p. 100).

Although operating in a highly competitive market, prior to the research undertaking described in this chapter, General Motors had not implemented UC&C technologies within its design, manufacturing or business operation functions and had not engaged in the development of **digital transformation** using an **Internet of Things (IoT)**-related digitization strategy.

Target Audience

As for the book, the content of this chapter is designed for business professionals, students and researchers in the field of services, and specifically in terms of the relationships between **digital transformation** and new *technologies*, as well as **new business models** and **customer experiences**. Examples of such an audience include managers, service or product developers, service or product designers, and executives.

Recommended Topics

Based on the **recommended topics** for the book, this chapter will focus on:

- Digital transformation
- Digital environments
- New technologies
- Business models
- Customer interactions
- Customer experiences

- Internet of Things (IoT)
- Services

Objective

"By empowering workforce efficiency, driving higher levels in the personalization of **customer experiences** and building **new business models** through *new technologies*, innovative **digital transformation** fuels disruption" (Bolton, et al., 2021b, p. 147). In the particular context of services, like the book, this chapter aims to provide relevant theoretical and empirical research findings and an innovative and multi-faceted perspective on how **digital transformation** and other innovative *technologies* can drive **new business models** and create value **experiences** for **customers at a global enterprise**. Specifically, it provides an understanding of the strategies that underpin **new business models** and how new *interactions* or experiences with the **customer** or enterprise are created and characterized in terms of antecedents, consequences, dynamics and value. It will be written for researchers or professionals, who want to improve their understanding in this area.

BACKGROUND

This section of the chapter and the next will provide broad definitions and discussions of the topic, on the impact of **digital transformation** on the development of **new business models** and **customer experiences** in terms of productivity and innovation at a global automotive enterprise, and incorporate the views of others (in the form of a *literature review*) into the discussion to support, refute, or demonstrate the authors' position on the topic.

A conference paper on enterprise digitization enablement through unified communication and collaboration (Bolton, Goosen, & Kritzinger, 2016, p. 4) provided a heading with particular relevance to the theme of this book, on the impact of **digital transformation** on the development of new business models and consumer experience: "**Connected Customer and Smart Services**".

The impact of unified communication and collaboration technologies on productivity and innovation towards promotion for the Fourth Industrial Revolution (4IR) can also not be discounted (Bolton, Goosen, & Kritzinger, 2020b).

The reader should note that this chapter only cites those references applicable to content provided here. However, the researcher had also participated in fieldwork, and, as such, had conducted an extensive literature review to support, explain and contribute to the **purpose** of the work - this is evidenced by e.g., the quantity of 96 references presented in Bolton, Goosen and Kritzinger (2021c).

Impact of Digital Transformation on the Automotive Industry

Regarding the impact of digital transformation on the automotive industry, technological forecasting and social change, Llopis-Albert, Rubio and Valero (2021, p. 1) indicated that digital "technologies are transforming the automotive industry and disrupting traditional business models." The impact of digital transformation on automotive organizations is also transforming industrial business (Piccinini, Hanelt, Gregory, & Kolbe, 2015), while insights from the European automotive industry are promoting understanding of digital transformation strategy formation (Chanias & Hess, 2016). In terms of digital transformation in the automotive industry and towards a generic value network, Riasanow, Galic and Böhm (2017, p. 3191) agreed that the "emergence of digital innovations is accelerating and" contributing to "existing business models by delivering opportunities for new services."

New Business Models

"**New business models**, new marketing channels and new markets are reached using" Information and Communication Technologies (ICTs) (Bolton, et al., 2021b, p. 134).

In their research, Marabelli, Hansen, Newell and Frigerio (2017) presented **emerging trends** related to **new business models** influenced by the emergence of the IoT and integration of digital sensor technologies into the daily lives of people and business processes in the form of sensor-supported automotive insurance *services*. These *services* support the interconnection of virtual sensor technologies and data with physical vehicle infrastructure, monitoring the performance and safety of human driving patterns.

A case study of the Indian restaurant industry presented by Sufi and Ahmed (2021, p. 303) indicated that across all "industries, incorporating internet-based digitalization strategies to start, expand or improve" a global enterprise "is one of the striking features of **new business models**."

Internet of Things

In a chapter on the integration and implementation of the **Internet of Things** through **digital transformation** and the impact thereof on productivity and innovation, Bolton, et al. (2021c) indicated that when building on the **Internet of Things** to implement new business models, a global enterprise needs to disrupt competitors to digitally transform the industry (Kranz, 2016).

The integration of people as a thing with the Internet and the enhanced contextual value that this brings to data and information gathered from machines and cyber-physical technologies are driving the evolutionary emergence of the cognitive **Internet of Things**. This evolved model of the Internet is enabling the development of context-aware systems and solutions, opening up **new business models** and intelligent proactive automated *services* with a higher degree of cyber-physical integration of people as a thing in the **Internet of Things**.

General Motors: An Automotive Case Study

The primary subject of the research case study was General Motors. The research study included the observation and analysis of the results of a full-feature unified communications and collaboration framework and technical **solutions** at the GM global enterprise.

General Motors Company Overview

The formation of General Motors occurred in September 1908 under the leadership of William C. Durant, and followed a strategy by Durant to consolidate several automobile companies, including Oldsmobile, Oakland (Pontiac), Buick, Cadillac, and W.F. Stewart Co. body makers, located in Flint, Michigan (Heitmann, 2009). Under the leadership of Durant, General Motors continued its expansion through mergers and acquisitions, most notably with the incorporation of Chevrolet and Delco Products into GM in 1918 (Chapman, 2011).

Dynamic Obsolescence Driving Rapid Innovation in Design

Alfred P. Sloan Jr. succeeded Durant in 1920. Among many other things, Sloan is recognized as introducing the concept of planned obsolesce as a strategy into production and marketing. After experiencing saturation of the automobile market through instalment sales, instituted as a strategy in 1916, Sloan introduced the concept of model year design changes to encourage car owners to upgrade and buy replacement vehicles (Axelrod & Phillips, 2008).

Pope (2017) suggested that this had contributed to the continuing focus of GM on the regular innovation of vehicle style and design as a core strategy aligned to product obsolescence. Product obsolescence (aesthetics and design) facilitates faster product and marketing cycles, as opposed to relying on technological innovation associated with functional obsolescence, where innovation tends to be slower.

General Motors Company Profile

Today, General Motors is one of the world's largest multinational companies, ranking number eight on the Fortune 500 list of United States (US) industrial corporations, as measured by gross income (Fortune, 2017). In 2016, General Motors generated $166 billion in worldwide net sales and revenue. GM sold over 10 million vehicles globally, with markets in North and South America, Europe and internationally (Barra, 2017). Figure 1 provides a visual summary of GM business operations, highlighting 2016 sales by region, 2016 total sales (millions of units) and US sales as a percentage of industry in primary product categories.

The primary factors that are influencing GM **customer** vehicle preferences within the markets that they operate in include vehicle safety, quality and reliability, fuel economy, functionality, retail price and overall vehicle design (United States Securities and Exchange Commission, 2017). GM primarily sells vehicles to retail **customers** through a global network of dealers and sells directly and through the dealer network to fleet **customers**, including auto rental companies, auto leasing companies and commercial fleet **customers**.

Figure 1. General Motors global business operations
Source: Barra (2017)

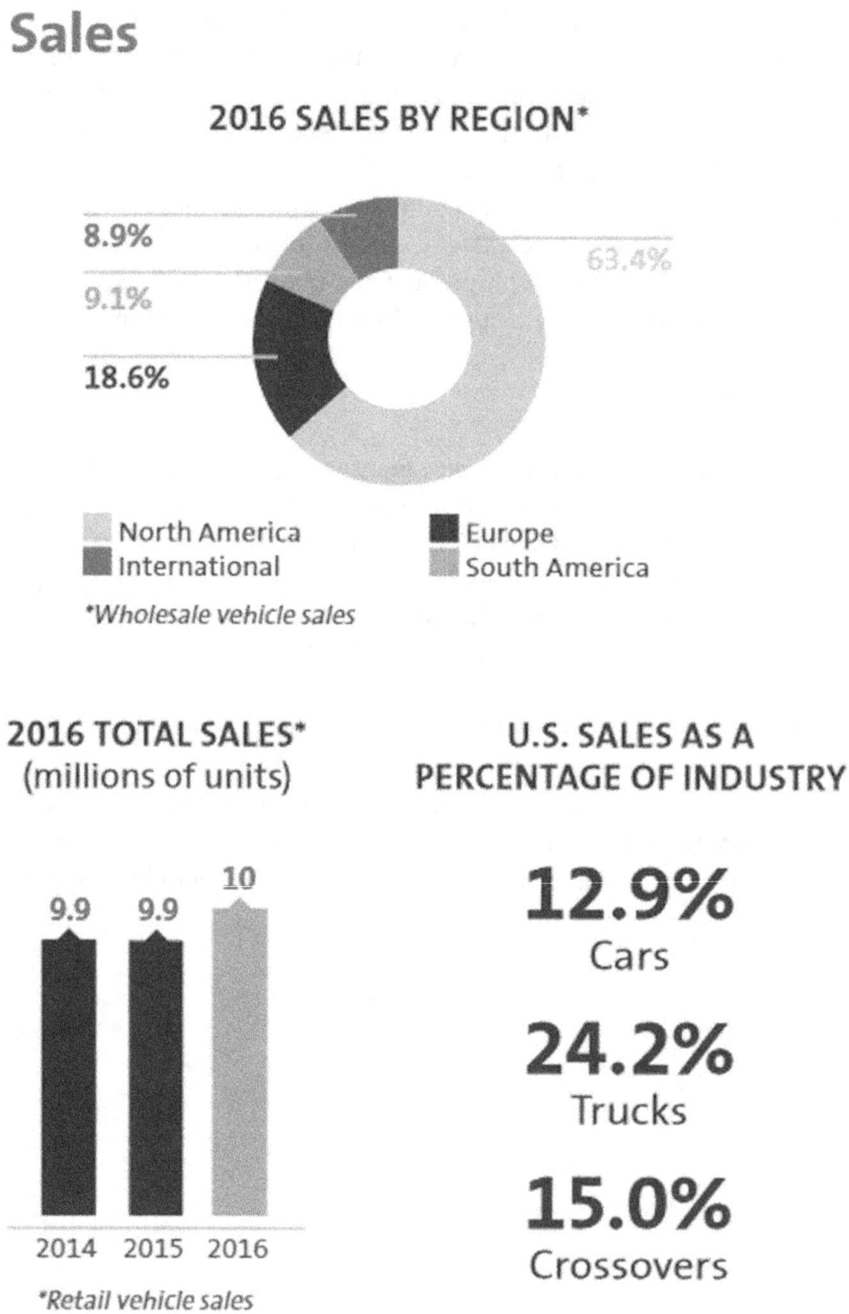

As featured in Figure 2, the distribution of employees is 55% in North America (124,000), 16% in Europe (38,000), 14% in Asia/Africa (32,000) and 10% in South America (22,000). General Motors represents a highly distributed modern enterprise of significant scale and operational complexity engaged in the process of automotive design, engineering, manufacturing and retail. General Motors had

225,000 global employees with operations spanning six continents, 396 facilities and leveraging more than 50 languages (General Motors, 2016). Sixty percent of GM employees are paid on an hourly basis (135,000), focused on operations in environments, such as GM manufacturing plants, and the remaining 40% are salaried professionals.

Figure 2. General Motors employee distribution 2016
Source: General Motors (2016, p. 11)

As an Original Equipment Manufacturer (OEM), General Motors develops products across eight brands, including Chevrolet, Buick, Holden, GMC, Baojun, Cadillac, Wuling and Jiefang. GM manages **customer** sales and marketing operations in over 140 countries.

General Motors is recognized as a pioneer and leader in IoT-connected vehicles through its Onstar brand and *services* (Sanchez & Carro, 2017). Onstar *services* and capabilities bring mobile connectivity to GM vehicles in the form of emergency service response, **consumer** mobile WiFi, remote vehicle operation and diagnostics. General Motors supports over 7 million Onstar connected subscribers globally.

MAIN FOCUS OF THE CHAPTER

Issues, Problems, Challenges

This subsection of the chapter will present the authors' perspective on the **issues**, **problems**, **challenges**, etc., as these relate to the main theme of the book, on the impact of **digital transformation** on the development of new business models and consumer experience, and arguments supporting the authors' position. It will also compare and contrast with what has been, or is currently being, done as it relates to the specific topic of the chapter, on the impact of **digital transformation** on the development of new business models and **customer experiences** in terms of productivity and innovation at a global automotive enterprise.

In contexts close to that of this chapter, Lu, Cheng, Zhang, Shen and Mark (2014) specifically considered the **challenges** related to connected vehicles, while Riepe and Pisano (2015) looked at **issues** regarding **new business models** in a digital culture through the open tail model. Bennet (2015) indicated that changing societies and media systems pose **challenges** for communication theory, research and education. "Establishing **new business models** to counteract the **risk** posed by commoditization through digital technology and an increasingly digital savvy and digital native **customer** base are key **challenges** facing any transforming enterprise" (Bolton, et al., 2021b, p. 140).

Case Study Methodology: Research Design Components and Scope Constraints

The **issues** targeted for investigation within the scope of the *case study methodology* align with the research questions outlined in Table 1. General Motors is representative of a large global automotive OEM enterprise. While phenomenon observed through the course of the *case study* may be representative of broader automotive OEMs, the focus of observation was limited to the operating environment unique to General Motors and its employees.

In addressing one of the core **issues** to enhancing and evaluating the **impact of digital transformation** within GM, a technical and end user framework and architecture was also specifically designed, implemented and monitored over a multi-year program and limited to the GM enterprise. The scope of the enterprise deployment was inclusive of over 120,000 end users, 65 countries and over 300 sites.

As part of the qualitative mode of inquiry, an interactive *research design*, in the form of a *case study*, was employed. E.g., a quantitative, non-experimental *research design*, including questionnaires as data gathering technique, was also selected for use in this study (Maree, 2020). Other data collection techniques (**research methods**) included interview schedules. In line with the *strategic focus* on *social responsibility* discussed later on in this chapter, trans-disciplinary approaches to action research for community engagement and ICTs for Development (ICT4D) were further considered (Goosen, 2018).

Business Priorities as Innovation Drivers

Per the letter from the chairperson (Barra, 2017), GM had placed the main focus on six key strategic areas to enhance, expand and establish new business opportunities (General Motors, 2016). These strategic elements include enhancing *vehicle quality and design*, strengthening *brand value and reputation*,

Table 1. Central components of the General Motors case study

Study Questions	• What are the drivers behind the digital transformation of a global automotive enterprise and how do these intersect with end user communication? • What are the characteristics of existing and **emerging** communication technologies associated with the digital enterprise? • What impact does the digital transformation of communication, delivered via unified communications and collaboration technologies, have on end user productivity and innovation within a global automotive enterprise?
Theoretical Propositions	• Development and assessment of theory aligned with the case study through leverage of data and observation of phenomenon before and after digital transformation of communication via UC&C. • Evaluation of the hypotheses associated with the work carried out at GM, reported on and analyzed in this study, which are outlined in more detail in Bolton, Goosen and Kritzinger (2021a).
Units of Analysis	• Sources of data and information central to theoretical development and hypothesis evaluation. • Leverage of multiple sources consistent with the cast study topic and embedded case study design using combined qualitative and quantitative data: Interviews, survey, adoption, consumption and system utilization metrics. • Chain of evidence for data collection, i.e., defined data collection protocol, data storage, citations for externally referenced data and supporting literature.
Logic Linking – Data to propositions	• Strategy for analyzing the results and evidence developed within the course of the case study. • Aligning analysis to the primary propositions around which the case study has formed. • Leverage of analytic techniques: Pattern matching, explanation building, time-series (how and why) analysis). • Description of general characteristics, relationships of the observed phenomenon.
Criteria and guidelines for selection and implementation towards interpreting case study findings (Goosen, 2004)	• Iterative development of associated propositions and data. • Identification, matching and contrasting patterns in data and observations.

establishing *new business* growth *opportunities*, *operational excellence*, *social responsibility* in terms of building a workplace of choice for its employees and partners, and defining the *innovative future of mobility*. Figure 3 depicts a visual summary of the GM strategic business priorities.

Megill (2013) suggested that integrated digital environments unite functions and concepts that may not usually appear to belong together and facilitate the development of new communities of practice. **Transformed digital** enterprise communication and collaboration technologies and processes serve to support GM operations, and through integrated communication and collaboration, enhance product development, engineering, manufacturing and support value chain efficiency and growth via sales, marketing and logistics functions.

Strategic Focus: Vehicle Quality and Design

General Motors maintains a focus on the continuous development and redesign of its vehicle fleet, across all brands. Core to the GM stated strategic focus relating to *vehicle design* is "high standards for safety,

Figure 3. General Motors strategic business priorities
Source: Barra (2017)

quality and performance" (General Motors, 2016, p. 139). Industry recognizes GM as having created automotive design as a distinct discipline from automotive engineering (Lewin & Borroff, 2010). Within the scope of its **digital transformation** of communication and collaboration, a strategy to increase the capability for design and manufacturing teams to collaborate visually with high-definition multi-party, mobile features were a foundational requirement.

Before the GM implementation of a unified communication and collaboration technologies framework and architecture, the ability for teams to communicate and collaborate across critical processes, such as new vehicle design review, was not possible. Within the scope of the **digital** communication and collaboration **transformation** program, new capabilities were developed and implemented, allowing global teams and selected external partners to visually communicate and collaborate via leverage of mobile high-definition video, audio and application sharing technologies that was integrated into the core design process.

UC&C client and core voice and video Session Initiation Protocol (SIP) technologies were leveraged to expand real-time communication and collaboration capability between mission-critical central office-based Engineering Design (ED) and Manufacturing Engineering (ME) staff, and remote manufacturing operations and engineering staff on plant floors. These technologies deployments supported enhanced communication and collaboration among design, engineering and manufacturing operations teams.

One of the GM goals with the implementation of UC&C technologies through a globally consistent and integrated framework was to increase opportunities for the enhancement of quality design and design-related productivity through pervasive, digitally transformed communication and collaboration technologies and processes. Within the research study, a focus was placed on assessing the **impact of** these attributes and validating the associated hypotheses via the analysis and assessment of pre- and post-end user production use cases, **experiences**, as well as **impact** on operational processes.

Strategic Focus: Brand Value and Reputation

General Motors maintains a robust global portfolio of brands and has been recognized as a leader in vehicle sales for 77 consecutive years from 1931 through 2007 (Parment, 2014). GM has historically managed the development and production of vehicles across 37 countries and 11 brands. Driving consistent performance, optimized shared platform production and choosing the best practices across a global production and brand landscape of this breadth presents many **challenges**, especially in cross-functional and team communication and collaboration. GM sees its digital brand components as company assets and has developed a Digital Asset Management (DAM) system, now integrated into its brand strategy (Glazer, Kenkins, & Schaper, 2005).

UC&C technologies enabled GM to enhance the DAM strategy by providing additional **digital** communication and collaborative capacities and functionality across sales and brand marketing teams. A single unified and intuitive digital collaboration cockpit transformed the capability for global distributed brand marketing and sales teams to communicate and collaborate on digital assets and marketing initiatives via a single intuitive UC&C tool and **customer experience** interface.

Strategic Focus: New Business Opportunities

GM focuses on *new business opportunities* as a source of revenue and business growth (Barra, 2017). Central to the continued expansion of the GM enterprise are the Onstar vehicle connectivity service, GM financial *services* and the expansion of after-market parts, service and accessories. These *new business* areas present high-margin *opportunities* for revenue growth in expanding markets, such as China. Growing *new business opportunities* is vital to the long-term profitability and sustainability of a global enterprise.

Porter (2008) suggested that expanding *services* makes it harder for **customers** to leave a chosen provider for a rival competitor. Similarly, the latter author argued that growing *new business opportunities* can help to shift and influence forces of profitability within a particular industry in the favor of a global enterprise. Instability and uncertainty are realities for global enterprises. According to Riepe and Pisano (2015), enterprises that embrace a new digital culture can realize **new business models** that proactively deal with the increasing demands for speed and change.

Integrated communication and collaboration, as well as **customer experiences** within OnStar's 12 million connected vehicles, represent increasingly rich *opportunities* for profitable *services* growth (Barra, 2017).

Strategic Focus: Operational Excellence

Per the letter from the chairperson (Barra, 2017), GM is committed to continue driving and improving operating efficiencies within its business. In 2016, GM increased its cost efficiency targets by $1 billion to $6.5 billion through 2018. The efficiencies gained through the GM *Operational excellence* (Opex) programs provided strategic financial and resource offsets against investments required to further critical technologies, engineering and marketing initiatives.

The unified communications and collaboration technologies framework and deployment initiative associated with this research study was a contributing component of the GM Opex program through several individual initiatives. Table 2 depicts a summary of primary and related secondary drivers for operating expense reduction associated with Opex projects that were aligned to the **digital transformation** initiative, focusing on the digitization of communication and collaboration technologies.

Applying digital communication and collaboration technologies across the value chain of a global enterprise offers the potential to leverage the benefits of rich communication and collaboration, integrate human intelligence to drive workforce **digital transformation** and increase opportunities for interactive **customer experiences** (Bolton, Murray, & Fluker, 2017). UC&C technologies and *services* implemented within the scope of the research case study contributed to over USD 10 million in annual cost efficiencies being delivered to the GM enterprise.

Table 2. GM UC&C and collaboration related Opex initiatives

Digital Communications Initiative	Primary Opex Driver	Secondary Opex Driver
Digital Conference and Collaboration Scheduling	Productivity	Cost Efficiency
On premise Global Video Collaboration platform	Cost Efficiency	Productivity
On premise Corporate Audio Collaboration platform	Cost Efficiency	Productivity
Integrated UC&C Audio, Video, App Sharing platform	Productivity	Cost Efficiency
Integrated Corporate and Dealership Digital Signage Platform	Cost Efficiency	Productivity
Digital Telecom Expense Management Automation	Cost Efficiency	Productivity
UC&C Integrated Scheduled Meeting Platform	Productivity	Cost Efficiency
Next Generation Industry 4.0 Factory Communication Platform	Productivity	Cost Efficiency

Financial and productivity efficiencies and benefits were captured and tracked within the scope of the formal Information Technology (IT) Plan of Record (PoR) and Opex projects, as well as within the formal program governance processes at GM. Tracking of program completion and financial/productivity achievements included senior executive review and validation.

Strategic Focus: Social Responsibility

Bennet (2015) suggested that some unforeseen consequences of the past four decades of *social* and economic globalization include *social* fragmentation, personalization of social structures and separation of individuals from *social* institutions, leading to the era described as being liquid modernity. Castells (2007, p. 3) posited that the battle for "the human mind is played out in the" processes of communication and collaboration. Castells (2007, p. 3) thus **defined** a networked society as one where *social* structures comprise "of networks powered by microelectronics-based information and communication technologies."

The introduction of unified communication and collaboration technologies, in the form of integrated voice, video and messaging *services* through desktop, mobile and fixed room infrastructure, is a crucial enabler within the employee engagement process within General Motors. The unified communication and collaboration framework developed within the scope of the research study was leveraged to enhance communication opportunities across the employee population and increase collaboration across functional domains within the enterprise. Through an intuitive interface and integrated design, UC&C technologies also aided in simplifying the process of employee communication and collaboration through the presentation of user interfaces that were common within popular, non-corporate *social* media platforms, such as Skype and Facebook.

In addition to the *strategic focus* on an *innovate **future** of mobility* discussed next, more clarity on *social responsibility* as it relates to employees are presented in the **future research directions** section before the conclusion.

Strategic Focus: Innovate Future of Mobility

General Motors is a leader in connected vehicle infrastructure and *services*, leading the automotive industry in 2016 with more vehicles connected via embedded 4G connectivity than the rest of the industry combined. Onstar, the GM integrated, connected vehicle **customer** service, supported more than 1.5 billion **customer** *interactions* through its integrated communication-enabled vehicular applications and adviser-based contact centers.

These embedded advanced technologies require integrated infrastructure to support the real-time application, voice and data transfer and communication between vehicles, back-end application *services* and **customer** call center *interactions*. The convergence of business functions within the scope of the GM IT transformation program required the optimized consolidation of technology *services* within the Global Connected **Customer Experience** (GCCX) service portfolio.

Case Study Structure and Timeline

Like Mengelkamp, et al. (2018), the research reported on in this chapter used a case study. The security aspects of the empirical case study into the impact of **digital transformation** via unified communication and collaboration technologies on the productivity and innovation at a global automotive enterprise was discussed in the journal article by Bolton, et al. (2020a).

Winkelhake (2017) suggested that IT plays a vital role in enabling the strategies for **digital transformation** within a global enterprise. According to Winkelhake (2017), the **digital transformation** of General Motors is a leading case study in a large scale, industry leading, original equipment manufacturer. Specifically, Winkelhake (2017) highlighted the **digital transformation** from disparate, outsourced systems to a consolidated internal innovation structure, fueled by self-competence and agility.

Preston (2016) highlighted that the **digital transformation** at General Motors, led by its formative transformation of IT, had resulted in a shift from 80% allocation of IT headcount investments in maintaining its digital infrastructure in 2013 to over 74% allocation of investment to internal innovation and development by 2016. Mott (as quoted in Preston, 2016), Chief Information Officer for General Motors at the time, suggested that a shift to internal service and integration was central to the ability of GM to strategically manage the scale, complexity and a significant number of 'integration points' within the business.

Mott (as cited in Wayland, 2017) also highlighted the importance of tightly coupled and connected communication and collaboration between employees and creating a seamless digitally integrated environment to foster productivity and innovation. In reference to the new GM digitally enabled workplace, Mott (as quoted in Wayland, 2017) stated that the "facilities work interchangeably and are tightly connected by telecommunications systems, allowing IT employees to choose where they would like to work and participate in day-to-day meetings".

The IT transformation within General Motors started in late 2012. Specific to this research study, the transformation of telecommunications and the development of an integrated UC&C framework started in October 2012. Figure 4 depicts the primary building blocks of the GM **digital transformation**. These elements were combined to structure and deliver a comprehensive **digital transformation** strategy and architecture guiding the development of individual programs for **digital** transformation. Programs, such as the **digital** transformation of communication and collaboration aligned to the research case study, were also aligned to the key priorities and strategic goals of the enterprise.

Programs specific to this research study were completed between the period of October 2012 and November 2017. The research activities, inclusive of digital communication and collaboration framework development, pilot evaluation, service and infrastructure deployment, end user migration and post-deployment impact analysis and evaluation, were carried out within the scope of the broader General Motors IT-driven digital transformation of communication and collaboration technologies.

Scope and Timeline

The scope of digital transformation within the communication and collaboration program was inclusive of all existing telecommunication infrastructure and *services*, including, but not limited to, cellular voice, cellular data, local, wide area and internet networking data transports, Telecom Expense Management (TEM), carrier commercial and life cycle management, video broadcast *services*, as well as back office and contact center voice, chat and integrated application *services*. To enable the digital transformation of the complex, integrated global voice, data and end user communication infrastructure and application *services* at GM, a framework was developed within the scope of this research study, and subsequently deployed within GM and leveraged as the catalyst and architectural guide for digital transformation.

Results from the system deployments associated with UC&C *services* is presented in a chapter on research data analysis and results.

Figure 4. Core strategic elements of the GM IT digital transformation, highlighting the communication and collaboration technologies

SOLUTIONS AND RECOMMENDATIONS

As Lu, et al. (2014) indicated that connected vehicles could provide **solutions** to the **challenges** experienced, this section of the chapter will discuss **solutions** as detailed in the GM automotive UC&C framework, developed under the scope of the research study, and outline the extension of the framework to core architectural and system dependencies. It will also provide **recommendations** for dealing with the **issues** and/or **challenges** presented in the preceding sections.

Solutions: Architectural Framework for Enhanced UC&C Technologies

The *research approach* employed within the General Motors **case study** to establish and build the proposed **solutions** framework for integrated communication and collaboration involved a review of the enterprise executive goals and objectives, assessment of requirements aligned to the functional departments and analysis of supporting user competencies. Leveraging existing enterprise knowledge and the acquisition of insight from end users before the establishment of the next generation framework for the digitally transformed communication and collaboration technologies was an essential component of the **solutions** development process.

Von Hippel (2016) offered the concept of user innovation and the functional relationship between innovators and the innovations that they develop. The latter author also suggested that engaging end users proactively is essential to the enterprise capability to develop user innovations and leverage internal knowledge and resources for innovation.

Figure 5 depicts how data from the four stages of pre-design analysis were synthesized to develop the framework for digital transformation that was subsequently implemented and iteratively improved within the GM case study. Di Gangi and Wasko (2009) suggested that research in user innovation showed that some of the most unique innovations are the result of developments stemming from attempts by users to adapt existing processes and products that they use to improve productivity and better suit their needs.

Figure 5. Production of IT strategy based on a synthesis of business drivers towards an ICT solution

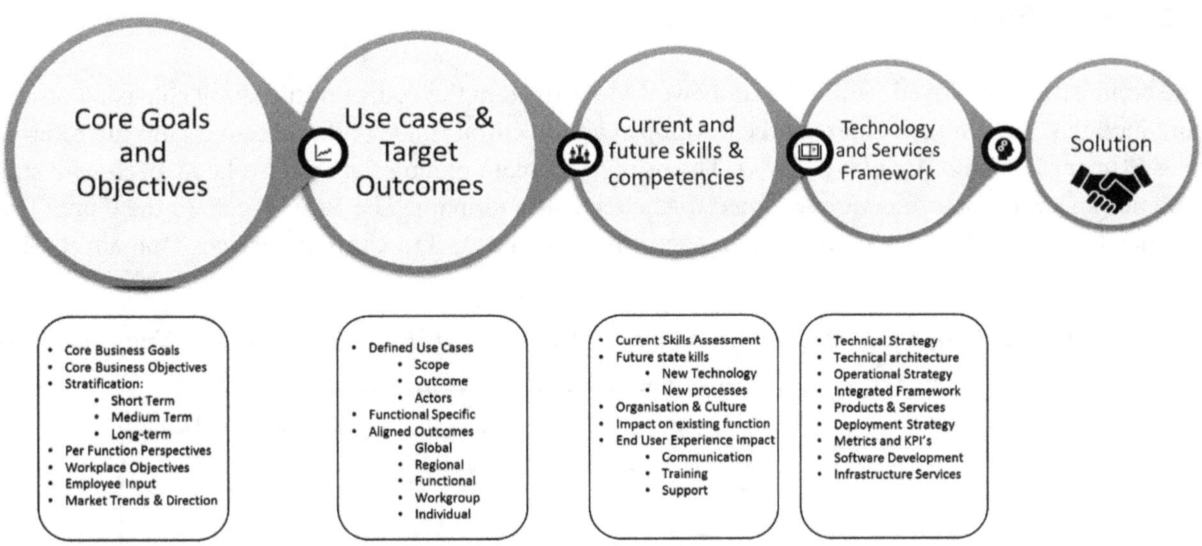

Research, such as that of Di Gangi and Wasko (2009), supported the research approach taken in the development of the GM case study framework, where enterprise goals and objectives were balanced with user input on real-life use cases and the consideration of required skills and competencies as core contributors to technical **solutions** and strategy development. The resulting designed framework represents a conceptual structure that includes the development of logical and physical technical services, operations and architectural models (Bolton, et al., 2016).

Enhanced Unified Communications and Collaboration Framework Design

The structure of the Enhanced UC&C (E-UC&C) framework developed within this study is depicted in Figure 6 and buildt on the foundational research by Jokonya, Kroeze and van der Poll (2012) and their proposed framework for decision-making regarding IT adoption. The resulting framework developed and adopted within the GM case study integrated technical **solutions** components aligned with an IT decision-making framework inclusive of IT governance, stakeholder and technology acceptance processes. The *research approach* combined IT decision and operational control processes with the technical **solutions**.

This *approach* ensured that consultation with end user and business stakeholders was achieved as an integrated part of the deployment planning, alignment of financial investment or service change, enabling ever-green iterative **solutions** improvements as the system evolved. The adopted *research approach* also avoided a framework implementation that is rigid and unable to flex to meet the changing nature and demands of the enterprise, its processes, end user culture and technologies. The framework developed was targeted for implementation within an existing enterprise ecosystem. To ensure alignment to enterprise goals and objectives, a process was required that ensured rigorous review of all decisions and actions that could adversely impact the GM enterprise or the productivity of employees (Bolton, et al., 2016). The implementation of governance and control processes embedded within the framework ensured that technical functionality did not take precedence over the enterprise priorities, recognizing how work is actually carried out within the enterprise and the needs of the end user.

Framework Structure

The architecture employed within the framework developed in the course of the study consisted of four core modules. Within the context of the developed architectural framework, these modules are referred to as Primary Domain Modules (PDMs). The primary domain modules are inter-related, each with sub-modules specific to the function assigned to each specific domain. The PDMs include the Core Governance Domain (CGD), Operational Management Domain (OMD), Unified Services Domain (USD)

Figure 6. Phase 1 draft of the GM framework, integrating concepts from IT decision-making framework

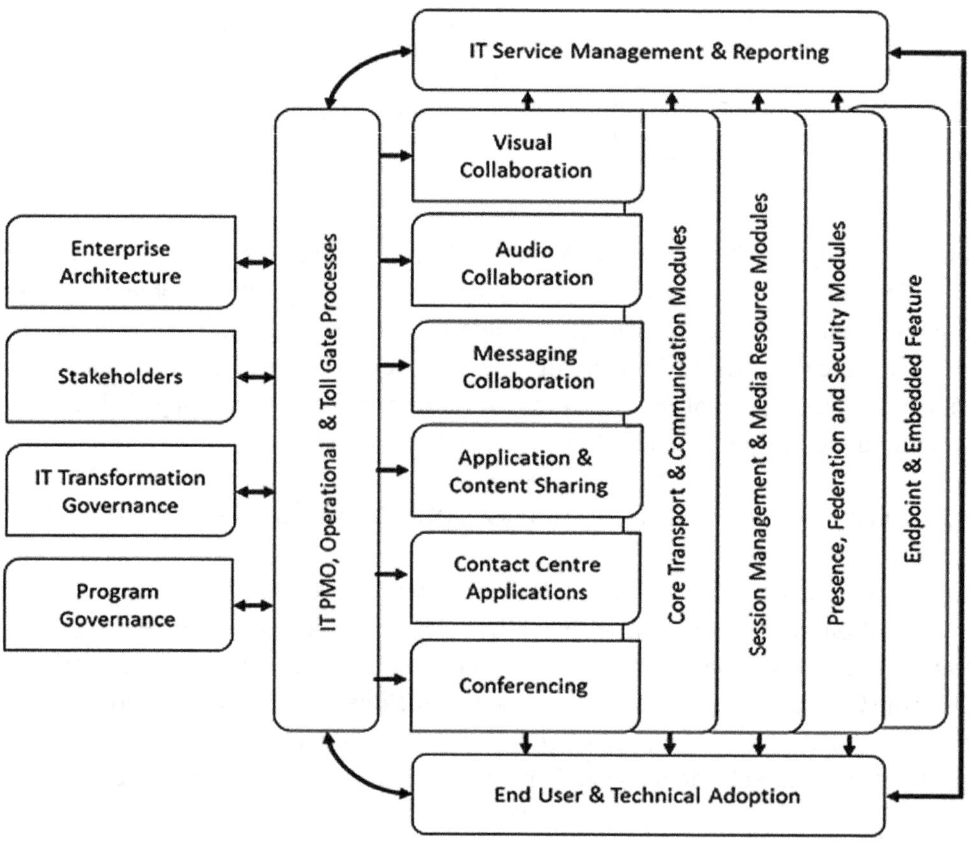

and Integrated Feature Domain (IFD). Combined, the modules within the framework represent a holistic architecture collapsing technology *services*, operations and end user processes and core service and IT governance into one consolidated framework, facilitating digitally transformed communication and collaboration.

In operation, the framework is not limited to delivering technical elements of the target digitally transformed communication and collaboration end state. The framework integrates governance and operational strategy in conjunction with all technical elements required to deliver a transformed unified communication and collaboration **solution** featuring iterative improvement as a core feature of the underlying architecture. The concepts of 'transferability module' and 'technology transferability maps' in the areas of patent analysis, Research and Development (R&D) planning and technology road mapping by Lee (2013, p. 280) was an influence in the design of the GM framework. The concept of technology transferability focuses on providing guidelines for the transference of technologies to target users (developers in the R&D context) to promote technological communication and collaboration, as well as facilitate diffusion, and maximize the applicability, of innovation and improvements within the framework over time.

In the method of application within the GM case study, the general framework developed was applied against some integrated technology and service strategies, facilitating the delivery of an end-to-end reference architecture and **solutions** deployed within the enterprise. Examples of specifically integrated **solutions** developed with overlap within the E-UC&C framework were reviewed in Bolton, et al. (2020a) and (2021a). Central to this research study was the unified communication and collaboration reference architecture and the subsequently deployed technical **solutions** developed and deployed under the E-UC&C framework.

Framework Primary Domain Modules

Operational subprocesses were aligned with the IT Infrastructure Library (ITIL) framework for the **definition** of associated IT service management and governance processes, such as service management. Benefits in the form of efficiency through reusable governance processes and low touch integration with existing operation is evidenced in the fact that GM already leverages the ITIL framework within its IT operations. ITIL and the five phases specified within the framework lifecycle are designed to accommodate constant change. Persse (2012) suggested that enterprises that leverage ITIL have an embedded ability to align IT operations with the needs of the enterprise and respond to change as technologies continually evolve. These characteristics make ITIL well-positioned for integration into a broader technical framework, such as the GM digitally transformed unified communication and collaboration framework for the global automotive enterprise.

Table 3 depicts how the general framework developed within the research study was leveraged to **define** the high-level technical architecture and operating model for digital transformation of communication and collaboration at General Motors. Table 3 further outlines the high-level process, infrastructure, software and integration components employed in the underlying detailed system reference architectures for discrete *services*. An example of the underlying reference architectures is discussed in the next subsection.

The framework as applied in Table 3 aligns a high degree of communication and collaboration integration across the primary domains with facilitating freedom in the use of evolving technologies and standards. Similar to the framework for the utilization "of global resources for knowledge creation and application through flexible" enterprises proposed by Lal (2014, pp. 164-172), the framework design considers a networked technology architecture integrated with a framework for governance and operational management and planned outcomes.

Example Application of Framework: Video Collaboration

A high-level example of how the framework as aligned to implementation within the GM case study is video collaboration. The modules of the core governance domain were leveraged to **define** and apply underlying processes focused on assessment of the legacy as-is state of video collaboration, identification and engagement of key stakeholders and establishment of the innovation roadmap for desired end state service technologies and user outcomes. Initial discovery in the as-is analysis identified limited existing capability (example, room-based video conferencing). The sub modules of the core governance domain were leveraged in this example to power enterprise architecture processes to assess the current state, identify gaps and align proposed high level technical and service architectures in the form of an integrated end state **solution**. The stakeholder sub module and associated processes was leveraged to identify and engage key business stakeholders to identify end state requirements, external technology partners on applicable technology **solutions** and IT operations, development and engineering on the establishment of detailed **solution** architecture and designs. The IT transformation and program governance sub modules were leveraged to align the technical and service plans emerging from the enterprise architecture teams, as well as to align financial, technology, sourcing, program implementation and reporting.

In the case of video collaboration, requirements within the GM case study specified a number of integrated capabilities focused on establishing an eco-system supporting individual, team and enterprise levels. The technical architecture derived from, and aligned within, the transformation to end state, the core governance domain detailed an eco-system centered around five core video technologies, Skype (core UC&C: Individual and Team Collaboration at the desk), Cisco room level video systems for in-person team collaboration, Cisco Acano for internal to external interfaces and room level to virtual team (Skype) integration and Kaltura for integrated mas audience broadcast functionality. Many other

integration elements were specified within the wider eco-system and architecture, supporting the implementation of video collaboration services. The core products of Skype, Cisco Telepresence, Cisco Acano and Kaltura had many peer and downstream system dependencies that needed to be delivered in order to effectively operate within the GM global enterprise. These interfaces and dependencies were identified through leverage of the framework specified sub modules within the integrated feature and unified services domains. For example, the identification and specification of video formats, transcoding requirements and specific media and control interfaces were identified and specified by a technical team focusing on the visual collaboration sub module. In parallel, the other sub modules for audio collaboration, application and content sharing, messaging collaboration, conferencing and scheduling were leveraged to define downstream requirements, new feature development and integration with adjunct systems. Capabilities resulting from functional design and integration/dependency mapping across the sub modules delivered **solution** specifications for real-time capabilities, such as cross platform content/presentation sharing between Skype, Cisco Acano, Cisco Room endpoints and Kaltura broadcast subscribers. Similar integrations were designed for cross platform audio and seamless integrated scheduling.

Table 3. Mapping of E-UC&C framework to the General Motors service reference model

Framework for Digitally Enhanced Embedded Unified Communication and Collaboration Automotive Enterprise Application			
Core Governance Domain	Operational Management Domain	Integrated Feature Domain	Unified Services Domain
Enterprise Architecture • Technology Models • System Models • Functional Models • Business Process Models • Workflow Models • Technical Standards • Standards Governance • Reference Architectures • Application Repository	**IT Service Management & Reporting** • Service & Feature Catalogue • Service performance Metrics • Supplier QBR & Management • Operational Financial Tracking • Service Operational Reviews • KPI Tracking & Dashboards • Core Service Roadmaps • Matrixed Operation Map	**Visual Collaboration** • Video Codec / Transcoding • Video Conference Bridges • Video Streaming (uni/multi) • Video CDN Optimisation • Video Platform Integration	**Network/App/Video** • IP Routing & Switching • Media Transcoding • Multicast AV Transmission • Unicast AV Transmission • VBSS/RDP/H.264 Sharing
Enterprise Stakeholders • IT Management & Function • Finance • Manufacturing Engineering • Design Operations • Sales & Marketing Operations • Corporate Function-HR/Legal • Sourcing & Procurement • Engineering Operations • Application Repository	**PMO, Operations & Toll Gate Processes** • Operational Support • Program Governance • Project Management • Pre-Production Validation • Change & UAT Process • Release Management • Asset Management	**Audio Collaboration** • Intra Enterprise Conferencing • External Audio Conferencing • Dial Plan and Session Mgt • MOS and Quality Monitoring • IVR and Speech Req Services	**Session & Media Mgt.** • RFC3261 SIP Signalling • IPT Clusters & Call Managers • Call Quality Recoding (CQN) • Video Border Gateway • B2BUA Mediation Services
IT Transformation & Program Governance • IT Plan Of Record (Program) • Technology Investment Plan • Program Prioritisation Process • Resource Allocation & Mgt • Benefit and Financial Tracking • Executive Level KPI Tracking • Transformation Council • End User Advocacy Groups	**End User Engagement & Service Adoption** • End User Training • End User Communication • End User Support • Usability Analysis and Support	**Application & Content Sharing** • Integrated White Boarding • Application / Desktop Sharing • CTI Application Integration • Embedded UC Services	**Presence & Federation** • Active Directory Integration • Skype Edge Server Services • XMPP Federation Service • Nextplane Ext. Federation • Front End Presence Servers
	Security, Risk Management & Data Loss Protection • Data Retention Policies • Data Loss Protection Strategy • Security Architecture • IT Security Policies	**Messaging Collaboration** • Standalone and Embedded IM • Chat & Conversation History • Cross platform integration • Internal/External Federation	**Endpoints & EmbeddedFeatures** • Unified Desktop Client • Unified Mobile Client • Integrated Room Devices • Embedded Web Services
		Conferencing & Scheduling Services • Multi-media bridging services • Media Services • External Interfaces • Common Scheduling Platform	**Transport & QOS** • SIP Session Border Controllers • Priority Queuing – WAN COS • Media Priority Segmentation • MPLS/Direct Internet/Cellular • H264AVC, G.722, SRTP, HTTPS
Outputs and Outcomes • Published Architecture • Strategic Alignment • Documented Standards • Aligned goals objectives • Technology & Process Assets • Organisational Alignment • Agreed Outcomes • Commercial Strategy • Benefit Tracking & Accounting • Prioritised Initiative Plan • Continuous End User Insights • Executive KPI Dashboards	**Outputs and Outcomes** • Product & Service Portfolio • Supplier Performance Metrics • Change Performance Metrics • Service Operation Dashboards • Product & Service Roadmaps • Integrated Operations Plan • Program Execution Tracking • Post Change Validation • SW/HW/IP Asset Tracking • End User Training Guide • End User Communication Plan • Security & Risk Assessment	**Outputs and Outcomes** • Video Codec Standards • Multi-Conference Arch. • Video Transmission Arch. • Video Distribution Arch. • Real-Time Media Monitoring • Carrier/Conference Interfaces • Integrated IVR/Speech Arch. • CTI Architecture & Platform • Service Integration Arch. • Back Office Chat Platforms • Secure Service Federation • Enterprise Scheduling Arch.	**Outputs and Outcomes** • Integrated Network Arch. • Media Transport Architecture • Approved Protocol Standards • Core Telephony Platforms • Core Video Platforms • Carrier Integration Platforms • Enterprise Dial Plan • Common UC&C Client Apps • Collaboration Room Arch. • IP based Carrier Transports • Transport Architecture • Class of Service Architecture

In the case of GM, a unique integrated eco-system was established through the custom integration of the core Cisco, Microsoft and Kaltura platforms, establishing a flexible **solution** that enabled seamless integration and scheduling of meetings between individuals, physically located, virtual teams and large internal and external audiences. The specification of lower-level interfaces and transports required to secure and delivery with quality, and the media associated with the video collaboration traffic was specified through an iterative review of the sub modules specified in the unified services domain. For example, the legacy network within General Motors had no reliable intra-regional, regional or site network Quality of Service (QoS) capability. Bandwidth on the network was also constrained. The specification of requirements associated with the video collaboration influenced the transformation and design of the underlying GM network, resulting in the implementation of global Software Defined Wide Area Network (SDWAN) design that delivered QoS-assured delivery of video traffic at reduced cost. Prior to the implementation of UC&C technologies at GM, all voice communication leveraged legacy analogue and digital telecommunications technologies. The migration to UC&C for voice and video collaboration influenced and led to the implementation of a global Internet Protocol (IP)-based SIP infrastructure and migration of all external carrier and partner telecommunications via a global session border controller infrastructure, delivering video and voice transcoding, session management and security. The integration designs were specified within the transport, QoS, session and media management modules.

Underpinning the delivery of video collaboration was a focus on end user experience. The resulting eco-system of integrated video collaboration had to work seamlessly for the end user, offer one integrated experience (with the elevation of modes from person-to-person through team and mass collaboration), and be delivered through a simple and intuitive front end. The end user experience story cards, interface design, testing and validation were managed by a team dedicated to the sub module function of end user management and service adoption within the operational management domain. In the example of video collaboration, this team ensured that the interface and operation of features, such as cross system scheduling of meetings between Skype, Cisco Acano and Kaltura, were designed to ensure ease of operation and a single method of scheduling. This drove custom design within the GM **solution**, as no common off-the-shelf **solution** existed that integrated these platforms. Investment and development needs were identified, proposed and aligned to ensure that the priority of end user experience took precedence and demanded overcoming **limitations** within the selected products prior to approval for implementation.

As the **solution** was implemented, a framework for operational reporting, program governance, financial benefit reporting, end user adoption and performance monitoring was established.

The framework sub-modules that were designed with alignment to ITIL, such as IT service management and Project Management Office (PMO) operations, provided a template for establishment of these services and processes. This example relating to video collaboration provides a high-level overview of the alignment and leverage of the framework in the establishing one element of the UC&C portfolio of services; others include direct inbound dial voice, digital signage, application sharing, desktop remote access and sharing, integrated file sharing, productivity application integration, conference federation and presence services. The example shows how the framework was used at a high level to identify, coordinate, guide and track design of the technical architecture from a conceptual level down to discrete interface level. The example also shows the unique integration of non-technical elements that facilitate the design of a **solution** tied to the organization needs and centered around end user experience and adoption.

Deployed Framework

Figure 7 depicts the framework implemented within the GM production environment, the results of which were evaluated within the scope of the research case study. The diagram provides a visual summary of the four core framework elements (domains) and their relationships. These domains, combined within the structure of the E-UC&C framework and summarized in Bolton, et al. (2016), (2020a) and (2021a), represent an adaptable modular framework integrating technologies, operations and governance. A differentiator of the E-UC&C model versus description of traditional UC&C models is the expansion and integration of non-technical elements. The core governance and operational management domains ensured that a focus was maintained on end user needs, outcomes and business priorities. Technology specifications, features, functionality and deployments within the framework were applied purposefully and aligned with business needs versus adopting a feature and technology first approach. This avoided an approach where the enterprise was expected to adapt and change to effectively utilize the deployed technologies.

Figure 7. General Motors framework for digitally transformed unified communication and collaboration

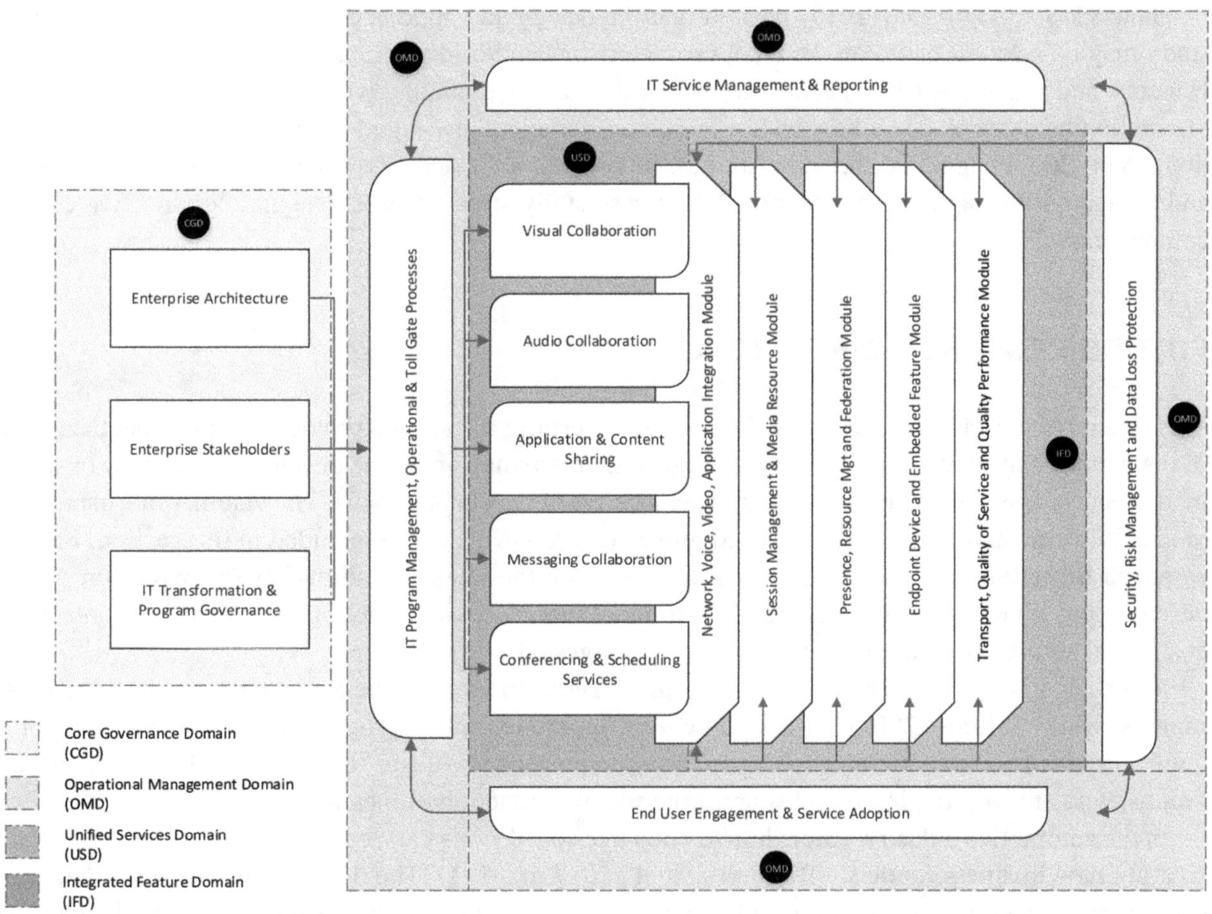

Core Governance Domain

According to Feher (2012), the purpose of enterprise architecture processes and models is to support the development of a common shared understanding within an enterprise.

Unified Services Domain

The underlying system components and applications were overlaid onto the E-UC&C primary domain structures. This system reference architecture was employed to map out the primary signaling protocol paths, sub-system relationships, border, internal and external endpoint elements and core communication integration and session management systems.

Recommendations

Lee and Saunders (2017) **recommended** that in order to theorize successfully about empirical evidence obtained through research case studies, it is essential to consider both the rationale for selection and how the case study aligns to subsequent proposed theories.

Hancock and Algozzine (2017) posited that the design and approach adopted for a particular case study may be selected based on the type, characteristics and/or disciplinary orientation of the subject. Hancock and Algozzine (2017) also **recommended** that selection of a particular case study design and orientation be determined by how well it facilitates complete investigation of the target research questions. Yin (2009) suggested that case studies, in general, are oriented around exploratory, descriptive and explanatory designs. The General Motors case study structure was designed around five central components.

FUTURE RESEARCH DIRECTIONS

This section of the chapter will discuss **future** and **emerging trends** and provide insight about the future of the theme of the book, on the impact of **digital transformation** on the development of new business models and consumer experience, from the perspective of the chapter focus. The viability of a paradigm, model, implementation issues of proposed programs, etc., may also be included in this section. **Future research directions** within the domain of the topic, on the impact of **digital transformation** on the development of new business models and **customer experiences** in terms of productivity and innovation at a global automotive enterprise, will finally be suggested.

Riepe and Pisano (2015) reported on **emerging trends** in terms of the management of **new business models**, while Castells (2007) argued that **emerging trends** in the progressive development of communication and collaboration technologies have the power to coalesce the thinking of individuals and groups, who are working in IT, and support the social production of meaning.

In the automotive industry, **emerging** "**trends** like self-driving cars, connectivity and car sharing are creating **new business models**" (Riasanow, et al., 2017, p. 3191). The development of new connected **customer** *services* and establishing leadership in terms of **emerging trends** with regard to the Internet of Vehicles (IoV) market leads towards having an integrated, digitally transformed UC&C infrastructure

(Lu, et al., 2014). Parment (2014) described Auto Brand as a solution towards building successful car brands for the **future**.

Through a *strategic focus* on *social responsibility*, General Motors is building and maintaining a world-class, industry leading workforce and establishing a workplace where current and **future** employees will identify as being a place from where they can make a difference and the world a better place. Underscoring this commitment, General Motors chairman and CEO, Barra (as quoted in General Motors, 2016, p. 6) stated that "we are investing in both our current and **future** employees. We want people to know that if they truly want to make the world a better place, they can make a real difference here".

General Motors also maintains a *strategic focus* on an *innovative* ***future*** *of mobility*: Barra (as quoted in General Motors, 2016, p. 7) specified that "nothing GM is doing today is more important for society's long-term **future** than leading the transformation of personal mobility".

The UC&C framework developed within the scope of the research study required comprehension of the connected vehicle technologies consolidation, **future** global expansion of *services* and optimized sharing of technologies and *services* across existing and **future** connected vehicle innovations. Examples of these consolidations and expanded business requirements included the consolidation and optimization of **customer** and dealer support contact center *services* with Onstar connected vehicle contact center *services* and infrastructure.

The technical architecture associated with the extended components of the UC&C architecture was designed with current and **future** core UC&C functional and technical integration incorporated. This approach ensured ongoing integration and compatibility of UC&C core technologies and functionality (chat, voice, video, mobile, file & screen sharing, reporting), while allowing a broad degree of independence in the specific architecture of extended components. For example, a network architecture based on software defined wide area network principles was elected, allowing for independence of the underlying network transport type (Multi-Protocol Label Switching (MPLS), frame relay, Virtual Private Local Area Network (LAN) Service (VPLS), Provider Backbone Bridge (PBB), and Metro-Ethernet) from upper layer UC&C transport requirements. Through this construct, a fixed quality of service architecture was extended end-to-end from the LAN through to General Motors core computer and carrier transport facilities. This approach allows for ongoing commercial and technical flexibility associated with the provider and network transport *services*, while assuring ongoing compatibility and quality delivery of UC&C core service.

Future research directions in the context of the study reported on in this chapter are especially discussed in Bolton, et al. (2021a).

CONCLUSION

This section of the chapter will provide a discussion of the overall coverage of the chapter and concluding remarks.

The chapter introduced the empirical research design and method of execution employed to evaluate the research questions and the developed research hypotheses. The **purpose** of the empirical study as a whole was to obtain real-life data and use it compared to theories.

The General Motors research case study was presented, providing an overview of the enterprise, priorities, enterprise and industry drivers and elements of strategic focus. The case study structure, scope, timeline and a summary of execution were also shown.

The empirical study enabled the researcher to develop and evaluate new concepts, processes, tools, methods and techniques. The outputs from empirical studies can facilitate improving existing processes by using evidence and evaluating the hypotheses formed during the study. Shdaimah, Stahl and Schram (2011) argued that one of the benefits derived from an empirical study is the establishment of facts about **problems** that can subsequently be analyzed and addressed.

The research study was carried out over a five-year period, leveraging General Motors, one of the world's largest automotive manufacturing and sales enterprises, as a case study focus. Demands to take the enterprise beyond the current horizon and changes in the enterprise landscape of General Motors, including a significant shift to globalized operations and increased infusion of technologies into enterprise processes, drove a reciprocal demand for **digital transformation** and the optimization of communication and collaboration among employees. Under the scope of the study, a unique E-UC&C framework was developed and tailored to guide the establishment of a technical and service architecture, facilitating broad **digital transformation** across multiple facets of employee-to-employee, employee-to-partner, employee-to-customer and enterprise-to-employee communication and collaboration.

The deployment of a digitally transformed and enhanced communication and collaboration system aligned to a unified enterprise system was displayed. The analysis of impact and summary of results attributed to the implemented system, deployed under the E-UC&C framework, will be represented in a chapter on results and analysis.

Study Limitations

Limitations of this study included the fact that the research design and case study focused on a global enterprise within the automotive industry. The study required observation and study of the transformation process and analysis of the pre- and post-transformation states in order to evaluate the established research hypothesis and question. To achieve this objective a global enterprise is leveraged as a case study subject and the General Motors Corporation selected. Opportunity for the researcher to engage with an enterprise at a global scale and influence the investment and transformation within such a company was limited. As an executive within General Motors, I was hired to transform the global telecommunication landscape of systems and services, and this opportunity was aligned with my academic pursuit, resulting in this thesis.

In this way, the unprecedented access that gained from my role within GM and the opportunity associated with guiding their transformation, while limited to a global automotive enterprise, represented unique research opportunity. The study was also limited in the timeframe provided for observation post-transformation. Due to the lengthy planning, investment and execution of such a broad transformation the post-transformation observation period was limited to approximately eight months of deployment of the UC&C tools to the general user population of GM. As indicated within the population of the user survey just under half of the respondents had IT experience and technical skills of varying levels. The process for deployment of the technologies was structured with a focus on delivery a pre-production cohort of users consisting of IT employees and business users. This pre-pilot was required to validate the production readiness of the new systems, tools and associated training and end-user communication material.

Some bias in responses relating to ease of use, for example, could have been introduced into the survey response data due to the more extensive than normal distribution of IT associated staff. It is reasonable to suggest that with 56% of respondents coming from non-IT functions within GM and little to no prior background in digital and virtual collaboration that any bias introduced by the IT skilled staff is offset.

The detailed interviews were not limited in this way as individual employees were specifically selected to ensure a broad and diverse inclusion of skills, experience and business functional knowledge. General Motors represents many global enterprises from the standpoint of global scale, business functions and manufacturing. It is not assumed that the pre-transformed technical environment within GM parallels that of other large enterprises as each business is unique in its history of technical development and maturity. GM does represent large enterprises that engage in multi-disciplinary industrial business processes at global scale who are transforming from a mostly non-digital environment with low levels of digital and virtual collaboration between functions.

REFERENCES

Axelrod, A., & Phillips, C. (2008). *What every American should know about American history: 225 Events that shaped the nation*. Zenda Inc.

Barra, M. (2017). *2016 Chairman's Letter*. Retrieved from General Motors: https://www.gm.com/content/dam/gm/en_us/english/Group4/InvestorsPDFDocuments/2016_Chairman%27s_Letter.pdf

Bennet, L. (2015). Changing Societies, changing media systems: Challenges for communication theory, research and education. In Can the media serve democracy? Essays in Honor of Jay G. Blumer (pp. 151-163). Palgrave MacMillan.

Bolton, A., Goosen, L., & Kritzinger, E. (2016). Enterprise Digitization Enablement Through Unified Communication and Collaboration. *Proceedings of the Annual Conference of the South African Institute of Computer Scientists and Information Technologists (SAICSIT)* 10.1145/2987491.2987516

Bolton, A., Goosen, L., & Kritzinger, E. (2020b). The Impact of Unified Communication and Collaboration Technologies on Productivity and Innovation: Promotion for the Fourth Industrial Revolution. In *Promoting Inclusive Growth in the Fourth Industrial Revolution* (pp. 44–73). IGI Global. doi:10.4018/978-1-7998-4882-0.ch002

Bolton, A., Goosen, L., & Kritzinger, E. (2021a). Unified Communication Technologies at a Global Automotive Organization. In Encyclopedia of Organizational Knowledge, Administration, and Technologies (pp. 2592-2608). IGI Global. doi:10.4018/978-1-7998-3473-1.ch179

Bolton, A., Goosen, L., & Kritzinger, E. (2021b). An Empirical Study into the Impact on Innovation and Productivity Towards the Post-COVID-19 Era: Digital Transformation of an Automotive Enterprise. In *Handbook of Research on Entrepreneurship, Innovation, Sustainability, and ICTs in the Post-COVID-19 Era* (pp. 133–159). IGI Global. doi:10.4018/978-1-7998-6776-0.ch007

Bolton, A., Goosen, L., & Kritzinger, E. (2021c). The Integration and Implementation of the Internet of Things Through Digital Transformation: Impact on Productivity and Innovation. In Integration and Implementation of the Internet of Things Through Cloud Computing (pp. 85-112). IGI Global.

Bolton, A., Murray, M., & Fluker, J. (2017). Transforming the Workplace: Unified Communications & Collaboration Usage Patterns in a Large Automotive Manufacturer. *Proceedings of the 50th Hawaii International Conference on System Sciences*, 5470-5479. 10.24251/HICSS.2017.661

Bolton, T., Goosen, L., & Kritzinger, E. (2020a, March 8). Security Aspects of an Empirical Study into the Impact of Digital Transformation via Unified Communication and Collaboration Technologies on the Productivity and Innovation of a Global Automotive Enterprise. *Communications in Computer and Information Science, 1166*, 99–113. doi:10.1007/978-3-030-43276-8_8

Castells, M. (2007). *The Network Society*. Edward Elgar.

Chanias, S., & Hess, T. (2016). Understanding Digital Transformation Strategy formation: Insights from Europe's Automotive Industry. In *Pacific Asia Conference on Information Systems*. Association for Information Systems.

Chapman, G. (2011). *The Car Book: The definitive visual history*. Dorling Kindersley Ltd.

Di-Gangi, P., & Wasko, M. (2009). Steal my idea! Organizational adoption of user innovations from a user innovation community: A case study of Dell IdeaStorm. *Decision Support Systems, 48*(1), 303–312. doi:10.1016/j.dss.2009.04.004

Feher, P. (2012). Integrating and Measuring Business and Technology Services in the Context of Enterprise. In Business Enterprise, Process, and Technology Management: Models and Applications (p. 148). Business Science Reference. doi:10.4018/978-1-4666-0249-6.ch008

Fortune. (2017). *Fortune 500 General Motors*. Retrieved from https://fortune.com/fortune500/general-motors/

General Motors. (2016). *Sustainability Report*. Retrieved from https://www.gmsustainability.com/_pdf/resources-and-downloads/GM_2016_SR.pdf

Glazer, D., Kenkins, T., & Schaper, H. (2005). *Enterprise Content Management Technology: Turning Content into Competitive Advantage*. Open Text Corporation.

Goosen, L. (2004). *Criteria and Guidelines for the Selection and Implementation of a First Programming Language in High Schools*. North West University.

Goosen, L. (2018). Trans-Disciplinary Approaches to Action Research for e-Schools, Community Engagement, and ICT4D. In Cross-Disciplinary Approaches to Action Research and Action Learning (pp. 97-110). IGI Global.

Goosen, L., & Naidoo, L. (2014). Computer Lecturers Using Their Institutional LMS for ICT Education in the Cyber World. In *Proceedings of the 43rd Conference of the Southern African Computer Lecturers' Association* (pp. 99-108). Nelson Mandela Metropolitan University.

Hancock, D., & Algozzine, B. (2017). *Doing Case Study Research: A Practical Guide for Beginning Researchers*. Teachers College Press.

Heitmann, J. (2009). *The Automobile and American Life*. McFarland & Company Inc.

Jokonya, O., Kroeze, J., & van der Poll, J. (2012). Towards a Framework for Decision Making Regarding IT Adoption. *Proceedings of SAICSIT Conference* (pp. 316-325). ACM. 10.1145/2389836.2389874

Kranz, M. (2016). *Building the Internet of Things: Implement new Business Models, Disrupt Competitors, Transform Your Industry*. John Wiley & Sons.

Lal, B. (2014). Framework for Utilization of Global Resources for Knowledge Creation and Application Through Flexible Organizations. In *The Flexible Enterprise* (pp. 164–172). Springer. doi:10.1007/978-81-322-1560-8_10

Lee, B., & Saunders, M. (2017). Conducting Case Study Research for Business and Management Students: Mastering Business Research Methods. *Sage (Atlanta, Ga.).*

Lee, S. (2013). Linking Technology Roadmapping to Patent Analysis. In Technology Roadmapping for Strategy and Innovation: Chartering the Route to Success (pp. 267-284). Springer. doi:10.1007/978-3-642-33923-3_17

Lewin, T., & Borroff, R. (2010). *How To Design Cars Like A Pro*. Motorbooks International.

Llopis-Albert, C., Rubio, F., & Valero, F. (2021). Impact of digital transformation on the automotive industry. *Technological Forecasting and Social Change*, *162*, 120343. Advance online publication. doi:10.1016/j.techfore.2020.120343 PMID:33052150

Lu, N., Cheng, N., Zhang, N., Shen, X., & Mark, J. (2014). Connected vehicles: Solutions and challenges. *IEEE Internet of Things Journal*, *1*(4), 289–299. doi:10.1109/JIOT.2014.2327587

Marabelli, M., Hansen, S., Newell, S., & Frigerio, C. (2017). The Light and Dark Side of the Black Box: Sensor-based Technology in the Automotive Industry. *Communications of the Association for Information Systems*, *34*, 555–580. doi:10.17705/1CAIS.04016

Maree, K. (2020). Planning a research proposal. In *First steps in research* (pp. 25–53). Van Schaik.

Megill, K. (2013). *Thinking for a Living*. Walter de Gruyter GmbH.

Mengelkamp, E., Gärttner, J., Rock, K., Kessler, S., Orsini, L., & Weinhardt, C. (2018). Designing microgrid energy markets: A case study: The Brooklyn Microgrid. *Applied Energy*, *210*, 870–880. doi:10.1016/j.apenergy.2017.06.054

Parment, A. (2014). *Auto Brand: Building successful car brands for the future*. Kogan Page. doi:10.4271/0749469293

Persse, J. (2012). *The ITIL Process Manual: Key Processes and their Application*. Van Haren.

Piccinini, E., Hanelt, A., Gregory, R., & Kolbe, L. (2015). Transforming industrial business: The impact of digital transformation on automotive organizations. *Proceedings of the International Conference on Information Systems*. Retrieved from https://aisel.aisnet.org/icis2015/proceedings/GeneralIS/5/

Pope, M. (2017). *Understanding Planned Obsolescence: Unsustainability through production, consumption and waste generation*. Kogan Page.

Porter, M. (2008). The five competitive forces that shape strategy. *Harvard Business Review*, *86*(1), 25–40. PMID:18271320

Preston, R. (2016). General Motors' IT Transformation: Building Downturn Resistant Profitability. *Forbes BrandVoice*. Retrieved from https://www.forbes.com/sites/oracle/2016/04/14/general-motors-it-transformation-building-downturn-resistant-profitability/#af9a51e1222f

Riasanow, T., Galic, G., & Böhm, M. (2017). Digital transformation in the automotive industry: Towards a generic value network. In *Proceedings of the 25th European Conference on Information Systems* (pp. 3191-3201). Academic Press.

Riepe, A., & Pisano, P. (2015). Business models in a new digital culture: The open tail model. *Symphonya Emerging Issues in Management, 75-88.*

Sanchez, A., & Carro, B. (2017). *Digital Services in the 21st Century: A Strategic and Business Perspective*. John Wiley & Sons. doi:10.1002/9781119314905

Shdaimah, C., Stahl, R., & Schram, S. (2011). *Change Research: A Case Study on Collaborative Methods for Social Workers and Advocates*. Columbia University.

Sufi, T., & Ahmed, S. (2021). Surviving COVID-19 Crisis by New Business Models: A Case Study of the Indian Restaurant Industry. In Handbook of Research on Entrepreneurship, Innovation, Sustainability, and ICTs in the Post-COVID-19 Era (pp. 301-316). IGI Global. doi:10.4018/978-1-7998-6776-0.ch015

United States Securities and Exchange Commission. (2017). *General Motors Company Form 10k, Annual Report.* US Securities and Exchange Commission. Retrieved from https://www.gm.com/content/dam/gm/en_us/english/Group4/InvestorsPDFDocuments/10-K.pdf

Von Hippel, E. (2016). *Free Innovation*. MIT Press. doi:10.7551/mitpress/9780262035217.001.0001

Wayland, M. (2017). Randy Mott built GM's IT engine. *Automotive News*. doi:https://www.autonews.com/article/20171002/OEM06/171009988/how-mott-built-gms-it-engine

Winkelhake, U. (2017). *The Digital Transformation of the Automotive Industry: Catalysts, Roadmap, Practice*. Springer.

Yin, R. (2009). Case Study Research: Design and Methods. *Sage (Atlanta, Ga.).*

ADDITIONAL READING

Wolf, G. (2017). New Challenges of the Digital Transformation: The Comeback of the Vision Mission System. In Out-thinking Organizational Communications: The Impact of Digital Transformation (pp. 113-128). Springer.

KEY TERMS AND DEFINITIONS

Information and Communication Technologies (ICTs): Technologies used for information and communication purposes.

Networked Society: A society where social structures comprise of networked microelectronics-based ICTs.

Compilation of References

A gamified marketing strategy to create emotional customer connection: Success factors for irresistible advergame design. (2021). *Strategic Direction, 37*(1), 25-27. doi:10.1108/SD-10-2020-0182

Aagaard, A. (2019). The Concept and Frameworks of Digital Business Models. In A. Aagaard (Ed.), *Digital Business Models Driving Transformation and Innovation* (pp. 1–26). Palgrave Macmillan. doi:10.1007/978-3-319-96902-2_1

Abou-Shouk, M., & Soliman, M. (2021). The impact of gamification adoption intention on brand awareness and loyalty in tourism: The mediating effect of customer engagement. *Journal of Destination Marketing & Management, 20*, 100559. Advance online publication. doi:10.1016/j.jdmm.2021.100559

Achtenhagen, L., Melin, L., & Naldi, L. (2013). Dynamics of Business Models – Strategizing, Critical Capabilities and Activities for Sustained Value Creation. *Long Range Planning, 46*(6), 427–442. doi:10.1016/j.lrp.2013.04.002

Agarwal, S., & Teas, R. K. (2001). Perceived value: Mediating role of perceived risk. *Journal of Marketing Theory and Practice, 9*(4), 1–14. doi:10.1080/10696679.2001.11501899

Alavi, S., & Habel, J. (2021). The human side of digital transformation in sales: Review & future paths. *Journal of Personal Selling & Sales Management, 41*(2), 83–86. doi:10.1080/08853134.2021.1920969

Albayrak, T., Caber, M., & Çömen, N. (2016). Tourist shopping: The relationships among shopping attributes, shopping value, and behavioral intention. *Tourism Management Perspectives, 18*, 98–106. doi:10.1016/j.tmp.2016.01.007

Ali, H. (2019). Building Repurchase Intention and Purchase Decision: Brand Awareness and Brand Loyalty Analysis (Case Study Private Label Product in Alfamidi Tangerang). *Saudi Journal of Humanities and Social Sciences, 4*(09), 623–634. doi:10.36348/SJHSS.2019.v04i09.009

Aljabali, R. N., & Ahmad, N. (2019). *A review on adopting personalized gamified experience in the learning context.* Paper presented at the 2018 IEEE Conference on e-Learning, e-Management, and e-Services, IC3e 2018. 10.1109/IC3e.2018.8632635

Almarashdeh, I., Jaradat, G., Abuhamdah, A., Alsmadi, M., Alazzam, M. B., Alkhasawneh, R., & Awawdeh, I. (2019). The difference between shopping online using mobile apps and website shopping: A case study of service convenience. *International Journal of Computer Information Systems and Industrial Management Applications, 11*, 151–160.

Alshamrani, M. (in press). IoT and artificial intelligence implementations for remote healthcare monitoring systems: A survey. *Journal of King Saud University - Computer and Information Sciences.*

Altimeter. (2016). *The Six Stages of Digital Transformation.* https://www.prophet.com/2016/04/the-six-stages-of-digital-transformation/

Alves, C., & Reis, J. L. (2020, February). The Intention to Use E-Commerce Using Augmented Reality-The Case of IKEA Place. In *International Conference on Information Technology & Systems* (pp. 114-123). Springer. 10.1007/978-3-030-40690-5_12

Alves, H., Fernandes, C., & Raposo, M. (2016). Value co-creation: Concept and contexts of application and study. *Journal of Business Research, 69*(5), 1626–1633. doi:10.1016/j.jbusres.2015.10.029

Amankwah-Amoah, J., Khan, Z., Wood, G., & Knight, G. (2021). Covid-19 and digitalization: The great acceleration. *Journal of Business Research, 136*, 602–611. doi:10.1016/j.jbusres.2021.08.011 PMID:34538980

Anker, T. B., Sparks, L., Moutinho, L., & Grönroos, C. (2015). Consumer dominant value creation: A theoretical response to the recent call for a consumer dominant logic for marketing. *European Journal of Marketing, 49*(3/4), 532–560. doi:10.1108/EJM-09-2013-0518

Appel, G., Grewal, L., Hadi, R., & Stephen, A. T. (2020). The future of social media in marketing. *Journal of the Academy of Marketing Science, 48*(1), 79–95. doi:10.100711747-019-00695-1 PMID:32431463

Apple Inc. (2020). *Augmented Reality-System Capabilities-IOS-Human Interface Guidelines - Apple Developer.* https://developer.apple.com/design/human-interface-guidelines/ios/system-capabilities/augmented-reality/

Arni, P., & Laddha, S. (2017). Adoption of digital marketing in health industry. *SIES Journal of Management, 13*(1).

Arnold, M. J., & Reynolds, K. E. (2003). Hedonic shopping motivations. *Journal of Retailing, 79*(2), 77–95. doi:10.1016/S0022-4359(03)00007-1

Arora, S., & Sahney, S. (2017). Webrooming behaviour: A conceptual framework. *International Journal of Retail & Distribution Management, 45*(7/8), 762–781. doi:10.1108/IJRDM-09-2016-0158

Axelrod, A., & Phillips, C. (2008). *What every American should know about American history: 225 Events that shaped the nation*. Zenda Inc.

Aydin, S., & Schnabel, M. A. (2016). The museum of gamers: Unmediated cultural heritage through gaming. In Cultural heritage in a changing world (pp. 125-141). doi:10.1007/978-3-319-29544-2_8

Azuma, R. T. (1997). A survey of augmented reality. *Presence (Cambridge, Mass.), 6*(4), 355–385. doi:10.1162/pres.1997.6.4.355

Azuma, R., Baillot, Y., Behringer, R., Feiner, S., Julier, S., & Macintyre, B. (2001). Recent advances in augmented reality. *IEEE Computer Graphics and Applications, 21*(6), 34–47. doi:10.1109/38.963459

Babin, B. J., Darden, W. R., & Griffin, M. (1994). Work and/or fun: Measuring hedonic and utilitarian shopping value. *The Journal of Consumer Research, 20*(4), 644–656. doi:10.1086/209376

Baday, H. M. (2011). *Tehnici de comunicare in social media*. Polirom Publishing House.

Bakos, Y. (1998). The emerging role of electronic marketplaces on the Internet. *Communications of the ACM, 41*(8), 35–42. doi:10.1145/280324.280330

Balagurunathan, Y., Mitchell, R., & Naqa, I. E. (2021). Requirements and reliability of AI in the medical context. *Physica Medica, 83*, 72–78. doi:10.1016/j.ejmp.2021.02.024 PMID:33721700

Ballantine, P. W. (2005). Effects of interactivity and product information on consumer satisfaction in an online retail setting. *International Journal of Retail & Distribution Management, 33*(6), 461–471. doi:10.1108/09590550510600870

Barra, M. (2017). *2016 Chairman's Letter.* Retrieved from General Motors: https://www.gm.com/content/dam/gm/en_us/english/Group4/InvestorsPDFDocuments/2016_Chairman%27s_Letter.pdf

Barreto, A. M. (2013). Do users look at banner ads on Facebook? *Journal of Research in Interactive Marketing.*

Başlangıç Noktası, W. (2019). *Getir'in Sosyolojisi* [The Sociology of Getir]. Retrieved July 25, 2021, from https://baslangicnoktasi.org/getirin-sosyolojisi/

Batra, R., & Ahtola, O. T. (1991). Measuring the hedonic and utilitarian sources of consumer attitudes. *Marketing Letters, 2*(2), 159–170. doi:10.1007/BF00436035

Bayuk, J., & Altobello, S. A. (2019). Can gamification improve financial behavior? The moderating role of app expertise. *International Journal of Bank Marketing, 37*(4), 951–975. doi:10.1108/IJBM-04-2018-0086

Bazaki, E., & Wanick, V. (2019). *Unlocking the potential of the salesperson in the virtual fitting room: Enhancing the online retail experience for fashion brands.* Academic Press.

Bechkoff, J. (2019). Gamification using a choose-your-own-adventure type platform to augment learning and facilitate student engagement in marketing education. *Journal for Advancement of Marketing Education, 27*(1), 13–30.

Becker, A. (2019). Artificial intelligence in medicine: What is it doing for us today? *Health Policy and Technology, 8*(2), 198–205. doi:10.1016/j.hlpt.2019.03.004

Beck, M., & Crié, D. (2018). I virtually try it… I want it! Virtual Fitting Room: A tool to increase on-line and off-line exploratory behavior, patronage and purchase intentions. *Journal of Retailing and Consumer Services, 40*, 279–286. doi:10.1016/j.jretconser.2016.08.006

Bego Jeans. (n.d.). Retrieved December 14, 2021, from https://www.begojeans.com/

Bellman, S., Treleaven-Hassard, S., Robinson, J. A., Varan, D., & Potter, R. F. (2013). Brand communication with branded smartphone apps: First insights on possibilities and limits. *NIM Marketing Intelligence Review, 5*(2), 24–27. doi:10.2478/gfkmir-2014-0014

Bencsik, A., Horváth-Csikós, G., & Juhász, T. (2016). Y and Z Generations at Workplaces. *Journal of Competitiveness, 8*(3), 90–106. doi:10.7441/joc.2016.03.06

Beninger, P. (2020). COVID-19: Regulatory Landscape of Medicinal and Medical Device Products for Human Use. *Clinical Therapeutics, 42*(8), 1444–1450. doi:10.1016/j.clinthera.2020.06.014 PMID:32651020

Benkler, Y. (2006). *The Wealth of Networks—How Social Production Transforms Markets and Freedom.* Yale University Press.

Bennet, L. (2015). Changing Societies, changing media systems: Challenges for communication theory, research and education. In Can the media serve democracy? Essays in Honor of Jay G. Blumer (pp. 151-163). Palgrave MacMillan.

Bennett, R., & Vijaygopal, R. (2018). Consumer attitudes towards electric vehicles: Effects of product user stereotypes and self-image congruence. *European Journal of Marketing, 52*(3-4), 499–527. doi:10.1108/EJM-09-2016-0538

Benwell, S. (2014). Capitalising on social media to grow your business. *The Guardian, 28.*

Berger, A., Schlager, T., Sprott, D. E., & Herrmann, A. (2018). Gamified interactions: Whether, when, and how games facilitate self–brand connections. *Journal of the Academy of Marketing Science, 46*(4), 652–673. doi:10.100711747-017-0530-0

Berman, S. J. (2012). Digital transformation: Opportunities to create new business models. *Strategy and Leadership, 40*(2), 16–24. doi:10.1108/10878571211209314

Bettany-Saltikov, J. (2016). *How to do a Systematic Literature Review in Nursing: A step-by-step guide* (2nd ed.). McGraw-Hill Education.

Bilgin, Y. (2017). Qualitative method versus quantitative method in marketing research: An application example at Oba restaurant. *Qualitative Versus Quantitative Research*, 1-28.

Bitrián, P., Buil, I., & Catalán, S. (2021). Enhancing user engagement: The role of gamification in mobile apps. *Journal of Business Research, 132*, 170–185. doi:10.1016/j.jbusres.2021.04.028

Blank, S. (2013). Why the Lean Start-Up Changes Everything. *Harvard Business Review, 91*(5), 63–72.

Boada, J. P., Maestre, B. R., & Genís, C. T. (2021). The ethical issues of social assistive robotics: A critical literature review. *Technology in Society, 67*, 101726. doi:10.1016/j.techsoc.2021.101726

Bolton, A., Goosen, L., & Kritzinger, E. (2021a). Unified Communication Technologies at a Global Automotive Organization. In Encyclopedia of Organizational Knowledge, Administration, and Technologies (pp. 2592-2608). IGI Global. doi:10.4018/978-1-7998-3473-1.ch179

Bolton, A., Goosen, L., & Kritzinger, E. (2021c). The Integration and Implementation of the Internet of Things Through Digital Transformation: Impact on Productivity and Innovation. In Integration and Implementation of the Internet of Things Through Cloud Computing (pp. 85-112). IGI Global.

Bolton, A., Goosen, L., & Kritzinger, E. (2016). Enterprise Digitization Enablement Through Unified Communication and Collaboration. *Proceedings of the Annual Conference of the South African Institute of Computer Scientists and Information Technologists (SAICSIT)* 10.1145/2987491.2987516

Bolton, A., Goosen, L., & Kritzinger, E. (2020b). The Impact of Unified Communication and Collaboration Technologies on Productivity and Innovation: Promotion for the Fourth Industrial Revolution. In *Promoting Inclusive Growth in the Fourth Industrial Revolution* (pp. 44–73). IGI Global. doi:10.4018/978-1-7998-4882-0.ch002

Bolton, A., Goosen, L., & Kritzinger, E. (2021b). An Empirical Study into the Impact on Innovation and Productivity Towards the Post-COVID-19 Era: Digital Transformation of an Automotive Enterprise. In *Handbook of Research on Entrepreneurship, Innovation, Sustainability, and ICTs in the Post-COVID-19 Era* (pp. 133–159). IGI Global. doi:10.4018/978-1-7998-6776-0.ch007

Bolton, A., Murray, M., & Fluker, J. (2017). Transforming the Workplace: Unified Communications & Collaboration Usage Patterns in a Large Automotive Manufacturer. *Proceedings of the 50th Hawaii International Conference on System Sciences*, 5470-5479. 10.24251/HICSS.2017.661

Bolton, T., Goosen, L., & Kritzinger, E. (2020a, March 8). Security Aspects of an Empirical Study into the Impact of Digital Transformation via Unified Communication and Collaboration Technologies on the Productivity and Innovation of a Global Automotive Enterprise. *Communications in Computer and Information Science, 1166*, 99–113. doi:10.1007/978-3-030-43276-8_8

Bonchek, M. (2017). A Good Digital Strategy Creates a Gravitational Pull. *Harvard Business Review*. Retrieved from https://hbr.org/2017/01/a-good-digital-strategy-creates-a-gravitational-pull

Bonetti, F., Pantano, E., Warnaby, G., & Quinn, L. (2019). Augmenting reality: Fusing consumers' experiences and interactions with immersive technologies in physical retail settings. *International Journal of Technology Marketing, 13*(3-4), 260–284. doi:10.1504/IJTMKT.2019.104592

Bonner, J. M. (2010). Customer interactivity and new product performance: Moderating effects of product newness and product embeddedness. *Industrial Marketing Management, 39*(3), 485–492. doi:10.1016/j.indmarman.2008.11.006

Boomsonar; Marketing Türkiye. (2017). *Social Medya Awards Turkey. Social Medya Awards.* https://www.socialmediaawardsturkey.com/

Boorstin, D. J. (2010). The Americans: The democratic experience (Vol. 3). Vintage. *Business Horizons, 53*(1), 59–68.

Brengman, M., Willems, K., & Van Kerrebroeck, H. (2018). Can't touch this: The impact of augmented reality versus touch and non-touch interfaces on perceived ownership. *Virtual Reality (Waltham Cross)*, 1–12.

Brownell, B., Cechanowicz, J., & Gutwin, C. (2015). Gamification of survey research: Empirical results from gamifying a conjoint experiment. In Gamification in education and business (pp. 569-591). doi:10.1007/978-3-319-10208-5_29

Brown, S., & Bessant, J. (2003). The manufacturing strategy-capabilities links in mass customisation and agile manufacturing—An exploratory study. *International Journal of Operations & Production Management, 23*(7), 707–730. doi:10.1108/01443570310481522

Bughin, J., Catlin, T., & Dietz, M. (2019, May 7). The right digital-platform strategy. *The McKinsey Quarterly.*

Burdea, G., & Coiffet, P. (2003). *Virtual reality technology.* MIT Press. doi:10.1162/105474603322955950

Burton, S., & Soboleva, A. (2011). Interactive or reactive? Marketing with Twitter. *Journal of Consumer Marketing, 28*(7), 491–499. doi:10.1108/07363761111181473

Caboni, F., & Hagberg, J. (2019). Augmented reality in retailing: A review of features, applications and value. *International Journal of Retail & Distribution Management, 47*(11), 1125–1140. doi:10.1108/IJRDM-12-2018-0263

Çağlar, İ., & Kılıç, S. (2005). *Pazarlama.* Nobel Yayın Dağıtım.

Călin, G. (2010). Advergames: Characteristics, Limitations and Potential. Annals of the University of Oradea. *Economic Science Series, 19*(1).

Canestrino, R., C'wiklicki, M., Kafel, P., Wojnarowska, M., & Magliocca, P. (2020). The digitalization in EMAS-registered organizations: Evidences from Italy and Poland. *The TQM Journal, 32*(4), 673–695. doi:10.1108/TQM-12-2019-0301

Canhoto, A. I., & Murphy, J. (2016). Learning from simulation design to develop better experiential learning initiatives: An integrative approach. *Journal of Marketing Education, 38*(2), 98–106. doi:10.1177/0273475316643746

Cappo, J. (2005). *Reklamcılığın geleceği* (Ö. Girnek, Ed.). MediaCat Kitapları.

Caputo, A., Pizzi, S., Pellegrini, M. M., & Dabić, M. (2021). Digitalization and business models: Where are we going? A science map of the field. *Journal of Business Research, 123*, 489–501. doi:10.1016/j.jbusres.2020.09.053

Carlson, J., & O'Cass, A. (2011). Creating commercially compelling website-service encounters: An examination of the effect of website-service interface performance components on flow experiences. *Electronic Markets, 21*(4), 237–253. doi:10.100712525-011-0073-z

Carmignani, J., & Furht, B. (2011). Augmented Reality: An Overview. In B. Furht (Ed.), *Handbook of Augmented Reality. Heidelberg/Dortrecht/London/NewYork* (pp. 3–46). Springer Verlag. doi:10.1007/978-1-4614-0064-6_1

Carr, N. G. (2003). IT Doesn't Matter. *Harvard Business Review.* Retrieved from https://hbr.org/2003/05/it-doesnt-matter

Casadesus-Masanell, R., & Ricart, J. E. (2011, Jan.). How to design a winning business model. *Harvard Business Review.*

Casteleyn, J., Mottart, A., & Rutten, K. (2009). How to use Facebook in your market research. *International Journal of Market Research, 51*(4), 439–447. doi:10.2501/S1470785309200669

Castells, M. (2007). *The Network Society*. Edward Elgar.

Catania, L. J. (2021). 6 - Current AI applications in medical therapies and services. In *Foundations of Artificial Intelligence in Healthcare and Bioscience*. Academic Press.

Caudell, T. P., & Mizell, D. W. (1992). Augmented reality: an application of heads-up display technology to manual manufacturing processes. *Proceedings of the 25th Hawaii International Conference on System Sciences, 2*, 659-669. 10.1109/HICSS.1992.183317

Çeker, E., & Özdaml, F. (2017). What" Gamification" Is and What It's Not. *European Journal of Contemporary Education, 6*(2), 221–228. doi:10.13187/ejced.2017.2.221

Chaffey, D., Ellis-Chadwick, F., Mayer, R., & Johnston, K. (2009). *Internet marketing: strategy, implementation and practice*. Pearson Education.

Chaffey, D., Hemphill, T., & Edmundson-Bird, D. (2019). *Digital business and e-commerce management* (7th ed.). Pearson Education.

Chandon, P., Wansink, B., & Laurent, G. (2000). A Benefit Congruency Framework of Sales Promotion Effectiveness. *Journal of Marketing, 64*(4), 65–81. doi:10.1509/jmkg.64.4.65.18071

Chanias, S., & Hess, T. (2016). Understanding Digital Transformation Strategy formation: Insights from Europe's Automotive Industry. In *Pacific Asia Conference on Information Systems*. Association for Information Systems.

Chapman, G. (2011). *The Car Book: The definitive visual history*. Dorling Kindersley Ltd.

Charan, R. (2016). How to Transform a Traditional Giant into a Digital One. *Harvard Business Review*. Retrieved from https://hbr.org/2016/02/how-to-transform-a-traditional-giant-into-a-digital-one

Charitsis, V., Yngfalk, A. F., & Skålén, P. (2019). 'Made to run': Biopolitical marketing and the making of the self-quantified runner. *Marketing Theory, 19*(3), 347–366. doi:10.1177/1470593118799794

Chatterjee, S. (2013). Simple rules for designing business models. *California Management Review, 55*(2), 97–124. doi:10.1525/cmr.2013.55.2.97

Chawla, R. N., & Goyal, P. (2021). Emerging trends in digital transformation: A bibliometric analysis. *Benchmarking*, 1463–5771. doi:10.1108/BIJ-01-2021-0009

Chen, R. (2020). *The Role of Augmented Reality in Retail Settings: A Systematic Literature Review and Research Agenda* (Doctoral dissertation). The University of Manchester.

Chen, C. F., & Chen, F. S. (2010). Experience quality, perceived value, satisfaction and behavioral intentions for heritage tourists. *Tourism Management, 31*(1), 29–35. doi:10.1016/j.tourman.2009.02.008

Cheng, Z. B., Huang, G., Wen, J. H., & Yan, J. H. (2021). Applications of artificial intelligence in nuclear medicine image generation. *Quantitative Imaging in Medicine and Surgery, 11*(6), 2792–2822. doi:10.21037/qims-20-1078 PMID:34079744

Chen, T., Drennan, J., Andrews, L., & Hollebeek, L. D. (2018). User experience sharing: Understanding customer initiation of value co-creation in online communities. *European Journal of Marketing, 52*(5/6), 1154–1184. doi:10.1108/EJM-05-2016-0298

Chesbrough, H. (2010). Business Model Innovation: Opportunities and Barriers. *Long Range Planning*, *43*(2–3), 354–363. doi:10.1016/j.lrp.2009.07.010

Chicca, J., & Shellenbarger, T. (2018). Connecting with Generation Z: Approaches in Nursing Education. *Teaching and Learning in Nursing*, *13*(3), 180–184. doi:10.1016/j.teln.2018.03.008

Childers, T. L., Carr, C. L., Peck, J., & Carson, S. (2001). Hedonic and utilitarian motivations for online retail shopping behavior. *Journal of Retailing*, *77*(4), 511–535. doi:10.1016/S0022-4359(01)00056-2

China Academy of Information and Communications Technology. (2021). *Artificial Intelligence Core Technology Industry White Paper*. Beijing: Author.

China Academy of Information and Communications Technology. (2021). *White Paper on China's Digital Economy Development*. Beijing: Author.

China Comprehensive Deepening Reform Commission. (2019). *Guiding Opinions on Promoting the Deep Smart Integration of Artificial Intelligence and the Real Economy*. China General Office of the State Council.

China Industry and Information Technology Department. (2016). Special Action for Innovative development of Smart Hardware Industry (2016-2018) (China Ministry of Industry and Information Technology [2016] No. 302). Beijing: China General Office of the State Council.

China Industry and Information Technology Department. (2017). Three-year Action Plan to Promote the Development of a New Generation of Artificial Intelligence Industry (2018-2020) (China Ministry of Industry and Information Technology [2017] No. 315). Beijing: China General Office of the State Council.

China International Capital Corporation (CICC). (2019). *China E-commerce Industry in 2019*. Retrieved August 2020 from https://research.cicc.com/index

China National Development and Reform Commission. (2016). Planning Guide on Pharmaceutical Industry Development (Beijing ICP No. 05070218). Beijing: China General Office of the State Council.

China National Development and Reform Commission. (2016). *The Development Plan in Robot Industry (2016-2020)* (Beijing ICP No. 05052393). Beijing: China General Office of the State Council.

China National Development and Reform Commission. (2016). The Three-year Action Implementation Plan on "Internet+" Artificial Intelligence (China Development and Reform Commission [2016] No. 1078). Beijing: China General Office of the State Council.

China National Development and Reform Commission. (2017). "Thirteenth Five-Year" Plan for National Population Health Information Development (Beijing ICP No. 05052393). Beijing: China General Office of the State Council.

China National Development and Reform Commission. (2019). *Catalogue for the Guidance of Industrial Structure Adjustment (2019)* (China National Development and Reform Commission Publication No. 29). Beijing: China General Office of the State Council.

China National Health Commission. (2018). Norms and Standards of National Hospital Informatization Construction (Trial Implementation) (China National Health Office Planning Publication [2018] No. 4). Beijing: China General Office of the State Council.

China National Health Commission. (2018). Notice on the In-depth Development of "Internet + Medical and Health" Activities to Facilitate the People and Benefit the People (China National Health Office Planning Publication [2018] No. 22). Beijing: China General Office of the State Council.

China Potion. (2020). *Breakdown of PDD's business model to overtake Alibaba.* https://www.kidostech.com/post/breakdown-of-PDDs-business

Chinanews. (2021). *Wuhan Zhongnan Hospital 5G mobile CT assists Hebei.* https://www.chinanews.com/sh/2021/01-11/9383897.shtml

Chiu, C. M., Wang, E. T., Fang, Y. H., & Huang, H. Y. (2014). Understanding customers' repeat purchase intentions in B2C e-commerce: The roles of utilitarian value, hedonic value and perceived risk. *Information Systems Journal, 24*(1), 85–114. doi:10.1111/j.1365-2575.2012.00407.x

Choi, J. A., & Lim, K. (2020). Identifying machine learning techniques for classification of target advertising. *ICT Express, 6*(3), 175–180. doi:10.1016/j.icte.2020.04.012

Choi, K., Gitelman, Y., Leri, D., Deleener, M. E., Hahn, L., & Lang, E. (2021). Insourcing and scaling a telemedicine solution in under 2 weeks: Lessons for the digital transformation of health care. *Health Care, 9*(3), 100568. PMID:34293616

Choudhury, A., Behl, A., Sheorey, P. A., & Pal, A. (2021). Digital supply chain to unlock new agility: A TISM approach. *Benchmarking, 28*(6), 2075–2109. doi:10.1108/BIJ-08-2020-0461

Cobbe, J., & Singh, J. (2021). Artificial intelligence as a service: Legal responsibilities, liabilities, and policy challenges. *Computer Law & Security Review, 42*, 105573. doi:10.1016/j.clsr.2021.105573

Colnar, S., Penger, S., Grah, B., & Dimovski, V. (2020). Digital transformation of integrated care: Literature review and research agenda. *IFAC-PapersOnLine, 53*(2), 16890–16895. doi:10.1016/j.ifacol.2020.12.1221

Cook, A. V. (2020). *Augmented shopping : the quiet revolution.* Deloitte. https://www2.deloitte.com/content/dam/insights/us/articles/6367_Augmented-shopping/DI_Augmented-shopping.pdf

Cossío-Silva, F.-J., Revilla-Camacho, M.-Á., Vega-Vázquez, M., & Palacios-Florencio, B. (2016). Value co-creation and customer loyalty. *Journal of Business Research, 69*(5), 1621–1625. doi:10.1016/j.jbusres.2015.10.028

Council, C. M. O. (2014). *Mastering Adaptive Customer Engagements.* Retrieved from https://www.cmocouncil.org/thought-leadership/reports/286

Cruz, E., Orts-Escolano, S., Gomez-Donoso, F., Rizo, C., Rangel, J. C., Mora, H., & Cazorla, M. (2018). An augmented reality application for improving shopping experience in large retail stores. *Virtual Reality (Waltham Cross)*, 1–11.

Csikzentimihalyi, M. (1975). Beyond boredom and anxiety: Experiencing flow in work and play. Academic Press.

Cusumano, M., Yoffie, D. B., & Gawer, A. (2020). The Future of Platforms. *MIT Sloan Management Review, 61*(3).

Dacko, S. G. (2017). Enabling smart retail settings via mobile augmented reality shopping apps. *Technological Forecasting and Social Change, 124*, 243–256. doi:10.1016/j.techfore.2016.09.032

DaSilva, C. M., & Trkman, P. (2014). Business Model: What It Is and What It Is Not. *Long Range Planning, 47*(6), 379–389. doi:10.1016/j.lrp.2013.08.004

Davenport, T. H., & Beck, J. C. (2002). *The attention economy: Understanding the new currency of business.* Harvard Business Press.

Davidavičienė, V., Raudeliūnienė, J., & Viršilaitė, R. (2019). User experience evaluation and creativity stimulation with augmented reality mobile applications. *Creativity Studies, 12*(1), 34-48.

Dawes, J. (2008). Do data characteristics change according to the number of scale points used? An experiment using 5-point, 7-point and 10-point scales. *International Journal of Market Research, 50*(1), 61–77. doi:10.1177/147078530805000106

Dawson, R. (2018). *The six elements of platform strategy.* Retrieved from https://rossdawson.com/new-framework-the-six-elements-of-platform-strategy/

Daxue Consulting. (2020). *The AI in China 2020 White Paper.* https://daxueconsulting.com/ai-in-china-white-paper/

De Canio, F., Fuentes-Blasco, M., & Martinelli, E. (2021). Engaging shoppers through mobile apps: The role of gamification. *International Journal of Retail & Distribution Management, 49*(7), 919–940. Advance online publication. doi:10.1108/IJRDM-09-2020-0360

de Jong, A., de Ruyter, K., Keeling, D. I., Polyakova, A., & Ringberg, T. (2021). Key trends in business-to-business services marketing strategies: Developing a practice-based research agenda. *Industrial Marketing Management, 93*, 1–9. doi:10.1016/j.indmarman.2020.12.004

de Ruyter, K., Heller, J., Hilken, T., Chylinski, M., Keeling, D. I., & Mahr, D. (2020). Seeing with the Customer's Eye: Exploring the Challenges and Opportunities of AR Advertising. *Journal of Advertising, 49*(2), 109–124. doi:10.1080/00913367.2020.1740123

Dellaert, B. G. C. (2019). The consumer production journey: Marketing to consumers as co-producers in the sharing economy. *Journal of the Academy of Marketing Science, 47*(2), 238–254. doi:10.100711747-018-0607-4

Deloitte Access Economics. (2013). *Connected Small Businesses: how Australian small businesses are growing in the digital economy.* Retrieved October 10, 2014 from https://www.deloitteaccesseconomics.com.au/uploads/File/Connected%20Small%20Busin ss.pdf

Deloitte. (2017). *Digital Future Readiness.* Retrieved from https://www2.deloitte.com/content/dam/Deloitte/ch/Documents/consumer-business/ch-cip-en-swiss-transformation.pdf

Delone, W. H., & McLean, E. R. (2003). The DeLone and McLean model of information systems success: A ten-year update. *Journal of Management Information Systems, 19*(4), 9–30. doi:10.1080/07421222.2003.11045748

Desai, V. (2019). Digital marketing: A review. *International Journal of Trend in Scientific Research and Development, 5*(5), 196–200. doi:10.31142/ijtsrd23100

Dholakia, U. M., Bagozzi, R. P., & Pearo, L. K. (2004). A social influence model of consumer participation in network-and small-group-based virtual communities. *International Journal of Research in Marketing, 21*(3), 241–263. doi:10.1016/j.ijresmar.2003.12.004

Dietrich, T., Mulcahy, R., & Knox, K. (2018). Gaming attribute preferences in social marketing programs: Meaning matters more than rewards. *Journal of Social Marketing, 8*(3), 280–296. doi:10.1108/JSOCM-06-2017-0038

Dietrich, T., Rundle-Thiele, S., Kubacki, K., Durl, J., Gullo, M. J., Arli, D., & Connor, J. P. (2019). Virtual reality in social marketing: A process evaluation. *Marketing Intelligence & Planning, 37*(7), 806–820. doi:10.1108/MIP-11-2018-0537

Di-Gangi, P., & Wasko, M. (2009). Steal my idea! Organizational adoption of user innovations from a user innovation community: A case study of Dell IdeaStorm. *Decision Support Systems, 48*(1), 303–312. doi:10.1016/j.dss.2009.04.004

Dijesh, P., & Babu, S. S. (2016, March). Electronic commerce process as a method to improve the product and process. In *Data Mining and Advanced Computing (SAPIENCE), Internationa Conference on* (pp. 378-381). IEEE. 10.1109/SAPIENCE.2016.7684126

Dikcius, V., Urbonavicius, S., Adomaviciute, K., Degutis, M., & Zimaitis, I. (2020). Learning marketing online: The role of social interactions and gamification rewards. *Journal of Marketing Education.* Advance online publication. doi:10.1177/0273475320968252

Dillon, K., & Olberding, J. C. (2016). Promoting events: Through cause marketing, social media, and "gamification." In Social enterprise and special events (pp. 37-51). doi:10.4324/9781315673219

Donio', J., Massari, P., & Passiante, G. (2006). Customer satisfaction and loyalty in a digital environment: An empirical test. *Journal of Consumer Marketing*, *23*(7), 445–457.

Drell, L. (2014). Let the gamification begin. *Marketing Health Services*, *34*(1), 24–27. PMID:24741765

Duffett, R. (2020). The YouTube marketing communication effect on cognitive, affective and behavioural attitudes among Generation Z consumers. *Sustainability*, *12*(12), 5075. doi:10.3390u12125075

Dünser, A., Grasset, R., Seichter, H., & Billinghurst, M. (2007, March). *Applying HCI principles to AR systems design* [Conference contribution]. MRUI'07: 2nd International Workshop at the IEEE Virtual Reality 2007 Conference, Christchurch, New Zealand.

Dwivedi, Y. K., Ismagilova, E., Hughes, D. L., Carlson, J., Filieri, R., Jacobson, J., Jain, V., Karjaluoto, H., Kefi, H., Krishen, A. S., Kumar, V., Rahman, M. M., Raman, R., Rauschnabel, P. A., Rowley, J., Salo, J., Tran, G. A., & Wang, Y. (2021). Setting the future of digital and social media marketing research: Perspectives and research propositions. *International Journal of Information Management*, *59*, 102168. doi:10.1016/j.ijinfomgt.2020.102168

Dymek, M. (2016). Inside the gamification case of a mobile phone marketing campaign: The amalgamation of game studies with marketing communications? In The business of gamification: A critical analysis (pp. 99-121). doi:10.4324/9781315740867

Dymek, M. (2018). Expanding the magic circle–gamification as a marketplace icon. *Consumption Markets & Culture*, *21*(6), 590–602. doi:10.1080/10253866.2017.1361153

Edelman, D. C., & Singer, M. (2015). Competing on Customer Journeys. *Harvard Business Review*. Retrieved from https://hbr.org/2015/11/competing-on-customer-journeys

Edelman, D. C. (2007). From the periphery to the core: As online strategy becomes overall strategy, marketing organizations and agencies will never be the same. *Journal of Advertising Research*, *47*(2), 130–134. doi:10.2501/S0021849907070146

Eggers, J. P., & Park, K. F. (2018). Incumbent adaptation to technological change: The past, present, and future of research on heterogeneous incumbent response. *The Academy of Management Annals*, *12*(1), 357–389.

Engeser, S., & Schiepe-Tiska, A. (2012). Historical lines and an overview of current research on flow. In Advances in flow research (pp. 1-22). Springer Publishing. doi:10.1007/978-1-4614-2359-1_1

Eppmann, R., Bekk, M., & Klein, K. (2018). Gameful experience in gamification: Construction and validation of a gameful experience scale. *Journal of Interactive Marketing*, *43*, 98–115. doi:10.1016/j.intmar.2018.03.002

Eppmann, R., Klein, K., & Bekk, M. (2018). WTG (way to go)! how to take gamification research in marketing to the next level. Marketing. *Zeitschrift Fur Forschung Und Praxis*, *40*(4), 44–52. doi:10.15358/0344-1369-2018-4-44

Ernst & Young. (2011) *The digitisation of everything*. Available at: https://www.ey.com/Publication/vwLUAssets/The_digitisation_of_everything_-_How_organisations_must_adapt_to_changing_consumer_behaviour/%24file/EY_Digitisation_of_everything.pdf

Eroğlu, O. (2019). *2018 Yılı Arama Motoru İstatistikleri* [Search Engine Statistics for 2018]. Retrieved September 22, 2021, from https://www.motionb.com/blog/2018-yili-arama-motoru-istatistikleri

Eshlaghy, A. T., Mashayekhi, A. N., Rajabzadeh, A., & Razavian, M. M. (2010). Applying path analysis method in defining effective factors in organisation agility. *International Journal of Production Research*, *48*(6), 1765–1786.

Essence Securities. (2021). *2021: Smart flowers bloom, AI is all over the world.* https://m-robo.datayes.com/report/summary?id=4421892

Essence Securities. (2021). *Welcome to the first year of AI medical commercialization-Smart Flower 2021 Series Report 4.* https://mp.weixin.qq.com/s/Gh8BLJsTqffeO5Hlzw37SA

Etgar, M. (2008). A Descriptive model of the consumer co-production process. *Journal of the Academy of Marketing Science*, *36*, 97–108.

Facebook. (2020). *Introducing The Spark AR Design Guidelines.* https://sparkar.facebook.com/blog/introducing-spark-ar-design-guidelines/

Facebook. (2021). *Connect 2021: Our vision for the metaverse*. Retrieved 28 November 2021, from https://tech.fb.com/connect-2021-our-vision-for-the-metaverse/

Falk, S., & Riemensperger, F. (2019, August 5). Three Lessons From Germany's Platform Economy. *MIT Sloan Management Review.* Retrieved November 2021 from https://sloanreview.mit.edu/article/three-lessons-from-germanys-platform-economy/

Fan, D. D. (2019). *Surgical robot is warned! FDA does not recommend robotic tumor surgery and mastectomy.* https://med.sina.com/article_detail_103_2_61748.html

Fan, Q., & Ouppara, N. (2021). Surviving Disruption and Uncertainty Through Digital Transformation: A Case Study on Small to Medium-Sized Enterprises (SME). In T. Semerádová & P. Weinlich (Eds.), *Moving Businesses Online and Embracing E-Commerce: Impact and Opportunities Caused by COVID-19* (pp. 1–22). IGI Global. doi:10.4018/978-1-7998-8294-7.ch001

Favaro, K. (2016). Don't Draft a Digital Strategy just because everyone else is. *Harvard Business Review.* Retrieved from https://hbr.org/2016/03/dont-draft-a-digital-strategy-just-because-everyone-else-is

Featherman, M. S., & Pavlou, P. A. (2003). Predicting e-services adoption: A perceived risk facets perspective. *International Journal of Human-Computer Studies*, *59*(4), 451–474. doi:10.1016/S1071-5819(03)00111-3

Feher, P. (2012). Integrating and Measuring Business and Technology Services in the Context of Enterprise. In Business Enterprise, Process, and Technology Management: Models and Applications (p. 148). Business Science Reference. doi:10.4018/978-1-4666-0249-6.ch008

Feng, Y., Liu, Z., Qian, W., Guo, M., & Chen, J. (2019). *Research on the influence mechanism of gamification elements on users' willingness to continue using in interest-based virtual communities - based on ECM-ISC model.* Paper presented at the 2019 16th International Conference on Service Systems and Service Management, ICSSSM 2019. 10.1109/ICSSSM.2019.8887645

Fernandes, J., Martins, J., Teixeira, M. S., Branco, F., Gonçalves, R., Au-Yong-Oliveira, M., & Moreira, F. (2018). Incorporating innovative ICT in child-oriented marketing - A retail sector case study. *Proceedings of the European Conference on Innovation and Entrepreneurship, ECIE*, 1006-1014.

Firat, D. (2019). YouTube advertising value and its effects on purchase intention. *Journal of Global Business Insights*, *4*(2), 141–155. doi:10.5038/2640-6489.4.2.1097

Flavián, C., & Guinalíu, M. (2006). Consumer trust, perceived security and privacy policy: Three basic elements of loyalty to a web site. *Industrial Management & Data Systems*, *106*(5), 601–620. doi:10.1108/02635570610666403

Flavián, C., Ibáñez-Sánchez, S., & Orús, C. (2019). The impact of virtual, augmented and mixed reality technologies on the customer experience. *Journal of Business Research*, *100*, 547–560. doi:10.1016/j.jbusres.2018.10.050

Fletcher, G., & Griffiths, M. (2020). Digital transformation during a lockdown. *International Journal of Information Management, 55*, 102185. doi:10.1016/j.ijinfomgt.2020.102185 PMID:32836642

Flint, D. J., Blocker, C. P., & Boutin, P. J. (2011). Customer value anticipation, customer satisfaction and loyalty: An empirical examination. *Industrial Marketing Management, 40*(2), 219–230.

Florenthal, B. (2019). Young consumers' motivational drivers of brand engagement behavior on social media sites: A synthesized U&G and TAM framework. *Journal of Research in Interactive Marketing, 13*(3), 351–391. doi:10.1108/JRIM-05-2018-0064

Ford, G., Compton, M., Millett, G., & Tzortzis, A. (2017). *The Role of Digital Disruption in Healthcare Service Innovation*. Academic Press.

Forrest, C. (2016). *Altimeter report outlines 6 stages necessary for digital transformation in business*. https://www.techrepublic.com/article/altimeter-report-outlines-6-stages-necessary-for-digital-transformation-in-business/

Forsythe, S. M., & Shi, B. (2003). Consumer patronage and risk perceptions in Internet shopping. *Journal of Business Research, 56*(11), 867–875. doi:10.1016/S0148-2963(01)00273-9

Fortune. (2017). *Fortune 500 General Motors*. Retrieved from https://fortune.com/fortune500/general-motors/

Fournier, S. (1998). Consumers and their brands: Developing relationship theory in consumer research. *The Journal of Consumer Research, 24*(4), 343–373. doi:10.1086/209515

Foye, L. (2018). *Global ad spend will reach $37bn in the next five years*. Retrieved from http://www.bizcommunity.com/Article/1/12/172893.html#more

Francisco, B. (2006). *Cracking the social network code*. Academic Press.

Fruchter, G. E., & Tapiero, C. S. (2005). Dynamic online and offline channel pricing for heterogeneous customers in virtual acceptance. *International Game Theory Review, 7*(02), 137–150. doi:10.1142/S0219198905000454

Fuentes, C., Bäckström, K., & Svingstedt, A. (2017). Smartphones and the reconfiguration ofretailscapes: Stores, shopping, and digitalization. *Journal of Retailing and Consumer Services, 39*, 270–278. doi:10.1016/j.jretconser.2017.08.006

Gangadharbatla, H. (2008). Facebook me: Collective self-esteem, need to belong, and internet self-efficacy as predictors of the iGeneration's attitudes toward social networking sites. *Journal of Interactive Advertising, 8*(2), 5–15. doi:10.1080/15252019.2008.10722138

Garaus, M., & Wagner, U. (2016). Retail shopper confusion: Conceptualization, scale development, and consequences. *Journal of Business Research, 69*(9), 3459–3467. doi:10.1016/j.jbusres.2016.01.040

García-Magro, C., & Soriano-Pinar, I. (2020). Design of services in servitized firms: Gamification as an adequate tool. *Journal of Business and Industrial Marketing, 35*(3), 575–585. doi:10.1108/JBIM-12-2018-0413

Garrett, J. J. (2010). *The elements of user experience: user-centered design for the web and beyond*. Pearson Education.

Gassmann, O., Kausch, C., & Enkel, E. (2010). Negative side effects of customer integration. *International Journal of Technology Management, 50*(1), 43–63.

Gatautis, R., & Vitkauskaite, E. (2014). Gamification in marketing activities. *Proceedings of the 23rd International Business Information Management Association Conference, IBIMA 2014, 1*, 1875-1881.

Gehani, R. R. (2010). Time-based management strategic roles. *International Journal of Operations & Production Management, 15*, 19–35.

General Motors. (2016). *Sustainability Report.* Retrieved from https://www.gmsustainability.com/_pdf/resources-and-downloads/GM_2016_SR.pdf

Gensler, S., Neslin, S. A., & Verhoef, P. C. (2017). The showrooming phenomenon: It's more than just about price. *Journal of Interactive Marketing, 38*, 29–43. doi:10.1016/j.intmar.2017.01.003

Gentile, C., Spiller, N., & Noci, G. (2007). How to sustain the customer experience: An overview of experience components that co-create value with the customer. *European Management Journal, 25*(5), 395–410. doi:10.1016/j.emj.2007.08.005

Getir. (2021). *Kurucularımız.* Retrieved July 25, 2021, from https://getir.com/hakkimizda/kurucularimiz/

Ghirvu, A. (2011). Advergames: marketing advantages and risks involved. *International Conference "Marketing – from information to decision"*, 174-183.

Glazer, D., Kenkins, T., & Schaper, H. (2005). *Enterprise Content Management Technology: Turning Content into Competitive Advantage.* Open Text Corporation.

Gobble, M. (2018). Digitalization, Digitization, and Innovation. *Research Technology Management, 61*(4), 56–59. doi:10.1080/08956308.2018.1471280

Google. (2020). *Augmented Reality Design Guidelines.* https://designguidelines.withgoogle.com/ar-design/augmented-reality-design-guidelines/introduction.html

Goosen, L. (2018). Trans-Disciplinary Approaches to Action Research for e-Schools, Community Engagement, and ICT4D. In Cross-Disciplinary Approaches to Action Research and Action Learning (pp. 97-110). IGI Global.

Goosen, L. (2004). *Criteria and Guidelines for the Selection and Implementation of a First Programming Language in High Schools.* North West University.

Goosen, L., & Naidoo, L. (2014). Computer Lecturers Using Their Institutional LMS for ICT Education in the Cyber World. In *Proceedings of the 43rd Conference of the Southern African Computer Lecturers' Association* (pp. 99-108). Nelson Mandela Metropolitan University.

Gorissen, L., Vrancken, K., & Manshoven, S. (2016). Transition Thinking and Business Model Innovation—Towards a Transformative Business Model and New Role for the Reuse Centers of Limburg, Belgium. *Sustainability, 8*(112), 1–23. doi:10.3390u8020112

Gould, S. J., Pola, B. G., & Grabner-Krauter, S. (2000). Product Placements in Movies: A Cross- Cultural Analysis of Austrian, French and American Consumers' Attitudes Toward This Emerging, International Promotional Medium. *Journal of Advertising, 29*(4), 41–58. doi:10.1080/00913367.2000.10673623

Graziani, T. (2017, June 13). WeChat Official Account: A Simple Guide. *WalktheChat.* Retrieved August 2019 from https://walkthechat.com/wechat-official-account-simpleguide/

Graziani, T. (2018). *PDD: A closer look at the Fastest Growing E-commerce App in China.* Retrieved October 10, 2014 from https://www.techinasia.com/talk/PDD-fastest-growing-appchina

Grewal, D., Gauri, D. K., Roggeveen, A. L., & Sethuraman, R. (2021). Strategizing Retailing in the New Technology Era. *Journal of Retailing, 97*(1), 6–12.

Grewal, D., Roggeveen, A. L., & Nordfält, J. (2017). The future of retailing. *Journal of Retailing, 93*(1), 1–6. doi:10.1016/j.jretai.2016.12.008

Grönroos, C. (2006). Adopting a service logic for marketing. *Marketing Theory, 6*(3), 317–333.

Grönroos, C. (2012). Conceptualising value co-creation: A journey to the 1970s and back to the future. *Journal of Marketing Management*, *28*(13-14), 1520–1534.

Grönroos, C., & Voima, P. (2013). Critical service logic: Making sense of value creation and co-creation. *Journal of the Academy of Marketing Science*, *41*(2), 133–150.

Guarnieri, O. L. (2018). The role of Instagram in Fashion Communication: Analyse of Dolce & Gabbana's profile. Academic Press.

Gultekin, B., & Erdem, S. (2021). Omni-Channel Strategy in the Framework of the Search Engines. In T. Dirsehan (Ed.), *Managing Customer Experiences in an Omnichannel World*. Emerald Publishing Limited.

Gultekin, B., & Kement, U. (2018). *Müşteri İlişkileri Yönetimi (Customer Relationship Management)* (1st ed.). Nobel Academic Publishing.

Gunasekaran, A., Marri, H. B., McGaughey, R. E., & Nebhwani, M. D. (2002). E-commerce and its impact on operations management. *International Journal of Production Economics*, *75*(1-2), 185–197. doi:10.1016/S0925-5273(01)00191-8

Guo, F. (2013). *More Than Usability: The Four Elements Of User Experience, Part IV, UX matters*. https://www.uxmatters.com/mt/archives/2013/11/more-than-usability-the-four-elements-of-user-experience-part-iv.php

Guo, Y. M., & Poole, M. S. (2009). Antecedents of flow in online shopping: A test of alternative models. *Information Systems Journal*, *19*(4), 369–390. doi:10.1111/j.1365-2575.2007.00292.x

Gupta, S. (2018). *Driving Digital Strategy: A Guide to Reimagining Your Business*. Harvard Business Review Press.

Gura, S., & Gura, K. (2016). The use of mobile advergame as brand communication tool: Case study "Vodafon City". *American Journal of Marketing Research*, *2*(2), 61–72.

Gürkan, G. C., & Tükeltürk, S. A. (2017). Strategies for Innovative Organization Structure: Innovative Culture and Open Innovation. In Ü. Hacioğlu, H. Dinçer, & N. Alayoğlu (Eds.), *Global Business Strategies in Crisis: Strategic Thinking and Development* (pp. 185–199). Springer. doi:10.1007/978-3-319-44591-5_13

Gutt, D., von Rechenberg, T., & Kundisch, D. (2020). Goal achievement, subsequent user effort, and the moderating role of goal difficulty. *Journal of Business Research*, *106*, 277–287. doi:10.1016/j.jbusres.2018.06.019

Habuza, T., Navaz, A. N., Hashim, F., Alnajjar, F., Zaki, N., Serhani, M. A., & Statsenko, Y. (2021). AI applications in robotics, precision medicine, and medical image analysis: An overview and future trends. *Informatics in Medicine Unlocked*, *24*, 100596. doi:10.1016/j.imu.2021.100596

Hadar, E. (2016). *Mobile gamification principles applied to social engagement: Short paper of industry experience*. doi:10.1007/978-3-319-40515-5_15

Hagberg, J., Jonsson, A., & Egels-Zandén, N. (2017). Retail digitalization: Implications for physical stores. *Journal of Retailing and Consumer Services*, *39*, 264–269.

Hagberg, J., Sundstrom, M., & Egels-Zandén, N. (2016). The digitalization of retailing: An exploratory framework. *International Journal of Retail & Distribution Management*, *44*(7), 694–712.

Hagiu, A. (2013). *Multi-Sided Platforms: Foundations and Strategy*. Academic Press.

Hagiu, A., & Altman, E. J. (2017, July). Finding the Platform in Your Product. *Harvard Business Review*.

Haleem, A., Javaid, M., & Khan, I. H. (2019). Current status and applications of Artificial Intelligence (AI) in medical field: An overview. *Current Medicine Research and Practice*, *9*(6), 231–237. doi:10.1016/j.cmrp.2019.11.005

Hamari, J. (2013). Transforming homo economicus into homo ludens: A field experiment on gamification in a utilitarian peer-to-peer trading service. *Electronic Commerce Research and Applications*, *12*(4), 236–245. doi:10.1016/j.elerap.2013.01.004

Hancock, D., & Algozzine, B. (2017). *Doing Case Study Research: A Practical Guide for Beginning Researchers*. Teachers College Press.

Hanelt, A., Bohnsack, R., Marz, D., & Antunes Marante, C. (2021). A systematic review of the literature on digital transformation: Insights and implications for strategy and organizational change. *Journal of Management Studies*, *58*(5), 1159–1197. doi:10.1111/joms.12639

Hansson, L., Wrangmo, A., & Søilen, K. S. (2013). Optimal ways for companies to use Facebook as a marketing channel. *Journal of Information, Communication and Ethics in Society*.

Harman, K., Koohang, A., & Paliszkiewicz, J. (2014). Scholarly interest in gamification: A citation network analysis. *Industrial Management & Data Systems*, *114*(9), 1438–1452. doi:10.1108/IMDS-07-2014-0208

Hartmans, A. (2021). *Jeff Bezos originally wanted to name Amazon "Cadabra," and 14 other little-known facts about the early days of the e-commerce giant*. Retrieved September 9, 2021, from https://www.businessinsider.com/jeff-bezos-amazon-history-facts-2017-4

Harwood, T., Garry, T., & Broderick, A. (2008). *Relationship Marketing: Perspectives, Dimensions and Contexts*. McGraw-Hill Higher Education.

Heinonen, K., Strandvik, T., Mickelsson, K., Edvardsson, B., Sundström, E., & Andersson, P. (2010). A customer-dominant logic of service. *Journal of Service Management*, *21*(4), 531–548.

Heitmann, J. (2009). *The Automobile and American Life*. McFarland & Company Inc.

Heller, J., Chylinski, M., de Ruyter, K., Mahr, D., & Keeling, D. I. (2019). Touching the untouchable: Exploring multi-sensory augmented reality in the context of online retailing. *Journal of Retailing*, *95*(4), 219–234. doi:10.1016/j.jretai.2019.10.008

Hellier, P. K., Geursen, G. M., Carr, R. A., & Rickard, J. A. (2003). Customer repurchase intention: A general structural equation model. *European Journal of Marketing*, *37*(11/12), 1762–1800. doi:10.1108/03090560310495456

Helmefalk, M., & Marcusson, L. (2019). Gamification in a servicescape context: A conceptual framework. *International Journal of Internet Marketing and Advertising*, *13*(1), 22–46. doi:10.1504/IJIMA.2019.097894

Hienerth, C., Keinz, P., & Lettl, C. (2011). Exploring the Nature and Implementation Process of User-Centric Business Models. *Long Range Planning*, *44*(5–6), 344–374. doi:10.1016/j.lrp.2011.09.009

Hilken, T., Chylinski, M., Keeling, D. I., Heller, J., de Ruyter, K., & Mahr, D. (2021). How to strategically choose or combine augmented and virtual reality for improved online experiential retailing. *Psychology and Marketing*, 1–35.

Hilken, T., de Ruyter, K., Chylinski, M., Mahr, D., & Keeling, D. I. (2017). Augmenting the eye of the beholder: Exploring the strategic potential of augmented reality to enhance online service experiences. *Journal of the Academy of Marketing Science*, *45*(6), 884–905. doi:10.100711747-017-0541-x

Hilken, T., Heller, J., Chylinski, M., Keeling, D. I., Mahr, D., & de Ruyter, K. (2018). Making omnichannel an augmented reality: The current and future state of the art. *Journal of Research in Interactive Marketing*, *12*(4), 509–523.

Hinings, B., Gegenhuber, T., & Greenwood, R. (2018). Digital innovation and transformation: An institutional perspective. *Information and Organization*, *28*(1), 52–61.

Hoch, N. B., & Brad, S. (2021). Managing business model innovation: An innovative approach towards designing a digital ecosystem and multi-sided platform. *Business Process Management Journal*, *27*(2), 415–438. doi:10.1108/BPMJ-01-2020-0017

Hofacker, C. F., de Ruyter, K., Lurie, N. H., Manchanda, P., & Donaldson, J. (2016). Gamification and mobile marketing effectiveness. *Journal of Interactive Marketing*, *34*, 25–36. doi:10.1016/j.intmar.2016.03.001

Hoffman, D. L., & Novak, T. P. (2009). Flow online: Lessons learned and future prospects. *Journal of Interactive Marketing*, *23*(1), 23–34. doi:10.1016/j.intmar.2008.10.003

Högberg, J., Ramberg, M. O., Gustafsson, A., & Wästlund, E. (2019). Creating brand engagement through in-store gamified customer experiences. *Journal of Retailing and Consumer Services*, *50*, 122–130. doi:10.1016/j.jretconser.2019.05.006

Högberg, J., Shams, P., & Wästlund, E. (2019). Gamified in-store mobile marketing: The mixed effect of gamified point-of-purchase advertising. *Journal of Retailing and Consumer Services*, *50*, 298–304. doi:10.1016/j.jretconser.2018.07.004

Holbrook, M. B., & Hirschman, E. C. (1982). The experiential aspects of consumption: Consumer fantasy, feelings and fun. *The Journal of Consumer Research*, *9*(2), 132–140.

Hong, I. B. (2015). Understanding the consumer's online merchant selection process: The roles of product involvement, perceived risk, and trust expectation. *International Journal of Information Management*, *35*(3), 322–336. doi:10.1016/j.ijinfomgt.2015.01.003

Horea, M. B. (2016). *Tehnici de comunicare în social media*. Elefant Online.Editura Polirom.

Houk, K. M., & Thornhill, K. (2013). Using Facebook page insights data to determine posting best practices in an academic health sciences library. *Journal of Web Librarianship*, *7*(4), 372–388. doi:10.1080/19322909.2013.837346

Huang, T. L., & Liao, S. (2015). A model of acceptance of augmented-reality interactive technology: The moderating role of cognitive innovativeness. *Electronic Commerce Research*, *15*(2), 269–295. doi:10.100710660-014-9163-2

Huang, X., & Wu, B. X. (2020). Impact of urban-rural health insurance integration on health care: Evidence from rural China. *China Economic Review*, *64*, 101543. doi:10.1016/j.chieco.2020.101543

Huatai Securities. (2020). *Internet Medical Industry Depth: Analysis Framework of Internet Medical Industry*. https://m-robo.datayes.com/report/summary?id=4173915

Huey, L. S., & Yazdanifard, R. (2014). *How Instagram can be used as a tool in social network marketing. Center for Southern New Hampshire University.*

Hulland, J., Wade, M. R., & Antia, K. D. (2007). The impact of capabilities and prior investments on online channel commitment and performance. *Journal of Management Information Systems*, *23*(4), 109–142. doi:10.2753/MIS0742-1222230406

Hume, M., Mort, G. S., & Winzar, H. (2007). Exploring repurchase intention in a performing arts context: Who comes? and why do they come back? *International Journal of Nonprofit and Voluntary Sector Marketing*, *12*(2), 135–148. doi:10.1002/nvsm.284

Huotari, K., & Hamari, J. (2017). A definition for gamification: Anchoring gamification in the service marketing literature. *Electronic Markets*, *27*(1), 21–31. doi:10.100712525-015-0212-z

Hu, X., & Wise, K. (2021). How playable ads influence consumer attitude: Exploring the mediation effects of perceived control and freedom threat. *Journal of Research in Interactive Marketing*, *15*(2), 295–315. Advance online publication. doi:10.1108/JRIM-12-2020-0269

Hwangbo, H., Kim, Y.S. & Cha, K.J. (2017). Use of the smart store for persuasive marketing and immersive customer experiences: a case study of Korean apparel enterprise. *Mobile Information System*, 1-17.

Iacobucci, D., Arabie, P., & Bodapati, A. (2000). Recommendation agents on the internet. *Journal of Interactive Marketing*, *14*(3), 2–11. doi:10.1002/1520-6653(200022)14:3<2::AID-DIR1>3.0.CO;2-J

Inkpen, A. C., & Tsang, E. W. (2005). Social capital, networks, and knowledge transfer. *Academy of Management Review*, *30*(1), 146–165. doi:10.5465/amr.2005.15281445

Insights, C. B. (2021). *China Industry Digital Development Report*. http://www.cbdio.com/node_2567.htm

International Organization for Standardization. (2010). *Ergonomics of human-system interaction — Part 210: Human-centred design for interactive systems* (ISO/DIS Standard No. 9241-210). Retrieved from: https://www.iso.org/obp/ui/#iso:std:iso:9241:-210:ed-1:v1:en

Irshad, S., & Rambli, D. R. B. A. (2014, September). User experience of mobile augmented reality: A review of studies. In *2014 3rd international conference on user science and engineering (i-USEr)* (pp. 125-130). IEEE. 10.1109/IUSER.2014.7002689

Işılar, H. B. (2021). Havayolu Endüstrisinde Dijital Pazarlama Uygulamalarının Değerlendirilmesi. *Havacılık ve Uzay Çalışmaları Dergisi*, *1*(2), 42–63.

ITIL4. (2022). *ITIL 4: the framework for the management of IT-enabled services*. https://www.axelos.com/certifications/itil-service-management

Jacoby, J., & Kaplan, L. B. (1972). *The components of perceived risk*. ACR Special Volumes.

Jain, R., & Bagdare, S. (2009). Determinants of customer experience in new format retail stores. *Journal of Marketing Communications*, *5*(2).

Jang, S., Kitchen, P. J., & Kim, J. (2018). The effects of gamified customer benefits and characteristics on behavioral engagement and purchase: Evidence from mobile exercise application uses. *Journal of Business Research*, *92*, 250–259. doi:10.1016/j.jbusres.2018.07.056

Jansen, B. J., Zhang, M., Sobel, K., & Chowdury, A. (2009). Twitter power: Tweets as electronic word of mouth. *Journal of the American Society for Information Science and Technology*, *60*(11), 2169–2188. doi:10.1002/asi.21149

Javornik, A. (2016). 'It's an illusion, but it looks real!'Consumer affective, cognitive and behavioural responses to augmented reality applications. *Journal of Marketing Management*, *32*(9-10), 987–1011. doi:10.1080/0267257X.2016.1174726

Javornik, A. (2016a). Augmented reality: Research agenda for studying the impact of its media characteristics on consumer behavior. *Journal of Retailing and Consumer Services*, *30*, 252–26.

Javornik, A. (2016b). It's an illusion, but it looks real! Consumer affective, cognitive and behavioural responses to augmented reality applications. *Journal of Marketing Management*, *32*(9-10), 987–1011.

Javornik, A., Kostopoulou, E., Rogers, Y., Fatah gen Schieck, A., Koutsolampros, P., Maria Moutinho, A., & Julier, S. (2019). An experimental study on the role of augmented reality content type in an outdoor site exploration. *Behaviour & Information Technology*, *38*(1), 9–27. doi:10.1080/0144929X.2018.1505950

Jefferies, J. G., Bishop, S., & Hibbert, S. (2019). Customer boundary work to navigate institutional arrangements around service interactions: Exploring the case of telehealth. *Journal of Business Research*, *105*, 420–433. doi:10.1016/j.jbusres.2019.03.052

Jiménez-Castillo, D., & Sánchez-Fernández, R. (2019). The role of digital influencers in brand recommendation: Examining their impact on engagement, expected value and purchase intention. *International Journal of Information Management*, *49*, 366–376. doi:10.1016/j.ijinfomgt.2019.07.009

Jin, Y. H., & Qiu, M. J. (2019). *China Artificial Intelligence Medical White Paper*. Shanghai: Artificial Intelligence Research Institute of Shanghai Jiaotong University.

Jin, S. A. A., & Sung, Y. (2010). The roles of spokes-avatars' personalities in brand communication in 3D virtual environments. *Journal of Brand Management*, *17*(5), 317–327. doi:10.1057/bm.2009.18

Johnson, M. W., Christensen, C. M., & Kagermann, H. (2008). Reinventing Your Business Model through Disruptive Innovation. *Innosight*. Retrieved from https://www.innosight.com/insight/reinventing-yourbusiness-model/

Johnson, M. W., Christensen, C. M., & Kagermann, H. (2008). Reinventing your business model. *Harvard Business Review*, *86*(12), 58–68.

Johnson, M.W., Christensen, C. M., & Kagermann, H. (2008). Reinventing Your Business Model. *Harvard Business Review*.

Joia, L. A. (2004). Developing Government-to-Government enterprises in Brazil: A heuristic model drawn from multiple case studies. *International Journal of Information Management*, *24*(2), 147–166. doi:10.1016/j.ijinfomgt.2003.12.013

Jokonya, O., Kroeze, J., & van der Poll, J. (2012). Towards a Framework for Decision Making Regarding IT Adoption. *Proceedings of SAICSIT Conference* (pp. 316-325). ACM. 10.1145/2389836.2389874

Jothi, P. S., Neelamalar, M., & Prasad, R. S. (2011). Analysis of social networking sites: A study on effective communication strategy in developing brand communication. *Journal of Media and Communication Studies, 3*(7), 234-242.

Joyce, A., & Paquin, R. L. (2016). The triple layered business model canvas: A tool to design moresustainable business models. *Journal of Cleaner Production*, *135*, 1474–1486. doi:10.1016/j.jclepro.2016.06.067

Kachniewska, M. (2015). Gamification and social media as tools for tourism promotion. In Handbook of research on effective advertising strategies in the social media age (pp. 17-51). doi:10.4018/978-1-4666-8125-5.ch002

Kang, M. J. Y. (2014). Augmented reality and motion capture apparel e-shopping values and usage intention. *International Journal of Clothing Science and Technology*, *26*(6), 486–499.

Kaplan, A. M., & Haenlein, M. (2010). Users of the world, unite! The challenges and opportunities of Social Media. *Business Horizons*, *53*(1), 59–68. doi:10.1016/j.bushor.2009.09.003

Kaplan, S., & Sawhney, M. (2000). E-hubs: The new B2B marketplaces. *Harvard Business Review*, *78*(3), 97–106. PMID:11183982

Kassabli Al Fakhry, C. (2019). *Marketing strategies in the age of technology*. doi:10.1007/978-3-030-30874-2_27

Kathan, W., Matzler, K., & Veider, V. (2016). The sharing economy: Your business model's friend or foe? *Business Horizons*, *59*(6), 663–672. doi:10.1016/j.bushor.2016.06.006

Katz, E., & Lazarsfeld, P. F. (1955). *Personal influence: The part played by people in the flow of mass communications*. Routledge.

Kavadias, S., Ladas, K., & Loch, C. (2016). The Transformative Business Models. *Harvard Business Review*, *94*(10), 90–98.

Kecskes, R. (2017). Brand communication in a digitalized world. *NIM Marketing Intelligence Review*, *9*(2), 55–58.

Kemell, K., Feshchenko, P., Himmanen, J., Hossain, A., Jameel, F., Puca, R. L., Vitikainen, T., Kultanen, J., Risku, J., Impiö, J., Sorvisto, A., & Abrahamsson, P. (2020). Software startup education: Gamifying growth hacking. In Fundamentals of software startups: Essential engineering and business aspects (pp. 269-277) doi:10.1007/978-3-030-35983-6_16

Kietzmann, J., Paschen, J., & Treen, E. (2018). Artificial intelligence in advertising: How marketers can leverage artificial intelligence along the consumer journey. *Journal of Advertising Research*, *58*(3), 263–267. doi:10.2501/JAR-2018-035

Kim, H. Y., Lee, J. Y., Mun, J. M., & Johnson, K. K. (2017). Consumer adoption of smart in-store technology: Assessing the predictive value of attitude versus beliefs in the technology acceptance model. *International Journal of Fashion Design. Technology and Education*, *10*(1), 26–36.

Kim, J. (2016). The platform business model and business ecosystem: Quality management and revenue structures. *European Planning Studies*, *24*(12), 2113–2132. doi:10.1080/09654313.2016.1251882

Kim, K., & Ahn, S. J. (2017). The Role of Gamification in Enhancing Intrinsic Motivation to Use a Loyalty Program. *Journal of Interactive Marketing*, *40*, 41–51. doi:10.1016/j.intmar.2017.07.001

Ko, H., Jung, J., Kim, J., & Shim, S. W. (2004). Cross-cultural differences in perceived risk of online shopping. *Journal of Interactive Advertising*, *4*(2), 20–29. doi:10.1080/15252019.2004.10722084

Komninos, N., Pallot, M., & Schaffers, H. (2013). Smart Cities and the Future Internet in Europe. *Journal of the Knowledge Economy*, *4*(2), 119–134.

Korper, S., & Ellis, J. (2001). *The E-Commerce Book: Building the E-Empire*. Morgan Kaufmann.

Kotler, P., Keller, K. L., & Martinović, M. (2008). *Upravljanje marketingom* (Vol. 14). Izdanje.

Kotter, J. (2012). Leading Change. *Harvard Business Review*.

Kozinets, R. V., Hemetsberger, A., & Schau, H. J. (2008). The wisdom of consumer crowds: Collective innovation in the age of networked marketing. *Journal of Macromarketing*, *28*(4), 339–354.

Kozinets, R. V., Sherry, J. F., DeBerry-Spence, B., Duhachek, A., Nuttavuthisit, K., & Storm, D. (2002). Themed flagship brand stores in the new millennium: Theory, practice, prospects. *Journal of Retailing*, *78*(1), 17–29. doi:10.1016/S0022-4359(01)00063-X

Kozlen, K. (2006). *The value of banner advertising on the web* (Doctoral dissertation). University of Missouri - Columbia.

Kranz, M. (2016). *Building the Internet of Things: Implement new Business Models, Disrupt Competitors, Transform Your Industry*. John Wiley & Sons.

Kraus, S., Schiavone, F., Pluzhnikova, A., & Invernizzi, A. C. (2021). Digital transformation in healthcare: Analyzing the current state-of-research. *Journal of Business Research*, *123*, 557–567. doi:10.1016/j.jbusres.2020.10.030

Kubala, M. (2019). *China's second biggest e-commerce player: PDD*. Retrieved October 10, 2014 from https://www.drwealth.com/chinas-second-biggest-e-commerce-player-PDD/

Kumar, G. A., & Ravi Kumar, A. (2019). Employing gamification methods to increase customer engagement in digital marketing. *International Journal of Recent Technology and Engineering*, *8*(2), 869-872. doi:10.35940/ijrte.B1366.0882S819

Kumar, D. (2021). *Marketing in the Digital Age*. Sage.

Kunaviktikul, W., Juntasopeepun, P., Soriano, G. P., Locsin, R. C., & Evangelista, L. S. (in press). Social transformation and social isolation of older adults: Digital technologies, nursing, healthcare. *Collegian (Royal College of Nursing, Australia)*.

Kuznetsova, E., & Sos, P. J. (2020). Management education for digital natives in the 21st century. *Proceedings of the 16th European Conference on Management Leadership and Governance, ECMLG 2020*, 106-112. 10.34190/ELG.20.034

la Cuadra, M. T., Vila-Lopez, N., & Hernandez-Fernández, A. (2020). Could gamification improve visitors' engagement? *International Journal of Tourism Cities*, *6*(2), 317–334. doi:10.1108/IJTC-07-2019-0100

Lal, B. (2014). Framework for Utilization of Global Resources for Knowledge Creation and Application Through Flexible Organizations. In *The Flexible Enterprise* (pp. 164–172). Springer. doi:10.1007/978-81-322-1560-8_10

Landers, R. N. (2019). Gamification misunderstood: How badly executed and rhetorical gamification obscures its transformative potential. *Journal of Management Inquiry*, *28*(2), 137–140. doi:10.1177/1056492618790913

Landers, R. N., Auer, E. M., & Abraham, J. D. (2020). Gamifying a situational judgment test with immersion and control game elements: Effects on applicant reactions and construct validity. *Journal of Managerial Psychology*, *35*(4), 225–239. doi:10.1108/JMP-10-2018-0446

Landers, R. N., Auer, E. M., Collmus, A. B., & Armstrong, M. B. (2018). Gamification science, its history, and future: Definitions and a research agenda. *Simulation & Gaming*, *49*(3), 315–337. doi:10.1177/1046878118774385

Lee, E. (2018, July 26). The Incredible Rise of Pinduoduo, China's Newest Force in E Commerce. *TechCrunch*. Retrieved August 2019 from https://techcrunch.com/2018/07/26/the-incredible-rise-of-pinduoduo/

Lee, H., & Leonas, K. (2018). Consumer experiences, the key to survive in an omni-channel environment: use of virtual technology. *Journal of Textile and Apparel, Technology and Management, 10*(3).

Lee, H., & Xu, Y. (2020). Classification of virtual fitting room technologies in the fashion industry: from the perspective of consumer experience. *International Journal of Fashion Design, Technology and Education, 13*(1), 1-10.

Lee, S. (2013). Linking Technology Roadmapping to Patent Analysis. In Technology Roadmapping for Strategy and Innovation: Chartering the Route to Success (pp. 267-284). Springer. doi:10.1007/978-3-642-33923-3_17

Lee, B., & Saunders, M. (2017). Conducting Case Study Research for Business and Management Students: Mastering Business Research Methods. *Sage (Atlanta, Ga.)*.

Lee, H., & Leonas, K. (2018). Consumer experiences, the key to survive in an omni-channel environment: Use of virtual technology. *Journal of Textile and Apparel Technology Management*, *10*(3), 1–23.

Lee, J. H., & Kim, S. I. (2019). Evaluation of User Experience in AR-based shopping Applications Focused on Ikea Place and Amazon AR View. *Journal of Digital Convergence*, *17*(10), 411–416.

Leinwand, P., & Mani, M. M. (2021). Digitizing Isn't the Same as Digital Transformation. *HBR Org*. Retrieved from https://hbr.org/2021/03/digitizing-isnt-the-same-as-digital-transformation

Leme, M., & Proenca, J. F. (2021). Digital Servitization as a New Research Stream: A Bibliometric Analysis. In *Digital Economy. Emerging Technologies and Business Innovation. ICDEc 2021. Exploring Service Science. Lecture Notes in Business Information Processing (LNBIP)*. Springer Nature Switzerland AG.

Lemon, K. N., & Verhoef, P. C. (2016). Understanding customer experience throughout the customer journey. *Journal of Marketing*, *80*(6), 69–96.

Lemon, K. N., & Verhoef, P. C. (2016). Understanding Customer Experience throughout the Customer Journey. *Journal of Marketing*, *80*(6), 69–96.

Levickaite, R. (2010). Generations X, Y, Z: How social networks form the concept of the world without borders (the case of Lithuania). *LIMES: Cultural Regionalistics*, *3*(2), 170–183.

Lewin, T., & Borroff, R. (2010). *How To Design Cars Like A Pro*. Motorbooks International.

Li, X. L. (2019). "Surgical robot" medical accident liability consultation. *Democracy and the Rule of Law Times*. Retrieved May 24,2021, from http://www.mzyfz.com/cms/benwangzhuanfang/xinwenzhongxin/zuixinbaodao/html/1040/2019-09-27/content-1406397.html

Lieberoth, A., Møller, M., & Marin, A. C. (2015). Deep and shallow gamification in marketing: Thin evidence and the forgotten powers of really good games. In Engaging consumers through branded entertainment and convergent media (pp. 110-126). doi:10.4018/978-1-4666-8342-6.ch006

Lim, D. H., Song, J. H., & Yoon, S. W. (2014). Trends and issues in integrating knowledge management and organizational learning for workplace performance improvement. In N. Chalosfki & M. L. Morris (Eds.), *Handbook of HRD: Theory and application* (pp. 369–385). Jossey-Bass.

Lindič, J., & Marques da Silva, C. (2011). Value proposition as a catalyst for a customer focused innovation. *Management Decision*, *49*(10), 1694–1708. doi:10.1108/00251741111183834

Lissitsa, S., & Kol, O. (2016). Generation X vs. Generation Y–A decade of online shopping. *Journal of Retailing and Consumer Services*, *31*, 304–312. doi:10.1016/j.jretconser.2016.04.015

Liu, D., Zhao, J., He, K. L., Wang, Z. Q., Wei, B., & Huang, Y. H. (2019). *White Paper on Smart Healthcare in the 5G Era*. Internet Healthcare Industry Alliance.

Liu, C., & Arnett, K. P. (2000). Exploring the factors associated with Web site success in the context of electronic commerce. *Information & Management*, *38*(1), 23–33. doi:10.1016/S0378-7206(00)00049-5

Liu, J., Tong, T. W., & Sinfield, J. V. (2021). Toward a resilient complex adaptive system view of business models. *Long Range Planning*, *54*(3), 102030. doi:10.1016/j.lrp.2020.102030

Llopis-Albert, C., Rubio, F., & Valero, F. (2021). Impact of digital transformation on the automotive industry. *Technological Forecasting and Social Change*, *162*, 120343. Advance online publication. doi:10.1016/j.techfore.2020.120343 PMID:33052150

Longhua District Health Bureau. (2020). *Longhua District Central Hospital's Bluetooth IoT body temperature monitoring system: one of China's Top 10 Technological Battles*. Government office of Longhua.

Lopatina, I. (2005). *Context-aware mobile gaming* (Unpublished Master's thesis). Faculty of Science, Department of Computer Science, University of Troms.

Luke, K. (2009). Marketing the new-fashioned way: Connect with your target market through social networking sites. *Journal of Financial Planning*, (November/December), 18–19.

Lu, N., Cheng, N., Zhang, N., Shen, X., & Mark, J. (2014). Connected vehicles: Solutions and challenges. *IEEE Internet of Things Journal*, *1*(4), 289–299. doi:10.1109/JIOT.2014.2327587

Lusch, R. F., & Vargo, S. L. (2006). Service-dominant logic: Reactions, reflections and refinements. *Marketing Theory*, *6*(3), 281–288.

Magretta, J. (2002). Why business models matter. *Harvard Business Review*, *80*(5), 86–92. PMID:12024761

Mahadevan, B. (2000). Business models for Internet-based e-commerce: An anatomy. *California Management Review*, *42*(4), 55–69. doi:10.2307/41166053

Maharani, N., Helmi, A., Mulyana, A., & Hasan, M. (2020). Factors Influencing Purchase Intention on Private Label Products. *The Journal of Asian Finance. Economics and Business*, *7*(11), 939–945. doi:10.13106/jafeb.2020.vol7.no11.939

Mankodiya, K., Martins, R., Francis, J., Garduno, E., Gandhi, R., & Narasimhan, P. (2013). Interactive shopping experience through immersive store environments. In *International Conference of Design, User Experience, and Usability*. Springer.

Mann, D. L. (2021). Will Artificial Intelligence Transform Translational Medicine: (Not So) Elementary, My Dear Watson. *JACC. Basic to Translational Science*, *6*(4), 400–401. doi:10.1016/j.jacbts.2021.03.005 PMID:33997527

Manovich, L. (2017). *Instagram and Contemporary Image*. Available at: http://manovich.net/index.php/projects/instagram-and-contemporary-image

Marabelli, M., Hansen, S., Newell, S., & Frigerio, C. (2017). The Light and Dark Side of the Black Box: Sensor-based Technology in the Automotive Industry. *Communications of the Association for Information Systems*, *34*, 555–580. doi:10.17705/1CAIS.04016

Maraun, D., Wetterhall, F., Ireson, A. M., Chandler, R. E., Kendon, E. J., Widmann, M., Brienen, S., Rust, H. W., Sauter, T., Themeßl, M., Venema, V. K. C., Chun, K. P., Goodess, C. M., Jones, R. G., Onof, C., Vrac, M., & Thiele-Eich, I. (2010). Precipitation downscaling under climate change: Recent developments to bridge the gap between dynamical models and the end user. *Reviews of Geophysics*, *48*(3), RG3003. doi:10.1029/2009RG000314

Mardani, A., Saraji, M. K., Mishra, A. R., & Rani, P. (2020). A novel extended approach under hesitant fuzzy sets to design a framework for assessing the key challenges of digital health interventions adoption during the COVID-19 outbreak. *Applied Soft Computing*, *96*, 106613. doi:10.1016/j.asoc.2020.106613 PMID:32834799

Maree, K. (2020). Planning a research proposal. In *First steps in research* (pp. 25–53). Van Schaik.

Marino, U. (2019). *Enrico Piaggio: Vespa (Enrico Piaggio: Un Songo Italiano)*. Moviheart RAI Fiction.

Matarazzo, M., Penco, L., Profumo, G., & Quaglia, R. (2021). Digital transformation and customer value creation in Made in Italy SMEs: A dynamic capabilities perspective. *Journal of Business Research*, *123*, 642–656. doi:10.1016/j.jbusres.2020.10.033

Mathur, N. (2019). *IEEE Spectrum: IBM Watson has a long way to go before it becomes an efficient AI doctor*. https://hub.packtpub.com/ieee-spectrum-ibm-watson-has-a-long-way-to-go-before-it-becomes-an-efficient-ai-doctor/

Matt, C., Hess, T., & Benlian, A. (2015). Digital Transformation Strategies. *Business & Information Systems Engineering*, *57*(5), 339–343. Advance online publication. doi:10.100712599-015-0401-5

Mattila, M., Yrjölä, M., & Hautamäki, P. (2021). Digital transformation of business-to-business sales: What needs to be unlearned? *Journal of Personal Selling & Sales Management*, *41*(2), 113–129. doi:10.1080/08853134.2021.1916396

McKeown, I., & Philip, G. (2003). Business transformation, information technology and competitive strategies: Learning to fly. *International Journal of Information Management*, *23*(1), 3–24. doi:10.1016/S0268-4012(02)00065-8

McKinsey & Company. (2020). *McKinsey COVID-19 US digital Sentiment Survey (April 25-28, 2020)*. McKinsey & Company. Retrieved from https://www.mckinsey.com

Megill, K. (2013). *Thinking for a Living*. Walter de Gruyter GmbH.

Meng, C. K., & Hamzah, M. (2014). A gamification model to motivate lecturers towards a satisfied job performance. *Proceedings of the 23rd International Business Information Management Association Conference, IBIMA 2014, 1*, 196-200.

Mengelkamp, E., Gärttner, J., Rock, K., Kessler, S., Orsini, L., & Weinhardt, C. (2018). Designing microgrid energy markets: A case study: The Brooklyn Microgrid. *Applied Energy*, *210*, 870–880. doi:10.1016/j.apenergy.2017.06.054

Merriam-Webster Dictionary. (n.d.). *Definition*. Retrieved September 22, 2021, from https://www.merriam-webster.com/dictionary

Merz, M. A., Zarantonello, L., & Grappi, S. (2018). How valuable are your customers in the brand value co-creation process? The development of a Customer Co-Creation Value (CCCV) scale. *Journal of Business Research*, *82*, 79–89.

Meyer, C., & Schwager, A. (2007). Understanding customer experience. *Harvard Business Review*, *85*(2), 116.

Meyer, C., & Schwager, A. (2007). Understanding Customer Experience. *Harvard Business Review*. PMID:17345685

Meyerson, M. (2010). *Success secrets of social media marketing superstars*. Entrepreneur Press.

Microsoft Corporation. (2019). *Retail trends report, 2019 Retail Trends Report.* https://info.microsoft.com/rs/157-GQE-382/images/2019%20Retail%20Trends%20Report.pdf

Mikalef, P., & Pateli, A. (2017). Information technology-enabled dynamic capabilities and their indirect effect on competitive performance: Findings from PLS-SEM and fsQCA. *Journal of Business Research*, (70), 1–16.

Ministry of Science and Technology of China. (2019). Guidelines for the Construction of the National New Generation of Artificial Intelligence Open Innovation Platform (Ministry of Science and Technology Publication [2019] No. 265). Beijing: China General Office of the State Council.

Mishra, D., Gunasekaran, A., Papadopoulos, T., & Childe, S. J. (2018). Big data and supply chain management: A review and bibliometric analysis. *Annals of Operations Research*, *270*(1), 313–336.

Mishra, S., & Malhotra, G. (2020). The gamification of in-game advertising: Examining the role of psychological ownership and advertisement intrusiveness. *International Journal of Information Management*. Advance online publication. doi:10.1016/j.ijinfomgt.2020.102245 PMID:33012944

Mitchell, R., Schuster, L., & Drennan, J. (2017). Understanding how gamification influences behavior in social marketing. *Australasian Marketing Journal*, *25*(1), 12–19. doi:10.1016/j.ausmj.2016.12.001

Mize, S. R. (2009). *Social network benefits*. Academic Press.

Molinari, L. K., Abratt, R., & Dion, P. (2008). Satisfaction, quality and value and effects on repurchase and positive word-of-mouth behavioral intentions in a B2B services context. *Journal of Services Marketing*, *22*(5), 363–373.

Moncrief, W. C., Marshall, G. W., & Rudd, J. M. (2015). Social media and related technology: Drivers of change in managing the contemporary sales force. *Business Horizons*, *58*(1), 45–55. doi:10.1016/j.bushor.2014.09.009

Moody, G. (2007). The Netscape Story: From Mosaic to Mozilla. *Computerworld UK*, *12*(1).

Morgeson, F. V., Mithas, S., Keiningham, T. L., & Aksoy, L. (2011). An investigation of the cross-national determinants of customer satisfaction. *Journal of the Academy of Marketing Science*, *39*, 198–215.

Morris, M., Schindehutte, M., & Allen, J. (2005). The entrepreneur's business model: Toward a unified perspective. *Journal of Business Research*, *58*(6), 726–735. doi:10.1016/j.jbusres.2003.11.001

Moscardo, G. (2020). The story turn in tourism: Forces and futures. *Journal of Tourism Futures*. doi:10.1108/JTF-11-2019-0131

Moshrefjavadi, M. H., Dolatabadi, H. R., Nourbakhsh, M., Poursaeedi, A., & Asadollahi, A. (2012). An analysis of factors affecting on online shopping behavior of consumers. *International Journal of Marketing Studies*, *4*(5), 81. doi:10.5539/ijms.v4n5p81

Muhuri, P. K., Shukla, A. K., & Abraham, A. (2019). Industry 4.0: A bibliometric analysis and detailed overview. *Engineering Applications of Artificial Intelligence*, *78*, 218–235.

Mulcahy, R. F., Russell-Bennett, R., Zainuddin, N., & Kuhn, K. (2018). Designing gamified transformative and social marketing services: An investigation of serious m-games. *Journal of Service Theory and Practice*, *28*(1), 26–51. doi:10.1108/JSTP-02-2017-0034

Mulcahy, R., Russell-Bennett, R., & Iacobucci, D. (2020). Designing gamified apps for sustainable consumption: A field study. *Journal of Business Research*, *106*, 377–387. doi:10.1016/j.jbusres.2018.10.026

Muniz, A. M. Jr, & O'Guinn, T. C. (2001). Brand community. *The Journal of Consumer Research*, *27*(4), 412–432. doi:10.1086/319618

Nadkarni, S., & Prügl, R. (2021). Digital transformation: A review, synthesis and opportunities for future research. *Management Review Quarterly*, *71*(2), 233–341. doi:10.100711301-020-00185-7

Nakamura, J., & Csikszentmihalyi, M. (2014). The concept of flow. In Flow and the foundations of positive psychology (pp. 239-263). Springer Publishing. doi:10.1007/978-94-017-9088-8_16

Nambisan, S., Lyytinen, K., Majchrzak, A., & Song, M. (2017). Digital innovation management: Reinventing innovation management research in a digital world. *Management Information Systems Quarterly*, *41*(1), 223–238.

National Internet Emergency Center. (2021). Digital China Development Report in 2020 (Beijing ICP No. 14042428). Beijing: China National Internet Information Office.

National Party Media. (2020). *2020 China Digital Transformation Successful Case Collection*. https://www.hubpd.com/c/2020-05-13/960082.shtml

Naughton, J. (2019). How Microsoft reinvented itself. *The Guardian*. Retrieved from https://www.theguardian.com/commentisfree/2019/may/12/how-microsoft-was-resurrected-as-the-third-most-valuable-tech-company-1-trillion-dollars

NAZIR, S. (2017). E-Commerce Perception and Adoption-A Study of Tour and Travel Operators of J&K State. *Amity Global Business Review*, *12*(2).

Nemat, R. (2011). Taking a look at different types of e-commerce. *World Applied Programming*, *1*(2), 100–104.

Newman, D. (2020). *Top ten digital transformation trends for 2021*. https://www.forbes.com/sites/danielnewman/2020/09/21/top-10-digital-transformation-trends-for-2021/?sh=3c85f180c6f4

Nguyen, D., & Meixner, G. (2020). *Comparison user engagement of gamified and non-gamified augmented reality assembly training*. doi:10.1007/978-3-030-37534-8_8

Nie, W., & Feng, Y. F. (2019, February). PDD: E-Commerce for the Underserved – A Chinese Online Merchant at the Crossroads. *IMD*. Retrieved October 2020 from https://www.imd.org/research-knowledge/articles/pdd-ecommerce-for-the-underserved/

Nielsen, J. (2000). *Why You Only Need to Test with 5 Users, NN/g Nielsen Norman Group*. https://www.nngroup.com/articles/why-you-only-need-to-test-with-5-users/

Niemimaa, M., Järveläinen, J., Heikkilä, M., & Heikkilä, J. (2019). Business continuity of business models: Evaluating the resilience of business models for contingencies. *International Journal of Information Management*, *49*, 208–216. doi:10.1016/j.ijinfomgt.2019.04.010

Nobre, H., & Ferreira, A. (2017). Gamification as a platform for brand co-creation experiences. *Journal of Brand Management*, *24*(4), 349–361. doi:10.105741262-017-0055-3

Noorbehbahani, F., Salehi, F., & Jafar Zadeh, R. (2019). A systematic mapping study on gamification applied to e-marketing. *Journal of Research in Interactive Marketing*, *13*(3), 392–410. doi:10.1108/JRIM-08-2018-0103

O'Fallon, C., & Sullivan, C. (2004). Personalised marketing-improving evaluation. *Transport Engineering in Australia, 9*(2), 85–101.

Obringer, L. A. (2007). *How Advergaming Works.* http://money.howstuffworks.com/ advergaming.htm

Ögel Aydın, S., & Argan, M. (2021). Understanding how gamification influences consumers' dietary preferences. *Journal of Social Marketing, 11*(2), 82–123. doi:10.1108/JSOCM-09-2019-0137

Olsson, T. (2012). *User expectations and experiences of mobile augmented reality services* (Doctoral dissertation). Tampere University of Technology.

Olsson, T., & Salo, M. (2011, October). Online user survey on current mobile augmented reality applications. In *2011 10th IEEE International Symposium on Mixed and Augmented Reality* (pp. 75-84). IEEE. 10.1109/ISMAR.2011.6092372

Olsson, T., Lagerstam, E., Kärkkäinen, T., & Väänänen-Vainio-Mattila, K. (2013). Expected user experience of mobile augmented reality services: A user study in the context of shopping centres. *Personal and Ubiquitous Computing, 17*(2), 287–304. doi:10.100700779-011-0494-x

Örnek, N. (2021). *Nasıl Olunur? Bego Abdulhalim Demir.* Retrieved December 18, 2021, from https://spoti.fi/3sbcF86

Osterwalder, A., & Pigneur, Y. (2010). *Business Model Generation A Handbook for Visionaries, Game Changers, and Challengers.* John Wiley & Sons, Inc.

Ovodenko, A. A., Peshkova, G. Y., & Zlobina, O. V. (2020). Digital Evolution of Consumer Behavior and its Impact on Digital Transformation of Small and Medium Business Sustained Development Strategy. In *2nd International Scientific and Practical Conference on Digital Economy (ISCDE2020)* (pp. 424-428). Atlantis Press. 10.2991/aebmr.k.201205.071

Ozturkcan, S. (2021). Service innovation: Using augmented reality in the IKEA Place app. *Journal of Information Technology Teaching Cases, 11*(1), 8–13. doi:10.1177/2043886920947110

Pachoulakis, I., & Kapetanakis, K. (2012). Augmented reality platforms for virtual fitting rooms. *The International Journal of Multimedia & Its Applications, 4*(4), 35–46. doi:10.5121/ijma.2012.4404

Paknejad, F., Mosaddad, S. H., & Naeini, H. S. (2021). Purchasing and consumption modification among Iranians throughout gamification. *International Journal of Industrial Engineering and Production Research, 32*(1), 121–132. doi:10.22068/ijiepr.32.1.121

Panasenko, S. V., Nikishin, A. F., Mayorova, E. A., Boris, O. A., & Murtuzalieva, T. V. (2018). Innovative approach to fitness industry development. *Espacios, 39*(41).

Pantano, E. (Ed.). (2020). Retail Futures: The Good, the Bad and the Ugly of the Digital Transformation. Emerald Group Publishing.

Pantano, E. (2010). New technologies and retailing: Trends and directions. *Journal of Retailing and Consumer Services, 17*(3), 171–172.

Pantano, E. (2014). Innovation drivers in retail industry. *International Journal of Information Management, 34*(3), 344–350.

Pantano, E. (2016). Benefits and risks associated with time choice of innovating in retail settings. *International Journal of Retail & Distribution Management, 44*(1), 58–70.

Pantano, E., & Gandini, A. (2017). Exploring the forms of sociality mediated by innovative technologies in retail settings. *Computers in Human Behavior, 77*, 367–373.

Pantano, E., & Gandini, A. (2018). Shopping as a 'networked experience': An emerging framework in the retail industry. *International Journal of Retail & Distribution Management*, *46*(7), 690–704.

Pantano, E., & Laria, G. (2012). Innovation in retail process: From consumers' experience to immersive store design. *Journal of Technology Management & Innovation*, *7*(3), 198–206.

Pantano, E., & Naccarato, G. (2010). Entertainment in retailing: The influences of advanced technologies. *Journal of Retailing and Consumer Services*, *17*(3), 200–204.

Pantano, E., Priporas, C. V., & Dennis, C. (2018). A new approach to retailing for successful competition in the new smart scenario. *International Journal of Retail & Distribution Management*, *46*(3), 264–282.

Pantano, E., Rese, A., & Baier, D. (2017). Enhancing the online decision-making process by using augmented reality: A two-country comparison of youth markets. *Journal of Retailing and Consumer Services*, *38*, 81–95.

Pantano, E., & Servidio, R. (2012). Modeling innovative points of sales through virtual and immersive technologies. *Journal of Retailing and Consumer Services*, *19*(3), 279–286.

Pantano, E., & Timmermans, H. (2014). What is smart for retailing? *Procedia Environmental Sciences*, *22*, 101–107.

Pantano, E., & Viassone, M. (2015). Engaging consumers on new integrated multichannel retail settings: Challenges for retailers. *Journal of Retailing and Consumer Services*, *25*, 106–114.

Parameswaran, M., Susarla, A., & Whinston, A. B. (2001). P2P networking: An information sharing alternative. *Computer*, *34*(7), 31–38. doi:10.1109/2.933501

Parasuraman, A., Zeithaml, V. A., & Malhotra, A. (2005). ES-QUAL: A multiple-item scale for assessing electronic service quality. *Journal of Service Research*, *7*(3), 213–233. doi:10.1177/1094670504271156

Parida, V., Sjödin, D., & Reim, W. (2019). Reviewing literature on digitalization, business model innovation, and sustainable industry: Past achievements and future promises. *Sustainability*, *11*(2), 1–18. doi:10.3390u11020391

Parise, S., Guinan, P. J., & Kafka, R. (2016). Solving the crisis of immediacy: How digital technology can transform the customer experience. *Business Horizons*, *59*(4), 411–420. doi:10.1016/j.bushor.2016.03.004

Parment, A. (2013). Generation Y vs. Baby Boomers: Shopping behavior, buyer involvement and implications for retailing. *Journal of Retailing and Consumer Services*, *20*(2), 189–199. doi:10.1016/j.jretconser.2012.12.001

Parment, A. (2014). *Auto Brand: Building successful car brands for the future*. Kogan Page. doi:10.4271/0749469293

Payne, A. F., Storbacka, K., & Frow, P. (2008). Managing the co-creation of value. *Journal of the Academy of Marketing Science*, *36*, 83–96.

Payne, A., Frow, P., & Eggert, A. (2017). The customer value proposition: Evolution, development, and application in marketing. *Journal of the Academy of Marketing Science*, *45*, 467–489.

Payne, A., Storbacka, K., Frow, P., & Knox, S. (2009). Co-creating brands: Diagnosing and designing the relationship experience. *Journal of Business Research*, *62*(3), 379–389.

PDD. (2019b, September 30). *PDD Inc. Q3 2019 financial report*. Retrieved March 2021 from https://investor.PDD.com/financial-information/quarterly-results

PDD. (2020a). *PDD Inc. 2019 annual report*. Retrieved March 2021 from https://investor.PDD.com/financial-information/annual-reports

PDD. (2020b, September 30). *PDD Inc. Q3 2020 financial report*. Retrieved March 2021 from https://investor.PDD.com/financial-information/quarterly-results

People's Daily. (2020). *China's Digital Transformation Successful Cases Announced in 2020*. http://ip.people.com.cn/n1/2020/0529/c136655-31728749.html

Perkin, N., & Abraham, P. (2017). *Building the Agile Business through Digital Transformation*. Kogan Page.

Perspectives, C. (2018). *Asian Paints: The Digital Odyssey of a Serial Reinventor*. Retrieved from https://www.cognizant.com/perspectives/asian-paints-the-digital-odyssey-of-a-serial-reinventor

Persse, J. (2012). *The ITIL Process Manual: Key Processes and their Application*. Van Haren.

Piccinini, E., Hanelt, A., Gregory, R., & Kolbe, L. (2015). Transforming industrial business: The impact of digital transformation on automotive organizations. *Proceedings of the International Conference on Information Systems*. Retrieved from https://aisel.aisnet.org/icis2015/proceedings/GeneralIS/5/

Piccinini, E., Gregory, R. W., & Kolbe, L. M. (2015). Changes in the producer-consumer relationship-towards digital transformation. *Changes (Hove, England)*, *3*(4), 1634–1648.

Pihir, I., Tomičić-Pupek, K., & Furjan, M. (2019). Digital Transformation Playground - Literature Review and Framework of Concepts. *Journal of Information and Organizational Sciences*, *43*(1), 33–48. doi:10.31341/jios.43.1.3

Piligrimiene, Z., Dovaliene, A., & Virvilaite, R. (2015). Consumer engagement in value co-creation: What kind of value it creates for company? *The Engineering Economist*, *26*(4), 452–460. doi:10.5755/j01.ee.26.4.12502

Pinduoduo (PDD). (2019a, June 28). *PDD Inc. Pinduoduo's "New Brand Initiative" Reshapes Retail Industry by Prioritizing Consumers' Needs*. Retrieved August 2021 from https://investor.pinduoduo.com/node/6831/pdf

Pine, B. J., & Gilmore, J. H. (2011). *The experience economy*. Harvard Business Press.

PingWest. (2018). *PDD's Factory of Creation*. Retrieved August 2019 from https://www.pingwest.com/a/160720

Pires, G., Stanton, J., & Eckford, A. (2004). Influences on the perceived risk of purchasing online. *Journal of Consumer Behaviour: An International Research Review*, *4*(2), 118–131. doi:10.1002/cb.163

Pizzi, G., Vannucci, V., & Aiello, G. (2020). Branding in the time of virtual reality: Are virtual store brand perceptions real? *Journal of Business Research*, *119*, 502–510.

Poncin, I., & Mimoun, M. S. B. (2014). The impact of "e-atmospherics" on physical stores. *Journal of Retailing and Consumer Services*, *21*(5), 851–859. doi:10.1016/j.jretconser.2014.02.013

Pope, M. (2017). *Understanding Planned Obsolescence: Unsustainability through production, consumption and waste generation*. Kogan Page.

Popescu, I. C. (2003). *Comunicarea in marketing: Concepte, tehnici, strategii*. Editura Uranus.

Porter, M. E. (2001). *Strategy and the Internet*. Ilustraciones Gibbs.

Porter, M. (2008). The five competitive forces that shape strategy. *Harvard Business Review*, *86*(1), 25–40. PMID:18271320

Poushneh, A., & Vasquez-Parraga, A. Z. (2017). Discernible impact of augmented reality on retail customer's experience, satisfaction and willingness to buy. *Journal of Retailing and Consumer Services*, *34*, 229–234.

Poushneh, A., & Vasquez-Parraga, A. Z. (2017a). Customer dissatisfaction and satisfaction with augmented reality in shopping and entertainment. *Journal of Consumer Satisfaction, Dissatisfaction & Complaining Behavior*, 30.

Prahalad, C. K., & Ramaswamy, V. (2000). *Co-opting customer competence.* https://hbr.org/2000/01/co-opting-customer-competence

Prahalad, C. K., & Ramaswamy, V. (2004). Co-creating unique value with customers. *Strategy and Leadership*, *32*(3), 4–9.

Preston, R. (2016). General Motors' IT Transformation: Building Downturn Resistant Profitability. *Forbes BrandVoice.* Retrieved from https://www.forbes.com/sites/oracle/2016/04/14/general-motors-it-transformation-building-downturn-resistant-profitability/#af9a51e1222f

Priem, R. L., Wenzel, M., & Koch, J. (2018). Demand-side strategy and business models: Putting value creation for consumers center stage. *Long Range Planning*, *51*(1), 22–31.

Proka, A., Beers, P. J., & Loorbach, D. (2018). Transformative Business Models for Sustainability Transitions. In L. Moratis, F. Melissen, & S. Idowu (Eds.), *Sustainable Business Models. CSR, Sustainability, Ethics & Governance.* Springer. doi:10.1007/978-3-319-73503-0_2

Puccinelli, N. M., Goodstein, R. C., Grewal, D., Price, R., Raghubir, P., & Stewart, D. (2009). Customer experience management in retailing: Understanding the buying process. *Journal of Retailing*, *85*(1), 15–30. doi:10.1016/j.jretai.2008.11.003

Punjaisri, K., & Wilson, A. (2011). Internal branding process: Key mechanisms, outcomes and moderating factors. *European Journal of Marketing.*

Qiao, X., Ren, P., Dustdar, S., Liu, L., Ma, H., & Chen, J. (2019). Web AR: A Promising Future for Mobile Augmented Reality-State of the Art, Challenges, and Insights. *Proceedings of the IEEE, 107*(4), 651–666. doi:10.1109/JPROC.2019.2895105

Qin, H., Osatuyi, B., & Xu, L. (2021). How mobile augmented reality applications affect continuous use and purchase intentions: A cognition-affect-conation perspective. *Journal of Retailing and Consumer Services*, *63*, 102680.

Qin, H., Peak, D. A., & Prybutok, V. (2021). A virtual market in your pocket: How does mobile augmented reality (MAR) influence consumer decision making? *Journal of Retailing and Consumer Services*, *58*, 102337.

Raimundo, R., & Rosário, A. (2021). Blockchain system in the Higher Education. *European Journal of Investigation in Health, Psychology and Education, 11*(1), 276-293. doi:10.3390/ejihpe1101002

Ramadan, Z. B., & Farah, M. F. (2017). The Pokémonisation of the first moment of truth. *International Journal of Web Based Communities*, *13*(2), 262–277.

Ranjan, K. R., & Read, S. (2016). Value co-creation: Concept and measurement. *Journal of the Academy of Marketing Science*, *44*, 290–315.

Ranjan, K. R., & Read, S. (2019). Bringing the individual into the co-creation of value. *Journal of Services Marketing*, *33*(7), 904–920.

Rao, V. R. (2011). Collaborative government to employee (G2E): Issues and challenges to e government. *Journal of e-Governance, 34*(4), 214-229.

Reeves, M., Zeng, M., & Venjara, A. (2015, June). The Self-Tuning Enterprise. *Harvard Business Review.*

Reinartz, W., Wiegand, N., & Imschloss, M. (2019). The Impact of Digital Transformation on the Retailing Value Chain. *International Journal of Research in Marketing*, *36*(3), 350–366.

Reinartz, W., Wiegand, N., & Imschloss, M. (2019). The impact of digital transformation on the retailing value chain. *International Journal of Research in Marketing*, *36*(3), 350–366. doi:10.1016/j.ijresmar.2018.12.002

Reinwald, F., Berger, M., Stoik, C., Platzer, M., & Damyanovic, D. (2014). Augmented reality at the service of participatory urban planning and community informatics – a case study from Vienna. *The Journal of Community Informatics*, *10*(3).

Ren, J., Yusuf, Y. Y., & Burns, N. D. (2009). A decision-support framework for agile enterprise partnering. *International Journal of Advanced Manufacturing Technology*, *41*(1–2), 180–192.

Rese, A., Baier, D., Geyer-Schulz, A., & Schreiber, S. (2017). How augmented reality apps are accepted by consumers: A comparative analysis using scales and opinions. *Technological Forecasting and Social Change*, *124*, 306–319.

Rese, A., Schreiber, S., & Baier, D. (2014). Technology acceptance modeling of augmented reality at the point of sale: Can surveys be replaced by an analysis of online reviews? *Journal of Retailing and Consumer Services*, *21*(5), 869–876. doi:10.1016/j.jretconser.2014.02.011

Rezaei, M., Vahid, J. S., Cao, D. M., & Mahdiraji, H. A. (2021). Key indicators of ethical challenges in digital healthcare: A combined Delphi exploration and confirmative factor analysis approach with evidence from Khorasan province in Iran. *Technological Forecasting and Social Change*, *167*, 120724. doi:10.1016/j.techfore.2021.120724

Riasanow, T., Galic, G., & Böhm, M. (2017). Digital transformation in the automotive industry: Towards a generic value network. In *Proceedings of the 25th European Conference on Information Systems* (pp. 3191-3201). Academic Press.

Richter, G., Raban, D. R., & Rafaeli, S. (2015). *Studying gamification: The effect of rewards and incentives on motivation*. Gamification in Education and Business. doi:10.1007/978-3-319-10208-5_2

Riepe, A., & Pisano, P. (2015). Business models in a new digital culture: The open tail model. *Symphonya Emerging Issues in Management, 75-88.*

Ring, J. (1996). *Reklam Dünyasının İçyüzü*. Milliyet Yayınları.

Rintamäki, T., Kanto, A., Kuusela, H., & Spence, M. T. (2006). Decomposing the value of department store shopping into utilitarian, hedonic and social dimensions: Evidence from Finland. *International Journal of Retail & Distribution Management*, *34*(1), 6–24. doi:10.1108/09590550610642792

Rintamäki, T., & Saarijärvi, H. (2021). An integrative framework for managing customer value propositions. *Journal of Business Research*, *134*, 754–764.

Ripeanu, M. (2001, August). Peer-to-peer architecture case study: Gnutella network. *Peer-to-Peer Computing, 2001. Proceedings. First International Conference on IEEE*, 99-100.

Ritchie, R. (2019). *Maersk: Springing back from a catastrophic cyber-attack*. I-CIO.com

Roberts, D., Hughes, M., & Kertbo, K. (2014). Exploring consumers' motivations to engage in innovation through co-creation activities. *European Journal of Marketing*, *48*(1/2), 147–169.

Robson, K. (2019). Motivating professional student behavior through a gamified personal branding assignment. *Journal of Marketing Education*, *41*(2), 154–164. doi:10.1177/0273475318823847

Rogers, D. (2016). *The Digital Transformation Playbook: Rethink Your Business for the Digital Age*. Columbia Business School Publishing. doi:10.7312/roge17544

Romano, B., Sands, S., & Pallant, J. I. (2021). Augmented reality and the customer journey: An exploratory study. *Australasian Marketing Journal*, *29*(4), 354–363. doi:10.1016/j.ausmj.2020.06.010

Rosário, A. (2021). Research-Based Guidelines for Marketing Information Systems. *International Journal of Business Strategy and Automation*, *2*(1), 1–16. doi:10.4018/IJBSA.20210101.oa1

Rosário, A., & Cruz, R. (2019). Determinants of Innovation in Digital Marketing, Innovation Policy and Trends in the Digital Age. *Journal of Reviews on Global Economics*, *8*, 1722–1731. doi:10.6000/1929-7092.2019.08.154

Rosário, A., Fernandes, F., Raimundo, R., & Cruz, R. (2021). Determinants of Nascent Entrepreneurship Development. In A. Carrizo Moreira & J. G. Dantas (Eds.), *Handbook of Research on Nascent Entrepreneurship and Creating New Ventures* (pp. 172–193). IGI Global. doi:10.4018/978-1-7998-4826-4.ch008

Rueckel, J., Sperl, J., Kaestle, S., Hoppe, B., Fink, N., Rudolph, J., Schwarze, V., Geyer, T., Strobl, F., Ricke, J., Ingrisch, M., & Sabel, B. (2021). Reduction of missed thoracic findings in emergency whole-body computed tomography using artificial intelligence assistance. *Quantitative Imaging in Medicine and Surgery*, *11*(6), 2486–2498. doi:10.21037/qims-20-1037 PMID:34079718

Ruffino, P. (2017). Engagement and the quantified self: Uneventful relationships with ghostly companions. In Self-tracking: Empirical and philosophical investigations (pp. 11-25). doi:10.1007/978-3-319-65379-2_2

Rundle, A. G., Torsiello, N. E., Davis, B. M., Griffin, B., Neugut, A. I., & Levy, D. L. (2020). Analyses of Employer Medical Claims Data to Assess Receipt of High-Priority Preventive Health Services. *American Journal of Preventive Medicine*, *58*(5), 715–723. doi:10.1016/j.amepre.2019.12.016 PMID:32173164

Sabri, E. (2019). *Technology Optimization and Change Management for Successful Digital Supply Chains*. IGI Global

Sahu, N., Deng, H., & Mollah, A. (2018). Investigating the Critical Success Factors of Digital Transformation for Improving Customer Experience. *CONFIRM 2018 Proceedings*. Retrieved from https://aisel.aisnet.org/confirm2018/18

Saleme, P., Dietrich, T., Pang, B., & Parkinson, J. (2020). A gamified approach to promoting empathy in children. *Journal of Social Marketing*, *10*(3), 321–337. doi:10.1108/JSOCM-11-2019-0204

Salo, J. (2009). Mobile games advertising in international marketing context. *Journal of International Marketing and Exporting*, 14.

Samar, R., & Mazuri, A. G. (2019). Does gamified elements influence on user's intention to adopt internet banking with integration of UTAUT and general self-confidence? *International Journal of Business Excellence*, *19*(3), 394–414. doi:10.1504/IJBEX.2019.102835

Sambamurthy, V., Bharadwaj, A., & Grover, V. (2003). Shaping agility through digital options: Reconceptualizing the role of information technology in contemporary firms. *Management Information Systems Quarterly*, *27*(2), 237–263.

Sanchez, A., & Carro, B. (2017). *Digital Services in the 21st Century: A Strategic and Business Perspective*. John Wiley & Sons. doi:10.1002/9781119314905

Sands, S., Ferraro, C., Campbell, C., & Pallant, J. (2016). Segmenting multichannel consumers across search, purchase and after-sales. *Journal of Retailing and Consumer Services*, *33*, 62–71. doi:10.1016/j.jretconser.2016.08.001

Sangvikar, B., Kolte, A., & Pawar, A. (2019). Competitive Strategies for Unorganised Retail Business: Understanding Structure, Operations, and Profitability of Small Mom and Pop Stores in India. *International Journal on Emerging Technologies*, *10*(3), 253–259.

Sarkar, R., & Das, S. (2017). Online shopping vs Offline shopping: A comparative study. *International Journal of Scientific Research in Science and Technology*, *3*(1).

Schiele, K. (2018). Utilizing gamification to promote sustainable practices: Making sustainability fun and rewarding. In Handbook of engaged sustainability (pp. 427-444). doi:10.1007/978-3-319-71312-0_16

Schneebergerb, D., Stögera, K., Kiesebergc, P., & Holzingerd, A. (2021). Legal aspects of data cleansing in medical AI. *Computer Law & Security Review*, *42*, 105587. doi:10.1016/j.clsr.2021.105587

Scholz, J., & Duffy, K. (2018). We are at home: How augmented reality reshapes mobile marketing and consumer-brand relationships. *Journal of Retailing and Consumer Services*, *44*, 11–23.

Scholz, J., & Duffy, K. (2018). We ARe at home: How augmented reality reshapes mobile marketing and consumer-brand relationships. *Journal of Retailing and Consumer Services*, *44*, 11–23. doi:10.1016/j.jretconser.2018.05.004

Scholz, J., & Smith, A. N. (2016). Augmented reality: Designing immersive experiences that maximize consumer engagement. *Business Horizons*, *59*(2), 149–161. doi:10.1016/j.bushor.2015.10.003

Schonfeld, E. (2009, Oct. 26). Twitter finds growth abroad with 58.4 million global visitors in September. *TechCrunch*.

Scopus. (n.d.). *Scopus (keyword: "business model")*. Retrieved December 14, 2021, from https://bit.ly/3DUwX86

Seetharaman, P. (2020). Business models shifts: Impact of Covid-19. *International Journal of Information Management*, *54*, 102173. doi:10.1016/j.ijinfomgt.2020.102173 PMID:32834338

Seifert, T., & Hedderson, C. (2010). Intrinsic motivation and flow in skateboarding: An ethnographic study. *Journal of Happiness Studies*, *11*(3), 277–292. doi:10.100710902-009-9140-y

Seiffert-Brockmann, J., Weitzl, W., & Henriks, M. (2018). Stakeholder engagement through gamification: Effects of user motivation on psychological and behavioral stakeholder reactions. *Journal of Communication Management (London)*, *22*(1), 67–78. doi:10.1108/JCOM-12-2016-0096

Seiffert, J., & Nothhaft, H. (2015). The missing media: The procedural rhetoric of computer games. *Public Relations Review*, *41*(2), 254–263. doi:10.1016/j.pubrev.2014.11.011

Senadeera, M. P., Quinn, T., Jacobs, S., Le, V., & Coghlan, S. (2021). The three ghosts of medical AI: Can the black-box present deliver? *Artificial Intelligence in Medicine*, 102158. PMID:34511267

Séraphin, H. (2019). *Marketing and diaspora tourism: Visual online learning materials as tools to attract the Haitian diaspora 'New generation'.* doi:10.1007/978-3-319-91095-6_25

Séraphin, H., Butcher, J., & Korstanje, M. (2017). Challenging the negative images of Haiti at a pre-visit stage using visual online learning materials. *Journal of Policy Research in Tourism, Leisure & Events*, *9*(2), 169–181. doi:10.1080/19407963.2016.1261146

Shafer, S. M., Smith, H. J., & Linder, J. C. (2005). The power of business models. *Business Horizons*, *48*(3), 199–207. doi:10.1016/j.bushor.2004.10.014

Shankar, V., Kalyanam, K., Setia, P., Golmohammadi, A., Tirunillai, S., Douglass, T., ... Waddoups, R. (2021). How technology is changing retail. *Journal of Retailing*, *97*(1), 13–27.

Shannon, R., Stabeler, M., Quigley, A., & Nixon, P. (2009). Profiling and targeting opportunities in pervasive advertising. *1st Workshop on Pervasive Advertising*.

Shao, A., & Li, H. (2021). How do utilitarian versus hedonic products influence choice preferences: Mediating effect of social comparison. *Psychology and Marketing*, *38*(8), 1250–1261. doi:10.1002/mar.21520

Sharma, M. (2014). Advergaming–The Novel Instrument in the Advertising. *Procedia Economics and Finance*, *11*, 249. doi:10.1016/S2212-5671(14)00193-2

Shdaimah, C., Stahl, R., & Schram, S. (2011). *Change Research: A Case Study on Collaborative Methods for Social Workers and Advocates*. Columbia University.

Sherehiy, B., Karwowski, W., & Layer, J. K. (2007). A review of enterprise agility: Concepts, frameworks, and attributes. *International Journal of Industrial Ergonomics*, *37*(5), 445–460.

Sholeh, A., & Rusdi, A. (2019). *A New Measurement of Instagram Addiction: Psychometric Properties of The Instagram Addiction Scale*. TIAS.

Shpakova, A., Dörfler, V., & MacBryde, J. (2019). *Gamifying innovation and innovating through gamification*. doi:10.1007/978-3-030-11542-5_10

Shpakova, A., Dörfler, V., & MacBryde, J. (2020). Gamifying the process of innovating. Innovation. *Organization and Management*, *22*(4), 488–502. doi:10.1080/14479338.2019.1642763

Sigala, M. (2015). Gamification for crowdsourcing marketing practices: Applications and benefits in tourism. In Advances in crowdsourcing (pp. 129-146). doi:10.1007/978-3-319-18341-1_11

Silva, R., Rodrigues, R., & Leal, C. (2019). Play it again: How game-based learning improves flow in accounting and marketing education. *Accounting Education*, *28*(5), 484–507. doi:10.1080/09639284.2019.1647859

Simonson, I. (1999). The Effect of Product Assortment on Buyer Preferences. *Journal of Retailing*, *75*(3), 347–370. doi:10.1016/S0022-4359(99)00012-3

Singh, J., & Sharma, G. (2013). Organizational agility: What it is, what it is not, and why it matters. *Academy of Management Proceedings*, *2013*(1), 1–40.

Singh, P., Singh, G., & Kaur, G. (2021). Integrating Artificial Intelligence/Internet of Things Technologies to Support Medical Devices and Systems. In G. Kaur (Ed.), *Artificial Intelligence to Solve Pervasive Internet of Things Issues* (pp. 331–349). Academic Press. doi:10.1016/B978-0-12-818576-6.00017-4

Sitkin, S. B., & Pablo, A. L. (1992). Reconceptualizing the determinants of risk behavior. *Academy of Management Review*, *17*(1), 9–38. doi:10.5465/amr.1992.4279564

Smith, M. J., & Bean, S. (2019). AI and Ethics in Medical Radiation Sciences. *Journal of Medical Imaging and Radiation Sciences*, *50*(4), S24–S26. doi:10.1016/j.jmir.2019.08.005 PMID:31563532

Snoj, B., Pisnik Korda, A., & Mumel, D. (2004). The relationships among perceived quality, perceived risk and perceived product value. *Journal of Product and Brand Management*, *13*(3), 156–167.

Snyder, C. R. (1992). Product scarcity by need for uniqueness interaction: A consumer catch-22 carousel? *Basic and Applied Social Psychology*, *13*(1), 9–24.

Solakis, K., Peña-Vinces, J., Lopez-Bonilla, J. M., & Aguado, L. F. (2021). From value co-creation to positive experiences and customer satisfaction. A customer perspective in the hotel industry. *Technological and Economic Development of Economy*, *27*(4), 948–969.

Sood, S. (2012). The death of social media in start-up companies and the rise of s-commerce: Convergence of e-commerce, complexity and social media. *Journal of Electronic Commerce in Organizations*, *10*(2), 1–15.

Soopramanien, D. G., & Robertson, A. (2007). Adoption and usage of online shopping: An empirical analysis of the characteristics of "buyers""browsers" and "non-internet shoppers". *Journal of Retailing and Consumer Services*, *14*(1), 73–82. doi:10.1016/j.jretconser.2006.04.002

Spyropoulos, C. D. (2000). AI planning and scheduling in the medical hospital environment. *Artificial Intelligence in Medicine, 20*(2), 101–111. doi:10.1016/S0933-3657(00)00059-2 PMID:10936748

Srinivasan, S. S., Anderson, R., & Ponnavolu, K. (2002). Customer loyalty in e-commerce: An exploration of its antecedents and consequences. *Journal of Retailing, 78*(1), 41–50. doi:10.1016/S0022-4359(01)00065-3

State Council of China. (2015). Guiding Opinions on Actively Promoting the "Internet +" Action (China National Publication [2015] No. 40). Beijing: China General Office of the State Council.

State Council of China. (2016). "Thirteenth Five-Year" National Informatization Plan (China National Publication [2016] No. 73). Beijing: China General Office of the State Council.

State Council of China. (2016). Guiding Opinions on Promoting and Regulating the Application and Development of Big Data in Health Care (China State Council [2016] No. 47). Beijing: China General Office of the State Council.

State Council of China. (2017). "Thirteenth Five-Year" Special Plan for Health and Health Technology Innovation (China National Publication [2016] No. 77). Beijing: China General Office of the State Council.

State Council of China. (2017). Plan for New Generation Artificial Intelligence Development (China National Publication [2017] No. 35). Beijing: China General Office of the State Council.

State Council of China. (2018). Opinions on Promoting the Development of "Internet + Medical Health" (China State Council [2018] No. 26). Beijing: China General Office of the State Council.

Steiber, A., Alänge, S., Ghosh, S., & Goncalves, D. (2020). Digital transformation of industrial firms: An innovation diffusion perspective. *European Journal of Innovation Management, 24*(3), 799–819.

Sterne, J. (2002). *World Wide Web marketing: integrating the Web into your marketing strategy*. John Wiley & Sons.

Stokes, R. (2013). *eMarketing: The essential guide to marketing in a digital world*. Quirk eMarketing.

Straw, I. (2020). The automation of bias in medical Artificial Intelligence (AI): Decoding the past to create a better future. *Artificial Intelligence in Medicine, 110*, 101965. doi:10.1016/j.artmed.2020.101965 PMID:33250145

Strickland, E. (2019). *How IBM Watson overpromised and underdelivered on AI health care*. https://spectrum.ieee.org/biomedical/diagnostics/how-ibm-watson-overpromised-and-underdelivered-on-ai-health-care

Strzębicki, D. (2017). Development factors for cross-border b2c e-commerce in the world and in Poland. *Acta Scientiarum Polonorum. Oeconomia, 16*(4), 161–168. doi:10.22630/ASPE.2017.16.4.55

Sufi, T., & Ahmed, S. (2021). Surviving COVID-19 Crisis by New Business Models: A Case Study of the Indian Restaurant Industry. In Handbook of Research on Entrepreneurship, Innovation, Sustainability, and ICTs in the Post-COVID-19 Era (pp. 301-316). IGI Global. doi:10.4018/978-1-7998-6776-0.ch015

Sugathan, P., Ranjan, K. R., & Mulky, A. G. (2017). Atypical shifts post-failure: Influence of co-creation on attribution and future motivation to co-create. *Journal of Interactive Marketing, 38*, 64–81.

Sun, R. J., Yu, Y., Zhang, Z. H., Liu, H. P., Yuan, S. W., Jiang, T., & … . (2021). AI-guided resource allocation and rescue decision system for medical applications. *Future Generation Computer Systems, 118*, 485–491. doi:10.1016/j.future.2020.12.010

Swani, K., Milne, G., & Brown, B. P. (2013). Spreading the word through likes on Facebook: Evaluating the message strategy effectiveness of Fortune 500 companies. *Journal of Research in Interactive Marketing, 7*(4), 269–294. doi:10.1108/JRIM-05-2013-0026

Sweeney, J. C., & Soutar, G. N. (2001). Consumer perceived value: The development of a multiple item scale. *Journal of Retailing, 77*(2), 203–220.

Szopa, Ł., & Cyplik, P. (2020). The concept of building a digital transformation model for enterprises from the SME sector – case study. *LogForum, 16*(4), 593–601.

Szymanski, D. M., & Hise, R. T. (2000). E-satisfaction: An initial examination. *Journal of Retailing, 76*(3), 309–322. doi:10.1016/S0022-4359(00)00035-X

Tabrizi, B., Lam, E., Girard, K., & Irvin, V. (2019). Digital Transformation is not about Technology. *HBR Org*. Retrieved from https://hbr.org/2019/03/digital-transformation-is-not-about-technology

Tabrizi, B., Lam, E., Girard, K., & Irvin, V. (2019). *Digital transformation is not about technology*. https://hbr.org/2019/03/digital-transformation-is-not-about-technology

Teece, D. J. (2010). Business models, business strategy and innovation. *Long Range Planning, 43*(2-3), 172–194.

Teece, D. J. (2010). Business Models, Business Strategy and Innovation. *Long Range Planning, 43*(2–3), 172–194. doi:10.1016/j.lrp.2009.07.003

Teece, D., Peteraf, M., & Leih, S. (2016). Dynamic capabilities and organizational agility: Risk, uncertainty, and strategy in the innovation economy. *California Management Review, 58*, 13–35.

The Economist. (2010, Jan. 30). A world of connections – a special report on social networking. *The Economist.*

The Economist. (2019). *What Microsoft's revival can teach other tech companies*. Retrieved from https://www.economist.com/leaders/2019/07/25/what-microsofts-revival-can-teach-other-tech-companies

Thorpe, A. S., & Roper, S. (2019). The ethics of gamification in a marketing context. *Journal of Business Ethics, 155*(2), 597–609. doi:10.100710551-017-3501-y

Timchenko, V. V., Trapitsin, S. Y., & Apevalova, Z. V. (2020). Educational technology market analysis. *Proceedings of the 2020 IEEE International Conference "Quality Management, Transport and Information Security, Information Technologies," IT and QM and IS 2020*, 612-617. 10.1109/ITQMIS51053.2020.9322982

To, P. L., Liao, C., & Lin, T. H. (2007). Shopping motivations on Internet: A study based on utilitarian and hedonic value. *Technovation, 27*(12), 774–787. doi:10.1016/j.technovation.2007.01.001

Toubia, O., & Stephen, A. T. (2013). Intrinsic vs. image-related utility in social media: Why do people contribute content to twitter? *Marketing Science, 32*(3), 368–392. doi:10.1287/mksc.2013.0773

Treadaway, C., & Smith, M. (2010). *Facebook marketing an hour a day*. Wiley Publishing.

Tsai, H. T., & Huang, H. C. (2007). Determinants of e-repurchase intentions: An integrative model of quadruple retention drivers. *Information & Management, 44*(3), 231–239. doi:10.1016/j.im.2006.11.006

Tseng, T. H., Hsieh, S. H., & Lee, C. T. (2021). How gamified branded applications drive marketing effectiveness? *Marketing Intelligence & Planning, 39*(5), 633–648. Advance online publication. doi:10.1108/MIP-09-2020-0407

Tumbas, S., Berente, N., & Brocke, J. V. (2018). Digital innovation and institutional entrepreneurship: Chief digital officer perspectives of their emerging role. *Journal of Information Technology, 33*(3), 188–202.

Tung, V. W. S., & Ritchie, J. B. (2011). Exploring the essence of memorable tourism experiences. *Annals of Tourism Research, 38*(4), 1367–1386.

Turner, A. (2015). Generation Z: Technology and social interest. *Journal of Individual Psychology, 71*(2), 103–113. doi:10.1353/jip.2015.0021

Tuten, T. L. (2008). *Advertising 2.0: Social Media Marketing in a Web 2.0*. ABC-CLIO.

Tuzii, J. (2017). Healthcare information technology in Italy, critiques and suggestions for European digitalization. *Pharmaceuticals Policy & Law, 19*(3/4), 161–176.

Tzeng, S.-Y., Ertz, M., Jo, M.-S., & Sarigöllü, E. (2021). Factors affecting customer satisfaction on online shopping holiday. *Marketing Intelligence & Planning, 39*(4), 516–532.

Ukwuani, N., & Bashir, E. (2017). Emerging technologies: An exploration of novel interactive technologies. *International Journal of Information Systems in the Service Sector, 9*(4), 30–43.

United States Securities and Exchange Commission. (2017). *General Motors Company Form 10k, Annual Report*. US Securities and Exchange Commission. Retrieved from https://www.gm.com/content/dam/gm/en_us/english/Group4/InvestorsPDFDocuments/10-K.pdf

Uzunoğlu, E., & Kip, S. M. (2014). Brand communication through digital influencers: Leveraging blogger engagement. *International Journal of Information Management, 34*(5), 592–602. doi:10.1016/j.ijinfomgt.2014.04.007

Van Alstyne, M. W., Parker, G. G., & Choudary, S. P. (2016). Pipelines, Platforms, and the New Rules of Strategy. *Harvard Business Review*, (April), 2–9.

Van Noort, G., Voorveld, H. A., & Van Reijmersdal, E. A. (2012). Interactivity in brand web sites: Cognitive, affective, and behavioral responses explained by consumers' online flow experience. *Journal of Interactive Marketing, 26*(4), 223–234. doi:10.1016/j.intmar.2011.11.002

Vargo, S. L., & Akaka, M. A. (2009). Service-dominant logic as a foundation for service science: Clarifications. *Service Science, 1*, 32–41.

Vargo, S. L., & Lusch, R. F. (2004). Evolving to a new dominant logic for marketing. *Journal of Marketing, 68*(1), 1–17.

Vargo, S. L., & Lusch, R. F. (2008). Service-dominant logic: Continuing the evolution. *Journal of the Academy of Marketing Science, 36*, 1–10.

Vargo, S. L., & Lusch, R. F. (2016). Institutions and axioms: An extension and update of service-dominant logic. *Journal of the Academy of Marketing Science, 44*, 5–23.

Vargo, S. L., & Lusch, R. F. (2017). Service-dominant logic 2025. *International Journal of Research in Marketing, 34*, 46–67.

Varma, M., Dhakane, N., & Pawar, A. (2020). Evaluation of Impact of Instagram on Customer Preferences: The Significance of Online Marketing. *International Journal of Scientific & Technology Research, 9*(2), 548–554.

Varshneya, G., & Das, G. (2017). Experiential value: Multi-item scale development and validation. *Journal of Retailing and Consumer Services, 34*, 48–57.

Vashisht, D., Royne, M. B., & Sreejesh, S. (2019). What we know and need to know about the gamification of advertising: A review and synthesis of the advergame studies. *European Journal of Marketing, 53*(4), 607–634. doi:10.1108/EJM-01-2017-0070

Vasilevski, N., Brand, J., & Birt, J. (2019). Optimizing augmented reality outcomes in a gamified place experience application through design science research. *Proceedings - VRCAI 2019: 17th ACM SIGGRAPH International Conference on Virtual-Reality Continuum and its Applications in Industry*. 10.1145/3359997.3365747

Veleva, S. S., & Tsvetanova, A. I. (2020). Characteristics of the digital marketing advantages and disadvantages. *IOP Conference Series. Materials Science and Engineering*, *940*(1), 012065. doi:10.1088/1757-899X/940/1/012065

Venkatesh, A., Sherry, J. F. J., & Firat, A. F. (1993). Postmodernism and the marketing imaginary. *International Journal of Research in Marketing*, *10*(3), 215–223. doi:10.1016/0167-8116(93)90007-L

Venkatesh, V., Thong, J. Y. L., & Xu, X. (2012). Consumer Acceptance and Use of Information Technology: Extending the Unified Theory of Acceptance and Use of Technology. *Management Information Systems Quarterly*, *36*(1), 157–178. doi:10.2307/41410412

Verhagen, T., & Van Dolen, W. (2009). Online purchase intentions: A multi-channel store image perspective. *Information & Management*, *46*(2), 77–82. doi:10.1016/j.im.2008.12.001

Verhoef, P. C., Broekhuizen, T., Bart, Y., Bhattacharya, A., Qi Dong, J., Fabian, N., & Haenlein, M. (2021). Digital transformation: A multidisciplinary reflection and research agenda. *Journal of Business Research*, *122*, 889–901.

Vial, G. (2019). Understanding digital transformation: A review and a research agenda. *The Journal of Strategic Information Systems*, *28*(2), 118–144.

Vieira, V., Santini, F. O., & Araujo, C. F. (2018). A meta-analytic review of hedonic and utilitarian shopping values. *Journal of Consumer Marketing*, *35*(4), 426–437. doi:10.1108/JCM-08-2016-1914

Viertola, W. (2018). *To what extent does YouTube marketing influence the consumer behaviour of a young target group* (Bachelor's thesis). Helsinki Metropolia University of Applied Sciences.

Villaronga, E. F., & Mahler, T. (2021). Cybersecurity, safety and robots: Strengthening the link between cybersecurity and safety in the context of care robots. *Computer Law & Security Review*, *41*, 105528. doi:10.1016/j.clsr.2021.105528

Vingilis, E., Yildirim-Yenier, Z., Vingilis-Jaremko, L., Seeley, J., Wickens, C. M., Grushka, D. H., & Fleiter, J. (2018). Young male drivers' perceptions of and experiences with YouTube videos of risky driving behaviours. *Accident; Analysis and Prevention*, *120*, 46–54.

Von Hippel, E. (2016). *Free Innovation*. MIT Press. doi:10.7551/mitpress/9780262035217.001.0001

Voorveld, H. A., Smit, E. G., Neijens, P. C., & Bronner, A. F. (2016). Consumers' cross-channel use in online and offline purchases. *Journal of Advertising Research*, *56*(4), 385–400. doi:10.2501/JAR-2016-044

Vos, L. (2015). Simulation games in business and marketing education: How educators assess student learning from simulations. *International Journal of Management Education*, *13*(1), 57–74. doi:10.1016/j.ijme.2015.01.001

Vukasovič, T. (2015). Brand developing relationships through social media. *Europe*, *21*(5).

Wai, K., Dastane, O., Johari, Z., & Ismail, N. B. (2019). Perceived risk factors affecting consumers' online shopping behaviour. *The Journal of Asian Finance. Economics and Business*, *6*(4), 246–260.

Wally, E., & Koshy, S. (2014). *The use of Instagram as a marketing tool by Emirati female entrepreneurs: An exploratory study*. University of Wollongong in Dubai.

Wang, K. W., Lau, A., & Gong, F. (2016, April 15). *How savvy social shoppers are transforming Chinese e-commerce*. McKinsey Survey.

Wang, Q., & Shi, Y. H. (2019). The Artificial Intelligence-Enabled Medical Imaging: Today and Its Future. *Chinese Medical Sciences Journal*, *34*, 71–75. PMID:31315746

Wang, X., Yu, C., & Wei, Y. (2012). Social media peer communication and impacts on purchase intentions: A consumer socialization framework. *Journal of Interactive Marketing*, *26*(4), 198–208.

Wang, Y. S., & Liao, Y. W. (2008). Assessing eGovernment systems success: A validation of the DeLone and McLean model of information systems success. *Government Information Quarterly*, *25*(4), 717–733. doi:10.1016/j.giq.2007.06.002

Wasan, P. (2017). Managing technologies for consumer engagement. In Hospitality marketing and consumer behavior: Creating memorable experiences (pp. 261-289) doi:10.1201/9781315366227-11

Watson, A., Alexander, B., & Salavati, L. (2020). The impact of experiential augmented reality applications on fashion purchase intention. *International Journal of Retail & Distribution Management*, *48*(5), 433–451.

Wayland, M. (2017). Randy Mott built GM's IT engine. *Automotive News*. doi:https://www.autonews.com/article/20171002/OEM06/171009988/how-mott-built-gms-it-engine

Web of Science. (n.d.). *Web of Science (keyword: "business model")*. Retrieved December 14, 2021, from https://bit.ly/3231OCd

Weber, E. U., & Bottom, W. P. (1989). Axiomatic Measures of Perceived Risk: Some Tests and Extensions. *Journal of Behavioral Decision Making*, *2*(2), 113–131. doi:10.1002/bdm.3960020205

Wedel, M., Bigné, E., & Zhang, J. (2020). Virtual and augmented reality: Advancing research in consumer marketing. *International Journal of Research in Marketing*, *37*(3), 443–465. doi:10.1016/j.ijresmar.2020.04.004

Weill, P., & Woerner, S. L. (2015). Thriving in an Increasingly Digital Ecosystem. *MIT Sloan Management Review*, *56*(4), 27–34.

Wendt, L. M., Griesbaum, J., & Kölle, R. (2016). Product advertising and viral stealth marketing in online videos: A description and comparison of comments on YouTube. *Aslib Journal of Information Management*, *68*(3), 250–264. doi:10.1108/AJIM-11-2015-0174

Westerman, G. (2014). Leading Digital: Turning Technology into Business Transformation. *Harvard Business Review*.

Westerman, G., Bonnet, D., & McAfee, A. (2014). *Leading Digital: Turning Technology into Business Transformation*. Harvard Business Review Press.

Whiting, T., Gautam, A., Tye, J., Simmons, M., Henstrom, J., Oudah, M., & Crandall, J. W. (2021). Confronting barriers to human-robot cooperation: Balancing efficiency and risk in machine behavior. *iScience*, *24*(1), 101963. doi:10.1016/j.isci.2020.101963 PMID:33458615

Widawska-Stanisz, A. (2018). Questing in city promotion on the example of the city of częstochowa. *Innovative Marketing*, *14*(1), 7–12. doi:10.21511/im.14(1).2018.01

Wikipedia. (2021). *Getir*. Retrieved July 25, 2021, from https://tr.wikipedia.org/wiki/Getir

Winkelhake, U. (2017). *The Digital Transformation of the Automotive Industry: Catalysts, Roadmap, Practice*. Springer.

Wirtz, B. W., Pistoia, A., Ullrich, S., & Göttel, V. (2016). Business Models: Origin, Development and Future Research Perspectives. *Long Range Planning*, *49*(1), 36–54. doi:10.1016/j.lrp.2015.04.001

Wisdom Innovation Development Institute. (2021). *In-depth, China's digital medical development trend and outlook*. Retrieved May 23,2021, from https://baijiahao.baidu.com/s?id=1688775674315855921&wfr=spider&for=pc

Wolfinbarger, M., & Gilly, M. C. (2001). Shopping online for freedom, control, and fun. *California Management Review*, *43*(2), 34–55. doi:10.2307/41166074

Wolf, T., Weiger, W. H., & Hammerschmidt, M. (2020). Experiences that matter? the motivational experiences and business outcomes of gamified services. *Journal of Business Research*, *106*, 353–364. doi:10.1016/j.jbusres.2018.12.058

Wu, K. (2016). YouTube marketing: Legality of sponsorship and endorsements in advertising. *JL Bus. & Ethics*, *22*, 59.

Xiao, Y., & Liu, S. Y. (2019). Collaborations of Industry, Academia, Research and Application Improve the Healthy Development of Medical Imaging Artificial Intelligence Industry in China. *Chinese Medical Sciences Journal*, *34*, 84–88. PMID:31315748

Xie, K. Y. (2018) *Uncover the secret of Pinduoduo popularity*. Retrieved July 2019 from http://finance.jrj.com.cn

Xie, C., Bagozzi, R. P., & Troye, S. V. (2008). Trying to prosume: Toward a theory of consumers and co-creators of value. *Journal of the Academy of Marketing Science*, *36*(1), 109–122.

Xi, N., & Hamari, J. (2020). Does gamification affect brand engagement and equity? A study in online brand communities. *Journal of Business Research*, *109*, 449–460. doi:10.1016/j.jbusres.2019.11.058

Xing, F., Peng, G. C., Zhang, B. Q., Li, S. Y., & Liang, X. T. (2021). Socio-technical barriers affecting large-scale deployment of AI-enabled wearable medical devices among the ageing population in China. *Technological Forecasting and Social Change*, *166*, 120609. doi:10.1016/j.techfore.2021.120609

Xingye Securities. (2021). *In-depth report on the pathological diagnosis industry: Tracing the origin, the long-ignored "fundamental of medicine"*. https://m-robo.datayes.com/report/summary?id=4526796

Xingye Securities. (2021). *Privacy Computing: The New Blue Ocean in the Era of Data Security*. https://mp.weixin.qq.com/s/VU4Zl4QK3mpzrhOTNAI6Xg

Xinhua News Agency. (2016). Outline of the Thirteenth Five-Year Plan for National Economic and Social Development (Beijing ICP No. 05070218). Beijing: China General Office of the State Council.

Xu, F., Buhalis, D., & Weber, J. (2017). Serious games and the gamification of tourism. *Tourism Management*, *60*, 244–256. doi:10.1016/j.tourman.2016.11.020

Xu, F., Tian, F., Buhalis, D., Weber, J., & Zhang, H. (2016). Tourists as mobile gamers: Gamification for tourism marketing. *Journal of Travel & Tourism Marketing*, *33*(8), 1124–1142. doi:10.1080/10548408.2015.1093999

Yadav, M. S., & Pavlou, P. A. (2014). Marketing in computer-mediated environments: Research synthesis and new directions. *Journal of Marketing*, *78*(1), 20–40. doi:10.1509/jm.12.0020

Yamakami, T. (2015). *A gap analysis of enterprise gamification applications with social servicenics theory: Challenges and implications*. Paper presented at the 2015 12th International Conference on Service Systems and Service Management, ICSSSM 2015. 10.1109/ICSSSM.2015.7170189

Yang, P., Xu, T., Feng, Y., Zhao, Y., & Wang, X. (2018). The impact of gamification elements on the evaluation of marketing activities. *Proceedings of the International Conference on Electronic Business (ICEB)*, 634-643.

Yang, P., Zhao, Y., Xu, T., & Feng, Y. (2019). *The impact of gamification element on purchase intention*. Paper presented at the 2019 16th International Conference on Service Systems and Service Management, ICSSSM 2019. 10.1109/ICSSSM.2019.8887654

Yang, T., Kim, D., & Dhalwani, V. (2008). Social networking as a new trend in e-marketing. In Research and Practical Issues of Enterprise Information Systems II (pp. 847-856). Boston: Springer. doi:10.1007/978-0-387-76312-5_7

Yang, S., Lu, Y., & Chau, P. Y. (2013). Why do consumers adopt online channel? An empirical investigation of two channel extension mechanisms. *Decision Support Systems*, *54*(2), 858–869. doi:10.1016/j.dss.2012.09.011

Yang, Y., Asaad, Y., & Dwivedi, Y. (2017). Examining the impact of gamification on intention of engagement and brand attitude in the marketing context. *Computers in Human Behavior, 73*, 459–469. doi:10.1016/j.chb.2017.03.066

Yang, Z., Algesheimer, R., & Dholakia, U. (2017). When ethical transgressions of customers have beneficial long-term effects in retailing: An empirical investigation. *Journal of Retailing, 93*(4), 420–439. doi:10.1016/j.jretai.2017.09.005

Yang, Z., Cai, S., Zhou, Z., & Zhou, N. (2005). Development and validation of an instrument to measure user perceived service quality of information presenting web portals. *Information & Management, 42*(4), 575–589. doi:10.1016/S0378-7206(04)00073-4

Yang, Z., & Peterson, R. (2004). Customer perceived value, satisfaction, and loyalty: The role of switching costs. *Psychology and Marketing, 21*, 799–822.

Yao, Y. B., Liu, Y., Li, Z., Yi, B., Wang, G. H., & Zhu, S. H. (2020). Chinese surgical robot micro hand S: A consecutive case series in general surgery. *International Journal of Surgery, 75*, 55–59. doi:10.1016/j.ijsu.2020.01.013 PMID:31982634

Yaoyuneyong, G., Foster, J., Johnson, E., & Johnson, D. (2016). Augmented reality marketing: Consumer preferences and attitudes toward hypermedia print ads. *Journal of Interactive Advertising, 16*(1), 16–30. doi:10.1080/15252019.2015.1125316

Yasmin, A., Tasneem, S., & Fatema, K. (2015). Effectiveness of Digital Marketing in the Challenging Age: An Empirical Study. *International Journal of Management Science and Business Administration, 1*(5), 69–80. doi:10.18775/ijmsba.1849-5664-5419.2014.15.1006

Yen, B. T. H., Mulley, C., & Burke, M. (2019). Gamification in transport interventions: Another way to improve travel behavioral change. *Cities (London, England), 85*, 140–149. doi:10.1016/j.cities.2018.09.002

Yim, M. Y. C., Chu, S. C., & Sauer, P. L. (2017). Is augmented reality technology an effective tool for e commerce? An interactivity and vividness perspective. *Journal of Interactive Marketing, 39*, 89–103.

Yim, M. Y. C., Chu, S. C., & Sauer, P. L. (2017). Is augmented reality technology an effective tool for e-commerce? An interactivity and vividness perspective. *Journal of Interactive Marketing, 39*, 89–103. doi:10.1016/j.intmar.2017.04.001

Yin, R. (2009). Case Study Research: Design and Methods. *Sage (Atlanta, Ga.).*

Yin, R. K. (1994). *Case Study: Design and Methods*. Sage Publications.

Yi, Y., Wang, Y., & Shu, C. (2020). Business model innovations in China: A focus on value propositions. *Business Horizons, 63*(6), 787–799. doi:10.1016/j.bushor.2020.07.002

Youn, S., Lee, M., & Doyle, K. O. (2003). Lifestyles of online gamers: A psychographic approach. *Journal of Interactive Advertising, 3*(2), 49–56. doi:10.1080/15252019.2003.10722073

Yüksel, M. (2007). Küreselleşme sürecinde yeni bir iletişim ortami. *Öneri Dergisi, 7*(28), 317-326. doi:10.14783/maruoneri.684439

Zacca, R., & Dayan, M. (2017). Entrepreneurship: An Evolving Conceptual Framework. *International Journal of Entrepreneurship and Innovation Management, 21*(1/2), 2–26. doi:10.1504/IJEIM.2017.081495

Zeng, M. (2018, Sept.). Alibaba and the Future of Business Lessons from China's innovative digital giant. *Harvard Business Review.*

Zhang, J. Y., Gao, F., & Ye, Z. W. (2020). Remote consultation based on mixed reality technology. *Global Health Journal, 4*(1), 31–32. doi:10.1016/j.glohj.2020.01.001 PMID:33614179

Zhang, M., Zhang, Z. C., Wang, X., Yu, H., Xia, Y. F., Tan, K. R., Wang, X., & Wang, F. Y. (2021). From AR to AI: Augmentation Technology for Intelligent Surgery and Medical Treatments. *IFAC-PapersOnLine*, *53*(5), 792–796. doi:10.1016/j.ifacol.2021.04.174

Zhao, W., Wang, A. Q., & Chen, Y. (2019, November). How to maintain the sustainable development of a Business Platform: A case study of PDD Social Commerce Platform in China. *Sustainability*. Retrieved August 2020 from https://www.mdpi.com/journal/sustainability

Ziaie, A., ShamiZanjani, M., & Manian, A. (2021). Systematic review of digital value propositions in the retail sector: New approach for digital experience study. *Electronic Commerce Research and Applications, 47*, 101053.

Zimmerman, C. A., & Kelley, C. M. (2010). I'll remember this! Effects of emotionality on memory predictions versus memory performance. *Journal of Memory and Language*, *62*, 240–253.

About the Contributors

Maria Antónia Rodrigues is a senior lecturer at the business school of Polytechnic of Porto. She is a director of Bachelor in Marketing, member of the school's Scientific Council, member of the scientific committee of the International Journal of Marketing, Communication and New Media, a researcher at CEOS.PP, and SIIS Porto. She has published several papers. Her main research interests are services, consumer behavior, and business relationships. Maria Antónia Rodrigues has also professional experience in business and services.

* * *

Vandana Ahuja is a Professor of Marketing at the Amity Business School. She has over 22 years of experience across the corporate sector and academia and is the author of the book on Digital Marketing – published by Oxford University Press. She is the proud recipient of the ILDC-AMP Women Excellence Award for exemplary contribution to Management Teaching. She has published several manuscripts in International and National journals and also serves on the editorial board of several international journals as an Associate Editor, Guest Editor and Review board member. She has organised and chaired several National and International Conferences and is part of several committees for NBA and AACSB accreditation at Amity Business School. Her teaching and research interests are Digital Marketing, Advanced Sales Management and Marketing Analytics and she has taught in several Management Development programs organised for the corporate sector. She has supervised 7 doctoral theses in the domain of management heads the Centre for Research Publications at Amity Business School.

Shirin Alavi has about 14 years of experience across the academia and corporate sector. She is currently working as an Associate Professor with Jaypee Institute of Information Technology, Noida. She has earlier worked with the Standard Chartered Bank and has work experience in the domain of CRM operations and International Business and Marketing. She has conducted research in the domains of customer relationship management, online communities, marketing, social media and mobile apps and has several years of research experience. She has published several manuscripts in international and national journals and also serves on the editorial review board of international journals. She has completed three Ph.D. guidance. She has completed one edited book of IGI global publications. She is member of NBA and NAAC accreditation committee of the university.

Eirini Bazaki is Senior Teaching Fellow in Fashion Management Marketing and MA Coordinator of MA Luxury Brand Management, MA Fashion Management, MA Fashion Marketing and Branding at the University of Southampton. Eirini is a graduate of Saïd Business School, University of Oxford, a Fellow of the Higher Education Academy UK, holds a PhD in Marketing from Adam Smith Business School, University of Glasgow, an MSc in Management Research from the University of Glasgow, an MSc Degree in Marketing Management from Aston University and a BSc (Hons) in Sociology from the department of Social Sciences, Panteion University. Eirini research interests lie in fashion marketing, e-branding and e-retailing for fashion and luxury fashion brands. Her research work is published in leading academic books and international journals and has previously been presented at the 2021 Global Fashion Marketing Conference, 2019 Academy for Design Innovation Management Conference UK, the European Academy of Marketing Conference and the Global Brand Conference. Eirini actively advises fashion and luxury fashion brands on how to build a strong brand identity, connect with customers and drive sales through digital channels.

Anthony Bolton is a graduate of University of South Africa, holding a PhD in Information Systems. Anthony is the CIO and CTO for Global Telecommunications, Infrastructure, End User Services and Immersive Technologies for General Motors. Anthony previously held executive IT positions leading IT Transformation and innovation in a career spanning over 30 years, working in Fortune 50 companies such as Dell, Hewlett Packard and Price Waterhouse. Anthony's focus in academic research centres on Unified Communication and Collaboration technology, Zero trust client security and Software Defined Networking.

Flávio Augusto Brito is a graduate in Information Science from the Faculty of Arts and Humanities (FLUC) of the University of Coimbra (2014-2018) and a postgraduate in Electronic Business from the Porto Accounting and Business School (ISCAP) of the Polytechnic Institute of Porto (2019-2021). His research interests include consumption habits, new technologies, social media, digital business models, marketing, informational practices, music and the phonographic industry.

Federica Caboni, PhD, is an Assistant Professor in Business Communication at the University of Cagliari, Department of Economic and Business Science (Italy). Since 2017 she is a visiting researcher at the Centre for Retailing, School of Business, Economics and Law at the University of Gothenburg. Her research interests focus on retail, consumer behavior, digitalization and new technology. She is an author of several scientific publications and book chapters edited by Emerald, Springer, Palgrave.

N. Meltem Çakıcı is Associate Professor of Marketing at Beykent University, Turkey. Her areas of interest are cross-cultural consumer behavior, international marketing strategy and brand management. Digital customer journey and business model development are also part of her research agenda. She has publications in top-tier marketing journals such as International Marketing Review.

Qiuyan Fan is a lecturer at Western Sydney University (WSU), Australia. Dr Fan has a particular research interest in the issues surrounding digital innovation, digital transformation and strategy for SMEs, digital government, digital business and cross-border e-commerce. Dr Fan has extensive industry experiences in government policy analysis and business strategy development and management. Over the last few years Dr Fan has published a number of referred Journal articles, book chapters and refereed conference papers in the areas above. Dr Fan has been supervising and co-supervising PhD students at WSU.

Leila Goosen is a full professor in the Department of Science and Technology Education of the University of South Africa. Prof. Goosen was an Associate Professor in the School of Computing, and the module leader and head designer of the fully online signature module for the College for Science, Engineering and Technology, rolled out to over 92,000 registered students since the first semester of 2013. She also supervises ten Masters and Doctoral students, and has successfully completed supervision of 43 students at postgraduate level. Previously, she was a Deputy Director at the South African national Department of Education. In this capacity, she was required to develop ICT strategies for implementation. She also promoted, coordinated, managed, monitored and evaluated ICT policies and strategies, and drove the research agenda in this area. Before that, she had been a lecturer of Information Technology (IT) in the Department for Science, Mathematics and Technology Education in the Faculty of Education of the University of Pretoria. Her research interests have included cooperative work in IT, effective teaching and learning of programming and teacher professional development.

Beyza Gultekin is an Associate Professor of Marketing at Hacettepe University, Turkey. She delivers Marketing, Retail Marketing Management, Customer Relationship Management, Distribution Channels, and International Economics and Business courses in undergraduate and graduate programs and supervises master's theses and doctorate level dissertations. Her main research interests include retailing, distribution channels, consumer behavior, customer relationship management, and consumer ethics. Her studies are published in the Journal of Retailing and Consumer Services, Social Behavior & Personality, and by Emerald Publishing.

Esra Güven is a lecturer at the University of Manisa Celal Bayar in Turkey. She holds a PhD on the impact of social media on consumer decision-makings. Her current interests include marketing communications, consumer behaviours and consumer communications in social media. Ph. Dr. Esra Guven is the author of several national and international papers and the marketing advisor of the Association of Strategic Researches in Turkey. The author still gives lectures on marketing, marketing researches, modern business, human resources at Manisa Celal Bayar University.

Johan Hagberg is professor of Business Administration specialising in Marketing at the Centre for Retailing and the Marketing Section at the School of Business, Economics and Law, University of Gothenburg. His research revolves around the digitalization of retailing, consumption and markets. In current research projects, he investigates digital ecosystems and intermediation of insurance as well as digital platforms and the structural transformation of retailing. His publications include articles in Industrial Marketing Management, Journal of Marketing Management, Urban Studies, Marketing Theory, Journal of Historical Research in Marketing, Consumption Markets & Culture, International Journal of Retail & Distribution Management, and Journal of Retailing and Consumer Services.

Roumiana Ilieva is Associate Professor Dr. Eng. on "Automated Systems for Data Processing & Management" at the Technical University of Sofia, Bulgaria. Head of Dept. Management and Business Information Systems. Specializes and teaches in the fields of Business Intelligence (BI) & eGovernance at the Universities of Amsterdam and The Hague (2007), Lancaster (2008, 2017), Southampton Solent (2010, 2013), Westminster and UCL, London (2009, 2011), Portsmouth (2016-2019), UK; Otto-von-Guericke-Universität Magdeburg (2013); Universidad Publica de Navarra, Pamplona, Spain (2015); eXchange Security, Donau-Universität Krems, Austria, (2011); "Space Challenges" (2010-2012), etc.

Major areas of research and teaching: Heterogeneous Intelligent Systems (AI, ML, BI) for Business Analytics, incl. Multimedia and Network Mining (DM) from Big Data; Robotic Process Automation (RPA); Interactive Multimedia and Agile Integration in Shared Environments, incl. Virtual, Augmented, Extended and Mixed Reality for Agile Digital Transformation of Modern Business, ITSM, Contemporary Research Methods in e-Gov and Business, etc. Author of over 100 scientific publications. Member of: the University Alliances of SAP Labs Bulgaria Ltd; IEEE: Computer Society; Robotics and Automation Society; Society for Systems, Man and Cybernetics, etc.; UDBC at USAID; Union of Automation and Informatics (UAI); National Key Expert at the STUME in IT & ERP Systems; Computer Science Expert in Machine Building, Biomechanics and Robotics at SOCOURT Ltd., Berlin /Innovative Products Development/; PC member of 11th & 12th International Workshops on Interactive Environments and Emerging Technologies for eLearning (IEETeL) in conjunction with IEEE 10th International Conference in Methodologies and Intelligent Systems for Technology Enhanced Learning, 2020, L'Aquila, Italy and IEEE 19th International Conference on Information Technology Based Higher Education and Training, 2021, Sydney, Australia; JeDEM and CeDEM & Asia '11-21, Austria, etc.

Elmarie Kritzinger joined the University of South Africa's College of Science, Engineering and Technology (CSET) in 2000 and currently holds the position of Professor in the School of Computing. Prof Kritzinger completed her PhD in 2006 and Post Graduate Certificate in Education in 2012. She is currently enrolled for her Master's in Education (Online Technology). Her research primarily focuses on Cyber Safety awareness, training and education for school learners, teachers and schools. The main aim is to establish and promote social responsibilities within communities to establish and grow a cyber-safety culture within South Africa. Prof Kritzinger has established herself as a mature researcher and has published in accredited national and international journals, contributed to a chapter in a book and presented at peer-reviewed conferences across the globe. Prof Kritzinger currently hold a NRF C3 rating within her research field.

Dinesh Kumar (PhD) is Associate Professor at Jagran Lakecity University, Bhopal. He has corporate experience for over 15 years after which he switched to teaching in 1995. He has taught at leading business schools in India. He has travelled widely and has published and presented many papers. He is the author of five major books on Marketing, including *Marketing Channels* (2012) and *Consumer Behavior* (2015), both published by Oxford University Press, *The Connected Consumer* published by Business Expert Press, New York, and *Rural Marketing*, which has been published by Sage (2017). His latest book is *Marketing in the Digital Era* published by Sage (2021).

Ana Lima is a Marketing Professor at Porto Polytechnic Institute in ISCAP – School of Accounting and Administration of Porto, since 2007. She has a PhD in Marketing Management and she is a research in CEOS (Center for Organizational and Social Studies of the Polytechnic of Porto) with a research work in retailing, digital marketing, branding, luxury and store equity. In research fields she has participated in international conferences and Eramus programs. She is also Director of a Business post-graduation course and responsible for professional technical course to improve employability among students.

Ramya Mahendran is the an managed innovation consultant. She is certified in design thinking, business modeling and jobs to be done. She has over 10 years of experience in the fields of managed innovation, startup incubation and acceleration, crowd sources idea management systems, design thinking and sustainability. She works with student entrepreneurs to build their business ideas into a successful business model. She works with some of India's leading Technology and Business Incubators, Institution Innovation Councils and Entrepreneurship Cells. She specializes in setting up innovation strategy, opportunity identification, large scale ideation campaigns and facilitating rapid prototyping events like design service jams and hackathons, organizing large-scale Innovation summits and global idea crowdsourcing events. Her current areas of research is - how can empathy be taught with the help of design tools for product, service, and policy designers.

João F. Proença is a full professor at the University of Porto and researcher at the Advance-CSG, ISEG, University of Lisbon, Portugal. He has been the Rector of the Universidade Europeia, Lisbon, Portugal, and the Dean of the Faculty of Economics, University of Porto, where he was also been in charge of relevant positions as Director of the Ph.D., MSc or BSc. He also held relevant professional positions in companies as administrator, CEO, managing director or sales manager. Furthermore, he has more than 150 papers published in several academic journals, for instance, at the Industrial Marketing Management, Journal of Service Management, Services Industry Journal, Journal of Services Marketing, or at the Journal of Business & Industrial Marketing, among many others. He also has published books, book chapters, conference papers, and opinion articles in newspapers and magazines. His research interests cover sustainability, services and B2B marketing, relationships and business networks, and the links between industry and services.

Albérico Travassos Rosário, Ph.D. Marketing and Strategy of the Universities of Aveiro (UA), Minho (UM) and Beira Interior (UBI). With affiliation to the GOVCOPP research center of the University of Aveiro. Master in Marketing and Degree in Marketing, Advertising and Public Relations, degree from ISLA Campus Lisbon-European University | Laureate International Universities. Has the title of Marketing Specialist and teaches with the category of Assistant Professor at IADE-Faculty of Design, Technology and Communication of the European University and as a visiting Associate Professor at the Santarém Higher School of Management and Technology (ESGTS) of the Polytechnic Institute of Santarém. He taught at IPAM-School of Marketing | Laureate International Universities, ISLA- Higher Institute of Management and Administration of Santarém (ISLA-Santarém), was Director of the Commercial Management Course, Director of the Professional Technical Course (TeSP) of Sales and Commercial Management, Chairman of the Pedagogical Council and Member of the Technical Council and ISLA-Santarém Scientific Researcher. He is also a marketing and strategy consultant for SMEs.

Diana Aguiar Vieira, PhD, is a psychologist, coach, trainer, Associate Professor at Porto Accounting and Business School (ISCAP), and researcher at the Centre for Organizational and Social Studies Polytechnic Institute of Porto (P.PORTO), Portugal. Former Vice-Dean of Porto Accounting and Business School (ISCAP). Founder and coordinator of the Coaching, Career and Personal Development Unit (2011-2018) and the Alumni Office (2012-2018), both at ISCAP. Former Pro-Rector of P.PORTO for employability and Alumni Strategy for all P.PORTO Schools. Founder of the ICAReAlumni community (https://icarealumni.com/). Her research interests include alumni relations, career development, employability, coaching, higher education, soft skills and self-efficacy. She has been involved in international research projects and partnerships with European and Brazilian universities. Her personal site (https://beyou-bemore.com/) aims to share her knowledge not only to the scientific community but also with the general public.

Vanissa Wanick is a Teaching Fellow in MA Design Management and Games Design & Art at Winchester School of Art, University of Southampton. Vanissa Wanick holds a PhD in design from the University of Southampton, MBA in Marketing from University Federal Fluminense (UFF), and a BA in Design at PUC-Rio, Rio de Janeiro, Brazil. Currently, she is teaching fellow at the University of Southampton (Winchester School of Art), teaching and researching games design and innovative applications in user experience design. She is also a Fellow of the Higher Education Academy (FHEA). Her research interests are multidisciplinary and include cross-cultural Human-Computer Interaction (HCI), games design, creativity and diversity, design innovation, games user research methods, gamification, immersive technologies like Virtual Reality (VR), games for behaviour change and sustainable consumer behaviour across cultures. Vanissa has more than 10 years of international experience in digital design and user experience design, working as a designer for several companies in Rio de Janeiro, Brazil. Vanissa has also published more than 20 papers in the area of games design, gamification, user interface design, brand experience, VR/AR, cross-cultural design and engagement. She is an active member of the Academy of Design Management Innovation (ADIM) and has collaborated to main conferences in her field such as CHIPlay, ADIM, Graphica and SBGames.

Wenye Xue is an independent researcher. Her research interests include FinTech, Chinese economy and business analytics.

Shuo-Yun Yang is a postgraduate student in Winchester School of Art, University of Southampton.

Yuanyuan Yin is an Associate Professor, Head of Research at Design Department, Winchester School of Art, University of Southampton. Yuanyuan completed her PhD in Design Research and MA in Design Strategy & Innovation and from Brunel University, UK. She earlier obtained her B. Eng degree in Industrial Design in China. She joined University of Southampton in 2009. Her research has been concentrated on promoting business performance through developing design and brand strategies, understanding customers and users, supporting design collaboration, and improving innovation in product design. In recent years, she focused on research in inclusive service design for the ageing population. Yuanyuan has published over 35 academic papers in the design research field, registered two product design patents with the UK Intellectual Property Office. She has received more than 560k grants income from ESRC, British Council, Confucius Institute Headquarter and the University of Southampton.

Poshan (Sam) Yu is a Lecturer in Accounting and Finance in the International Cooperative Education Program of Soochow University (China). He is also an External Professor of FinTech and Finance at SKEMA Business School (China), a Visiting Professor at Krirk University (Thailand) and a Visiting Researcher at the Australian Studies Center of Shanghai University (China). Sam leads FasterCapital (Dubai, UAE) as a Regional Partner (China) and serves as a Startup Mentor for AIC RAISE (Coimbatore, India). His research interests include financial technology, regulatory technology, public-private partnerships, mergers and acquisitions, private equity, venture capital, start-ups, intellectual property, art finance, and China's "One Belt One Road" policy.

Index

A

B

C

D

www.ingramcontent.com/pod-product-compliance
Lightning Source LLC
LaVergne TN
LVHW060414300926
849162LV00006B/1424